**Readings in
Educational Psychology:
Contemporary Perspectives**

Readings in Educational Psychology: Contemporary Perspectives

1976-77 edition

edited by
Robert A. Dentler
and
Bernard J. Shapiro

series editor Phillip Whitten

HARPER & ROW

New York   Hagerstown   San Francisco   London

Cover design by Helen Dentler.

Photograph of Paul Klee's ''Puppentheater'' from Kunstmuseum Bern.

ISBN: 0-06-047083-6

ACKNOWLEDGMENTS

I. THE CONCERNS OF EDUCATIONAL PSYCHOLOGISTS
IS THERE A DISCIPLINE OF EDUCATIONAL PSYCHOLOGY?
by David P. Ausubel is reprinted by permission of EDUCA-
TIONAL PSYCHOLOGIST and David P. Ausubel.
EDUCATIONAL PSYCHOLOGY AND MODES OF INQUIRY by
Thomas F. Jordan is reprinted by permission of EDUCA-
TIONAL PSYCHOLOGIST and Thomas F. Jordan.
HOW PSYCHOLOGY STIMULATES EDUCATION by Jacob
Kagan is reprinted by permission from PSYCHOLOGY IN
THE SCHOOLS.
MEASURING YOUNG MINDS by David Elkind. Copyright ©
1971, American Heritage Publishing Company, Inc. Re-
printed by permission from HORIZON (WINTER, 1971).
DON'T USE THE KITCHEN SINK APPROACH TO ENRICH-
MENT by David Krech is reprinted by permission from
TODAY'S EDUCATION: Journal of the National Education
Association, and from David Krech.
HOW CHILDREN LEARN: A DEVELOPMENTAL APPROACH
by Raymond E. Keel and G. Thomas Rowland. Copyright ©
1974 THE ELEMENTARY SCHOOL JOURNAL, The University
of Chicago Press and the author.

II. DEVELOPMENT
A CHILD'S MIND IS SHAPED BEFORE AGE TWO by Maya
Pines, LIFE Magazine, Copyright © 1971 by Time Inc.
Reprinted with permission.
KINDERGARTEN IS TOO LATE by Esther P. Edwards. Copy-
right 1968 SATURDAY REVIEW. Photograph by Phillip
Whitten.
PLAY IS SERIOUS BUSINESS by Jerome S. Bruner from the
book CHILD ALIVE! edited by Roger Lewin. Copyright ©
1974, 1975 by IPC Magazines, Ltd. Reprinted by permission
of Doubleday & Company, Inc.
IMPLICATIONS OF CHILD DEVELOPMENT THEORIES FOR
PRE-SCHOOL PROGRAMMING by Sharon and Thomas
Cooke is reprinted by permission from EDUCATION and
Sharon and Thomas Cooke.
PIAGET'S THEORY OF CHILD DEVELOPMENT AND ITS
IMPLICATIONS by Robbie Case is reprinted by permission
from PHI DELTA KAPPAN and Robbie Case.

III. COGNITION
THE MYSTERY OF THE PRELOGICAL CHILD by Joachim F.
Wohwill. Copyright © 1967 Ziff-Davis Publishing Company.
Reprinted by permission of PSYCHOLOGY TODAY
MAGAZINE.
ATTENTION AND PSYCHOLOGICAL CHANGE IN THE
YOUNG CHILD by Jerome Kagan is reprinted by permission
from SCIENCE, Vol. 170, pp. 826-832, November 20, 1970,
and Jerome Kagan.
CONCEPTUAL AND ROTE LEARNING IN CHILDREN by

John D. Nolan is reprinted by permission from TEACHERS
COLLEGE RECORD and John D. Nolan.
LANGUAGE AND THE MIND by Noam Chomsky. Copyright ©
1968 Ziff-Davis Publishing Company. Reprinted by per-
mission of PSYCHOLOGY TODAY MAGAZINE.
TOWARD A COGNITIVE THEORY OF TEACHING by Nathaniel
Gage is reprinted by permission from TEACHERS COLLEGE
RECORD.
LOST: OUR INTELLIGENCE, WHY? by Quinn McNemar.
Copyright © 1964 AMERICAN PSYCHOLOGIST. Reprinted
by permission from the American Psychological Association
and Quinn McNemar.
ARE IQ TESTS INTELLIGENT? by Raymond Bernard Cattell.
Copyright © 1968 Ziff-Davis Publishing Company. Reprinted
by permission of PSYCHOLOGY TODAY MAGAZINE.
THE INTELLIGENT MAN'S GUIDE TO INTELLIGENCE by
Morton Hunt. Originally appeared in PLAYBOY Magazine;
copyright © 1971 by Morton Hunt.
IQ: FAIR SCIENCE FOR DARK DEEDS by Jerome Kagan.
Copyright 1972, Radcliffe College. Reprinted by permission
from RADCLIFFE QUARTERLY.
ONE INTELLIGENCE INDIVISIBLE by Constance Kamii.
Reprinted by permission from YOUNG CHILDREN, Vol. 30,
No. 4, May 1975. Copyright © 1975, National Association
for the Education of Young Children, 1934 Connecticut Ave.
N.W., Washington, D.C. and by Constance Kamii.
ASSESSING NATIONAL LEVELS OF ACHIEVEMENT IN A
SYSTEMATIC MANNER by John Stanley Ahmann is re-
printed by permission from EDUCATIONAL HORIZONS.
WHY JOHNNY CAN'T WRITE by Merrill Sheils. Copyright ©
1975 by NEWSWEEK, INC. All rights reserved. Reprinted by
permission.
Photographs by Jeff Lowenthal, NEWSWEEK.

V. THE BODY
PHYSICAL, MENTAL, AND CRITICAL PERIOD by John Money.
Copyright © 1969 by JOURNAL OF LEARNING DISABILI-
TIES. Reprinted by permission. Reprinted by permission
from John Money.
BIOLOGICAL INDIVIDUALITY by Rene Dubos is reprinted by
permission from THE COLUMBIA FORUM, Volume XII, No. 1
(Spring 1969) Copyright © 1969 by the Trustees of Columbia
University in the City of New York. All rights reserved.
MOVEMENT AND LEARNING by Alice Yardley is reprinted by
permission from TODAY'S EDUCATION; Journal of the
National Education Association. Also reprinted by permis-
sion from Alice Yardley author of nine books on early learn-
ing and development (Evans Bros. U.K.) eight of which are
published by Citation Press, New York.
Photographs by Trent Polytechnic, Nottingham, England.
THE MOVEMENT MOVEMENT by Lorena R. Porter is reprinted
by permission from TODAY'S EDUCATION: Journal of the
National Education Association, and the author.

CONTENTS

David Ausubel defines educational psychology as
that special branch of psychology concerned with
the nature of school learning. He points to the
difficulty of a tendency among educational
psychologists to uncritically extrapolate findings
from laboratory studies to classroom learning
environments and comes to the conclusion that the
principles of school learning can only be discovered
through applied research that takes into account
both the kinds of learning that occur in the classroom and the salient characteristics of the learner.

Do educational psychologists apply the concepts of
psychology to the circumstances of children's
learning or is this speciality little more than psychological talk about educational matters? Thomas
Jordan considers this common questions but concludes that it is not a helpful one. He feels that the
term psychologist is an accident of terminology and
that it would be more appropriate to distinguish
between two classes of educational empiricists.
One of these consists of practice-centered people.
The other — the group of educational psychologists
— uses the same mode of inquiry but chooses a
better conceptual representation of educational
reality as the desired end product.

Skinnerian psychology views learning as a three-
step process: preceding stimulus, response, and
consequent stimulus. Almost all applications of this
view to education have focused on response and
consequent stimulus — the last two steps. Jacob
Kagan — drawing on the work of William James —
works within the framework of operant psychology
both to downplay the model of animal learning and
to affirm the critical role of preceding stimuli in the
teaching act.

David Elkind introduces in this short article the
seminal figure, Jean Piaget. Working in Binet's
laboratory school in Paris, Piaget found that he
could combine his biological and philosophical
interests by testing the child's understanding of the
physical, biological, and social worlds at successive age levels. Piaget found that the child's ideas
about the world were "constructions" that involved
both mental structures and experience, and Elkind
recounts the major stages of this natural history as
Piaget has stated them.

In considering his psycho-physical and chemical
studies of animal behavior, Professor Krech concludes that (a) the psychological environment is of
crucial importance for the development of the brain,
and (b) the manipulation of the educational and
psychological environment is a more effective way
of inducing brain changes than is the direct administration of drugs. However, not every experience or
stimulation contributes equally to the development
of the brain. The challenge to the educator is to
select those variables that will make a positive
difference, and David Krech concludes the article
with a number of his specific suggestions.

Keel and Rowland attempt to focus some of the
findings of educational psychology in terms of their

meaning and import to the classroom teacher. They define education as the guided changing of behavior, and restrict their concern to behaviors that are observable. Assuming that survival is the long term goal of human behavior and that knowledge seeking is the means to that objective, they suggest how the teacher can structure the learning environment so that it helps the pupils to reach this goal.

In examining the differences between more and less competent pre-school children between three and six years of age, the researchers of the Harvard Pre-School Project found that whatever produced the differences between these two groups had occurred before the age of three. Apparently something happened between the ages of ten and eighteen months which propelled children into one line of development or another, and the results are very much dependent upon the role of the mother. Ms. Pines outlines the role of the "consultant" mother and suggests possible parent and school roles in preventing educational handicaps from developing in this early period.

This article is an impassioned plea for greater emphasis on the development and availability of pre-school education. Edwards outlines the basis for the importance of pre-school experience in the research work of Piaget, Vygotsky, Hebb, and Bloom relative to child development. A number of specific approaches to early childhood education including those of Head Start, O.K. Moore, and Bereiter and Engeleman are discussed, and the author concludes that the partisanship prevalent between these groups is more apparent than real. She argues that we determine how best to employ each approach: when, with whom, for what reasons, and under what circumstances.

Findings from animal studies have long suggested that play does not merely provide practice of instinctive survival behaviors; it also makes possible the practice of behaviors that later come together in useful problem solving. Further, with young children, the more intensive and exploratory they have been in their previous play, the higher their apparent creativity in later years. Bruner argues that, in fact, play is the principal business of childhood. He sees it developmentally as the first carrier of rule systems through which a world of cultural restraint replaces the operation of childish impulse.

The Cookes review and critique three schools of child development theory: the cognitive, the maturational, and the behavioral. Each position is analyzed in terms of its potential application to early childhood educational programming. The authors stress the commonalities of the three approaches: that is, the importance of the environment, the evolution of all mature behavior from infancy, and developmental processes from simple to complex, and they suggest that these common assumptions provide a core around which pre-school programming should be built.

Robbie Case begins by providing a brief outline of the philosophical foundations of Piaget's work. He then provides a succinct description of some of Piaget's important studies and an outline of the four major developmental stages which Piaget posits: sensorimotor, preconceptual, concrete operations, and formal operations. Then, stressing the difficulty of moving from Piaget's work to direct classroom applications, Case discusses a number of such current attempts and concludes that most of them depend for their justification on an additional set of assumptions which are either untested as yet, or inherently untestable.

B. F. Skinner and Sigmund Freud have been the preeminent figures in learning psychology and personality theory respectively. In the theory of cognitive development, the outstanding figure is Jean Piaget. Although differing interpretations have been made, Wohlwill feels that Piaget's emphasis is on the innate and biological rather than the learning and environmental factors. The thrust of American research on cognitive development has been to test the age-stage correspondence as outlined by Piaget and to establish how much development can be accelerated by specific types of teaching interventions. The author contends that teaching can hasten the development of logical thinking and that knowledge of a student's logical capacities can help to guide the teacher's selection of cognitive tasks.

Kagan begins by suggesting that different processes are likely to mediate alterations in cognitive structure and that conditioning principles do not seem sufficient to explain all such changes. He points out that better understanding of the forces that control selectivity and duration of attention should provide insight into the nature of changes in cognitive structure. He argues that events with a high rate of change in their physical characteristics, that were moderately discrepant from established schematia, and that activated hypotheses in the service of assimilation had the greatest power to recruit and maintain attention in the young child.

Although rote learning and conceptual learning have traditionally been thought of as antithetical, Nolan attempts to blur this customary distinction. He points to research that indicates that rote learning requires conceptualizing and conceptual learning requires considerable rote repetition. A teacher may think that a concept has been taught because the pupils retrieve together those items which the teacher sees as related. However, the pupils who may not yet be capable of forming the particular concept, may have been "chunking" rather than categorizing. Professor Nolan feels that this is all to the good. When the child is ready for the concept, he will have what he remembers from his "chunk" to work with. The younger child needs to learn by rote as a preparation for conceptual learning.

How does the mind work? In response to this question, Noam Chomsky's theory of language acquisition is a serious challenge to behavioral studies of learning. According to Chomsky, a child's competence for generating an infinite number of novel sentences is innate and consists of an intuitive, tacit, and unconscious grasp of the relevant rules. He refers to the grammar of a language as a transformational grammar, which describes the operations we use to relate to its deep structure. Traditional grammar — according to Chomsky — analyzes only surface structure. For teachers, the question is if language capacity is innate, rather than learned, what is the role of language teaching in the school?

Gage points out that 'teaching' is a misleadingly generic term that covers too much to be made the subject of theory development. For fruitful theory development, 'teaching' needs to be broken down into simpler, more unitary elements. He offers a number of such possibilities but selects for focus that aspect of teaching whose objective is bringing about comprehension of the academic disciplines. In considering this area, he points to the need to focus just as sharply on the cognitive aspects of teacher behavior as the students of programmed instruction have focused on the cognitive aspects of their programs.

Quinn McNemar argues that the concept of general intelligence, despite being maligned by a few and discarded or ignored by others, still has an important place in the study of psychology and the practical affairs of the world. He does not argue that the nature of general intelligence is well understood. Rather, he suggests that in studying intelligence, we have focused too much on stimulus-response (S-R) models. McNemar argues that progress in the further study of intellect is doomed to failure unless the simple S-R paradigm is modified to include variables relating to both organism (O) and process (P).

In considering the current controversies over the meaning of intelligence and intelligence testing, Dr. Cattell does not concentrate on specific problems of test reliability and validity. Rather, he moves to a discussion of different types of intelligence making the distinction between fluid and crystallized intelligence. He argues that this society must make some kind of policy decision on which kind of intelligence should be given emphasis in this period, but that whatever the decision, the distinction which he draws will facilitate the development of culture-fair tests and thus respond to the need to open equal educational opportunity to all of our subcultures.

Morton Hunt provides an excellent general introduction to the concept of intelligence in the light of the controversy regarding "race" and intelligence. The initial work of Alfred Binet is summarized, and special attention is given to the recurrent environment vs. heredity arguments, with special attention to the studies of identical twins. In trying to assess the apparently contradictory evidence, Hunt stresses the possible synthesis arising from the work of I. I. Gottesman. That is, intelligence is not a lump sum to which heredity and environment each contribute so many units. Heredity and environment do not add up, they interact — and the result is not a sum but a product.

In this article, Jerome Kagan suggests that our society has created a specialized style of problem solving which it summarizes under the concept 'intelligence.' Further, since we use this skill as a rite of passage to power and wealth, we can easily be seduced into the conclusion that those without power and wealth are of fundamentally inferior intellectual competence. Kagan argues that the genetic contributions to IQ is unknown and that the observed IQ differences between American blacks and whites is likely to be due to the strong cultural biases contained in the IQ tests.

In trying to develop the implications of ideas about intelligence for practice in the schools, Kamii attempts to show how profoundly one's conception of intelligence affects the formulation of educational objectives. She suggests that a mechanistic conception of intelligence leads to the definition of objectives as a collection of fragmented cognitive skills that have little to do with children's development of intelligence. By contrast, she recommends the Piagetian conception which she feels leads to attempts to develop children's intelligence as an organized whole.

Stanley Ahmann describes the general organization of the National Assessment of Educational Progress (NAEP). His description includes the learning areas selected and both the sampling and analysis of data designs. Finally, he provides the reader with summaries of representative findings in social studies, citizenship, science, reading, writing, literature, and music. In terms of general trends, Ahmann finds that there is a large degree of consistency in the findings from one learning area to another. That is, the differences in relative achievement among subgroups of the sample are largely consistent in direction although not always in size.

This article is a consideration of the NAEP's latest studies which show that the essays of 13- and 17-year-olds are far more awkward, incoherent, and disorganized than the efforts of those tested in 1969. Various social and educational trends that may account for this result are discussed. The author concludes that there is a necessity for some fixed rules in writing, however tedious, if the codes of human communication are to remain decipherable. Are too many people intent on being masters of their language and too few willing to be its servants?

V. THE BODY

Overview

John Money argues against what he sees as existing Aristotelian dichotomies such as the physical and the mental, the constitutional and the acquired, the inherited and the environmental, the instinctual and the learned. In an attempt to bridge these dichotomies, he points to the critical period concept in which there is no clear distinction between body and mind.

All human beings have the same physiological processes and are driven by the same biological urges, yet no two human beings are precisely alike. Dr. Dubos accepts the assumption of this special uniqueness and focuses on defining the biological mechanisms through which each person develops his or her own behavioral singularity. He maintains that individuality is a product of the total environment, and he proposes that society provide environmental conditions so diversified that each person has a wide range of opportunities from which to develop his or her own potentiality.

Alice Yardley's concern with movement relates not merely to the improvement of one's motor and psycho-motor skills, but is centrally related to more general learning. Thus, for example, Yardley suggests that the child's opportunity to experience environments through the senses enhances the meaning value of words. Further, the author feels that important communication skills cannot be learned without exploratory experiences with the environment, including many forms of bodily movement. Children, she argues, use movement as a natural mode of expression, and, therefore, movement, is a mode which must be taken into account in the planning of educational programs.

Lorena Porter emphasizes the importance both of providing individualized child-centered physical education programs and of extending movement education to everyone in the school program. She provides guidelines for structuring movement experiences explaining types of equipment which can be used to stimulate creativity and exploration of the environment. Warning against the uncritical acceptance of preconceived adult notions of competition and rules, she offers a number of teaching techniques — such as body awareness in space — which are discussed both from theoretical and practical viewpoints.

VI. AFFECT

Overview

Lawrence Kohlberg outlines his three-level scheme describing the development of the structures and form of moral thought. He specifies the characteristics of the preconventional, the conventional, and the autonomous levels of moral reasoning, and discusses his own research findings regarding how young children — from a number of different cultures — progress from one stage to another. In particular, Kohlberg describes the 'trading up' phenomenon characteristic of his experimental moral discussion classes, and he further suggests that his studies demonstrate that youths who understand justice act more justly.

Junell outlines a critique of the scientific method in terms of its enabling children to cope with feelings. He argues that it is naive to assume that children will select what is demonstrably true over what is demonstrably false, for he suggests that it is feeling, not reasoning, that provides the motivation to act on our most widely held beliefs. In this context, the school's major objective is seen as one of combining children's need for a life of freedom with the amount of emotional conditioning that seems imperative to the maintenance of social stability.

Richard Farson argues that the development of technology relieves education of the needs to be either irksome and/or limited to cognitive and verbal skills. He defines technology broadly to include not only educational hardware but also systems engineering, social technology, classroom simulation, and sensitivity-training groups. He suggests that these developments need not turn students into mechanical idiots but may offer teachers and students the time and freedom to have more meaningful person-to-person relationships and more concern with noncognitive and nonverbal dimensions.

Gordon stresses the importance of synthesizing affect and cognition rather than treating them as mutually exclusive territories of human behavior. In his view, any teaching act or learning behavior is an inextricable mix.

Setting aside complex questions of methodology and validity, Dentler summarizes the major findings of the landmark survey, *Equality of Educational Opportunity,* conducted for the federal government by James S. Coleman and associates. The study found that even when background factors were held constant, teacher influences on verbal achievement of students was extremely limited. Teacher differences on such factors as socioeconomic status, years of teaching experience, and attitudes, among other measures, made about a two percent contribution to accounting for differences in the achievement of sixth graders.

Kohn shows that teachers have preconceptions about the abilities of many of their pupils and that these get communicated to most pupils. He summarizes studies that indicate how these preconceptions get translated into expectations and how the expectations often influence the achievement performances of students.

Spicker summarizes the evidence of the effects of various kinds of instruction upon the development of mental ability among preschool children. In marked contrast to evidence of slight effects upon older children, those taught by several different methods show marked gains in intelligence and achievement test scores. Where children then entered conventionally taught elementary programs, these gains tended to disappear over time, but where the elementary programs were designed to reinforce the gains, they were maintained. Spicker's evidence suggests that where they are well designed, very early teacher interventions have great, positive influence upon learning.

Hawkins "de-psychologizes" the meaning of teaching by placing it in historical, moral, and philosophical perspective, and by emphasizing how the teaching act is extended into and through subject matter. Through the participation of the learner in his transactions with subject matter, Hawkins believes, the teacher goes through repeated cycles of diagnosing, designing, responding, and then rediagnosing the mental as well as observable physical successes and failures of the learner. The article attacks simplistic approaches to the question of the teaching act.

Elkind analyses teacher-student interaction in terms of a model of interpersonal relations, whose form he calls the contractual relationship. This model releases us from undue attention to the personalities of teacher and student and emphasizes the mutual expectations that obtain between them. The expectations of demonstrated responsibility in exchange for autonomy, loyalty and commitment in exchange for support, and respect in exchange for teacher competence, among others, are described as basic to the interaction. Elkind suggests ways to use this model to understand events in the classroom, in preference to personality concepts or studies of background factors.

Behavior modification guided by teacher interaction with students is defined and analysed by Risley in this report on his use of Skinnerian theories of reinforcement. The rewards used in his experiments ranged from M&M candies to warm soup to expressions of praise. His premise was that disadvantaged preschool children of the urban poor could be prepared effectively for elementary school success by proper preliminary changes in behavior. He proved that the changes were accomplished, without taking up whether the changes were pertinent to future school experiences.

In exploring the uses of play as a learning resource of great importance for all children, Arnaud emphasizes how this importance is mediated in the classroom by the interactions of teachers and aides. Crucial as play is to cognitive and overall personality development, it is the teacher who facilitates or impedes, who integrates or fractures the role of play in the curriculum. Thus, teacher interaction with concepts of human nature that include or deny the value of play are as important in early childhood as teacher-student interaction itself.

Hamblin and associates show that the behavior of hyper-aggressive, immature, and even autistic children can be modified significantly through informed use of reinforcement schedules and strategies by teachers and other adults. Expressed praise and approval were not powerful enough as modifiers, but a token-exchange system leading to movies, snacks, and toys, used sparingly, and connected directly with the content of tasks, proved very adequate. With autistic children, token exchange produced permanent behavior changes where these were reinforced intermittently later on. The experiments illuminate some of the conditions under which teacher interaction may have very powerful effects on learning.

This essay summarizes the evidence on the theory, methods, and effectiveness of Omar Khayyam Moore's invention, the automated Edison Responsive Environment machine and related systems for individualizing teaching and learning. The invention was intended to enable children from preschool age upward to learn to typewrite and read. The E.R.E. entails minimal programmed instruction and maximal self-instruction through spontaneous exploration, with verbal reinforcements, of a typewriter keyboard. The environment simulates play conditions. Fast, accurate learning with high, positive side effects for problem-solving and creativity results. Direct teacher interaction is minimized.

This article summarizes the purposes of the open education movement as an alternative to conventional classroom-bound education. In open education, the mobility of both learners and teachers is greatly increased. Teachers collaborate with one another and with teams of students. Students participate in defining their studies. Drawbacks of the movement are sketched in.

A companion piece to Barth and Rathbone's, this article explains the origins of the open education movement in the English Infant Schools.

Marshall's article on how, as a teacher in a Boston public school, she experimented with alternative methods of instructions, planning, and classroom controls, exemplifies the large and growing clinical literature pertinent to educational psychology. No systematic or objective research and evaluation is recorded, but the self-report includes vital observations of innovative strategies that are varied as students interact with them more or less successfully.

Strom reports on simple experiments designed to train parents to strengthen interaction, verbal communication, and self-concept in their children, using toys and vocabulary as stimulus materials. Mothers and children in low income, urban minority families showed significant gains in both self-concepts and vocabulary.

Rice presents a series of models for concept teaching for use by parents with very young children. Concepts are defined as words which stand for a general idea or thing. The words chosen are drawn from among hundreds of common household objects. Deductive and inductive models are outlined for teaching, with specific steps and procedures for both. Other words drawn from vacation travel are used, as well. The feasibility of preparing Home Demonstration Teachers is explored.

Cohen summarizes some of the findings of the Pre-School Project at the Harvard University Laboratory of Human Development: Children initiate 80 percent of their own learning situations, but mothers do affect the quality of learning powerfully, especially through degree of restriction of exploratory activity, disciplinary firmness and consistency, and quality and frequency of reinforcement of child's interaction. Criteria for excellence in parenting are identified.

This article enlarges upon the findings summarized by Martin Cohen from the Harvard Pre-School Project, and offers a checklist of do's and don'ts for parents.

The authors hypothesize that children with reading problems develop the art of being stupid as one of their contributions to maintaining an upset or communications-disordered family system. The hypothesis is tested using tape recordings of family member verbal interaction and decision making. The findings suggest that the hypothesis has some validity, as families of children with reading problems manifest significant differences on pre-selected variables.

A series of reports from school districts in Des Moines, Iowa, Nashville, Tennessee, Boise, Idaho, and Owensboro, Kentucky, give strong evidence of innovations toward improved ties between families and public schools, with collaborative teaching and learning and counselling activities for parents and teachers.

Overview

Cooperation and competition between students in classrooms is defined and previous research findings summarized in this study. Cooperation is said to stimulate higher achievement while competition generates aggressiveness and higher anxieties. Individual differences are introduced to qualify these findings. New data are then analyzed and found to support the generalizations, even when individual differences are considered. Most children studied preferred cooperative structures.

Rardin and Moan studied 81 children, ranking them on measures of popularity, cognitive and social development. They supported the hypothesis that peer relations develop in a manner parallel to the development of concepts. Peer group popularity was found to associate closely with social skill development but not with physical concept development.

In a field study of a residence cottage for young boys within a state training school for mentally retarded children and youth, Dentler and Mackler used sociometric measures and intelligence tests to show that adult cottage sides and staff professionals negatively reinforce peer interaction so that avoidance learning results. Social learning through social expansiveness is restricted. The peer group is nearly eliminated as a force while compliance with school routines is internalized.

Overview

Some of the findings and implications for schooling of the International Association for the Evaluation of Educational Research (IEA) are summarized by Featherstone. The comparative results from IEA suggest that in certain subject and skill areas, schools affect learning outcomes significantly.

Philadelphia public schools, that achievement was significantly affected by student body composition, racial balance, class size, quality of teacher preparation, and length of teacher experience. The authors argue that school resources can be used to attain greater equity in educational opportunity.

PREFACE

In retrospect, educational psychology seems once to have been a rather tight little island of knowledge, set slightly offshore from the mainland of the behavioral and social sciences and bounded by a preoccupation with theories of school and classroom-based learning, and with tests and measurements of formal teaching and classroom learning behavior. A bridge was thrown to the mainland during World War II, when the knowledge of educational psychology proved essential to the design of mass instruction of military personnel. When the Russians lofted Sputnik in 1957, the bridge was widened and improved as educational psychologists in North America were called upon to help speed up the processes of educational innovation.

As most of the readings in this collection indicate, educational psychology became fused with developmental and social psychology, and infused with sociological and anthropological ideas during the 1960's, when the winds of cultural change swept across education with hurricane force. With very few exceptions, the readings we have selected are dated within the last five and at most ten years for this reason, for the field has been opened and transformed in recent years.

No one author and no one text can cover this field adequately any more. Moreover, teachers, counselors, and other practitioners, along with students concentrating in education, want to sense the conflict, controversy, and fertile developments in educational psychology by direct access to current writings. Therefore, we have selected articles, reports, and essays that address current issues, yet do so in ways that illuminate the basic questions in the field. We have also tried to select writing that was reflective of diverse points of view, yet balanced rather than polemical, in the spirit of an applied science. And, we have looked for writing that was readable for the beginning student. Many — but not all — of the selections are from the public press for this reason.

While the readings have been classified into thirteen sections appropriate to the concerns of educational psychologists, they cut across one another in both theme and content. New concepts and findings from early childhood education, for example, appear in nearly every section because this is the *frontier* of the field.

While there is a section on the school as a variable, there are entries in nearly every other section that bear on the nature and reality of schooling.

Acknowledgements

All flaws in this book are ours alone, while whatever is excellent is the result of collaboration with others. Special thanks go to Phillip Whitten, for pioneering in the conception of the series of which this book is a part; to Leslie Palmer for her editorial assistance; to Cheryl Lurye for resourceful library work; and to Helen H. Dentler for the cover design.

Robert A. Dentler
Bernard J. Shapiro
Boston University School of Education

I. THE CONCERNS OF EDUCATIONAL PSYCHOLOGISTS

Education is not synonymous with schooling, for children and adults learn outside schools as well as in them. To study education means, in fact, to study society and culture, but if we take this notion too far, education all but disappears, becoming synonymous with enculturation. We therefore define education more narrowly as *the deliberate evocation or transmission of knowledge, abilities, skills, and values.* Psychology is the scientific study of the behavior of human beings. The purpose of such study is to attain understanding of human behavior in order that it may be described, predicted, and influenced.

What is educational psychology? The usual answer—the application of the principles of psychology to the phenomena of education—appears quite straightforward. It is, however, deceptively simple, for it masks a basic problem that has plagued the definitional boundaries of this field. The difficulty is that psychology and education are not perfectly suited to each other. Thus psychology as a discipline uses methods and selects variables that tend to focus on the behavioral characteristics of individuals, and it studies phenomena from the perspective of individual differences. Education, however, even though it is vitally concerned with individual development as well, is also a very complex and fascinating matrix of social practices. Explanations based solely on individual differentiation are never adequate to fully explain an educational problem, for individuals also bring to the educational setting a vast social history.

This is not, of course, to argue that the focus of psychology on education is unproductive. Rather, it is to suggest that the lack of agreement on the precise definition of educational psychology finds its root in the attempt of educational psychologists to find more complete explanations for educational phenomena than their 'psychological' findings generally provide. In taking this step, they inevitably begin to consider the possible contributions of other variables—particularly those more commonly associated with sociology. Thus, educational psychology as a field becomes blurred at its edges. The two articles which begin this section are illustrative. David Ausubel begins by defining educational psychology traditionally as that branch of psychology concerned with the nature of school learning. He finds difficulty, however, with the simple psychological model as he considers the problems associated with extrapolating laboratory results to classroom learning environments, and he finally concludes that the characteristics of the learner are not sufficient for the discovery of the principles of school learning. By contrast, Thomas Jordan begins with the widest possible view. He viually abandons the label of 'psychology' as an accident of history, and he defines educational psychologists as those empiricists in education who choose a better conceptual representation of educational reality as the desired end product of their work.

Jordan's view may be adequate to the full complexities of education, but it is not helpful to actual educational psychologists attempting both to do justice to the multi-dimensionality of the educational context and yet to limit the range of their work in the interests of possible progress. A selection must, in fact, be made. Further, this selection must be carefully considered. As David Krech points out in his article, the kitchen-sink model is unlikely to be very productive. It is not the number of variables being considered but their relevance and quality that matter most. Jacob Kagan, working within the standard framework of operant conditioning—i.e., the stimulus-response-consequence model, points out that our emphasis is too frequently on the response and consequence notions. He argues that the social phenomena inherent in the stimuli which precede these two are also necessary to our understanding of the teaching act. From a Piagetian point of view, David Elkind stresses the importance of the interaction of the physical, biological, and social worlds in the development of the child as learner.

Turning from the concerns of educational psychologists in their study of education, Keel and Rowland, in the last article of this section, try to focus on the meaning of some of the findings in educational psychology for classroom practice. Assuming that survival is our most basic human goal and that knowledge is the road to survival, these two authors discuss how the teacher can structure the learning environment so as to facilitate knowledge acquisition.

IS THERE A DISCIPLINE OF EDUCATIONAL PSYCHOLOGY?

David P. Ausubel

Is there such a discipline as educational psychology? It is certainly not the case that I perceive this question as irrelevant or irreverent. Quite the contrary, it follows very pertinently if one examines many textbooks of educational psychology that were written during the past thirty years. In fact, from the conception of educational psychology inferable from analysis of the contents of these textbooks—that is, as a superficial, ill-digested, and typically disjointed and watered-down miscellany of general psychology, learning theory, developmental psychology, social psychology, psychological measurement, psychology of adjustment, mental hygiene, client-centered counseling and child-centered education—one would be hard put to give a negative answer to the question raised by the title of my paper.

Definition of the Field

My thesis, in brief, is that educational psychology is that special branch of psychology concerned with the nature, conditions, outcomes, and evaluation of school learning and retention. As such, the subject matter of educational psychology, in my opinion, consists primarily of the theory of meaningful learning and retention and the influence of all significant variables—cognitive, developmental, affective, motivational, personality and social—on school learning outcomes, particularly the influence of those variables that are manipulable by the teacher, by the curriculum developer, by the programmed instruction specialist, by the educational technologist, by the school psychologist or guidance counselor, by the educational administrator, or by society at large.

Psychology versus Educational Psychology

Since both psychology and educational psychology deal with the problem of learning, how can we distinguish between the special theoretical and research interests of each discipline in this area? As an applied science, educational psychology is not concerned with general laws of learning *per se,* but only with those properties of learning that can be related to efficacious ways of *deliberately* effecting stable cognitive changes which have social value (Ausubel, 1953). Education, therefore, refers to guided or manipulated learning directed toward specific practical ends. These ends may be defined as the long-term acquisition of stable bodies of knowledge and of the capacities needed for acquiring such knowledge.

The psychologist's interest in learning, on the other hand, is much more *general.* Many aspects of learning, other than the efficient achievement of the above-designated competences and capacities for growth in a directed context, concern him. More typically, he investigates the nature of simple, fragmentary, or short-term learning experiences, which are allegedly more representative of learning in general, rather than the kinds of long-term learning involved in assimilating extensive and organized bodies of knowledge.

IN WHAT SENSE IS EDUCATIONAL PSYCHOLOGY AN "APPLIED" DISCIPLINE?

Few persons would take issue with the proposition that education is an applied or engineering science. It is an *applied science* because it is concerned with the realization of certain practical ends which have social value. The precise nature of these ends is highly controversial, in terms of both substance and relative emphasis, To some individuals the function of education is to transmit the ideology of the culture and a core body of knowledge and intellectual skills. To others, education is primarily concerned with the optimal development of potentiality for growth and achievement—not only with respect to cognitive abilities, but also with respect to personality goals and adjustment. Disagreement with respect to ends, however, neither removes education from the category of science, nor makes it any less of an applied branch of knowledge. It might be mentioned in passing that automobile engineers are also not entirely agreed as to the characteristics of the "ideal" car: and physicians disagree violently in formulating a definition of health.

Regardless of the ends it chooses to adopt, an applied discipline becomes a science only when it seeks to ground proposed means to ends on empirically validatable propositions. The operations involved in such an undertaking are commonly subsumed under the term "research." The question under discussion here relates to the nature of research in applied science, or, more specifically, in education. Is educational research a field in its own right with theoretical problems and a methodology of its own, or does it merely involve the operation of applying knowledge from "pure" scientific disciplines to practical problems of pedagogy?

Despite the fact that education is an applied science, educational psychologists have manifested a marked tendency uncritically to extrapolate research findings from laboratory studies of simplified learning situations to the classroom learning environment. This tendency reflects the fascination which many research workers feel for the "basic-science" approach to research in the applied sciences, as well as their concomitant failure to appreciate its inherent limitations. They argue that progress in educational psychology is made more rapidly by focusing indirectly on basic-science problems in general psychology, than by trying to come to grips directly with the applied problems that are more indigenous to the field. Spence (1959), for example, perceived classroom learning as much too complex to permit the discovery of general laws of learning, and advocated a straightforward application to the classroom situation of the laws of learning discovered in the laboratory: he saw very little scope, however, for applying the latter laws to problems of educational practice. Melton (1959) and E. R. Hilgard (1961) take a more eclectic position. They would search for basic-science laws of learning in both laboratory and classroom contexts, and would leave to the educational technologist the task of conducting the research necessary for implementing these laws in actual classroom practice.

My position, in other words, is that the principles governing the nature and conditions of school learning can be discovered only through an applied or engineering type of research that actually takes into account both the kinds of learning that occur in the classroom as well as salient characteristics of the learner. We cannot merely extrapolate to classroom learning general basic-science laws that are derived from the laboratory study of qualitatively different and vastly simpler instances of learning.

Laws of classroom learning at an applied level are needed by the educational technologist before he can hope to conduct the research preparatory to effecting scientific changes in teaching practices. He can be aided further by general principles of teaching which are intermediate, in level of generality and prescriptiveness, between laws of classroom learning and the technological problems that confront him. Contrary to Spence's (1959) contention, the greater complexity and number of determining variables involved in classroom learning does not preclude the possibility of discovering precise laws with wide generality from one educational situation to another. It simply means that such research demands experimental ingenuity and sophisticated use of modern techniques of research design.

Prerequisites for a Discipline of Educational Psychology

The foregoing historical considerations and substantive propositions regarding the definition of the field of educational psychology, its relationships to general psychology, and its status as an applied discipline lead to the conclusion that a minimum number of crucial prerequisites must first be met before educational psychology can emerge as a viable and flourishing discipline. First, the acquisition of certain basic intellectual skills, the learning and retention of subject-matter knowledge, and the development of problem-solving capabilities must be regarded as the principal practical concerns toward which theory and research in this area of inquiry are directed. Second, the attainment of these objectives must be conceptualized as products of meaningful verbal or symbolical learning and retention, and a cogent theory of such learning and retention must be formulated in terms of manipulable independent variables. Third, the elaboration of this theory implies the delineation of unambiguous distinctions between meaningful learning, on the one hand, and such other forms of learning as classical and operant conditioning, rote verbal and instrumental learning, perceptual-motor and simple discrimination learning, on the other, as well as clear distinctions between such varieties of meaningful verbal learning as representational or vocabulary learning, concept learning, and propositional learning, and between reception and discovery learning. Finally, meaningful verbal learning must be studied in the form in which it actually occurs in classrooms, that is, as the guided, long-term, structured learning in a social context of large bodies of logically organized and interrelated concepts, facts, and principles, rather than as the short-term and fragmented learning of discrete and granulated items of information such as is represented by short-frame and small-step-size teaching machine programs.

CONCLUSION

In conclusion, educational psychology, in my opinion, is unequivocally an applied discipline, but it is *not* general psychology applied to educational problems—no more so than

mechanical engineering is general physics applied to problems of designing machinery, or medicine is general biology applied to problems of diagnosing, curing, and preventing human diseases. In these latter applied disciplines, general laws from the parent discipline are not applied to a domain of practical problems; rather, separate bodies of applied theory have evolved that are just as basic as the theory undergirding the parent disciplines, but are stated at a lower level of generality and have direct relevance for and applicability to the applied problems in their respective fields.

The time-bound and particular properties of knowledge in the applied sciences have also been exaggerated. Such knowledge involves more than technological applications of basic science generalizations to current practical problems. Although less generalizable than the basic sciences, they are also disciplines *in their own right,* with distinctive and relatively enduring bodies of theory and methodology that cannot simply be derived or extrapolated from the basic sciences to which they are related. It is simply not true that only basic-science knowledge can be related to and organized around general principles. Each of the applied biological sciences (e.g., medicine and agronomy) possesses an *independent* body of general principles underlying the detailed knowledge in its field, in addition to being related in a still more general way to basic principles in biology.

In the same way, educational psychology, in my view, must evolve as an autonomous discipline, with its own theory and methodology, but must obviously continue to be related to and be influenced by the parent discipline of psychology—as an independent adult peer rather than as a dependent child with a wholly derivative status.

REFERENCES

Ausubel, D. P. The nature of educational research. *Educ. Theory,* 1953, 3, 314-320.

Hilgard, E. R. A perspective on the relationship between learning theory and educational practices. In *Theories of learning and instruction,* 63rd Yearbook, *Nat. Soc. Stud. Educ.,* Part I. Chicago: Univer. Chicago Press, 1964, pp. 402-415.

Melton, A. W. The science of learning and the technology of educational methods. *Harvard Educ. Rev.,* 1959, 29, 96-106.

Spencer, K. W. The relations of learning theory to the technology of education. *Harvard Educ. Rev.,* 1959, 29, 84-95.

EDUCATIONAL PSYCHOLOGY AND MODES OF INQUIRY

Thomas E. Jordan

There are several ways to look at the field of educational psychology, with the most common being that employed by Professor Denny in the November 1966 issue of *Educational Psychologist*. In that approach analysis starts with two domains, educational events, and psychological events, and the patterns which evolve when the relative emphasis on each is altered. In this brief space I would like to sketch some outcomes of changing the connotations we give to the phrase "educational psychology."

People who identify with educational psychology identify only minimally with each other; that is, they generally feel their account of the proper business of educational psychology is more fundamental, productive and wholesome, than someone else's. Even so, they generally agree that science and the scientific movement describe the way they *do* their business. Pushed beyond that generality agreement evaporates. Some people feel they approach educational events psychologically, applying the concepts of that discipline to the circumstances of children's learning. Others see in the speciality of educational psychology little more than psychological talk about educational matters. In both instances we see a proportion of one domain balanced against the other, that is, good-to-bad psychologizing is added to good-to-bad educationizing. The formulation is not really productive since the outcomes are not really satisfactory to people in educational psychology or out of it. Some view educational psychologists about the way the A.M.A. views chiropractors; others are jumped-up educationists with nothing but pretentious language. There is, I feel, an alternative to these dyspeptic notions, a formulation that may ease the tensions.

Modes of Inquiry. There are many ways by which we arrive at stable beliefs, be they accepted hypotheses in a climate of cool heads or options on the flatness of the earth and the dangers of going too far. Some men rely on experience, others employ intuition, while the majority employ authority in some form. Grouping people by their mode of inquiry leads to some interesting observations about how educational procedures are conducted. We find that children start school at six because everyone "knows" that is the right age, and children learn to read by processes justified in research. In this instance we recognize that not everyone "knows" nor is any particular way of teaching reading justified by unequivocal facts. Tactical decisions about learning are made in many ways and by very different processes which are at times strange companions. People in administrative positions tend to use tradition and appeal to the authority of tradition to settle organizational problems—every county needs a county superintendent. Curriculum workers tend to feel that group experiences are valuable to children because, to use their rhetoric, masses of children somehow are a microcosm of the body politic. They use groups because, among other reasons, mass experience parallels their value preferences, and they organize the tactics of instruction as alternatives in values. Others—anonymous for the moment —reach their stable beliefs about what is best by applying reason to some experiential formulation of reality.

The examples just presented are instances of inquiry into problem areas by means of appeals to the authority of tradition, to value discriminations, and to empiricism. On occasions all three are employed by people, but traditionally the first two have been preferred. Over the years educationists engaged in developing consistent ways of doing things have turned to authority, to value judgments, but rarely to empiricism. The

adequacy of the first two approaches was rarely questioned. Since rigorous questions are themselves not encouraged within the first two modes, one knows by tradition that schools are not really supposed to take care of slum children; one readily discriminates that men teachers have little place in the elementary school. Empiricism and its commitment to the fallibility of knowledge has been the quickest index of potential for disloyalty.

Sputnik altered things and thereby set in motion a train of events leading all the way to this paper. First, the curriculum was questioned and found wanting; value discrimination based on slogans rather than reason wilted. The ascendants of the sciences elevated their empirical modes of inquiry into prominence, and gave encouragement to the role of empiricism in educational affairs. Educational empiricists most frequently in departments of educational psychology began to flourish.

However, in other fields of education empiricism began to appear too. School administration has grown remarkably and has profited considerably from the use of empiricism rather than appeal to authority. Curriculum workers are no longer satisfied to learn that children have had a nice experience. Evidence and reason have supplanted personal preferences to some degree. Educational psychology departments have found all kinds of people taking their courses in quantitative methods. In short, empiricism is no longer identified peculiarly with educational psychology; it is found in all aspects of education.

Consideration of the relationship between empiricism both conceptual and operational, and educational psychologists suggests that it was once particular but accidental. It was their forte by default, but it is now a mode of operation which is employed by other groups.

It may well be that educational psychology has acquired fairly permeable boundaries and that the identity of the discipline based on the way of doing its business is no longer stable. Professors of elementary education now measure, co-vary, and program. They use empirical techniques comfortably, introducing the self consciousness of methodology once rather clearly identified with educational psychology.

Conversely, educational psychologists have pushed their empiricism from procedural to conceptual planes, they taxonomize, build models and examine the epistemological properties of their ideas. In this last case empiricism has overtones of science which are clearly philosophical.

The situation appears as follows: Educational psychologists are no longer identifiable by a special relation to science, since other workers have discovered it. Further, educational psychologists have moved empiricism into theoretical realms traditionally identified as pedagogy or philosophy of education.

What then is an educational psychologist? What is the role on the basis of how he does his business? My opinion is that there are two components to an answer. The first component is work style, the peculiar way of approaching problems, e.g. formulation of issues in manageable ways and a decent respect for evidence. In this regard there are a lot of people who can be identified as educational empiricists or psychologists. More sharply put there now are educational empiricists in many fields. Empiricism has been about the only common characteristic of educational psychologist, but it is no longer a distinguishing trait. To answer the questions posed earlier, it seems that people in fields traditionally distinct from educational psychology can claim some identity with that phrase because of the use of a common mode of inquiry, empiricism.

The second component to the answer emerges from the residue of the previous remarks. We are left with little when we say that half the educators use our work style in problems of education. The little that remains after the mode is generally and widely adopted is large, but in a different sense. A mode can be applied at a practice-centered level or at a level we can consider conceptual. This last element is the basis for distinguishing educational empiricists generally from the subgroup who are educational psychologists. Conceptual analyses are those intellectual ventures whose pay-off is some generalized form of knowledge rather than a pay-off restricted to a change in educational tactics.

Inferentially, the discriminations I am making are not be-

tween educational psychologists and other adjectival psychologists. I feel the word psychologist is an accident of terminology entirely too particular for this day, apart from its connotations of empiricism and social science. Rather, I wish to distinguish between two groups of educational empiricists, one of which consists of practice-centered people, the other consists of people using the same mode of inquiry, adhering to the same falliblistic theory of truth, but choosing better conceptual representation of educational reality as the desired end-product. As educational psychologists press the epistemological aspects of their enterprise, they deal with the long neglected conceptual stratum of educational data. In so doing they give a little more structure and character to their domain at a time when it can seem all too often blurred and indistinct.

HOW PSYCHOLOGY STIMULATES EDUCATION NOW (B. F. SKINNER) AND THEN (WILLIAM JAMES)

Jacob M. Kagan

In a recent address dedicated to B. F. Skinner on the occasion of his sixty-fifth birthday, Bijou (1970) cited many applications of Skinnerian psychology to education. This psychology views learning as a three-step process: preceding stimulus, response, and consequent stimulus. The "response" and "consequent stimulus" components were well treated but, strangely, no applications were seen to stem from preceding stimuli, which common sense tells us constitute the heart of teaching. The purpose of this paper is to affirm the role of preceding stimuli in teaching in a manner consistent with operant psychology and to speculate upon causes for neglect by modern operant psychologists if not by teachers. For a preferable treatment we shall refer frequently to William James, whose lectures on education, delivered some 80 years ago, may still be read for profit and pleasure (see Barzun, 1963 and Gates, 1967). Curiously Skinner holds the William James Professorship at Harvard.

There are four principal reasons why preceding stimuli are of great importance in education:

1. *To reinforce a pupil's approach behavior.* In education, approach behavior refers to activity preparatory to actual learning of subject matter. Such activity includes coming to class, opening a book, paying attention, etc. A teacher or author should not take these responses for granted because, unfortunately, responses antagonistic to school learning and proper conduct often provide strong competing reinforcement. Students may drop out or tune out before they are reinforced in educationally desirable ways. Chilling statistics on drop-out rates as well as the commentary of many educational reformers regarding the dullness of school life suggest that teachers ought actively to capture or recruit pupils' spontaneous interest from the very outset, before it is too late. James' (1899) sound advice was to employ fascinating and engrossing antecedent stimuli.

". . . in teaching, you must simply work your pupil into such a state of interest in what you are going to teach him that every other object of attention is banished from his mind; then reveal it to him so impressively that he will remember the occasion to his dying day; and finally fill him with devouring curiosity to know what the next steps in connection wth the subject are . . . [p. 4]."

2. *To condition desirable emotional reactions.* Even operant theorists reserve a small but legitimate role for classical Pavlovian conditioning of emotions. While they emphasize overt operants, these theorists recognize the existence of feelings, emotions and attitudes. In education, positive emotions are obviously desirable for short- and, in particular, long-range objectives. The teacher who entertains and fascinates his students from the very outset should be the best conditioner of positive emotions.

In a description of this Pavlovian paradigm, Bugelski (1971) placed the teacher in the position of the unconditioned stimulus and the schoolwork in the position of the conditioned stimulus. If the teacher naturally evokes feelings of enjoyment, excitement and hope in his students, these feelings should become associated with originally neutral or even insipid school work. In Bugelski's view of Mowrer's theory, the teacher's primary function is that of a conditioner of emotional responses. Primary or not, the teacher certainly does play such a role whether or not he wants to. Interesting stimulus inputs can only serve to produce more positive emotional conditioning toward subject matter.

This is a far cry from the impersonal teaching role connoted by Skinner's phrase, "manager of instructional contingencies." No doubt Skinner is correct to caution against excessive dependence upon personal reinforcers, yet this caution itself may be too extreme. A pedagogy that specifically excludes natural and acquirable personal attributes of teachers neglects a powerful ally in the quest to make the learning situation a pleasant one. The importance of a happy, optimistic outlook toward learning is self-evident and undeniable, particularly for younger students. One way to facilitate the development of such a healthy outlook is to have vibrant and fascinating stimulus presentations *before* the student responds. Another way, preferred by Skinner, is to provide lots of positive reinforcement *after* correct responses. The two are by no means incompatible, but neither is one a substitute for the other. Let teachers do both, either personally or with assistance from technology.

3. *To secure automatic, effortless attention.* Operant psychologists treat attention as a free operant subject to modification through shaping. Numerous studies *(e.g.,* Packard, 1970) have demonstrated that the frequency of operant attention increases as a result of external reinforcement. Unfortunately, these studies fail to discuss the duration of attention, the relative ease or strain involved, and the utter dependence on consequential external reward or fear of punishment. James characterized operant attention as a momentary affair that soon dies and must be revived by a violent wrench back to concentration, but he also distinguished another kind of attention far more important to education. It is *passive* rather than active, *involuntary* rather than voluntary and *spontaneous* rather than forced. To the beholder, the focal stimuli are interesting in themselves and permit long periods of easy but unfailing attention.

Clearly the preferred kind of attention for teaching is the effortless, automatic kind: "In all respects, reliance upon such attention as this [strained] is a wasteful method, bringing temper and nervous wear and tear as well as imperfect results. The teacher who can get along by keeping spontaneous interest excited must be regarded as the teacher with the greatest skill . . . [James, 1899, p. 53]." To secure this kind of attention the teacher must use a fascinating array of antecedent stimuli.

Spontaneous attention seems like respondent or reflexive behavior. However, consequential feedback also may be present. As James (1899) stated with regard to the sustained automatic attention of a genius deeply immersed in thought, "The subject of thought, once started, develops all sorts of *fascinating consequences.* The attention is led along one of these to another in the most interesting manner, and the attention never once tends to stray away . . . [p. 53, emphasis added]." It thus would appear that this form of behavior is triggered automatically but is maintained by intrinsic rewards.

Skinner (1968) recognizes the reinforcing properties of such stimulus inputs and recommends that they come *after* the student has actually learned (or done) something:

> "In good instruction interesting things should happen *after* the student has read a page or listened or looked with care. The four-color picture should *become* interesting when the text which it accompanies has been read. . . . In general, naturally attractive and interesting things further the primary goals of education only when they enter into much more subtle contingencies of reinforcement than are usually represented by audio-visual aids . . . [p. 106, emphasis added]."

In the writer's view, operant psychologists also might recognize the need to arouse spontaneous attention even at the cost of squandering some rich stimulus material prematurely. Otherwise "we might lose our pigeon" or, more accurately, we might never entrap him without resort to strong aversive control, which nobody favors. Surely teaching is a performance art, as James insisted (see the first of his *Talks* entitled "Psychology and the Teaching Art"). Even Skinner (1968) refers in passing to "the art of teaching [p. 223]." Every good performer knows the importance of "starting off with a bang," and every resourceful performer will have an ample supply of good material left over to carry the day. These stimuli should be part of the treatment to induce good work rather than restricted to rewards or treats after good work was done.

4. *To get the pupil interested in the topic.* Interest and attention are closely related so this point is similar to that just made, but there is a difference. The automatic elicitation of attention by means of attention-compelling stimuli was just discussed; now the point is to associate material to be learned with previously conditioned topics or activities. Thus, the skillful teacher will teach arithmetic

averages by means of examples from baseball. Interest in sex or drugs can spur a teenager's study of physiology. James refers to this techniques as Herbart's "Doctrine of Borrowed Interest." The idea is so well known, if not by that name, that little more need be said. It is very basic: to facilitate learning, select antecedent stimuli that are pleasant, important, or interesting to the learner and associate them with the required curriculum.

Reasons for Neglect

Why have operant theorists tended to underestimate the significance of preceding stimuli in education? In the writer's opinion, this is a result of a literal, but not entirely correct, transposition of successful procedures for training animals to the training of humans. Skinner undoubtedly is correct in his view that some behavioral laws of educational significance can be learned from the analysis of the behavior of a single animal under controlled conditions, perhaps even better than from the typical "ed psych" experiment. But with regard to preceding stimuli at least, the writer believes that animal learning is *not* a good model for school learning. An attempt now will be made to demonstrate why the above four reasons for the importance of preceding stimuli in classroom learning are inapplicable to animal learning.

1.   There usually is little concern with approach behavior in animal experiments because the subjects are physically placed into task situations and physically prevented from leaving. In other situations approach behavior is shaped directly, but there are no incompatible responses with strong competing reinforcement. The animal trainer has an easier task in this regard than the teacher, who typically has much less control over students' drive states, responses, and reinforcement.

2.   In animal studies generally no one cares how the subject feels about the present task or later ones, the present experimenter or later ones, or the present situation or similar ones. This cannot be the case in teaching.

3.   The attention span of animals is extremely short and precarious, and the primary way to maintain it is through arousal of physiological needs. Spontaneous attention based on intellectual curiosity or thought simply does not exist at the animal level. The problem of motivation is solved by starving the subject. If these animals have any "devouring curiosity," it is curiosity about what they can devour! Higher apes may be an exception, but Skinnerians tend to study rats and pigeons.

4.   To what former interests, other than primary drives, can one appeal in animal learning? In this sense, as well as in the previously mentioned sense, teaching is easier than training animals.

The writer agrees with Bugelski (1971) that for the practical purposes of education, it is no longer advisable to experiment on lower animals. "Psychologists probably should dispense with rat studies altogether as far as human learning is concerned, except for some extremely primitive kinds of conditioning at the very early ages . . . [p. 148]." Insofar as the practical aspects of education are concerned, further study of lower organisms is probably a blind, dead-end alley.

What is the Skinnerian Approach to the Problem of Motivation?

We have stressed the motivational functions of preceding stimuli in human learning. Without resort to such techniques and without resort to aversive control, which Skinner categorically rejects, it is difficult to see how the teacher can motivate a class! What then is operant psychology's answer if it is not imaginative and significant input-stimulation?

Skinner's answer to the problem of motivation lies in reinforcement schedules: to get the learner to work for leaner and leaner schedules of unpredictable reinforcement. There is indeed ample evidence from the laboratory that animals will emit thousands upon thousands of responses without consequential reinforcement if they have been trained to respond under gradually thinning, unpredictable schedules. Therefore, argues Skinner, humans also should be subjected to the same kinds of training schedules. He actually suggests to teachers, lecturers and writers that they should gradually but firmly increase the amount of work their students, listeners, or readers must do in order to obtain reinforcement. The ideal is long stretches of unreinforced behavior maintained by infrequent and unpredictable reinforcers. The present writer is skeptical about this analogy because of two differentiating factors: drive state and intrinsic confirmation in meaningful learning.

To the writer's knowledge, the partial reinforcement effect depends on a high-drive state. Even in humans, the effect is found in such behaviors as vigilance, gambling, search etc., in which the person usually is quite excited and eager. Remove the excitement or the stakes and behavior will become lethargic and extinction will soon ensue. As any teacher knows, the typical student is not terribly enthusiastic about most school work. To be sure there are exceptions, but most youngsters from all social and economic strata find school per se rather dull. Where drive state is low, partial reinforcement should be used with extreme caution. Every non-reinforced trial runs the risk of "turning off" the none-too-eager learner. With highly motivated learners the risk is less, but should the exceptionally motivated student be the model for all? Skinner (1968) himself cautions against the "Idol of the Good Student [p. 112]."

Ironically, Skinner appears guilty of what he criticized in James. James, as cited earlier, said that the key to effective teaching was to arouse in the student a "devouring curiosity." Skinner (196, p. 145) claims that James never revealed *how* to do this[1] and then proceeds to solve the problem by means of partial reinforcement schedules. However, in so doing he appears to attribute to students an equally devouring drive for reinforcement by the teacher that is capable of maintaining educationally relevant behavior over long periods of no reinforcement. Where did this drive come from?

The other differentiating factor is the causal relationship between response and reinforcement. At best, an animal sees only a means-ends-relationship between his response and the possibility of reward. The most direct human analogy is to games of chance where indeed, as Skinner often has noted, great resistance to extinction does occur. However, in meaningful human learning, the acquisition of verbal or motor skills and the subsequent rewards are not related capriciously, and is *not* a guessing game. To the contrary, the student gets continuous intrinsic feedback as to the efficacy of his performance. It is true that at very early stages in learning the student may not have an intrinsic basis for the evaluation of his own work, but this comes with many reinforced trials. Certainly in motor skills there is an abundant opportunity for feedback, *i.e.*, the ball goes in the basket. It is precisely through the nonarbitrary cause-and-effect relationship between response and consequence that the child learns about the regularities and systematic nature of the world around him as well as the world of schol learning. Why then should one advocate that human skills ought to be taught by means of partial schedules of reinforcement?

In a guessing situation the individual does not control the events; where the roulette wheel stops or when the radar scope blurps has nothing to do with his efforts. Under intermittent schedules, the individual is rewarded for responding in the face of failure and frustration. He even believes that his chances of success increase after failure. The gambler's fallacy is a psychological truth; with experimenter-determined ratio schedules it is also a statistical truth (except during extinction). In meaningful learning, success depends for the most part on the learner's skill. Particularly with overt expression, the learner knows that he knows or does not know. Even external reinforcement is not haphazard—success usually does not depend on luck or magic. This writer finds the notion of partial schedules inapplicable to non-chance human performance.

It is fortunate that Skinner does not practice what he preaches. His well-earned influence and stature result from the continuous reinforcement to his students that is provided by his writing, teaching and filmed appearances. The "small minority" (Bijou, 1970) of educational psychologsts who identify completely with his views might well increase if greater emphasis were given to preceeding stimuli in education and if less emphasis were placed on an animal model of learning. Then William James' chair would be filled in the same admirable spirit as it now is with regard to overt expression and consequential feedback.

---

[1] In the writer's opinion, James did suggest the way to arouse curiosity, particularly in the *Talks* on Interest and Attention, chapters 10 and 11.

REFERENCES

BARZUN, J. Review of J. S. Bruner's Essays for the Left Hand. *Science,* 1963, *25,* 323.

BIJOU, S. W. What psychology has to offer education now. *Journal of Applied Behavior Analysis,* 1970, *3,* 65-71.

BUGELSKI, B. R. *The psychology of learning applied to teaching.* New York: Bobbs-Merrill, 1971.

GATES, A. I. Education class: talks to teachers, *NEA Journal,* 1967, *56,* 34-35.

JAMES, W. *Talks to teachers on psychology.* New York: Henry Holt, 1899. (Republished: New York: Dover, 1962).

PACKARD, R. G. The control of "classroom attention:" a group contingency for complex behavior. *Journal of Applied Behavior Analysis,* 1970, *3,* 13-28.

SKINNER, B. F. *The technology of teaching.* New York: Appleton-Century-Crofts, 1968.

MEASURING YOUNG MINDS

The venerable Swiss savant Jean Piaget

keeps learning more about the way human beings acquire

knowledge. How? By talking to children

By DAVID ELKIND

He is still, at seventy-four, a familiar sight in the streets of Geneva, pedaling by on his bicycle or trudging along—tall, stoop-shouldered, and somewhat portly—as he mulls over some new problem arising out of his most recent investigations into the mystery of how knowledge develops in the young human being. A pipe juts from between his teeth, and a mass of fine white hair billows out around his blue beret. Indoors and close up, the beret is gone, but the pipe remains, the meerschaum lining of its bowl burned a deep amber; as he puffs on it, a forefinger locked around the stem, the eyes behind the horn-rimmed glasses narrow with interest when a question is being put to him. He answers—in French—in clear and unambiguous language, perhaps interjecting a mild joke; and although his manner is one of Old World charm (unless he feels his precious time is being imposed on to no good purpose, when he can turn direct and abrupt), he also seems to emanate an aura of intellectual presence not unlike the aura of dramatic presence emanated by a great actor.

Does this sound like the description of a revolutionary? Hardly: the famous Swiss psychologist Jean Piaget appears, in person, more like a benign if startlingly percipient paterfamilias; and indeed, he is the father of three grown children. (More significantly, he possesses a remarkable degree of empathy for children and ability to communicate with them—qualities that have helped him very considerably in his work.) Yet the findings he has gleaned, and the theory he has constructed after more than forty years of studying the development of intelligence, are effecting a veritable Copernican revolution in our understanding of the growth and functioning of the human mind.

Jean Piaget showed his scientific promise early: at ten, he observed a rare part-albino sparrow and wrote a note about it, which he submitted to a scientific journal. The journal published the note—the first of the vast

number of articles and more than thirty books Piaget has authored and seen into print. Soon after, he became an apprentice of the curator of the museum in his native town of Neuchâtel. The curator, a biologist, had a fine collection of mollusks, Piaget began to observe mollusks on his own and again published his findings in Swiss scientific journals. By the time he was sixteen he had quite a respectable bibliography; indeed, so respectable that he was offered, sight unseen, the post of curator of the mollusk collection at the museum in Geneva—an offer he had to turn down because he was still in high school.

Although biology was Piaget's first love, and the discipline in which he received his doctorate with a thesis on mollusks, he did not find it entirely satisfying. For one thing, he was interested in philosophical questions regarding the problem of "how we know," and his work in biology was not a sufficiently direct route to solving that problem. Then, too, he realized that he lacked the dexterity—and perhaps the stomach—for such activities as dissection.

After receiving his doctorate, Piaget tried out a number of occupations that he hoped might prove better suited to his talents and interests. He flirted with psychoanalysis and spent six months at the Burghölzli Psychiatric Clinic in Zurich (where Jung once worked). While Piaget was intrigued by Freudian theory (he presented a paper on dreams at a conference that Freud attended), clinical practice had little appeal for him. After this he went to Paris, where he worked at the school in which Alfred Binet had originated the intelligence test. It was while testing children in Binet's laboratory school that Piaget discovered—or invented—his own scientific discipline.

Piaget found that in administering mental tests to children he could not only combine his biological and philosophical interests but could perform experiments that required little in the way of dexterity. The child is, first of

all, a growing organism to whom all the principles of biological development apply. He is a thinking organism, who comes to know, in one way or another, about the social and physical reality within which he functions. By testing the child's understanding of the physical, biological, and social worlds at successive age levels, Piaget hoped to find an answer to the question of how we acquire knowledge. In effect Piaget had created an experimental philosophy that sought to answer philosophical questions by putting them to empirical test. He called this new discipline genetic epistemology.

To put Piaget's enterprise in perspective we must know something about the scientific *Zeitgeist,* or spirit of the times. In the twenties and early thirties social science in America and England had become rigidly environmentalist: in contrast to the theories of hereditary taint that still predominated in European discussions of mental retardation and criminal behavior, the environmentalists stressed the brutal conditions under which criminals and familial retardates were reared.

In America the emphasis on environmental factors was reflected in an almost total preoccupation with learning, which psychologists defined as the modification of behavior due to experience. Psychology textbooks spent pages laying to rest the ghost of so-called instincts, the innate behavior patterns. While animals had instincts, the student was taught, man for the most part did not: even maturation, conceived as the unfolding of genetically determined (in part, at least) behavior patterns, was regarded as unscientific. Not surprisingly, maturationists such as Arnold Gesell, whose careful observations were a model of good descriptive psychology, fell into scientific disrepute.

In sharp contrast to the environmentalism of American social science was the nativism of European psychology. This nativism, a belief in the hereditary determination of personal and social traits, was later subverted into the racist doctrines of Nazism. From Europe had come Gestalt psychology, which suggested that experience never came to us "in the raw" but always in an organized fashion; that, for example, notes played in sequence are heard as a melody and not just as a sequence of notes. Such organizations were, according to Gestalt psychologists, determined by innate organizers or mental structures. When many Gestalt psychologists immigrated to America to escape Hitler, they ran head on into environmentalism. And the winds of the nature-nurture controversy blew hot and strong.

Piaget declined to take sides; he saw himself as "the man in the middle," the man who viewed nature and nurture as always relative to each other. His early experiments with mollusks had suggested that the influences of environment and heredity were reciprocal, with neither absolute, and his first observations of children convinced him that this relativism of nature and nurture extended to the development of human intelligence as well. He discovered that children harbored notions concerning nature and the physical world that they had neither inherited nor learned in the classic sense. He found, for example, that young children believed the moon followed them when they went for a walk at night, that dreams came in through the window while they were asleep, and that anything that moved, including waves and wind-blown curtains, was alive.

Where did such ideas come from? They were not inborn; because something that is inborn does not change and most children give up these ideas as they grow older. Likewise, the ideas could not have been learned from adults, because adults do not think in this way and would hardly teach such things to children. And since children everywhere, from completely different backgrounds, harbor such ideas, the ideas could not have been learned.

Piaget's answer to this puzzle was that the child's ideas about the world were "constructions" that involved both mental structures and experience. Like the Gestalt psychologists, Piaget argued that experience does not come to us raw but is organized by our intelligence. His advance over Gestalt psychology was his argument that the organizing structures are not fixed at birth but develop in a regular sequence of stages related to age. While the changes with age imply the role of experience, their orderliness reflects an interaction between nature and nurture. Piaget set out to discover the principles that govern this interaction.

One of the developmental principles revealed by Piaget's work is that mental growth occurs by integration and substitution and not solely by the addition of new facts. The child of three or four already has an elementary concept of quantity: confronted with two identical glasses of orangeade filled to the same level, he would say that both had the "same to drink." But if the orangeade from one glass were poured into a tall, narrow beaker while he looked on, the child would say, Piaget found, that the tall glass had "more to drink" than the shorter one. Not until about six or seven do most children understand that changing the shape of a quantity does not change its amount. The young child has a concept of quantity, but it is clearly a different concept from the one held by older children and adults: he thinks the amount of liquid can be gauged by its level without taking its width into account. Older children and adults, however, assess liquid quantities by taking both height and width into consideration.

This is mental growth by integration, wherein a new, higher-level idea (amount is determined by height and width) is formed by the integration of two lower-level ideas (amount is determined by height *or* width). It suggests that mental growth is an expanding upward spiral in which the same problems are attacked at successive age levels but are resolved more completely and more successfully at each higher level. Something similar occurs in science generally. The ancient Greeks talked about "atoms," but their concept of atoms was quite different from that held by modern physicists; even so, some of their ideas about atoms coincide, or are integrated, with our own. Growth by integration means the progression from a primitive to a more mature, differentiated, and elaborate concept.

The principle growth by integration is particularly important in its application to education. By and large, our educational system is concerned with growth by the accretion of facts. Now, certain facts—the capital of Greece, the number of days in a week, and the meaning of the abbreviation C.O.D.—are either right or wrong: the capital of Greece is Athens, and no other answer is correct. But a child who thinks that quantity is gauged by one dimension alone does not have a "wrong" idea; he simply has a *different* one from ours. Piaget's work indicates that we must expand our view of knowledge to include not only facts that are correct but also concepts that may be the same as or different from ours without being either right or wrong.

Mental growth also occurs by substitution. In areas such as moral judgment and ideas about nature, the primitive ideas held by young children are simply replaced by more mature ideas as the children grow older. Piaget found, for example, that young children judge a person according to the amount of damage he does rather than on the basis of his intentions. He told children two stories: in the first a child helping his mother to set the table trips and breaks twelve cups, and in the second a child who has been forbidden to climb up to a cupboard for jam does so and breaks one cup. Young children feel that the first child needs punishing the most since he broke twelve cups, while older children tend to find the second child more worthy of punishment because he intentionally disobeyed his mother.

Piaget obtained similar results when he queried children about lying. Again, children of different age groups were presented with two stories. In one story a boy told his mother he had seen a pink elephant dancing in the street to the tune of an organ played by a monkey. In the other a boy reported that he had received a grade of one hundred on an arithmetic test when in fact he had received only a sixty-five. Young children said the child who told the elephant story was more to be blamed because his lie was "bigger." Older children said that the boy who told the story about the elephant had meant to amuse his mother and was therefore less culpable than the one who said he had received a perfect grade in order consciously to deceive his mother.

In these studies and in many others like them, Piaget found that young children have an "objective morality," based on the amount of damage done, whereas older children have a "subjective morality," based on the subject's intentions. This developmental progression from objective to subjective morality is, however, only relative, and we adults often slip into an objective morality—particularly when we are dealing with children. A child, for example, who deliberately smashes an old record of no special interest is likely to receive a milder verbal blast than one who accidentally breaks his father's favorite record. In such cases we revert to judging the "badness" of an action in terms of material damage done rather than in terms of intention. In mental growth by substitution, therefore, there is always the possibility of a reversion to an earlier level of mental functioning.

Piaget's initial findings regarding the evolution of mental growth and the principles of integration and substitution were not well received. His method of talking to children about a particular topic was widely criticized, his results were questioned, and his interpretations were ridiculed and dismissed. In America as recently as ten years ago Piaget was seen as a quaint old man who sat around on the shores of Swiss lakes talking to children about nature and the physical world.

In spite of the unfavorable reaction, Piaget persevered, extending his investigations to the study of infants—particularly his own three children—and adolescents. In this work, carried out during the 1930's and 1940's, he concerned himself mainly with the phenomena of "conservation," which in Piaget's vocabulary refers to the child's awareness that a quantity remains the same—that is, the quantity is "conserved"—despite a change in its appearance. In the example of the orangeade being poured from one size container into another, a child who recognizes that the quantity stays the same is said to "have" conservation.

What Piaget discovered during this second phase of his work was the widespread absence of quantity conservation in young children. Before the age of five or six, for example, most children believe that six pennies in a pile are fewer than six in a row, and that if one of two identical clay balls is rolled into a sausage, it increases in mass, weight, and volume. By seven or eight, however, children recognize that a change in appearance does not mean a change in amount. Piaget argued that the child's discovery of conservation in the realm of quantity was the reflection of new mental structures and new modes of organizing experience.

During this period a second principle of mental growth became evident; namely, that the emergence of new mental structures for organizing experience is accompanied by an increased ability to distinguish between appearance and reality, between how things look and how they really are. Once again, this principle of mental growth parallels what has occurred in history. Early man believed that the sun circled the earth and that the earth was flat. Such ideas come from an uncritical acceptance of information received through the senses: the sun does appear to move around the earth, and the land about us does appear flat.

We overcome the deceptive appearances of things with the aid of reason. It is the appearance of reasoning in the child that enables him to discover the conservation of quantity, number, and length. To demonstrate that reasoning is, in fact, involved, consider the following situation. Suppose an adult is presented with a clay ball and a clay sausage and asked whether they are the same weight. Without actually weighing the two objects he would have no way of knowing, but if he knew that the clay sausage had previously been a ball, and that as a ball it had been equal in weight to the other clay ball, the weight equality of ball and sausage could easily be deduced.

It is with the emergence of elementary reasoning structures, at about six or seven, that the child begins to distinguish between how things look and how they really are. But at this age his ability is limited to material things—the conservation of the length of sticks, the number of elements in a group, or the amount of liquid poured from one container into another. There remains another level at which the distinction between appearance and reality is still closed to the child; that is, the symbolic level—the level of metaphor, illusion, and double-entendre.

Piaget found that it is only during adolescence that human beings become capable of making such distinctions. For example, children cannot grasp the satirical significance of political cartoons or the metaphorical significance of proverbs; only during adolescence, when still more new mental structures and mental organizations appear, do young people begin to appreciate the double meanings, the social significance, of books like *Gulliver's Travels* and *Alice in Wonderland*. Adolescents can also use irony and metaphor to belittle their enemies; they become skilled in making the apparently innocent yet cutting remark.

Thus Piaget's findings demonstrated two levels of distinction between appearance and reality: the concrete level, at which reason enables the child to discover that quantities do not change despite a change in appearance, and the symbolic level, at which adolescents discover the multifaceted meanings implicit in words and learn that the apparent meaning of words may mask their real meaning and intent. Although much of this research was done in the thirties and forties, it did not become widely known until the late 1950's, when the *Zeitgeist* once again affected the reception of Piaget's work.

Even before sputnik, critics of education in America had begun to demand that educators abandon the goal of achieving the "personal adjustment of the whole child" and devote themselves to teaching children "how to think." This new emphasis led to a search for new curricula and curricular materials. When curriculum builders turned to psychology for information about how the mind grows and how children think, they found that the psychologists had little to offer. In their zeal to keep psychology a strictly experimental science, psychological researchers had performed most of their work on learning with lower organisms, and the results were hardly applicable to the kind of learning that children in school were engaged in.

It was through the efforts of men like Jerome Bruner at Harvard, and the late David Rapaport at the Austen Riggs Center in Stockbridge, Massachusetts, that Piaget's work first came to the attention of curriculum builders. In Piaget's books educators read about the child's view of space, time, and numbers, about children's reasoning processes and their ability to classify and relate things. The curriculum planners discovered that Piaget had been studying how *children* learn, and that he had come to define learning in a new way, a way they tried to incorporate (not always successfully) into their new curricula.

Traditional psychology had always defined learning as "the modification of behavior as the result of experience."

Such a definition makes the learner a more-or-less passive recipient of environmental happenings. While this may be true of rats, it is certainly not true of children. Piaget turned the definition around and spoke of learning as, in part, "the modification of experience as the result of behavior." He argued that the child's actions upon the world changed the nature of his experience. This is another way of stating the relativity of nature and nurture. If experience is always a product (to some extent) of the child's behavior, any modification of behavior as a result of experience must be relative to the child's actions. Human experience, then, must be relative to human action.

This theory has been one of the most difficult for American educators and psychologists to accept, even those who are sympathetic to Piaget's views. It has been difficult to accept because of a lack of familiarity with Piaget's third principle of mental growth. Our tradition has been one of empiricism, which assumes a complete separation of mind and reality. Implicit in empiricism is a kind of "copy" theory of learning that says that our minds simply copy what exists in the outside world, much as a photograph copies the light patterns conveyed to the exposed film. Piaget argues that the mind never copies reality but instead organizes it and transforms it, reality, in and of itself, being—as Kant made clear—unknowable.

Everyone has had the experience of looking at the clouds drifting by and seeing in them castles, horses, airplanes, and the like. Since different people see different things in the same cloud pattern, it is apparent that what is being seen is a product of the individual's own organizing processes. This is the principle upon which the Rorschach inkblot test is based: inkblots provide an ambiguous configuration, which allows individuals to reveal the organizing patterns of their minds.

Now, a characteristic of all such organizing activities is that the person is unaware of his own part in con-

structing what he sees; this is Piaget's third principle of mental growth. Many a patient confronting an inkblot has accused the examiner of showing him "dirty pictures." What Piaget has shown is that our role in organizing experience is much larger than we realize, and is a major cause of misunderstanding between adults and children. When an adult watches a quantity of liquid being poured from a short, wide container into a tall, narrow one, his organizing and deductive processes are so rapid that he literally *sees* that the quantity in the taller container is the same as it was before. The equality seems to be a property of the liquid, like its fluidity or its wetness, and to have nothing to do with his own mental processes. Yet the difficulty this problem presents to the young child shows that this awareness arises from the reasoning ability of the subject, and not from perceptible attributes of the object.

The adult actually sees the world around him in a very different way than a child who does not have conservation, but the adult is not aware of this. It is because we adults take for granted that children see the world as we do that we are often upset and angered by their behavior, and it is also the reason children often find adults unpredictable and incomprehensible. The same holds true in education, and teachers often make erroneous assumptions about how children view the world.

Piaget's fourth principle of mental growth, which is just coming to be appreciated in America, concerns motivation. On the basis of their work in animal learning, in which external rewards are required to train an animal in certain behaviors, psychologists assumed that the same held true for all learning. One of the main reasons grades are used in school, for example, is that they provide children with rewards for achievement. Children, particularly middle-class children, work hard to get good grades.

Not all learning has to be rewarded from without, however, and the structures Piaget describes lead to a kind of spontaneous learning that does not require any special rewards. If, on a certain day, one asks an adult what he has done since breakfast that morning, he will be able to give a fairly good account of his activities: though he does not set out to "remember" his activities as he might, say, a poem, and though no rewards are provided for remembering what has occurred, learning has obviously been going on. It is, however, a different kind of learning than memorizing a poem or the date of a historical incident.

Three aspects of this kind of learning should be noted. First, it involves the organization of material into a spatial or temporal or causal sequence. Second, the person is not conscious of the fact that he is processing or organizing the material. Third, and most important, such learning always involves the subject's own activity. These features of what might be called "structural learning" are present not only when we recalled how we spent the morning but also in the child's attainment of the conservation of quantity and number and in his understanding of classes and logical relations. In each case the learning involves some logical ordering of information, is unconscious as far as the learner is concerned, and involves the learner's own activities, including mental activities such as reasoning.

Accordingly, it is not really appropriate to ask "why" a child attains conservation in the same way that we might ask "why" he knocked his brother down. The latter question presupposes conscious intention and demands an "answer" in dynamic terms: the reply could be "his brother hit him," or "his brother took his toy," or something to that effect. It is an entirely different matter to ask why a child has *not* attained conservation. The question is analogous to asking "why doesn't a fish walk?" In both cases an intentional answer is inappropriate. To say that the child does not attain conservation because he is too lazy or too busy with other things is like saying that a fish doesn't walk because it prefers to swim. For both questions the appropriate answer is one of structure and function.

To explain why a fish swims you must describe the natural history of the fish, the structure and shape of its body and gills, and the functioning of its breathing apparatus. Likewise, to explain why a child attains conservation, his mental structures and their functions must be described. If a fish cannot walk, it is because it lacks the necessary physical structures, and if a child has not attained conservation, then, other things being equal, he must lack the necessary mental structures. Conservation is thus as natural a function of elementary reasoning abilities as swimming is a natural function of the fish's organs and body conformation.

It is because Piaget stresses this sort of "motivation" that he has spent a good part of his career in formulating in more specific terms the mental structures that characterize the development of intelligence from infancy through adolescence. Piaget has described four stages of mental growth, which he summarizes in terms of the major cognitive task each seems designed to accomplish. During the first two years of life (the sensory-motor period) the mental structures are mainly concerned with the mastery of concrete objects. The second stage, from about two to six or seven (the preoperational period), concerns the mastery of symbols, including those that occur in language, fantasy, play, and dreams. During the third stage, from about six or seven to about twelve (the concrete operational period), children learn the mastery of classes, relations, and numbers and how to reason about them. Finally, from about twelve to fifteen (the formal operational period), young people are concerned with the mastery of thought and can think about their own and other people's thinking.

These stages of mental growth, and the principles manifested in their development, are gradually impressing themselves on American psychology and education but not always in undistorted form. Now that Piaget's name has become well known, it is often invoked in support of many viewpoints and practices that are in opposition to the real direction of Piaget's work. Piaget, for example, is cited as an authority by those who advocate formal preschool instruction for young children *and* by those who argue for the value of play and informal methods of education for young children. Piaget is both criticized for views he does not hold and praised for positions he has never taken.

In 1969 the American Psychological Association presented Piaget with an award for his distinguished contribution to psychology. Despite this formal recognition, Piaget retains the ambiguous position of the intellectual innovator. It will probably be decades before his ideas become firmly rooted within the canons of psychology, and then Piaget, like Freud, will be dismissed because the valuable part of his work will have become part of the established modes of psychological thought. Piaget knows this, but he has always had the indifference to fame, the independence of mind, the steadfastness of purpose, and the dedication to truth that mark the true intellectual innovator. And though Piaget has not always been treated generously by his colleagues, he retains his sense of humor, his pleasure in work, his wonder at the world, and his delight in people. Not the least of Piaget's contributions is the example he provides to his students and, indeed, to all young people, of a life well lived in the service of science and mankind.

David Elkind spent a year at Jean Piaget's Institute for Educational Science in Geneva before he joined the faculty of the University of Rochester, New York, in 1966, as a professor of psychology.

Don't use the kitchen-sink approach to enrich-ment

☐ **Some time ago, we in the Berkeley laboratories** decided to test the validity of the following hypothesis: If the laying down of memories involves the synthesis of chemical products in the brain, then an animal whose life had been replete with opportunities for learning and memorizing would end up with a brain chemically and morphologically different from that of an animal who had lived out an intellectually impoverished life. For almost two decades now, Drs. E. L. Bennett, Marion Diamond, M. R. Rosenzweig, and I, together with technical assistants and graduate students, have experimented with thousands of rats to find such evidence. Let me tell you some of what we found.

We divided our experimental rats into two groups at weaning time. We placed half of the sibs in an "intellectually enriched" environment; the other half, in a deprived environment. Although both groups received an identical diet, their psychological environments differed greatly. The animals in the first group lived together in one large cage, had many rat "toys" (tunnels to explore, ladders to climb, levers to press), and were cared for by graduate students who gave them loving attention and kindness, taught them to run mazes, and in general provided them with the best and most expensive supervised higher education available to any young rat at the University of California.

While these rats were thus being encouraged to store up many and varied memories, their brother rats in the deprived group lived in isolated, barren cages, devoid of stimulation by either their environmental appurtenances, fellow rats, or graduate students. After about 80 days of this differential treatment, we sacrificed all the animals, dissected their brains, and performed various chemical and histological analyses. The results are convincing. The brain of a rat from the enriched environment (and presumably, therefore, with many more stored memories) has a heavier and thicker cortex, a better blood supply, larger brain cells, more glia cells, and increased activity of two brain enzymes—acetylcholinesterase and cholinesterase—than does the brain from an animal whose life has been less memorable.

We can draw several conclusions from these experiments. First, the growing animal's psychological environment is of crucial importance for the development of its brain. By manipulating the environment of the young, one can truly create a "lame brain"—with lighter cortex, shrunken brain cells, fewer glia cells, smaller blood vessels, and lower enzymatic activity levels—or one can create a more robust, a healthier, a more metabolically active brain. If what is true for the rat brain should turn out to be also true for the human brain—if by careful manipulation of this or that group's early environment we can develop among them bigger and better brains or smaller and meaner ones—then the wondrous promises of a glorious future or the monstrous horrors of a Huxleian *Brave New World* are fairly self-evident.

The second conclusion I draw from our experiments is this: Since the effect of any chemical upon an organ is, in part, a function of the beginning chemical status of that organ, and since—as we have just seen—the chemical and anatomical status of the individual's brain is determined by his educational experience, then the effectiveness of the biochemist's "get smart pill," predicted for the future, will depend upon how the educator has prepared the brain in the first instance. Indeed, a review of all the data indicates that manipulating the educational and psychological environment is a more effective way of inducing long-lasting brain changes than is direct administration of drugs.

We have learned several more lessons from subsequent experimentation. When we first tried to create a psychologically enriched environment for our Berkeley rats, we did not really know what we were up to, so we threw everything into the environment including, almost, the kitchen sink. We kept the cages in brightly lighted, sound-filled rooms; we gave the rats playmates to relate to, games to manipulate, maze problems to solve, new areas to explore. We fondled them and tamed them and chucked them under the chin. In other words, we provided our happy rats with almost every kind of stimulation we could think of—or afford. And it seems to have worked. But, of course, we were aware that, quite possibly, many of the things we did were not at all necessary; indeed, that some may have had an adverse effect. And so we undertook a series of experiments to discover which elements of our environment were effective and which were not. Let me skip the details of our many experiments, past and present, and list some of the tentative conclusions that we have already been able to draw from them.

First: Sheer exercise or physical activity alone is not at all effective in developing the brain. A physical training director seems not to be an adequate substitute for a teacher.

Second: Varied visual stimulation or, indeed, any kind of visual stimulation is neither necessary nor sufficient to develop the brain, as we were able to demonstrate by using some blind rats.

Third: Handling, or taming, or petting are also without effect in developing the growing rat's brain. Love is not enough.

Fourth: The presence of a brother rat in the cage of our intellectually deprived rat helps him not a whit. *Bruderschaft* is not enough.

Fifth: Teaching the rat to press levers for food—that and only that—seems to help somewhat, but only minimally.

The only experience we have thus far found really effective is freedom to roam around in a large object-filled space. Experiments in Dr. Diamond's laboratory suggest that if you give the young rat continuous and varied maze problems to solve—that and little else—he will develop a number of the same brain changes (at least the morphological ones) we observed in rats from our randomly "enriched" environment.

Clearly, then, not *every* experience or variation in stimulation contributes equally to the development of the brain. But of even greater interest is the suggestion in the above data that the most effective way to develop the brain is through what I will call *species-specific enrichment experiences*. Here is what I mean: The ability of a rat to learn its way through tunnels and dark passages—to localize points in a three dimensional space full of objects to be climbed upon, burrowed under, and crawled through—is, we can assume, of particular survival value for the rat as he is now constituted.

Presumably, through the selective evolutionary process, the rat has developed a brain peculiarly fitted to support and enhance the above skills. The effective rat brain, therefore, is one that is a good "space brain"—not a lever-pressing brain or an arithmetic-reasoning brain. The effective stimulating environment, correspondingly, would be one that makes spatial learning demands on that brain—which "pushes" that particular kind of brain in that particular way. To generalize *this* hypothesis, I would suggest that *for each species there exists a set of species-specific experiences that are maximally enriching and maximally efficient in developing its brain.*

If there be any validity to the above hypothesis, then the challenge to the human educator is clear, for the educator also has been using the kitchen-sink approach when he seeks to design a psychologically or educationally enriched environment for the child.

Some educators advocate bombarding the child, practically from infancy on, with every kind of stimulus change imaginable. They would advocate festooning his crib with jumping beads and dangling colored bits and pieces of wood (all sold at a high price to his affluent parents); giving him squishy, squeaking, squawking toys to play with, to fondle, to be frightened by, to choke on. They would have him jounced and bounced and picked up and put down. And when he goes to school, they confront him with the same blooming, buzzing confusion. He is stimulated with play activities, with opportunities for social interaction, with rhythmic movements, with music, with visual displays, with contact sports, with tactual experiences, and with anything and everything the school system can think of—or afford.

But maybe a "stimulating environment" and an "enriched environment" are not one and the same thing. It is not true that a brain is a brain is a brain. The rat is a rat and he hath a rat's brain; the child is a child and he hath a child's brain. And each, according to my hypothesis, requires its own educational nutrient. What, then, are the species-specific enrichments for the human child?

Of course, I do not know the answer to this question, but let me share with you my present enthusiastic guess that in the language arts you will find part of the answer.

I can start with no better text than a quotation from my teacher—Edward Chace Tolman, who was a completely devoted rat psychologist. "Speech," he wrote, ". . . is in any really developed and characteristic sense, the sole prerogative of the human being. . . . It is speech which first and foremost distinguishes man from the great apes." In my opinion, it is in the study of language, above anything else, that the psychologist will discover the psychology of man, and that the educator will discover how to educate man.

In the first place, in my opinion, human language, with its complex and abstract structure, has *nothing* in common with animal communication. Language is probably the clearest instance of a pure species-specific behavior. This is true whether you study language as a neurologist or as a psychologist. Let us look at some brain research first.

In 1967, Robinson, at the National Institute of Mental Health, attempted to discover which areas of the monkey's brain controlled its vocalizations. Now the monkey most certainly uses vocalization for communication, but principally for communication with emotional overtones, such as threat, fear, pain, and pleasure. Using 15 animals, Robinson stimulated 5,880 different loci or spots in the brain by electrodes to see whether such stimulation could bring forth vocalization. He explored loci that included neocortical areas as well as areas in the limbic system—that older part of the mammalian brain which is most intimately involved with motivational and emotional responses.

Robinson's results were clear-cut: First, despite exploration of several hundred different neocortical sites he was unable to raise a single sound from his animals by stimulating their *neocortex;* second, stimulation of the limbic system brought forth regular, consistent, and identifiable vocalizations.

These results differ sharply from those found with the human brain. While there is some evidence that human cries and exclamations uttered in moments of excitement are also controlled by the limbic system, *speech and language clearly depend upon neocortical areas*—areas for which there simply are no analogues in the brain of any other animal. These areas are, of course, the well-known Broca and Wernicke areas in the left hemisphere of the human brain. It seems clear, as Robinson says, that "human speech did not develop 'out of' primate vocalization, but arose from *new tissue* (italics my own) which permitted it the necessary detachment from immediate, emotional situations." Man's brain, and his alone, is a language-supporting brain.

Corresponding to the neurological picture is the psycholinguist's view of language. Almost every psycholinguist is impressed not only with the unique nature of language itself, but with its unique mode of achievement by the child. Whatever value so-called reinforcement or stimulus-response theories of learning may have for describing acquisition of motor skills by people, maze learning by rats, and bar pressing by pigeons, these theories are assessed as completely trivial and utterly irrelevant when it comes to understanding what McNeill refers to as that "stunning intellectual achievement"—the acquisition of language by the child.

Indeed, in reading the psycholinguists' work, one is left with the impression that we will have to develop a species-specific learning theory for this species-specific behavior of language. I must confess that I agree with them. And if we ever achieve an understanding of language development, and if we learn how to push the *human* brain with this *human* experience, then we will indeed be on our way.

Now I know that other people have proposed other ways with which to enrich the child's education. Some plug for what are referred to as "cognitive" experiences or "productive thinking" experiences. Let me hasten to record that I quite agree with them. As a matter of fact, I am not at all certain that I am saying anything other than what my cognitive friends propose. For I hold with McNeill's judgment that ". . . the study of how language is acquired may provide insight into the very basis of mental life." And, I would go on, being human *means* having an effective mental, cognitive life.

For these and many, many other reasons I would urge the educator to turn to the psycholinguist—as well as to Piaget and Crutchfield and Bruner—for his major guides in designing a rational educational enrichment program.

Now, whether my guess merits this enthusiasm or not will perhaps eventually be determined by research. But here is the challenge and here is the promise for the educator: Drop your kitchen-sink approach, and specify and define for us the species-specific, psychologically enriching experiences for the child—and we will be off and running! □

How Children Learn: A Developmental Approach

Raymond E. Keel

G. Thomas Rowland

The question of how children (or people of any age) learn has long concerned teachers and other professionals. Any teacher who has been frustrated by the problems of a "slow learner" or a "problem child" has asked this question and searched back over his professional preparation for an answer, usually with little or no success.

Scientists in education, psychology, biology, sociology, and anthropology have advanced many theories, philosophies, hypotheses, and just plain guesses about the nature of the fascinating and critical human function called "learning." In the barrage of conflicting ideas, the classroom teacher may question the value of science and research. For while the battles over theory rage on, the teacher continues to face the same problems on Monday that she faced on Friday without, it seems, any more cogent answers.

Yet, with the advent of the developmental approach to human learning, many of the earlier difficulties associated with education—such as evaluation, objectives, goals, and strategies—have taken on a semblance of clarity. Simply stated, the developmental approach restricts education and research to behaviors that are observable. Such an approach will be familiar to the teacher who has read of or used objectives stated in behavioral terms. Developmentalism eliminates obscure or indefinite terms, such as "understanding," "appreciating," and even "knowing," and replaces them with precise terms, such as "listing," "sorting," and "stating" (1). The latter terms describe actions the teacher can readily observe and evaluate.

What is education? Education is the guided changing of behavior. After a learning encounter, the pupil should do something differently than he did it before—something that the teacher wanted him to do. First, it is necessary to determine what the pupil is doing (or not doing) that needs transformation. Then, an educational intervention must be developed and attempted. Finally, it is necessary to determine whether the behavior has changed. If a pupil is unable to divide correctly, as evidenced by mistakes on a written exercise, the teacher initiates a program to overcome the pupil's deficiency and then checks the effectiveness of the program by retesting, using the same or comparable problems. The teacher is not concerned with whether the pupil understands division, but rather with whether the pupil can perform in a way that is developmentally different from his earlier performance.

This approach to teaching is much like the evaluation procedure used in educational research. The research scientist selects at random a number of subjects for his study. The subjects are divided into two groups that are similar in developmental level, age distribution, experiential background, and other characteristics.

The first group, called the "experimental group," undergoes some type of experimental teaching situation, known as an "intervention." The second, or control, group does not experience the intervention, but is given the same pre- and posttest as the experimental group. Test gains (or losses) for the control group reflect the impact of environmental events not related to the intervention. By comparing changes in the scores of the two groups, the researcher can evaluate the effect of the intervention alone.

A class of thirty children might be selected for a study. Half the class is designated as the experimental group, and the other half the control group. The intervention could be a social studies series, and the chosen topic "Africa." During a week-long experiment many class members might see a television special on the topic, a television special that is not a planned part of the study. Because of the television program, even the control group would conceivably score higher on the posttest than on the pretest. Scores of the experimental group would be affected by the planned intervention and the television special. The researcher can isolate the impact of the intervention by subtracting the gain of the control group from the gain of the experimental group.

The classroom teacher who is concerned with the quality of teaching (that is, with whether children are learning) can use the research approach to evolve more effective curriculums. In a real way the teacher functions as a behavioral scientist.

Why do children learn? One major point of contention has been the nature of human motivation. Why do people learn some things and not others? Some have said that we learn only when we are compelled to do so by some external power.

The learning theory of B. F. Skinner, of Harvard University, relies almost completely on external control of behavior. This school of thought is sometimes known as "behavior modification" or "operant conditioning."

The Skinnerian model holds that behaviors are learned in response to rewards, which are dispensed in a predetermined manner by some controlling agent. The social implications of Skinner's work are clearly brought out in his novel *Walden Two* (2) and his more recent book *Beyond Freedom and Dignity* (3), in which he contends that as far as individuals are concerned, freedom in making decisions is an illusion, as is the concept of human dignity.

Skinner's hypotheses have drawn varied and extreme reactions, but in truth he is describing ancient cultural, social, and individual strategies for controlling the behavior of others. Women control the behavior of men and *vice versa;* companies control the behavior of their employees; governments control their populations; and in the past churches have controlled the value systems and the behavior of their members. There is little to contest in Skinner's observations; and there is not much to challenge in his research, which uses controlled laboratory conditions.

The real question is whether external controls compromise the fundamental nature of the human mind. In contrast, the principles of guided discovery (1, 4) allow for maximum decision-making and minimum error, and lack the rigidity of the Skinnerian model or the behavioral anarchy of Illich (5), Elkind (6), or Zigler (7), who propose that learning may be more a matter of chance than plan and in general urge a romantic renewal of the "noble savage" concepts of Rousseau as expressed in *Emile* (8).

The great scientists of the past and the present share one quality: a need to know, an exhilarating pursuit of the unknown in any subject area. The same need to know may be observed in an infant as he explores a new toy or "discovers" his toes, intently manipulating and studying them until his interest is exhausted. A teacher may seek out and study information about "disadvantaged" children in the same way, not necessarily because he has to, but because he is interested.

This curiosity, this insatiable need to know about the environment in which an individual must survive, has emerged as the fundamental element in human motivation (9). In science, knowledge-seeking is known as "epistemic behavior" (10).

The fairly recent understanding of epistemic behavior as the fundamental motive has led to a slight restatement of Darwin's hypothesis that survival is man's basic motivation. Now we may say that survival is the long-term goal of behavior, and knowledge-seeking is the means to that objective (11, 12).

For the teacher such a simple understanding of curiosity, or epistemic behavior, encourages a sympathetic appreciation of the needs of children as they try to explore their environment. For example, the seemingly interminable questions of children are manifestations of each child's natural desire to understand what he needs to know to survive in the classroom environment.

The individual learner's perception of how to survive in a particular environment is affected by several factors. Certainly the physical environment has some effect. A person in the Philippines, for example, would not perceive clothing and shelter as having the same significance as someone coping with a Canadian winter.

As a social creature, man derives much of his learning from the people he encounters. These people may be parents, peers, or teachers. All of them are teachers, for from every human encounter we learn something that is useful in developing life-styles, attitudes, habits, and methods of operation. However, for purposes of differentiation, "teachers" are understood to be individuals that society selects to transmit learning to the young.

A mother plays a powerful role in developing her child's patterns of behavior, attitudes, and self-concept, simply because she is near the child almost constantly during his first six critically formative years (1). Even in the first months of life the child recognizes voice inflections and touch responses that result from certain behaviors, such as crying, bed-wetting, or laughing, and he begins to control his behaviors accordingly (13).

One problem that faces teachers in the form of so-called deviant classroom behavior seems to stem from very early learning. The self-rejection manifested by many children frequently seems to be the result of parental attitudes toward simple bodily functions, such as defecation. The infant has no reason to consider the need to defecate as "bad," for it is a natural and necessary part of the human digestive process. Yet he may learn that, to the power-figure (mother) in his early environment, it is a repulsive function. Recognizing the mother's reaction, the child can only conclude that he is naturally evil, a medieval concept seldom held today even among theologians.

How do children learn? Learning seems to be accomplished by a process of individual experimentation with the environment (14, 15). The individual does something, checks to see whether the behavior results in a satisfactory effect or response, then, using that feedback, confirms or rejects the behavior. If a child wants to pick up a toy, he reaches out in a particular direction. If the direction is correct, he will grasp the toy; otherwise, he will reach out in a new direction. In this process of trial and error the infant is learning to coordinate eye and hand movements, a crucial process in the development of intelligent behavior (16).

A child in the classroom may decide that he is not receiving an adequate amount of the teacher's attention, a common problem in many of today's crowded classrooms. To solicit attention, the child may try any or all of several behaviors, including conforming to the teacher's demands, crying, talking, fighting, or withdrawing. The behavior that works—the behavior that causes the teacher to notice and respond—will become the pupil's mode of operation for

survival, even if the form of attention is punishment or reprimand.

One seemingly obvious implication is that pupils learn from every behavior the teacher manifests, whether in the classroom, on the playground, in an assembly, or in the lunchroom, simply because the pupil is constantly seeking knowledge and does not recognize the artificial boundaries between the classroom and other areas.

The process of learning can be represented in a simple yet powerful tool known as a "behavioral model." First, a model is proposed that seems to describe a given problem. Then, each new related set of behaviors is checked to see whether the model continues to hold for any given set of circumstances. Thus, models are always in a state of evolution or change, as new circumstances expose problems and changes are made to compensate.

The model that forms the basis for this article is the Dyadic Model developed primarily by Rowland and McGuire (14). This model depicts the strategic dynamics of the individual learning process in a sociocultural context. The individual learner manifests a particular behavior, evaluates the results of that behavior in terms of prevailing goals, and then reinforces or alters plans for future behaviors. He is learning how to behave or act in that particular situation. The goals are determined by the cultural factors (parents, peers, and teachers) and the individual's own perceptions and concept of self.

The model applies in any learning situation. The learner may be a pupil, a teacher, the superintendent, or the school system as a whole. This flexibility makes the model a powerful evaluative tool.

What, then, is the teacher's role? Because the teacher is the dominant power-figure in the classroom, he is responsible, first, for clearly defining the goals of the educational encounter. After the goals have been defined, he must structure the learning environment so that it helps the pupil to reach those goals.

Educational goals should be constantly changing, or evolving, to meet the needs of the developing learner. If the goal of learning to add is achieved, a new goal takes its place—learning to subtract. In this way the teacher serves as the instigator in the early developmental learning sequence, constantly changing the requirements for success as each new level of competence is reached. If the sequence of encounters has been logical, and the "learning" appropriate, the pupil will at some point be adequately prepared to set developmental goals for himself—he will have become autonomous.

What part does genetics play? One of the most critical understandings that arises from the behavioral approach to learning and education is that it is nearly impossible to determine a "maximum potential" or "genetically endowed limitation" for a given individual or group, as Jensen (17) and his associates contend. Each individual has had a unique set of experiences that have retarded or facilitated learning in each of many areas of development. A child from a minority group, for example, may suffer language difficulties as a result of limited home exposure to standard English. It should not be assumed that his difficulties are due to an inability to learn. Similar problems exist among "advantaged" children, who often have limited personal interaction with family members or who have learned value systems not necessarily conducive to educational goals.

For the teacher, who may have little knowledge of a pupil's repertory of experience, there is only one reliable guideline for determining where to begin a developmental program. That guideline is to begin where the pupil is at the time the program is to be initiated. This is the essence of individualized instruction, which is simply offering each pupil educational opportunities appropriate to his level of experience and need.

If the indications of research are correct, we as teachers can assume that, given an appropriate set of learning experiences, all children can learn. The responsibility for providing appropriate circumstances falls to us.

The teacher has direct control of goals and classroom environment. This control, which is nearly absolute from the pupil's viewpoint, carries with it considerable responsibility. To meet this challenge, the educator needs, first, to understand the dynamics of learning. His understanding will be greatly facilitated by a study of the behavior of children, for they are our teachers. What they learn tells us a great deal about ourselves.

References

1. J. L. Frost and G. T. Rowland. *Curricula for the Seventies.* Boston: Houghton Mifflin, 1969.
2. B. F. Skinner. *Walden Two.* New York, New York: Macmillan Company, 1948.
3. B. F. Skinner. *Beyond Freedom and Dignity.* New York, New York: A. A. Knopf, 1971.
4. J. S. Bruner. "The Act of Discovery," *Harvard Educational Review, 31* (Winter, 1961), 21-32.
5. I. Illich. "The Alternative to Schooling," *Saturday Review, 54* (June 19, 1971), 44-48*f.*
6. D. Elkind. "Misunderstandings about How Children Learn," *Today's Education, 61* (March, 1972), 18-20.
7. E. Zigler. "The Environmental Mystique," *Childhood Education, 46* (May, 1970), 402-12.
8. W. Boyd. *The Emile of Jean Jacques Rousseau.* New York, New York: Teachers College Press, 1956.
9. G. T. Rowland and J. L. Frost. "Human Motivation: A Structure Process Interpretation," *Psychology in the Schools, 7* (October, 1970), 375-83.
10. D. E. Berlyne. *Structure and Direction in Thinking.* New York, New York: John Wiley and Sons, 1965.
11. E. G. Patterson and G. T. Rowland. "Developmental Nursing," *Journal of Continuing Education in Nursing, 2* (March-April, 1971), 14-22.
12. G. T. Rowland. "Goals and Their Developmental Significance." Paper prepared for the United Cerebral Palsy Associations, Staff Training Workshop of the Collaborative Infant Project, The University of Texas at Austin, June, 1972.
13. T. G. R. Bower. "The Object in the World of the Infant," *Scientific American, 225* (October, 1971), 30-38.
14. G. T. Rowland and J. C. McGuire. *The Mind of Man.* Englewood Cliffs, New Jersey: Prentice-Hall, Inc., 1971.
15. J. McV. Hunt. *Intelligence and Experience.* New York, New York: Ronald Press, 1961.
16. J. S. Bruner. "Eye, Hand and Mind," *Studies in Cognitive Development: Essays in Honor of Jean Piaget,* pp. 223-35. Edited by D. Elkind and J. H. Flavell. New York, New York: Oxford University Press, 1969.
17. A. R. Jensen. "How Much Can We Boost I.Q. and Scholastic Achievement?" *Harvard Educational Review, 39* (Winter, 1969), 1-123.

II. HUMAN DEVELOPMENT

Although both biologists and psychologists seem to agree on the ultimate uniqueness of each human being, they would also agree that we have large shared commonalities The human organism develops through time. The nature of the common pattern in this development has long been one of the central concerns of psychological inquiry. The developmental method of investigation is characterized by the continuous or extended observation of behavior as a function of time. Developmental psychology seeks both to record the changing characteristics of the child with age and to develop explanations for the observed changes. Illustrative of this tradition is the work of Sir Francis Galton in the later nineteenth century, in describing the variability of human traits, the work of Freud in the early twentieth century, in describing the psycho-sexual basis of human personality development, and the more recent work of Piaget in cognitive development.

Why has development also been of paticular concern to educational psychologists? Why has it been important for us to approach an understanding of the mechanisms which explain the developmental patterns of the human organism? On the simplest level, the answer is that since the individual at any stage is the product of both organic and environmental factors, the teacher must understand the nature and mechanisms of these two bases of behavior in order to diagnose and guide the growth and development of children. The school, after all, wishes to provide a milieu that will encourage a student to respond, learn, and create, and it cannot do so without the knowledge of what makes students what they are. The school, dramatically concerned with the modification of human behavior, must be based on an understanding of the factors that influence human development.

Where, however, does nature end and nurture begin? To what extent can the school and the teacher be proactive and influential in fostering development as opposed to simply providing a context for its natural unfolding? In educational psychology, this question has centered on the concept of readiness. It appears that teachable moments occur in the sequence of development, moments when the child may be optimally ready to learn certain skills. There is, however, disagreement on the way in which educational programs should be structured to allow for this readiness. There are those who hold the "natural" view exemplified in the work of Arnold Gessell. Here, the stress is on maturation. By contrast, there are those working in the tradition of D. O. Hebb, J. McV. Hunt, and Jerome Bruner who take note of the typical developmental trends but advocate that we systematically lead all children through them. These are the advocates of enriched early experience whether it be speeded sense development in infants, the teaching of two-year-olds to read, or the generally more comprehensive programmed curriculum.

These two approaches need not be mutually exclusive, but if we had to choose between them, it is with the more proactive group that we would be associated. We would agree with Maya Pines that the role of the parent is critical in the early development of the child although we would not go so far as to claim that a child's mind is entirely shaped before he or she reaches the age of two. Much remains to be determined by the influences which the society and the school can bring to bear on both the growing child and the older adult. Esther Edwards, Jerome Bruner, and the Cookes are clearly identified in their articles with the proponents of enriched early experience. Professor Edwards may go too far in claiming that kindergarten is too late, but she does find an important basis for pre-school—or early childhood—education in the work of Piaget, Vygotsky, Bloom and Hebb. Jerome Bruner's suggestive paper explores the possibilities of play as an important educative device in the development of problem solving skills. Sharon and Thomas Cooke approach the problem from a more general perspective. They rather convincingly argue that the common assumptions underlying otherwise competing theories of child development provide a common core around which school programming can be built.

The final article in this section brings an important caveat to bear on our enthusiasm for bringing the work in child development to apply importantly to classroom learning. In considering the particular work of Jean Piaget—but the point has, in fact, more general application—Robbie Case points out that the move from psychology to educational practice frequently depends upon an additional set of untested assumptions. It is in this area that the most important future work of educational psychologists lies.

A child's mind is shaped before age 2

MAYA PINES

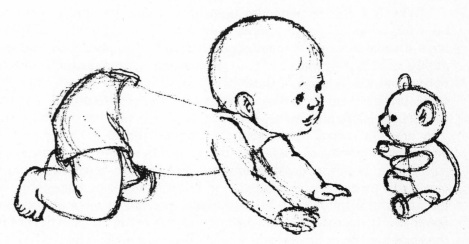

Ask any parent what period in a child's life is most decisive for his intellectual development, and you'll get a variety of answers: the years from 3 to 6, the first grade of school, the prenatal period or, perhaps, the first few weeks after birth. Hardly anyone will come up with the answer now clearly emerging from a major study of young children: the time from 10 months to 1½ years of age, an eight-month period which so far has no name.

In this brief span of life, it appears, the mother's actions do more to determine her child's future competence than at any time before or after. She can turn him into a highly successful human being who—short of catastrophe—stands excellent chances of doing well at whatever he undertakes, or she can produce an intellectual and social failure who might be changed only with difficulty. Yet nobody warns her of the dangers of this period, nor of its promise. Nobody offers her useful guidelines for this time. She makes her daily decisions about the child's routines purely on instinct, without the least inkling of their enormous importance, because until recently even the professionals were unaware of it.

The Harvard Pre-School Project, a gigantic research operation started by psychologist Burton L. White in 1965, never expected to focus on this specific period. When the project began, the nation was just awakening to the fact that children's success or failure in school seemed somehow determined even before they entered the first grade at 6. In a book published in 1964, *Stability & Change in Human Characteristics*, Dr. Benjamin S. Bloom of the University of Chicago pointed out that by 4 as much as 50% of a person's intelligence is set. Before the age of 4, a child's intelligence is highly flexible, Bloom declared, but after that the chances of raising a child's intelligence diminish, and more and more powerful forces are required to produce a given amount of change.

Suddenly, then, parents were saddled with a new burden. In the '50s they had been made to feel guilty if they gave any special attention to their young children's intellectual development—this was supposed to take care of itself, following a built-in timetable, as long as the mother was loving and warm. In the mid-'60s it was

becoming apparent that love was not enough, and that something more was needed to prepare a child to learn well in school. Besides worrying about their child's early emotional and social development, parents were now held responsible for his intellectual growth as well.

But what were they to do? Here, unfortunately, nobody could help them. There was no Spock of the intellect to turn to. Few scientists had given much thought to this problem in preceding decades—they were too busy studying the pros and cons of breast-feeding, early toilet training and other burning issues of the Freudian era. In their concern about "emotional blocks," they had made no attempt to find out what caused either educational handicaps or exceptional competence. A few experimental programs in this general area existed, but a really satisfying solution to the question of how to raise intellectually competent children remained to be found.

The Harvard Pre-School Project set out to find one. But first it had to decide how you recognize "competent" youngsters. "What specifically *is* competence at 6?" asked Dr. White. "If you don't know the answer to that, you can't have any idea of what you're trying to achieve."

White and a dozen other researchers set to work like naturalists observing a strange species. They went to watch children once a week in a variety of kindergartens and Head Start centers, tested a large number of them, discussed them with their teachers, and eventually selected two groups of normal 3-to-6-year-olds for contrast. One, the "A" group, rated exceptionally high on all aspects of competence—not just in readiness for first grade but in dealing with problems in the school yard as well as in the classroom. The other, the "C" group, never seemed quite able to cope. Then, as described in *Major Influences on the Development of Young Children*, a book just finished by White and co-director Jean Carew Watts, they studied the two groups with great care to find out how they differed.

In motor and sensory skills, it turned out, the children were all pretty much alike. The real differences appeared in a set of intellectual and social skills, broken down into 17 specific abilities which the A children had but the others lacked. The most able children always knew how to get the attention of adults for information or help as they needed it, while the more inept generally remained unnoticed, or else disrupted the whole classroom. The A children anticipated consequences. They planned and carried out complicated projects. They understood more complex sentences.

Each of these abilities could be tested in some form at all ages, and before long the researchers were forced to a startling conclusion: the youngest members of their A group, who were barely 3 years old, had exactly the same cluster of abilities as the 6-year-old A's. They also seemed well ahead of the 6-year-old C's in both social and intellectual skills. In other words, the researchers had come too late: whatever produced the differences between the two groups had occurred well before the age of 3.

'A' mothers seldom give a child their undivided attention

At that point, the Pre-School Project abandoned the "older" children, withdrew from such places as kindergartens and nursery schools, and deployed to the homes of toddlers between the ages of one and 3.

The researchers weren't particularly interested in the family's race, income, education or residence—the kind of information which some social scientists think explains everything—but in the experiences which actually made up the small child's world: How often did his mother talk to him? What did she teach him, what sort of encouragement or restrictions did she convey? Who initiated most activities—the child or his mother? What kind of toys were used, and how? Armed with tape recorders, one team of observers noted the child's moment-to-moment behavior while another team, under Dr. Watts, studied the role of the mother and the objects around the child.

During two years of painstaking work, the staff nearly drowned in details about the activities of 40 mothers and their children. But at last the project tracked down what it was looking for: the point at which the paths of A and C toddlers began to diverge.

The differences between A's and C's were already clear by the age of 2. Even at 1½, the child seemed set—his path was predictable. But when observing children 10 months old, the researchers were unable to find enough differences to divide the children into A and C groups. Apparently, something very important happened between the ages of 10 months and 1½ years which propelled children into one line of development or another.

"We have become pretty confident about this divergence—and we've begun to see the reasons for it," declares Professor White. According to him, it all depends on the mother. "The mother is right on the hook, just where Freud put her," he says. Children change radically between the ages of 10 and 18 months, he points out. Suddenly they can walk, move around the house, get into everything. At the same time they begin to understand language and to assert themselves. It is a stressful time for the mother, a testing time, and the way she responds then determines how her child will do by 3.

What do the mothers who produce A children do during this period? Surprisingly, they don't spend a great deal of time "interacting" with each child—they are far too busy, and some of them even have part-time jobs. Dr. White estimates that the mothers seldom give the child their undivided attention for more than 10% of his waking time (for a baby who sleeps 12 hours a day, that's only 1.2 hours). Nor do they do much deliberate teaching.

However, they are superbly effective in two roles: (1) indirectly, as organizers, designers and rulers of the child's physical environment; and (2) directly, as consultants to their children "on the fly."

The two roles may be equally important, since one-year-old children seem far more interested in exploration than in social relations. "It's man against nature," explains White. Nobody could have guessed, until his researchers clocked it, that one-year-olds spend more than one-fifth of their waking hours "gaining information by looking"—that is, staring at various things intently, as if to memorize their features. Probably this is their dominant activity. They also try little scientific experiments, like the 13-month-old girl who accidentally dropped a piece of meat in her milk, seemed startled to see it sink, then deliberately put a potato chip in and looked puzzled when it floated. Later on, the child screeched when her mother removed the

The dominant activity of a one-year-old is staring intently

glass before she had finished her experiments. The A mothers provide a rich variety of toys and household objects to play with, and allow their children to roam all over the living area. Usually they place poisons or sharp utensils beyond the toddler's reach, so that nearly everything else may be used. The C mothers, on the other hand, "protect" their children (and their possessions) by ruling a large number of places out of bounds. They restrict the child's instinct to explore. According to White, the use of playpens, high chairs or gates for long periods of time every day can stunt a child's curiosity severely enough to impede his intellectual development by the age of 1½.

The mother's consultant role comes in when the wandering one-year-old runs into something particularly exciting, or an obstacle which he can't overcome. In most cases, White notes, the A mother will pause for the few seconds it takes and (a) get in some language, (b) beef up the child's curiosity, (c) give him some related ideas which will start him thinking, and (d) unwittingly teach him an important skill: using adults as a resource.

"She does all that, in little 10- or 20-second episodes, many times during the day," says White admiringly. "Note that the initiative comes from the child—but she encourages him to master the tasks he gives himself." The C mothers make themselves much less available, he points out. They may be loving, patient and well-meaning, but they don't share their baby's excitement, they talk much less to him, and they fail to stimulate him intellectually. Some of the A mothers manage to turn even the dullest everyday situation—diaper changing—into occasions for "intellectually promising" games such as peek-a-boo, which teaches the baby that things exist even when they are hidden from sight. The C mothers, on the other hand, seldom encourage their babies' attempts at making sense of the world.

The 10-to-18-months period seems so critical because it is a time when mothers reveal their style. "By their words and actions they begin to emphasize different values in bringing up their children, and this difference in emphasis

will become greater and greater," explains Jean Watts. This does not mean that the children's fate is fixed forever at the age of 1½. Given a different environment, they could probably change radically for better or for worse. However, if the babies stay with their mothers—as they are likely to do—and if the mothers continue in the same manner, the children's lines of development are clear. In all their follow-ups so far, the original A children have continued to excel, while the C children have remained at the bottom of the heap.

The project did not attempt in any way to change the mothers' child-rearing methods. "This was a natural experiment," emphasizes White. "So far, we've learned from *them*." One thing he learned is that "you don't need an awful lot of resources to do a good job with a child at that age—not even a marvelous marriage!" What you do need, in most cases, are some practical guidelines, some knowledge about how a baby's mind develops—both of which can be acquired—and vast reserves of energy, because raising a child of that age is extremely demanding. To the extent that she has these qualities, a caretaker can do as good a job as a good mother.

The idea, then, is to try to get to young women before their child-rearing patterns are set. Next year White plans to talk with expectant mothers to make them aware of what an "A" mother is and what she can do to foster A characteristics in her child. He will urge them to fill the world of the 10-to-18-month-old child with small, manipulatable, visually detailed objects (either toys or household articles) and things to climb and move on, all freely available. This freedom may conflict with a spotless home—but A mothers are not meticulous housekeepers. He will tell them to pack the maximum into their brief snatches of consulting "on the fly"; to first try to understand what the child's activity means to him and what he might be learning from it, then give him something new and interesting to think about or do along the same lines. Though mothers need not *always* drop whatever they are doing to attend to the child's requests, he will explain, they should respond with help or shared enthusiasm *most of the time*, stimulating the child's desire to do things well and perhaps suggesting a related task or game that he could try next. If a little girl comes to show off how she dressed her doll, for instance, the mother may occasionally do more than praise her—she might take her to a mirror, where the child can see her finished product from another angle while learning about reflections. If a child wants help because he can't put a big block on a little one without its toppling, she might show how to reverse his operation, putting the little block safely over the big one and then add a third one on top. In every case the mother should talk to the child a great deal —even before the mother is certain the child can understand, White insists—for this will nourish the child's intellect.

Today parents are no longer afraid to teach their children the sounds of letters, or how to trace the shape of a sandpaper letter, or how to put two letters together and make a word

—when this fits in with the child's interest at the moment. They realize the dangers of teaching too much, beyond the child's ability or desires, and producing frustration. They don't push, but they no longer cop out, either. As a result, middle-class youngsters now come to school far better prepared, in the opinion of first-grade teachers, and they have fewer reading problems in school. At a time when *Sesame Street*, the educational TV program for preschoolers, enjoys phenomenal success and any toy that is labeled "educational" sells swiftly (only ten years ago this label guaranteed poor sales), early learning is definitely "in"—at least among many middle-class parents.

Nevertheless, millions of children still fail miserably in school, especially those who are black and poor. This has led some people to ask whether it isn't all due to genetic differences. In a widely quoted article, Prof. Arthur R. Jensen of the University of California argued that IQs are more a matter of inheritance than environment and therefore cannot be changed by any form of compensatory education. At first glance, a recent study by Dr. Rick Heber of the University of Wisconsin would seem to confirm this: in a poor area of Milwaukee, 80% of the children with IQs under 80 (which placed them in the mentally retarded category) were found to come from a group of mothers with equally low IQs—an apparently clear case of inherited stupidity. Yet when Dr. Heber organized a program of special training for newborn babies of similar mothers, they scored well above 100 IQ within three years. Equally startling improvements have been found in Israel among the children of poor immigrants from North Africa and Yemen, who, when reared at home, have extremely low IQs (an average of 85)—but when raised in communal nurseries from birth on, have IQs of 115.

Even in the best environment, some 10% of all children are held back by various kinds of perceptual handicaps. These are insidious be-

Certainly by age 2 educational handicaps can be' picked up

cause the parents may be totally unaware of them. They range from subtle hearing losses, which stunt the child's acquisition of language, to the strange disabilities and coordination problems lumped under the name of "dyslexia," which interfere with reading or writing. Unrecognized and uncorrected, any one of these can poison a child's life, making him feel worthless as he encounters constant failure despite a high IQ.

"We can now pick up educational handicaps very early—certainly by the age of 2," says White. "This calls for a commitment from so-ciety to move into this age range. We cannot let things go until a child starts school."

In the town of Brookline, Mass., the school system is reaching down to the first year of life. It hopes someday to offer a whole range of services to children from birth to 5, with special programs for those with learning handicaps, including C children. It will try new curricula for normal youngsters. Next fall it will open a neighborhood information center where parents can get dependable answers to any question involving young children. Both before and during these programs, it will assess each child's social competence, intellectual skills and receptive language (what he understands, not what he says), so as to develop a blueprint of what works best for whom, at what age and at what cost. The California legislature recently provided funds for a program of early diagnosis, designed to reach children before the age of 3.

As research in child development focuses on increasingly younger age groups, scientists have begun to uncover fragments of what happens to the child's mind even before the 10-to-18-month period. Conceivably, the differences which *seem* to appear during the 10-to-18-month period may have their roots even earlier in the baby's development. But so far, the first weeks and months of life have defied systematic analysis. When scientists learn more about this period, they may see how different methods of caring for newborns affect their later development, and tell us how the A mothers promote competence by 10 months.

Meanwhile, however, parents can produce much happier and more intelligent children by applying what is known about the time of clear divergence—10 to 18 months—and the stages that follow. Within ten years, it won't seem at all strange for babies to get educational checkups as regularly as they now receive physicals, and for parents to learn to track the stages of early mental growth as naturally as they now learn to sterilize their babies' bottles.

"The young human creature spends months and years completing the intellectual structures which at his birth are present only as possibilities."

KINDERGARTEN IS TOO LATE

By ESTHER P. EDWARDS, *associate professor, The Eliot-Pearson Department of Child Study, Tufts University.*

EDUCATION of the young child has come with a rush and a swirl out of the quiet backwater where it sat so long in its own reflection and has swept into the mainstream of American concern and controversy. At last we are hit hard with the fact that young children's experiences in their first years are of crucial creative importance for their total future lives. The heredity-environment dilemma having been laid to rest with the recognition that both are significant in continual interaction, we are ready to accept the thesis that intelligence is not fixed once and for all at birth but can be shaped by experience. We are just beginning to look seriously at the kinds of stimuli we provide for children. What should these be? When should they occur? How should they be presented? By whom? In what setting?

But what is the basis for this growing awareness that the early years are of incalculable significance? Any attempt to give a capsule explanation will be an oversimplification; yet the attempt must be made.

The word "cognition"—knowing—became respectable in American psychology in the Fifties. Piaget in Switzerland and Vygotsky in Russia had shown as long ago as the Twenties and Thirties that human intellectual functioning could not be sufficiently explained in any purely mechanical fashion. American psychology of the ruling behaviorist school came more reluctantly to recognize that thinking, learning, and behaving as we know them cannot be reduced wholly to a direct stimulus-response hookup.

What gives an intelligent adult the ability to focus his attention on *this* rather than on *that*? What allows him some degree of choice, of voluntary control? What gets him out from under the domination of his environment—not always, not entirely, but in part, and part of the time? Why can the absorbed reader fail even to hear the clock tick in the corner, the rain on the roof, the hiss of the fire, yet leap to instant attention when his child cries out softly in its sleep? Why, and how, have we human beings attained waking consciousness, that demanding burden and endless delight? What gives us alone of all life on this planet symbolic language—created, shared, used to build and sustain our cloud-palace cultures that float from generation to generation on the mind of man?

D. O. Hebb of McGill University has shown that there is a relation between the level of complexity of a species, the slowness and difficulty of early learning in its members, and the ease and speed with which they can deal at maturity with complex ideas. Whatever an ant learns—if it learns anything at all, functioning as it does chiefly through instinct—may be learned in the first moments of its life, learned once and for all. Thereafter it functions well as an ant, but with no possibility of varying its set pattern. "Go to the ant, thou sluggard"—but not for help with calculus. A rat reared in darkness, Hebb tells us, is capable of a selective visual discrimination, definitely learned, after a total visual experience of less than fifteen minutes; within an hour or so it has learned to function as well as its peer reared normally. A rat is an ingenious and canny beast, but calculus is not its meat either.

The young human creature spends

months and years completing the intellectual structures which at his birth are present only as possibilities. Slowly he develops, with little visible change from hour to hour or day to day. His early learning is more laborious than that of neurologically simpler creatures. It is not only that the baby's period of development is longer than the ant's or the rat's, but that the human child is involved in a more difficult task. So difficult, indeed, that his first learning is less efficient, less fluent than any other creature's. It has been said: "The longest journey in the world is the journey from the back of the head to the front of the head." The infant is building the pathways that will make this journey at first possible, then easy, then lightning swift and marvelously effective. What pathways these, through what trackless jungle? Connected and interconnected systems of neurons, branching and coiling back, going off in new directions and returning, making patterned avenues through the forest of nine billion nerve cells that lies between the incoming sensory areas of the brain and the outgoing motor centers. Without this development, conceptual thought is forever impossible.

So at maturity the intelligent adult, whose potential has thus been translated into reality, perceives with understanding, speaks and thinks symbolically, solves problems, categorizes, appreciates, and does all this with an instantaneous flash of insight that is alone of its kind in nature. He deals conceptually with the universe—a universe he first had to construct for himself. How does he do this? As each of us must, he has built it during his earliest years out of the myriad perceptual cues coming into the nervous system from "out there"—cues impinging continually on nerve endings, but meaningless until his system has built the structures that allow a reading of the signals and a response to them.

This is what the infant in his cradle is doing. We adults, rushing about harassed and busy, look at the baby and think: "How restful—to be fed, kept warm and clean, to have nothing to do but play with a toe, eat, cry a little, sleep. . . ." But the infant lying there is building his universe, and building himself. He must do both of these things, do them *then*, do them *at once* (for one is the converse of the other), or never do them at all. Never to do them is never to develop, to be cut off, to be a thing and not a man.

How construct a universe? The newborn baby possesses a nervous system which already receives and responds reflexively to signals from the outer world —to light, sound, temperature, pressure, and other stimuli. But though he responds through reflex action, the baby does not yet understand the signals: he cannot *read* them. He must learn to interconnect sets of cues—to see what he hears, for instance, and to learn that a light and a sound may describe one and the same object. So he begins to define reality. He must develop ability to deal with more and more signals at once. In time, perceptual cues gain meaning: the baby has begun to know what they signify. Memory, judgment, intention all stem from this moment in his intellectual life. First he acts as a purely physical being and learns how to solve problems by means of bodily acts. Then he learns to represent physical action by mental symbol, and thought has begun.

His first symbols are images, pictures which allow him to hang on to fleeting reality ("I remember my mother's face though she is out of the room"). Then the child learns a word, and another, and another, and begins to put words together. At eight months, or a year, he has begun to grasp the shorthand which allows him to hold in his head the whole of reality and to manipulate it, to solve the problems it sets him, through mental operations. Until he is five or six or older, the chief intellectual task of his life will be the creation of a symbolic vocabulary, or several of them (words, numbers images, musical notes), which become the medium of his life as a human being.

HOW vital this is to human development is implied by the linguists' suggestion that the supremely difficult feat of building language recognition and response which takes place during the first years of life can occur because there is a built-in neurological mechanism for language learning present in every normal human organism. But like the image on the sensitized negative, this potential will not appear as reality unless the proper circumstances develop it. Experience—the right experience—is essential.

Heredity and environment interact. Hereditary possibilities are shaped by the influences that only human culture can provide; they are potentialities that must be developed while the young neurological organism is still rapidly growing, malleable, open to stimulus. If the "critical periods in learning" hypothesis applies to human beings (as we know it does to other creatures—dogs, for instance—and as evidence increasingly indicates it does to us), then the right experience must come at the right time, or the potential must remain forever unrealized.

Benjamin Bloom of the University of Chicago implies this when he says that the early environment, during the first five to seven years of life, is the significant one for intellectual development. This is why we are finally realizing that the young child's experience is of indelible importance, not only for his emotional life, but also in the formation of that aspect of man which is perhaps most crucially his own—his sapience.

If all this can be accepted as in some degree reflecting truth, where are we? We are at a point where we can see why education for the young child can matter enormously. It matters not as much as the family. The family is basic. But the good family is good precisely because it provides so much of the young child's education. Still, other appropriate experiences can add to what even the best family can do.

For the child born into a family which cannot give him what he needs in emotional security or intellectual stimulus, such experiences may act as a lifeline to essential development. What early education is offered to what children becomes, therefore, of first importance. Perhaps the right choices here can make a difference comparable to the release of nuclear energy—a release of human potential energizing our whole society.

This sense that the choices matter tremendously is why the present debate as to what constitutes good education for young children is more a battle than a scholarly discussion: Montessori—or not; "Teach your child to read at two"—or don't; imaginative play as the focus of the preschool experience vs. structured cognitive stimulation. Every aspect of the preschool is up for reconsideration, defended with zeal, attacked with fury. Partisanship is prevalent, the grounds for decision-making uncertain.

PART of this malaise stems from the attempt of psychologists and teachers to create activities appropriate for the thousands of urban — and rural — slum children who have come into preschool classes through such programs as Head Start. Once these children would never have seen the inside of a nursery school classroom. Now they are here. Teachers are responsible for them. And teachers have found that their tried and true techniques don't work with these children. How do you make contact with a nonverbal, uncooperative, frightened, dirty, doleful, thumb-sucking four-year-old dragged to school by a slightly older sister who can't tell you anything about him except that his name is Buzzer?

So it is perfectly true that many Head Start programs are not making a significant difference in the intellectual capacities or the academic readiness of children thrust into them for a brief six to eight weeks the summer before they go to "real" school. Head Start has been oversold in an effort to enlist citizen support: "It will bring the slum child up to the level of his middle-class age mates in one quick and easy exposure." That was a line that saved the taxpayer's conscience with a minimum of damage to his bank account. But it was a lie. No one with the faintest understanding of the realities of mental, social, and emotional growth ever thought it could do any such thing. Head Start may be better than nothing (in some cases even this is questionable), but it is vastly less good—and *less* than is needed.

The solution, however, is not to damn previous educational goals and means across the board. New circumstances and children with new needs do not prove that the established ways of going at the education of young children are valueless—only that we now are dealing with a wider range of children and must supplement the older ways with different aims, content, and techniques. We need a more varied repertoire. We need to know when to do what, and why. That's all. But that's a tall order.

THE situation, then, calls for a plea to the embattled camps in preschool education to beat a few swords into plowshares, to leave their respective strongholds, to stop maintaining that each holds all the truth, and to begin to share questions and insights. A vast amount of hostility can be dissipated if we can accept two basic truths:

1) There is no one method of teaching young children which is ideal for all of them. Like the rest of us, they differ in temperament, in background, in needs, in readiness for this or that experience. As children vary, so must educational approaches.

2) Human beings are totalities: they have bodies, and they have minds; they exist in social contexts within which they act and feel. Small children are people, and their life in school needs to be a whole life in which physical, emotional, intellectual, and social aspects of the self are all given adequate nourishment. It is wrong to leave out any major segment, though emphasis can and should vary with the particular set of circumstances.

Perhaps the first step is acceptance of the individual differences among children. Some of these are genetic in origin; others are caused by environmental accidents. Within groups of children from similar cultural and social strata are wide ranges in health, energy, temperament, aptitudes, and innate potential. Even among children in the same family this is so. Dozens of factors can affect the quality of early experience. One child's mother was sick when he was at a vulnerable stage; another child had an illness that required hospitalization; for a third, everything went along smoothly and success bred success. The gap between one socioeconomic group and another magnifies the differences. The early life histories of children living

within a few blocks of each other in an American city may be as remote from one another as is the Arabia Desert from Manhattan. How foolish then to think that any one approach can be the best, much less the only one for such diverse bits of mortality, so variously shaped by their three or four years of life.

Proponents of cognitive preschool experience have recently leveled severe criticism at the less-structured types of nursery school curricula. "Only play," they say, "only messing around with finger paints . . ." The Montessori schools point to their abundance of graded materials which can be used by the individual child to move step by step from growing mastery of sensory-motor skills to a knowledge of letters, of numbers, of ordering and labeling. The child's attention span increases. He learns to work independently, systematically, following a coherent pattern established by materials and setting. For children from the often chaotic homes of poverty this may mean a significant gain.

O. K. Moore, of the University of Pittsburgh, uses his "talking typewriter" (actually a total language environment, rather than a typewriter in an ordinary sense) as a tool whereby children as young as three years have learned to read and write in the natural way in which they learn to talk—inductively—with personal choice of activity and pace. Carl Bereiter and Siegfried Engelmann, formerly of the University of Illinois and now of the Ontario Institute for Studies in Education, have created what is perhaps at the moment the most controversial program in preschool education. It has been called a "pressure-cooker approach." In this setting, under direct academic force-feeding, groups of four- and five-year-olds from lower-class families are taught verbal and number patterns:

This is a ball.
This is a piece of clay.
Is this a ball?
Yes, this is a ball./No, this is not a ball.
This is a what? This is a ball. . . .

The aim of this exercise is to develop the ability not merely to label "ball" and "clay," but to know the use and significance of such essential carriers of meaning as the simple word "not." Verbal skills, numbers, and reading are taught. Drill is the medium. The adults unashamedly pressure children to learn. Hopefully their own desire to achieve competence will be fired by the sense that they are doing something tough and important, but praise, exhortation, and tangible rewards and punishment are freely used. The atmopshere is intense. These children have no time to lose. They must move into the world created

by adult society. The whole thrust of the program is to make this possible for them.

These and other preschool programs focused on cognitive development add a dimension that was underplayed if not lacking in the older nursery schools, organized as these were around the child's social and emotional growth, his creative activity in the graphic arts and in music, and (with varying degrees of effectiveness) around introductory experiences in those areas recognized at a higher level as the basic disciplines (literature, mathematics, sciences, social sciences). Such a curriculum assumed that the young child entering preschool brought with him a fund of organized sensory and motor learnings. His language development was already well under way, chiefly through many months of interaction with an intelligent, loving, verbal, and attentive mother. Often what he needed most was to be a child among children in an environment which allowed him to explore and to play. He had already been molded and stimulated by the adult world, represented by his vitally concerned parents, and every day he went home to continue this part of his education.

But the Head Start children come from homes which have failed to nourish them in health, in emotional stability, in intellect. They need desperately to develop language, to learn to think. For these children such a program as Bereiter and Engelmann's can perhaps give the all-essential forward thrust without which nothing else can have meaning. They come to school late in the day to establish basic learnings. Their tendency is *not* to listen, *not* to focus. They know in their bones that no one is paying attention to them. They have to undo false beginnings. From a mile behind the starting line they have to start the race their more fortunate peers are already running. Under such circumstances, if pressured instruction will get them ready for school, blessings on it and let them have it.

But young children are being made ready for more than the first grade, and there is more to them than a brain, however vital that may be. William C. Rhodes of the National Institute of Mental Health writes in *Behavioral Science Frontiers in Education*:

The imposition of culture upon the child, without relating the culture to his inner substance, is forcing a foreign body into his being . . . He will only mobilize defenses against the culture in an attempt to neutralize its harsh, abrasive denials of what he is.

This we must not make children do by being too demanding in our concern for cognitive growth. There are other values also of major importance.

Maya Pines, in her October 15, 1967, *New York Times Magazine* article "Slum Children Must Make Up for Lost Time," quotes disparagingly from the Head Start *Guide to a Daily Program*, which advocates that children:

> . . . learn to work and play independently, at ease about being away from home, and able to accept help and direction from adults . . . . learn to live effectively with other children, and to value one's own rights and the rights of others . . . . develop self-identity and a view of themselves as having competence and worth.

This is not mere cant. It is not necessarily accomplished, but these are worthy goals. Anyone who has worked with young children, whether they be culturally deprived or not, knows it to be the most sober of cold facts that such children do need to develop independence, social competence, and a sense of self. Until they do, their growth toward other sorts of learning is enfeebled. The child who lacks adequate ego development neither cares nor dares to learn.

Hopefully children can learn both to use their minds and to become more fully human. Social and intellectual growth are not mutually exclusive. The valid criticism of the Bereiter and Engelmann program is not made on the ground that it gives drill in cognitive patterns, but that it gives little else except such drill, in a setting where teacher imposes and child conforms. This is too narrow a segment of experience. It ignores vital components of the totality that is a child. What the end result for these children after some years will be, no one knows. But one must wonder whether so intense a focus on the growth of knowledge and the means of its verification will not diminish other aspects of personality.

Preschool educators criticize the Bereiter and Engelmann program because of its frank admission of dependence on rewards (cookies, praise) and its use of punishment (physical coercion, isolation in unpleasant surroundings). These are gross inducements toward learning. If they are used only to prime the pump, as is recommended, then one may consider them symptomatic not of the program so much as of the damage already done to the child by his stultifying early experience, a damage demanding heroic measures to overcome. But if they must remain in the teacher's repertoire, if they are not left behind in favor of satisfaction from the achievement itself, then they form an indictment of the meaningfulness of this approach to children. A learning that takes place only when the teacher doles out candy or brandishes a switch (hypothetical or not) is a learning without intrinsic satisfaction. Performance can be evoked temporarily through pressure, but will not last. This is one touchstone of valid education.

BUT why must we wait so long, and then resort to pressure? Already there are several experimental programs which are attempting significant intervention before the age of two in the lives of "high risk" children (the younger brothers and sisters of academically retarded children from deprived homes, or children from markedly nonverbal backgrounds). Appropriate education must be made available to every child as soon as he can benefit from it. We know that as early as eighteen months disadvantaged children start trailing their middle-class age mates in tests of general intelligence and language development. Already the subtle undermining brought about by inadequate experience has begun. It is simply not true that all lower-class children are lacking in potential compared with their middle-class peers. Some, no doubt, are. But for many, if not most, the deficit that so early becomes visible is more likely caused after conception by various environmental lacks (poor nutrition, the mother's ill health during the baby's intrauterine life, and inadequate sensory-motor stimulation after birth). Such lacks can be reversed, and they ought to be.

We are going to have to make educational stimulation available from babyhood on for the children whose families cannot provide it for them. Whether tutors should go into the homes, whether children should be brought into carefully planned, well staffed *educational* (as distinct from baby-sitting day-care) programs, we do not now know. Experiments going on in several places in the country should help us decide. But however we do it, intervention by the age of eighteen months should be the rule for the children of deprived inner-city or poor rural families. As it is now, few children reach Head Start before the age of four. We are not making use of the golden period when we can most easily and effectively work with children without using pressure, without having to force on them a culture already so foreign that it cannot be learned unless, as William Rhodes says, we make the child "give up completely the content of the self." We are not coming to children when there is still time to help them build effective roadways through the neurological labyrinth, to help them create a universe rich, diverse, satisfying. We can, if we will. And we must.

We must build programs designed to amplify the child's world as the middle-class child's parents do, when he is still an infant in the crib. We must do this not to cut the lower-class child off from his home and his family, but to assist his overburdened mother, to help make the family milieu better for the child. We must create kinds of stimulation that become a constant part of his life, involving him daily in meaningful interactions, just as the child from a more fortunate home interacts with his mother every day for years, until the time that the thousands of exchanges, each modifying and adding to his understanding, give him mastery of thought and speech. We know that this is the most deeply meaningful education for the one-, two-, or three-year-old child. We must try to approach it for every child.

Such special interventions are not yet widely available. Large numbers of deprived children remain, in a sense, accident victims in need of first aid. Perhaps the Bereiter and Engelmann type of program is that first aid. Perhaps it is the best solution to an unfortunate situation. Perhaps it can build in children who have missed out on the normal growth toward competence some of the abilities they would have developed more gradually had their backgrounds been more intellectually stimulating. Perhaps it cannot. We do not know, but surely it is worth trying, with the sobering thought that force-feeding programs, though they rescue the starving, do not make up for deficits already incurred.

But because people who have been hurt need first aid is no reason to prescribe first aid as the all-important component of everyone's experience. Because deprived children may benefit from intensive work in the cognitive areas where they lack development does not mean that a broader, more inclusive type of program which meets the equally real needs of the intellectually advanced child deserves ridicule. What we really want is to bring into our repertoire a much wider range of experience from which we may select intelligently those aspects which are most useful and appropriate for each group of children—indeed for each child.

HERE we take issue with Miss Pines's description of the "established" nursery school, quoted from her *New York Times Magazine* article but similar in tone to what she writes in her new book, *Revolution in Learning: The Years from Birth to Six.* Miss Pines states:

> Middle-class nursery schools operate on the theory that they can directly influence only the child's emotional and social development—not his mental growth. They assume that if they build up a shy child's confidence, or redirect

an angry one's aggression, the child's intellectual development will take care of itself, following a sort of built-in timetable. Therefore they concentrate on teaching children to "get along with others" and "adjust to the group."

Undoubtedly this neglect of the cognitive dimension is true of many preschools, but it is not true of the good ones, and certainly it is false to the philosophy behind early education. It overlooks a range of experience which is very present when young children are well taught by intelligent teachers who are themselves cultivated and concerned people. Children do not get over being shy; they do not learn to redirect their anger or interact with others in a vacuum. They are able to develop as people, in the social and emotional sense, most effectively when their minds are occupied with challenging ideas. "Why does the ice cube melt? What is *melting*? Why does the wind blow, and what is air, and what are the words that let me talk about it? How can I draw a picture of what I felt like when I was in the hospital? What is a dream? Why am I afraid? How many nickels do we need to buy fresh food for our guppies if a box of fish food costs a quarter? What makes my baby brother cry at night and wake me up? How can a rocket go around the world so fast? When is tomorrow? How far is far?" These, and the millions of other questions small children ask every day, are *intellectual* challenges. The preschool exists to help children formulate them, examine them, and, in some degree, answer them. It can only do this by giving children some of the multiplicity of interlocking experiences through which they can move slowly toward mature answers. As nursery-school children they will not arrive, but they make progress.

BECAUSE in the past the intellectual component of the preschool has been implicit rather than explicit, this does not mean that it has been lacking. It means that the skilled preschool teacher has done a good job only when she has turned every experience to the benefit of intellectual growth as much as to social or emotional growth. It has given her the task of picking up the children's leads and building her program about these, on the presumption that children are readiest to learn in areas where they already show interest.

Let us not be so foolish as to say that the established nursery school curriculum—if it is taught well—lacks intellectual content, or that it ignores children's growth toward cognitive ability, for it does not. It has been subtle in its approach to these. Perhaps it has been too subtle to allow the critics to recognize the presence of these strands of experience, but not too subtle for children to learn from them—provided the children were ready to do so.

But let us also admit that children who have lacked the requisite preparatory growth are *not* ready for such a program and need something else, something with a more explicit structure, something which is geared specifically to their level of attainment and their deficits. If these children are not always to be accident victims, they need educational intervention years sooner than we are giving it to most of them now. But in trying to do this, we must also bear in mind that to teach is not to bulldoze. Nonverbal, immature, dirty Buzzer is still a person, not a thing to be obtusely shoved into any mold we choose. This is why we need teachers to create programs that as yet do not exist, programs which can combine structured cognitive stimulation with full respect for the inalienable right of each human being to be himself.

LET us admit, also, that when we create these new approaches to cognitive growth, they may also be able to add something vital to the multiple stimuli offered by the middle-class nursery school. To object to an exclusive focus on structured intellectual learning for the middle-class child is not to say that he cannot gain from some of it. No one is talking in terms of taking the bloom off frail butterfly wings. Children who have learned how to learn are eager and resilient, and gobble up new information, skills, and insights in every conceivable way. If they are given some leeway to choose those aspects of a program on which they will spend most of their time, they can only benefit from encountering a wider range of possibilities. Teachers should know all the materials—the fullest spectrum of approaches—and should not be afraid to use them.

We are wasting time and energy, good humor and understanding, in opposing each other. No school of thought has all the light. There is no one ideal approach to learning for all young children. Instead, there are many possible variations of emphasis which can make the preschool experience maximally valuable for a wide range of children from differing family backgrounds, social strata, and levels of development. Let's stop this fruitless squabbling and instead fight ignorance (our own as well as that of others) and the limitations to children's potential growth, however these may occur. Let's be grateful for every addition to the armament of techniques and tools which we can use to help children. Let us try to find out how best to employ each approach: when, with whom, for what reasons, under what circumstances. And for heaven's sake, let's get going.

The random play of infants, from monkeys to human beings, is the first business of child-hood and the forerunner of adult competence. Play allows practice for the problem-solving and creativity that come later.
by Jerome S. Bruner

CHILD DEVELOPMENT
Play Is Serious Business

EXPERIMENTAL psychologists are a rather sobersided and tough-minded breed. They prefer to study topics that are scientifically manageable and precisely defined. No surprise, then, that when they began to study early human development, they steered clear of so antic a phenomenon as play. Everyone recognizes play when he sees it, but one cannot frame it into a single, impeccable definition. Play encompasses a motley, very unsober set of activities, from childish punning, to cowboys-and-Indians, to the construction of building-block towers.

Fortunately, the progress of research is subject to accidents of opportunity and the availability of data. A decade ago, while the methodologically vexed were still rejecting play as an unmanageable laboratory topic, primate ethologists began to raise new questions about the nature and role of play in primate evolution. On closer inspection, play turned out to be less diverse a phenomenon than had been thought, particularly when observed in its natural setting. Nor was it all that antic in its structure, if analyzed properly.

Most important, primatologists found that play seems to serve a crucial function during immaturity, a function that increases in importance as one moves up the evolutionary scale from Old World monkeys, through great apes, to man. Play, they found, is a precursor of adult competence.

Some of the pioneering observations came from Jane van Lawick-Goodall and her colleagues, who studied free-ranging chimpanzees at the Gombe Stream Reserve in Tanzania. They found that during the first four or five years of life, a chimp is in close contact with his mother, and is her only offspring. Unlike the offspring of Old World monkeys, who are supplanted by new progeny within a year, young chimpanzees have plenty of time to observe adult behavior and incorporate what they observe into their play.

Termites With Relish. Van Lawick-Goodall reported a striking example of how this early observation together with play leads to skilled adult behavior. Adult chimps develop a very skilled technique for catching termites. They wet stripped sticks in their mouths, insert the sticks into the opening of a termite hill, and wait a bit for the termites to adhere to the sticks. Then they remove the fishing instruments with the termites on them and devour the insects with great relish.

Young chimps learn the art of termiting by trying it out in play. Seated by the mother, buffered from external pressures, they learn the individual acts that make up termiting. Though they do not obtain the usual reward of food, they nonetheless learn to play with sticks, strip leaves from twigs, and pick the right length of twig for getting into different holes. The chimps perform these steps, which eventually must combine into the final act, in all kinds of antic episodes of play.

Merlin, a young chimp who lost his mother in his third year and was raised by older siblings, did not learn to termite as well as the others, reported Van Lawick-Goodall. He lacked the opportunity to observe an adult closely, and probably did not get the buffering from distraction and pressure that a mother normally provides. As a result, at four and a half years he was still inept and ill-equipped for the task.

Observations like this one suggest that play does not merely provide practice of instinctive behavior relevant to survival. Rather, it makes possible the playful practice of subroutines of behavior that later come together in useful problem solving. What appears to be at stake is the chance to assemble and reassemble sequences of behavior that lead to skilled action. At least, that is one function of play.

More generally, play seems to reduce or neutralize the pressure that comes from

> **Even when their initial approach was misguided, they ended by solving the problem because they were able to resist frustration and the temptation to give up. They were playing.**

having to achieve. There is a well-known rule in the psychology of learning, the Yerkes-Dodson Law, that states that the more complex a skill is, the lower the optimum level of motivation required to learn it. That is, too much motivation arousal can interfere with learning. By deemphasizing the importance of the goal, play may serve to reduce excessive drive and thus enable young animals and children to learn more easily the skills they will need when they are older.

Playful Solutions. With my colleagues Kathy Sylva and Paul Genova at Harvard University, I studied the effects of play on the problem-solving abilities of three- to five-year-olds. The children's task was to fish a prize from a box that was out of reach. The only tools available were two short sticks and a clamp. The solution was to extend the sticks by clamping them together to make a pole.

We gave the children various kinds of training before they tried to solve the problem themselves. Some of them watched an adult demonstrate the principle of clamping sticks together, others practiced fastening clamps on single sticks, and a third group watched the experimenter carry out the entire task. A fourth group of children received no

special training, but had an opportunity to play with the materials, while a fifth group had no exposure to the materials at all.

The play group did as well on the problem as those who saw the complete task demonstrated, and did significantly better than the other three groups. The chart summarizes the differences in performance, in terms of the number of solutions spontaneously achieved without help from the experimenter.

We were quite struck by the tenacity with which the children in the play group stuck to the task. Even when their initial approach was misguided, they ended by solving the problem because they were able to resist frustration and the temptation to give up. They were playing.

There are comparable experimental results for primates below man. One technique for removing the pressure to achieve a goal is semidomestication; the experimenter puts out food in the animals' natural habitat, and thus relieves them of the necessity to search out their own sustenance. This has the effect of increasing innovation.

In Japanese studies of semi-domestication, macaque monkeys have taken to washing yams, and have learned

to separate maize from the sand on which it has been spread by dropping a handful of the mix into sea water and letting the sand sink. Once in the water, the younger animals begin to play, learn to swim, and finally migrate to nearby islands.

In all of these activities, it is the playful young who are most involved, even though they are not always the innovators of the new "technologies." The young are game for change, and their gameness predisposes the troop as a whole to change its ways. The full-grown males are often most resistant, or at least most out of touch, since the new enterprises get a first tryout in the groups that play around the mother monkeys, and adult males are not part of these groups. However, French primatologist Jean Claude Fady has shown that even ordinarily combative adult males will learn to cooperate with each other to move heavy rocks under which food has been hidden, when pressure is removed through semidomestication.

Play also has other functions that are less utilitarian but equally important. Erik Erikson recently reported that in a 30-year follow-up of people who had been studied as children, those subjects who had the most interesting and fulfilling lives were ones who had managed to keep a sense of playfulness at the center of things. And Corinne Hutt of the University of Keele has shown that the opportunity for play affects a child's later creativity.

Hutt designed a supertoy for children three to five years old. The toy consisted of a table with a lever, buzzers, bells and counters attached. Different movements of the lever caused buzzers to sound, bells to ring, etc.

When children encounter this toy, they first explore its possibilities, tentatively trying things out, and then, having contented themselves, they go on to richer, more combinatorial play. Hutt rated the children on how inventive they were in their play, and divided them into nonexplorers, explorers and inventive ex-

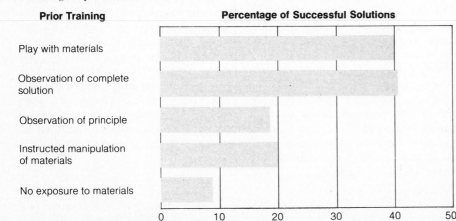

Prior Training	Percentage of Successful Solutions

PLAY AND PROBLEM-SOLVING. Young children had to solve a problem that involved clamping two sticks together. Children who merely played with the materials beforehand did as well as or better than children who saw a demonstration or received special training.

**quickly discovered
that if one young
animal failed to
notice the play
signal of another who
sought to play-fight
with him, a real
fight broke out.**

plorers. The latter group went from initial exploration to full-blown play.

Unplayful and Tense. Four years later, when the children were seven to 10 years old, Hutt gave them a number of personality tests, including one for creativity. The more inventive and exploratory the children had been in their previous play with the supertoy, the higher their originality scores were four years later. In general, the nonexploring boys viewed themselves as unadventurous and inactive, and their parents and teachers felt they lacked curiosity. The nonexploratory and unplayful girls turned out to be rather unforthcoming in social interactions, as well as more tense than their more playful comrades.

As we examine play and its functions more closely, we are discovering that even the simplest play activities, far from being "random," are structured and governed by rules. In subhuman primates, play is always preceded by certain physical signals. These include a "play face," a particular kind of open-mouthed gesture that signals the message "this is play," as well as a slack but exaggerated gait and galumphing movements.

When Stephen Miller and I analyzed Irven DeVore's films of juvenile play in East African Savanna baboons, we quickly discovered that if one young animal failed to notice the play signal of another who sought to play-fight with him, a real fight broke out. But once the signal was perceived by both parties, the fight changed into the clownish ballet of monkeys feigning a fight. They obviously knew how to do it both ways.

New studies by psycholinguist Catherine Garvey show how three- to five-year-old children, playing in pairs, manage even in their simplest games to create and recognize implicit rules and expectancies, all the while distinguishing sharply between the structure of make-believe and the real thing.

For instance, one common rule is to respond to your playmate by copying what he says. A violation of the rule evokes a reprimand:

Child one: *Bye Mommy*
Child two: *Bye Mommy*
Child one: *Bye Mommy*
Child two: *Bye Daddy*
Child one: *You're a nut.*

At other times, a complement rule prevails, and the expected response to "*Bye Mommy*" is "*Bye Daddy.*"

The rules also specify the situation in which the play takes place. These rules may be subject to some discussion and negotiation:

Child one: *I have to go to work.*
Child two: *You're already at work.*
Child one: *No I'm not.*

Young children are usually well aware of the line between fantasy and reality. In the following exchange, the first child is seated on a three-legged stool that has a magnifying glass at its center:

Child one: *I've got to go to the potty.*
Child two: *Really?*
Child one: (Grins) *No, pretend.*

These simple exchanges have a concise, almost grammatical quality, and reveal an extraordinary sensitivity to violations of implicit expectancies. In them, children work out variations and combinations according to unspoken rules. The combination of elements is an essential feature of language, and one wonders, though we can never know, whether play has some deep connection with the origins of language in man.

Play certainly has a part in a child's first mastery of language. In our studies at Oxford, we have observed how, in exchange games such as "peek-a-boo," young children learn to signal and recognize certain expectancies. They delight in the primitive rules that come to govern their encounters with other children. And they learn to manipulate features of language that they must later put together in complicated ways.

An episode from one study illustrates how play can serve as a vehicle for language acquisition. At nine months, Nan begins to play an exchange game with her mother; she offers her mother an object, withdraws it excitedly, then hands it over and says "Kew," her version of "Thank you." She does not say "Kew" when she herself receives an object. Nan has not yet learned the adult language code for giving and receiving.

Three months later, "Look" has replaced "Kew" in the giving phase of the game, and "Kew" has moved to its correct position in the receiving phase. Nan has used the order of steps in the game to sort out the proper order for the language she uses now in play and will use later to communicate.

We have come a long way since Piaget's brilliant observation that play helps the child assimilate experience to his personal schema of the world, and more research on play is underway. We now know that play is serious business, indeed, the principle business of childhood. It is the vehicle of improvisation and combination, the first carrier of rule systems through which a world of cultural restraint replaces the operation of childish impulse.

IMPLICATIONS OF CHILD DEVELOPMENT THEORIES FOR PRE-SCHOOL PROGRAMMING

SHARON COOKE AND THOMAS COOKE

George Peabody College for Teachers, Nashville, Tennessee 37203

This paper reviews and critiques three major schools of child development theories: the cognitive, the developmental, and the behavioral. These theoretical positions are analyzed in terms of their potential application to preschool educational programming. An attempt is made to highlight commonalities and consistencies across the various positions in an effort to reveal some constants for programming.

There exists today a number of varied ideas of how children develop and subsequently grow into adults. Many theorists have presented hypotheses which they feel reveal a reasonable outline of normative developmental patterns and sequences. Unfortunately, not all child development theorists approach the study of child development from the same perspective. Some theorists are concerned with social development exclusively, many focus on personality formation, and still others have chosen to concentrate on intellectual maturation. In addition, none of the theories available provide all the answers to the "hows," "whens," and "whys" of child development.

This lack of contiguity in explaining child development has recently become of even greater concern. Some Educators are now suggesting that a meaningful curriculum for preschool children should be based upon major developmental sequences. This introduces problems of interpretation.

Despite the surface abstract nature of many child development theories, it is possible to identify contributions each can provide for preschool programming. Due to the number of theorists and theories available, those who study early childhood development will be divided into three major categories for this discussion: the Cognitive theorists who support an "interactionist theory" of development, the Maturational theorists who conceive of development as an unfolding of prepatterned stages, and the Behavioral theorists who present an "environmental-contingency" theory of development. This paper will attempt to highlight the functional relevance the cognitive, maturational, and behavioral theories of child development may have for preschool educational programming.

Cognitive Theorists

Generally speaking, Piaget, Dewey, Montessori, and Bruner have been considered cognitive developmental theorists.[1] Due to the recent focus on the educational significance of Piaget's theories,[2] he seemed an appropriate representative of the cognitive theorists.

Piaget does not conceive of mature thought as developing from fixed genetic factors, direct biological maturation, or direct learning, but rather views it as a result of organism-environment interactions.[3] He stresses the importance of continuity and experience in intellectual growth, and the dependence of each future stage of development upon the successful implementation of past stages. Piaget views cognitive and affective (social) development as parallel aspects of a child's total development.[4] He draws a distinction between development (spontaneous processes tied to the process of embryo-genesis) and learning (that which is provoked by situations).

Piaget also defines motivation for learning as the intrinsic desire to exercise the assimilation-accommodation processes for the purpose of developing cognitive structures for dealing with the environment.[5]

Unfortunately, Piaget himself has little to say about operationalizing his theories for educational purposes.[6] However, others have been successful in operationalizing Piaget's theories. For example, Ginsberg and Opper have organized the following cursory outline of Piagentian theory and how it relates to education:[7]

1. *Piaget regards the language and thought of the child as qualitatively different from that of an adult's.* Teachers can deal with this phenomenon by encouraging children to teach themselves through experimenting and "discovery-learning."[8] The Madison Project of Syracuse University and Webster College has investigated the learning of mathematical ideas by children (CA 3-19) based on this Piagetian 'difference concept.'[9] The Ontario Institute for Educational Studies has investigated also the match between the conceptual levels of pupils and teachers.[10]
2. *Piaget believes that children learn from activity.* According to Piaget, the child is an active rather than a passive learner.[11] The processes of finding out, testing, and manipulating should be encouraged. Teachers can support this learning pattern by focusing on the *process* of a task by asking questions which call for predictions, and evaluations of a child's predictions.[12]
3. *Piaget indicates that the notion of "interest" and motivation for learning are primarily intrinsic and are dependent upon the degree to which subject matter is matched to a child's intellectual level.*

For Piaget, both the way children learn and what they learn is determined by their level or stage of mental development.[13] It would appear to follow then, that a structured environment at a child's developmental level would maximize discoveries and subsequently create greater interest.

The cognitive theorists, Piaget specifically in this case, could have other practical inputs for the field of education. There is a present dissatisfaction with traditional intelligence tests.[14] New scales based on (Piagetian) developmental tasks could prove to be more efficient predictors of academic success. This type of scale would definitely have greater value for the classroom teacher than the usual I.Q. scores. The new scales would measure the possession of a core concept, not the speed and quality with which the concept was expressed.[15]

Maturational Theorists

Many have considered Freud, Erikson, Gesell and Adler to be maturational developmental theorists.[16] The maturational theorists consider developmental stages to be "embryological;" that is, a stage represents the total state of an organism at any given time.[17] Stage descriptions are essential components of the maturationists' theories. For instance, Gesell provides stage descriptions of normative behavior patterns for various age periods.[18] Freud and Erikson postulated specific psychosexual stages. Within the construct of Freud and Erikson's psychosexual stages it is possible to progress from one stage to the next regardless of experiences or organization in earlier stages.[19] Generally, the mateurational theorists assume that cognitive and affective development unfolds through hereditary or prepatterned stages. This group also consider that the difference in individual development can be explained as being largely inborn.[20]

Richard Jones in his book, *An Application of Psychoanalysis to Education,* defined education as "ideally inspiring or allowing free play to the natural, health-seeking symbolic processes of ego synthesis."[21] Like some psychoanalysts and maturational theorists, Jones believes that intellectual development and creativity will continue to be seriously inhibited unless emotional maturity is also established as a firm goal of education.[22] Many maturationists consider education and experience important because of their potential fo rencouraging "successful integration" of the concerns of a present development stage.[23] These theorists assume that enrichment will not necessarily accelerate development.[24]

Erikson's work with a child's association modality suggests that play behavior and a child's general approach to his body, space, and time reveal his inner developmental preoccupation.[25] Since healthy integration of a stage is contingent on experience, and play is regarded as the major function of a child's ego, it would appear that play therapy and play analysis offer viable additions to the affective realm of a comprehensive preschool program. It is believed that non-directed play operates within a child's natural medium of self-expression, offering the child growth experiences and opportunities to play out frustrations, tension, insecurity, fear and confusion.[26] By playing out these feelings a child brings them to the surface, faces them, learns to control them, or abandons them in a "quality ego experience."[27] It has been suggested that teachers do not intervene during these sessions—no praise, no comments, no criticisms—so that maximal therapeutic potential may be achieved.[28]

Behavior Theorists

When discussing the behavioral theory of child development the names of Skinner, Sears, Thorndike, Bijou and Baer commonly come to mind.[29] In this "environmental-contingency" theory of child development the environment is seen as a source of energy or information which is directly or indirectly transmitted to, and accumulated in, the child.[30] The child, in turn, emits observable behavior. Bijou and Baer describe the child as a interrelated cluster of responses and stimuli.[31] Within this stimulus-response or

interactionist theory, the progressive development of a child is dependent upon the opportunities in a child's past and future history.[32] Sears places special importance on the parents' influence in developing the personality of a child.[33] He states that as long as behavior essentially represents reinforced actions, development may be viewed as a mere training process. A child's behavior and development, consequently, is the outcome of how he is reared.[34] Behaviorists assume that environmental conditions dictate the existence of developmental phases.[35]

In terms of tools—operationalized techniques—the behaviorists have spoken more directly to the issue of education than the cognitists or maturationists. The behaviorists focus on observable behavior which immediately denies other emphases based on opinion. Behaviorists regard faulty learning largely as the product of a faulty environment, rather than a faulty child.[36] Since behaviorists regard cognitive development as the result of guided learning, "teaching" cognition would demand a careful statement of desirable behavior patterns, described in terms of specific responses.[37] Behaviorists advocate direct education for building skills rather than trying to pinpoint and operationalize arbitrary "stages" of development.[38] One system of education that rests firmly on the experimental findings of Skinner is Precision Teaching.[39] This educational technique emphasizes contingent environments which promote predictable, stable climates, provides continuous feedback, and establishes correction based on data.[40] Numerous studies have shown the effectiveness of reinforcement techniques in handling school-related problems such as eliminating disruptive behavior, increasing "on-task" behavior, teaching functional reading to trainable mentally retarded students, and programming speech and language training.[41]

Discussion

Despite apparent differences in these theories of child development, many commonalities exist. For example, in each theory all mature aspects of behavior evolve from infancy.[42] Further, development progresses from simple to complex and growth is assumed to occur in an orderly fashion.[43] Each group, in addition, credits the environment and experience for significant influences over a child's development.[44] The cognitivists and maturationists are similar in their conception of developmental phases and their emphasis on the importance of play.[46]

Kohlberg and Mayer in their article entitled, "Development as the Aim of

Education," strongly advocate applying current knowledge of child development to all educational programming.[46] It would appear that programming based on developmental movements would hold special significance for handicapped preschool populations as well.

It seems clear that many child development theories have viable practical applications for preschool teachers and educational programming. Programs developed around these developmental assumptions could produce more satisfying results than those which are arbitrarily founded on tradition, intuition and personal opinion. Kohlberg and Mayer state: "Developmental criteria are the best ones for defining educationally important behavior changes."[47] Perhaps this is a preview of future preschool programming trends.

Footnotes

[1] Ripple, R., and Rockcastle, V. N. (Eds.). *Piaget Rediscovered: A Report of the Conference on Cognitive Studies and Curriculum Development.* A report of the Jean Piaget Conference at Cornell University and the University of California; March, 1964.

Kohlberg, L., and Mayer, R. Development as the Aim of Education. *Harvard Educational Review.* 1972, *42,* 449-446.

Kohlberg, L. Montessori with the Culturally Disadvantaged: A Cognitive-Developmental Interpretation and Some Research Findings. In Hess, R., and Baer, R. M. *Early Education: Current Theory, Research, and Action.* Chicago: Aldine Publishing Co., 1968.

[2] Garrison, M. *Development of a Piagetian Curriculum for Exceptional Children: Final Report.* Pennsylvania: The Wood Schools and Residential Treatment Center, 1968.

Ripple, et al., *op. cit.*

Elkind, D. Cognition in Infancy and Early Childhood. In Brackbill, Y. (Ed.) *Infancy and Early Childhood.* New York: The Free Press, 1967.

Kohlberg, et al., *op. cit.* (1972).

[3] Athey, I. J., and Rubadeau, D. O. *Educational Implications of Piaget's Theory.* Massachusetts: Ginn-Blaisdell Co., 1970.

Kohlberg, et al., *op. cit.* (1972).

[4] *Ibid.*

[5] Ripple, et al., *op. cit.*

Schiamberg, L. B. Piaget's Theories and Early Childhood Education. *Children.* 1970, May-June, 114-116.

Furth, H. G. *Piaget for Teachers.* New Jersey: Prentice-Hall, 1970.

[6] Sonquist, H., Kamii, C., and Derman, L. *A Piaget-Derived Preschool Curriculum.* Ypsilanti, Michigan; Public Schools, August, 1968.

[7] Ginsberg, H., and Opper, S. *Piaget's Theory of Intellectual Development—An Introduction.* New Jersey: Prentice-Hall, 1969.

[8] Ripple, et al., *op. cit.*

Sonquist, et al., *op. cit.*

Schiamberg, *op. cit.*

[9] Ripple, et al., *op. cit.*

[10] Ginsberg, et al., *op. cit.*

[11] Athey, et al., *op. cit.*

Hammerman, A., and Morse, S. Open Teaching: Piaget in the Classroom. *Young Children.* 1972, October, 41-54.

[12] *Ibid.*

[13] Sonquist, et al., *op. cit.*

[14] Kohlberg, et al., *op. cit.*

Athey, et al., *op. cit.*

Maier, H. W. *Three Theories of Child Development.* New York: Harper and Row, 1965.

Garrison, *op. cit.*

[15] Kohlberg, et al., *op. cit.* (1972).

[16] *Ibid.*

Coles, R. *Erik H. Erikson: The Growth of His Work.* Boston: Little, Brown and Company, 1970.

Maier, *op. cit.*

Munroe, R. L. *Schools of Psychoanalytic Thought.* New York: The Dryden Press, 1955.

[17] Kohlberg, et al., *op. cit.* (1972).

Coles, *op. cit.*

Maier, *op. cit.*

Mussen, et al., *op. cit.*

[18] Kohlberg, et al., *op. cit.* (1972).

[19] Kohlberg, et al., *op. cit.* (1972).

Coles, *op. cit.*

[20] Kohlberg, et al., *op. cit.,* 1972.

Maier, *op. cit.*

[21] Jones, P. M. *An Application of Psychoanalysis to Education.* Springfield: Charles C Thomas, 1960, p. 15.

[22] *Ibid.*

[23] Kohlberg, et al., *op. cit.* (1972).

Jones, *op. cit.*

[24] Stone, L. J., and Church, J. *Childhood and Adolescence.* New York: Random House, 1951.

[25] *Ibid.*

Klein, M. *The Psycho-Analysis of Children.* London: The Hogarth Press Ltd., 1959.

[28] Maier, *op. cit.*

Coles, *op. cit.*

[26] Axline, V. M. *Play Therapy.* Boston: Houghton-Mifflin Co., 1947.

Klein, *op. cit.*

[27] Maier, *op. cit.*

Axline, *op. cit.*

[28] *Ibid.*

[29] Kohlberg, et al., *op. cit.* (1972).

Bijou, S. W., and Bear, D. M. *Child Development I: A Systematic and Empirical Theory.* New York: Appleton-Century-Crofts, 1961.

Maier, *op. cit.*

Ulrich, R., Stachnik, T., and Mabry, J. *Control of Human Behavior: From Cure to Prevention.* New York: Scott, Foresman and Co., 1970.

[30] Kohlberg, et al., *op. cit.* (1972).

Bijou, et al., *op. cit.*

[31] *Ibid.*

[35] *Ibid.*

[33] Maier, *op. cit.*

[34] *Ibid.*

[35] Bijou, et al., *op. cit.*

[36] Ulrich, et al., *op. cit.*

Meacham, M. L., and Wissen, A. E. *Changing Classroom Behavior: A Manual for Precision Teaching.* Pennsylvania: International Textbook Co., 1969.

[37] Kohlberg, et al., *op. cit.*

[38] Ulrich, et al., *op. cit.*

[39] Meacham, et al., *op. cit.*

[40] *Ibid.*

[41] Brown, L., and Sontag, E. (Eds.). *Toward the Development and Implementation of an Empirically Based Public School Program for Trainable Mentally Retarded and Severely Emotionally Disturbed Students—Part II.* Madison Public Schools, June, 1972.

[42] Maier, *op. cit.*

[43] *Ibid.*

[44] *Ibid.*

Kohlberg, et al., *op. cit.* (1972).

[45] *Ibid.*

Maier, *op. cit.*

[46] *Ibid.*

[47] Kohlberg, et al., *op. cit.,* p. 485 (1972).

PIAGET'S THEORY OF CHILD DEVELOPMENT AND ITS IMPLICATIONS

A succinct description of Piaget's pioneering studies — studies that brought the great Swiss psychologist into direct conflict with American behaviorists — and their meaning for education.

Should the elementary school curriculum be overhauled? Should formal instruction in reading be delayed until the third grade? Is didactic pedagogy at all suited to the natural reasoning processes of young children? Are conventional IQ tests invalid?

Questions such as these are not new in education. What *is* relatively new is the extent to which educators are basing their answers on the work of Swiss psychologist Jean Piaget. The purpose of this article is to summarize Piaget's research and theory, and to take a critical look at its implications for education.

Philosophical Foundations

In order to put Piaget's work in perspective, it is worthwhile to point out that it stems from a very different philosophic position from the work of many American psychologists. The latter, particularly the behaviorists, draw heavily upon the philosophy of the British empiricists, Locke and Hume. Both Locke and Hume were concerned with formulating ideas about the way in which man comes to acquire knowledge of the world. They both came to a conclusion that, although somewhat heretical at the time, seems almost commonplace now: Man acquires his knowledge of the world not from God or from logic but from the impressions he receives through his various sense organs. At birth, man is essentially a "blank slate," but as sensa-

tions are etched into this slate, he acquires knowledge of the world. The process by which this knowledge is acquired is essentially that of association: the association of one set of sensations or stimuli with another.

By contrast, the work of Piaget was based on the writings of the German philosopher, Immanuel Kant. Although Kant was impressed by much of what Locke and Hume asserted, he decided that their conceptualization of the knowing process was incomplete.

One of the main dimensions of human knowledge on which Kant focused was its organization. He concluded that, while it is true that human beings cannot acquire any knowledge of the world *without* their sense organs, it is impossible to explain the universal organizational properties of their knowledge by assuming their sense organs to be the *only* source of this knowledge. All human beings have certain basic notions — of space, for example, and of time — which they do not simply "receive" from their senses but which they in a way possess already, and which they use to give order and meaning to what they *do* receive. Consider the simple fact that objects have a permanence independent of our own sensations. For Kant this truth could not simply be "etched in" to our minds by sensation, since it refers to something which must by definition always lie *beyond* our sensation. Rather than being a perceivable fact, then, it is a precondition which is necessary for what *is* perceived to have any meaning, or coherent organization. The human mind does not accept the registration of total chaos, as a blank slate might. In effect, it *demands* that the world be

organized, and it has the inherent capacity to make that demand come true.

When Piaget began his pioneering studies, it was with this basic philosophic perspective. Like Kant, he assumed that human beings are not blank slates which passively receive the world; rather, that they actively structure it. Like Kant, he assumed that the structure of man's knowledge depends on certain universal notions which he is never explicitly taught: notions concerning space, time, causality, the permanence of objects, and so on. What Piaget became interested in was the *development* and *origin* of these basic notions. As he himself described it, what he became interested in was *genetic epistemology*.

Perhaps because the notions Piaget was interested in *were* so very basic, and were so "taken for granted" by adults all over the world, the results of his investigations were often quite surprising.

Experimental Findings and Theory

The Sensorimotor Stage – From the first days of life, the infant exhibits basic reflexes when confronted by certain stimuli. If a nipple is placed in his mouth, he will suck; if something enters his hand, he will grasp; if a shape moves into his field of vision, he will track it. But his appreciation of causality, or of the permanence of objects, does not appear to be as inborn as these basic reflexes. In fact, it does not appear to be really *finely* developed until he is about two years of age.

Consider the following simple facts. If an interesting object enters his field of vision, even the youngest infant will

ROBBIE CASE is assistant professor of education, University of California, Berkeley.

track it. However, if it goes out of his field of vision repeatedly and then immediately returns, he will not wait for it: His glance will move to other things. Time does not appear to be represented the same way for a child as it is for an adult. When something is out of sight, it is out of mind.

When he is somewhat older, the infant's glance *will* linger in a situation such as that mentioned above. In other situations, however, he will still act as though that which is not immediately present does not exist. For example: Hold a rattle out to a six-month-old child. Then, as he starts to reach out, conceal it behind something he could easily move, such as a handkerchief. All his signs of intention will vanish and he will not try to retrieve it. In fact, he may not try to retrieve it even if it is only *partially* hidden.

When one thinks about it carefully, one can appreciate that a half-hidden object does not look exactly the same as one that is completely in view. How is the child to know it is not "half-made," as it were? When one thinks about it carefully, one can appreciate that a covered object is not present to sensation at all. How is the child to know it has not been completely *un*made? Piaget's interpretation is that this is exactly how infants do see the world — things are made and unmade, and a half-hidden object is only half an object.

Consider another example. There is a stage in the first year of life when a baby will make no attempt to rotate a baby bottle that is presented to him bottom first instead of nipple first. Once again, how is he supposed to know that they are the same object? The bottom certainly doesn't look like the top. The knowledge that an object looks different at different times but is actually a constant thing seems to be one that the infant has to *develop*. In short, the world as we see it is not something that is automatically *given* to the infant by sensation at all; it is something that he has to construct.

In constructing his world, the small child seems to follow a definite series of steps, or successive approximations, to the world we know. When he is just beginning to toddle, one can hide his favorite toy under a bright red handkerchief (in his full view) and he will remove the handkerchief with great glee. Aha, you say, he has learned that an inanimate object continues to stay where it was put. But has he? After you have played this game a few times, place the favorite toy, again in full sight,

under a yellow handkerchief. Then watch as he looks under the red one again and appears baffled that the toy is not there. What he appears to have learned is only a first approximation — that when someone causes something to disappear, it will always continue to exist under a red handkerchief.

Piaget invented a number of these sorts of "trick" situations, and he found that it was not until about the age of 18 months to 2 years that the child ceased to be fooled by any of them. Piaget's inference was that it is not until this time that the child has a really strong intuitive notion of the fact that objects have a permanence independent of his perception and that cause and effect can operate independently of his willing them.

How does the child acquire this knowledge? If you watch an infant, you will note that he is continually exploring things with his mouth, his hands, his eyes, and so on. At first these explorations occur independently of each other; later they are coordinated; and finally they are extended to include shaking, throwing, and other actions. Such exploration and testing may not be too easy on parents, but the indications are that it is universal.

For Piaget, this activity is the key mechanism by which an organized view of the world is constructed. An action, even if it is a reflex, is represented in the brain by some sort of plan. You could call it a program. You could call it a neural impulse: the firing of some cells in the brain. It doesn't matter. Piaget calls it a *scheme*. Consider what happens when the child looks at his bottle or a matchbox. The visual configuration of the top activates something in the brain, called a *schema* by Piaget, and the child then acts on the object himself by manipulating it. Presto! A brand new visual configuration appears. Furthermore, when he manipulates the bottle again the first configuration reappears.

In Piaget's terminology, the first schema, or the representation in the brain of the top of the box, is assimilated by (or actually incorporated into) the scheme representing the child's action. Then the reciprocal event occurs: The second schema or visual pattern is assimilated by the same action scheme. As this happens time and again, a compound schema is built up, composed of all the various ways the matchbox can look (all the various schemata) and bound together, as it were, by all the ways it can be acted upon (the schemes). Thus the top of the box is no

longer a floating, isolated pattern. It becomes part of a series of patterns, which are intimately connected by virtue of the fact that any one can be produced from any other by simply acting on it. It becomes part of a coordinated whole. Because Piaget sees the product of the child's first two years of life as the result of this sensorimotor integration, he labels this first phase of the child's development the sensorimotor stage.

Preconceptual and Intuitive Thought — The toddler now uses the achievements of the first stage of his life as building blocks to reduce the chaos of the world even further. Now that objects are perceived as entities, and reflexes are integrated into coordinated movements, they can be given names. A little later they can be grouped together in different ways and the whole group can be named.

However, once again, none of these accomplishments occurs overnight. To begin with, the child's language reflects that his psychological units are still objects very different from adult units, which tend to be concepts. At first he seems very uncertain as to the difference between particular objects (for example, his brother), and whole classes of objects (for example, boys). He is not always sure if objects are actually in the same group. When he does build rules about general categories, they tend (as with the rules built in the sensorimotor stage) to be only first approximations to the ones used by adults. They tend to focus on only one attribute of a class and then not necessarily on the adult one. We are all familiar with the child who delights his parents by labeling a dog as "doggie," and who goes on to label a cow as doggie, a cat as doggie, and maybe even his younger brother as a doggie too. By degrees, of course, the child's organization and classification of the world becomes more refined. By the age of 5 or 6, although he cannot yet answer such tricky questions as whether there are more red roses or more roses in a flower bowl, he does appreciate that all the flowers are roses, and that some are red and some are white.

According to Piaget, the mechanism at work is very similar to that in the first stage. By forming things into classes and dividing them again, by calling a certain pattern a cow at one time and an animal at another, the child's mental activity begins to tie together the separate labels and the separate groups into an organized hierarchical framework. At first, during the preconceptual stage, a moving object is gradually tied together with other similar moving things until they all may be called cows. Then, in the intuitive stage, cows are tied together with cats and put into the category of animals, and the whole classification system is bound together as a whole.

In short, between the second and seventh year of his life, the child builds on objects to form concepts and on concepts to form classes of concepts. He does this by grouping things together, regrouping them, naming them, and continuing to explore. By the age of 7 or 8, he is capable of making some remarkably sophisticated observations about the world. His thinking begins to take on quite a logical character. However, it still depends heavily on interacting with the concrete world and it is still different from adult thought in many interesting respects.

Concrete Operations – The building blocks are now not just individual objects or people but classes of objects or people. Not only does a lump of Plasticine remain in existence when hidden but it remains Plasticine, able to be differentiated from other similar objects such as mud by certain properties, and itself containing subcategories depending, say, on whether or not it will harden overnight.

Once more, by acting on the world, the child begins to reduce the remaining chaos. He begins to extract higher-order features of groups that do not change, even though the groups change drastically. For example, having learned by the age of 5 or 6 to classify objects as long or short, heavy or light, and so on, and to relate perceptual properties of objects by using categories like more and less, he begins to appreciate that there are such higher-order categories as length and amount, which remain constant even though the perceptual input (on which the classification is originally made) may change drastically.

Probably the most famous of Piaget's experiments concerns just this sort of achievement. Take your bright-eyed little 5-year-old daughter who has just learned to count. Have her count out five beads in one row, then five in another row right beside it, and ask her if there are the same number in each row. She will tell you – perhaps proudly – that there are. However, spread out one row a little farther so it looks longer and ask her if there are still the same number in each row. Again, perhaps

proudly, she will tell you that there are not, that there are more beads in the long row of five than in the short row of five. What we see once more is that her first understanding is only an approximation of the adult one and that it is based more on changing sensations.

By age 7 she will no longer make this mistake. However, her understanding will not yet be complete; once again it will proceed in definite steps. If we take two balls of Plasticine that she agrees are equal in size, and roll one into a sausage, she will not think that the long one has more Plasticine than the short one, but she *will* still think that the long one weighs more.

Although the kind of activity taking place is no longer one of sensorimotor manipulation, or of grouping and naming, Piaget sees the mechanism by which these higher-order adult constancies are introduced as essentially the same as the mechanism operating in the first two stages. The child learns that although one can always transfer two arrays of five into states where they appear different, the number you get by counting each array will still be five. Furthermore, you can always conduct the reciprocal operation: You can always transform them back into a state where they *are* in one-to-one correspondence. Once again, then, the various possible perceptual configurations of "five" all get tied together into an organized whole, connected by the internalized operations, the mental schemes. The result is that one label can eventually be applied to any array of the same number, no matter how different they look.

Formal Operations – With such higher-order concepts of the properties of objects as number, quantity, and weight, with a good intuitive grasp of causality, and with an understanding of the various possible ways things can be transformed, the child is ready to begin creating an order that is more formal. He is ready to begin relating things – for example, such concepts as mass and number – in terms of invariants which are of a higher order still, such as scientific laws. In addition, his activity in noting the things that actually happen in the world and in producing changes appears to enable him to begin thinking about what *might* happen and to envision all the changes that are possible. It enables him to reason without visual props. This in turn enables him to deduce an appropriate method

for scientific procedure.

Consider the following problem: A spinning wheel has holes of various sizes in it and marbles of various sizes on it. A child is asked to figure out why some marbles fall off before others and then to test to see if he is correct.

The child who is in the concrete stage can classify the holes quite accurately and can even cross-classify them. He can see that there are big and small holes and that in both categories there are some near the center and some near the edge. He also has an intuitive notion of causality. However, he appears restricted to noting what actually occurs. If you ask why the big one fell off first, he will say, "Because it's bigger." Then, if you arrange them so that a small one falls off first, he will sometimes say, "Because it's smaller," without being overly upset by the contradiction. If you ask him to *prove* that big ones fall off first, he will not always bother to keep other things constant.

For Piaget, this child has not internalized a system in which *any* relevant attribute may vary and in which many different combinations of possibilities can all produce the same result. The child sees a big marble in a small hole near the edge and concludes that it fell off so soon because it was big. He does not imagine that one could put a small marble in a small hole near the edge and that it might fall off too, so he does not see the need to control other factors before he draws a conclusion about size. In short, although he has an internalized classification system, it is still bound to the concrete things he sees before him. The organization of his knowledge is not yet complex enough to represent conditions of the world accurately which are not before him.

In describing the sequence of stages, I have been referring with confidence to *the* child rather than to *some* children. This is because a remarkable uniformity has been found in the things children can and cannot do (the knowledge they have and don't have) and in the order in which they learn to do them. The exact age at which an individual child may begin to appreciate that weight does not change if nothing is added or subtracted may vary, but it never occurs before he learns that objects have a permanence or after he learns that all other things must be equal in a scientific experiment. Within substages the same is true; a child will always learn the conditions under which weight remains constant before he learns the conditions under which displaced volume remains constant and after he learns the conditions under which number and amount remain constant. We may thus talk about *the* child, since in these most basic interactions with the world and in the constructions of reality, all children achieve an identical series of accomplishments in an identical order.

What Piaget has described, then, is a series of stages through which all children develop. What he has postulated is that the process which propels them through these stages is a highly active one: At each stage the child starts with a world that is ordered in some respects and chaotic in others. And at each level, by acting on the world, by executing transformations, by reversing these transformations, and so on, he builds some further element of order into it. He constructs something that remains unchanged in the face of change – a coordinated whole.

I would now like to turn to the influence Piaget's theory has had, or is having, on education.

Educational Applications and Influences

Basis for the Content of New Curricula – One of the first applications of Piaget's theory, dating back almost a decade, was to suggest the content for new curricula. The reasoning of the curriculum developers probably went something like this: If these are the stages of development through which a child passes, if the abilities he acquires are really the crucial ones from a cognitive viewpoint, and if one of our jobs as educators is to assist in intellectual development, then maybe we should start providing some assistance to the child in precisely the processes and achievements which Piaget has concentrated on. Furthermore, since one stage appears to be built on the prior stage and to incorporate its achievements, maybe we should start this assistance at an early age. Whether or not this has been the precise reasoning, a number of different curricula have been developed, all aimed at providing activities to assist the preschool or elementary school child in representing number, space, and time, or to help him in classifying the world around him. Curricula have also been developed for elementary and high school students to better prepare them to understand formal and experimental reasoning in science. Particular attention has been paid to making these programs suitable for disadvantaged children. It is felt that such children may benefit more than others from programs aimed not at specific rote skills or the acquisition of factual knowledge but at broader cognitive development.

Exciting as it may seem on the surface, however, the attempt to make Piaget's stages the basis for new curriculum content is not one which, in my opinion, should be accepted uncritically. When one sees how painfully inadequate (by adult standards) is the knowledge of some children, there is a great temptation to rush out and prove that one is a really good teacher: that one can teach the child what he doesn't know or, at least, "help him in his attempts to teach himself." There is an equally strong pull to take something new and exciting and clearly intellectual and, because it *is* all these things, put it in the classroom. But, even if we assume that intellectual development is important – which I *do* assume – I submit that this extension of Piagetian theory into classroom practice can be justified only on the basis of one of two further assumptions: that children would not achieve the stages of development unless they had our help or that (if they *could* achieve the stages without our help) they could not achieve them as early.

Let us consider these assumptions separately. There is some evidence to suggest that not all adults reach the stage of formal operations. Estimates of adults who do not reach this stage vary between about 30 and 90%. The people trying to teach formal operational skills would seem, then, to be on the right track. Assuming that these skills are important and that 50% of the people in the world never achieve them, here is a definite task in which the schools might help.

But what about concrete operational activity and the insights about the world that result from it? Here the evidence (literally, from around the world) is very different. Children appear to acquire these insights and skills on their own almost universally. Why, then, should we expend effort and money teaching them these skills in the classroom?

The only possible justification I can see is the second assumption: that for some reason children should learn these things a little earlier. But this assumption cannot be accepted simply on faith.

What reasons are there for rushing a child toward a goal he will reach in a year or so anyway? The only reason I can think of is that the skills in question are somehow necessary for success in the *other* things that the school must teach and that the child who is missing them will therefore be handicapped. Yet, although I stand to be corrected, I know of no evidence to indicate that this is the case or that any conventional elementary school subject cannot be taught until children have reached the stage of concrete operations. I have seen studies quoted which suggest that children often learn to perform certain kinds of arithmetic problems at the same time as they learn to solve certain concrete operational problems, but this is obviously not the same thing.

A crucial study would be to take a group of children who were low in general development, to accelerate or broaden their development with a Piaget-based curriculum, and to show not only that they could *now* learn the required material or generalize it to the required variety of situations, but also that they could do so with less effort than a group for whom the same amount of time had been spent teaching the specific lower-order subject skills prerequisite to mastering the later

> "[Advocates of alternative schools reason that] Piaget has shown that the child's own activity is what is responsible for his intellectual development. . . . It is therefore a mistake to make him enter a classroom . . . and absorb facts for 15 years, as though he were a blank slate."

material. Until such a study is done, I see no reason to support the investment of money in Piagetian elementary school curricula other than in the hope that they *might* help the children and might be fun. But similar reasoning could support the abolition of curricula completely.

Basis for New Assessment Procedures – A second school-related use to which Piaget has been put has been the development of a new intelligence scale. So far, the results have correlated well with those obtained on regular intelligence scales. The Piagetian items, although they probably can be influenced by specially enriching experiences, are said by those developing them to have the advantage of being linked to a theory of intelligence, which normal IQ tests are not. Also, they are said to draw on experience which varies less widely from subculture to subculture; they do not appear to depend on linguistic sophistication, for example, or on any particular knowledge unique to middle-class North Americans.

The attempt to construct and validate an intelligence scale based on Piaget's tests seems to me to be a basically worthwhile one. The only comment I would offer is that any decision as to which sort of test should actually be used in a school should depend on which sort of test proves to be the most useful. This means that criteria other than those of academic or developmental psychologists have to be invoked. Is the test any better at predicting school success? Does it arouse any less hostility in the community at large? Does it provide any more clues as to what help should be given to a child whose poor school performance is associated with a low IQ, and so on?

Justification for a "Readiness" Approach – A third educational influence I feel Piaget is having is that of providing people who believe in "readiness" with some additional ammunition for their arguments. This influence is not so easy to demonstrate as the first two I mentioned. I cannot point to particular teachers or particular programs and say, "There. They are doing that because they believe in readiness, and one of the reasons they believe in readiness is clearly Jean Piaget's work." Yet in the discussions I have had with teachers and have seen in the literature on Piaget's discussions with teachers, his developmental findings are often cited in precisely this connection.

The argument generally goes something like this: The stages of intellectual development have been discovered across a wide variety of tasks. Furthermore, they have always emerged in a definite order; the consolidation of activity and knowledge at one stage is clearly a prerequisite for the progression to activity and knowledge at the next. Since the base of these stages *is* so

broad, since one stage *is* the prerequisite for the next, and finally, since the child must actively restructure his world at each stage *for himself,* one should therefore not try to lead the child too much. The best that a school can hope to do is to offer an environment that maximizes readiness-related experience; then, when the child appears to be ready, the teacher can introduce him to those activities that will produce the desired learning. "We can get more mileage from five minutes of teaching at this time than from five hours of teaching before he is ready" is the kind of argument put forward by proponents of readiness.

However, once again, arguments using Piaget to support a laissez faire approach should not be accepted uncritically. Ironically, one can uncover exactly the same unsupported assumption in them as is present in the arguments of those who advocate acceleration. That the achievements of one stage normally depend on massive general experience is probably true. That the achievements of one stage are prerequisite for those of the next stage may also be true. One can even assert the opposite of that which is claimed by those who have developed Piagetian curricula: that the school cannot provide a program which is much superior to normal general experience from an intellectual point of view. However, even if one assumes all three of these propositions, it does not follow that one should avoid teaching a child some specific subject (for example, reading) until he has reached a certain developmental stage – unless one also assumes that some general level of intellectual development is vital to achievement in this subject. And, as I have mentioned already, there is really no strong evidence either way on this point.

Given the pressures inherent in our present system – the stigma and frustration, for example, that are attached to not being able to read until grade five – it would seem that the greatest short-term payoff for our children would be to adopt a chain of reasoning something like this: If some children do not appear "ready" to profit from our current teaching methods, let us not stigmatize them by waiting four years to teach them. Let us find out what specific skills they can be taught so that they *will* be able to profit from our methods. Either that or change the methods.

Justification for Activity-Learning and Self-Discovery Approaches – A fourth use to which Piaget's theory has been put is similar to the third, in that it is not easy to demonstrate and also represents an attempt to justify a teaching method in which – perhaps for other reasons – people already believe. Since early in the century, "progressive" educators have believed that children should learn from their own spontaneous activity, that they should discover facts about the world for themselves, and that education should not be some tight little ticky-tacky compartment set off from the rest of children's experience. Renewed life has been added to this philosophy recently, with student unrest, with liberal criticism of our mechanized, uncreative way of life, with the advent of open plan schools, and so on. One of the bodies of evidence to which people interested in alternative education have turned has been the work of Jean Piaget.

Their reasoning has been roughly as follows: Piaget has shown that the child's own activity is what is responsible for his intellectual development, that he has to rediscover what the adult world already knows. It is therefore a mistake to make him enter a classroom, sit down in one of five rows of eight desks per row, and absorb facts for 15 years, as though he were a blank slate. In so doing, conventional education, like conventional psychology, is employing an understanding of human knowledge that has not evolved since the time of Locke and Hume. What we should be doing is encouraging activity or discovery learning.

The only comment I would make on this point is that one must be very careful about what one means by "activity" and "discovery," and one must be very precise in one's thinking about goals, before one can come to a decision as to whether Piaget's work is even relevant to this argument. Piaget's point, as has been stressed by Vinh Bang (his colleague most closely connected with education), is that when school children do learn something that really becomes a part of their view of the world or their way of thinking, it is by internalized activity. In the early years this activity must have a concrete base, but, nevertheless, it is still internalized, i.e., thinking. This would certainly imply that if one's goal was to produce such learning, one should not merely talk to young children or have them recite rules.

However, this probably happens (even in traditional schools) much less often than liberal educators think. Teachers have got the message that rote learning is not the most desirable kind. Rote learning is not at issue.

What is at issue is whether, by setting tasks for children, especially tasks that are done at desks and in which the goal is not to discover something but to demonstrate or apply it, one can really bring about this sort of "constructive" mental activity — whether one can get the child to rediscover what one has just told him and to make it a part of himself. What is at issue is not the *nature* of thought, which would certainly appear to be active, but whether children can genuinely be stimulated to think without being left on their own, taken to the zoo, told to choose a project, or asked to discover a principle. My suspicion is that they *can* be stimulated to think and that this is what good traditional schools have always attempted to do. However, what is needed to answer this sort of question is a Piaget-type study about concepts that are taught in school rather than concepts that are never taught in school.

Even if this type of study were conducted, however, the implications for education would not be automatic. Let us suppose it was discovered that a proper mix of didactic instruction and interaction with concrete props produced a greater amount of mental ac-

tivity and a greater depth of conceptual understanding than an activity or discovery method. This finding could still not be used as sufficient evidence to argue that traditional methods are more desirable than progressive ones. A question of desirability like this — like the one about IQ tests — simply cannot be answered purely on the basis of psychological investigations. All that can be shown is that A does or does not produce X, not whether X is or is not desirable. It could well be, for example, that although a discovery method turned out to be inferior at eliciting scientific understanding, it might nevertheless be more desirable than a lecture method from other viewpoints — perhaps motivation, recall after 30 years, training in independent work, absence of anxiety, sense of controlling one's own destiny, and so on. And these other standpoints might well be more important to parents, students, and teachers alike than scientific understanding.

Questions of desirability do not depend only on empirical facts about their consequences. They also depend on value judgments about the desirability of those consequences. And one simply cannot ask psychology — or, for that matter, science — to make these value judgments for one.

Summary

The research and theory of Jean Piaget takes as its point of departure the philosophy of Immanuel Kant — in particular, Kant's proposition that some knowledge of the world is universal and inborn in the human species and not stamped in by sensation. Piaget has shown that, while a certain kind of knowledge is indeed universal, it is not present at birth but is, rather, constructed in a series of stages over the course of the first 16 years of human life. Piaget has also theorized that the mental process through which these stages are achieved is a highly active one, with origins in the first reflexes that the human infant exhibits.

Since one of the universal functions of education is to ensure that the younger generation does not lose the knowledge and perspective that the older generation went to so much trouble to acquire, it would be hard to argue that any theory related to the nature of that knowledge or the processes by which it is acquired could be dismissed as irrelevant. However, what I have attempted to show is that most of the current "applications" of Piaget's work actually go a good deal beyond what he has established empirically, or even what he has theorized. At a deeper level, most of them depend for their justification on an additional set of assumptions, which are either untested as yet, or inherently untestable.   □

III. COGNITION

Cognition is related to thought but is a wider concept in that it refers to all of the ways in which a person comes to know about the world. For the psychologist, cognitive development involves describing and examining the psychological processes that give rise to knowledge. Understanding the student's cognitive development, therefore, is a prerequisite to an understanding of the educational process. A teacher can use the most advanced teaching methods, employ the most highly regarded formal curriculum, be ideally attuned to the desires of the students, and still be unsuccessful in communicating material. If the level of presentation is either too advanced or too simple, relative to the student's cognitive development, failure is more or less assured. In order to accomplish many of the goals of the school, educators need to match the contents of the curriculum, and the ways in which these contents are structured, with the entering capabilities and educational readiness of individual children. The task of relating the abilities of individual pupils to the demand of the school curriculum requires an understanding of cognitive growth.

The "nature-nurture" controversy remains an interestingly open question in cognitive development. Noam Chomsky's article on language represents the "nature" end of this continuum in that he contends that a child's competence for generating an infinite number of novel sentences is innate and consists of an intuitive, tacit, and unconscious grasp of the relevant rules. By contrast, the cumulative learning model put forward by Robert Gagne attempts to explain cognitive growth and the development of new capabilities exclusively as the result of learning. According to Gagne, children develop because they learn a progressively more complex set of rules. Stages of development are seen to be related to the age of the child only because learning takes time, and society can determine or regulate the rate at which information is conveyed to children. For Gagne, competence merely awaits the appropriate training.

None of the articles in this section is reflective of quite so exclusively an environmental view. We would argue that the framework provided by Jean Piaget, one which relies heavily on both hereditary and environmental factors in explaining cognitive growth, is more appropriate to understanding the reality of classroom learning. Piaget's is a "nature" theory in that the particular sequence of stages through which children pass is determined by genetic mechanisms related to intellectual growth. It is, however, a "nurture" theory in that the child's experiences with the environment are crucial in terms of the age at which each stage is entered. Thus, Joachim Wohlwill's article on the prological child is written very much within the Piagetian model. It accepts some stress on innate and biological factors in development, but it suggests that teaching can hasten the deevlopment of logical thinking and that knowledge of a student's logical capacities can help to guide the teacher's selection of cognitive tasks. Similarly, although not from a Piagetian point of view, John Nolan in trying to bring together the notions of conceptual and rote learning, allows not only for important pedagogical contributions to learning but also for developmental maturation as a prerequisite for certain conceptual understandings. Teachers must, in a sense, agree with both Nolan and Wohlwill in this particular respect. Assuming that there are some innate constraints on development, only a conception which also provides for environmental influences is capable of providing possibilities for imaginative instructional input.

In thinking about particular applcations of cognitive theory to educational practice, it is important not to focus too narrowly. For example, Nathan Gage points in his article to the need to focus just as sharply on the cognitive aspects of teacher behavior as we do on the cognitive aspects of students and their curricula. Jerome Kagan underlines the importance of non-cognitive considerations. He stresses how important attention—essentially an affective dimension—is in mediating alterations in cognitive structure, and he tries to characterize the kinds of stimuli that will be successful in eliciting attention in a learning situation.

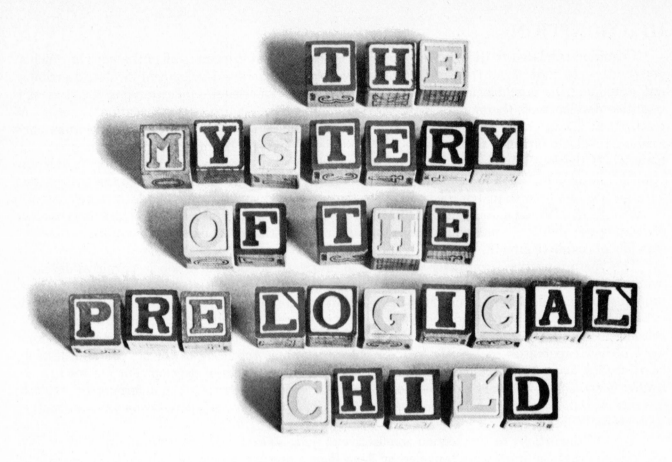

THE MYSTERY OF THE PRELOGICAL CHILD

A five-year-old girl, Mary,
has been taken out of her kindergarten class to participate
in a psychological experiment. She is seated in front of
a table on which two brightly colored necklaces lie side
by side; they are of equal length, and their ends are neatly aligned.
"Let's pretend that the blue one is yours," the psychologist tells her,
"and the red one is mine. Who do you think has the longer necklace,
you or me?" Mary slightly puzzled, replies with conviction, "We
both do!"—her way of asserting that the two lengths are equal.
"That's right, but watch carefully," says the experimenter as she picks
up her own necklace and forms a circle out of it. "Now tell me, Mary,
whose necklace is longer, or is mine still just as long as yours?"
Mary stretches out her arms to illustrate length, and beams:
"Mine is longest! You made yours into a ring, and mine is all *this* long."

By Joachin F. Wohlwill

In schools, psychological laboratories, and child-study centers across the country and throughout the world, children are participating in such experiments in our attempts to answer one of the most difficult and puzzling questions about child development: How does the uniquely human capacity for logical thought develop? How does the child's thinking evolve from a pre-logical stage to one defined by the rules of adult logic? Children are being asked questions about lengths, weights, amounts, and numbers, and about space, time, and probability to see if they use a qualitatively different type of reasoning from that used by adults, or if children—naive realists that they are—place undue trust in appearances.

By the time she is six or seven, Mary will know that the length of a string of beads is conserved—that is, its length will not change even if its longness disappears when both ends are joined in a circle. How does she gain the concept of length as a dimension so that she ignores the perceptual cues presented by changes in shape? Does understanding of dimension, class, probability, and the like come from a natural process of maturation or from extensive teaching and experience? A generation ago the child-mind was pictured either as an empty shell that gradually fills with knowledge picked up piece by piece from the environment, or as an adult-mind-in-miniature which grows to its full size as the child develops. Today, many psychologists believe that neither view is correct. Instead, they see a structured mind, internally consistent yet externally illogical—a kind of Alice-in-Wonderland world where lengths, weights, and distances have as much constancy as the shape of "silly putty."

This new picture has aroused widespread and vigorous debate, not only among child psychologists, but also among educators because it raises a host of questions about our understanding of mental processes in general and about child development in particular. Do we develop in specific stages on our way to adult reasoning? Is this development "pre-set" as is a child's physical growth, or can it be speeded up by teaching and experience? If so, by what methods of teaching and by what kinds of experiences? Since what we call intelligence involves to a large extent conceptual thinking, our inquiry holds important implications for our understanding of this much-debated subject.

Jean Piaget— Explorer of a New World

The current concern with the conceptual world of childhood and with the child's mode of reasoning has been inspired very largely by the work of Jean Piaget at the Institute Jean-Jacques Rousseau in Geneva, Switzerland. During the past 30 years, Piaget and his collaborators have mapped out, step by step and book by book, the dimensions of the curious and fascinating world which exists in the child's mind.

Let us sit in on one of Piaget's experiments. On the table in front of Johnny, a typical five-year-old, are two glasses identical in size and shape. Piaget's glass is half full of orange soda and Johnny's glass is half full of lemonade. Piaget puts a tall, thin glass on the table and pours Johnny's lemonade into it [*see illustration, page 26*]. "Now who has more to drink, you or me?" the famous experimenter asks the five-year-old. "I have," Johnny says. "There's more lemonade in mine because it's higher in the glass." The five-year-old is convinced that he has more lemonade in his new glass even when he is asked: "Are you sure it just doesn't look as though there is more?" Piaget points out that his own glass is wider than Johnny's new glass, but the child replies, "Yes, but this one goes way up to *here*, so there's more." Pointing to the original lemonade container, the experimenter then asks: "Suppose we pour your lemonade back into the glass it came from—then what?" Johnny remains firm: "There would still be more lemonade."

The responses of Lonny, a typical six-year-old, are interestingly different. When the lemonade is poured into the taller, narrower glass and Piaget asks, "Do we both have the same amount to drink?" Lonny, on thinking it over, says, "Well, no." Asked to explain why, he says, "Your glass is bigger." But he becomes confused when the experimenter points out that the new glass is taller: "I guess there's more lemonade in the tall glass." Piaget asks, "Suppose we poured your lemonade back into the glass it came from?" Shades of Alice-in-Wonderland, the answer is, "Then we'd have the same amount to drink."

But now here is Ronny, a year older than Lonny. When the lemonade is poured into the narrow glass, Ronny is sure that there is still the same amount of lemonade as there was before. The conversation goes this way:

"How do you know it is still the same?"

"Well, it was the same before."

"But isn't this new glass higher?"

"Yes, but the old glass is wider."

What do these three tests tell us? Five-year-old Johnny's insistence that there is more to drink in the tall, narrow glass comes from his preoccupation with the most salient fact about the liquids—the difference in their heights. He blithely ignores the difference in the widths of the two glasses. Six-year-old Lonny shows some confusion. He seems to recognize that both the height of the liquid and the width of the glasses must be taken into account, but he can focus only on one aspect of the situation at a time. He recognizes, however, that if the lemonade is poured back into its original container, equality will be restored. But seven-year-old Ronny has no doubts. He *knows* the amount of liquid remains the same because he understands the compensatory relationship between height and width; he understands the concept of conservation of amount.

The Idea of Logical Necessity

Ronny's *understanding* is the critical point for Piaget. It is not merely that Ronny, at seven, can simultaneously perceive both the height and the width of the containers, but also that he can understand the inverse relationship between the two dimensions and can thus recognize that conservation of amount is a logical necessity. Some children may express this recognition without referring to dimensions at all: "You only poured my lemonade into that glass; it's still just as much." Or, "Well, it's the same as it was before; you haven't given me any more lemonade."

The conservation of amount—which Ronny understands at seven—is but one of a set of dimensions for which children acquire the concept of conservation at different ages. The more important of the "conservations" and the ages at which children, on the average, first show understanding of them, are the following:

Conservation of number (6-7 years): The number of elements in a collection remains unchanged, regardless of how the elements are displaced or spatially rearranged.
Conservation of substance (7-8 years): The amount of a deformable substance such as dough, soft clay, or liquid remains unchanged, regardless of how its shape is al-

tered (as in transforming a ball of clay into a long, narrow snake).

Conservation of length (7-8 years): The length of a line or an object remains unchanged, regardless of how it is displaced in space or its shape altered.

Conservation of area (8-9 years): The total amount of surface covered by a set of plane figures (such as small squares) remains unchanged, in spite of rearranging positions of the figures.

Conservation of weight (9-10 years): The weight of an object remains unchanged, regardless of how its shape is altered.

Conservation of volume (14-15 years): The volume of an object (in terms of the water it displaces) remains unchanged, regardless of changes in its shape.

It must be emphasized that the ages given above are only gross averages; first, because children vary considerably in the rate at which their thinking develops, and second, because their recognition of the concept depends to a certain extent on the way the problem is presented. For example, children may recognize that the number of checkers in a row remains unchanged when the length of the row is expanded, but fail to recognize it when the checkers are stacked in a pile.

The Stage of Concrete Operations

The responses of young children to tests such as those I have described give us a fascinating glimpse into processes which we, as adults, take so much for granted that they scarcely seem to involve thinking at all. But what is the significance of the conservation problem for an understanding of mental development? Piaget holds that the attainment of conservation points to the formation of a new stage in the child's mental development, the stage of concrete operations. This stage is manifested by conservation, and in a variety of other ways which attest to a new mode of reasoning.

For example, if children who have not yet reached the stage of concrete operations are presented with a set of pictures [*see illustration, right*] comprised of seven dogs and three horses, and are asked, "How many animals are there?" they will readily answer, "Ten." They are quite able to recognize that both the subsets—dogs and horses—are part of a total set—animals. But if asked, "Are there more dogs or more animals?" these

"pre-operational" children will maintain there are more dogs. They translate the question into one involving a comparison of majority to minority subsets and have difficulty in comparing the elements of a single subset with those of the total set.

For Piaget this indicates that these children as yet lack mental structure corresponding to the logical operation of adding classes—or to use modern jargon, they are not "programmed" to carry out this operation.

The various manifestations of the stage of concrete operations do not necessarily appear at the same time. As we saw, concepts of conservation are attained for various dimensions at different age levels, and one concept may consistently lag behind another closely related concept. Suppose we present a child with two balls of modeling clay, identical in appearance and weight. Let us flatten one of the balls and roll it out into the form of a sausage. Now we will ask the conservation question for two different dimensions, *substance*—"Is there still as much clay in the ball as in the sausage?"—and *weight*—"Does the ball still weigh as much as the sausage?" The same child often will give opposite answers to these questions, and in such cases the child almost invariably asserts conservation for substance while denying it for weight. Thus it appears that the mode of reasoning involved in recognizing conservation of substance precedes that for weight.

The Young Child: Pre-Logical or Merely Naive?

Piaget holds, first, that these phenomena represent qualitative developmental changes in the child's mode of thinking; and second, that they are largely spontaneous and occur independently of teaching or of specific experiences. His views have aroused controversy as vigorous and at times as heated as did the views of Freud. Piaget's descriptions of the phenomena themselves—the diverse ways in which children respond to conceptual tasks—have been on the whole verified and accepted as essentially correct. The controversy rages over the explanation for them. Can the young child's lack of conservation be explained as resulting from a qualitatively different mode of reasoning, characteristic of the pre-operational stage? Or is it merely the result of a naive trust in perceptual cues, combined with a strong tendency to respond to the most obvious, or per-

ceptually salient, aspect of a situation?

For example, the sight of liquid rising in a narrow glass to a height well above that of the shorter, wider glass from which it came conveys a compelling impression of difference in quantity. It is easy to lose sight of the compensating difference in the width of the two glasses. Moreover, in the child's everyday life, glasses tend to be fairly similar in size; thus the height of liquid in a glass is a reasonably reliable index to its amount. There is indeed some evidence to support "naiveté" as an explanation. Studies carried out at Harvard suggest that children who initially lack the notion of conservation can recognize it if the misleading perceptual cues are screened out—that is, if the child cannot see the level of liquid as it is poured into the new container. It must be said, however, that other investigators who replicated this experiment did not obtain similar results.

Martin Braine of Walter Reed Medical Center conducted experiments using the ring-segmented illusion [*see illustration, right*] which showed that children can learn to resist perceptual cues when they are induced to differentiate between appearance and fact. Two shapes, A and B, are first superimposed so that the child can see that B is bigger. A is then placed above B; the child now will assert that A both looks bigger and really is bigger. As a result of a series of such problems in which the experimenter corrects all erroneous responses, the child will learn to pick B as really bigger than A, in the face of the contrary evidence of the senses.

These experiments suggest that the child is inclined to respond naively to perceptual clues, but is this really the whole truth? In collaboration with a student, Michael Katz, I recently carried out the following experiment on the class-inclusion (set-subset) problem described earlier. Instead of presenting pictures of animals, we asked five- and six-year-old children, "Suppose that on a farm there are seven dogs and three horses. Are there more dogs or more animals?" Lo and behold, when the problem was presented in purely verbal form, avoiding perceptual cues, many of the children did consistently better than they did when asked to solve the problem on the basis of pictures [*see illustration, right*].

On the face of it, this finding is the reverse of what might be expected. It is generally considered that at this age

Top illustration: When children are shown a picture containing seven dogs and three horses, and then asked whether there are more dogs or animals, "pre-operational" children maintain there are more dogs. However, when asked the same question in purely verbal form—without visual "aids"—many of these same children do considerably better.

Bottom illustration: In the ring-segmented illusion—in which segment B is really larger than segment A—children gradually learn to resist perceptual cues when they are induced to differentiate between appearance and fact.

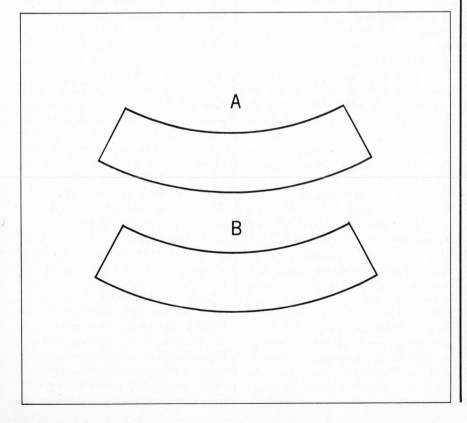

children's thinking is highly concrete, making it difficult for them to deal with purely hypothetical situations. However, it may be that the children did better when the problem was presented verbally because the pictures offered perceptual cues which strongly impelled the children to compare the two subsets. This explanation is in line with the view that children have difficulty with such tasks not because their reasoning is faulty but simply because they focus on the compelling aspects of appearance.

Nevertheless, further data uncovered in our studies seem to show that the interpretation is at best a gross oversimplification of the situation. When we tabulated the results for each child and compared scores on the verbal and the picture tests, we found the following: Among the large number of children who did not give any correct answers at all on the picture test, almost half also failed to give any correct answers in the verbal test. But of those who did give at least one correct answer to the picture test, 90 percent scored higher on the verbal test.

Eliminating the perceptual factor did *not* guarantee that a child could relate the subsets to the total set. These children seemed quite incapable of recognizing that an object can belong to two classes at once. Improved performance on the verbal test seems to indicate that there is an intermediary phase in the establishment of the class-inclusion concept. During this phase the perceptual cues are still dominant enough to bias the child's recognition of the concept.

Moreover, it is difficult to interpret the results of Piaget's experiment with the two balls of clay on the basis of perceptual cues alone. Why should the change in shape from sphere to sausage, with length becoming salient, bias the child toward thinking that the *weight* has changed and yet not bias the same child with respect to the *amount of substance?* The question becomes even more significant when we ask ourselves why one concept precedes another.

If we assume that conservation concepts are acquired primarily through experience, we would be led to the conclusion that weight-conservation should be acquired first. The weight of an object, or more particularly the difference in weight between two objects, can be verified directly by weighing an object in one's hand; experiencing differences in the weight of objects begins in infancy. On the other hand, how does one *know* that amount-of-substance is conserved with change in shape? Yet the child recognizes that this "unexperienced" abstraction, "amount of clay," is conserved and does so well before he agrees that the readily-defined, often-experienced entity, *weight*, is conserved.

Conceptual Development—
Taught or Spontaneous?

The problems just discussed raise a more general question. Let us return to the types of reasoning displayed by Johnny, Lonny, and Ronny. I did not choose these names just to create a nursery-rhyme effect; I intended to suggest that the three boys could very well have been the same child at five, six, and seven years old. For, in the normal course of events, we expect Johnny to come to think as Lonny did, and Lonny, as he matures, to reason as Ronny did. Yet these changes usually occur spontaneously. In the course of play activities and everyday experience, children pour liquid from one container to another, roll balls of modeling clay into snakes, form rings with strings of beads. But five- and six-year-olds rarely ask themselves questions—or are asked questions by others—which lead them to ponder about things like the conservation of length. They are even less likely to be given direct information about such questions involving conservation.

Somehow, therefore, these logical notions must be acquired indirectly, by the back door, as it were. The question is, where *is* the back door? If we assume that these seemingly spontaneous changes in mode of thinking do not occur in a vacuum, what sorts of experiences or activities can we postulate that may mediate them? What facets of his experience play a role in the child's acquisition of logical principles? It is this question which has been the subject of a great deal of concentrated discussion and research the world over.

Can such rules be taught before the child has discovered them for himself? A great deal of ingenuity has been expended to devise approaches aimed at teaching children "the logical facts of life," especially the conservations. Many such attempts have met with indifferent success, although recent studies have been more encouraging. Nevertheless, even where the zealous psychologist has succeeded in demonstrating the beneficial effect of this or that type of training, the results have been quite limited. That is, the learning has rarely been shown to have much transfer, even to similar concepts or tasks.

There is a real question, then, whether such restricted, short-term training offers sufficient conditions for establishing the basic rules of thought which, according to Piaget, are "of the essence" in the child's mental development. At least equally important, however, is the question—do such experiences represent *necessary* conditions for the development of logical thought?

If we look at what children actually do during the years in which changes in their mode of thinking take place, the answers to our questions may not be quite so difficult to find. For example, children do gain considerable experience in counting objects and so it does not seem unreasonable to suggest that the child comes to realize—quite implicitly—that *number* is a dimension, totally independent of the perceptual aspects of a situation. But doesn't this directly contradict the suggestion that such concepts are not established through knowledge gained from experience? What I am suggesting is this: Through his experience in measuring, counting, and the like, the child may develop a *conceptual attitude* toward dimension in general. Then, confronted with a conservation-type question, he is able to ignore the perceptual cues which had previously been predominant, and can respond only to those aspects which, as a result of his experience, have now become dominant. Thus for Johnny, at five, the situation was dominated by a single perceptual cue—height of liquid in the glass. By the time he is seven, Ronny has, one might say, become an operationist; his concept of quantity is determined by the criteria he utilizes in measuring—for instance, as with the number of glasses of equal size that could be filled with the contents of a jar.

Ronny has developed a concept of quantity, furthermore, which may be of sufficient generality to encompass related dimensions that cannot be directly measured. This is particularly true if the dimension that is difficult to measure—for example, amount-of-substance—is assimilated to one that is easily measured —for example, quantity-of-liquid. Indeed, conservation for substance and liquid do appear at about the same time! It is interesting to note that the conservation-promoting attitude can go astray by dint of overgeneralization—a square and a circle made from the same piece of string do not have the same areas, counter to what even many adults assume.

Counting, Measuring, Ordering, Classifying

This interpretation of the way young children form logical concepts suggests that we may better understand their development by looking at activities such as counting and measuring and ordering or seriating, for these are clearly relevant to concepts of quantitative attributes like weight, length, area, and the like. In a similar vein, classifying or sorting are relevant to understanding class and subclass relationships.

Counting, measuring, sorting, and the like are usually part of children's spontaneous, unprogrammed, everyday experience along with the more formal instruction they may receive in school. In research currently under way at Clark University, we are focusing on an intensive study of these activities and on their possible relationships to concepts like conservation and class-inclusion.

For instance, we want to see the extent to which children will arrange spontaneously a set of stimuli according to some plan or order. Children are offered a set of nine blocks with different pictures on each face representing six classes of pictured objects—houses, birds, flowers, vehicles, stars, and dolls. Each class is subdivided according to size, color, and type; for example, there are three kinds of flowers, each pictured in one of three colors. The child is given a board divided into nine compartments in a 3 × 3 layout, into which he can place the blocks in whatever way he thinks they should go, though he is asked to do so in successively different ways. [*See illustration, page 33.*]

We are interested in seeing how many categories the child constructs and how much internal order is displayed in each arrangement. In addition, we want to see how actively and systematically he handles the blocks (for example, in searching for a particular face). Not surprisingly, there is a close relationship between the two aspects of a child's performance: Children who receive high scores for recognition of categories and

In this experiment the child's ability to recognize and order categories is tested by having him place nine blocks—with different pictures on each face representing six classes of pictured objects—into a 3 × 3 layout of compartments. One interesting finding was that the performance of a group of lower-class children was greatly improved by providing them with extensive experience in responding to dimensions of order.

internal order generally go about their task in a much more systematic manner and manipulate the blocks more actively than the low scorers.

A perfectly consistent arrangement, showing three rows and three columns filled with pictures belonging to the same category, would earn a score of six. The five- to seven-year-olds we have studied thus far tend to be relatively unsystematic in their handling of the blocks, and lacking in consistency and order. On any one trial the median number of rows or columns filled with pictures in the same category is only 0.6. In one study carried out with a group of lower-class children from a day-care center, we found, however, that their scores could be substantially raised by intensive experience in responding to dimensions of order and to relationships of identity and difference in a set of stimuli.

Thus far, we have not found an unequivocal correlation between these measures of block-sorting behavior and conservation. However, we did find that of those children who were very poor in ordering the blocks, only 25 percent showed number conservation. Whereas among the children who did somewhat better at ordering the blocks, 64 percent did show number conservation. The relation between block-sorting scores and performance on the class-inclusion task is much closer, as would be expected, since the two tasks are similar.

In other experiments we looked at children's approach to comparing and measuring lengths, heights, and distances. In general, almost no kindergartners and few first-graders showed awareness of the function of a unit of distance or a reference object. They failed to make use of a plastic ruler to measure distance. In many instances they did not even think of placing two objects side by side

to see which was longer. In other words, since they had as yet no real understanding of length as a dimension, it is not surprising that many lacked conservation.

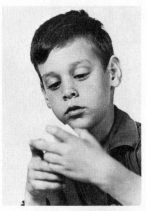

When faced with the set of dowels at the left, most children place the dowels of varying lengths into the constant-size holes in the base—and form an ordered pattern of decreasing heights. However, when faced with the set of dowels on the right in which both the lengths of the dowels and the depths of the holes vary, most children become confused—and cannot produce either of the two ordered arrangements shown.

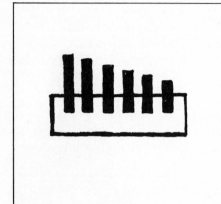
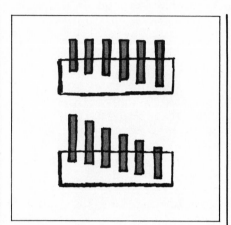

Other interesting insights were provided by experiments with the dowel-board [*see illustration, at left*]. When children are given a set of red dowels of different lengths and asked to put them any way they like into the holes of the accompanying wooden base, a majority come up with an ordered series. They are then given an identical set of blue dowels, but the holes in the accompanying base vary in depth, matching the variations in the lengths of the dowels. Thus, if they like, the children can arrange the blue dowels in a series identical to that of the red dowels or, by matching the lengths of the dowels with the depth of the holes, they can produce a series of equal height. Many children find this "problem" highly puzzling. Their behavior often becomes so disorganized and erratic that they produce no sort of order whatsoever. Of the 35 children we tested, 25 were unsuccessful. Again, comparing this kind of ordering ability with conservation-of-number ability, we found that, of the 25 unsuccessful children, 16 lacked number conservation, whereas among the 10 successful children, only 2 lacked conservation of number.

Though our research is still in its early stages, the results thus far obtained encourage us to believe that our approach may help solve the mystery of the prelogical child, and tell us something about how the conservations and other concepts manifested in the stage of concrete operations come into existence.

Our finding that children's scores could be raised by intensive experience suggests a profitable focus for instruction in the primary grades, where little attention is generally given to cultivating the child's measuring and classifying skills. Our guess is that concerted efforts to encourage and guide children's activities in this area might well pay handsome dividends. Beyond merely speeding the development of the skills themselves, an imaginative approach should provide children with a sounder, more broadly based foundation on which subsequent learning of mathematical and scientific concepts can be built. ◘

Attention and Psychological Change in the Young Child

Analysis of early determinants of attention provides insights into the nature of psychological growth.

Jerome Kagan

One of the great unanswered psychological questions concerns the mechanisms responsible for the transformations in organization of behavior and cognitive structure that define growth and differentiation. Until recently most of these changes were viewed as the product of learning. The child was presumably born unmarked, and the imposing hand of experience taught him the structures that defined him. Hence, many behavioral scientists agreed that learning was the central mystery to unravel, and conditioning was the fundamental mechanism of learning. There is a growing consensus, however, that conditioning may be too limited a process to explain the breadth and variety of change characteristic of behavioral and psychological structures. What was once a unitary problem has become a set of more manageable and theoretically sounder themes.

Category of Change

It is always desirable to categorize phenomena according to the hypothetical processes that produced them. But since psychology has not discovered these primary mechanisms, it is often limited to descriptive classifications. One category includes alterations in the probability that a stimulus will evoke a given response, which is a brief operational definition of conditioning. Half a century of research on the acquisition of conditioned responses has generated several significant principles, some with developmental implications. It is generally true, for example, that the acquisition of a conditioned response proceeds faster as the child matures (1). Although the explanation of this fact is still not settled, it is assumed that, with age, the child becomes more selectively attentive and better able to differentiate the relevant signal from

background noise. Thus a newborn requires about 32 trials before he will turn his head to a conditioned auditory stimulus in order to obtain milk; a 3-month-old requires about nine trials (2, 3).

A second category of change refers to the delayed appearance of species-specific behaviors after exposure to a narrow band of experience. A bird's ability to produce the song of its species (4) or a child's competence with the language of his community (5) requires only the processing of particular auditory events, with no overt response necessary at the time of initial exposure. The environment allows an inherited capacity to become manifest. Close analysis indicates that the development of these and related behaviors does not seem to conform to conditioning principles, especially to the assumption that the new response must occur in temporal contiguity with the conditioned stimulus. This class of phenomena suggests, incidentally, the value of differentiating between the acquisition of a disposition to action and the establishment of and successive changes in cognitive structures not tied directly to behavior. This distinction between behavioral performance and cognitive competence is exemplified by the difference between a child's learning to play marbles and his ability to recognize the faces of the children with whom he plays.

A third category of change, and the one to which this essay is primarily devoted, involves the initial establishment and subsequent alteration of representations of experience, called schemata (singular: schema). A schema is a representation of experience that preserves the temporal and spatial relations of the original event, without being necessarily isomorphic with that event. It is similar in meaning to the older term "engram." Like the engram,

the construct of schema was invented to explain the organism's capacity to recognize an event encountered in the past. Although the process of recognition is not clearly understood, the neurophysiologist's suggestion that a cortical neuronal model is matched to current experience captures the essential flavor of the concept (6). It is important to differentiate between the notion of schema as a representation of a sensory event and the hypothetical process that represents the organism's potential action toward an object. Piaget (7) does not make this differentiation as sharply as we do, for his concept of *sensory-motor scheme* includes the internal representation of the object as well as the organized action toward it.

There is some evidence that some form of primitive representation of experience can be established prior to or soon after birth. Grier, Counter, and Shearer (8) incubated eggs of White Rock chickens (*Gallus gallus*) from 12 to 18 days under conditions of quiet or patterned sound. Within 6 hours after hatching, each chick was tested for responsiveness to two auditory stimuli, the 200-hertz tone presented prenatally and a novel 2000-hertz sound. The control chicks moved equivalent distances toward both sounds; the experimental chicks moved significantly closer to the 200-hertz sound than to the novel one. Similarly, infant laughing gulls (*Larus atricilla*) 6 to 13 days old seem able to form representations of their parents' calls, for they orient toward and approach the calls of their own parents but orient away from the calls of other adult gulls (9).

A central assumption surrounding early schema formation states that the first schemata represent invariant stimulus patterns that are part of a larger context characterized by high rate of change (movement, contour contrast, and acoustic shifts). Hence a schema for the human face should develop early, for the face is characterized by an invariant arrangement of eyes, nose, and mouth within a frame that moves and emits intermittent, variable sounds. Experimental observations of young infants suggest that the face is one of the earliest representations to be acquired. Since the establishment of a schema is so dependent upon the selectivity of the infant's attention, understanding of developmental priorities in

53

schema formation should be facilitated by appreciation of the principles governing the distribution of attention. These principles will be considered in the sections that follow.

Contrast, Movement, and Change

Ontogenetically, the earliest determinant of duration of orientation to a visual event is probably inherent in the structure of the central nervous system. The infant naturally attends to events that possess a high rate of change in their physical characteristics. Stimuli that move, have many discrete elements, or possess contour contrast are most likely to attract and hold a newborn's attention. Hence, a 2-day-old infant is more attentive to a moving or intermittent light than to a continuous light source; to a solid black figure on a white background than to a stimulus that is homogeneously gray (10, 11). The newborn's visual search behavior seems to be guided by the following rules (12):

If he is alert and if light is not too bright, his eyes open up.

If his eyes are open but no light is seen, he searches.

If he sees light but no edges, he keeps searching.

If he sees contour edges, he holds and crosses them.

The preference for the study of contour is monitored, however, by the area of the stimulus field, and there seems to be an optimum amount of contour that maintains attention at a maximum. Four-month-old infants exposed to meaningless achromatic designs with variable contour length were most attentive to those with moderately long contours (13). Karmel (14) has reported that, among young infants, duration of attention to meaningless achromatic figures is a curvilinear function of the square root of the absolute amount of black-white border in the figure.

The behavioral addiction to contour and movement is in accord with neurophysiological information on ganglion potentials in vertebrate retinas. Some cells respond to movement; others, to onset of illumination, to offset, or to both. Objects with contour edges should function better as onset stimuli than do solid patterns, because the change in stimulation created by a sharp edge elicits specialized firing patterns that may facilitate sustained attention (15).

There is some controversy over the question of whether contour or complexity exerts primary control over attention in the early months, where complexity is defined in terms of either redundancy or variety or number of elements in the figure and where contour is defined in terms of the total amount of border contained in the arrangement of figures on a background. Existing data support the more salient role of contour over complexity. McCall and Kagan (13) found no direct relation, in 4-month-olds, between fixation time and number of angles in a set of achromatic meaningless designs. Rather, there was an approximate inverted-U relation between attention and total length of contour in the figure. Similarly, fixation time in 5-month-old infants was independent of degree of asymmetry and irregularity in the arrangement of nine squares; however, when these indices of complexity were held constant but area and amount of contour were varied, fixation times were a function of contour (16). Finally, the average evoked cortical potentials of infants to checkerboard and random matrix patterns were independent of redundancy of pattern, but they displayed an inverted-U relation with density of contour edge (17).

Although indices of attention to auditory events are considerably more ambiguous than those used for vision, it appears that stimuli that have a high rate of change, such as intermittent sounds, produce more quieting and, by inference, more focused attention than continuous sounds (18). Nature has apparently equipped the newborn with an initial bias in the processing of experience. He does not, as the 19th-century empiricists believed, have to learn what he should examine. The preferential orientation to change is clearly adaptive, for the locus of change is likely to contain the most information about the presence of his mother or of danger.

Discrepancy from Schema

The initial disposition to attend to events with a high rate of change soon competes with a new determinant based largely on experience. The child's attentional encounters with events result, inevitably, in a schema. Somewhere during the second month, duration of attention comes under the influence of the relation between a class of events

and the infant's schema for that class. One form of this relation, called the discrepancy principle, states that stimuli moderately discrepant from the schema elicit longer orientations than do either minimally discrepant (that is, familiar) events or novel events that bear no relation to the schema. The relation between attention and magnitude of discrepancy is assumed to be curvilinear (an inverted U). Although an orientation reflex can be produced by any change in quality or intensity of stimulation, duration of sustained attention is constrained by the degree of discrepancy between the event and the relevant schema. Consider some empirical support for the discrepancy principle.

One-week-old infants show equivalent fixations to an achromatic representation of human faces (see Fig. 1) and a meaningless achromatic design, for contour is assumed to be the major determinant of attention at this early age. Even the 8-week-old shows equivalent fixations to a three-dimensional representation of a face and an abstract three-dimensional form (19). But a 4-month-old shows markedly longer attention to the regular achromatic face than to the design (13), presumably because he has acquired a schema for a human face and the laboratory representation is moderately discrepant from that schema. If the representation of the face is too discrepant, as when the facial components are rearranged (see Fig. 1), fixation times are reduced (20, 21).

Fixation times to photographic representations of faces drop by over 50 percent after 6 months and are equivalent to both regular and irregular faces during the last half of the first year (20, 21). This developmental pattern is in accord with the discrepancy principle. During the opening few weeks of life, before the infant has established a schema for a human face, photographs of either regular or irregular faces are so discrepant from the infant's schema that they elicit equivalent epochs of attention. As the schema for a human face becomes well established, between 2 and 4 months, the photograph of a strange face becomes optimally discrepant from that schema. During the latter half of the first year, the face schema becomes so well established that photographs of regular or irregular faces, though discriminable,

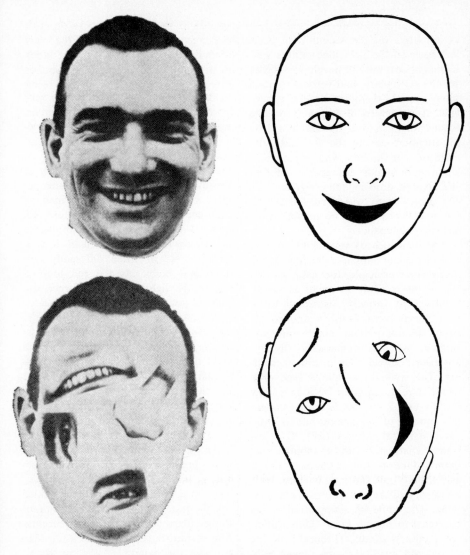

Fig. 1. Achromatic representations of four facelike stimuli shown to infants.

are easily assimilated and elicit short and equivalent fixations.

A second source of support for the discrepancy principle comes from research designs in which familiarity and discrepancy are manipulated through repeated presentation of an originally meaningless stimulus, followed by a transformation of the standard. Fixation times are typically longer to the transformation than to the last few presentations of the habituated standard (*22*). For example, 4-month-old infants were shown three objects in a triangular arrangement for five repeated trials. On the sixth trial, infants saw a transformation of the standard in which one, two, or three of the original objects were replaced with new ones. Most infants displayed longer fixations to the transformation than to the preceding standard. When the analysis was restricted to the 42 infants who displayed either rapid habituation or short fixations to the last four presentations of the standard trials 2 through 5), an increasing monotonic relation emerged between amount of change in the standard (one, two, or three elements replaced) and increase in fixation from the last standard to the transformation (*23*).

Although fixation time cannot be used as an index of sustained attention to auditory stimuli, magnitude of cardiac deceleration, which covaries with motor quieting, provides a partial index of focused attention. Melson and McCall (*24*) repeated the same eight-note ascending scale for eight trials to 5-month-old girls; this repetition was followed by transformations, in which the same eight notes were rearranged. The magnitude of cardiac deceleration was larger to the discrepant scale than to the preceding standard. The curvilinear form of the discrepancy principle finds support in an experiment in which 5½-month-old male infants were shown a simple stimulus consisting of five green, three-dimensional elements arranged vertically on a white background (far left in Fig. 2). The order of stimulus presentation was SSSSSS-SSTSSTSSTS, in which S was the standard and T was one of three transformations of differing discrepancy from the standard. Each infant was shown only one of the three transformations in Fig. 2. The magnitude of cardiac deceleration was larger to the moderate transformation of the standard (oblique arrangement of the five elements in Fig. 2, second from left) than to the two more serious transformations (*22*). This finding is partially congruent with an earlier study on younger infants that used the same stimuli but established the schema over

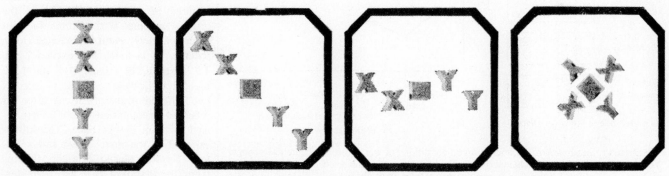

Fig. 2. Standard (far left) and three transformations shown to infants in study of reaction to discrepancy.

a 4-week period. The girls, but not the boys, displayed larger decelerations to the transformations than to the standard (*25*).

The most persuasive confirmation of the curvilinear relation between attention and discrepancy was revealed in an experiment in which firstborn, 4-month-old infants were shown a three-dimensional stimulus composed of three geometric forms of different shape and hue for 12 half-minute presentations (*26*). Each infant was then randomly assigned to one of seven groups. Six of these groups were exposed to a stimulus at home that was of varying discrepancy from the standard viewed in the laboratory. The seventh was not exposed to any experimental stimulus. The mother showed the stimulus to the infant, in the form of a mobile above his crib, 30 minutes a day for 21 days. The seven experimental groups are summarized in Fig. 3.

Three weeks later each subject returned to the laboratory and saw exactly the same stimulus he viewed initially at the age of 4 months. The major dependent variable was the *change in fixation time* between the first and second test sessions. Figure 4 illustrates these change scores for total fixation time across the first six trials of each session.

The infants who saw no mobile at home showed no change in fixation time across the 3 weeks, which indi-

cates that the laboratory stimulus was as attractive on the second visit as it had been on the first. The infants who had an opportunity to develop a schema for the asymmetric and vertical rotation mobiles and, therefore, could experience a moderate discrepancy on the second visit, showed the smallest drop in attention across the 3 weeks. By contrast, the infants who experienced a minor or major discrepancy showed the greatest drop in interest ($F = 5.29$, $P < .05$). There was a curvilinear relation between attention and stimulus-schema discrepancy.

The incidence of smiling to familiar and discrepant stimuli also supports the discrepancy principle. It is assumed that the infant is likely to smile as he assimilates an initially discrepant event (*7*). Hence, very familiar and totally novel stimuli should elicit minimum smiling, whereas moderately discrepant events should elicit maximum smiling. The smile to a human face or a pictorial representation of a face during the first 7 months is most frequent at 4 months of age among infants from varied cultural settings (*27*). It is assumed that, prior to 4 months, the human face is too discrepant to be assimilated, and after this time it is minimally discrepant and easily assimilated. The smile of assimilation is not restricted to human faces. Three different auditory stimuli (bronze bell, toy piano, and nursery rhyme played by a music box) were presented to 13-week-

old infants in two trial blocks on each of 2 successive days (*28*). Frequency of smiling was lowest on the first block of trials on day 1, when the sounds were novel, and on the second block on day 2, when they had become very familiar, but highest on the two intermediate blocks, when the infant presumably was able to assimilate them after some effort.

A final illustration of the display of the smile as a sign of assimilation comes from a study in progress in which 60 children, 5½ to 11½ months old, watched a hand slowly move an orange rod clockwise in an arc until it contacted a set of three differently colored light bulbs. As the rod touched one of the lights, all three turned on. This 11-second sequence was repeated eight or ten times (depending upon the age of the child) during which most children remained very attentive. Each child then saw only one of four transformations for five successive trials: (i) the bulbs did not light when the rod touched them, (ii) the hand did not appear, (iii) the rod did not move, or (iv) no hand appeared and no bulbs lit, but the rod moved. After the fifth presentation, the original sequence was repeated three more times. The proportion of infants who smiled was largest on the sixth repetition of the standard and on the third presentation of the transformation. Figure 5 illustrates the pattern of smiling to this episode for one 7½-month-old girl who displayed maximum smiling on trials 4 and 5 of the initial familiarization series and trials 3, 4, and 5 of the transformation series, during which the hand did not appear. Thus both duration of fixation and probability of smiling seem to be curvilinearly related to degree of discrepancy between an event and the child's schema for that event. Moreover, the child seems to become most excited by moderately discrepant events that are perceived as transformations of those that produced the original schema. If the infant does not regard a new event as related to a schema, he is much less excited by it. To illustrate, 72 infants, 9½ and 11½ months old, were exposed to one of two different transformations after six repeated presentations of a 2-inch (5-cm) wooden orange cube. The infants exposed to the novel event saw a yellow, rippled, plastic cylinder differing from the standard in color, size, texture, and shape. The infants exposed

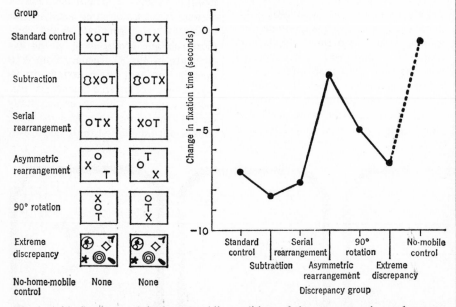

Fig. 3 (left). Summary of the home mobile conditions of the seven experimental groups. The drawings illustrate in schematic form the stimulus to which each child was exposed at home.   Fig. 4 (right). Change in mean total fixation time across the two test sessions for each of the seven experimental groups.

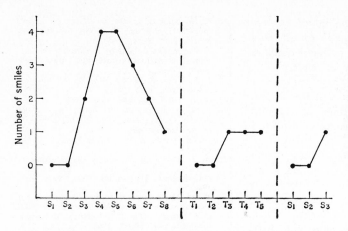

Fig. 5. Frequency of smiling to the light episode for a 7½-month-old girl (*S*, standard presentation; *T*, transformation).

to the moderate transformation saw a 1-inch (2.54-cm) wooden orange cube, in which only size was altered. Almost half (43 percent) of the females in the moderate group displayed an obvious increase in vocalization when the smaller cube appeared, suggesting they were excited by this transformation. By contrast, only one female exposed to the novel yellow form showed increased vocalization, and most showed no change at all ($P < .05$). There was no comparable difference for boys.

The onset of a special reaction to discrepancy at about 2 months may reflect the fact that structures in the central nervous system have matured enough to permit long-term representation or retrieval of such representations. It is probably not a coincidence that a broad band of physiological and behavioral phenomena also occur at this time. The latency of the visual evoked potential begins to approach adult form, growth of occipital neurons levels off, alpha rhythm becomes recognizable (*29*), the Moro reflex begins to disappear, habituation to repeated presentations of a visual event becomes a reliable phenomenon (*30*), and three-dimensional representations of objects elicit longer fixations than two-dimensional ones (*11*).

Activation of Hypotheses

Two empirical facts require the invention of a third process that influences attention and, subsequently, produces change in cognitive structures. The relation between age and fixation time to masklike representations of a human face (see Fig. 6) decreases dramatically across the period from 4 to 12 months, but it increases, just as dramatically, from 12 to 36 months (*21*). If discrepancy from schema exerted primary control over attention, increased fixation times after 1 year should not have occurred, for the masks should have become less discrepant with maturity. Furthermore, educational level of the infant's family was independent of fixation time prior to 1 year but was positively correlated with fixation time (correlation coefficient of 0.4) after 1 year (*21*). These data suggest the potential usefulness of positing the emergence of a new cognitive structure toward the end of the first year. This structure, called a *hypothesis*, is the child's interpretation of a discrepant event accomplished by mentally transforming it to a form he is familiar with, where the "familiar form" is the schema. The cognitive structure used in the transformation is the hypothesis. To recognize that a particular sequence of sounds is human speech rather than a series of clarinet tones requires a schema for the quality of the human voice. Interpretation of the meaning of the speech, on the other hand, requires the activation of hypotheses which, in this example, are linguistic rules. The critical difference between a schema and a hypothesis is analogous to the difference between the processes of recognition and interpretation and bears some relation to Piaget's complementary notions of assimilation and accommodation (*7*).

It is assumed that the activation of hypotheses to explain discrepant events is accompanied by sustained attention. The more extensive the repertoire of hypotheses, the longer the child can work at interpretation and the more prolonged is his attention. The interaction between discrepancy and the activation of hypotheses is illustrated in the pattern of fixation times of 2-year-olds to four related stimuli: a doll-like representation of a male figure; the same figure with the head placed between the legs; the same figure with the head, arms, and legs rearranged in an asymmetric pattern; and an amorphous free form of the same color, size, and texture as the other three. Duration of fixation was significantly longer to the two moderately discrepant forms (8.5 seconds) than to the regular figure (7 seconds) or to the free form (5.5 seconds) (*21*).

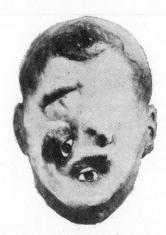

Fig. 6. Facelike masks shown to infants from 4 to 36 months of age.

In sum, events that possess a high rate of change, that are discrepant from established schemata, and that activate hypotheses in the service of interpretation elicit the longest epochs of attention. These events are most likely to produce changes in cognitive structures, for the attempt to assimilate a transformation of a familiar event inevitably leads to alterations in the original schema.

Summary

This article began by suggesting that different processes are likely to mediate alterations in behavior and cognitive structure and that conditioning principles do not seem sufficient to explain all the classes of change. Although the acquisition of conditioned responses, the potentiation of inborn capacities, and the establishment of schemata probably implicate different processes, all three involve selective attention to sensory events, whether these events function as conditioned stimuli, releasers of innate response dispositions, or the bases for mental representations. Hence, better understanding of the forces that control selectivity and duration of attention should provide insights into the nature of psychological growth, especially the lawful alterations in cognitive structure that seem to occur continually as a function of the child's encounter with discrepant events. The heart of this article was devoted to this theme. It was argued that events that possessed a high rate of change in their physical characteristics, that were moderately discrepant from established schemata, and that activated hypotheses in the service of assimilation had the greatest power to recruit and maintain attention in the young child.

Unfortunately, quantification of the fragile process of attention is still inelegant, for an infant displays a small set of relatively simple reactions to an interesting event. The infant can look at it, vocalize, be quiet, thrash, smile, or display changes in heart rate, respiration, or pattern of electrocortical discharge. Each of these variables reflects a different aspect of the attention process. Fixation time provides the clearest view and seems controlled by movement, contour, discrepancy, and the activation of hypotheses. Smiling seems to reflect the state that follows effortful assimilation. Cardiac deceleration occasionally accompanies attention to discrepant events, but not always, and vocalization can index, among other things, the excitement generated by a stimulus that engages a schema. It is important to realize, however, that a specific magnitude for any of these responses serves many different forces. The future mapping of these magnitudes on a set of determinants will require a delicate orchestration of rigorous method, ingenious theory, and a keen sensitivity to nature's subtle messages.

References and Notes

1. L. P. Lipsitt, in *Advances in Child Development and Behavior*, L. P. Lipsitt and C. C. Spiker, Eds. (Academic Press, New York, 1963), p. 147.
2. H. Papousek, in *Early Behavior*, H. W. Stevenson, E. H. Hess, H. L. Rheingold, Eds. (Wiley, New York, 1967), p. 249.
3. Infants over 3 months old who had learned the conditioned response continued to turn their head to the auditory stimulus even though they were completely satiated for milk and did not drink. This phenomenon replicates similar observations with pigeons and rats who, after having acquired a conditioned response to obtain food, continued to respond even though ample food was available without any effort [see B. Carder and K. Berkowitz, *Science* 167, 1273 (1970); A. J. Neuringer, *ibid.* 166, 399 (1969)]. One interpretation of this phenomenon assumes that when an organism is alerted or aroused, for whatever reason, he issues those responses that are prepotent in that context. This view is congruent with the demonstration that intracranial stimulation of the hypothalamus elicits behaviors appropriate to the immediate situation [E. S. Valenstein, V. C. Cox, J. W. Kakolewski, *Psychol. Rev.* 77, 16 (1970)]. If food is available, the rat eats; if water, he drinks; if wood chips, he gnaws. Intracranial stimulation, like transfer from the home to the experimental chamber, alerts the animal, and prepotent behavior is activated.
4. F. Nottebohm, *Science* 167, 950 (1970).
5. R. W. Brown and U. Bellugi, *Harvard Educ. Rev.* 34, 135 (1964).
6. H. W. Magoun, in *On the Biology of Learning*, K. H. Pribram, Ed. (Harcourt, Brace & World, New York, 1969), p. 171.
7. J. Piaget, *The Origins of Intelligence in Children* (International Universities Press, New York, 1952).
8. J. B. Grier, S. A. Counter, W. M. Shearer, *Science* 155, 1692 (1967).
9. C. G. Beer, *ibid.* 166, 1030 (1969).
10. P. Salapetek and W. Kessen, *J. Exp. Child Psychol.* 3, 113 (1966); R. L. Fantz and S. Nevis, *Merrill-Palmer Quart.* 13, 77 (1967); M. M. Haith, *J. Exp. Child Psychol.* 3, 235 (1966).
11. R. L. Fantz, in *Perceptual Development in Children*, A. H. Kidd and J. L. Rivoire, Eds. (International Universities Press, New York, 1966), p. 143.
12. M. M. Haith, paper presented at the regional meeting of the Society for Research in Child Development, Clark University, Worcester, Massachusetts, March 1968.
13. R. B. McCall and J. Kagan, *Child Develop.* 38, 939 (1967).
14. B. Z. Karmel, *J. Comp. Physiol. Psychol.* 69, 649 (1969).
15. S. W. Kuffler, *Cold Spring Harbor Symp. Quant. Biol.* 17, 281 (1952); *J. Physiol. London* 16, 37 (1953).
16. R. B. McCall and W. H. Melson, *Develop. Psychol.*, in press.
17. B. Z. Karmel, C. T. White, W. T. Cleaves, K. J. Steinsiek, paper presented at the meeting of the Eastern Psychological Association, Atlantic City, New Jersey, April 1970.
18. R. B. Eisenberg, E. J. Griffin, D. B. Coursin, M. A. Hunter, *J. Speech Hear. Res.* 7, 245 (1964); Y. Brackbill, G. Adams, D. H. Crowell, M. C. Gray, *J. Exp. Child Psychol.* 3, 176 (1966).
19. G. C. Carpenter, paper presented at the Merrill-Palmer Infancy Conference, Detroit, Michigan, February 1969.
20. R. A. Haaf and R. Q. Bell, *Child Develop.* 38, 893 (1967); M. Lewis, *Develop. Psychol.* 1, 75 (1969).
21. J. Kagan, *Change and Continuity in Infancy* (Wiley, New York, in press).
22. R. B. McCall and W. H. Melson, *Psychonom. Sci.* 17, 317 (1969).
23. R. B. McCall and J. Kagan, *Develop. Psychol.* 2, 90 (1970).
24. W. H. Melson and R. B. McCall, *Child Develop.*, in press.
25. R. B. McCall and J. Kagan, *J. Exp. Child Psychol.* 5, 381 (1967).
26. C. Super, J. Kagan, F. Morrison, M. Haith, J. Weiffenbach, unpublished manuscript.
27. J. L. Gewirtz, in *Determinants of Infant Behaviour*, B. M. Foss, Ed. (Methuen, London, 1965), vol. 3, p. 205.
28. P. R. Zelazo and J. M. Chandler, unpublished manuscript.
29. R. J. Ellingson, in *Advances in Child Development and Behavior*, L. P. Lipsitt and C. C. Spiker, Eds. (Academic Press, New York, 1963), p. 53.
30. C. Dreyfus-Brisac, D. Samson, C. Blanc, N. Monod, *Etud. Neo-natales* 7, 143 (1958).
31. This work was supported by grants from the National Institute of Child Health and Human Development (HD 4299) and the Carnegie Corporation of New York. I thank Robert McCall, Marshall Haith, and Philip Zelazo for comments on the manuscript.

Centerpieces

Conceptual and Rote Learning in Children

John D. Nolan

This paper will attempt to dull the distinction between conceptual and rote learning. While the two have traditionally been considered antithetical, psychological research indicates that rote learning involves a good deal of what is commonly considered conceptualizing, and conceptual learning demands a large amount of what is often considered rote repetition. In school, therefore, the child, of necessity, is doing more rote learning than his teacher may suspect.

Conceptual learning has long, if not always, been considered superior to rote learning. The principal who berated his primary teachers for not teaching concepts may have been undiplomatic in his approach but surely justified in his concern. Who would want to head a school where rote learning seemed to take precedence over conceptual learning? But later in the year the principal's attitude changed from concern to delight. To his surprise, statewide testing of fourth graders indicated that students in his school were "overachieving" so spectacularly that a state department team of observers was sent to find out what the teachers were doing that was so right. Could it have been rote teaching?

The growing emphasis on an information processing approach to the study of learning over the past two decades has convinced psychologists and other educators that a passive learner is a contradiction in terms—that all learning is a very active process, whether it be associating a sound with a letter, learning the addition tables, or grasping the general theory of relativity. Though Jerome Bruner's

John D. Nolan is associate professor of psychology and education at Teachers College. This is the second in a series of papers to appear in TCR *whose purpose is to explicate and interpret for educators the significance of psychological research in their work. The papers have been organized by Dr. Mary Alice White and her colleagues at The Center for the Behavioral Analysis of School Learning, Teachers College.*

contention that ". . . all perceptual experience is necessarily the end product of a categorization process" is rejected by some as a bit too extreme, it is widely accepted that the perception, the storage, and the retrieval of information are all constructive processes. This view is not new. F.C. Bartlett was conducting experiments to test such a position during World War I. However, the plethora of research on perception and memory in recent years has refined our knowledge of how the constructive process works.

That a certain pattern of light waves impinges upon the retina does not necessarily lead to the source of the waves being perceived. We are all aware that we can look at a familiar word printed on a page and read it as a different word. That the source is perceived does not mean that information about it will or even can be stored and retrieved. Work on both visual and auditory perception indicates that, even in the first one-fourth of a second, information which has actually been perceived is lost. Information which survives the twofold danger of (a) not being perceived and (b) being lost immediately may be available for retrieval for only a few seconds; it may be so available many years later; or it may be available for any time period in between. What is to eventuate depends upon what is done with the information.

An oversimplification of one model of human memory may help explain the process. The perceived stimulus first enters a *sensory register* somewhere in the brain (its life span here is about one-fourth of a second) from which it may or may not be read out into *short-term storage*. What is in short-term storage may or may not enter *long-term storage*. The bottleneck in the information processing system is short-term storage because it can hold very few items of information, and can hold these few for only a few seconds unless the items are rehearsed. In this model there is a direct relationship between the length of rehearsal and the probability that an item will enter long-term storage. Of course, factors other than rehearsal time also affect the probability of an item entering long-term storage.

Another important factor concerns what is already in long-term storage. Items related to a new item may be retrieved from long-term storage and rehearsed with the new item. The few items which will be rehearsed are determined by the processor. If he begins to process new information before he has had time to rehearse the old sufficiently, he will lose the old. How then can some people seemingly process and retain so much information rapidly? The answer is that they are processing very few items of information, though each item is informationally rich. For example, when an expert reads a well-written treatise in his field, he can read rapidly with excellent comprehension because most of the ideas presented are familiar. Since the technical phrases are redolent with meaning, the expert need not bother with many of the author's explanations. He can easily pick out and store the new information in the article because there is so little of it that even a rapid reading allows him ample rehearsal time. Moreover, the few new items are informationally rich because they have ramifications for the expert. The novice, on the other hand, must read slowly and carefully if he is to comprehend. There is much information new to him. Each item contains little information because the ramifications are lacking. Thus he has many items to learn.

Chunking and Categorizing   We know that there is a severe limitation on the number of items of information which can be rehearsed. We know that some rehearsal is necessary if the information is to be retained. Miller suggested that the way to overcome the limitation is to "chunk" information. This is a divide-so-as-to-conquer approach. If a person needs to learn a long list of items, he can segment the list into sections of about five items. These five items can then be rehearsed until they form a chunk, that is, a single unit or item. The original five items, now unitized, can be stored or rehearsed as a single item.

For purposes of discussion, let the items be English words. With the single exception of the indefinite article, any English word is an example of unitization or chunking. Each polysyllabic word is a concatenation of syllables. Most syllables are concatenations of phonemes. The series of letters e-d-u-c-a-t-i-o-n is a unit to us; it may not be a unit for a third grader. G. H. Bower is just one of many experimenters who have substantiated the chunking or unitization hypothesis. For example, Bower demonstrated that twelve three-word clichés (each a unit), e.g., "stitch in time," could be learned by adults as rapidly as twelve unrelated words.

There is learning which involves material so unfamiliar that the most efficient approach is to divide it into manageable segments and then form a chunk out of each segment. However, most learning involves material with which the learner already has some familiarity. He can simplify the learning process by organizing the material, that is, putting together those items which share some common attribute, and then rehearsing together what has been organized together. For example, if for some reason one wished to learn the fauna in Yellowstone National Park, one would probably organize them. Birds, mammals, and reptiles would be learned separately. In the class of mammals one would be more likely to learn elk with the various species of deer than with the grizzly bear. Organizing on the basis of a common attribute is usually called categorizing. Bruner suggested that there is a need to categorize in order to reduce the cognitive load. In other words, categorizing reduces how much one must learn.

To categorize incoming information is really equivalent to concept formation. To form a concept one must extract from items those attributes which they share. It is on the basis of common attributes that one places several items of information into a single category. Chunking differs from categorizing precisely on this dimension. The only attribute common to items in the same chunk is spatial or temporal contiguity, that is, the items are seen together or seen or heard one right after the other. The minority who learn their social security numbers do so by chunking. In fact, the number is presented chunked into three digits, two digits, and four digits.

The major difference, then, between conceptual learning and rote learning is the difference between categorizing and chunking. The latter consists of grouping items together because they are experienced together temporarily or spatially, the former because they share common attributes. While the term organizing is usually taken to mean categorizing, it really applies to chunking also. G. Mandler demonstrated that organizing in the sense of categorizing was equivalent to learning. He also demonstrated that there is a limit on the number of items, about five, which can be recalled from a single category. If a person puts more than this number of items into a category, he must subcategorize—form two or more subcategories with the same limitation of about five items. The categories themselves, because they too are items, are subject to the same limitation as their members. About five categories can be retrieved from a supercategory, which in turn forms a unit subject to the same limits. Bower and others demonstrated that, if all information is simultaneously available to the learner, the information organized in an hierarchical fashion is learned far more rapidly than the same information presented in an unorganized manner. However, if the information is presented item-by-item to adults, an organized presentation does not necessarily lead to more rapid learning than does an unorganized presentation. The reason is that if the semantic basis of the organization is sufficiently clear, and if presentation is sufficiently slow, adults can organize and learn the material just as well if it is presented in an unorganized manner as when it is presented in an organized manner. This is not true, however, if the organizational basis is not readily apparent or if presentation is too rapid. The Bower et al. experiment involved a rather rapid presentation.

The picture we obtain of the adult learner is that of a very active individual selectively choosing a limited amount of information from his environment, acting upon that information to organize it on the basis of common attributes (conceptual learning), and rehearsing together the items he has categorized as well as rehearsing the categories. He can also organize the information on the basis of spatial/temporal contiguity by dividing it into segments of a few items and rehearsing the items in each segment until they have formed a chunk, that is, a single item, and then rehearse the chunks (rote learning). For an adult learner, this last approach is a last resort. He can usually find some attribute common to several items and upon this basis organize the seemingly most unrelated information.

E. Tulving asked adults to learn a list of what appeared to be unrelated words. Across a number of learning trials (a single word-by-word presentation of the list followed by a recall in any order the subject wished to recall), he measured the consistency in order of recall when the order of presentation of the words varied on each trial. Tulving called this consistency "subjective organization," that is, an organization chosen by the subject without any preconceptions on the part of the experimenter about how the subject should organize. He found not only a significant correlation between each subject's index of subjective organization and the rate at which the subject learned, but also a commonality in the way the different subjects organized the words. This latter finding suggests that there exists an objective basis for organizing information among people with the same language and cultural backgrounds. Organization is so important to an adult who is attempting to learn that he can be kept from learning if he is forced to keep reorganizing on every learning trial.

Semantic Markers   It is known that adults categorize items on the basis of common attributes. A decade ago researchers suggested that a word be considered a symbol for a sequence of what was called semantic markers. For example, the word "boy" is a symbol for the following sequence: +entity, +object, +living, +animal, +human, -adult, +male; "girl" has the same sequence of markers, but is -male, while "woman" differs from "boy" by being +adult, and -male; since "boy" and "girl" differ only on the sign of the last marker, they are more closely associated than "girl" and "woman" which differ on the sign of the penultimate marker. "Boy" and "tree" are related because they share the markers +entity, +object, +living, so they should be associated, but not as closely associated as "boy" and "cat" which also share the marker +animal. Miller made an empirical study of the way people organize words in an attempt to define the semantic markers. Though there are some difficulties with looking at a word as a well-defined sequence of semantic markers, the notion has produced worthwhile research and will aid the present discussion.

Adults can organize. Adults do organize, and their rate of learning is related to their organization. Children are another story. The younger they are, the more slowly they learn and the more poorly they organize. Young children are particularly poor at organizing on a semantic basis, at least on the semantic basis defined for adults. However, if they are forced to organize on a semantic basis, even kindergarten children increase the amount they can recall.

Unfortunately, kindergarteners do not learn from such an experience, since they immediately go back to an unorganized (at least from an adult view) approach to learning. Third graders profit from the experience of being forced to organize and subsequently will organize (and learn) better on a similar task than they had before being forced to organize, but not as well as when they were being forced. Even ninth graders, though they spontaneously organize much better than younger children, profit from being forced to organize; there is a transfer of organizing to similar learning situations.

We do not know all the reasons why children do not spontaneously organize on a semantic basis when they obviously recognize the basis to some extent and profit from using it. We do know that a particular word is not the same sign for a young child as it is for an adult. In other words, for the child the full set of semantic markers for a word have not yet developed. For example, when a two-year-old boy with a twin sister is told "good boy" by his mother and responds, "No. Me good girl. Her bad boy," he obviously has not developed the marker for gender for the words "boy" and "girl." In this instance, the child apparently differentiated "good" and "bad," but for him "good," when applied to a person was labelled "good-girl" and "bad" labelled "bad-boy." Evidently, he had rarely heard "good-boy."

It is not clear in what order the semantic markers develop. Did the boy in question have fully developed the +living for "boy"? In a series of experiments addressed to the controversy over the order of development of semantic markers, J.M. Anglin obtained inconclusive results. He did, however, clearly demonstrate that the growth of the markers, or at least the ability to use the markers to see relationships between words, and to organize words, continues into young adulthood (mid-twenties), the limit of his investigation. Anglin's results suggest that the younger a person is, the less basis for organization is available to him. That these findings regarding words can be generalized to other concepts is suggested by experiments on hierarchical organization done by Piagetians. For example, a child not yet in the Piagetian stage of formal operations will not see that bird is superordinate of duck, though he can use "bird" and "duck" correctly in a sentence and comprehend that a duck is a bird but a bird is not necessarily a duck.

That there is a definite shift in the way children organize at about the time they move from elementary school to junior high has been demonstrated. For example, Mandler and Stephens found that second and fourth graders not only organize less than sixth and eighth graders (and are able to recall less), but that the basis of organization for the younger children is different. In learning a list of words, the older children tended to organize by putting the nouns together, verbs together, and adjectives together. Moreover, there was more uniformity in organization among the older children. What organization the younger children showed tended to be more idiosyncratic. As the authors remark, it is at about the sixth grade that American children begin entering the Piagetian stage of formal operations.

Implications The investigations cited above have several implications for education. First, we know that the younger a child is, the less apt and the less able he is to organize information in a manner which increases his rate of learning and aids his retention. Because the child's concepts are quite limited, he does not see the relationships adults see, and thus must carry a heavier cognitive load to retain the same items of information. Where the adult can place five items in the same category because they share many semantic markers, and thus has only to recall the category and differentiate a few final semantic markers, the child may place the five items in the same category because, for him, they share just a few markers, and thus he must retrieve the category plus many markers for each item. This also makes it less likely that the child will be able to relate the category to many other categories on the basis of shared semantic markers.

Where the adult is actually forming concepts (seeing the same semantic markers in different items of information), the child may instead be forming chunks, putting items together because they occur together. This makes both his learning slower (he has more to learn) and his retention poorer (items are not as interrelated.) Chunking rather than categorizing may account for some of the rather strange associations primary grade children make. They have experienced semantically unrelated items together and thus formed associations which adults would never form.

A teacher may think that he has successfully taught concepts to a class because the pupils retrieve in juxtaposition those items which the teacher sees as related. Yet the pupils may simply have been chunking, not categorizing. Their learning may be more rote than the teacher thinks it is. This is not bad. In fact, it shows good teaching. The child is not yet capable of forming the full concept, but when he is, he will have what he remembers from his chunk with which to work.

If the younger child is actually forming more of a chunk than a concept, then it is more important for him than for the older child that information be presented in an organized manner. It is also more important that the presentation be slower and more repetitious, for in learning the same material he is processing more information. In other words, the younger child needs to learn by rote as a preparation for conceptual learning.

References

Anglin, J. M. *The Growth of Word Meaning.* Cambridge, Mass.: M.I.T. Press, 1970.
Atkinson, R. C. and Shiffrin, R. M., "Human Memory: A Proposed System and its Control Processes," in K.W. Spence and J.T. Spence, eds. *The Psychology of Learning and Motivation,* Vol. 2. New York: Academic Press, 1968, pp. 89-195.
Bartlett, F.C. *Remembering.* Cambridge, England: Cambridge University Press, 1932.
Bower, G.H., "Chunks as Interference Units in Free Recall," *Journal of Verbal Learning and Verbal Behavior,* No. 8, 1969, pp. 610-613.
Bower, G.H., Clark, M.C., Lesgold, A.M., and Winzenz, D., "Hierarchical Retrieval Schemes in Recall of Categorized Word Lists," *Journal of Verbal Learning and Verbal Behavior,* No. 8, 1961, pp. 323-33.
Bower, G.H. and Lesgold, A.M., "Organization as a Determinant of Part-to-Whole Transfer in Free Recall," *Journal of Verbal Learning and Verbal Behavior,* No. 8, 1969, pp. 501-506.
Bruner, J.S., "On Conceptual Readiness," *Psychological Review,* Vol. 64, 1957, pp. 123-152.
Bruner, J.S., Goodnow, J.J., and Austin, G.A. *A Study of Thinking.* New York: John Wiley, 1956.
Cofer, C.N., Bruce, D.R., and Reicher, G.M., "Clustering in Free Recall as a Function of Certain Methodological Variations," *Journal of Experimental Psychology,* Vol. 71, 1966, pp. 858-877.
Darwin, C.J., Turvey, M.T., and Crowder, R.G., "An Auditory Analogue of the Sperling Partial Report Procedure: Evidence for Brief Auditory Storage," *Cognitive Psychology,* Vol. 3, 1972, pp. 255-267.
Katz, J.J. and Fodor, J.A., "The Structure of Semantic Theory," *Language,* Vol. 39, 1963, pp. 170-210.
Lange, G.W., "The Effectiveness of Conceptual and Rote Verbal Learning Strategies in Children: A Developmental Analysis," unpublished doctoral thesis, The Pennsylvania State University, 1970.
Mandler, G., "Organization and Memory," in K.W. Spence and J.T. Spence, eds. *The Psychology of Learning and Motivation,* Vol. 1. New York: Academic Press, 1967, pp. 327-372.
Mandler, G. and Pearlstone, A., "Free and Constrained Concept Learning and Subsequent Recall," *Journal of Verbal Learning and Verbal Behavior,"* No. 5, 1966, pp. 126-131.
Mandler, G. and Stephens, D., "The Development of Free and Constrained Conceptualization and Subsequent Verbal Memory," *Journal of Experimental Child Psychology,"* Vol. 5, 1967, pp. 86-93.
Miller, G.A., "The Magical Number Seven Plus or Minus Two: Some Limits on our Capacity for Processing Information," *Psychological Review,* Vol. 63, 1956, pp. 81-97.
Miller, G.A., "Psycholinguistic Approaches to the Study of Communication," in D.L. Arm, ed. *Journeys in Science: Small Steps—Great Strides.* Albuquerque, New Mexico: University of New Mexico Press, 1967.
Niemark, E.D., Slotnick, N.S., and Ulrich, T., "Development of Memorization Strategies," *Developmental Psychology,* Vol. 5, 1971, pp. 427-432.
Neisser, Ulric. *Cognitive Psychology.* New York: Appleton-Century-Crofts, 1967.
Rock, I., Halper, F., and Clayton, T., "The Perception and Recognition of Complex Figures," *Cognitive Psychology,* Vol. 3, 1972, pp. 655-673.
Sperling, G., "The Information Available in Brief Visual Presentations," *Psychological Monographs,* Vol. 74, No. 11, Whole No. 498, 1960.
Tulving, E., "Subjective Organization in Free Recall of 'Unrelated' Words," *Psychological Review,* Vol. 69, 1962, pp. 344-354.
For a review of the current state of knowledge on perception and memory of interest to educators, see Kumar, V.K., "The Structures of Human Memory and Some Educational Implications," *Review of Educational Research,* Vol. 41, 1971, pp. 379-417.
For a well worked out set of rules of association based on the concept of semantic markers, cf. Clark, H.H., "Word Associations and Linguistic Theory," in J. Lyons. *New Horizons in Linguistics.* Harmondsworth, Middlesex, England: Penguin Books, 1970.

Language

And The Mind

By Noam Chomsky

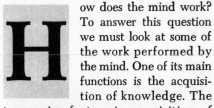 ow does the mind work? To answer this question we must look at some of the work performed by the mind. One of its main functions is the acquisition of knowledge. The two major factors in acquisition of knowledge, perception and learning, have been the subject of study and speculation for centuries. It would not, I think, be misleading to characterize the major positions that have developed as outgrowths of classical rationalism and empiricism. The rationalist theories are marked by the importance they assign to *intrinsic* structures in mental operations—to central processes and organizing principles in perception, and to innate ideas and principles in learning. The empiricist approach, in contrast, has stressed the role of experience and control by environmental factors.

The classical empiricist view is that sensory images are transmitted to the brain as impressions. They remain as ideas that will be associated in various ways, depending on the fortuitous character of experience. In this view a language is merely a collection of words, phrases, and sentences, a habit system, acquired accidentally and extrinsically. In the formulation of Williard Quine, knowledge of a language (and, in fact, knowledge in general) can be represented as "a fabric of sentences variously associated to one another and to nonverbal stimuli by the mechanism of conditioned response." Acquisition of knowledge is only a matter of the gradual construction of this fabric. When sensory experience is interpreted, the already established network may be activated in some fashion. In its essentials, this view has been predominant in modern behavioral science, and it has been accepted with little question by many philosophers as well.

The classical rationalist view is quite different. In this view the mind contains a system of "common notions" that enable it to interpret the scattered and incoherent data of sense in terms of objects and their relations, cause and effect, whole and part, symmetry, gestalt properties, functions, and so on. Sensation, providing only fleeting and meaningless images, is degenerate and particular. Knowledge, much of it beyond immediate awareness, is rich in structure, involves universals, and is highly organized. The innate general principles that underlie and organize this knowledge, according to Leibniz, "enter into our thoughts, of which they form the soul and the connection . . . although we do not at all think of them."

This "active" rationalist view of the acquisition of knowledge persisted through the romantic period in its essentials. With respect to language, it achieves its most illuminating expression in the profound investigations of Wilhelm von Humboldt. His theory of speech perception supposes a generative system of rules that underlies speech production as well as its interpretation. The system is generative in that it makes infinite use of finite means. He regards a language as a structure of forms and concepts based on a system of rules that determine their interrelations, arrangement, and organization. But these finite materials can be combined to make a never-ending product.

n the rationalist and romantic tradition of linguistic theory, the normal use of language is regarded as characteristically innovative. We construct sentences that are entirely new to us. There is no substantive notion of "analogy" or "generalization" that accounts for this creative aspect of language use. It is equally erroneous to describe language as a "habit structure" or as a network of associated responses. The innovative element in normal use of language quickly exceeds the bounds of such marginal principles as analogy or generalization (under any substantive interpretation of these notions). It is important to emphasize this fact because the insight has been lost under the impact of the behaviorist assumptions that have dominated speculation and research in the twentieth century.

In Humboldt's view, acquisition of language is largely a matter of maturation of an innate language capacity. The maturation is guided by internal factors, by an innate "form of language" that is sharpened, differentiated, and given its specific realization through experience. Language is thus a kind of latent structure in the human mind, developed and fixed by exposure to specific linguistic experience. Humboldt believes that all languages will be found to be very simi-

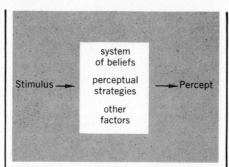

MODEL FOR PERCEPTION. Each physical stimulus, after interpretation by the mental processes, will result in a percept.

lar in their grammatical form, similar not on the surface but in their deeper inner structures. The innate organizing principles severely limit the class of possible languages, and these principles determine the properties of the language that is learned in the normal way.

The active and passive views of perception and learning have elaborated with varying degrees of clarity since the seventeenth century. These views can be confronted with empirical evidence in a variety of ways. Some recent work in psychology and neurophysiology is highly suggestive in this regard. There is evidence for the existence of central processes in perception, specifically for control over the functioning of sensory neurons by the brain-stem reticular system. Behavioral counterparts of this central control have been under investigation for several years. Furthermore, there is evidence for innate organization of the perceptual system of a highly specific sort at every level of biological organization. Studies of the visual system of the frog, the discovery of specialized cells responding to angle and motion in the lower cortical centers of cats and rabbits, and the somewhat comparable investigations of the auditory system of frogs—all are relevant to the classical questions of intrinsic structure mentioned earlier. These studies suggest that there are highly organized, innately determined perceptual systems that are adapted closely to the animal's "life space" and that provide the basis for what we might call "acquisition of knowledge." Also relevant are certain behavioral studies of human infants, for example those showing the preference for faces over other complex stimuli.

These and other studies make it reasonable to inquire into the possibility that complex intellectual structures are determined narrowly by innate mental organization. What is perceived may be determined by mental processes of considerable depth. As far as language

learning is concerned, it seems to me that a rather convincing argument can be made for the view that certain principles intrinsic to the mind provide invariant structures that are a precondition for linguistic experience. In the course of this article I would like to sketch some of the ways such conclusions might be clarified and firmly established.

here are several ways linguistic evidence can be used to reveal properties of human perception and learning. In this section we consider one research strategy that might take us nearer to this goal.

Let us say that in interpreting a certain physical stimulus a person constructs a "percept." This percept represents some of his conclusions (in general, unconscious) about the stimulus. To the extent that we can characterize such percepts, we can go on to investigate the mechanisms that relate stimulus and percept. Imagine a model of perception that takes stimuli as inputs and arrives at percepts as "outputs." The model might contain a system of beliefs, strategies for interpreting stimuli, and other factors, such as the organization of memory. We would then have a perceptual model that might be represented graphically [*see illustration at left, above*].

Consider next the system of beliefs that is a component of the perceptual model. How was this acquired? To study this problem, we must investigate a second model, which takes certain data as input and gives as "output" (again, internally represented) the system of be-

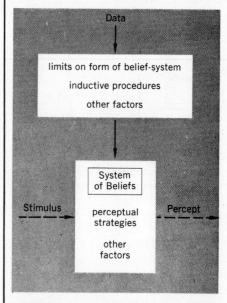

MODEL FOR LEARNING. One's system of beliefs, a part of the perception model, is acquired from data as shown above.

liefs operating in the perceptual model. This second model, a model of learning, would have its own intrinsic structure, as did the first. This structure might consist of conditions on the nature of the system of beliefs that can be acquired, of innate inductive strategies, and again, of other factors such as the organization of memory [*see illustration at left, below*].

Under further conditions, which are interesting but not relevant here, we can take these perceptual and learning models as theories of the acquisition of knowledge, rather than of belief. How then would the models apply to language? The input stimulus to the perceptual model is a speech signal, and the percept is a representation of the utterance that the hearer takes the signal to be and of the interpretation he assigns to it. We can think of the percept as the structural description of a linguistic expression which contains certain phonetic, semantic, and syntactic information. Most interesting is the syntactic information, which best can be discussed by examining a few typical cases.

he three sentences in the example seem to be the same syntactic structure [*see illustration at right*]. Each contains the subject *I,* and the predicate of each consists of a verb (*told, expected, persuaded*), a noun phrase (*John*), and an embedded predicate phrase (*to leave*). This similarity is only superficial, however—a similarity in what we may call the "surface structure" of these sentences, which differ in important ways when we consider them with somewhat greater care.

The differences can be seen when the sentences are paraphrased or subjected to certain grammatical operations, such as the conversion from active to passive forms. For example, in normal conversation the sentence "I told John to leave" can be roughly paraphrased as "What I told John was to leave." But the other two sentences cannot be paraphrased as "What I persuaded John was to leave" or "What I expected John was to leave." Sentence 2 can be paraphrased as: "It was expected by me that John would leave." But the other two sentences cannot undergo a corresponding formal operation, yielding: "It was persuaded by me that John would leave" or "It was told by me that John should leave."

Sentences 2 and 3 differ more subtly. In Sentence 3 *John* is the direct object of *persuade,* but in Sentence 2 *John* is not the direct object of *expect.* We can

show this by using these verbs in slightly more complex sentences: "I persuaded the doctor to examine John" and "I expected the doctor to examine John." If we replace the embedded proposition *the doctor to examine John* with its passive form *John to be examined by the doctor,* the change to the passive does not, in itself, change the meaning. We can accept as paraphrases "I expected the doctor to examine John" and "I expected John to be examined by the doctor." But we cannot accept as paraphrases "I persuaded the doctor to examine John" and "I persuaded John to be examined by the doctor."

The parts of these sentences differ in their grammatical functions. In "I persuaded John to leave" *John* is both the object of *persuade* and the subject of *leave.* These facts must be represented

(1)	I told John to leave
(2)	I expected John to leave
(3)	I persuaded John to leave

First Paraphrase:

(1a)	What I told John was to leave (ACCEPTABLE)
(2a)	What I expected John was to leave (UNACCEPTABLE)
(3a)	What I persuaded John was to leave (UNACCEPTABLE)

Second Paraphrase:

(1b)	It was told by me that John would leave (UNACCEPTABLE)
(2b)	It was expected by me that John would leave (ACCEPTABLE)
(3b)	It was persuaded by me that John would leave (UNACCEPTABLE)

(4)	I expected the doctor to examine John
(5)	I persuaded the doctor to examine John

Passive replacement as paraphrase:

(4a)	I expected John to be examined by the doctor (MEANING RETAINED)
(5a)	I persuaded John to be examined by the doctor (MEANING CHANGED)

SUPERFICIAL SIMILARITY. When the sentences above are paraphrased or are converted from active to passive forms, differences in their deep structure appear.

in the percept since they are known, intuitively, to the hearer of the speech signal. No special training or instruction is necessary to enable the native speaker to understand these examples, to know which are "wrong" and which "right," although they may all be quite new to him. They are interpreted by the native speaker instantaneously and uniformly, in accordance with structural principles that are known tacitly, intuitively, and unconsciously.

These examples illustrate two significant points. First, the surface structure of a sentence, its organization into various phrases, may not reveal or immediately reflect its deep syntactic structure. The deep structure is not represented directly in the form of the speech signal; it is abstract. Second, the rules that determine deep and surface structure and

their interrelation in particular cases must themselves be highly abstract. They are surely remote from consciousness, and in all likelihood they cannot be brought to consciousness.

 study of such examples, examples characteristic of all human languages that have been carefully studied, constitutes the first stage of the linguistic investigation outlined above, namely the study of the percept. The percept contains phonetic and semantic information related through the medium of syntactic structure. There are two aspects to this syntactic structure. It consists of a surface directly related to the phonetic form, and a deep structure that underlies the semantic interpretation. The deep structure is represented in the mind and rarely is indicated directly in the physical signal.

A language, then, involves a set of semantic-phonetic percepts, of sound-meaning correlations, the correlations being determined by the kind of intervening syntactic structure just illustrated. The English language correlates sound and meaning in one way, Japanese in another, and so on. But the general properties of percepts, their forms and mechanisms, are remarkably similar for all languages that have been carefully studied.

Returning to our models of perception and learning, we can now take up the problem of formulating the system of beliefs that is a central component in perceptual processes. In the case of language, the "system of beliefs" would now be called the "generative grammar," the system of rules that specifies the sound-meaning correlation and generates the class of structural descriptions (percepts) that constitute the language in question. The generative grammar, then, represents the speaker-hearer's knowledge of his language. We can use the term *grammar of a language* ambiguously, as referring not only to the speaker's internalized, subconscious knowledge but to the professional linguist's representation of this internalized and intuitive system of rules as well.

ow is this generative grammar acquired? Or, using our learning model, what is the internal structure of the device that could develop a generative grammar?

We can think of every normal human's internalized grammar as, in effect, a theory of his language. This theory provides a sound-meaning correlation for an infinite number of sentences. It provides an infinite set of structural descriptions; each contains a surface structure that determines phonetic form and a deep structure that determines semantic content.

In formal terms, then, we can describe the child's acquisition of language as a kind of theory construction. The child discovers the theory of his language with only small amounts of data from that language. Not only does his "theory of the language" have an enormous predictive scope, but it also enables the child to reject a great deal of the very data on which the theory has been constructed. Normal speech consists, in large part, of fragments, false starts, blends, and other distortions of the underlying idealized forms. Nevertheless, as is evident from a study of the mature use of language, what the child learns is the underlying ideal theory. This is a remarkable fact. We must also bear in mind that the child constructs this ideal theory without explicit instruction, that he acquires this knowledge at a time when he is not capable of complex intellectual achievements in many other domains, and that this achievement is relatively independent of intelligence or the particular course of experience. These are facts that a theory of learning must face.

A scientist who approaches phenomena of this sort without prejudice or dogma would conclude that the acquired knowledge must be determined in a rather specific way by intrinsic proper-

ties of mental organization. He would then set himself the task of discovering the innate ideas and principles that make such acquisition of knowledge possible.

It is unimaginable that a highly specific, abstract, and tightly organized language comes by accident into the mind of every four-year-old child. If there were not an innate restriction on the form of grammar, then the child could employ innumerable theories to account for his linguistic experience, and no one system, or even small class of systems, would be found exclusively acceptable or even preferable. The child could not possibly acquire knowledge of a language. This restriction on the form of grammar is a precondition for linguistic experience, and it is surely the critical factor in determining the course and result of language learning. The child cannot know at birth which language he is going to learn. But he must "know" that its grammar must be of a predetermined form that excludes many imaginable languages.

The child's task is to select the appropriate hypothesis from this restricted class. Having selected it, he can confirm his choice with the evidence further available to him. But neither the evidence nor any process of induction (in any well-defined sense) could in themselves have led to this choice. Once the hypothesis is sufficiently well confirmed, the child knows the language defined by this hypothesis; consequently, his knowledge extends vastly beyond his linguistic experience, and he can reject much of this experience as imperfect, as resulting from the interaction of many factors, only one of which is the ideal grammar that determines a sound-meaning connection for an infinite class of linguistic expressions. Along such lines as these one might outline a theory to explain the acquisition of language.

s has been pointed out, both the form and meaning of a sentence are determined by syntactic structures that are not represented directly in the signal and that are related to the signal only at a distance, through a long sequence of interpretive rules. This property of abstractness in grammatical structure is of primary importance, and it is on this property that our inferences about mental processes are based. Let us examine this abstractness a little more closely.

Not many years ago, the process of sentence interpretation might have been described approximately along the fol-

lowing lines. A speech signal is received and segmented into successive units (overlapping at the borders). These units are analyzed in terms of their invariant phonetic properties and assigned to "phonemes." The sequence of phonemes, so constructed, is then segmented into minimal grammatically functioning units (morphemes and words). These are again categorized. Successive operations of segmentation and classification will lead to what I have called "surface structure"—an analysis of a sentence into phrases, which can be represented as a proper bracketing of the sentence, with the bracketed units assigned to various categories [*see illustration, page 51*]. Each segment—phonetic, syntactic or semantic—would be identified in terms of certain invariant properties. This would be an exhaustive analysis of the structure of the sentence.

With such a conception of language structure, it made good sense to look forward hopefully to certain engineering applications of linguistics—for example, to voice-operated typewriters capable of segmenting an expression into its successive phonetic units and identifying these, so that speech could be converted to some form of phonetic writing in a mechanical way; to mechanical analysis of sentence structure by fairly straightforward and well-understood computational techniques; and perhaps even beyond to such projects as machine translation. But these hopes have by now been largely abandoned with the realization that this conception of grammatical structure is inadequate at every level, semantic, phonetic, and syntactic. Most important, at the level of syntactic organization, the surface structure indicates semantically significant relations only in extremely simple cases. In general, the deeper aspects of syntactic organization are representable by labeled bracketing, but of a very different sort from that seen in surface structure.

There is evidence of various sorts, both from phonetics and from experimental psychology, that labeled bracketing is an adequate representation of surface structure. It would go beyond the bounds of this paper to survey the phonetic evidence. A good deal of it is presented in a forthcoming book, *Sound Pattern of English*, by myself and Morris Halle. Similarly, very interesting experimental work by Jerry Fodor and his colleagues, based on earlier observations by D. E. Broadbent and Peter Ladefoged, has shown that the disruption of a speech signal (for example, by a superimposed click) tends to be perceived at the

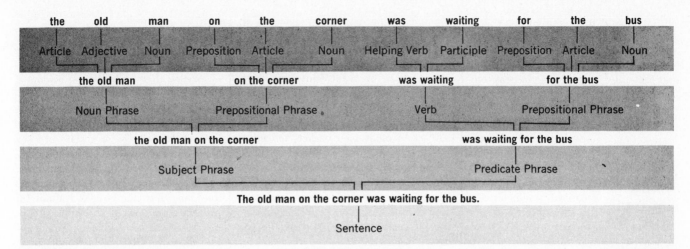

the	old	man	on	the	corner	was	waiting	for	the	bus
Article	Adjective	Noun	Preposition	Article	Noun	Helping Verb	Participle	Preposition	Article	Noun

the old man	on the corner	was waiting	for the bus
Noun Phrase	Prepositional Phrase	Verb	Prepositional Phrase

the old man on the corner	was waiting for the bus
Subject Phrase	Predicate Phrase

The old man on the corner was waiting for the bus.

Sentence

SURFACE STRUCTURE ANALYSIS. A type of sentence analysis now abandoned as inadequate at every level is this labeled bracketing which analyzes the sentence by successive division into larger units with each unit assigned to its own category.

boundaries of phrases rather than at the point where the disruption actually occurred, and that in many cases the bracketing of surface structure can be read directly from the data on perceptual displacement. I think the evidence is rather good that labeled bracketing serves to represent the surface structure that is related to the perceived form of physical signals.

Deep structures are related to surface structures by a sequence of certain formal operations, operations now generally called "grammatical transformations." At the levels of sound, meaning, and syntax, the significant structural features of sentences are highly abstract. For this reason they cannot be recovered by elementary data-processing techniques. This fact lies behind the search for central processes in speech perception and the search for intrinsic, innate structure as the basis for language learning.

ow can we represent deep structure? To answer this question we must consider the grammatical transformations that link surface structure to the underlying deep structure that is not always apparent.

Consider, for example, the operations of passivization and interrogation. In the sentences (1) John was examined by the doctor, and (2) did the doctor examine John, both have a deep structure similar to the paraphrase of Sentence 1, (3) the doctor examined John. The same network of grammatical relations determines the semantic interpretation in each case. Thus two of the grammatical transformations of English must be the operations of passivization and interrogation that form such surface structures as Sentences 1 and 2 from a deeper structure which in its essentials also un-

derlies Sentence 3. Since the transformations ultimately produce surface structures, they must produce labeled bracketings [*see illustration above*]. But notice that these operations can apply in sequence: we can form the passive question "was John examined by the doctor" by passivization followed by interrogation. Since the result of passivization is a labeled bracketing, it follows that the interrogative transformation operates on a labeled bracketing and forms a new labeled bracketing. Thus a transformation such as interrogation maps a labeled bracketing into a labeled bracketing.

By similar argument, we can show that all grammatical transformations are structure-dependent mappings of this sort and that the deep structures which underlie all sentences must themselves be labeled bracketings. Of course, the labeled bracketing that constitutes deep structure will in general be quite different from that representing the surface structure of a sentence. Our argument is somewhat oversimplified, but it is roughly correct. When made precise and fully accurate it strongly supports the view that deep structures, like surface structures, are formally to be taken as labeled bracketings, and that grammatical transformations are mappings of such structures onto other similar structures.

ecent studies have sought to explore the ways in which grammatical structure of the sort just described enters into mental operations. Much of this work has been based on a proposal formulated by George Miller as a first approximation, namely, that the amount of memory used to store a sentence should reflect the number of transformations used in deriving it. For example, H. B. Savin and E. Perchonock

investigated this assumption in the following way: they presented to subjects a sentence followed by a sequence of unrelated words. They then determined the number of these unrelated words recalled when the subject attempted to repeat the sentence and the sequence of words. The more words recalled, the less memory used to store the sentence. The fewer words recalled, the more memory used to store the sentence. The results showed a remarkable correlation of amount of memory and number of transformations in certain simple cases. In fact, in their experimental material, shorter sentences with more transformations took up more "space in memory" than longer sentences that involved fewer transformations.

Savin has extended this work and has shown that the effects of deep structure and surface structure can be differentiated by a similar technique. He considered paired sentences with approximately the same deep structure but with one of the pair being more complex in surface structure. He showed that, under the experimental conditions just described, the paired sentences were indistinguishable. But if the sequence of unrelated words precedes, rather than follows, the sentence being tested, then the more complex (in surface structure) of the pair is more difficult to repeat correctly than the simpler member. Savin's very plausible inference is that sentences are coded in memory in terms of deep structure. When the unrelated words precede the test sentence, these words use up a certain amount of short-term memory, and the sentence that is more complex in surface structure cannot be analyzed with the amount of memory remaining. But if the test sentence precedes the unrelated words, it is, once understood, stored in terms of deep structure, which is about the same in both cases. Therefore the same amount of memory remains, in the paired cases, for recall of the following words. This is a beautiful example of the way creative experimental studies can interweave with theoretical work in the study of language and of mental processes.

n speaking of mental processes we have returned to our original problem. We can now see why it is reasonable to maintain that the linguistic evidence supports an "active" theory of acquisition of knowledge. The study of sentences and of speech perception, it seems to me, leads to a perceptual theory of a classical rationalist sort. Representative of this school, among others, were the seventeenth-century Cambridge Platonists, who developed the idea that our perception is guided by notions that originate from the mind and that provide the framework for the interpretation of sensory stimuli. It is not sufficient to suggest that this framework is a store of "neural models" or "schemata" which are in some manner applied to perception (as is postulated in some current theories of perception). We must go well beyond this assumption and return to the view of Wilhelm von Humboldt, who attributed to the mind a system of rules that generates such models and schemata under the stimulation of the senses. The system of rules itself determines the content of the percept that is formed.

We can offer more than this vague and metaphoric account. A generative grammar and an associated theory of speech perception provide a concrete example of the rules that operate and of the mental objects that they construct and manipulate. Physiology cannot yet explain the physical mechanisms that affect these abstract functions. But neither physiology nor psychology provides evidence that calls this account into question or that suggests an alternative. As mentioned earlier, the most exciting current work in the physiology of perception shows that even the peripheral systems analyze stimuli into the complex properties of objects, and that central processes may significantly affect the information transmitted by the receptor organs.

The study of language, it seems to me, offers strong empirical evidence that empiricist theories of learning are quite inadequate. Serious efforts have been made in recent years to develop principles of induction, generalization, and data analysis that would account for knowledge of a language. These efforts have been a total failure. The methods and principles fail not for any superficial reason such as lack of time or data. They fail because they are intrinsically incapable of giving rise to the system of rules that underlies the normal use of language. What evidence is now available supports the view that all human languages share deep-seated properties of organization and structure. These properties—these linguistic universals—can be plausibly assumed to be an innate mental endowment rather than the result of learning. If this is true, then the study of language sheds light on certain long-standing issues in the theory of knowledge. Once again, I see little reason to doubt that what is true of language is true of other forms of human knowledge as well.

There is one further question that might be raised at this point. How does the human mind come to have the innate properties that underlie acquisition of knowledge? Here linguistic evidence obviously provides no information at all. The process by which the human mind has achieved its present state of complexity and its particular form of innate organization are a complete mystery, as much of a mystery as the analogous questions that can be asked about the processes leading to the physical and mental organization of any other complex organism. It is perfectly safe to attribute this to evolution, so long as we bear in mind that there is no substance to this assertion—it amounts to nothing more than the belief that there is surely some naturalistic explanation for these phenomena.

There are, however, important aspects of the problem of language and mind that can be studied sensibly within the limitations of present understanding and technique. I think that, for the moment, the most productive investigations are those dealing with the nature of particular grammars and with the universal conditions met by all human languages. I have tried to suggest how one can move, in successive steps of increasing abstractness, from the study of percepts to the study of grammar and perceptual mechanisms, and from the study of grammar to the study of universal grammar and the mechanisms of learning.

In this area of convergence of linguistics, psychology, and philosophy, we can look forward to much exciting work in coming years.

Toward a cognitive theory of teaching

by Nathan L. Gage

Let me begin with the assertion that, before we can undertake to develop theories of teaching, we need to analyze the concept of teaching. "Teaching" is a misleadingly generic term that simply covers too much. It falsely suggests a single, unitary phenomenon that can fruitfully be made the subject of theory development.

Learning theory, in my opinion, has long been hung up on a similar fallacy. Because the same term, "learning," has been applied to an enormous range of phenomena, psychologists have been misled into believing that single theory can be developed to explain the whole gamut. Animal learning in puzzle boxes and Skinner boxes, human learning of meaningless paired associates, and the learning of school subjects in classrooms have all been termed "learning." And because all these activities have been given the same name, some psychologists have attempted to account for all of them by a single, general, unified theory.

I shall support my references to this enterprise as a fallacy in learning theory by merely quoting Tolman, who said in 1949,

> I wish to suggest that our familiar theoretical disputes about learning may *perhaps* . . . be resolved, if we can agree that there are really a number of different kinds of learning. For it may then turn out that the theory and laws appropriate to one kind may well be different from those appropriate to other kinds (*5*, p. 144).

What Tolman saw as a saving possibility in learning theory is what I see as an absolute necessity at the present early beginnings of our concern with theories of teaching. We must guard against what I see as inevitably futile attempts to develop a single theory that will embrace all the phenomena that go under the single name of teaching.

Toward Analysis

If so, then the concept of teaching must be analyzed into processes or elements that might properly constitute the subject of theories. What kinds of analyses can be made? I want to offer some illustrative analyses about whose fruitfulness I have as yet almost no conviction but which do indicate what I have in mind.

First, teaching can be analyzed according to *types of teacher activity*. Rather than use my own examples, let me draw upon those listed in a recent paper by Sorenson and Husek (*3*). In developing an instrument for assessing teacher role expectations, they identified the following six role dimensions: information-giver, disciplinarian, adviser, counselor, motivator, and referrer. Their set omits such other dimensions as explainer, demonstrator, housekeeper, curriculum planner, and evaluator. My point is simply that teaching consists of many kinds of activity and that it is unreasonable to expect a single theory to explain all of them.

A second way to analyze teaching goes according to the *types of educational objectives*, the things to be learned. One well known categorization of objectives puts them into the cognitive, affective, and psychomotor domains. Tolman (*5*) classified the things to be learned—or the connections or relations that get learned—into six types, which he named cathexes, equivalence beliefs, field expectancies, field-cognition modes, drive discriminations, and motor patterns. No matter how we do it, we must recognize that teachers teach different things, different not only from one course to another, but even within a single class session; the same theory of teaching should not be expected to apply to all things taught.

A third way to analyze teaching might proceed on the basis of the *different families of learning theory* that now seem useful. My own favorite way of classifying these families refers to them as conditioning, identification, and cognitive theories. Each of these can be stood on its head to suggest a corresponding view of the teaching process. At the moment, I see such views not as competing but as complementary. Hence, again, I see them as providing alternative ways of analyzing the phenomena called teaching.

My fourth and last illustration of an analysis of teaching draws upon *components of the learning process* as formulated by any of the learning theories. The well known paradigm developed by Neal Miller (*2*) sets up four components of learning: drive, cue, response, and reward. Corresponding components of teaching would be "motivating," "cue-providing," "response-eliciting," and "rewarding." It may well be that we shall have to develop separate theories for each of such components of the teaching process.

Thus far, I have argued that teaching as such is too broad, vague, and unwieldy to provide the proper subject of attempts at theory development. And I have then offered some examples of ways in which it can perhaps be broken down into components that will support valid attempts at theory development. I have considered all this necessary as an introduction to my main concern in this paper, which is an attempt to outline a special—as against a general—theory that applies to just the kind of delimited concern that I am advocating.

Engendering Comprehension

Here I want to offer a point of view, a program, concerning aspects of research on teaching that I consider important, neglected, and promising. I have in mind the promotion of theory and research on engendering comprehension in the academic disciplines. This is a much narrower concern than all of teaching. I mean to omit from this focus such matters as motivating students, evaluating their achievement, promoting their mental health, increasing their store of information, improving their motor skills, developing their effectiveness as group members, and so on. Even within the realm of school subjects, my concern omits such matters as handwriting, spelling, woodshop, and physical education. I propose to focus, in short, on one relatively specific, although still immensely broad, aspect of all teaching: the teacher's role in engendering comprehension of concepts and principles as they are found in such so-called academic subjects as English, mathematics, science, and social studies. In doing so, I intend no value judgment either about school subjects or about other aspects of the learning process even within a single academic discipline. I grant that motivation, mental health, social relationships, and the like are important even in the acquisition of comprehension in the academic disciplines. But for the moment, I choose to regard them as merely subservient to the present focus, to the moment of truth in any classroom when the teacher has the attention of his well-motivated, emotionally and socially secure, and otherwise fully ready students, and faces the task of producing in them a comprehension of some concept or principle in the academic discipline with which he is concerned. What should he do? What *must* he do, if his behavior is to have the desired effect on the comprehension of his youngsters? How can the behavior of one person, a teacher, have an effect on another person's comprehension of a concept or principle? Here, at last, is the question to which I wish to address myself.

71

My answer, in very general terms, is that the teacher will manipulate the learner's environment, in accordance with the laws of logic and cognition, in the same way that he can influence another person's perceptions by manipulating the environment in accordance with the laws of perception. The latter kinds of laws are familiar to all of us; they refer to such matters as the constancies of perceived size and shape, the determiners of figure and ground, grouping and patterning, proximity, similarity, continuity, and closure. We can to a great extent compel others to perceive what we want them to perceive by controlling the patterning and structure of stimuli in their environment. We are compelled to see motion in stationary objects when lights go on and off in certain temporal and spatial patterns, *i.e.*, we are compelled to see the phi phenomenon or moving pictures by the manipulator of our visual environment. We are compelled to see the Big Dipper by someone who points it out to us because he calls our attention to it and gives us a set for a certain perception of this particular pattern of stars.

Cognition in the Classroom

The teacher, by the same token, can compel us to comprehend concepts and principles, depending on whether the stimuli or ideas themselves exist in certain patterns, whether they have certain relationships to one another, and, of course, on whether the pupil has certain cognitive capacities, sets, and the like.

Such an approach to the function of the teacher in engendering comprehension must rest on the assumption that what is to be learned does have a logical structure and organization, analogous to the structuring of dots and lines in the classical discussions of visual perception. It is because of this necessary assumption that I have restricted this discussion to the teaching of comprehension in the academic disciplines, which I define as those bodies of knowledge that have well formulated, clearly articulated, logical structures of powerful concepts and principles.

There happens to be a movement within educational psychology at present that is concerned with exactly the aspect of teaching to which I am restricting this discussion. I am referring to the efforts now being made to develop principles of programing instructional materials. For various reasons, at least some of which seem to be merely incidental and irrelevant, these efforts are currently being made on the basis of a stimulus-response, conditioning, or reinforcement paradigm of the learning process. Yet it seems to me that, at the heart of the programed instruction movement, where principles of programing are being developed, there lies not a reinforcement psychology but a cognitive psychology of which its users often seem to be oblivious. Consider the following statement from a discussion of the Ruleg (rule-example) system of programing:

> The third step is to arrange the ru index cards in an approximate order for program presentation. . . . Ordering may be according to a continuum of complexity . . . , chronology . . . , spatiality . . . , or dependence on other ru's. Interdependent relationships among rules should be carefully considered, because the understanding of one rule may depend upon the mastery of some other rules (*4*, p. 72).

Later, in describing another way of systematizing the programer's task, the same authors discuss outlining the material to be taught and state that the major headings should be "ordered in some *rational* sequence" (*4*, p. 74, my italics).

It is not only in the broad structuring of the subject that cognitive properties of instruction are invoked. Within the frames, or small units, of a program, the programers are also advised to give heed to laws of cognition. Thus, we are told that, in all good frames, "the response is evoked in the presence of a *meaningful* context which is new to the student" (*4*, p. 87, my italics). In discussing prompts, or stimuli in a frame intended to make it more effective in evoking the desired response, the authors say they provide "context" (*4*, p. 89). Presumably, a prompt depends for its effectiveness on such perception-relevant or cognition-relevant properties as its similarity to, proximity to, contrast, or continuity with the other stimuli in the frame and the response to be evoked by the frame. Formal prompts work because of their mere visual or auditory similarity, while thematic prompts depend on their similarity in meaning to the desired response. Without saying so, the authors refer to perceptual and cognitive properties of stimuli throughout their discussion of the many different kinds of prompts that they describe and illustrate.

Finally, it would be easy to identify references to ideas about perception and cognition in the programer's treatments of sequences of frames and general program characteristics. Such ideas as that of the "generalization sequence," aimed at broadening the range of stimuli to which a given response will be made, are described as including statements describing the "common properties" of the stimulus class involved. The notion of common property is a perceptual or logical one, and principles of perception and cognition enter into the determination and communication of a common property in a class of stimuli.

From Programs to Teachers

My purpose in identifying what seems to me to be a saturation of the programed instruction movement with cognitive psychology is not the invidious one of detracting from the power and relevance of reinforcement approaches to teaching. For some aspects of teaching, reinforcement models seem pertinent indeed. For other aspects of teaching, however, and particularly for understanding and improving the work of live teachers in promoting comprehension within the academic disciplines, we need to focus just as sharply on the cognitive aspects of teacher behavior as the students of programing principles have focused, however unwittingly, on the cognitive aspects of their programs. This kind of concern has been most notable by its absence in the research on teaching conducted by psychologists. Such research has often been concerned with who talks to whom and how much in the classroom. Or it has dealt with the teacher's warmth, permissiveness, or authoritarianism. Or it has dealt with the amount of organization and systematization that a teacher displayed in his preparation for and conduct of classroom work. But only rarely, it seems to me, have we been concerned with the actual intellectual content, the cognitive organization, and the logical validity of what teachers say to their pupils and of what the pupils say to their teacher and to one another. When we examine a textbook, of course, these aspects of its content and organization come to the fore. We pay close attention to the logic of its arguments and the aptness and compelling power of the data and examples that the authors adduce. I am saying that we ought to look in the same way at what teachers do in the classroom. The laws of logic and the principles of cognition, analogous to the principles of perception, give us a convenient point of entry into such an enterprise. If teaching gets studied in this way, it may eventually be possible to formulate a cognitive theory of teaching that will yield us the power we need to understand, predict, and improve the ability of teachers to engender comprehnsion in the academic disciplines. And that ability is not the least important or intriguing of the components of the complex of phenomena that we call teaching.

I have attempted two things: First, I have tried to demonstrate that the phenomenon called teaching is too broad and complex to support any attempt at a single, general theory that will embrace all of it. The concept of teaching needs to be analyzed, and I have offered examples of such analyses according to teacher functions, teaching objectives, families of learning theory, and components of the learning process. A valid theory of teaching had better be concerned with only a specific component resulting from such analyses.

Second, focusing on one part of teaching, the teacher's function of engendering comprehension in the academic disciplines, I have tried to indicate what cognitive theory has to offer toward a theory of teaching. Using analogies from perception and drawing upon recent efforts to develop principles for programing instructional materials, I have indicated the kinds of properties of teaching that would be the concern of such a theory of teaching. Finally, I have concluded by urging that more research on teaching deal with cognitive variables, in contrast to the affective, social, and motor variables to which it has in recent decades been almost exclusively devoted.

REFERENCES

1. Gage, N. L. Theories of teaching. In E. R. Hilgard (Chmn.) Theories of learning and education. *Yearb. Natl. Soc. Stud. Educ.,* 1964, *63.*
2. Miller, N. E., & Dollard, J. *Social learning and imitation.* New Haven: Yale Univer. Press, 1941.
3. Sorenson, G., & Husek, T. Development of a measure of teacher role expectations. *Amer. Psychologist,* 1963, *18,* 389 (Abst.).
4. Taber, J. I., Glaser, R., *et al. A guide to the preparation of programed instructional material.* Pittsburgh: Dept. Psychol., Univer. Pittsburgh, 1962 (Mimeo.).
5. Tolman, E. C. There is more than one kind of learning. *Psychol. Rev.,* 1949, *56,* 144-155.

IV. MENTAL ABILITY

In at least some ways, there is consensus among psychologists concerning mental ability. Thus, in terms of the measurement of intelligence, the Galton idea that intellectual ability manifests itself in simple, discrimination functioning has been abandoned—at least pending the possibilities of the more direct observation of thought taking place in the brain—in favor of the Binet notion that it reflects itself in more complex functioning. Further, intelligence tests are seen as moderately good predictors of school achievement, at least in terms of our present schooling arrangements. On more basic levels, however, despite the fact that for at least the past two thousand years there seems to have been recognition of the fact that individuals differ in mental ability, ambiguity continues to surround the definition, etiology, and social significance of the word, intelligence.

For many years, the basic conceptual controversy over intelligence or mental ability was whether or not it could be considered a unitary phenomenon. It was Charles Spearman who suggested that there was a single general intelligence, g, which lay behind various s's, specific abilities. By contrast, J. P. Guildford abandoned the notion of g altogether in favor of the identification of 120 highly specialized mental abilities each of which was conceptualized as independent of every other one. Louis Thurstone offered an intermediate view, identifying eight "primary" mental abilities. Raymond Cattell's article in this section represents another intermediate position. Professor Cattel distinguishes between two kinds of g or general intelligence: one provides the power for routine learned abilities while the other provids for less teachable and more complex abilities such as abstract reasoning.

In more recent years, the debate over intelligence has been in response to the frequently observed fact that the *measured* intelligence of various subgroups within the population differs. In the early phases of this debate, interest focused on the nature of the intelligence tests themselves. Were the subtests and individual items composed in such a way as to discriminate against and be unfair to children and adults from different social classes and/or cultural groups? Many investigators felt that this was, in fact, the case, and a number of attempts were made to construct essentially non-verbal culture-free or culture-fair instruments. It may have been the disappointing results of these efforts which led to the present form of the debate in which the question being discussed is whether observed IQ differences are genetically or environmentally determined.

It is probably true that more heat than light has been generated in this socially explosive controversy. In Morton Hunt's article, special attention is given to the environment vs. heredity arguments and the especially relevant studies of identical twins. In attempting to synthesize the apparently contradictory evidence, Mr. Hunt offers the middle-road solution. That is, intelligence is not a lump sum to which heredity and environment each contribute so many units. In this view, heredity and environment do not add up, they interact. The result is not a sum but a product. Jerome Kagan's article reinforces this position but makes an even stronger argument with which we essentially concur. That is, the genetic contribution to IQ is unknown. Further, intelligence can best be seen as simply a specialized style of problem solving valued by our particular society. Since we also use this skill as a rite of passage, we have been too easily seduced into the false belief that those without it were of fundamentally different intellectual competence.

As we have pointed out in discussing the general concerns of educational psychologists and the particular problems that arise in considering both development and cognition, the application of psychological ideas to educational contexts requires a certain breadth of view, one that is commensurate with the actual complexity of the process. The same is true in the consideration of mental ability or intelligence. Even without direct reference to educational applications, Quinn McNemar's article argues that further progress in the study of the intellect is unlikely unless we expand the traditional stimulus-response model to include the sociobiological dimensions of both organism and process. Constance Kamii also wishes to push our consideration of intelligence beyond simple cognition. She points out that Piaget's notion of intelligence as a living, growing thing functioning in the various stages of the mind's development is intimately related to both cognitive and affective considerations. Further, the very holistic conception is shown to have important implications for the formulation of educational objectives and classroom practices.

In terms of classroom practice, both mental ability and the effect of the educational program should reveal themselves in specific pupil achievement. Achievement data are the central focus of the last two articles in this section, both of which are based on reports of the National Assessment of Educational Progress (NAEP). Stanley Ahmann describes the nature of the NAEP project and the overall results. Interestingly, as with general intelligence, there are some consistent achievement differences between population subgroups. As a reading of Merrill Sheils' Newsweek article makes clear, however, differences in general intelligence are hardly an adequate explanation. Social variables, not simply the psychological ones, must be taken into account.

Lost: Our Intelligence? Why?[1]

by Quinn McNemar

THE Greeks had a word for it, but the Romans had a word with better survival properties. Regardless of the word, what is now called intelligence has been talked about for at least 2,000 years. And as long as 2,000 years before the advent of attempts to measure intelligence, there seems to have been recognition of the fact that individuals differ in intellectual ability.

The earlier attempts at measuring were based on either of two quite distinct conceptions: the Galton-Cattell idea that intellectual ability manifests itself in simple, discrimination functioning, and the Binet notion that cognitive ability reflects itself in more complex functioning. The Binet concept proved to be more fruitful, and by 1925 there was on the market, in addition to various versions of the Binet scale, a flood of group tests of so-called general intelligence.

A few words about definition may be in order. First, it might be claimed that no definition is required because all intelligent people know what intelligence is—it is the thing that the other guy lacks. Second, the fact that tests of general intelligence based on differing definitions tend to intercorrelate about as highly as their respective reliabilities permit indicates that, despite the diversity of definitions, the same function or process is being measured—definitions can be more confusing than enlightening. Third, that confusion might have been anticipated is evident from a recent reexamination of the problem of definition by Miles (1957). This British chappie found himself struggling with the awful fact that the word "definition" itself has 12 definitions. Perhaps the resolution of this problem should be assigned to the newly formed Division of Philosophical Psychology, or maybe the problem should be forgotten since psychologists seem to have lost the concept of general intelligence.

Why has the concept been abandoned? Was it replaced by something else? By something better?

Must we admit that the millions who have been tested on general intelligence tests were measured for a nonexistent function? If it is possible that the notion of general intelligence is not lost but merely gone astray, in what corners of what psychological fields should we search for it?

REASONS FOR DISCARDING THE IDEA OF GENERAL INTELLIGENCE

Apparently one reason why concepts are either discarded or modified beyond recognition is that too much is claimed for them. Among the supposed strikes against general intelligence are the following: the earlier false claims about IQ constancy; prediction failures in individual cases; unfounded claims that something innate was being measured by the tests; equally unfounded assertions that nothing but cultural effects were involved; the bugaboo that IQ tests reflect middle-class values; the notion that an IQ standing fosters undesirable expectations regarding school achievement; the idea that IQ differences are incompatible with democracy and lead to educational determinism; and, finally, the great stress on general intelligence caused us to ignore other possible abilities.

This last point leads us right into the problem of factor analysis. Spearman died in battle defending his theory of g. Under pressure he reluctantly conceded that factors other than g might exist, and he frequently said, in effect, I told you so as long ago as 1906. Actually, Spearman was on the run before the invention of modern factor analysis, but it was not until Thurstone's (1938) first major application of his centroid factor method that Spearman's g became, seemingly, nonexistent. Thurstone said, "We have not found the general factor of Spearman" and "We cannot report any general common factor in the battery of fifty-six tests [p. vii]." As anticipated by some, Spearman was not prone to admit defeat. He reworked Thurstone's data and a g was found, plus some group factors. He charged that Thurstone's rotational process had submerged the general factor.

[1] Address of the President to the Seventy-Second Annual Convention of the American Psychological Association, Los Angeles, September 5, 1964.

American factorists found Thurstone convincing. The description of abilities in terms of seven primaries was an attractive package. The so-called primaries were more amenable to specific definition than the old hodgepodge called general intelligence. Despite the fact that Thurstone was able to replicate his findings on samples from two other populations, thus giving credence to his method and results, there were a couple of events that led to some turbulence in his seven-dimension rarified atmosphere. The first of these was a minor study, by one of his own students, based on the intercorrelations of 1916 Stanford-Binet items, in which the *g* refused to be rotated out. But rather than admit that this might be some kind of general intelligence, the author renamed it "maturational level." Incidentally, this illustrates the first cardinal Principle of Psychological Progress: *Give new names to old things*.

The second disturber of the neat little set of primaries, sans a *g*, resulted when Thurstone took the next logical step, that of constructing tests to measure the primaries. It was found that the primaries were themselves intercorrelated whereas it had, at the time, been expected and hoped that they would be independent. The Thurstones (1941, p. 26) readily admitted that a general factor was needed to explain the interrelatedness of the primaries. This eventually led to the idea of oblique axes, which axes were regarded as representing the primaries as first-order factors, whereas the general factor pervading the primaries was dubbed a second-order factor. It began to look as though Spearman was being revisited, except for the little matter of labeling: anything called second-order could not possibly be regarded as of much importance. Furthermore, it could always be said that, in the ability domain, it is less difficult to attribute psychological meaningfulness to first-order than to second-order factors, so why pay much attention to the latter? Thus it was easy for most American factorists to drop the concept of general intelligence and to advocate that tests thereof, despite their proven usefulness over the years, should be replaced by tests of the primaries. Hence the emergence of differential aptitude batteries, about which more later.

Meanwhile, our British cousins did not tag along with the factor methods preferred on this side of the Atlantic. After all, it is possible to use factor methods that permit a sizable general factor, if

such exists, to emerge as the very first factor. Being first, it is, presto, the most important, as indeed it is as a factor explaining, for the starting battery as a whole, more variance for more tests than attributable to any American-style primary factor. The methods preferred by the British also yield group factors, apt to bear the same name as the primaries, but of attenuated importance. Apparently the British are skeptical of the multitude of ability factors being "discovered" in America. The structure of intellect that requires 120 factors may very well lead the British, and some of the rest of us, to regard our fractionization and fragmentation of ability, into more and more factors of less and less importance, as indicative of scatterbrainedness. This statement presumes that intellectual abilities are brain centered.

In practically all areas of psychological research the demonstration of trivially small minutia is doomed to failure because of random errors. Not so if your technique is factor analysis, despite its being based on the correlation coefficient—that slipperiest of all statistical measures. By some magic, hypotheses are tested without significance tests. This happy situation permits me to announce a Principle of Psychological Regress: *Use statistical techniques that lack inferential power*. This will not inhibit your power of subjective inference and consequently will progress you right back to the good old days when there was no strangling stat or sticky stix to make your insignificant data insignificant.

It may be a long time before we have an ivory tower, strictly scientific resolution of the issue as to whether a scheme involving primary abilities plus a deemphasized *g* is preferable to one involving an emphasized *g* plus group factors. With bigger and better computers we will have bigger, though not necessarily better, factor-analytic studies, but it seems unlikely that such further studies will, in and of themselves, settle the issue under discussion. Until such time as some genius resolves the broader question, so ably discussed by Lee Cronbach in 1957, of the place, if any, of correlational method in a science that aspires to be experimental, we may have to turn to the criterion of social usefulness as a basis for judging whether it is wise to discard general intelligence. Like it or not, much of our heritage in this area is that earlier workers, from Binet on, had as their motivation the solution of social problems, and currently many in the area have a similar motivation.

THE BEARING OF SOCIAL USEFULNESS

In practice, if you believe that the concept of general intelligence has outlived its usefulness, you may choose from among several differential, or multiple, aptitude batteries, which will provide measures of some of the so-called primary mental abilities. If you happen to believe that there is something to general ability, you can find tests to use. The novice looking for these latter tests may have to alert himself to the first Principle of Psychological Progress—the test labels may have changed from "general intelligence" to "general classification" or "scholastic aptitude." If you enjoy riding the fence, you might become a devotee of the practice of the College Board, and others, and measure just two abilities: Verbal and Quantitative.

This is certainly not the place to review the voluminous literature that amply demonstrates the practical utility of tests of general intelligence. Nor is it the place to catalog the misuses of the Stanford-Binet for purposes which Terman never claimed for it, or the misuses of the Wechsler scales for purposes which Wechsler *has* claimed for his scales. Neither the Binet nor the Wechsler provides a factorially pure, unidimensional measure of a *g*. The current Stanford-Binet was in reality constructed too early to benefit from the implication of factor analysis for test purity, whereas the Wechsler scales were based on the impossible premise that 10 or 11 subtests can simultaneously provide diagnostic subscores and a meaningful total score. Of the many group tests that appeared between 1920 and 1945 it can be said that few, if any, provide unidimensional measures of general intelligence. The chief difficulty is that most of them lead to a total score based on a mixture of verbal and mathematical material. Thus, with two main sources of variance, marked qualitative differences can exist for quantitatively similar total scores. The College Board–Educational Testing Service people have justifiably refrained from giving a total score involving verbal plus math, but there are those who question the usefulness of the Board's math score and there are those who criticize the Educational Testing Service for failing to change over to a differential aptitude battery.

Let us next turn to a somewhat more detailed examination of the various so-called multiple aptitude batteries. What and who influenced whom in the development of these batteries is difficult to disentangle. At the risk of oversimplification, it might be said that two prime influences operated.

First, the early factor studies by the Thurstones, by Holzinger, and by Guilford are the progenitors of the Science Research Associates' Primary Mental Abilities (PMA) Test, the Holzinger-Crowder Unifactor Tests, the Guilford-Zimmerman Aptitude Survey, and the Segel-Raskin Multiple Aptitude Tests (MAT).

The second influence, which seems to have emerged from testing experience in the Armed Services during World War II, is the job-element approach, an approach which may or may not differ from the old job-analysis method. For whatever jobs you are dealing with, you study the activities involved in order to decide what aptitudes are called for. Whether or not these aptitudes have been previously isolated by factor analysis is totally irrelevant. It is hoped that some jobs will have aptitudes in common so that the needed number of tests will be less than the number of jobs. The one battery that is built on this approach is the Flanagan Aptitude Classification Tests, a battery that just happens to have the catchy abbreviation, FACT. If we cannot muster any facts in psychology, we can at least have FACT scores!

A cross between testing for factorially defined abilities and job-element derived aptitudes is apparently involved in the General Aptitude Test Battery (GATB) of the United States Employment Service and the Differential Aptitudes Tests (DAT) of the Psychological Corporation, since in both batteries some of the tests seem to have sprung from factor-analysis results and some tests seem to have been thrown in as possible predictors of specific performances.

It is not our purpose to rank order the seven above-mentioned multitest batteries, but a few remarks may be relevant as background for the sequel. Apparently the Employment Service's GATB was made available (but not put on the commercial market) with the idea that there would be a continuing program of validities studies—the accumulation is now impressive. For the DAT of the Psychological Corporation there is an overabundance of data on validity, collected and analyzed prior to marketing the test. Both the Science Research Associates' PMA and FACT were made available without backing for the claimed usefulness of the tests. Belatedly, that is, 6 years after its appearance, some evidence on the predictive validity of FACT has been reported. Validity information for the other three batteries is not entirely lacking, though far from ample. Some will have noted that that fuzzy dodge called factor validity is being ignored here.

Now to get back to our main theme, to what extent have the seven batteries contributed to the demise of general intelligence? In attempting to answer this, one encounters a paradox: Some test authors want to eat their cake and have it too— they attempt to measure factors and g with the same instrument. This is understandable in a couple of instances. Three of the 15 tests of the Employment Service GATB were included to provide a measure of general intelligence, apparently because the authors still saw some merit in a g and were not committed to the factor schemata. Holzinger and Crowder suggest a weighted score for a measure of g, perhaps because of Holzinger's long-time alignment with Spearman. The real teaser is why Thurstone ever sanctioned, if he did, the summing of Science Research Associates' PMA scores to obtain an IQ. One has the uncomfortable feeling that his publishers wished to g garnish the factor cake to make it more palatable in the market place.

Although Segel says nothing in his 1957 article about a general score from the Segel-Raskin MAT, the test publishers say that, in addition to yielding scores for four factors, it also provides a "Scholastic Potential" score. Perhaps Flanagan has not completely broken with tradition since he states that four tests of the FACT battery measure "General College Aptitude"—a statement made with the same lack of empirical validity as the claim, which should be anxiety producing for those of you who fly a certain airline, that your highly paid pilot shares four of the aptitudes of a plumber!

Apparently, Guilford and Zimmerman and the test people at the Psychological Corporation are willing to stick to the sound principle that a differential test battery cannot provide factor scores that can be summed to obtain a meaningful IQ, or measure of a g.

Parenthetically, it might be said that the California Test of Mental Maturity (CTMM), which, according to the publisher's 1963 catalog, was originally "designed as a group test of intelligence patterned after the individual Stanford-Binet," serves as an illustration of factor icing a g cake. Some multitest batteries and the CTMM have a Madison Avenue advantage: The advertising claims the measurement of not only factors but also g; not only g but also factors. This measurement absurdity is all too apt to go unrecognized by many test users, and hence a sales advantage for the aptitude battery that produces both factor scores and an IQ.

Just how successful have the multitest batteries been? Since by far the most extensive social use of tests has been, and continues to be, in the schools, let us look at the evidence of validity studies therein. As indicated previously, little is known about the predictive usefulness of some of the seven batteries discussed above. The DAT of the Psychological Corporation is the only battery for which adequate predictive (and concurrent) validity data, derived from school sources, are available. It is also the battery that has fared best in the hands of the test reviewers; therefore if we allow the case for differential batteries to rest thereon, we will be looking at the best. So, what is the story?

Recall that the hoped-for advantage of a multitest battery over the old-fashioned general intelligence test was that it would have greater predictive power, a power which could manifest itself in higher validity coefficients for specific subject matter and, perhaps, for overall achievement. It was hoped that such a battery would be truly differential in that particular factors (or subtests) would correlate higher with achievement in some areas than in other areas. Presumably each factor (or subtest) should have unique usefulness. If a battery were truly differential, it would be a boon to school guidance personnel.

Now the manual of the DAT of the Psychological Corporation contains a staggering total of 4,096, yes I counted 'em, validity coefficients. With such a large pool to draw from, one could by gracious selection "show" that the DAT is the answer to the prayer of every counselor, male or female, or by malicious selection one could "prove" that the DAT is far worse than any test ever published. The validity coefficients range all the way down to $-.37$, which is presumably a chance deviation downward from 0, and all the way up to .90, which is likely not a chance deviation downward from unity. But ranges tell us nothing. After a careful perusal of the 4,096 correlations, it seems safe to summarize DAT validities as follows:

1. Verbal Reasoning (analogies to most of you) is the best single predictor; Language Usage, as represented by a sentence test dealing with grammar and word usage, and admittedly more achievement than aptitude, is a close second.

2. Numerical Ability, as measured by a test of simple arithmetic operations, designed to tap arithmetic reasoning without the usual verbal component, is the best predictor of achievement in school mathematics. It does not, however, correlate as well with grades in science as does Verbal Reasoning.

3. Aside from the Numerical Ability test, the only other test that shows differential power as a predictor is the Spelling test—if you cannot spell you may have trouble learning shorthand.

4. The remaining five tests in the battery simply fail to show compelling evidence that they are good in the differential predictive sense. For the Mechanical Reasoning and the Clerical Speed and Accuracy tests this may be understandable in that little of school curricula for Grades 8 through 12 requires such abilities, but one would expect that Abstract Reasoning and Space Relations would fare better than they seem to.

Such data as we have been able to locate for the other six multitest batteries tend to support these findings on the DAT. Aside from tests of numerical ability having differential value for predicting school grades in math, it seems safe to conclude that the worth of the multitest batteries as differential predictors of achievement in school has not been demonstrated. Incidentally, the fact that the Verbal and Numerical tests stand out as the only two useful predictors tends to provide some support for the Educational Testing Service–College Board practice of providing scores for just these two abilities.

And now we come to a very disturbing aspect of the situation. Those who have constructed and marketed multiple aptitude batteries, and advocated that they be used instead of tests of general intelligence, seem never to have bothered to demonstrate whether or not multitest batteries provide better predictions than the old-fashioned scale of general intelligence. Be it noted that we are not discussing experimental editions of tests. Some may say that insofar as a test publisher provides validity data for a new battery it is not necessary

to show that the validities are, for the given school condition, better than those of other tests. With this one can agree, but only in case no claims are made, explicitly or implicitly, regarding superior merits for the new battery.

It is far from clear that tests of general intelligence have been outmoded by the multitest batteries as the more useful predictors of school achievement. Indeed, one can use the vast accumulation of data on the validity of the Psychological Corporation's DAT to show that better predictions are possible via old-fashioned general intelligence tests. Consider the fact that a combination of the tests Verbal Reasoning (analogies) and Numerical Ability would be, in terms of content, very similar to many group tests of general intelligence. Consider also that an equally weighted combination of these two tests correlates in the mid-.80s with the Otis S-A, Higher Form. Then, when you turn to a careful study of the empirical validities, as reported in the DAT manual, you will not be surprised at the outcome of the application of a little arithmetic, which leads to the definite conclusion that a simple unweighted combination of the Verbal Reasoning and Numerical Ability tests predicts as well as or, in most instances, better than any subtest taken singly, or in the differential sense.

The manual for the DAT contains the following statement (Bennett, Seashore, & Wesman, 1952):

Apparently the *Verbal Reasoning* and *Numerical Ability* tests can serve most purposes for which a general mental ability test is usually given in addition to providing differential clues useful to the counselor. Hence, the use of the so-called intelligence test is apparently unnecessary where the *Differential Aptitude Tests* are already being used [p. 71].

Anyone who disagrees with this quotation could, with better justification, say that an intelligence test can serve nearly all, if not all, the purposes for which a multiple aptitude battery is given in the schools because the former, in general, is a better predictor and because, as we saw earlier, the differential clues are too fragmentary to be of use to the counselor. And there is a bonus: one classroom period of testing, compared to six periods. A second bonus: much less costly. A third bonus: fewer scores to confuse the already confused minds of most school counselors.

Thus, we come to the conclusion that general intelligence has not been lost in the trend to test more and more abilities; it was merely misplaced by a misplaced emphasis on a hope that a lot of us, including the speaker, once entertained, a hope that in turn was based on a misplaced faith in factor analysis: *the* hope that factors, when and if measured, would find great usefulness in the affairs of society. By the criterion of social usefulness, the multiple aptitude batteries have been found wanting. Now, I have no desire to furnish ammunition for those test critics who would have us stop all testing merely because they find a trivially faulty item in a standardized test. At a time when there is shouting about the tyranny of the testers and the brass of the brain watchers, at a time when school people are showing resentment at the disruption caused by too many national testing programs, at a time when federal and state legislators are all too willing to write legislation that places restrictions on the use of tests, and at a time when both majorities and minorities are being denied the benefits of test-based guidance because certain well-intentioned persons fail to realize that scores for the underprivileged minorities are useful indices of *immediate,* or present, functioning—at a time when all these and other forces are operating to throw out the tests, it is high time for the profession to establish a bureau of standards to test the tests instead of coasting down a road that is tinged with some of the trappings of Madison Avenue. Better to have informed internal control than ignorant, hostile, external control.

Intelligence Elsewhere?

Aside from the near loss of the idea that progress in school may depend on general intelligence, one wonders whether intelligence has come to be regarded as unimportant in other areas.

Any of you who have money invested in stocks and wish some reassurance regarding the intelligence level of business and industry managers should read Edwin Ghiselli's (1963) Bingham Lecture. His summary of his own work indicates that the average intelligence of those in the upper and middle management levels falls at the ninety-sixth percentile of the population. Thomas Harrell (1961) came to a similar conclusion. Furthermore, management level is correlated with intelligence—you can be too dumb to succeed as a manager. Also you can be too bright to be a managerial success! Now it must be admitted that little, if anything, is known about whether man-

agement success might be better predicted by measures of factor-analytic defined abilities. On this you are free to guess—most of you will have already guessed my guess.

A one-by-one cataloguing of what we know or do not know about what abilities contribute to success within various occupational and professional groups would merely add to the dullness of this presentation, so let us turn to some of the more esoteric fields of psychology to see whether the concept of general intelligence has or has had any relevance. One such field, and a very broad one, is creativity. Anyone who peeks over the fence into this field is apt to be astonished at the visible chaos. The definition of creativity is confounded by the diversity of subareas within the field, the criterion problems are far from licked, and so little is known about the creative process that measuring instruments are, seemingly, chosen on a trial-and-error basis.

We might presume that the role, if any, of general intelligence in creativity would increase as we pass from art to music, to architecture, to literature and drama, to science. Your presumption about the ordering may be different and more nearly correct. I would like to discuss briefly the extremes of my ordering.

At the risk of being called a heretic and a has-been statistician, I would like first to resort to the single case of a painter, examples of whose works were reproduced in color recently by Desmond Morris (1962) in a journal called *Portfolio and Art News Annual.* To my uncultured eye these paintings have the general appearance of the so-called school of modern art, and the running comment on the paintings involves what I must presume is the jargon of contemporary art critics: talk about self-rewarding activities, compositional control, calligraphic differentiation, thematic variation, optimum heterogeneity, and universal imagery. Since authors may use pen names, I would guess that this painter is using "Congon" as a "brush" name. Supposedly by now some of you will be guessing that this single case is of interest in the context of this paper because of Congon's IQ. Well, because of this painter's underprivileged cultural background, no test scores are available. Congon, despite striking contribution to art, happens to be a chimp. Aside from a rather obvious conclusion, one wonders what would emerge from a blind (as to source) analysis of Congon's paintings by the personality boys. We might even tell them that Congon was breast fed.

Without in any way implying that creativity in the arts is unimportant, we hasten on to scientific creativity, a specific area in which it seems likely, because of the Sputnik-inspired spurt of interest, that we can learn something of the role, if any, of general intelligence. But immediately we encounter skulls that have been cracked on the criterion problem.

One elaborate study (C. Taylor, Smith, Ghiselin, & Ellison, 1961), on a sample of 166 physical scientists working at Air Force research centers, came up with 150, yes, believe it or not, 150 *criteria* of scientific productivity and creativity. By combining some scores and eliminating others, the number of criteria was reduced to 48. A factor analysis of the intercorrelations of the 48 reduced the number to 14 "categories." Apparently the 150 original criterion measures included everything except success at turning on a kitchen faucet, so one need not be surprised at the outcome of the factor analysis. For example, one factor-derived criterion of scientific productivity and creativity is "likableness," another is "status seeking," another is extent of membership in scientific and professional societies—the joiners, no doubt.

The fact that the intercorrelations among the 14 criterion categories, derived from factor analysis, range from −.08 to +.55, with a median of only .18, indicates either criterion complexity or else a whale of a lot of vagueness as to what is meant by productivity and creativity in science. Now this criterion mess emerged from a study of interview results of 166 "physical scientists," but nearly half of these so-called scientists were engineers, and the education of the total group indicates only 2 years of graduate work on the average; so when is a scientist a scientist a scientist?

The next step in this study was to collect data on 107 of these so-called scientists for a whopping total of 130 potential predictors, which, when pitted against 17 criterion measures, produced 2,210 "validity coefficients." The distribution of these, excluding 30 values involving un-cross-validated empirical keys, almost restores one's faith in the random-sampling distribution of correlation coefficients around zero! There were 16 predictors based on aptitude tests, hence 16×17, or 272, "validities" for this area. Since only 4% of them reach the 5% level, we can do no more than accept the null hypothesis: Aptitude ain't important in scientific productivity and creativity. The idea that some scientists are more equal in ability than others apparently is not true.

But this criterion-based study did not contribute to my worry about the role of general intelligence— the failure to include a general intelligence measure as a potential predictor may be interpreted as indicating that the authors already had the answer.

Let us turn to another criterion-based study (D. Taylor, 1961). The criterion measures for creativity and productivity were based on the checking by supervisors of statements that had been scaled by Thurstone's equal-appearing interval method. Creativity and productivity, so gauged, correlated .69 with each other on a sample of 103 researchers (electronic scientists and engineers). For this same group, intelligence, as measured by the Terman Concept Mastery Test (CMT), correlated only .20 or less with the criteria. Two Psychological Corporation tests and an American Institute for Research test did a little better. Creativity is slightly more predictable than productivity. Insofar as these two criteria are themselves valid, the findings indicate that within a group of research workers, precious little of the variance in creativity, and still less in productivity, can be predicted by the tests.

A third study (MacKinnon, 1962) based on criterion (rated) measures of performance was concerned with the creativity of architects. Although the author reports that *within* a creative sample the correlation is essentially zero between intelligence (CMT) and rated creativity, it is not clear from the context what is meant by "within" sample. If this means within the sample of 40 creative architects selected as the "most creative" in the country, then we indeed have such a drastic restriction in range on the *criterion* variable that little, if any, correlation can be expected for any and all predictors. Now the author says, without presenting any evidence, that "Over the whole range of intelligence and creativity there is, of course, a positive relationship between the two variables [p. 488]." One wonders just what is meant by creativity in architecture as rated either by fellow architects or by editors of architectural journals. If judged creativity reflects engineering-structural innovation, then intelligence would likely be a correlate; if judged creativity depends on new artistic designs, then the intelligence component would likely be of less importance. It would seem that when the author says we "may have overestimated . . . the role of intelligence in creative achievement [p. 493]," he should have included some marked qualifications as to what type of creativity he had in mind.

That such qualification is indeed necessary is supplied by a finding of still another investigator (Barron, 1963). For a group of highly creative writers it was estimated, by way of the Terman CMT, that their average IQ is about 140, which we interpret as meaning that a high IQ is a necessary, though not sufficient, condition for outstanding success as a writer. On the basis of his own studies and those of other persons, this same investigator suggests that "over the total range of intelligence and creativity a low positive correlation" of .40 probably obtains. This sweeping generalization is for all areas of creativity.

And speaking of sweeping generalizations, consider the suggestion in a 1961 study (Holland, 1961) that "we need to use nonintellectual criteria in the selection of students for scholarships and fellowships [p. 146]." The author did not say so, but presumably he meant in addition to intellectual ability; maybe he did not, since he had previously concluded that "intelligence has little or no relationship to creative performance in arts and science . . . [p. 143]" at the high school level. His data back up this conclusion, as might have been expected when correlations are based on groups restricted in range to the top 1%!

If the foregoing examples of criterion-based studies of creativity seem to indicate that general intelligence is relatively unimportant for creativity, it should be remembered that drastic but unknown or unspecified curtailment of range exists for both ability and criteria. Why do correlational studies under such adverse circumstances?

Next we turn to a few studies of creativity which cannot be criticized because of restriction of range on the criteria—these studies simply avoid this problem by never having actual criterion information. The approach is to claim that certain tests, which typically are scored for novel responses or novel solutions to problems, *are* measures of creativity, with no evidence whatsoever that the tests have predictive validity for nontest, real-life creative performance. This bit of ignorance does not prove to be a handicap to those who think that creativity can be studied without the nuisance of obtaining criterion measures. We reluctantly accept the test-based criteria solely for the sake of seeing what happens to general intelligence as a part of the picture. Time permits only three examples.

We first note that general intelligence has not manifested itself as a correlate of so-called creativity tests in the factor-analytic studies of creativity. The explanation for this is easily found— no measures of general intelligence are used in these studies. When discussing his plans for studying creativity, a certain author (Guilford, 1950) said that "we must look well beyond the boundaries of the IQ if we are to fathom the domain of creativity [p. 448]." He went on to say, the conception "that creative talent is to be accounted for in terms of high intelligence or IQ . . . is not only inadequate but has been largely responsible for lack of progress in the understanding of creative people [p. 454]." With a part of this one can agree, but does it follow that one should prejudge the role of general intelligence as a source of variance in creativity tests or factors derived therefrom? Does the failure to include an IQ test help one learn the extent to which one must go beyond the boundaries of the IQ to fathom creativity? Apparently the author, although willing to predict that the correlations between IQ and the many types of creativity tests "are only moderate or low," was unwilling to include an IQ test for the sake of finding out. However, negation by omission is not very convincing.

That at least one test bearing the label "creativity" is correlated more than moderately with IQ is evidenced by the value of .67 (average for boys and girls) for the carefully chosen sample of 15-year-olds in Project Talent (Shaycoft, Dailey, Orr, Neyman, & Sherman, 1963). This sample-stable r (based on a total N of 7,648) becomes .80 when corrected for attenuation.

In a recent extensive study (Getzels & Jackson, 1962), already extensively criticized, creativity is defined as the sum of scores on five tests (median intercorrelation of only .28). Although the investigators use the sum score for most of their analyses, they do not bother to report the correlation of creativity, so defined, with IQ. From the published report I have ascertained (via the correlation-of-sums formula) that creativity and IQ correlate to the extent of .40 for the total of 533 cases. Now this r of .40 has been greatly attenuated because of three things: first, the usual measurement errors;

second, the cases were highly selected on IQ (mean of 132); third, the IQs are a mixture from the Stanford-Binet, Henmon-Nelson, and Wechsler Intelligence Scale for Children (the use of regression-estimated Binet IQs from the other two scales aggravates rather than improves the mixture). We deduce that intelligence and the creativity tests used here have far more common variance than the authors believe.

Much is made of the finding that the creativity tests tended to correlate higher than did IQ with verbal-content school achievements. Again the IQ comes in for an unfair drubbing because of the same mixture of IQ scores and, what is more pertinent, because of explicit selective curtailment on the IQ variable and only incidental selection on the creativity variable.

Of more importance to the present paper is the analysis, by these same authors, based on a high IQ group and a high creative group, these groups being selected as the top 20% for each variable but excluding those who were in the top 20% on both variables. These two selected groups were then contrasted on total school achievement (and a host of other variables that are of no interest here). The mean IQ for the high IQ group was 150 whereas the mean IQ for the high creative group was 127, yet the achievement means of the two groups were "unexpectedly" equally superior to the school population mean despite the 23-point difference in mean IQ. The authors say that it *"is quite surprising"* that the high creativity group achieved so well. From this it is concluded that the "creative instruments account for a significant portion of the variance in school achievement [p. 24]," and the subsequent argument implies that creativity is more important for ordinary school achievement than is the IQ. Now anyone who is at all familiar with a three-variate problem will not be "unexpectedly" surprised at the foregoing results—indeed, if the authors had bothered to give the three basic correlations among the three variables (IQ, creativity, and total school achievement) for the entire group, any person versed in simple multivariate analysis could deduce the results. Furthermore, he could deduce a further result (and this one has been overlooked by the critics) which might be unpleasantly surprising to the thesis of these authors: namely, the high IQ and the high creative groups did equally well in school achievement despite an unreported differ-

ence in mean creativity that is of the same order as the much stressed difference in IQ.[2] Utilizing the half-blind logic of the authors, one can say that creative ability is not as important as IQ for school achievement—just the opposite of their position.

Now the fact that seven of nine replications of this study confirm the original findings merely indicates that repetition of the same faulty design and false logic will lead to the same false conclusions. The design being used is such that, if two variables are equally correlated with a third, the conclusion will be reached that the two are actually unequally correlated with the third. This is the neatest trick of the decade for supplying educationists with an antidote for the IQ virus. I cannot refrain from saying at this point that, although discouraged, I am still hopeful that people who do statistical studies will first learn a modicum of elementary statistics!

Time does not permit a discussion of other studies in which creativity is defined in terms of test performance instead of being based on actual creativity of the sort prized by society. In summary of this brief on creativity studies, I would like to offer a few dogmatic-sounding observations. First, one need not be surprised at the fact that so-called creativity tests do not yield high correlations with IQ tests—but the correlations are generally far higher than those found in typical studies with range restrictions. I would anticipate that for normalized scores, the uncurtailed scatters for IQ versus creativity tests will be bivariate normal. Second, if we have honest to goodness criterion measures of literary or architectural or scientific creativity, the scatter diagram between IQ and such creativity (not normalized, since it makes sense to expect a skewed distribution for actual creativity) will be triangular in shape for unselected cases. That is, at the high IQ levels there will be a very wide range of creativity, whereas as we go down to average IQ, and on down to lower levels, the scatter for creativity will be less and less. Having a high IQ is not a guarantee of being creative; having a low IQ means creativity is impossible. Third, it remains to be seen whether or not the so-called creativity tests and/or factors derived therefrom have appreciable value as predictors of

[2] Since this was written, the replication study of Yamamoto (1964) gives data that corroborate this deduction.

actual creative performance. Such tests may or may not yield better predictions than a test of general intelligence. Fourth, as far as I am concerned, to claim factorial validity for creativity tests, along with definitions of creativity in terms of tests, is an unwarranted avoidance of the fundamental problem of validity.

The recently renewed interest in "gifted" children, along with the flurry of creativity studies, has led to a reexamination of methods for identifying the gifted. It has long been recognized that identification in terms of high IQ is too narrow—those gifted in such areas as art and music would be overlooked. The argument against the IQ is now (Torrance, 1962) being reinforced by the claim that the selection of the top 20% on IQ would mean the exclusion of 70% of the top 20% on tested creativity. This startling statistic, which implies a correlation of only .24 between IQ and creativity, is being used to advocate the use of creativity tests for identifying the gifted. Be it noted that these creativity tests will also miss those gifted in art and music.

We are being told that it is important "to identify creative talent early in life," hence you need not be surprised that the search goes down to the kindergarten level, with claims of successful identification. The creativity tests are presumed to be better for this purpose than the IQ tests because of the failure of the IQ to be constant, an argument that completely overlooks the fact that the IQ does have some constancy whereas absolutely nothing is known about the stability of standings on creativity tests. The IQ tests, known to be imperfectly valid as predictors of outstanding achievement in life, are to be replaced by the creativity tests, known to be of unknown validity as predictors. Anyway, progress, defined as change, is in the offing.

The IQ is being linked with *learning* as an outmoded educational objective; the new objective involves an emphasis on *thinking*. Somehow or other creativity, not general intelligence, is being associated with thinking. The horrible idea of underachievers and overachievers, in terms of expectancies based on the IQ, will be abolished. But no thought is given to the fact that the use of creativity tests will simply define a new crop of under- and overachievers.

In an apparent zeal to rid us of general intelligence, it is argued that measured creativity is significantly related to ordinary school achievement. Maybe so, but never, never does one find complete data reported as to the relative sizes of validity coefficients. And, as we have seen, the technique being used will show that equal coefficients are unequal. Why not the full facts, free of fantasy?

An additional difficulty is not being faced by those who would replace IQ tests by creativity tests, or creative-thinking tests. The factor-analytic studies indicate either no, or a trivially small, general creativity factor in these tests, yet these self-characterized "bold, adventurous" reformers (see Torrance, 1963) do not hesitate to advocate a total score which is nearly devoid of meaning. Changing the curriculum to the teaching of creativity and creative thinking will not overcome this measurement difficulty. Again, I express the hope that the IQ is replaced by something better rather than by something worse.

There are other areas, such as reasoning, problem solving, and concept formation, in which one might expect to find some consideration of intelligence as an aspect. One might also expect that investigators of thinking would have something to say about individual differences in thinking being dependent upon intelligence, but for some unintelligent reason these people seem never to mention intelligence. Surely, it cannot be inferred that thinking about thinking does not involve intelligence!

In Conclusion

It has been the thesis of this paper that the concept of general intelligence, despite being maligned by a few, regarded as a second-order function by some, and discarded or ignored by others, still has a rightful place in the science of psychology and in the practical affairs of man. It has not been argued that the nature of general intelligence is well understood. Much, however, has been written about its nature. Over 40 years ago (Intelligence, 1921a, 1921b), an editor secured and published the reasoned views of 13 well-known test psychologists. Later, Spearman set forth his speculations about the nature of *g*. Prior to these, Binet had, of course, given much thought to the problem.

More recent discussions exist. Hebb (1949) has considered the problem from the viewpoint of neurology and brain functioning. Cyril Burt (1955), always a vociferous defender of the concept of general intelligence, has reviewed the evidence for a *g* and restated the idea, dreadful to some, that intelligence is innate. Perhaps it was inevitable that Raymond Cattell (1963), who has camped with the general intelligence contingent, should gaze into his crystal *n*-dimensional factor ball and find evidence for crystallized as opposed to fluid general intelligence. Joseph McVicker Hunt's (1961) book on *Intelligence and Experience* is in large part devoted to questions pertaining to the nature of intelligence.

By far the most provocative recent discussion that I have encountered is the closely reasoned 44-page paper by Keith Hayes (1962). He puts forth a motivational-experiential theory of intelligence. In essence, he presumes that there are hereditary differences in motivation. "Experience-producing drives" and environmental differences produce differences in experience, which in turn, by way of learning, lead to differences in ability. Therefore, differences called intellectual are nothing more than acquired abilities. I think that Hayes has ignored the possibility of individual differences in learning ability, but if such a formulation leads to experimental manipulation of variables, we may eventually make progress in an area that has too long been dominated by ever increasing fractionization by factor analysis, with little thought as to how the fractured parts get put together into a functioning whole.

Abilities, or capacities, or aptitudes, or intellectual skills, or whatever you choose to call them, are measured in terms of response products to standardized stimulus situations. The *stimulus* is presented to an *organism* which by some *process* comes up with a *response;* thus any attempt to theorize and/or study intellect in terms of a simple stimulus-response (S-R) paradigm seems doomed to failure unless drastically modified and complicated by the insertion of O for organism and P for process.

There have been thousands of researches on the multitudinous variations from organism to organism, and the results fill books on individual differences. These studies can be roughly classified into two types. First, those that ascertain the inter-correlations among scaled response products to various stimulus situations, known as tests, have to do with the structure of intellect; and whether the resulting factors are anything more than dimensions for describing individual differences need not concern us here. The second type of study

seeks the nontest correlates of test performance, and whether or not any of the found correlates can be regarded as explaining individual differences is not of interest here. Both types of studies certainly force one to stress the overwhelming diversity exhibited among the organisms.

But these studies of individual differences never come to grips with the *process*, or operation, by which a given organism achieves an intellectual response. Indeed, it is difficult to see how the available individual difference data can be used even as a starting point for generating a theory as to the process nature of general intelligence or of any other specified ability.

As a basis for a little speculation, let us conceive of a highly hypothetical situation in which the two members of a pair of identical twins, with identical experiences, find themselves cast up on an uninhabited tropical island. Let us assume that they are at the supergenius level, far beyond that of your favorite man of genius. Let us also assume that, though highly educated in the sciences, they have been fortunate enough to have had zero exposure to psychology. In addition, we presume that, being highly involved and abstracted in the pursuit of science, they have never noticed what we call individual differences in abilities.

A quick exploration of the island assures them that food is plentiful, that shelter is available, and that clothing is not a necessity. To allay the boredom that they foresee as an eternity in this laborless heaven, they decide to spend their time in the further pursuit of science, but the lack of the wherewithal for constructing gadgets rules out any research in the physical sciences. Having had a college course in Bugs and Bites they proceed to study the life of the island's insects, then the habits of the birds, and the antics of a couple of monkeys. The manner in which the monkeys adjust to the environment leads them to set up some trial situations for more systematic observation. Needless to say, the monkeys show evidence of what we call learning and what we call problem solving.

Eventually they decide that attempting to outwit each other might be more fun than being outwitted by the monkeys, so they begin to cook up and use games and problems for this purpose. This activity leads each to speculate and introspect about how problems are invented and how solved. Then by cleverly designed experiments, preceded of course by theory, they set forth highly developed laws and principles about what we call reasoning and problem solving. Incidentally, they switch back and forth between the roles of experimenter and subject, there being no college sophomores available. They continue for years the study of their own mental operations, constantly on the alert for new phenomena to investigate.

And now with apologies to the ancient Greeks, who did have some ideas along these lines, we leave with you the 64-million drachma question: Will our two identical supergeniuses, being totally unaware of individual differences, ever hit upon and develop a concept of intelligence?

REFERENCES

BARRON, F. *Creativity and psychological health.* Princeton, N. J.: Van Nostrand, 1963.

BENNETT, G. K., SEASHORE, H. G., & WESMAN, A. G. *Differential Aptitude Tests, manual.* (2nd ed.) New York: Psychological Corporation, 1952.

BURT, C. L. The evidence for the concept of intelligence. *Brit. J. educ. Psychol.,* 1955, **25**, 158–177.

CATTELL, R. B. Theory of fluid and crystallized intelligence: A critical experiment. *J. educ. Psychol.,* 1963, **54**, 1–22.

CRONBACH, L. J. The two disciplines of scientific psychology. *Amer. Psychologist,* 1957, **12**, 671–684.

GETZELS, J. W., & JACKSON, P. W. *Creativity and intelligence.* New York: Wiley, 1962.

GHISELLI, E. E. Managerial talent. *Amer. Psychologist,* 1963, **18**, 631–642.

GUILFORD, J. P. Creativity. *Amer. Psychologist,* 1950, **5**, 444–454.

HARRELL, T. H. *Manager's performance and personality.* Cincinnati, O.: South-Western, 1961.

HAYES, K. J. Genes, drives, and intellect. *Psychol. Rep.,* 1962, **10**, 299–342.

HEBB, D. O. *The organization of behavior.* New York: Wiley, 1949.

HOLLAND, J. L. Creative and academic performance among talented adolescents. *J. educ. Psychol.,* 1961, **52**, 136–147.

HUNT, J. McV. *Intelligence and experience.* New York: Ronald Press, 1961.

Intelligence and its measurement: A symposium. *J. educ. Psychol.,* 1921, **12**, 123–147. (a)

Intelligence and its measurement: A symposium. *J. educ. Psychol.,* 1921, **12**, 195–216. (b)

MACKINNON, D. W. The nature and nurture of creative talent. *Amer. Psychologist,* 1962, **17**, 484–495.

MILES, T. R. On defining intelligence. *Brit. J. educ. Psychol.,* 1957, **27**, 153–165.

MORRIS, D. The biology of art. *Portfolio art News Annu.,* 1962, No. 6, 52–63, 122–124.

SEGEL, D. The multiple aptitude tests. *Personnel guid. J.,* 1957, **35**, 424–432.

SHAYCOFT, M. F., DAILEY, J. T., ORR, D. B., NEYMAN, C. A., JR., & SHERMAN, S. E. Project Talent: Studies of a complete age group—age 15. Pittsburgh: University of Pittsburgh, 1963. (Mimeo)

TAYLOR, C. W., SMITH, W. R., GHISELIN, B., & ELLISON, R. Explorations in the measurement and predictions of contributions of one sample of scientists. *USAF ASD tech. Rep.,* 1961, No. 61-96.

TAYLOR, D. W. Variables related to creativity and productivity among men in two research laboratories. In C. W. Taylor & F. Barron (Eds.), *Scientific creativity.* New York: Wiley, 1961.

THURSTONE, L. L. *Primary mental abilities.* Chicago: Univer. Chicago Press, 1938.

THURSTONE, L. L., & THURSTONE, T. G. *Factorial studies of intelligence.* Chicago: Univer. Chicago Press, 1941.

TORRANCE, E. P. *Guiding creative talent.* Englewood Cliffs, N. J.: Prentice-Hall, 1962.

TORRANCE, E. P. *Education and the creative potential.* Minneapolis: Univer. Minnesota Press, 1963.

YAMAMOTO, K. Role of creative thinking and intelligence in high school achievement. *Psychol. Rec.,* 1964, **14**, 783–789.

Are I.Q. TESTS Intelligent?

By Raymond Bernard Cattell

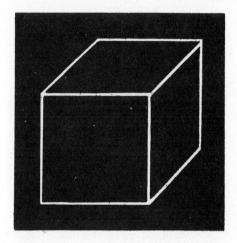

THE DILEMMA OF THE MENSA SOCIETY dramatizes the current upheaval in intelligence testing. Roughly three out of four of the prospective members selected on one kind of intelligence test failed to be selected by a second test, and three out of four of those chosen by the second type could not meet the standards of the first test. This international society, which limits entry to those at the 98th percentile or above in intelligence, was forced to make a policy decision on *which* kind of intelligence the society would consider.

Present controversy on the meaning of intelligence and of intelligence testing has erupted only in the past decade. It centers on whether there is a single factor of general intelligence and on the adequacy of present tests to measure it. My research indicates that there are two kinds of intelligence, fluid and crystallized, and that the former, which is independent of culture, can be measured as accurately as the latter.

To grasp what we now know of intelligence and the devices which attempt to measure it, one first must understand the background of the current dispute. In the first decade of this century, Charles Spearman brought to a field crowded with untutored, arbitrary, and generally naive definitions of intelligence, the theory of the "g" factor, a unitary, objectively defined, general-intelligence factor. For 50 years, Spearman's g factor has remained the only firm basis for the objective determination and measurement of intelligence.

This factor was defined by weights applied to different kinds of intellec-

tual performances, and its existence was proved by the peculiar form of correlation coefficients that appeared in correlations of ability measurement. If correlation coefficients show that four abilities, a, c, e, and g, are mutually positively related when measured over a group of 300 people, whereas the correlations are essentially zero on the abilities b, d, and f, we can assume some underlying unity behind a, c, e, and g.

There is no reason that there could not be two, three, or more such correlation clusters in a large group of abilities. But Spearman argued that the squared table of all possible correlations among a widely sampled set of abilities had a uniform slope which pointed to the existence of only one factor. To support this argument, he went beyond correlation clusters and developed factor analysis—a means of discovering the influences behind clusters.

Factor analysis is a method of calculating—from the various correlation coefficients of measured individual performances—the number and the general natures of the influences that account for observed relations. Through such an analysis, Spearman found the tests that bore most heavily on his general intelligence factor were those that had to do with reasoning and judgment. He therefore defined this factor as the capacity to educe relations and correlates.

Factor analysis also tells us how much of the individual variation in some particular performance is accounted for by each of the several factors that combine to produce that kind of behavior. Spearman concluded that g had about

a 9:1 ratio to special abilities in determining mathematical learning rate; about 7:1 in accounting for the size of one's properly used vocabulary; about 2:1 in determining musical ability; and about 1:4 in judging drawing ability.

Decades later, Louis Thurstone developed a multiple-factor analysis. This improvement over Spearman's methods led to Thurstone's discovery and definition of a dozen primary abilities, among them verbal comprehension, word fluency, number, space, and reasoning. Neither g nor the I.Q. were invalidated by Thurstone's work. On the contrary, advances in factor analysis rectified the only known statistical and structural flaw in Spearman's work. General intelligence now emerged from multiple-factor analysis as a single *second-order factor,* based on the intercorrelation among primary factors. The general intelligence concept was strengthened, for the pyramids of primary factors provided a far more reliable base than did the grains of innumerable small variables.

The question of how Thurstone's primary abilities grew out of Spearman's general ability remained unanswered, but researchers tended to neglect its importance. Instead of investigating the natural structure of abilities, the experts devised tests to fill the holes in a subjective framework. And so, for 30 years, there has been only trivial consolidation in this field, with a consequent hardening of attitudes and custom among professional intelligence testers.

As one who investigated with both Spearman and Thurstone, I at first was as much disturbed as intrigued when I thought I saw flaws in their monolithic structure. The first signs appeared in data on the second-order analysis of primary abilities. There was evidence that *two* general factors rather than one were involved. On rather slender evidence, I put forward in 1940 the theory of two g's. Those original disquieting conceptions since have been strengthened by the accumulation of evidence.

The breadth of a factor and the number of factors depend upon what tests an experimenter uses to gather his data. From the 20 primary abilities surveyed by John French, John Horn obtained some four or five broad abilities, such as fluid intelligence, crystallized intelligence, speed, and visualization. But the broadest of all such abilities, and the ones with a semantic claim to the label "intelligence," are fluid and crystallized.

Crystallized general ability, "g_c," shows itself in judgmental skills that have been acquired by cultural experience: vocabulary, good use of synonyms, numerical skills, mechanical knowledge, a well-stocked memory, and even habits of logical reasoning. G_c is high on the subtests that traditionally have been built into intelligence tests: vocabulary size, analogies, and classifications involving cultural knowledge of objects in the problem. Crystallized ability stretches across the whole range of cultural acquisitions. Mechanical knowledge—which is negligible or even negative on fluid ability—has a measurable effect on crystallized ability.

Tests of fluid ability, "g_f," have little relation to a well-stocked memory. They are culture fair perceptual and performance tests and those specially developed tests of judgment and reasoning which have been considered relatively culture free. They involve solutions to tests of classifications, analogies, matrices, topology, and problems that do not involve much educational acquisition. Fluid ability does have a role in numerical reasoning and even in verbal skills. It is fairly powerful in spatial reasoning and very powerful in inductive reasoning. [*See illustration, upper right.*]

The difference between fluid and crystallized general abilities becomes apparent when the intellectual responses of two persons who contrast in them are described. To find a person high in fluid ability but low in crystallized, we should have to take someone who accidentally has missed schooling. I have measured deck-hands and farmers who scored much higher than average professors in fluid ability but who acquired no com-

Primary Abilities of Specific Batteries	Research I: Boys (57) and Girls (5) of 6½ Years Old		Research II: Boys (151) and Girls (154) of 9, 10, & 11 Years Old		Research III: Boys and Girls (277) of 12 & 13 Years Old		Research IV: Men and Women (297) Adult Range	
	g_f	g_c	g_f	g_c	g_f	g_c	g_f	g_c
Verbal	−17	74	22	63	15	46	10	69
Spatial			73	03	32	14	30	−07
Reasoning	10	72			08	50	23	30
Number	43	49	47	35	05	59	24	29
Fluency					07	10	−03	25
Series: Culture Fair					35	23		
Classification; Culture Fair	58*	−11*	78*	09*	63	−02	48*	−08*
Matrices: Culture Fair					50	10		
Topology: Culture Fair					51	09		
Perceptual Speed							20	06
Flexibility							−03	03
Induction							55	12
Intellectual Speed							51	10
Mechanical Information							−15	48
Ego Strength	−07	−09					01	43
Self Sentiment							01	43
Super Ego								
Surgency								
Anxiety	10	−33	·04	−04			−05	−26

Fluid and Crystallized General Ability Factors at Various Ages. Crystallized general ability shows itself in those judgmental skills dependent upon cultural experience, while fluid ability affects tests unrelated to well-stocked memory. Flexibility is distinct from either g_c or g_f. Note the consistent level of g_f scores throughout all the age groups.

parable level of crystallized ability because they had not systematically applied their fluid intelligence to what is usually called culture. Such men will astonish you in a game of chess, or by solving a wire puzzle with which you have struggled in vain, or in swift insights into men and motives. But their

vocabularies may be arrested at a colloquial level, their knowledge of history negligible, and they never may have encountered algebra or geometry. These men often excel at the strategy of games, and one suspects they are naturally good soldiers. Lord Fisher, who designed the Dreadnought battleship, said, "In war

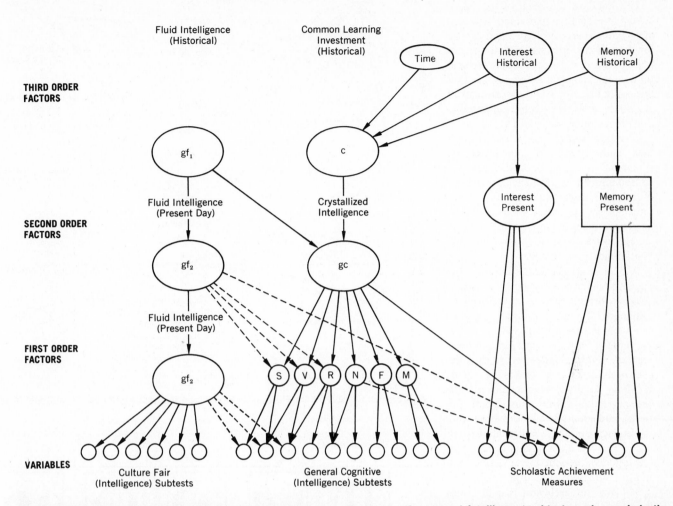

THIRD ORDER FACTORS

SECOND ORDER FACTORS

FIRST ORDER FACTORS

VARIABLES

Causal Relations Between Fluid and Crystallized Ability Factors. Scores on the general intelligence subtests and on scholastic achievement measures are the result of time, interest, memory and both fluid and crystallized intelligence. Arrows indicate the direction of influence and solid arrows show major lines of influence. Note the lack of other influence on culture fair subtests.

you need surprise." Surprise bursts from situations in which crystallized intelligence is useless. Napoleon claimed that he would make his despairing opponents "burn their books on tactics." The characteristic of fluid intelligence is that it leads to perception of complex relationships in new environments.

The individual with a high level of crystallized intelligence has different capacities. He will have learned many intelligent responses to problem situations. He will recognize an engineering problem as requiring solution by differential calculus, and he will diagnose a defective sentence by pointing to a dangling participle. He could not have acquired these skills, however, unless he had the fluid ability to see them.

To illustrate a case where crystallized ability is clearly higher than fluid ability, we must take either a person in whom there has been some recession of fluid ability, as through aging or brain damage, or a person who has been over-educated for his ability—say, someone like Sheridan's Mrs. Malaprop, taught

a bigger vocabulary than natural judgment permits handling.

Crystallized and fluid intelligence abilities could not be isolated until technical progress in factor analytic experiments made their recognition possible. These two structures have been confirmed repeatedly by researchers over the whole age range, from five to 50.

Fluid and crystallized ability factors are positively correlated. According to the theory of two broad intelligences, fluid intelligence is a general relation-perceiving capacity, independent of sensory area, and it is determined by the individual's endowment in cortical, neurological-connection count development. It is a broad factor because such integrating power can be brought to bear in almost any perceptual or reasoning area. Crystallized ability, on the other hand, appears as a related circle of abilities—verbal, numerical, reasoning—that normally are taught at school. The extent to which an individual takes or leaves what he is taught depends on his fluid ability, on his years of formal education,

and on his motivation to learn. Thus, crystallized general ability reflects both the neurological integrative potential of the individual and his fortune in cultural experience.

Crystallized ability is not identical with scholastic achievement. Many scholastic skills depend largely on rote memory, whereas what factor analysis shows is crystallized ability in that section of school learning involving complex judgmental skills that have been acquired by the application of fluid ability. [*See illustration above.*]

Once these two general abilities are located and independently measured, further distinguishing characteristics appear. The age curve of growth for the two abilities turns out to be quite different. Fluid ability follows a biological growth curve and approaches a plateau at about 14 years, whereas crystallized ability shows an increase to 16, 18, and beyond. The evidence points to some steady decline in fluid intelligence after about 22 years of age, but crystallized intelligence keeps its level as far into later years as adequate samples have been taken. [*See illustration, right.*]

The standard deviation of the calculated I.Q.—mental age divided by actual age—is almost exactly 50 per cent greater for fluid than for crystallized ability, 24 points instead of 16 points. Socio-educational research might determine whether arranging brighter and duller streams of classroom instruction would permit more divergence of crystallized I.Q.

There are substantial indications that fluid and crystallized intelligence respond differently to brain damage. Localized injury may produce localized loss of skills, while leaving other abilities untouched. By the nature of fluid ability, an impairment in any cortical locality should produce some loss of general fluid-ability performance.

A pilot study on nature-nuture ratios suggests that heredity bears a greater relation to fluid than to crystallized intelligence. Tentative estimates of relative variance are 90 per cent for g_f and 70 per cent for g_c. An independent demonstration of the higher hereditary influence of fluid-ability levels has been given by John Loehlin, who compared the primary factor within pairs of both fraternal and identical twins. Verbal ability, fluency, and reasoning primaries naturally showed environmental influence, but a general genetic factor corresponding to fluid ability was apparent.

My own research and that of others indicates that day-to-day changes do occur in intelligence. Our subjective conviction that we are brighter on some days than we are on others is borne out by measures of g_f variability over time, as might be expected from the closer dependence of fluid intelligence upon total physiological efficiency.

Many of the puzzling phenomena in intelligence testing are explained if we consider that the traditional intelligence test actually is a mixture of fluid and crystallized factors. Discoveries of different ages for the end of intelligence growth, significant differences in the standard deviation of I.Q.'s, and different ratios of the weight of heredity and environment on the I.Q. all result from a confusion of the two factors in the usual intelligence test.

When I first called attention to the flaws in the general intelligence theory, I at once proceeded to investigate the correlations with the general fluid ability factor of a variety of "perceptual" tests. From my research came the culture fair intelligence test associated with present uses in cross-cultural studies and Head-

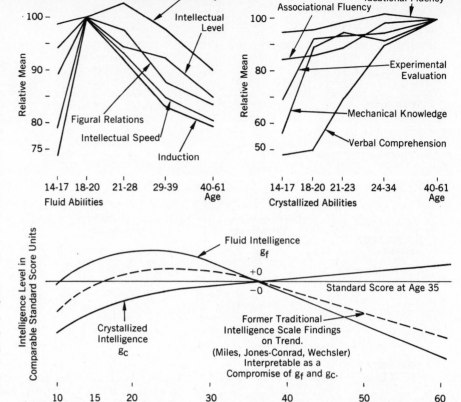

Age Curves Compared for Fluid and Crystallized General Ability and Traditional Tests.

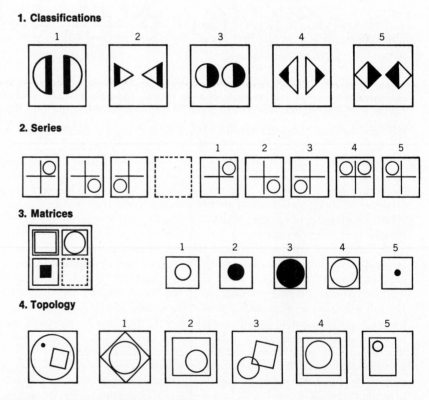

Sample Items from a Culture Fair Test.

1 Which one of these is different from the remaining four? (No. 3)
2 Which of 5 figures on right would properly continue 3 on left, i.e., fill blank? (No. 5)
3 Which of figures on right should go into square on left to make it look right? (No. 2)
4 At left, dot is outside the square and inside the circle. In which of the figures on the right could you put a dot outside the square and inside the circle? (No. 3)

1. Comparison of American and Chinese Children, 10 Years of Age, by IPAT Culture Fair Scale 2 (Rodd, 1960).

	American (1007)		Chinese (Hong Kong) (1007)	
	Mean	Stand. Dev.	Mean	Stand. Dev.
Culture Fair Form 2A	24.10	6.66	24.04	5.70

2. Comparison of American and Chinese College Students (Mean Age 18 yrs.) by IPAT Culture Fair Scale 3 (Rodd, 1960).

	American (1100)		Taiwanese (765)		Chinese Mainland Chinese (525)	
	Mean	Stand. Dev.	Mean	Stand. Dev.	Mean	Stand. Dev.
Culture Fair Form 3A	21.99	4.50	21.99	4.50	22.88	4.47
Culture Fair Form 3B	26.90	4.50	26.95	4.47	27.23	4.53

3. Correlation of Culture Fair and Traditional Tests with Social Status (McArthur and Elley, 1964).

1. Traditional Test (California Test of Mental Maturity)	+0.38
2. Traditional Test (Modified) (Lorge-Thorndike)	+0.27
3. Fluid Ability (IPAT Culture Fair) (On 271 12-and 13-Year-Olds)	+0.24

Cultural Differences and Culture Fair Scores. That culture is no barrier when a culture fair test is used shows in American and Chinese scores on the same test. The correlation between c_f and social status measures the relation of real ability to the status.

start programs. But whatever its present practical importance, the origin of these culture fair tests was in the first place the theoretical goal of defining the new form of intelligence.

In our first attempt at developing a fluid-ability test appropriate to all cultures, I took such common elements as parts of the human body, sun, moon, rain, and stars, as well as random blotches. But only the perceptual forms have been retained in later tests, for experiment has shown that these give accurate results. [*See illustration, lower right, page 60.*]

In choosing test elements, the effect on the score of cultural experience can be reduced by taking either what is over-learned in all cultures or what is absolutely strange to all. Anything in between these extremes is bound to show the influence of the culture in the test scores. To take overlearned items is more practicable, because valuable test time is wasted in getting responses on completely strange items.

To avoid pointless sociological arguments, we called fluid-ability measures culture *fair* rather than culture *free*. Objection from teachers to a culture-free concept arises from confusion between the cultural familiarity and test sophistication effects on test scores. *All* tests, culture fair tests included, are susceptible to test sophistication, and scores may continue to improve for some four to six retests. Scores increase due to familiarity with instructions, with layout, with timing, and with the tricks any good person being tested can learn. Studies by Sarason, Feingold, and me have shown that practice in the culture-fair type of spatial and analogies perception produced no real gain, unlike training in the verbal and numerical fields that dominate the traditional intelligence test. But with subjects unused to paper-and-pencil tests, and with subjects from other cultures, it would be ideal always to repeat testing several times and to throw away the results of the first three or four encounters.

The culture fair concept does not imply that no significant differences ever should be found between different populations living in different cultures or

	Correlation with School Total Achievement								Other Intelligence Tests		
	Validity General Factor	Marks by Teacher Amer.	Chin.	Stand. Ach. Test	English Amer.	Chin.	Reading	Math Amer.	Chin.	Calif. Test of Mental Maturity Verb.	Numer.	Wisc. I.Q.
Fluid Abil. (IPAT Cult. Fair Scale 2)	.79*	.34*		.35*		.52++						.72++
Fluid Abil. (IPAT Cult. Fair Scale 3)	.78°	.35**	.35**	.59 .49	40	30+		64	47+	42	56	
Crystal. Abil. (Cal. Test Ment. Mat.)	.58*	.66*	0?	.65*		0?			0?			
Crystal. Abil. (Lorge-Thorndike)	.52*	.43*	0?	.35*		0?			0?			
Army Beta					25			34		27	58	
Henmon Nelson				.81								
Pintuer						.85++						.80++

* McArthur & Elley, 271, 12 and 13 year olds
** Domino, 94 college students
+ Rodd & Goodman (Atten. corrected on school test)
++ 79 children in Bridge Project School
° Bajard

Correlations of Fluid and Crystallized Intelligence Tests with other Measures. The validity in terms of general ability saturation is highest for the culture fair scales, but correlation with school grades is higher when the traditional intelligence test is used.

subcultures or social classes. The bright people in most societies tend to migrate to higher socio-economic levels. The correlation of .20 to .25 between fluid ability measures and social status presumably is a measure of the relation of real ability to status, but the correlation of .38 found with traditional intelligence tests represents also the scholastic gain of those with the luck to be born into more-educated families.

Where ulterior evidence suggests that peoples *are* equally gifted, a culture fair test must show absolutely no difference of score despite profound differences of culture. No differences have been demonstrated on the culture fair scales among American, British, German, French, and Italian samples. A more severe test was made by William Rodd, who compared Chinese (Taiwanese) and American school children and university students on identically printed culture fair tests. The raw scores are identical to three significant figures for Midwestern American and Taiwanese school children. American college students do not differ from the Taiwanese, but there is a significant difference between Taiwanese and mainland Chinese, which could be the result of differences in methods of student selection. [See illustration, upper left, page 61.]

But testing does suggest that significant mean population differences *can* exist. Samples have shown higher means in the south than in the north of Japan, in the north than in the south of Italy, and in New Zealand migrants as compared with unselected British Isles stock. Further research might develop a world map of intelligence resources.

For school-age children, when intelligence tests are most used, the correlation between g_f and g_c scores is positive and substantial. It will probably become even higher if regular school attendance becomes universal and methods used in more efficient school systems become uniform. From this high correlation, casual administrators may argue that one kind of test—the old kind, of course —is enough. Indeed, hard-headed realism may assert that the traditional I.Q. test is preferable, because the g_c test predicts this or next year's scholastic performance slightly but systematically better than does the g_f test. [See illustration, bottom, page 61.]

But if a maximum prediction of next year's academic achievement were all that one desired, one would not use an intelligence test at all! For a higher correlation can be obtained from *this* year's grades, or from a proper combination of intelligence, personality, and motivation measures, as our research has shown.

The purpose of an intelligence test is different. It should help us to understand the causes of a given person's good or poor grades or to predict what he will do in the future in radically changed circumstances. Over an interval of a year or so we can expect habits and situations and the momentum of interest to make scholastic performance *now* the best predictor of grades in the future. But when a person's life turns a corner, as when he goes from liberal education in the school to technical education in a career, the crystallized-ability measure may be quite misleading. A fluid-ability I.Q. from a culture fair test is likely to be a better predictor of performance.

The same principle holds if we compare children of fundamentally different backgrounds. The Binet in French, administered to a mixed group of 100 French, 100 American, and 100 Chinese children, would show a correlation of I.Q. with French language skills, but the Binet score would be no general predictor of language ability among the Americans and Chinese. In the same situation, a culture fair test would correlate with the native-language performance about equally in each of the three language groups.

During the school years, culture fair tests are both theoretically and practically useful, especially in localities with language or cultural differences. But the dual I.Q. becomes indispensable almost anywhere when testing adults. The two I.Q. values for a given person may be very different, and the kinds of prediction made from each will differ. Crystallized ability may remain steady or even climb, for it increases with age and experience, but fluid ability falls after age 22. A middle-aged man handles most situations in our culture more intelligently than he would have when he was 20, but if a younger and an older man were transferred to an absolutely new society, the probably higher fluid-intelligence level of the younger man would be likely to show itself. Where performance in radically different situations is involved, the man of 50 will perform very differently from what would be predicted for him on the basis of his g_c mental age. The g_f mental age would have predicted this difference.

Despite the tremendous accumulation of experience concerning intelligence testing between 10 and 20 years of age, there has been comparatively little over the 20- to 70-year range, and we know little about what happens to age trends, distribution, or sex differences of intelligence in that period.

Our society, which values high intelligence, must make some kind of policy decision on *which* kind of intelligence should be given emphasis in this period. A decision on culture fair and traditional test usage becomes even more imperative for the psychologist whose testing helps determine jobs and clinical outcomes. As men leave school and go into their special occupational fields, the statistical general factor begins to disintegrate, or to persist only as an historical relic. Vocabulary tests for the average man reveal a distinct falling off in ability after school. And if women in middle age are tested by intelligence tests (at least as mostly designed by men), they undergo an apparent drop in crystallized ability not shown by men.

To continue to regard the traditional intelligence tests as a general intelligence measure when applied after the age of 20 is pure illusion. If a g_c score predicts relation-perceiving capacity in new fields, it does so indirectly by harking back to the fact that scholastic ability at 18 was a measure of g_f intelligence. If that happens not to be true for a person, or if such things as brain damage have occurred since, the g_c prediction can be badly in error.

The need for a dual I.Q. score is rooted not only in what happens to the man but in what happens to the culture. A comparison that I made of all 11-year-olds in a city of 300,000 before World War II with 11-year-olds in the same city after the war and 13 years later showed no trace of any significant difference on a culture fair test. Yet Godfrey Thomson's comparisons on the British Binet at about the same period showed a very significant upward shift. Results in America by Frank Finch with various traditional crystallized-ability tests showed an even greater upward shift. The standardization of a traditional test becomes unanchored from the moment it is made, and it drifts in whatever direction the tide of educational investment happens to take. In this more prosperous age, the direction is upward. Since no such drift is demonstrable with culture fair, fluid-ability measures, error of prediction is less flagrant.

New answers to educational, political, and social questions may be reached through culture fair intelligence testing. Culture fair tests are not toys for anthropologists to take to remote cultures. They need to be used here and now to open equal educational opportunity to all our subcultures of class and race. ∎

THE INTELLIGENT MAN'S GUIDE TO INTELLIGENCE

article **By MORTON HUNT** *what it is, how we get it, how much we have, how much we can have and what we can do with it*

AS IF THERE weren't enough controversy in our time, people are now fighting about *intelligence*—not the CIA type but the kind that *Webster's Dictionary* defines as: "the faculty of understanding; the capacity to know or apprehend." What could be debatable about that? Listen:

• Sir Charles Snow, the eminent British novelist and scientist —and a liberal—says in March 1969 that the astonishing disproportion of Jews among Nobel Prize winners and other outstandingly intelligent groups suggests that "there [is] something in the Jewish gene-pool which produces talent on quite a different scale from, say, the Anglo-Saxon gene-pool." For this, he draws a fierce barrage of criticism from non-Jews and Jews—many of *them* liberals—who call his suggestion "benign racism" and a "mirror image" of Nazi racist theories.

• The Los Angeles City Council, following the lead of New York City and Washington, D. C., votes in early 1969 to eliminate I. Q. testing from the lower grades of public schools. The cause: pressure by militant Negroes and other disadvantaged people, who regard I. Q. testing as one of Whitey's tricks to keep them out of college and the better schools. They have some odd bedfellows: The John Birch Society has been attacking I. Q. testing for years, on the ground that it is an effort by Big Government to control the minds of Americans.

• Psychologist Arthur Jensen, of the University of California at Berkeley, publishes a long, dense, scholarly paper in the *Harvard Educational Review*, using statistical methods to show that heredity is far more responsible than environment for differences in tested intelligence and suggesting that this may account for most of the 15-point difference between average white and Negro I. Q. scores. Dozens of newspapers and magazines find this article "inflammatory" and "incendiary." In the staid, academic pages of the *Harvard Educational Review*, various scholars and educators term his article "mischievous" and "unforgivable" and label him a "high priest of racism." At Berkeley, his office is picketed by the SDS, black students try to disrupt his classes and his safety is threatened via mail and phone.

• In October 1969, physicist William Shockley, of Stanford University, arises to deliver an address to a National Academy of Sciences meeting held at Dartmouth College. Shockley, a Nobel Prize winner as coinventor of the transistor, wants the academy to support research on the inheritance of intelligence. As soon as he is introduced, some 40 Negro students begin clapping loudly—and keep it up for 90 minutes, until Shockley and the administrative staff call the meeting off.

• A militant social-reform group named American Psychologists for Social Action circulates an anti-Jensen, anti-I. Q.- testing petition. One of the more vocal members of the organization, Dr. Martin Deutsch, of New York University, tells me: "There's no scientific definition of intelligence at this time. It's a convenient label for certain kinds of behavior; but I suspect that, in actual fact, the thing itself doesn't really exist."

Intelligence doesn't exist? What's he talking about? Don't we all *know* it exists? Even when we were children, we could tell which kids around us were smart and which were dumb. As adults, we have a fair idea, after a few minutes of conversation, whether a new acquaintance is bright or stupid and, after spending some time with any person, we *know* which he is. But our everyday experiences of intelligence do not tell us exactly what it is; they do not even prove its existence.

However, we have more than everyday experiences to go by; indeed, in the past 66 years, no subject in all of psychology has been so extensively researched and put to practical use as has intelligence. Each year, millions of I. Q. tests are given to school children, college students, draftees and job applicants. Articles, monographs and books on new research in intelligence appear at the rate of one a day. Current research concerns a wide variety of topics: the development of many new kinds of tests; the relationship of intelligence scores to social class, to ethnic origins, to the time and place of testing and even to the sex of the tester; the chemistry of the brain; problem-solving ability in pigeons, rats, cats, dogs, ·WASPs and Negroes; and such arcana as the representation of the structure of intellect by a three-dimensional matrix. Dr. Deutsch must be wrong; some of these people must know *something* about the subject.

And they do; the trouble is that they disagree about the meaning of most of what they know. Incompatible theories of intelligence exist in embarrassing profusion. The oldest was formulated half a century ago by English psychologist Charles Spearman, who noted that many mental abilities are statistically correlated: A person who does well in vocabulary is likely to do well in arithmetic, pencil-and-paper mazes and so on; a person who does poorly in one of them is likely to do poorly in the others. To Spearman, this clearly suggested that an unseen general intelligence, or g, lay behind the various specific abilities, or s's, and made all the scores go one way or the other. But what was g itself? Spearman could only suggest that it was the ability to perceive relationships or connections between things.

Most psychologists accepted g as a reality; a number of them, in fact, set about improving upon, and complicating, Spearman's basic theory. Louis Thurstone, of the University of Chicago, an authority on intelligence, and others found "group factors" common to bunches of s's—higher than s's, but still subordinate to g. Raymond Cattell, now with the University of Illinois, and various others found not one but two kinds of g; one provides the brain power for routine learned abilities such as vocabulary, another provides the brain power for less teachable and more complex abilities such as abstract reasoning. Some psychologists eventually decided that g doesn't really explain anything and that the theory might as well be junked. J. P. Guilford and his students at the University of Southern California identified many highly specialized mental abilities—more than 80, at last count—and organized them into a kind of three-dimensional structure, in which all are of equal merit and there is no overriding unseen "pure" intelligence. The brilliant Swiss psychologist Jean Piaget has, meanwhile, ignored practically the entire business of g, s, I. Q. and testing; instead, he has studied intelligence as a living, growing thing and described its functions in the various stages of the mind's development.

Those are some of the theories at the present time. Each answers some questions, raises others, ignores yet others. But not all is chaos. There are two distinct sides in the intelligence war and, on nearly every debated issue, psychologists are in one camp or the other. The two are those old classic opposites, nature versus nurture, heredity versus environment, instinct versus experience—the very same polarization of views that exists in the field of animal-behavior studies, between the instinct-oriented ethologists and the developmentalists. (See *Man and Beast*, PLAYBOY, July 1970.)

Hereditarians think that intelligence is essentially based on the individual's brain structure and chemistry, and hence is largely predetermined by his genetic make-up. Environmentalists think intelligence consists primarily of acquired or learned abilities to understand, to think and to solve problems; they consider it largely determined by experience.

Many adherents of one side or the other, however, are repelled by the company they find themselves in: hereditarians by racists who maintain that the Negro is an inferior species of human being; environmentalists by those liberals who refuse even to consider genetic knowledge. As a result, psychologists often equivocate. One distinguished member of this discipline, who publicly is a convinced environmentalist, privately told me, "Arthur Jensen has done us a real service —we needed to pin down the genetic contribution." But Jensen himself, having argued at great length in print that racial I. Q. differences are largely inherited, states that he has never labeled Negro intelligence "inferior."

Some hard facts do, nevertheless, exist and are generally accepted. They are nearly all derived from I. Q. testing; for despite its limitations, it is still the only means we have of measuring intelligence. To date, no one has observed the actual phenomenon of thought taking place in the brain, nor seen any record of its having occurred. Physiologists know a

fair amount about the brain—that it weighs about three pounds in the adult; that thought takes place in the cortex, a paint-thin outer layer of gray matter consisting of some 12 billion nerve cells, or neurons; that each neuron is almost, but not completely, connected to many other neurons at contact points called synapses; and that remembering, learning and problem solving involve the transmission of electrical impulses through the cells. At present, it is thought that the cell, when excited, produces a chemical, acetylcholine, that permits the electrical impulse to pass across the gap at the synapse to the next cell, exciting it, in turn; the moment the message has passed, however, another chemical, cholinesterase, destroys the acetylcholine and ends the transmission—all this within 4/10,000ths of a second.

A group of researchers at the University of California at Berkeley have been rearing bright rats and stupid rats, chopping off their heads and chemically analyzing their brains —and finding different ratios of acetylcholine to cholinesterase in the brains of the two strains. It may be that one ratio makes for faster transmission than the other: that is, faster thinking. But this still leaves many questions unanswered. Where and how is information stored and how is it drawn upon in the thinking process? Why are some men superb thinkers in some areas, such as music and mathematics, but not in others? Why have we never found any indication, under the microscope, of the "memory trace"—the record of permanent change due to learning or experience? Why is there no perceptible difference between the neurons of a genius and those of an idiot, those of the learned man and of the ignoramus, those of the dominant (operative) half of the brain and of the subordinate (unused) half?

But if we cannot yet observe intelligence directly, at least we can observe its effects in the form of intelligent behavior. This is why testing has been the principal source of information on the subject. It began 66 years ago, when the Ministry of Public Instruction in Paris commissioned psychologist Alfred Binet to design a test that would identify in advance the children who lacked the capacity to follow the regular curriculum and who should, therefore, be put in special schools. Binet's test consisted of numerous tasks and questions that graded those perceptual, verbal, arithmetical and reasoning abilities necessary for success in school; yet, it seemed obvious to him, and to most other psychologists, that he was measuring not only achievement but over-all intelligence.

Known in its various American revisions as the Stanford-Binet, it is still the most widely used individual intelligence test, although there are at least 40 others in print, including the well-known Wechsler-Bellevue test. All of them, however, are unsuited to large-scale use because they have to be given to one person at a time. Group tests, therefore, in which the subjects read questions to themselves and check off multiple-choice answers, have become a big business; there are close to 200 of them in print, with the Otis-Lennon Mental Ability Test (used in many schools) and the Armed Forces Qualification Test the best-known.

Originally, Binet scored each tested child as to his mental age, depending on how far the child got in the test compared with other children. But since a bright child might have a mental age of ten when he was only eight—and a dull one a mental age of ten when he was chronologically 12—the important figure was the *ratio* between mental age and chronological age; this ratio was his intelligence quotient, or I. Q. For the bright eight-year-old, it would be $\frac{10}{8}$ (x 100 to get rid of decimals), or 125; for the dull 12-year-old, it would be $\frac{10}{12}$ x 100, or about 83.

The tasks in all I. Q. tests are arranged in the order of their increasing difficulty. In the Stanford-Binet, for instance, three-year-olds are asked to do simple things such as building a bridge with three blocks or copying a circle. The four-year-old begins to get simple verbal and reasoning problems, such as "Why do we have cars?" or "Father is a man, mother is a _____." The ten-year-old, in the

Otis-Lennon test, has to do much more advanced reasoning, involving questions such as this:

The opposite of *easy* is:
hard slow tiresome simple short

or this:

Which number should come next in this series?
2   3   5   6   8   9   ?

or this:

Questions for teenagers and adults are, naturally, even harder and call upon anywhere from seven different mental abilities to scores of them. In The Psychological Corporation's Multi-Aptitude Test, which is much like other tests of general intelligence, there are, for instance, items testing verbal ability, such as:

What word *means most nearly the same* as IMBUE:
distort refute abstain inoculate allege

Others deal with quantitative (arithmetic) reasoning, such as:

Find the rule according to which this number series is formed, and write the next *two* numbers of the series:
5 −7 10 −14 19 −25 ___ ___

Still others deal with abstract reasoning, such as:

These four figures are alike in some way:

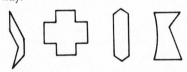

Which one of these five goes with the four above?

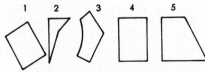

("Inoculate" comes closest in meaning to imbue; the rule for the number series is —the difference gets larger by one each time, but also the sign changes every other time, hence the last two numbers are 32 and −40; figure 3 is the only one that goes with the set of four because it alone has more than four angles.)

Using various I. Q. tests, psychologists have learned that intelligence is "normally" distributed in the general population—that is, the great majority of people have I. Q.s of 100, give or take a few points. More than two thirds have I. Q.s between 85 and 115; less than three percent score under 70 and less than three percent score 130 or above. The former are the mentally retarded; the latter are the gifted.

Such statistics are helpful as guides to planning the size of the school system, institutions for the mentally retarded, manpower needs and the like. More important, they enable us to ask what makes for intelligence; for when we find out what kinds of people are at the upper end and at the lower end of the I. Q. curve, we may begin looking for cause-and-effect relationships. For instance, most of the people at the high end are in the higher socioeconomic strata of society and most of those at the low end are in lower and impoverished ones. Hereditarians, by and large, think that intelligent persons make their way to the upper levels, unintelligent ones remain behind or sink in the scale. Environmentalists feel that children of poverty—and especially of minority groups—never have a chance to develop their intelligence and that, moreover, I. Q. tests are built on middle-class values and do not give a fair picture of the talents of the poor.

Equally indisputable are facts about the average I. Q. of various ethnic groups —and equally moot are the explanations offered. Scots in the British Isles and Jews in America have higher average I. Q.s than the populations around them (Jews, for instance, run five to eight I. Q. points above the average of non-Jews in their same social and economic positions). Americans of northern-European origin average somewhat higher than those of southern-European origin. Oriental children, in some West Coast school surveys, come out consistently higher than white children. Why? Innate superiority? Social factors making for greater striving? The particular cultural tradition or kind of family life in which the child is reared? Every possible view has some adherents and some supporting data.

I. Q. is, as might be expected, as good a predictor of success in life as it is in school. The distinguished psychologist Lewis Terman followed a number of highly gifted children through decades of their lives; as a group, they turned out to be uncommonly successful in terms of career, social position, creative output, health, marriage and similar criteria. More generally, people with high I. Q.s

tend to have careers of high social status and, indeed, careers that tend to require high I. Q.s: Ph.D.s have a median I. Q. close to 140; accountants, 128; lawyers, 127; salesmen and managers of retail stores, 116; auto mechanics, 102; farmers, 94; and teamsters, 89. (These are only averages; some farmers have scored as high as 147, some accountants as low as 94.)

The field of intelligence studies is full of curiosa of this sort. Here is a sampling:

• Despite all the clichés concerning the mental dullness of the criminal population, it seems to have about the same intelligence as the population at large.

• Males are consistently more intelligent than females, but only by a negligible amount—and only beyond the onset of adolescence; in childhood, girls score slightly higher than boys. In adulthood, though women score a little lower overall, they definitely surpass men in vocabulary and verbal fluency as well as straight memory; men are superior in arithmetical reasoning, mechanical aptitude and spatial relationships.

• Leadership among children, and probably among adults, is correlated with high I. Q., but only up to a point. When a person is 30 or more points brighter than most of the people in his group, he does not become a leader; it's anybody's guess why not. (There have been notable exceptions, however; Jefferson was evidently a highly intelligent man, and so were Churchill and Woodrow Wilson, among others.)

• Of all the measured similarities between man and wife, such as economic background, education and the like, the highest correlation is that of intelligence; spouses are even more alike in intelligence than brothers and sisters. Love evidently can't grow or survive where one lover is painfully dumb, or the other objectionably smart.

• The first-born child in a family is likely to be brighter than the last-born child by a little over three points. The difference could be due to the better intra-uterine or other biological advantages of being first in line; it might, however, be due to the greater attention and training first-borns get from their parents.

• Not all children of high-I. Q. parents are bright and not all children of low-I. Q. parents are dumb; in fact, on the average, children are part way between their parents' level and the average of the whole population.

• Creativity is not an automatic accompaniment of high I. Q.; in fact, some creative people have modest I. Q.s. A high I. Q. *is* essential for creativity in nuclear physics, mathematics and architecture; but numerous studies have shown that among painters, sculptors and designers, the correlation between creativity and intelligence is, oddly enough, zero or even slightly negative. (This does not mean that highly creative artists are stupid; rather, they are all fairly intelligent, but among them the *more* creative are not necessarily the *more* intelligent.)

• Twins average four to seven I. Q. points lower than singly born children. The psychological explanation: They get less individual attention from their parents. The biological explanation: They had less room in the womb, hence got a poorer start.

• Children born of incestuous matings between brothers and sisters, or parents and their own children, have, on the average, considerably depressed I. Q.s, plus an inordinate number of physical ailments. The genetic explanation: Inbreeding increases the chance of inheriting the same recessive hidden defects from both parents, in which case they become dominant. The environmental explanation: Incestuous connections are most common among people of extremely poor social position and defective home life, both of which cripple the offspring. Perhaps both genetics and environment play a part. But in Japan, where cousin marriages are perfectly acceptable and occur in all classes, the children of such marriages average eight I. Q. points below children of comparable noncousin marriages. Here, at least, there is no choice of alternative explanations—only the genetic makes sense.

Such is the more-or-less solid ground in intelligence; all the rest is a slough of conflicting data and contradictory hypotheses. Environmentalists hold that intelligence tests do not measure "innate" intelligence, because there is no such thing. Dr. Alexander Wesman, director of the Test Division of The Psychological Corporation, maintains, "Intelligence is the summation of the learning experiences of the individual; that's what the tests measure and that's all they measure. It is possible that some people do have a greater neurological potential for learning than others, but I haven't yet seen it proved or disproved—least of all by the existing intelligence tests." Others are completely skeptical. Says Dr. Jack Victor of the Institute for Developmental Studies at New York University: "Intelligence tests measure a variety of subskills, but whether these, taken together, really equal intelligence is highly debatable. The subskills are real, but intelligence may be a fictitious concept, a convenient label with which to refer to a number of disparate traits."

Hereditarians, however, insist that the tests do measure something innate and very real—an over-all potential capacity to learn, to recall, to discriminate, to think and to solve problems—and that this capacity deserves the name of intelligence. They admit that in most I. Q. tests, it is expressed through learned materials; but they insist that the "neurological substrate"—the individual's nervous structure and biochemistry—largely determines the ease with which he learns them and the effectiveness with which he uses them.

Variations in the neurological substrate are obvious enough, if one compares different species of animal. The brain of the worm is almost nonexistent, while that of the rat is well developed; the worm can learn only the simplest mazes; the rat, highly complex ones. But even within any given species, there are inherited differences in skeletal and body type, in excitability, in blood type, in hair color and the shape of the features, in the sensitivity to various pathogens; how could there not also be differences in the innate responsiveness and educability of the brain? Thus far, they have not been anatomically identified, but their presence is felt by every animal trainer and every teacher: Puppies of a given breed, children from very similar backgrounds, do not learn with equal ease or apply their training with equal success. In cloud chambers, physicists study unseen particles by means of the trails of droplets that condense along the paths they take; in I. Q. testing, psychologists study unseen innate intelligence by means of its effects on verbal, arithmetical and logical performance.

Some hereditarians go further; they argue that it *is* possible to measure "pure" or innate intelligence directly by omitting verbal and other culturally loaded materials and building tests around designs and shapes so familiar to persons of all classes and all cultures that learning is of no consequence. One such "culture-fair" test was constructed by Dr. Cattell (he of the two-*g* theory); it uses problems such as these:

Which one of these is different from the other four?

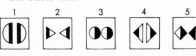

Which of the figures on the right goes in the missing square on the left?

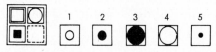

(Number three is different from the other four. Figure two goes into the missing square.)

Dr. Cattell says that in countries as different as the U. S., India and Taiwan, his test has yielded quite comparable results, indicating that it is unaffected by culture and is, indeed, measuring innate intelligence.

The environmentalists maintain that such tests, even if they are really culture-fair, measure only very special abilities rather than the broad sweep of intelligence. Says J. P. Guilford (he of the three-dimensional matrix of 80 or more mental abilities), "In ruling out verbal tests, probably the most important aspects of intelligence have been lost." The Psychological Corporation used to publish Dr. Cattell's test, but gave it up, and Dr. Wesman explains: "We came to the conclusion that although such a test may use learnings common to different cultures and subcultures, it ignores the relevance of those learnings to survival and success. That being the case, it can hardly provide an adequate measure of intelligence."

But even if the standard I. Q. tests are the best measures of intelligence now available, and even if they do measure something genuine, those measurements are very frequently distorted by variables in the testing process. Taking a test, for instance, is more productive of anxiety for some people than for others, and anxiety decreases problem-solving ability. When Negro children from impoverished homes take an I. Q. test under the supervision of a neatly dressed white examiner, they are very likely to feel strange, awkward and uneasy—and consequently do not do as well as they might. Recently, psychologist Irwin Katz, of the Graduate Center at New York University, deceived black students taking an I. Q. test into thinking they were being tested merely in eye-hand coordination. Freed of anxiety, they registered significantly higher I. Q.s—and did better when the test giver was white than when he was black. Katz's explanation: Well aware of the low opinion most whites have of black intellectual ability, the blacks' motivation to do well on the I. Q. test was low. But when the test was disguised as something else, the desire to do well took over and scores improved. And the challenge to do well in the eyes of the white examiner was greater than for one of their own.

The Katz study is backed up by the findings of British psychologist Peter Watson, who tested black West Indian students in a London working-class neighborhood. When the test was identified as an I. Q. test, scores dropped by ten points. Watson is convinced that the variation can account for the average 15 points by which blacks fall behind whites in I. Q. tests—the basis for the claim that whites are, genetically speaking, superior intellectually to blacks. Interestingly enough, both Watson and Katz admit that heredity no doubt contributes to intelligence —but that the science of genetics is not advanced enough to state precisely how much. (Incidentally, even Arthur Jensen has reported that Negro children, when they feel at ease with the examiner, will score eight to ten points higher on an I. Q. test.)

Most important in the Negro subculture, when it comes to the matter of I. Q. testing, is the fact that grammar and vocabulary in common use are markedly different from those in white middle-class society. Moreover, Negro mothers in the more disadvantaged levels of society are not explainers, as are white middle-class mothers. Negro children may, in consequence, simply be unacquainted with the words, the grammatical usages and many of the elemental concepts (such as categorization) that are needed to think about the questions asked. A social worker in Watts satirically constructed the "Chitling Test"—a mock I. Q. test using only words and problems familiar to the Negro poor—and few middle-class whites who saw it could answer most of the questions correctly. So, too, a French-Canadian guide might score moronic on verbal ability and abstract reasoning, yet completely outclass his examiner at outthinking wild animals or surviving in a midwinter storm.

For these and similar reasons, many of the findings of researchers on intelligence are contradicted by the findings of others. It is not just a matter of varying interpretations of the data; it is a matter of two or more studies of the same subject yielding different and even opposite findings.

Take the matter of intelligence and age. Various early studies indicated that it declines steadily from early adulthood onward. In the Thirties, for instance, researchers tested almost everybody in one New England town and found that the older the adults were, the lower they scored on reasoning ability. But whenever particular persons are tested and retested over a period of years, they show no such decline before the onset of senility; indeed, in one study a number of people were retested in middle age with an intelligence test they had taken 30 years earlier in college and got *better* scores in everything except arithmetic.

Just as bewildering is the case of our rapidly growing national intelligence. During World War Two, a large group of average soldiers took a test much like one given soldiers in World War One; if the 1917 standards for computing I. Q. had been used on their raw scores, they would have come out an average of 15 points higher than the World War One soldiers. The rise has continued: Since the end of World War Two, raw scores have gone up half as much again. What are we to think? Are the bright outbreeding the dull? Are we better informed because of improvements in education? Or have we merely become test-sophisticated; that is, skilled at getting better scores—but not any more intelligent than we were?

Assuming higher I. Q. scores would mean more than mere test-taking skill, the big question is: Can intensive education significantly increase the I. Q. in low-scoring children? Project Head Start, the nationwide Federally funded program of nursery-school experience for poor children, did not appreciably raise the school performance of the children involved—the I. Q. gains of five to ten points frequently reported for Head Start children did not hold up after the first year of regular schooling. But other efforts at compensatory education have used other techniques, and with more success: Colleagues of Dr. Deutsch at the Institute for Developmental Studies at New York University claim that their intensive-education experiments with small groups of New York City Negro children have resulted in average I. Q. gains of nearly eight points in a year of three-hours-per-day schooling. Whether these gains will endure is not yet known; to judge by some similar experiments, once the children return to ordinary classrooms, the discouraging milieu of Negro slum life may make them lose interest in schooling and cause them to drop back.

Such preschool compensatory programs are designed to bring the underprivileged up to par with the rest of American society, but could early education also benefit those who already have normal advantages? Some experts think so and certain experiments in which preschool children have been taught to read and to use typewriters lend credence to their arguments.

But equally eminent psychologists, including Jean Piaget and the late Arnold Gesell, have been convinced that children cannot grasp certain problems until their neural organization is ready—and that the maturation of the neural system cannot be accelerated. In a typical Piaget test, when children under seven see water poured from a short, wide glass into a tall, thin one, they think it has become "more." Even though they can be persuaded to *say* that it is the same, they cannot be taught to *feel* that it is the same. Beyond the age of seven, however, they become educable on the matter. Similarly, though it takes a good deal of effort, children can be taught to read a year or two before first grade; but those who are not taught until several years later catch on so rapidly and easily that they soon are abreast of the early learners, and often have a more positive and joyous feeling about reading.

These are only facets of the unanswered central question: Is the individual's intelligence primarily a product of his perceptions, experiences and the influence of other persons upon him, or is his intelligence primarily determined by his genotype, the unique mixture of genes he has inherited from his father and mother?

Time and research have amassed impressive evidence on both sides. A very few examples will give some idea how thoroughly convincing each argument is, and how hopelessly contradictory they appear to be.

First, evidence for the supremacy of environment:

• In Israel, children of European-Jewish origin have an average I. Q. of 105, while those of Oriental-Jewish origin (Yemenites and other Mideastern Jews) have an average I. Q. of only 85, or borderline normal. But when both groups of children are brought up in a kibbutz, where they spend most of their time in communal nurseries run by dedicated nurses, both groups—according to informal reports by some observers—end up with an average I. Q. of 115.

• Some 30 years ago in Iowa, a small group of mentally retarded year-old orphans was experimentally placed in a hospital ward for feeble-minded women. In an orphanage, the children had had a minimum of individual attention; in the hospital, they were "adopted" by the feeble-minded women, who fed and bathed them, played with them and talked to them. In less than two years, their average I. Q. leaped from 64 to 94 and all had become good prospects for adoption. By the age of six, all were in adoptive homes, where they made small additional gains averaging two I. Q. points. Many years later, a follow-up found that they were almost all living normal married lives and that their own children had an average I. Q. of 105.

• Gypsy and canal-boat children in England, and Appalachian and Negro children in the U. S., have normal or near-normal I. Q.s when very young but drift downward thereafter. All four groups get a normal amount of stimulation at the infant level, but in childhood and the teens suffer "stimulus deprivation," because of their impoverished homes, their barren cultural surroundings and their poor school experiences. A number of studies show marked I. Q. losses for these various groups, averaging 20 to 30 points between their preschool years and their late teens.

To the environmentalists, scores of such studies seem proof positive that I. Q. is not genetically fixed and does not follow an inevitable course of development as do such traits as skin color and blood type.

Now, evidence for the supremacy of the genotype:

• First, recall what we learned earlier about the offspring of cousin marriages: Their average I. Q. is eight points lower than that of other children in their own socioeconomic class. The phenomenon has no explanation other than the matching up of recessive genetic defects inherited from both sides.

• Even when socioeconomic factors are reversed, Negro children do not surpass or even equal whites: Negro children born of parents in the *highest* of four socioeconomic groupings (the professional-managerial) average nearly four I. Q. points below white children born of parents in the *lowest* of the four groupings (unskilled labor). The over-all socioeconomic status of American Indian children is as poor (and perhaps poorer) as that of Negro children, yet the Indian children average seven or eight I. Q. points higher.

• Unrelated children reared in the same home ought to have very similar I. Q.s if environment were the dominant factor in intellectual development. But their I. Q.s show a correlation only half as large as that between real siblings *reared in different homes.* Similarly, the I. Q.s of foster children correlate more closely with those of their biological parents than with those of their foster parents.

• Identical twins have exactly the same complement of genes; when they are reared together, therefore, both their genotypes and their environments are substantially identical. Not surprisingly, the correlation between their I. Q.s is very high: Various studies report it close to the 90 percent mark. In a few score of known cases, however, identical twins have been separated soon after birth and adopted into different homes; if environment were the major factor in determining their I. Q.s, the correlation should drop almost to zero but, in fact, it remains very high. Even in different environments, identical twins grow up far more alike in I. Q. than ordinary twins reared in the same home.

Scores of such studies seem proof positive to hereditarians that biological endowment is a far more significant

determinant of the intelligence of the individual than is environmental influence. They will admit, if pressed, that environment does affect mental development for good or ill in measurable ways, but having said so, they do their best to minimize its role, arguing that it accounts for 20 percent or less of the variance in I. Q. scores.

It seems obvious that one point of view must be correct, the other incorrect; but what seems obvious is not necessarily true. Most human phenomena are neither wholly good nor wholly bad, nor is a single doctrinaire explanation usually wholly true or wholly false. The truth lies not just in the middle but in a synthesis of the two sides. And so it is in the matter of intelligence. A unifying synthesis does exist.

It begins, as the noted psychologist I. I. Gottesman, of the University of Minnesota, points out, with the recognition that intelligence is not a lump sum, to which heredity contributes so many I. Q. points and environment the rest. The genotype and the environment do not *add up,* they *interact*—and the result is not a sum but a product.

But if we cannot separate the two interacting factors, at least we can ask how much difference it makes to modify one while keeping the other constant. We can ask, "Given any one genotype, how much can we modify the I. Q. by changing the environment?" And we can ask, "Given any one environment, how great are the variations heredity yields within it?"

As yet, there are no relevant research data that settle these questions for human I. Q.—but answers do exist for animals. Groups of genetically bright and genetically dull rats were reared in "restricted," "natural" and "enriched" environments, and then tested on maze-solving ability; various breeds of dogs were reared both indulgently and strictly, and then tested for their ability to obey a difficult command (not to eat). In both cases, the relative contributions of heredity and of environment varied for each combination of breed and rearing. For some breeds, changing the environment made little difference, while for others, it made a lot; and, conversely, within some environments, differences in heredity didn't amount to much, while within others, differences in heredity assumed considerable proportions.

Professor Gottesman believes that these results will prove to apply to human I. Q. and will make sense of what seem to be major contradictions in existing data. He offers the following diagram (from *Handbook of Mental Deficiency,* edited by N. Ellis) by way of illustrating the varying interactions (all of them speculative at this point) among a series of different environments and four hypothetical genotypes.

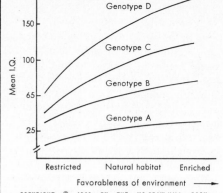

For genotype A, which might represent Mongolism, the "reaction range" is very narrow; that is, its various interactions with environments ranging from the worst to the best are all much alike, with a difference of only 50 percent or so between lowest and highest. For genotype D, which might represent hereditary genius, the reaction range is very broad; that is, its interactions with environments ranging from the worst to the best are very dissimilar, with a difference of some 300 percent between lowest and highest. Genotypes B and C are more nearly average and cover intermediate ranges.

Thus, it is clear that there is not one answer, not two answers, but a number of answers to the nature-nurture problem. It is clear, too, that both sides of the old argument have been right, and wrong, at the same time. For it is true that intelligence is the sum total of what has been learned—if we add: *learned by a given mind, which can utilize its experiences only within its own biological limits.* And it is also true that intelligence is a trait carried by the individual's genotype—if we add: *as it develops in the environment available to it.*

Applying this approach to the subject, we can make sense of many of the seeming contradictions in the existing findings. The contradictory results, for instance, of the intensive schooling of low-scoring children is not surprising: We have many genotypes being tested in many varied environments—and without anything like scientific control of either. Jewish children of two different backgrounds and I. Q. levels wind up, in a kibbutz, rising to the same higher level of I. Q.—but perhaps their genotypes were not really as dissimilar as one might suppose from their external traits. Negro and white children in the same schools, and even in the same socioeconomic class, remain widely separated, the Negro children being distinctly lower in I. Q.—but perhaps their environments were not really as similar as one might imagine. Negro and white children, even in the same schools and in the same socioeconomic class, do not actually have the same environment if, by environment, we mean the totality of the individual's experiences. Growing up black in a white society *feels* so different from growing up white in that society, even when class and income are equal, that we cannot fairly ascribe the remaining 10- or 11-point difference in I. Q. to heredity.

If Negroes were ever to experience thoroughgoing equality—social, economic and emotional—the average Negro I. Q. would very likely rise: perhaps only a little, still remaining distinctly below that of the white; perhaps enough for the two to coincide; perhaps enough to outstrip the white. We can't predict the outcome at this point, for blacks in America have never achieved genuine equality. Until they do, both those who say it will make no appreciable difference and those who are positive that all races have equal mental gifts are being demagogic in proclaiming as scientific fact

ideologies that may be based on political sentiment.

What is tragic is that they are both serving vicious ends while pursuing noble ones. Jensen and the behavioral geneticists are carrying on legitimate and potentially very important research, but some of them—Jensen, in particular—have unscientifically extended their tentative and speculative findings into firm and fixed policy recommendations. Jensen, for instance, in urging special schooling for many Negroes on the basis of their supposedly irremediable inferiority, is going far beyond anything his own work justifies. Deutsch and other environmentalists, on the other hand, are also doing important research, but most of them are so powerfully moved by their own egalitarian feelings and their desire to help the underprivileged that they have tried to block the publication of pro-Jensenist papers and condemned all further research on the

genetics of intelligence on the ground that whatever information it yielded would be "irrelevant" and "inflammatory."

Yet scientific inquiry and democratic progress are not, or at least need not be, antithetical. If the synthesis that resolves the nature-nurture controversy could be heard over the din of ideological battle, it might bring the two into harmonious alliance. Men did not learn to fly by ignoring gravity or denying that it existed but by learning the laws of aerodynamics and overcoming gravity. Men will make the most of their intelligence neither by denying the role of genetics nor by denigrating the importance of environment but by learning all they can about both and about the interaction of the two—and then applying the knowledge so as to give every man in society the maximum opportunity to develop his own potential.

IQ: fair science for dark deeds

by Jerome Kagan

Jerome Kagan, professor of developmental psychology of Harvard University, attacks the validity of the IQ test as a true measure of human intelligence. He takes issue with colleagues Arthur R. Jensen, professor of educational psychology at the University of California at Berkeley, and Richard J. Herrnstein, professor of psychology at Harvard University, both of whom uphold the integrity of the IQ. For their views Professors Jensen and Herrnstein have been vilified as racists and made the victims of abuse and harassment. Writing in the Winter, 1969, edition of the Harvard Educational Review, *Professor Jensen maintained that since intelligence is largely hereditary, compensatory education for the "culturally deprived" is a waste of national resources. More recently, in the September, 1971,* Atlantic, *Prof. Herrnstein predicted that a new "hereditary meritocracy" would arise, with class distinctions based on intelligence. However painful these conclusions are for those who yearn for an egalitarian society, we agree with the 107 Harvard professors, including Professor Kagan, who asserted in an ad in the* Crimson *that Professor Herrnstein has a right to be heard and threats against him "must be judged brutish by any civilized society."*

The concept of intelligence is among the most confused ideas in our lexicon, for ambiguity surrounds its definition, etiology, and social significance. A central issue turns on the degree to which scores on standard intelligence tests reflect generalized quality of memory and reasoning that is not limited to a particular cultural setting. It is our view that the relation between a person's score on a contemporary IQ test and his ability to think logically and coherently is poor. Moreover, the psychological trait "intelligence," which unfortunately has become equated with the IQ score, has become a primary explanation for the unequal access to power in our society.

Our own view, which we have explained in detail in other places, is that the white middle class Western community, like any moderately isolated social group, has created over the years a specialized vocabulary, reservoir of information, and style of problem solving and communication which it summarizes under the concept "intelligence." Since it uses possession of these skills as a rite of passage to positions of power and wealth in the society, many have been easily seduced into the conclusion that those without power or wealth were of fundamentally different intellectual competence. This view ignores the fact that there are enormous social class differences in a child's access to the experiences necessary to acquire the valued intellectual skills. But our society has been doing this for so long that the faulty logic has gone unnoticed, much like the Bushmen mothers who believe that a child will not walk unless he is placed erect in sand from the earliest weeks of life. Since no Bushman mother bothers to test this hypothesis, and all children walk by 18 months, the false idea continues to live.

Let us state the issue in kernel form. Every society, or large cohesive group within a society, recognizes that in order to maintain stability a small group must possess some power over the much larger citizenry. This power can be inherited, awarded, attained, or seized. In actual practice, this lean and rather raw description is usually disguised by a clever strategy — much like a magician's wrist movement — which makes select psychological traits symbolic of highly valued, status-conferring attributes and, hence, the vessel from which power is inevitably drawn.

Tenth-century Europe awarded power to those who were assumed to be more religious than their brothers. The presumption of a capacity for more intense religiosity provided a rationale that allowed the larger society to accept the fact that a privileged few were permitted entry into marble halls.

At other times and in other places sexual abstinence, sexual potency, hunting skill, a capacity for silent meditation, good soldiering, or efficient farming have been dimensions along which men were ordered and, as a consequence of that ranking, divided into unequal groups. Contemporary American society uses intelligence as one of the bases for ranking its members, and it makes the same arguments that educated Athenians uttered 2500 years ago.

We celebrate intelligence the way the Islamic Moroccan celebrates the warrior-saint. Moreover the cultural similarity extends to our explanations of the unequal distribution of either intelligence or saintliness. The majority of Americans believe that children are born with a differential intellectual capacity and, as a result, some are destined to assume positions of status and responsibility. A much smaller group believes that this psychological capacity has to be attained — through the right combination of early experience and will. These opposing hypotheses are identical in substance to the two interpretations of differential "capacity for religiosity" held by Islams in Morocco and Indonesia. The Moroccans believe that some are born with a greater capacity for strong and intense religious experience. The Javanese believe it is attained following long periods of meditation. And they, as we, discover the small proportion of their population that fit the description of the pure, and allow them ascent.

We are not contesting the obvious fact that there are real differences among individuals in psychological traits that our society values. But there is insufficient information on the causes of these differences.

Let me try to support this rather strong statement with a partial analysis of what an intelligence test is made of; for the widely publicized announcement that 80 percent of intelligence is inherited and 20 percent environmentally determined is based on information from two similarly constructed standardized IQ tests invented by Caucasian middle class Western men at the request of Caucasian middle class Western men for use by Caucasian middle class Western men to rank order everyone.

The most important set of test questions (important because scores on this set have the highest correlation with the total IQ) asks the testee to define words of increasing rarity. Rarity is a relative quality, depending always on the language community one selects as referent. *Shilling* is a rare word in the language space of the American child, but so is *fuzz*. The test constructors decided that rarity would be defined with respect to the middle class Caucasian experience. And a child reared in a middle class home is more likely to learn the meaning of shilling than the meaning of fuzz. If contemporary black psychologists had accepted the assignment of constructing the first intelligence test they probably would have made a different choice. A second set of questions poses the child some everyday problem and asks him to state what he would do in that situation. For example, one question asks a 7 year old, "What should you do if you were sent to buy a loaf of bread and the grocer said he didn't have any more?" Clearly, this question assumes a middle class urban or suburban environment with more than one grocery store within safe walking distance of the home for, believe it or not, the only answer for which maximal credit is given is, "I would go to another store." It is not surprising that rural and ghetto children less likely offer that answer. I examined recently a set of protocols gathered on poor black children living in a large Eastern city and found that many of them answered, "Go home," which is a perfectly reasonable — even intelli-

gent — answer for which they were not given credit. One task, which does not favor middle class white children, asks the testee to remember a list of four or five numbers read at the rate of one per second. It is relevant to add that this test usually yields minimal differences between class and ethnic groups in the United States.

These biases in the selection of questions comprise only part of the problem. There is also a serious source of error in the administration of the test. White middle class examiners usually administer the tests to children of different linguistic backgrounds. The test protocols of the black children mentioned above, gathered by well-intentioned, well-trained examiners, indicated that the children often misunderstood the examiner's pronunciation. When asked to define the word "fur" some said, "That's what happens when you light a match." Clearly, the child had interpreted the word to be "fire" and received no credit. Similarly, when requested to define "hat" some children said, "When you get burned," indicating they perceived the word as "hot," and, again, received no credit.

These few examples, which comprise only a small proportion of all the sources of error that could be documented, are persuasive of the view that the IQ test, upon which Arthur Jensen's argument and the statement that "80 percent of IQ is inherited" are based, is a seriously biased instrument that almost guarantees that middle class white children will obtain higher scores than any other group of children in the country, and that the more similar the experiences of two people the more similar their scores should be.

However, most citizens are unaware both of the fundamental faults with the IQ test, as well as the multiple bases for differences in tested intelligence. But like the Greeks, Islamic Moroccans, and medieval Christians, we too need a trait whose content can form a rational basis for the awarding of power and prizes. It is our modern inter-

pretation of saintliness, religiosity, courage, or moral intensity, and, of course, it works. It works so well that when we construct an intervention project, be it a major effort like Headstart or a small study run by a university scientist, we usually evaluate the effects of the intervention by administering a standard intelligence test or one very similar to it, a practice that reflects the unconscious bias that a child's IQ must be the essential dimension we wish to change.

What implications are to be drawn from this acerbic analysis of the IQ? The first may seem paradoxical, considering our apparently hostile critique of the IQ test. Despite the injustice inherent in awarding privilege, status, and self-esteem to those who possess more of some attribute the society happens to value, this dynamic seems to be universal, perhaps because it is necessary. Power — and we mean here benevolent power — probably has to be held unequally. Therefore the community must invent a complex, yet reasonable rationale that will both permit and explain the limited distribution of this prized resource. Knowledge of Western language, history, and customs is one basis on which to base part of the award. But let us be honest about the bases for this arbitrary decision and rid ourselves of the delusion that those who temporarily possess power are biologically more fit for this role because their brains are better organized. Sir Robert Filmer made this argument in 1680 to rationalize the right of kings to govern, and John Locke's political philosophy was shaped on a brilliant critique of Filmer's thesis.

We do not deny the existence of biological differences between and within ethnic and racial groups, many of which are inherited. But we do not regard inherited characteristics like eye color or tendency to perspire as entitling anyone to special favor. Similarly, we should reflect on the wisdom of using fifteen point differences in IQ between blacks and whites on a culturally biased test — regardless of the magnitude of the genetic contribution to the IQ — as a weapon to sort some children into stereotyped categories that impair their ability to become mayors, teachers, or lawyers. It is possible to defend the heretical suggestions that for many contemporary occupations — note that I did not say all — IQ should not be the primary attribute upon which a candidate is screened. Of course, biological factors determined a person's muscle mass, brain size, and adrenalin secretion to stress. But let us not unfairly exploit these hard won facts to rationalize the distribution of secular power, which is a political and sociological dimension. That is using fair science for dark deeds she is ill prepared to carry out.

Those who insist that IQ is inherited base their conclusion on a mathematical model of heritability which assumes that the statistical variation in IQ scores is additive, some of it due to genetic and some to environmental factors. That assumption is questionable and has been criticized by some psychologists and mathematicians. Hence, all one can say at the moment is that the genetic contribution to IQ is still unknown. The second fact that has led some to the conclusion that intelligence is controlled in a major way by genetic factors is that American blacks, who are of a different gene pool than whites, have lower IQ scores. We have argued that the ten to fifteen point average difference between American blacks and whites is likely to be due to the strong cultural biases contained in the IQ test. Hence, given the current knowledge no one can be sure of the determinants of variation in IQ score, a conclusion that is even more applicable to intelligence. □

CONSTANCE KAMII

One Intelligence Indivisible[1]

The title of my address is inspired by the theme of this conference, **One Child Indivisible.** It gives me an opportunity to express my growing concern about recent trends in curriculum and evaluation toward dividing intelligence into parts to be educated and evaluated separately. These trends can be seen in fragmentary or compartmentalized definitions of cognitive objectives such as "information-processing skills," which imply that information processing can be taught separately from other cognitive skills. Such a view now seems to be buttressed by the pseudoscientific respectability of psychometric tests which define so-called competencies in criterion-referenced tests. I am very distressed by the halo put around these competencies by program evaluators who use them to show quantitatively how much children have learned.

I would like to show that one's conception of intelligence and its development profoundly affects the formulation of educational objectives. A mechanistic conception of intelligence leads to the definition of objectives as a collection of fragmented "cognitive skills" that have little to do with children's development of intelligence. A Piagetian conception, on the other hand, leads to attempts to develop children's intelligence as an organized whole.

Most people now recognize the futility of trying to stuff children's heads with encyclopedic facts. In turning from content to process, however, some

[1]This is a revised version of one of the keynote addresses at the annual conference of the National Association for the Education of Young Children, November 25, 1974, in Washington, D.C. The author's work is supported by the Urban Education Research Program, College of Education, University of Illinois at Chicago Circle. The assistance of Rheta DeVries, also of UICC, is gratefully acknowledged. Copyright © 1974, Constance Kamii.

educators came to view the mind more and more like a machine. This view is especially clear in the recent preoccupation with the teaching of "cognitive skills" and "concepts." The term *skill* is justifiable when it refers to motor skills, such as walking, penmanship, swimming, skiing, and typing which become perfected with practice. However, I object strongly to the implication that the nature of intellectual learning is no different from the learning of motor skills. Motor skills can be developed by repetition and practice, but intelligence simply cannot be developed in these ways. Consider the following skills I found in one Head Start list of educational objectives:

Classification skills

Sensory skills

Attentional skills

Sequencing skills

Information-processing skills

Basic learning skills

Basic conceptual skills

Abstracting and mediating skills.

If objectives are conceptualized in terms of such separate skills, it is no wonder that curriculum activities reflect the same fragmentation.

Closely related to the teaching of cognitive skills is the teaching of a collection of so-called concepts such as the following:

Three, five, and ten

Constance Kamii, Ph.D., is currently Associate Professor of Education at the University of Illinois at Chicago Circle, Chicago, Illinois, and Chargée de Cours, Faculty of Psychology and Sciences of Education, University of Geneva, Switzerland. Formerly, she was curriculum Director for the Ypsilanti (Michigan) Early Education Program and Research Association for the Perry Preschool Project, both in the Ypsilanti Public Schools.

Squares and circles

Red and blue

Big and little

Before and after

Over and under

In and out

On and off

Behind and in front of.

It is true that one can often teach children to understand and produce these words correctly. However, one cannot say that children learn number, classes, sizes, or spatial or temporal relationships by learning these words. In fact, if one is successful in teaching children these words, it is usually because they already know the relationship. The teaching of concepts is generally equated with the teaching of words. While I have nothing against the teaching of words, I do object to attempts to teach relationships by teaching a collection of words that are believed to add up to intellectual development.

Let me turn now to a specific example. Recently, I received an announcement of a test called the "Cognitive Skills Assessment Battery" (Boehm and Slater 1974). The stated purpose of this test is curriculum planning for young children. One of the two items shown as examples of a competency worth teaching is the following: The child is shown a picture of some toys and a couple of chairs and is told, "Here are some toys. Listen carefully. Show me the dog in the box and the doll on the chair." I fail completely to see the importance of being able to find in a picture the dog that is *in* the box and the doll that is *on* the chair. It is not by learning to decipher pictures and other symbols on paper that children become more competent intellectually.

Piaget's notion of intelligence is very different from the view of intelligence as a collection of specific skills and concepts. When he taught a course on intelligence, he began by asking what is meant by *intelligence*. Like most teachers, he answered his own question by saying that, for him, "acts of intelligence" consist of "adaptation to new situations." He went on to say that, although intelligence enables us to adapt to new situations, situations are never entirely new, and we understand new ones in terms of the knowledge that we bring to them. There are thus two aspects in any act of intelligence: (1) the comprehension of the situation and (2) the invention of a solution based on how we comprehend the situation. In other words, our comprehension of reality, or the way in which we understand reality, precedes and largely determines how we adapt to it. A most important part of intelligence is, therefore, the ability to read reality, structure it, and get meaning out of what is observable. I think many educators are far too preoccupied with children's ability to manipulate symbols. I would like to see less worry about this and more worry about children's ability to read and structure reality in an intelligent way.

Let me discuss a classical Piagetian task to give an example of children's ability to read things from reality. The task I am referring to is known as *class inclusion*. In this task, the child is given, for example, six blue blocks and two yellow ones as shown in Figure 1. He is first asked, "What do we call these?", so that the examiner can proceed with whatever word came from the *child's* vocabulary. If he says, "Blocks," he is asked to show *all* the blocks. The examiner then asks the child to show "*all*

the blue blocks" and "*all* the yellow blocks." Only after making sure that the child understands the words "all the blocks," "all the blue blocks," and "all the yellow blocks" does the examiner ask the following question: "Are there more blue blocks or more blocks?" Five-year-olds typically answer, "More blue ones," whereupon the examiner asks, "Than what?" The five-year-old's typical answer is "Than yellow ones." In other words, the question the examiner asks is "Are there more blue blocks or more blocks?" but the question the child "hears" is "Are there more blue blocks or more yellow ones?"

Children "hear" a question that is different from the question the adult asks because once they mentally cut the whole into two parts, the only thing they can think about is the two parts. For them, at that moment, the whole does not exist any longer. They can think about the whole, but not when they are thinking about the parts. In order to compare the whole with a part, the child has to mentally do two opposite things at the same time—cut the whole into two parts and put the parts back together into a whole. This is precisely what young children cannot do. This inability to think simul-

---

Fig. 1. The arrangement of blocks in the class-inclusion task.

taneously about the whole and a part explains why, when they are asked, "Are there more blue blocks or more blocks?" the only "blocks" they can see while thinking about the blue ones are the yellow ones.

Note that the child has all the sensory information and all the language needed to answer this question correctly. Yet the reality the child *sees* is not the same reality the adult sees. We never see reality as it is "out there" in the external world. We know it by assimilating it to the intelligence that we bring to each situation. Piaget coined the term *logicization* to refer to this process of putting observable elements of the external world into relationships. The blocks are all "out there" and can be observed both by children and adults. Yet, the logical relationships the child can construct by looking at the blocks are not the same logical relationships the adult constructs.

I would like to discuss another famous task to illustrate what Piaget means by the logicization of reality. The task is known as the *conservation of weight*. When we show the seven-year-old child two clay balls of the same size,

roll one of them into a sausage,

and ask whether the ball has "the same amount" as the sausage, he is likely to say that, of course, the two have the same amount. When we ask him to explain the answer, he may shrug and say, "You didn't add anything or take anything away." If you then ask the child whether the two objects weigh the same, the seven-year-old usually says that the ball is heavier than the sausage! Note again that the child has all the observable information and all the language he needs to conclude that the two objects have the same weight. In fact, the child even told the examiner, just before saying that the ball is heavier, that nothing has been added or taken away.

To explain what Piaget means by the logicization of reality in this context, I would like to discuss a fundamental distinction he made between physical knowledge and logico-mathematical knowledge. *Physical knowledge* is knowledge of objects that are "out there" and observable in the external world. In the conservation of weight task, for example, the color of the clay is "out there" in the object and is observable. The weight of the clay ball, too, is in the object and observable. *Logico-mathematical knowledge*, by contrast, consists of relationships created by the individual. The numerical relationship "two," for example, is neither in this object

nor in this object,

and if the individual could not put these objects into a relationship, the two would remain unrelated. While physical knowledge comes mainly from outside the individual, logico-mathematical knowledge is constructed by the individual from the inside. Other examples of relationships created by the individual are "the same size," "bigger than," "longer than," and "heavier than." The relationship "heavier than" is neither in this object

nor in this object.

This is a creation by the individual who puts observable things into a relationship.

What is the relationship between physical knowledge and logico-mathematical knowledge? Three characteristics of this relationship illustrate the indivisibility of intelligence. The first is the mutual dependence and inseparability of physical and logico-mathematical knowledge. Piaget believes that physical knowledge cannot exist without logico-mathematical knowledge, and that the converse is also true. For example, when we think about the physical property of an object, such as the color of a pen which is red, we can think about this redness only by putting it into a relationship with "things that are not red." Without this classificatory scheme, in other words, it would not be possible even to have the idea that the pen is red. The shape of the pen can likewise be observed only by putting it into a relationship with other shapes that are *not* long. If there were no network of relationships in the mind of the observer, each observation would remain isolated and unrelated to every other observation. There can thus be no physical, i.e., empirical, knowledge without a logico-mathematical framework. There would, likewise, be no logico-mathematical framework if there were

no objects in the world to put into relationships.

Secondly, the relationship between physical and logico-mathematical knowledge is characterized by circular causality, in which the development of one contributes to the development of the other, and this development, in turn, contributes back to the first, and so forth in a continuous way from birth to adulthood. In other words, the better an individual can structure logico-mathematical relationships, the better she or he can read from reality whatever is observable.

Thirdly, knowledge begins in infancy mainly as physical knowledge, and the role of logico-mathematical knowledge becomes increasingly greater as the child becomes capable of concrete and formal operations. Babies and very young children spend most of their waking hours acting on objects to find out their physical properties. They examine everything in sight by turning it over, putting it in their mouths, squeezing it, dropping it, and so on, to find out about its properties. To put this development in anthropomorphic terms, logico-mathematical knowledge has a "tough row to hoe" because it comes into existence later than physical, i.e., empirical, knowledge, and has to subjugate it by logicizing it.

Let us return to the time lag between the conservation of amount of clay and the conservation of weight to illustrate the difficulty the child has in logicizing his physical, empirical knowledge. The size of the clay is visible, and therefore amount is easier to put into a logical relationship than weight. Since weight is invisible, the only way the child can observe it is by holding it and feeling its weight. When the seven-year-old compares the weight of the clay ball with that of the sausage, he usually compares the *pressure* exerted at the one point of contact between the ball and the table with the pressure that is distributed all the way along the bottom of the sausage. He thus confuses the *weight* of the object with the *pressure* he would feel if the table were his hand. This is why he says that the ball is heavier than the sausage, even though he knows that nothing has been added or taken away. Since weight is much harder to logicize than amount, the child can think of the amount of clay in logico-mathematical terms, but he continues to think about the weight of clay in physical terms. In other words, the seven-year-old's logico-mathematical framework is powerful enough to logicize visible amounts, but not powerful enough to logicize the invisible weight. Even adults can be found in situations where their logic is not powerful enough to be rational, especially when emotions and social pressures are involved. Politicians are particularly good at using emotional appeals to influence our evaluation of facts and sway our opinions.

So far, I have been talking about children's ideas about very intellectual things, such as class inclusion and the conservation of weight. What about more mundane things such as children's notions of "sisters," "mothers," and "grandmothers"? In the following excerpt from *The Child's Conception of Time*, Piaget (1946) was interviewing a four-and-a-half-year-old who had a younger sister. He asked:

> Who is the older of you two? *Me.* Why? *Because I'm the bigger one.* Who will be older when she starts going to school? *Don't know.* When you are grown up, will one of you be older

than the other? ... *Don't know.* Is your mother older than you? *Yes.* Is your Granny older than your mother? *No.* Are they the same age? *I think so.* Isn't she older than your mother? *Oh no.* Does your Granny grow older every year? *She stays the same.* And your mother? *She stays the same as well.* And you? *No, I get older.* And your little sister? *Yes!* (Categorically). (p. 221)

Note that there was a consistently good empirical reason for everything this child said. She believed that her grandmother was no older than her mother *because* the two were the same size. She also believed that neither was growing older because they did not become bigger. The child indeed had some notion of time, but it was all related to observable phenomena. Her time was not structured to the point of being a deductive system. Thus, the child could not deduce that the interval between her age and her sister's age would always remain the same. This is an example of how "simple" concepts like "sister," "mother," and "grandmother" are in fact extremely complex because they depend on children's structuring of logical, deductive systems. The intelligence that constructs all these interdependent notions is simply not a collection of separate cognitive fragments.

I have attempted so far to argue that intelligence is a highly interrelated network of concepts and relationships which develops as an indivisible whole. This development takes place not only indivisibly but also inseparably from the child's social and moral development because the child uses the same intelligence in making social and moral judgments. I would like to cite a few examples from *The Moral Judgment of the Child* (Piaget 1932) to support this point. Piaget asked children which act was the naughtier of two acts of breaking things: breaking 15 cups by flinging open a door without knowing that a trayful of cups was behind the door, or breaking only one cup while getting something that one is not supposed to get? Six-year-olds tended to say that it is worse to break 15 cups unintentionally than to break one cup while intentionally committing a "no-no." Older children, on the other hand, tended to say that intention is what counts in questions concerning morality. Young children here again showed the same way of making judgments on the basis of what is observable. The way young children read reality and get meaning out of it is simply not the same as older children's way of reading reality. This ability to read reality is simply not a collection of cognitive skills. Older children assimilate the reality of broken cups into a network of relationships such as the context within which the breakage occurred and whether there were any attenuating circumstances.

What about children's ideas about lies? Piaget made up pairs of stories and asked children which of the two lies was the worse. Here is an example of a story.

> A little boy (or a little girl) goes for a walk in the street and meets a dog who frightens him very much. So then he goes home and tells his mother he has seen a dog that was as big as a cow. (p. 148)

The second story was:

> A child comes home from school and tells his mother that the teacher had given him good marks, but it was not true; the teacher had given him no marks at all, either good or bad. Then his mother was very pleased and rewarded him. (p. 148)

Six-year-olds tended to say that it is worse to say, "I saw a dog as big as a cow." Why? Because dogs are never as big as cows, and mothers do not believe such statements! In other words, for six-year-olds, the more the lie deviates from what is plausible, the less believable it is, and the worse it is, because the greater the likelihood of punishment. Older children, in contrast, invoke the same empirical facts to support the opposite opinion. For them, the more believable the lie is, the worse it is *because* other people believe it. Given exactly the same external reality, young children read different "facts" from reality.

If you are saying to yourself that young children say the cute things they say only because they have not had all the experience of an adult, I would like to mention the attempts to cover up the Watergate affair. This is an example of how acts of intelligence are determined largely by how people understand a situation. Having read reality in a certain way, Mr. Nixon and his associates adapted to *their* reality as they understood *their* reality. These are highly intelligent people who were intelligent enough to get through law school and rise to power and wealth. Yet, their desires, ambitions, and social relationships reduced their ability to read reality to the point of lying in ways that were scarcely less transparent than the lies of four-year-olds.

If intelligence develops as an indivisible whole, and this development is inseparable from social and moral development, the objectives of early childhood education must be formulated in terms of *development as a whole*. This formulation is in contrast with lists of specific objectives, such as the ability to show "the dog *in* the box and the doll *on* the chair." It is also in sharp contrast with the objective of "success in school." "Success in school" and "intellectual and moral development for adaptation to the reality of adult life" are not mutually exclusive, but they overlap only partially as can be seen in the intersection of the two circles in Figure 2.

The part of "success in school" which does not overlap with "development" includes all the things we memorized just to succeed in school. We can all remember memorizing lots of irrelevant words we did not understand or care about, just to pass one test after another. To quote Piaget (1972), "Everybody knows how little remains of the knowledge acquired in school, five, ten, or twenty years after the end of secondary schools" (p. 88). This problem continues to be a very serious one, especially for compensatory education programs such as Head Start and Follow Through, whose perspective is limited to short-term adaptation to traditional schools.

The part of "development" in Figure 2 which does not overlap with "success in school" refers to the social, moral, and intellectual development which takes place outside the school or, sometimes, in spite of schools. It is sad to

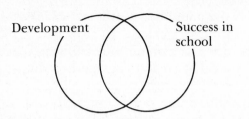

Fig. 2. The relationship between two conceptions of objectives.

note that formal operations and a high level of moral development are not always found among university students. Piaget (1972, p. 51) observes that when we look at normal adults, we are forced to conclude that people who are masters of their reason are as rare as people who are truly moral.

If we take intellectual, social, and moral development as our long-range goal (the circle on the left in Figure 2), how can we define short-range objectives for early childhood education? Many of you have already heard me objecting to my earlier juxtaposed conceptualization that circulated most widely in the *Handbook on Formative and Summative Evaluation* (Kamii 1971). In that book I delineated educational objectives by juxtaposing socioemotional and cognitive objectives as shown in Figure 3. Within the socioemotional realm, I further juxtaposed a variety of

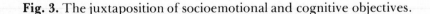

Fig. 3. The juxtaposition of socioemotional and cognitive objectives.

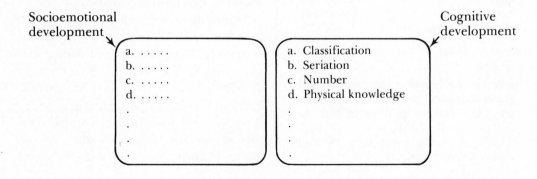

objectives that I now prefer not to recall. Within the cognitive realm, too, I juxtaposed all the areas of knowledge studied by Piaget, e.g., classification, seriation, number, space, time, physical knowledge, etc. In retrospect, this was an empiricist-mechanistic assimilation of Piaget's theory and a distortion of it. I subsequently found out that, in the psychological reality of the child, classification, seriation, number, physical knowledge, etc., are related not in this neat, mutually exclusive way as shown in this itemized list, but, rather, in the messy, inseparable way shown in Figure 4.

My colleagues and I nowadays define educational objectives by putting these cognitive objectives within the context of socioemotional objectives as shown in Figure 5. Since the child's social and moral development is beyond the scope of this paper, I would like to limit the rest of the discussion to the reason for putting cognitive objectives in the following socioemotional context:

Curiosity and initiative in pursuing curiosities

Alertness in putting things into relationships

Confidence to figure things out

Confidence to speak one's mind with conviction

Autonomy and ability to resist what does not make sense

Openness to consider different points of view.

This list may seem to some like a set of arbitrary values pulled out of what Kohlberg and Mayer (1972) call "a bag of virtues." While I agree that curiosity, alertness, confidence, and open-mindedness are highly valued in our culture, it is not for this reason that I consider them important educational objectives. My reason for valuing curiosity, alertness, etc., is that, without these, according to Piaget, human intelligence cannot develop. If intelligence develops as a whole by the child's own construction, then what makes this construction possible is the child's curiosity, interest, alertness, desire to communicate and exchange points of view, and a desire to make sense out of it all. Anyone who watches babies in light of *The Origins of Intelligence* (Piaget 1936) and *The Construction of Reality in the Child* (Piaget 1937) becomes convinced that curiosity, initiative, and alertness are what enable them to build all of their sensorimotor intelligence, which is truly a vast amount of knowledge. If curiosity, initiative, and alertness are present in young children, the rest of what are too often found in lists of cognitive objectives, such as "red"

Fig. 4. The areas of cognition studied by Piaget.

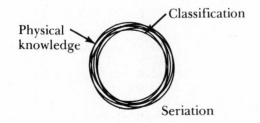

Fig. 5. The definition of cognitive objectives in the context of socioemotional ones.

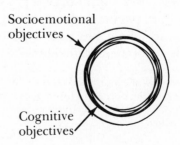

and "blue," are bound to be learned incidentally.

Logico-mathematical knowledge is especially dependent on the child's initiative, since it develops by the child's own creation and coordination of relationships. Logico-mathematical objectives are, therefore, better formulated in terms of encouraging the child's alertness than in terms of developing his "skills" such as "classification skills." The following example illustrates this point. A group of four-year-olds went on a walk one day when there were many puddles on the ground. The teacher cautioned the children by saying, "Anyone who steps in a puddle is a wet noodle." The next day was very cold, and the puddles were half frozen. When the group went outside again, one of the children said, "Anyone who steps in the ice is a frozen noodle!" This remark was typical of this alert child, who came up with similar statements all the time. Alert children thus think of relationships that do not even occur to adults. The child's alertness is, therefore, a richer, more fruitful objective than a list of preconceived "skills." While structuring the observable data in his reality, this child was perfecting his classifcatory scheme of "a puddle is to an icy puddle, what a wet noodle is to a frozen noodle."[2]

In conclusion, I would like to refer back to the examples given earlier of class inclusion, the conservation of weight, children's notions of "sister," "mother," and "grandmother," their moral judgments about breaking things and telling lies, and Mr. Nixon and his associates. Intelligence is not something that we can educate separately by pasting it onto the child. It is rooted in the biological origins of a whole organism and develops as a highly interdependent whole. To cite Piaget once again, our comprehension of reality, or the way in which we understand reality, precedes and largely determines how we react to it. Whatever specific objective we may define in education must, therefore, support and enhance qualities such as autonomy, so that intelligence can develop as a coherent, powerful whole. If we want this intelligence to develop into something powerful enough to overcome the natural human tendencies to see reality in terms of emotional needs and to accept easy ready-made answers, we must educate children to deal logically with reality itself. By compartmentalizing academic skills and separating them from the development of intelligence, schools too often produce passive students who wait to be told what to think next. Evaluators have been busy evaluating all kinds of things, but what they have yet to evaluate is the conceptualization of objectives from the standpoint of how human intelligence develops.

---

[2]Those who are interested in an explanation of the rest of the objectives listed above are referred to C. Kamii and R. DeVries in *The Preschool in Action.*

References

Boehm, A. E., and Slater, B. R. *Cognitive Skills Assessment Battery.* New York: Teachers College Press, 1974.

Kamii, C. "Evaluation of Learning in Preschool Education: Socio-Emotional, Perceptual-Motor, Cognitive Development." In *Handbook on Formative and Summative Evaluation of Student Learning,* edited by B. Bloom, J. Hastings, and G. Madaus. New York: McGraw-Hill, 1971.

Kamii, C., and DeVries, R. "Piaget for Early Education." In *The Preschool in Action,* edited by M. C. Day and R. K. Parker. 2nd ed. Boston: Allyn and Bacon, forthcoming.

Kohlberg, L., and Mayer, R. "Development As the Aim of Education." *Harvard Educational Review* 42 (1972):449-498.

Piaget, J. *The Child's Conception of Time.* New York: Ballantine Books, 1971. (First published as *Le Développement de la Notion de Temps chez l'Enfant.* Paris: Presses Universitaires de France, 1946.)

Piaget, J. *The Construction of Reality in the Child.* New York: Basic Books, 1954. (First published as *La Construction du Reel chez l'Enfant.* Neuchâtel: Delachaux et Niestlé, 1937.)

Piaget, J. *The Moral Judgment of the Child.* New York: The Free Press, 1965. (First published as *Le Judgement Moral chez l'Enfant.* Paris: Alcan, 1932.)

Piaget, J. *The Origins of Intelligence in Children.* New York: International Universities Press, 1952. (First published as *La Naissance de l'Intelligence chez l'Enfant.* Neuchâtel: Delachaux et Niestlé, 1936.)

Piaget, J. *Où Va l'Éducation?* Paris: Denoël, 1972.

ASSESSING NATIONAL LEVELS OF ACHIEVEMENT IN A SYSTEMATIC MANNER

J. STANLEY AHMANN

Less than a decade ago, the National Assessment of Educational Progress was established for the purpose of providing reliable information describing what young Americans (at the ages of 9, 13, 17, and 26-35) know and can do. More precisely, the assessment was designed to (1) obtain census-like data on the knowledge, skills, concepts, understandings, and attitudes possessed by these selected American subpopulations at regular intervals and (2) measure the growth or decline in educational attainments that occur over time in the learning areas.

The four age levels were selected to correspond to the end of primary, intermediate, secondary, and formal post-secondary education. Currently ten learning areas are assessed: Art, Career and Occupational Development, Citizenship, Literature, Mathematics, Music, Reading, Science, Social Studies, and Writing. For a task or question to be included in the assessment, it must be judged as important by scholars and lay people and accepted by educators as something that should be taught in American schools. Table 1 presents the assessment time-table through 1975. It should be noted that by 1974-75 all ten of the learning areas will have been assessed for the first time. Each of the ten areas will be reassessed regularly, that is, about every four to eight years.

Within each of the learning areas, National Assessment determines the percentages of the age levels who can acceptably answer a question or successfully perform a task. Through successive assessments in a learning area, it

Table 1. Assessment Timetable

Assessment Year	Learning Areas Assessed
1969-70	Science, Writing, Citizenship
1970-71	Reading, Literature
1971-72	Music, Social Studies
1972-73	Mathematics, Science°
1973-74	Career and Occupational Development, Writing°
1974-75	Art, Basic Mathematics

° Second Assessment

will be possible to determine changes in these percentages that will reflect the magnitude of change in the educational attainment of the various age groups for which data have been collected. This will provide valuable data to all levels of the educational decision-making community and the general public.

Learning Area Development

For each of the areas, the first stage of assessment is the development of objectives and subobjectives. The objectives for an area, which are developed and reviewed by panels of scholars, educators, and concerned lay persons, must be considered (1) meaningful to subject matter specialists, (2) reflective of teaching goals acceptable to educators, and (3) valuable and important for a young person in contemporary society.

Once a set of objectives has been established to meet these criteria, exercises are constructed to represent each of the objectives. These exercises serve as instruments through which National Assessment gathers data to determine the extent to which the objectives are being met by the subpopulation(s) for which the various objectives were designed. The exercises employed by National Assessment are unlike the more common educational instruments in that the exercises are not designed to discriminate between individuals or groups of individuals. Considerable effort is made to obtain exercises whose construction, wording, mode of administration, and scoring rationale do not make any particular subset of individuals more or less likely to respond correctly to the content of the exercise. One example is the presentation of exercises on paced tapes to standardize administration and to minimize the influence of reading difficulties. As with the objectives, each exercise is developed and reviewed by specialists in exercise construction within the area to be assessed and subjected to the scrutiny of other scholars, educators, and concerned lay people.

From the pool of exercises developed to represent the subject area, a set of exercises is selected for use in the actual assessment.

The set that is selected will require between 150 and 250 minutes of administration time at each age level. No student enrolled in school is allowed to take more than 45 minutes of assessment materials. Because of this restriction, the selected exercises are typically divided into 12 different booklets or packages. Nine of these packages are usually devoted to exercises that can be administered to groups of 12 students at a time; the remaining three packages are administered to one student at a time. The individually administered packages include performance exercises, such as playing a musical instrument or conducting a science experiment, and exercises that require a "mini-interview" of the respondent. The actual number of different packages will vary according to the areas and age level being assessed. Each package contains exercises that are unique to an age and exercises that are administered at two or more adjacent age levels. It should be noted that the out-of-school testing is the same as the in-school testing except that all exercises are individually administered, that is, one administrator for each respondent, and a respondent can answer four packages of exercises if he or she wishes.

Sampling and Administration

It is the policy of National Assessment to provide data at a national level. It is also the policy of National Assessment to avoid making comparisons of the data between states, school districts, schools, teachers, and individuals. A national probability sample of approximately 2,500 to 2,600 individuals per group-administered package and 2,100 to 2,200 individuals per individually-administered package for each age level are assessed annually. The samples are selected by use of a multistage design and are stratified by region, size of community, and socioeconomic status. A school frame is used for the 9s, 13s, and 87 percent of the 17s. A household frame is used for young adults, while 17s not enrolled in school are assessed through both the household frame and a specially designed frame of dropouts and early graduates. The total sample size for each of the three younger age groups is approximately 29,000. Because young adults are allowed to take up to four assessment packages per person, the sample size required for adults is approximately 4,800. During the last two assessments, approximately 95 percent of the selected schools and 82 percent of the selected eligible young adults have agreed to participate in the assessment.

All of the assessment packages are administered by specially trained exercise administrators. Group administered packages are presented on tape to standardize procedures and to facilitate the understanding of respondents with reading difficulties. Individually administered packages are presented in an interview mode following specific instructions for administration. The 13s are assessed during October and November, the 9s during January and February, and the 17s in-school during March and April. The supplementary frame for 17s out-of-school is completed during May through July. The young adult assessment is conducted from October through May.

Analysis of Data

Completed packages are carefully edited for errors resulting from either the administration or scoring of the packages. With exercises using a multiple-choice format, the respondent records his own answer by darkening an oval. Other exercises require scoring by specially trained personnel with subject-matter background in the area being assessed. After editing and machine scoring, the data are weighted in accordance with the respondents' probability of selection. The weighted data serve as the basis for all analyses. The proportion of acceptable and unacceptable responses is then estimated for each age level on an exercise-by-exercise basis.

Approximately 50 percent of the assessed exercises are retained for future assessments and are thus not released. These exercises were reserved to measure change over time. They are selected in such a way as to provide reasonable coverage across all objectives, difficulty levels, and age levels.

The concept of a "total score" is wholly inappropriate to National Assessment data as no respondent receives all of the packages. Each in-school respondent is randomly assigned one package (less than 10 percent of the assessed exercises). Thus, each package is administered to separate samples of the age population and each provides an estimate of the number of individuals at each age level who can respond correctly to an exercise. Results are reported by individual exercises, as well as by some summary value (e.g., the median) for small subsets of exercises having the same objective, similar content, or a meaningful element of communality.

The estimated percentages of acceptable and unacceptable responses are reported by age groups, and, within age groups, by geographic region, sex, size and type of community, level of parental education, and race. Table 2 presents a more detailed breakdown of these classifications.

Representative Findings

The number of exercises (or test items) used in each assessment varies according to the learning area. It ranges upward to over 500. The primary manner of reporting National Assessment results is to report the percentage of success and failure for various subgroups of students for each exercise. Consequently, literally thousands of pieces of data are available about the performance level of American youth in terms of the seven learning areas now being reported. The following are illustrative of some of these findings.

Table 2.
Major Reporting Categories Presently Used by National Assessment

Classification	Number of Subgroups	Subgroups
Age Level	4	9, 13, 17, 26-35
Sex	2	Male, Female
Geographic Region	4	Northeast Southeast Central West
Level of Parental Education	4	No high school Some high school Graduated high school Post high school
Size and Type of Community	7	Low metropolitan High metropolitan Extreme rural Main big city Urban fringe Medium cities Small places
Race	2	Black, White

Social Studies (1971-72)
1. Young Americans lacked knowledge of the fundamentals of politics and civil rights. For example, less than half of the nation's 17-year-olds and young adults could accurately read all parts of a ballot. Only 17 percent of the 13-year-olds, 49 percent of the 17-year-olds, and 60 percent of the young adults knew that the presidential candidate for each political party is formally nominated at a national convention. Many young people expressed reservations about granting constitutional rights when faced with specific circumstances.

2. Relatively few young Americans could read and interpret graphs, maps, or tables.
3. Most respondents had little knowledge of the contributions of minority groups to American culture and history.

Citizenship (1969-70)
1. An overwhelming majority of 17-year-olds (77 percent) and young adults (86 percent) knew one or more ways citizens can influence the actions of their government, but fewer (54 percent and 61 percent, respectively) felt that they personally could influence decisions of their state government.
2. A rough indicator of how well informed young people are about what is happening currently in government can be found in the fact that only 15 percent of the 17-year-olds could name their United States senators; 31 percent knew the name of the congressman from their district; and 7 percent could name the Secretary of State of the United States. Of the young adults, 31 percent could name both senators from their state; 39 percent knew who their congressmen were; and 16 percent could name the Secretary of State.
3. The vast majority of 17-year-olds (88 percent) and young adults (95 percent) could name the two major political parties, but substantially fewer (41 percent and 54 percent) could name a third political party.

Science (1969-70)
1. Male respondents at all ages achieved better in Science than female respondents. At age 9, male overall performance was only 1.8 percent above females; but at age 13, males were 2.9 percent above females; at age 17, 5.0 percent above females; and between the ages of 26 and 35, 9.9 percent above females.
2. At all four age levels, males demonstrated a more thorough knowledge of physical science, and females seemed to have a better knowledge of biological science. This trend was particularly apparent at the young adult level, where women appeared to know a good deal more about human reproduction.
3. Black Americans demonstrated the lowest science achievement of all groups reported. They were, overall, 15 percentage points below white Americans.

Reading (1970-71)

1. In general young Americans achieved better in Reading than the specialists who built the exercises had anticipated. Certainly they were able to read well enough to accomplish simple, practical kinds of tasks.
2. School-age males read less well than school-age females, but adult men and women had about the same levels of reading achievement.
3. Young people from families where neither parent had gone to high school and those from inner city areas read less well than most other groups assessed.
4. The overall reading ability of blacks was lower than that of whites in the survey.

Writing (1969-70)

1. Males were more adventurous and free in writing essays, although females demonstrated a better command of writing mechanics.
2. The writing skills that proved most difficult for young Americans were word choices, punctuation, and spelling.
3. Young adults had greater difficulty with punctuation than 9-, 13-, or 17-year-olds. Only 14 percent of the adults could write letters with no punctuation errors.
4. Commas were the most difficult form of punctuation to master for all age levels.
5. Application blanks are a common writing task for Americans, but results showed 50 percent of the nation's young adults actually filled in all the information required.

Literature (1970-71)

1. Seventeen-year-olds overwhelmingly believed that the study of literature was a positive experience, 90 percent believed literature should be part of every high school curriculum, about 10 percent thought that the study of literature increases one's tolerance for new and different ideas.
2. Responses to literary works varied, depending upon the age and sex of the individual as well as upon the kind of work he or she was reading. Girls wrote better essays about literature than did boys.
3. Inner city young people seemed to respond more completely to works that relate to their experiences or surroundings.

Music (1971-72)

1. Individuals of all ages are interested in and like music. Over 80 percent of all age groups either play or would like to learn to play a musical instrument. Far fewer individuals can actually play an instrument, however.
2. Less than 15 percent of any age group can sight read even the simplest line of music.
3. Judged on their ability to maintain pitch and rhythm and hit the right notes, fewer than half of the nation's youth can give an acceptable vocal performance of their own choosing.
4. Black Americans demonstrated a greater ability to repeat rhythmic patterns than did whites. Black 9-, 13-, and 17-year-olds scored 7 to 8 percentage points above whites when repeating and improvising rhythmic patterns.

General Trends

When the learning areas are considered as a composite, one finds a large degree of consistency of National Assessment findings from one learning area to another. This is to say that the differences in relative achievement among subgroups of the sample are largely consistent in direction even though they were not totally consistent in size.

The foregoing can be illustrated by examining the achievement levels of some of these subgroups. For instance, the level of performance of the northeastern portion of the country was typically higher than that of the other three regions in the seven learning areas assessed. The lowest level of performance was consistently found in the southeastern region. It should be noted, however, that these differences were comparatively modest, for example, the southeast deficit normally was no more than 5 percent below the national average.

Consider for a moment the performance of young Americans from the inner city, the rural areas, and the affluent suburb. The first group typically performed least well, and by a wide margin. The rural students did somewhat better but still well below the national average. Finally, the affluent suburb students exceeded the national average consistently by an important margin.

It is clear from the National Assessment data that the educational level of the parent of the respondent was also a vital factor in his/her level of achievement. Young Americans with parents who had only a grade school education performed least well of all. As the level of the parents' education increased to some high school, then to completion of high school, and ultimately to post-high school education, the performance level of the respondent increased markedly in the seven areas of achievement assessed.

The performance of black respondents was consistently below the national average, typically by a sizable margin. Male-female differences in achievement varied. For instance, the Science data revealed that male respondents generally perform better than female respondents. The reverse was true in the case of Writing, Reading, and Literature, and almost no difference was found in the case of Citizenship. These and other findings raise challenging questions for educators, textbook writers, curriculum specialists, and school board members.

———————————————

STANLEY AHMANN (B.A., *Trinity College; B.S., M.S., Ph.D., Iowa State University) is on leave from his position as professor of psychology and head of the Department of Psychology at Colorado State University to serve as staff director, National Assessment of Educational Progress for the Education Commission of the States; he is also adjunct professor of psychology and education at the University of Denver. Earlier, Dr. Ahmann served on the faculties of Iowa State University and Cornell University.*

In addition to Dr. Ahmann's teaching of general psychology, psychological testing, statistical methodology, educational psychology, methods of research in the behavioral sciences, and evaluative research, he has done research in the areas of construction and validation of psychological tests and evaluation of the effectiveness of educational programs and products.

—18-year-old college freshman

—17-year-old high-school student

WHY JOHNNY CAN'T

If your children are attending college, the chances are that when they graduate they will be unable to write ordinary, expository English with any real degree of structure and lucidity. If they are in high school and planning to attend college, the chances are less than even that they will be able to write English at the minimal college level when they get there. If they are not planning to attend college, their skills in writing English may not even qualify them for secretarial or clerical work. And if they are attending elementary school, they are almost certainly not being given the kind of required reading material, much less writing instruction, that might make it possible for them eventually to write comprehensible English. Willy-nilly, the U.S. educational system is spawning a generation of semiliterates.

Nationwide, the statistics on literacy grow more appalling each year. In March, the Department of Health, Education and Welfare revealed the results of a special study that showed a steady erosion of reading skills among American students since 1965. Last month, the College Entrance Examination Board announced the formation of a panel of top educators who will study the twelve-year-long decline in Scholastic Aptitude Test scores; the fall-off has been especially sharp in verbal skills. Students' SAT scores this year showed the biggest drop in two decades. According to the National Assessment of Educational Progress, the majority of Americans of all ages tend to use only the simplest sentence structure and the most elementary vocabulary when they write. Among teen-agers, writing performance appears to be deteriorating at the most alarming rate of all. The NAEP's latest studies show that the essays of 13- and 17-year-olds are far more awkward, incoherent and disorganized than the efforts of those tested in 1969.

To Marshall McLuhan, the signs were clear a decade ago: "Literary culture is through," he said, summing up the prospective long-term impact of television. The United States, says poet Karl Shapiro, "is in the midst of a literary breakdown." "We have ceased to think with words," observes historian Jacques Barzun. "We have stopped teaching our children that the truth cannot be told apart from the right words." Ronald Berman, chairman of the National Endowment for the Humanities, thinks that the decline of written English is only one among many symptoms of a massive "regression toward the intellectually invertebrate" among American academics. And philologist Mario Pei warns that

already much of academia is controlled by "a school preaching that one form of language is as good as another; that at the age of 5 anyone who is not deaf or idiotic has gained a full mastery of his language; that we must not try to correct or improve language, but must leave it alone; that the only language activity worthy of the name is speech on the colloquial, slangy, even illiterate plane; that writing is a secondary, unimportant activity."

The cries of dismay sound even louder in the halls of commerce, industry and the professions, where writing is the basis for almost all formal business communication. Computer print-outs and the conference call may have altered forever the pace and nature of information exchanged, but transactions for the record—from interoffice memorandums to multinational corporate contracts—all depend on the precision and clarity of the written word.

Increasingly, however, officials at graduate schools of law, business and journalism report gloomily that the products of even the best colleges have failed to master the skills of effective written communication so crucial to their fields. At Harvard, one economics instructor has been so disturbed at

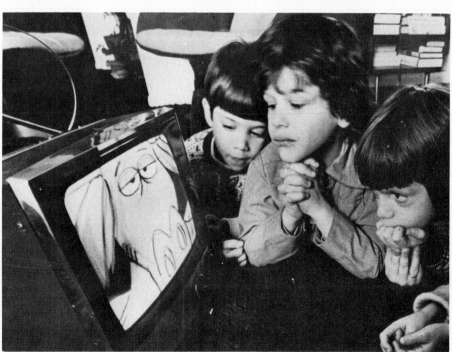

Passive voice: TV entertains, but demands no really active learning

122

My famous person whom I admire the most is John Wayne. He is a famous person in many people's eyes of America.

—-17-year-old high-school student

The old brige was a swing brige and it was a real old brige. The bords was roten in the brige and you could see right through the brige and some places the bord was missing.

Fenga & Freyer

—13-year-old junior-high student

WRITE

the inability of his students to write clearly that he now offers his own services to try to teach freshmen how to write. Businessmen seeking secretaries who can spell and punctuate or junior executives who can produce intelligible written reports complain that college graduates no longer fill the bill. "Errors we once found commonly in applications from high-school graduates are now cropping up in forms from people with four-year college degrees," says a personnel official for the Bank of America. Even the Civil Service Commission, the Federal government's largest employer, has recently doubled its in-house writing programs in order to develop adequate civil servants.

The colleges and universities complain that many of the most intelligent freshmen, in some ways more articulate and sophisticated than ever before, are seriously deficient when it comes to organizing their thoughts on paper. By the time they reach college, the professors complain, it is almost too late to help them. The breakdown in writing has been in the making for years, they say, and the causes for it range from inadequate grounding in the basics of syntax, structure and style to the popularity of secondary-school curriculums that no longer require the wide range of reading a student must have if he is to learn to write clearly.

There is no question in the minds of educators that a student who cannot read with true comprehension will never learn to write well. "Writing is, after all, book-talk," says Dr. Ramon Veal, associate professor of language education at the University of Georgia's College of Education. "You learn book-talk only by reading." But as the standard tests suggest, students' reading ability is declining—and the effects of this erosion are readily apparent. For example, when the Association of American Publishers prepared a pamphlet to help college freshmen get the most from their textbooks, they found that its "readability level"—calculated for twelfth-grade skills—was far too high for students entering college. The pamphlet had to be rewritten at the ninth-grade level.

The reading and writing skills of most Americans have never been remarkable, and the inability of the average high-school graduate to write three or four clear expository paragraphs has been the object of scornful criticism at least since the time of Mark Twain, when only 7 per cent of the population managed to earn high-school diplomas. What makes the new illiteracy so dismaying is precisely the fact that writing ability among even the best-educated young people seems to have fallen so far so fast.

The evidence is massive. At the University of California at Berkeley, where students come from the top 12.5 per cent of high-school graduates, nearly half of last year's freshmen demonstrated writing skills so poor that they were forced to enroll in remedial courses nicknamed "bonehead English." Officials at Michigan State University are so concerned about writing incompetence that they may soon require all undergraduates to pass a writing exam demonstrating "minimal literary skills" before they receive diplomas. The Georgia Board of Regents, distressed at the lack of writing skill demonstrated by graduates of the state's 32 colleges, already requires such a test—and demands remedial writing programs of those who cannot pass. At Temple University in Philadelphia, the proportion of freshmen failing an English placement exam has increased by more than 50 per cent since 1968. Harvard's freshman course in expository writing—the only class every Harvard student is required to take—has been expanded to such an extent in the past two years that some faculty members now call it a "pseudo-department."

Since 1969, the National Assessment of Educational Progress has been testing and evaluating the writing skills of Americans between the ages of 9 and 35. In its first appraisal of writing skills six years ago, it found that 9-year-olds showed almost no mastery of basic writing mechanics, that 17-year-olds demonstrated serious deficiencies in spelling, vocabulary and sentence structure and that participants over 18 were reluctant to write at all. Last month's announcement that writing skills have slipped steadily ever since indicated that older students in particular now show "increases in awkwardness, run-on sentences and incoherent paragraphs."

The judges, a panel of English teachers and scholars from across the country, suggest that most of those tested in the assessment have been strongly influenced by the simplistic spoken style of television. E.B. White, essayist emeritus of

Photos by Jeff Lowenthal

Active voice: To write, first learn to read

Jeff Lowenthal

Shakespeare	Standard English	Dialect
Alas! Poor Yorick. I knew him, Horatio; a fellow of infinite jest, of most excellent fancy; he hath borne me on his back a thousand times; and now, how abhorred in my imagination it is!	Poor Yorick! I really knew him, Horatio—a man of great good humor, of fantastic imagination; he helped me through many hard times, and I feel just terrible about this.	My man Yorick. We was real tight, Horatio. I mean, the dude be crazy but he saved my ass many times. What you think, man? It really took me on out.

Flasch and students: Teaching standard English as a second language

The New Yorker, puts it this way: "Short of throwing away all the television sets, I really don't know what we can do about writing." No one has yet produced a thorough study of the effect of TV on a generation of students raised in its glare, but on at least two points most language experts agree: time spent watching television is time that might otherwise be devoted to reading; and the passiveness of the viewing—"letting the television just sink into one's environment," in the words of Barzun—seems to have a markedly bad effect on a child's active pursuit of written skills. "The TV keeps children entertained," complains Albert Tillman, director of a writing clinic at the University of Illinois. "It does not demand that they take active part in their learning."

Even the effects of television might be counteracted if students were required to learn the language in the classroom. There, however, the past decade has produced a number of changes that in some school systems have all but terminated the teaching of the written language. Over-crowded classrooms and increased workloads have led many teachers to give up assigning essays and to rely, instead, on short-answer exercises that are easier to mark. As a result, many students now graduate from high school without ever having had any real practice in writing.

The 1960s also brought a subtle shift of educational philosophy away from the teaching of expository writing. Many teachers began to emphasize "creativity" in the English classrooms and expanded their curriculums to allow students to work with contemporary media of communication such as film, videotape and photography. In the process, charges Dorothy Matthews, director of undergraduate English at Illinois, they often short-changed instruction in the written language. "Things have never been good, but the situation is getting a lot worse," she complains. "What really disturbs us is the students' inability to organize their thoughts clearly." An essay by one of Matthews's Illinois freshmen stands as guileless testimony to the problem: "It's obvious in our modern world of today theirs a lot of impreciseness in expressing thoughts we have."

Even where writing still is taught, the creative school discourages insistence on grammar, structure and style. Many teachers seem to believe that rules stifle spontaneity. Dr. Eliott Anderson, professor of English at Northwestern University,

reports that many highschool teachers have simply stopped correcting poor grammar and sloppy construction, and he is inclined to think that these creative teachers have subverted their own goals. "You don't get very interesting creative results," he notes, "from students who can't use the language as a tool in the first place."

In the opinion of many language experts, another major villain is the school of "structural linguistics." Writing is far less important than speech, the structural linguists proclaim, because only about 4 per cent of the world's languages have a written form; they believe that there are no real standards for any language, apart from the way it is commonly spoken. Philologist Pei traces the predominance of this school to the 1961 publication of Webster's Third International Dictionary, the first English dictionary that did not give preference to the way the language is used by its best-educated writers. Since then, he suggests, teachers in the classrooms have come increasingly under the sway of the structural-linguistic dogma: that the spoken idiom is superior to the written, and that there is no real need for students to study the rules of their language at all. "If you will scoff at language study," asks Pei, "how, save in terms of language, will you scoff?"

The pervasive influence of the structural linguists, coupled with the political activism of the past decade, has led many teachers to take the view that standard English is just a "prestige" dialect among many others, and that insistence on its predominance constitutes an act of repression by the white middle class. Last year, after a bitter dispute within its own ranks, the Conference on College Composition of the National Council of Teachers of English adopted an extraordinary policy statement embodying that philosophy. Entitled "Students' Rights to Their Own Language," the document is more a political tract than a set of educational precepts. "Linguistic snobbery was tacitly encouraged by a slavish reliance on rules," it argues, "and these attitudes had consequences far beyond the realm of language. People from different language and ethnic backgrounds were denied social privileges, legal rights and economic opportunity, and their inability to manipulate the dialect used by the privileged group was used as an excuse for this denial."

The supporters of this argument reject the notion that public education is designed to help those who do not use standard English to survive in a society that does. "We tend to exaggerate the need for standard English," insists Elisabeth McPherson, an English teachers at a St. Louis community college who helped draft the declaration. "You don't need much standard English skill for most jobs in this country." True enough. But won't students, denied the opportunity to master standard English because their teachers refuse to teach it, also lose the chance at higher-ranking jobs where standard English does prevail? McPherson, who calls herself "idealistic," replies that "the important thing is that people find themselves through their own language."

But, "prestige dialect" or not, standard English is in fact the language of American law, politics, commerce and the vast bulk of American literature—and the traditionalists argue that to deny children access to it is in itself a pernicious form of oppression. They also emphasize that the new attempt to stress the language as it is spoken rather than as it is written has significance far beyond the basics of jobs. or social mobility. "Learning to write is the hardest, most important thing any child does," says Dr. Carlos Baker, chairman of the English department at Princeton University and author of a best-selling biography of Ernest Hemingway. "Learning to write is learning to think."

Baker and like-minded colleagues stress that setting down thoughts in writing forces students to examine the actual meaning of their words and the logic—or the lack of it—that leads from one statement to another. "You just don't know anything unless you can write it," says semanticist S.I. Hayakawa. "Sure, you can argue things in your head and bring them out at cocktail parties, but in order to argue anything thoroughly, you must be able to write it down on paper." The late James Knapton, a former supervisor of remedial English at Berkeley, quit the university in disgust eight years ago when officials dropped the school's essay requirement for admission. "I really worry about the great unwashed mass of students sloshing around out there," said Knapton, who before his death last summer was teaching English at a San Francisco high school. "Diagraming sentences is out, no one teaches Shakespeare any more, and there are all those kids talking and rapping with each other, not knowing how to examine what they think in one discursive sentence."

How to stop the rot is a matter of increasingly vigorous debate. Knapton, for one, thought the first step must be to teach the English teachers themselves how to write. "If *they* don't know," he asked, "how on earth are they supposed to teach the children?" Knapton's point is well taken. According to the National Council of Teachers of English, it is now possible for an aspirant who wants to teach high-school English to go all the way through high school, college and advanced-education degrees without taking a single course in English composition.

Some researchers estimate that more than 50 per cent of the nation's secondary-school English teachers did not specialize in English at all during their college years. School officials in Maryland were horrified by the results of a recent study which showed that half of the teachers who apply for English-teaching jobs in Montgomery County fail a basic test of grammar, punctuation and spelling. Just last week, the Board of Education of Stamford, Conn., passed a resolution requiring all teachers now employed in the district to pass a test in written and spoken English—or to take remedial courses. The board member who pushed the ruling through explained that he was alarmed at the number of incomprehensible communications he had recently received from those responsible for teaching English to Stamford children.

Many of the critics also point out that the worst debasement of the language to date is probably "educationese" itself, the jargon in which prospective teachers are taught to teach. English professor Peter Neumeyer of the State University of New York at Stony Brook cites several "deadly examples" of the prose produced by educators. Their subject? Teaching children to write. A few samples:

■ *"The behaviors can be taught or encouraged to happen spontaneously in a content context."*
■ *"Her result was a confusion matrix showing how often these children confused each letter with every other letter."*
■ *"The major dimensions of a teaching prescription are illustrated below in relation to the prescribed terminal behaviors described above."*

Last year, educators in San Francisco decided to do something about the teaching gap. The Bay Area Writing Project (BAWP), founded with money from Berkeley's School of Education and College of Letters and Sciences, invited teachers from nine California counties to spend a five-week summer session with a coalition of Berkeley professors. Six days a week, eight hours a day, the teachers studied current research on writing, examined practical approaches to teaching it, developed curriculum materials and wrote extensively on their own. Each then returned to his school district to offer similar training to his colleagues. The workshop was such a success that it was repeated this summer, and as a result, 31 Bay Area school districts have funded their own writing workshops and a consortium of California colleges and universities is considering plans for more such programs.

In other areas, a number of schools have come up with their own methods of improving writing skills. At Phillips Academy in Andover, Mass., the traditional four years of required English courses have been thrown out altogether and replaced with a school-wide requirement for competence in reading and writing. Every student, regardless of his grade level, must take the course—called, simply enough, "Competence"—until he passes it. The focus is on sentence and paragraph construction and the elements of style (box). The premise, says headmaster Theodore Sizer, is elementary: "Until a youngster can demonstrate that he is competent in reading and writing, you just cannot pass him along to more advanced studies."

In some inner-city schools, many teachers seem to be getting better results in reading and writing by teaching standard English as a second language. "When I first started teaching," says Betty Flasch, an English teacher at Dusable High School in Chicago's black ghetto, "I was always saying, 'No, Joan, you don't mean you ain't got no more, you mean you don't have any more'." That approach, she reports, built up "incredible hostility" among her students, who resisted and denounced her efforts to make them use "honky talk," a dialect literally foreign to their families and friends. Today, Flasch tells her students that she will teach them a new language—standard English—and that when they have mastered it, they will be bilingual. To teach them how their everyday speech is related to ordinary English, for example, she has her pupils translate Shakespeare's Elizabethan dialect both into modern prose and into their own "street" language (page 60). Her results, she reports, have been remarkable. And interestingly enough, she finds that the youngsters respond particularly well to traditional drills for teaching standard English. "They get a big kick out of diagraming sentences," says Flasch, "whereas they seem to be turned off by a lot of the audiovisual techniques."

But audiovisual techniques, as well as television itself, are here to stay, and now a number of concerned teachers and researchers are beginning to suggest that they be used to promote—not replace—the study of the written language. "Kids spend three to four hours watching TV every day," says Peter Almond, who has been studying children and television for the Carnegie Council on Children. "Why not learn to use it more wisely?" Almond reports that many of the best teachers already assign reading and writing exercises based on television shows their students watch, and in that way try to channel the "quick impression" talents developed by television into the more reflective skills demanded by the written language.

Educators agree that it is absolutely essential to make students write. "That's the only way they learn," says Eunice Sims, coordinator of English for the Atlanta school system. "Let them write about whatever interests them and teach from that. You can always move a student from essays on street fighting to essays on Shelley." Sims thinks that even in overcrowded classrooms where teachers cannot possibly analyze every single paper, the students still should write as often as possible. "If a teacher reads every fifth paper a child writes, he or she knows pretty well how the student's doing."

Most of the experts, in fact, applaud the modern notion that grammar and syntax are most successfully taught through a child's own writing, not by handing him a set of abstract rules and expecting him to conform once he has learned them by rote. "The main principle is to get a student deeply involved in the materials of his past and memory and have him write about them," says James Dickey, resident poet at the University of South Carolina. "Then the teacher must become a kind of coach. In football, if someone is slow of foot the coach makes him do wind sprints. In writing, if a student is weak on how the language is put together I have him get an elementary grammar book and *exercise.*"

Despite the laudable coaching efforts of some individual teachers, however, very little improvement in the writing skills of American students is likely unless the educational establishment recaptures the earlier conviction that the written language is important. One thing that is clearly needed is a renewed emphasis on reading as both a discipline and a diversion. Those who would teach English must also once again insist that not all writing is equally admirable. "At some point you have to stop a kid, tell him that that string of epithets masquerading as a poem was garbage twenty years ago and it's garbage now," says Princeton's Baker. "You have to direct good writing, sluice it, build banks around it."

The spoken word, while adding indisputable richness and variety to the language as a whole, is by its very nature ephem-

eral. The written language remains the only effective vehicle for transmitting and debating a culture's ideas, values and goals. "Every lover of the language knows that its glory resides in the recurring infusions of new elements . . . and that change is constant, continual, and will never cease," wrote Lincoln Barnett in his classic work "The Treasure of Our Tongue." "But the written word is the brake on the spoken word. The written word is the link between the past and the future."

The point is that there have to be some fixed rules, however tedious, if the codes of human communication are to remain decipherable. If the written language is placed at the mercy of every new colloquialism and if every fresh dialect demands and gets equal sway, then we will soon find ourselves back in Babel. In America today, as in the never-never world Alice discovered on her trip through the looking-glass, there are too many people intent on being masters of their language and too few willing to be its servants.

"There's glory for you!"

"I don't know what you mean by 'glory'," Alice said.

Humpty Dumpty smiled contemptuously. "Of course you don't—till I tell you. I meant 'there's a nice knock-down argument for you'!"

"But 'glory' doesn't mean 'a nice knock-down argument'," Alice objected.

"When I use a word," Humpty Dumpty said in rather a scornful tone, "it means just what I choose it to mean, neither more nor less."

"The question is," said Alice, "whether you can make words mean so many different things."

"The question is," said Humpty Dumpty, "which is to be Master—that's all."

—MERRILL SHEILS with bureau reports

WRITER'S GUIDE: WHAT NOT TO DO

At Phillips Academy in Andover, Mass., teachers have devised their own "English Competence Handbook" *(Independent School Press)* which, among other things, offers the following examples of some of the most common current errors in usage:

SENTENCE FRAGMENT: A phrase or dependent clause punctuated as a full sentence. (Sometimes writers use fragments intentionally for emphasis.)

The reason being that he did, however, neglect to look behind the door, for there he would have found the awful culprit, with weapon in hand, ready to smite his youthful victim.

MISPLACED MODIFIER: Placing a modifying word, phrase, or clause somewhere in the sentence other than next to the element it is meant to modify.

Bill uses the tennis balls for practice with no fuzz on them.

FAULTY AGREEMENT OF SUBJECT AND VERB: Subjects and verbs which do not agree in number.

The performance of the madrigals precede the intermission.

FAULTY AGREEMENT OF NOUN AND PRONOUN: Pronouns which do not agree with antecedents in number.

Everyone should check their coat before going into the dance.

VAGUE PRONOUN REFERENCE: Use of pronouns (especially *this* and *which*) without specific antecedents or with remote antecedents.

Similar to the telescope, the microscope has an uncertain origin lost in improbable legends of the Middle Ages which, if true, could have been the ancestor of the first magnifying glass.

MIXED METAPHOR: Use of conflicting or inconsistent metaphors.

Young man, if you have a spark, water it and watch it grow.

FAULTY PARALLELISM: Repeated constructions which are not equivalent in syntax (for balance and proper parallelism, follow a word with a word, a phrase with a phrase, a clause with a clause).

Superman fought for truth, justice, and keeping crime out of Metropolis.

SHIFT OF PERSON: Mixing first, second, and third person in the use of pronouns.

A person is bound to feel resentment when your car is vandalized.

V. THE BODY

Beginning with such pseudo-scientific systems as phrenology and physiognomy, the body has long been a subject of study in psychology. In the course of these studies, developmental norms have been established for height, weight, body proportion, etc. In addition, the available research on physique and behavior has revealed no well established relationships strong enough to be of practical value in assessing abilities or personality through physical signs, although some such casual explanations have been found for a few pathological conditions. The body, has not, however, been widely studied by educational psychologists. In many standard texts, in the field, the word *body* does not even appear in the subject index, and although such texts generally include major sections on thinking, concept formation, verbal learning, etc., there is rarely any significant amount of material on motor learning or other topics that might relate body issues to other areas of the school curriculum. In constructing the Taxonomy of Educational Objectives for the classification of educational goals, it was not simply fortuitous that work on the cognitive and affective domains was completed and published well before formal work on the psychomotor behaviors had even begun.

This relative neglect of potentially exciting material may only be a reflection of the almost exclusively cognitive orientation of our schools. This in turn may be grounded in our more or less unconscious acceptance of the Aristotelian dichotomy between body and mind. This is certainly the underlying reason offered by John Money in his editorial entitled "Physical, Mental, and Critical Period." Dr. Money attempts to bridge this constraining dichotomy by developing the concept of *critical period*, in which there is no clear distinction between body and mind. He argues convincingly that the events of life, as assimilated by the mind, are also assimilated by the brain, which is affected by what it assimilates as well as affecting, in turn, the events outside of itself in social life. Approaching the problem from a very different perspective, Rene Dubos' article also suggests the productive interaction between biological-body processes and the external environment. He notes that although all human beings have the same physiological body processes, no two are precisely alike. He maintains that this individuality is the product of the total environment—both physical and mental. Although Dr. Dubos does not himself make any direct application of his ideas to education, his concern for a society which provides each person with a very wide range of opportunities from which to develop his or her own potentitality implies for us an educational context in which the traditional dichotomies are eschewed.

Simply more comprehensive body or physical education programs would not represent a major advance. The mind/body dichotomy would only be further reinforced, and in the discussions of educational psychology, the physical bases of behavior would be even further separated from the psychological processes of development. More to the point is Alice Yardley's approach in "Movement and Learning." In this article, Professor Yardley tries to relate the movement curriculum not only to the development of motor and psychomotor skills but also to areas of more general learning. She suggests that the child's opportunity to experience environments through the senses, i.e., through movement, facilitates the learning of many tasks traditionally seen as wholly cognitive in nature. In a sense, although she does not put it in this way. Ms. Yardley is extending over a longer age-span the kind of learning model that Piaget has found particularly characteristic of very young children in their sensori-motor period. We would agree and extend the concept even further to the affective domain. For example, since self-awareness is first manifested in a bodily sense of self, we might hypothesize that physical processes are an important influence in shaping the self-concept. Several studies have, in fact, found significant relationships between the timing of physical maturation, physical disabilities, body physique, and the self-concept.

Lorena Porter's article, the last one in this section, gets down to rather precise details in terms of the development of a movement curriculum within the school. She provides guidelines for structuring movement experiences, and she explains the types of equipment which can be used to stimulate creativity and exploration of the environment. Finally, she discusses a number of possible teaching techniques from both theoretical and practical perspectives.

Physical, Mental and Critical Period

John Money

Because we are heirs to Plato, the Bible and the nineteenth century, we irresistably dichotomize the physical and mental, the organic and functional, the constitutional and acquired, the inherited and the environmental, the instinctual and the learned. In addition, we irresistably feel that an explanation that is physical, organic, constitutional, inherited or instinctual is more basic, more real and even more morally respectable. For example, it is easier to announce that one's child is brain damaged than that he is mentally retarded or emotionally disturbed. The mental, functional, acquired, environmental or learned explanation irresistably has the feel of not being so deeply set, so pervasive or so permanent and unmodifiable as its dichotomous counterpart. Yet, this is not so.

Every embryologist knows that a genetic trait may not properly express itself in a hostile environment, and that the environment itself can modify the genetic code at the critical embryological period when the code should be unfolding. Thalidomide, taken at the critical embryological period when the limbs are budding, changes the pattern of development as written in the genetic code, so that the baby is born with deformed arms and legs. Rubella (German measles) virus in utero also creates defects and deformities.

Every psychologist should know — but he doesn't — that events in the social environment can permanently alter the brain. The findings of the new era of work on sensory deprivation of young animals provide many examples. Another example is not new, but its import has been overlooked: it is the example of cerebral dominance. At birth, the two hemispheres of the brain are equipotential for language dominance in the sense that, if the left hemisphere, typically the language hemisphere, is removed, the right hemisphere will substitute for it. Left in place, the left hemisphere for the majority of people becomes the language-dominant hemisphere, as the native language is learned. Thereafter, if this language hemisphere is removed (as in the case of a tumor), then the patient will never again recover fluent speech usage. It is too late for the right hemisphere to take over. The critical period for right hemisphere dominance has passed. Thus, one may infer that during the critical period of language development, the actual structure and/or molecular chemistry of one hemisphere of the brain is permanently altered under the influence of environmental events entering the brain by way of the ears.

In a new paper on the electroencephalogram, behavior disorder and minimal brain damage in children, Stevens,

Sachdev and Milstein (1968) studied EEG, neurological, psychological and historical characteristics of 97 children referred with severe behavior disorders typical of the so-called minimal brain-damage syndrome and compared them with 88 control children. Contrary to the traditional brain-damage hypothesis, adverse family environment led all other predisposing factors differentiating behavior-problem children from controls. They suggested that certain slow-developing regions of the brain "may be peculiarly subject to the vicissitudes of the social and physical environment both by reason of late maturation and functional specialization for social and intellectual action." According to this hypothesis, an adverse environment during an early critical period may leave a permanent adverse effect on the undeveloped brain, the likelihood being increased if the brain is already adversely affected by heredity and prenatal impairment.

The critical period concept is new in the philosophy of science as applied to social science, education and psychology. It bridges the gap between the old nineteenth century dichotomies. The essential elements of the concept are: 1) that a developmental readiness of the organism must be met by a suitable stimulus-environment before the given phase of development can take place; 2) there is a time limit, after which the developmental opportunity is lost, often forever; 3) the events of the developmental phase leave a permanent, or at least very durable, residue or imprint; 4) defective or impaired development may leave a permanent residual defect; 5) as applied to social science, there is no clear distinction between body and mind, for the events of social life as assimilated by the mind are also assimilated by the brain which is affected by what it assimilates as well as affecting, in turn, the events outside of itself in social life.

Eventually all social scientists and educators will have no choice but to incorporate this interactional way of thought into the breakfast, lunch and dinner of their workaday theories, assumptions, sentences and idioms. Meantime everyone still must struggle against the ingrained philosophical thought-habits of Plato, the Bible and the nineteenth century.

REFERENCE

Stevens, J. R., Sachdev, K. and Milstein, V. 1968. Behavior disorders of childhood and the electroencephalogram. *Archives of Neurology, 18:160-177.*

Biological Individuality

Rene Dubos

All human beings have fundamentally the same anatomical structure, operate through the same physiological processes, and are driven by the same biological urges. Yet no two human beings are alike, and what is perhaps more important, the individuality of a person living now is different from that of anyone who has ever lived in the past or will live in the future. Each person is unique, unprecedented, and unrepeatable, and my purpose here will be to try to define the biological mechanisms through which each person develops his own behavioral singularity.

Some of these mechanisms have their roots deep in the evolutionary past of the human race itself and have similar effects in all human beings. Other mechanisms are derived from the peculiarities of the genetic endowment of each person, and still others—these are perhaps the most important —concern the relationships that make each individual respond to his total environment and be modified in an irreversible manner by these responses. Some people may feel that this does not give due importance to genetic characteristics, so I would like to clarify this point at the beginning. Genes do not determine traits. Genes only govern the responses of the person to environmental stimuli. Individuality, therefore, is as much the product of the total environment as of the genetic endowment; the biological and mental characteristics are conditioned at every moment of life by the whole history of the person. Individuality can be regarded as the incarnation of the responses that the organism has made to the influences that have impinged on it in the course of its development.

From his Paleolithic past man has retained certain patterns of response to environmental stimuli that still exert profound influences on the biological and mental aspects of his life in the modern world. Just as the long-domesticated dog still retains the fundamental characteristics of the wolf, so modern man retains many biological characteristics of his Paleolithic ancestors. The evidence is now overwhelming that man's body and brain have not changed significantly during the past 100,000 years. The same set of genes that governed man's life when he was a Paleolithic hunter or a Neolithic farmer still govern his anatomical development, physiological needs, and emotional drives. There are, therefore, a number of genetic attributes that are common to the human race as a whole. They reflect the conditions that prevailed before man began civilized life, and their universal existence provides an explanation for similarities in the behavior of all human beings irrespective of the conditions under which they live.

Today, even in an environment that can be air-conditioned, and in which we can have as much light as we want at any hour of the day or night, most functions of the body continue to exhibit daily and seasonal cycles, as well perhaps as cycles of other periodicities. (There is, for example, some evidence of lunar cycles in human physiology.) Even though the ideal of technology is to create a constant and uniform environment, physiological functions still undergo cyclic changes because these are linked to the cosmic forces under which human evolution took place. When modern life carries day into night, and imposes rapid changes of latitude, as in a jet aircraft, it creates physiological conflicts because man's body continues to function according to the cosmic

order. We really are still operating with the physiological equipment that had fitted us to the natural environment prevailing during the Late Stone Age.

Many classical scholars have written extensively upon the fact that earlier civilizations had tried to discipline the expressions of ancient physiological traits. Eric R. Dodds in his extraordinary book *The Greeks and the Irrational* says of the religious celebrations in Greece that many of the rituals serve as release mechanisms for fundamental urges that did not find expression in the rational aspects of Greek life. Many such ancient traditions still persist in our own countries, though in distorted form. In the most modern city, as among the hills of Acadia 3,000 years ago, men and women perceive in springtime that nature is awakening. It is no accident that the world over Carnival is celebrated at the time when the sap starts running in the trees.

In all times, writers and artists have been aware of the immense role played by these unconscious biological processes in human life. One of the most extraordinary expressions of this awareness is in Plato's dialogue *Phaedrus*. Here Socrates speaks of the creative forces released in man by what Plato calls a "divine madness." The text makes it clear that the word madness, as used by Plato, does not refer to a diseased mental state but rather to the deep attributes which are almost beyond the control of reason because they are woven into the fabric of man's biological nature. These attributes remain unexpressed in the ordinary circumstances of life, but they profoundly influence behavior under many conditions. And, as Plato suggested, they can be powerful sources of inspiration and motivation. Another expression of the awareness of the persistence of these ancient traits is Pascal's famous statement in his *Pensées: Le coeur a ses raisons, que la raison ne connait pas.* The heart does indeed have its own reasons, which reason does not know.

The heart of which Pascal spoke includes all those determinants of individuality that do not originate from conscious reason and often escape its control. Some of these determinants survive from man's evolutionary past and are inscribed in the genetic code of the human species. But others are acquired by each person in the course of his own life, and usually very early in life. Such acquired determinants of physiological responses and mental attitudes naturally differ from culture to culture and from person to person; thus they greatly magnify the individual differences of genetic origin.

I should like now to direct attention to the obvious fact —and yet not sufficiently obvious to have inspired as much biological study as it deserves—that the total environment affects individuality through the influences it exerts on the organism during the crucial phases of development, including the intrauterine phase. These early influences affect lastingly and often irreversibly practically all anatomical, physiological, and behavioral characteristics throughout the whole life span.

I realize that the phrase "early influences" is most commonly used to denote the conditioning of behavior by the experiences of early life. At least as important is that early experiences also affect practically all other biological characteristics, practically all phenotypic expressions of the adult. This kind of conditioning is well known, but what is less well known is that it is possible to analyze in the laboratory the effects of these early influences through a great variety of experimental models.

Among the many environmental factors that have been manipulated in the laboratory to change irreversibly the characteristics of the animal by early influences is nutrition —both its quantitative and qualitative aspects, as well as the rate at which the diet is administered. This has an enormous effect on what the adult becomes. Infections so minor that they are not detected except on very careful examination of an animal will determine whether the creature will become a very large or a very small animal. An infection of that sort occurring during the first two or three days of life, and not having any detectable clinical manifestation, will also affect the size of the brain—and probably, as we are now learning, the composition of the brain. By that I do not mean an infection invading the brain, but an infectious agent that, as far as we can judge, multiplies only in the intestinal tract.

Other factors that can be manipulated are: the temperature at which the animal is maintained early in life, the humidity, the type of caging, and of course the extent and variety of stimuli—degree of crowding and extent of association with animals of the same and other species. The effects of these factors, observed in laboratories, include the rate of growth, the ultimate size of the adult animal, resistance to various forms of stress, learning ability, behavioral patterns, emotional responses, indeed almost any attribute of an animal that one wishes to examine. The principle of these experiments is to manipulate the animal only at the very beginning of its life, either during the intrauterine phase or during the first few days of life, and from then on to expose the animal to the most optimal conditions possible.

Do these observations apply only to mice and rats and pigs and not to human beings? One need only look around the world to know that the same is happening everywhere to human beings. We all know that Japanese teenagers are now much taller than their parents, not as a result of genetic change but because the postwar environment in Japan is very different from what it was in the past. One is quite familiar by now with the extraordinary changes that have occurred in the Israeli kibbutzim where children were raised under conditions very different from those experienced by their parents in the ghettos of Europe. Within one generation these children tower over their parents and are completely different from them in many behavioral characteristics. These changes in the rate of maturation in Japan and in Israel are but particular cases of a constant trend toward earlier maturation of children in all countries that have followed the Western way of life. It is not only that growth is being accelerated; some other physiological characteristics also accompany this anatomical acceleration. Many studies, for example, have been made of the change in age of first menstruation, which has been advanced by more than four years in many of the countries of Western Europe during the past 50 to 100 years.

As far as I know no systematic study has been made of the long-range consequences of this acceleration in the rate of maturation. But it is a disturbing fact that our society tends increasingly to treat young men and women as children and to deny them the chance to engage in responsible activities precisely at the time when their physiological development is so markedly accelerated. There is a dissociation between social responsibility and biological development which is truly one of the most peculiar aspects of our society.

We are not quite clear as yet about the reasons for this extraordinary acceleration of physical and physiological maturation, but studies with experimental animal models make it possible to formulate several kinds of hypotheses— each one of which can be put to the test. One is that acceleration of development is due to improvement in nutrition and the control of infection, both in the mother and in the child, and that this in turn is responsible for the much larger size achieved by the adult. The evidence for this is overwhelming in animals, even though it is not as easy to establish in man. Then there has recently come to light another kind of

evidence, which deserves further study; mainly that the wider range in the choice of a mate results in hybrid vigor through increase in heterosis. And this has implications for humans. Some studies of human populations carried out in England and in France have shown that the bicycle increases by some tenfold the range in the choice of a mate. With the automobile, of course, the choice has increased by a hundred or a thousandfold. There is no doubt, as one can show in animals, that this can result in greater hybrid vigor.

The conditioning of early life with regard to almost any physiological activity is much more lasting than anyone had anticipated. For example, it can be demonstrated with rats that animals used to having a diet low in protein during the first few weeks of their lives tend to continue eating this diet even when a better one is made available to them later in life. In some experiments an animal's mother was given a deficient diet during gestation or lactation, or the animal itself was given a decent diet very early in life. If later that animal was given all the food it wanted, of the richest quality, it could not metabolically make use of the better food; and therefore it could never correct for this initial deficiency. There are indications that the same happens in human beings. From some reports published in underdeveloped countries, it seems to be certain that persons who early in life had been used to a certain kind of metabolic level in food utilization will retain from then on that level even though much food is offered to them. They achieve a certain form of physiological and behavioral adaptation to low food intake. They tend to restrict their physical and mental activity and thereby reduce their nutritional needs. Evidently there is really no sharp demarcation between the behavioral and metabolic physiological conditions, and for all I know both are part of the same mechanism.

These observations refer to undernutrition, but malnutrition can take many other forms, including perhaps excessive feeding of the infant. There are indications, not only behavioral but again also physiological, that infants fed an extremely rich and abundant diet tend to become large eaters as adults. Such acquired dietary habits are probably objectionable from the physiological point of view, and I would be surprised if they did not have some behavioral manifestations.

There is now fairly good evidence, from both human and animal studies, that the obese person or the obese animal has become obese because very early in life it had been fed a very rich diet. The organism is obese because it contains a much larger number of lipogenic (fat producing) cells. This fact—that the number of certain types of cells that are produced in a given person or animal is the expression of the conditions of early life—is probably a very general fact, and one that I believe applies also to the development of the brain.

Now let me turn for a minute to the phenomena of crowding. Everybody knows that crowding commonly results in disturbances in endocrine function and of behavior, but the fact is that the precise effects of crowding differ profoundly depending upon the conditions under which high population density occurs. If adult animals, who were born and raised in uncrowded conditions, are suddenly brought together in large numbers they exhibit extremely aggressive behavior, and a large percentage of them die. But in contrast—and this is an experiment that as far as I know has been done in only two place—animals born and allowed to multiply within a given enclosure can reach very high population densities without displaying destructive aggressiveness. Crowding, therefore, cannot be defined only in terms of population density, but must be defined in terms of the past experience. I was so impressed by these experiments with animals that I was particularly interested to observe last summer in Hong Kong and in Taiwan that people in these cities can live peacefully and apparently happily under conditions that we would call unbearable crowding.

Though I have been discussing human problems largely from the biological point of view, I am aware of course that the effects of the environment on the emergence of individuality are greatly complicated by the fact that man tends to symbolize everything that happens to him, and then to react to the symbols themselves. But a person does not create the symbols to which he responds; he receives most of the elements of his symbolic system from the group to which he belongs. His views of the physical and social universe are impressed upon him very early in life by rituals and myth, taboos and parental training, traditions and education. What is most extraordinary, as one reads the literature in social anthropology, is that the symbolic system of a group of people can persist essentially unchanged for many generations, perhaps thousands of years, within a given culture. In such a stable system the person's views of the total universe are transmitted as a social heritage through the same kinds of mechanisms that operate for other early influences. Furthermore, they are not subject to question. This stability of the symbolic system minimizes differences in individuality and thus gives greater homogeneity to the population.

But in contrast, any profound and especially sudden social change—as caused, for example, by economic forces, scientific discoveries, and the arrival of new ethnic groups—weakens the transmission of the symbolic system and thereby allows for greater freedom of expression of the genetic endowment. The tragedy of this situation is that a wider spread of individuality is essential for greater social creativity, but usually it also results in social unrest. I have a very strong suspicion that many of the great periods of history have been at the same time creative and very disturbing. It is one of the reasons I am not as troubled as many people are about our own time. I believe that the social unrest we are now experiencing is the price we must pay for greater social creativity.

It appears, in summary, that whether we look at the biological or the cultural aspects of development, the body and the mind are simultaneously being affected by the physical, chemical, and mental stimuli that impinge on the organism. This interdependence of body and mind that the students of psychosomatic medicine have discussed at such length has deep roots in the evolutionary aspects of the human past and also in the experiential past of each individual person. In the course of human evolution, the brain, the body, and the culture developed simultaneously under one another's influence through the operation of complex feedback processes. Integrated interrelationships of constitution and of function necessarily resulted from this evolutionary interdependence. It seems to me that the activities of the human brain implied certain characteristics of the body and also certain patterns of culture. Likewise, the individual development of each person consists of an integrated series of responses to environmental stimuli. In most life situations the effects of the total environment on the body and on the mind are interrelated because exposure to almost any kind of stimulus evokes into activity associated patterns of physical and mental response simultaneously established by past experiences. It accounts for the fact that human nature in health and in disease is the historical expression of the adaptive responses made by man during his evolutionary past and his individual life. Genetic and experiential factors operate in an interrelated manner in all biological and behavioral manifestations of human life and thereby shape individuality.

An impoverished environment results almost inevitably in biological and mental deficiency. Since human potentialities can be realized only to the extent that conditions favor the phenotypic expression, it seems to me that diversity within a given culture is an essential component of true functionalism. The latent potentialities of human beings have a better chance to emerge in a living form when the social environment is sufficiently diversified to provide a variety of stimulating experience, especially for the young. This variety of experience need not depend on economic position; it is very likely that the farm in the past did provide such a variety of experience through the exposure of the child to the events of nature and the varied activities of the farm. The Lower East Side in New York City, despite its poverty, offered the children who were brought up there an extraordinary range of experience because they were exposed to the multifarious activities of an environment where people came from all parts of the world. I think it is no accident that so many distinguished people came from the Lower East Side. In contrast, most people raised in a featureless environment and limited to a narrow frame of experiences will be crippled intellectually and mentally. For this reason we must shun uniformity of surroundings as much as absolute uniformity in behavior.

Creating diversified environments may result in some loss of efficiency but in my opinion diversity is vastly more important than efficiency because it is essential for the germination of the seeds dormant in man's nature. Since the physical and social environments play such a crucial role in the shaping of individuality, environmental design should aim at enlarging the range of choices as much as possible. The word *design* as I use it applies to social planning, urban or rural development, and all the practices that affect the conduct of life.

Now, all forms of conditioning naturally interfere in some degree with the manifestations of free will; there cannot be conditioning without interference with free will. This is particularly true of the very early influences which, as we have seen, have such a lasting effect on all physical and mental characteristics. The effectiveness of this early conditioning makes it, in my opinion, theoretically impossible to design any form of social life that will provide absolute social freedom. The child is programmed by the conditions of intrauterine and early post-natal life over which he has no control. He can never change his past and all manifestations of his free will during adult life are thus conditioned by this early programming. The most and best that society can do is to provide environmental conditions so diversified that each person has a wide range of opportunities from which to select. From this point of view, it seems to me that, contrary to what has been said, the modern world is probably at least as favorable to the expression of biological freedom and the development of individuality as any period in the history of mankind.

Movement and Learning

By ALICE YARDLEY
Principal Lecturer in Education, Nottingham College of Education, Clifton, Nottingham, England; Author of several books on the ways children develop and learn.

Movement is the very essence of childhood. If we require five-year-olds to stand still, we are asking them to do something entirely foreign to their nature. They may try to oblige, but they find the feat extremely difficult, if not impossible, and exert great effort in their attempts to achieve it. Relaxed stillness is a quality of later bodily control.

Given the opportunity, young children move with obvious joy, and those who are close to young children are deeply aware that movement is of far greater significance than mere physical and psychological satisfaction. It is inextricably interwoven with every aspect of development, and movement in one of its many forms provides the basis of everything young children learn. It has as much to do with their thinking as it does with developing muscular skill.

In his prespeech days, the child's knowledge of his surroundings depends on his sensory and emotional experiences. He learns about the world through his skin, his eyes, and his ears. His mouth is one of the most sensitive and responsive parts of his body, and the feel and taste of objects referred to his mouth act as his guide to them. Each sensory experience is embodied in how he feels at the moment of experience, and the impressions he retains of events are colored by his feelings.

The child's opportunities to exercise his senses and emotions depend on the extent and variety of his environment and on the opportunity he has to reach out in it. Even when speech makes verbal communication possible, what the child is told needs to be grafted on to what he understands through personal contact, for he has no other means of bringing meaning to words.

The child's drive to explore is very active at birth. The size and quality of the environment from which he learns is the responsibility of those in charge of him, and we must do all we can to ensure that he has plenty from which to learn. As the child grows, he becomes more mobile, and the range of his exploratory adventures is directly related to his mobility.

Because the child's learning environment is what he finds at his fingertips, his movements must be given unfettered opportunity to bring his skin in contact with as much of the world as possible. If we limit the child's world to the size of a high chair, a playpen, or a single room, then we limit his learning accordingly.

When Sue was about a year old, her father died, and by the time she could toddle, her mother was forced to work, leaving Sue in the care of kind, but elderly, Mrs. Jones. Sue was given every possible physical care and attention, and she was clean and ready to go to bed when mother fetched her in the evening. "I don't want any harm to come to her," Mrs. Jones explained, "so I keep her in her chair or take her out in the pram. I try to keep her out of mischief by giving her lots of things to play with on her table."

For a time all was well. Then Sue became increasingly listless. She was very much overweight, subject to colds, and whimpered frequently for no apparent reason.

"She seems to have lost interest in her toys," Mrs. Jones complained to Sue's mother. "I'm sure I can't think why. She used to play so energetically." Mrs. Jones was obviously worried and raised no objection when the mother suggested, "I can see she's a bit of a problem for you. She's really old enough to join a play group. I'll take her off your hands for a week or two."

A few weeks in the play group, where she was encouraged to engage in plenty of vigorous movement and play with other children, brought an amazing change in Sue. What she previously lacked was the chance to "get into everything," and this the solicitous Mrs. Jones had unwittingly denied her.

In a literate society, great emphasis is placed on the development of communication skills and facility in the use of words. Sometimes, in order to accelerate linguistic progress, a child is subjected to intensive programs in which word skills are forced on him. What is often forgotten is that the meaning with which his words are endowed grows from experience, not through merely hearing and saying words.

Communication has three main components: experience, or that which gives rise to the need for communication, suitable symbols through which impressions may be

◀*What a child is feeling is very clearly expressed through his body.*

represented, and a vehicle for these symbols. In his early years, while his vocabulary and modes of using words are limited, the child resorts to nonverbal ways of expressing himself. His exploratory adventures provide the incentive to communicate impressions of people or events. The vehicle he uses is one of the many forms of bodily movement. These include mime, dance, gesture, play, creative work, facial expression (accompanied by laughing, crying, shouting, and the like), and the symbols he fashions from what he finds in the way of dressing-up equipment and other miscellaneous materials and objects. The skills he acquires in nonverbal ways he later transfers to the verbal situation, and if these opportunities for learning to communicate through his body are curbed or fettered, then the uses he ultimately makes of words may be impaired.

Doing and meaning are inseparable in developing the use of words. A child can be taught to say, to write, and to "read" words such as *drip, flow, gush, dribble, squirt,* and *cascade,* but they hold meaning only when understood as part of water play.

A group of six-year-old children were handling a tricorn shell. One boy was fascinated by the shape of it, and he talked as he explored it with his hands. "It's so smooth and strong. If I lived inside, it would keep all the sea out. It's got a pattern, and it goes round and round like this," his body echoed the movement of his finger, "until it gets to nothing at the top." At this point, the teacher provided the word *spiral.*

Two hours later, the group of children were found in a corner of the cloakroom. Not a word was spoken as they swirled and twirled, weaving in and out in the pattern of their "Spiral Dance." It was through their bodies that these children provided *spiral* with meaning.

In my opinion, mathematical ideas and logical reasoning have their roots in early movement. As an example of the way in which highly abstract notions are formed, take the child's concept of space.

The child first experiences space as a small enclosed place which shelters him during his prenatal days. Although he is ejected into a vast outside space at birth, during the early months of his life, his perception of space remains bound by what he can touch. As he becomes aware of his own body as a separate shape in space, his idea of space expands, but, from his point of view, it is still enclosed. He reaches for the moon, or the clouds, convinced he can touch them as easily as the toy suspended from the canopy of his pram.

He crawls, toddles, runs, climbs, and swings, but he still doesn't reach the limits of space. Once he is able to walk, outdoor space experience is added to experience of more confined space, and he makes his discoveries of the great outside by racing round, rolling, skipping, and jumping up and down.

He finds that he can make different shapes in space and take up different positions in it. He can explore space by moving at differing speeds and with varying emphasis. Awareness of either indoor or outside space develops through bodily movement. The child may eventually travel by car or airplane and find that space goes on and on and is high up as well as a long way off.

On television, he watches man land on the moon. He learns that space extends further than he can go, but in his view it is still a place you can reach, and this view is confirmed when man lands on the moon.

The concept of space as immeasurable and unlimited is not available to the child until a much later stage in his cognitive growth.

In a similar way, other abstract ideas grow from the child's exploratory movements. Even his later ability to reflect and reason depends on the opportunity he has in early life to learn through his body and through manipulative experience.

He learns about the invariable nature of objects or amounts of matter by what he physically does with them. He learns through manipulating objects that a process can be reversed. It is not a foregone conclusion to a six-year-old for instance, that if he lends the boy next door two of his five toy cars, he will have five again when the two he lent are returned. He needs to perform the operation in a physical sense before the idea can be formed and accepted.

These notions of invariance and reversibility are fundamental to reasoning skill, and the child who is restricted in his physical exploration and manipulation of the world may have difficulty attaining higher thinking and reasoning skills.

Observation of children aged four to six provides us with ample evidence of the way in which bodily movement contributes to social, emotional, intellectual, and spiritual development, as well as to physical growth. Children communicate with others through sharing physical experiences such as play, dance, skin contact, and even fighting. It would be difficult to imagine how immobilized young children would be if they were not allowed to make adequate social contact with their peers.

Children also use movement as a means of exploring or expressing their emotions. What a child is feeling is very clearly expressed through his body. He jumps for joy, cowers in fear, walks tall when he is confident, fights when he is frustrated, and shrinks away when he is unhappy.

The child's spiritual development stems from his growing awareness of the wonderful world of physical things and phenomena and from his growing interest in and knowledge of the people who live in it. The child's later attitudes and beliefs are firmly rooted in the inner impressions he retains of his contact with the world of external things. His understanding of what life is about can be enhanced by the opportunity he has for living fully at the level he understands, that of bodily awareness.

We can best help the child in his magnificent task by making a start with what he already possesses. He needs to explore bodily experience for his own purposes and should have ample freedom to move in his own way.

Once he is knowledgeable about his body and confident in what he can do with it, we can then begin to expect him to move in the ways we ask of him.

In practical terms, this means that when, for example, we first introduce a group of five-year-old children to an unfamiliar large indoor space, we should leave them free to move in it in the way which comes easily to those particular children.

One child may race round and round, another roll on the ground, a third bounce about on his bottom or jump up and down, while their companions may crawl, stretch, squirm, try to stand on their hands, or simply lie on their backs and kick. The observant teacher will quickly discover the movements each child can perform well, and this information provides her with starting points for planned improvement later on.

Too often, teachers are afraid that, given such freedom, children get out of hand. However, if we restrict a child to what we tell him to do, then what he can do well may not be revealed. If we require a child to use a ball or apparatus or to work with a partner before he has sufficient control of his movements to enable him to relate them to an external object or to another person, then his movements may become somewhat clumsy and stilted.

This does not mean that the child's movement development should be left to chance, but that he needs to explore fully the uses of his own body for his own purposes before we ask him to use it in ways that we design.

The more we learn about the child, the easier it is to perceive that during the early years of his living, the quality of his movement experience determines the quality of his total learning. □

LORENA R. PORTER, *professor, Department of Physical Education for Women, Northern Illinois University, DeKalb. Dr. Porter has been a counselor for physical education and a special teacher of physical education in public schools in Missouri and Illinois.*

□ **"If you want to teach physical** education to children, you need to bone up on motivational techniques. You may know what *you* want to teach, but all the kids want to do is run, hop, skip, jump, and climb!"

This comment reflects the activity-centered approach to physical education long emphasized in most teacher-training programs. For years, we've tried to push children into learning skills before they can control basic movement patterns; thrust them into complex games and dances before they learn the necessary patterns and skills.

The new trend in physical education calls for an individualized, child-centered program that enables each boy and girl to explore movement in many situations. Once they learn to control the ways in which their bodies can move, children can participate with confidence in any new learning situation, in work or in play.

The effort to extend movement education to everyone in the school program is another important trend. Contemporary research reinforces a finding of the early 1930's —that motor development plays an important part in an individual's total development. Only if a child can move freely, is he able to learn about himself and his world. When this philosophy permeates the entire school, younger children are not denied the use of physical education facilities as is often the practice when such facilities are in scarce supply.

Unfortunately, as many as one-fourth of the pupils in any given school may achieve only limited success because of minimal neurological problems or perceptual-motor deprivation. Those who have such deficiencies need remedial help. Children whose developmental sequence is lagging or whose previous activities have been limited should have enrichment experiences in addition to those provided their peers.

The guidelines for structuring movement experiences come from two sources—our knowledge of how youngsters learn and our understanding of the nature and structure of movement. A teacher gains insight into both of these by watching children at play.

Let's suppose, for example, that a group of boys and girls are playing in an area with natural environ-

THE MOVEMENT MOVEMENT

by
Lorena R. Porter

mental stimuli—trees to climb, a brook to jump across, hanging vines for swinging. In this self-motivating situation, we'd see members of the group constantly testing themselves, responding with sensitivity and ingenuity to the various challenges.

Children have always learned through exploration, but in our urban-suburban society fewer have the chance for free bodily movement. They *want* to move and explore, but they live in an environment requiring little physical effort. For this reason, the school program must offer the kind of movement experiences found in natural play situations—with guidance as an extra ingredient.

The first step is to set the stage for learning. Unfortunately, the typical school offers only limited opportunities for exploration of movement potentials. Even when ample space is provided, play equipment is of the traditional sit-and-ride variety—swings, teeters, slides, and merry-go-rounds.

The new stress is on equipment that encourages vigorous movement, adventure, and creativity—that simulates natural environmental challenges. The equipment includes ropes, ladders, and frames for climbing; beams and benches for balancing; planks for sliding and scrambling; tables and boxes for jumping; and tunnels for creeping through and over.

Manipulatory equipment should also be available and in sufficient quantity so that each pupil can select tasks for which he is ready. This equipment includes hoops, bean bags, fluff balls, scoops, paddles, wands, targets, and objects of all sizes and shapes for throwing, catching, propelling, and striking.

As children explore their new environment during their early years at school, the teacher must help them do so safely and with consideration for others. (Important aspects of safety include suitable clothing and footwear, splinter-free floors, and rubble-free playgrounds; ample space around apparatus so that collisions are avoided; mats for landings from heights; strong boxes, tables, saw-

horses, planks, benches.)

The teacher fosters respect for individual differences by encouraging pupils to observe the creative movements of their peers. When this is done, we begin to hear such comments as, "Look at Susie! She can reach the rings today!" or "John is moving upside down under the trestle."

The next stage of movement education calls for guiding the children's experimentation into more definite channels. The teacher sets specific movement tasks and encourages each member of the class to find ways of solving them within his own capacity. As the child widens his experiences, he develops awareness of *what* his body can do and *where* in space it can move. He also develops conscious control of *how* he moves—analyzing his movements in terms of the motion factors:

- Weight. How much force do I use? What is the degree of my muscular tension?
- Space. What is the direction of my motion in space? Straight? Roundabout?
- Time. Is my motion quick or slow, sudden or sustained? Is it accelerating or slowing down?
- Flow. Is my motion continuous? Is it bound and restricted or free flowing?

A skilled movement is one in which there is an appropriate blend of the motion factors.

Experimentation in a lesson is ordinarily focused on tasks pertaining to a particular theme or concept. For example, in a lesson in which emphasis is on body awareness, the teacher may challenge a child to discover ways in which different parts of his body can support his whole weight. Or he may be asked to experiment with ways of traveling with weight being transferred on only one part or from one body part to another. Since there are innumerable right answers to these basic movement ideas, all the children have the opportunity to discover a movement pattern new to them.

As children select, practice, and refine a motion pattern of their own invention, they achieve safe and sensitive use of their bodies in various modes of locomotion—running, skipping, sliding, or rolling in various ways. Later, they may experiment with ways of traveling by transferring weight to distant body parts—from feet, to hands, to feet, for example. Children especially enjoy experimenting with flight, that specialized form of locomotion in which one leaves the ground and flies through the air. Control of body weight is a prerequisite to safe and efficient movement involved in everyday play as well as in games, apparatus work, and dance.

After pupils learn control of body weight in safe and easy situations, the teacher may encourage them to experiment with similar challenges on the apparatus, and to add interest to their patterns by using contrasting motion factors—fast or slow, strong or light, with restricted or free flow. They may also experiment with the use of space, changing directions or levels.

Teachers must avoid imposing preconceived adult notions of competition and rules on young children. Their proposal, "Let's play football," is likely to mean "Let's play kicking and catching"—a game calling for a loose association of youngsters interested in increasing their range of skill.

The concepts of "trying to beat others" and the ability to follow rules usually develop when children are eight or nine. During this stage, they should have opportunity to invent and play games which emphasize cooperation as well as competition. Size of groups should be kept sufficiently small so that there is opportunity for maximum involvement of all children.

Helping the child discover how he can use his body in expressive ways is another appropriate theme. Hands or feet may be used in beating on the floor, clapping or tapping, shaking or grasping. Pupils can experiment with various forms of locomotion, individually at first, and then in combinations—stepping and running, galloping and skipping, spinning and turning.

As the children refine these movement sequences, repeating them until a natural rhythm evolves, they enjoy dancing for its own sake. Spontaneous rhythmic movement is exhilarating, and they will like to accompany themselves or each other with percussive instruments.

Children develop expressiveness as they learn to color a phrase with their own variations of motion factors. For example, let's suppose they learn a simple sequence comprised of three stepping actions interspersed with periods of stillness. When all can perform this sequence rhythmically and in unison with the teacher, they can experiment with different speeds and changes of direction. With guidance, each pupil creates his own phrase, and a dance is in process.

Children may work in pairs and experiment with various relationships—advancing and retreating, moving in turn or simultaneously, matching or contrasting action. What begins as a simple movement phrase evolves into significantly different forms of expression as ideas are exchanged and feelings are evoked from action patterns.

Some patterns may convey feelings of aggression; others, of mysteriousness; still others, of happiness or sadness. In this way, boys and girls develop a language of action. They are not asked to *be* a giant or ghost, or to move as the music makes them feel—practices which may arouse dislike of dancing. Instead, they are challenged to experiment with movement and relationships in which they discover a resemblance to feelings, persons, or objects experienced in real life. Movement can serve as an integrating factor in the related arts program in which music, art, language, and dance serve as sources of creative expression.

The content of the physical education lesson has long been viewed in terms of activities to be learned—games, dances, stunts, and so on. But in many schools today, young people have the chance to create new forms of expression as well as to discover their talents in important cultural activities. □

VI. AFFECT

Affective learning is the acquisition of valuative meanings for ideas, objects, persons, or events. Affective learnings are manifested in tastes, preferences, attitudes, and values. Affective goals in education are those which emphasize a feeling tone, an emotion, or a degree of acceptance or rejection. They may vary from simple attention to selected phenomena to complex qualities of character and conscience.

It is axiomatic that all educational programs have implicit affective outcomes—this is the forceful arena of the hidden curriculum. The degree to which educators have been explicitly concerned with affective outcome seems to be a cyclical phenomenon. Not too many years ago, when the "whole child" philosophy was the most popular theory of education, attitudes were frequently considered more important than subject matter. When, however, the excitement over the Progressive Education movement abated, educational programs became more classic and academic in character. The 1960's witnessed a resurgence of interest in affective value-oriented curricula, but in the middle of the present decade, there appears to be another return to more exclusively cognitive concerns—generally referred to as a return to the "basics."

Lawrence Kohlberg's approach to moral education would seem to have the best of both worlds. Although moral education is concerned with value-laden behavior, Kohlberg's approach is based on Piaget's theory of cognitive development. Further, the structure of Kohlberg's moral education classes reinforces very intellectualized behaviors. We, however, are not as convinced as he that youths who understand justice will necessarily feel motivated to act more justly. Joseph Junell is even more distrustful of Kohlberg's scientific method in terms of its enabling children to cope with the central issues of value. He argues that it is naive to assume that children will select what is demonstrably true over what is demonstrably false, for it is feeling, not reasoning, that provides the motivation to act on belief. Junell might argue that Kohlberg's approach leads inevitably to moral anarchy. Kohlberg would probably respond that Junell has only benign brain-washing to offer as an alternative. No easy solution recommends itself. Is the life of freedom compatible with the maintenance of social stability?

Just as much cognitive learning takes place outside the school, a great deal of affective learning rises from nonschool experiences. Nevertheless, we feel that educators should deal with the affective components of their programs explicitly, and, thus, we are encouraged by Richard Farson's article. He argues that the development of technology relieves education of the need to be limited to cognitive and verbal skills. We may now be free to offer teachers and students the time and freedom to develop affectively, without fearing that we are in a "zero-sum" game with respect to important cognitive outcomes to which we also aspire. This outcome is also in accord with our understanding that to analyze the affective area separately from the cognitive is not intended to suggest that there is a fundamental separation. As Scheerer puts it, ". . . behavior may be conceptualized as being embedded in a cognitive-emotional-motivational matrix in which no true separation is possible. No matter how we slice behavior, the ingredients of motivation-emotion-cognition are present in one order or another."

It is this fundamental unit of the organism that Ira Gordon advocates in his article dealing with affect and cognition. In his understanding, the learner will devour intellectual activities when they are matched to his present resolution; these will challenge him because they create some disequilibrium in his present system. As Professor Gordon puts it: ". . . to be competent is motive to behave competently. Knowing self and world heightens affect and creates that measure of discontent which, in turn, can spur us on to achieve our human potentialities."

The Child as a Moral Philosopher

By Lawrence Kohlberg

How can one study morality? Current trends in the fields of ethics, linguistics, anthropology and cognitive psychology have suggested a new approach which seems to avoid the morass of semantical confusions, value-bias and cultural relativity in which the psychoanalytic and semantic approaches to morality have foundered. New scholarship in all these fields is now focusing upon structures, forms and relationships that seem to be common to all societies and all languages rather than upon the features that make particular languages or cultures different.

For 12 years, my colleagues and I studied the same group of 75 boys, following their development at three-year intervals from early adolescence through young manhood. At the start of the study, the boys were aged 10 to 16. We have now followed them through to ages 22 to 28. In addition, I have explored moral development in other cultures — Great Britain, Canada, Taiwan, Mexico and Turkey.

Inspired by Jean Piaget's pioneering effort to apply a structural approach to moral development, I have gradually elaborated over the years of my study a typological scheme describing general structures and forms of moral thought which can be defined independently of the specific content of particular moral decisions or actions.

The typology contains three distinct levels of moral thinking, and within each of these levels distinguishes two related stages. These levels and stages may be considered separate moral philosophies, distinct views of the socio-moral world.

We can speak of the child as having his own morality or series of moralities. Adults seldom listen to children's moralizing. If a child throws back a few adult cliches and behaves himself, most parents—and many anthropologists and psychologists as well—think that the child has adopted or internalized the appropriate parental standards.

Actually, as soon as we talk with children about morality, we find that they have many ways of making judgments which are not "internalized" from the outside, and which do not come in any direct and obvious way from parents, teachers or even peers.

Moral Levels

The *preconventional* level is the first of three levels of moral thinking; the second level is *conventional,* and the third *postconventional* or autonomous. While the preconventional child is often "well-behaved" and is responsive to cultural labels of good and bad, he interprets these labels in terms of their physical consequences (punishment, reward, exchange of favors) or in terms of the physical power of those who enunciate the rules and labels of good and bad.

This level is usually occupied by children aged four to 10, a fact long known to sensitive observers of children. The capacity of "properly behaved" children of this age to engage in cruel behavior when there are holes in the power structure is sometimes noted as tragic (*Lord of the Flies, High Wind in Jamaica*), sometimes as comic (Lucy in *Peanuts*).

The second or *conventional* level also can be described as conformist, but that is perhaps too smug a term. Maintaining the expectations and rules of the individual's family, group or nation is perceived as valuable in its own right. There is a concern not only with *conforming* to the individual's social order but in *maintaining,* supporting and justifying this order.

The *postconventional* level is characterized by a major thrust toward autonomous moral principles which have validity and application apart from authority of the groups or persons who hold them and apart from the individual's identification with those persons or groups.

Moral Stages

Within each of these three levels there are two discernable stages. At the preconventional level we have:

Stage 1: Orientation toward punishment and unquestioning deference to superior power. The physical consequences of action regardless of their human meaning or value determine its goodness or badness.

Stage 2: Right action consists of that which instrumentally satisfies one's own needs and occasionally the needs of others. Human relations are viewed in terms like those of the marketplace. Elements of fairness, of reciprocity and equal sharing are present, but they are always interpreted in a physical, pragmatic way. Reciprocity is a matter of "you scratch my back and I'll scratch yours" not of loyalty, gratitude or justice.

And at the conventional level we have:

Stage 3: Good-boy—good-girl orientation. Good behavior is that which pleases or helps others and is approved by them. There is much conformity to stereotypical images of what is majority or "natural" behavior. Behavior is often judged by intention —"he means well" becomes important for the first time, and is overused, as by Charlie Brown in *Peanuts.* One seeks approval by being "nice."

Stage 4: Orientation toward authority, fixed rules and the maintenance of the social order. Right behavior consists of doing one's duty, showing respect for authority and maintaining the given social order for its own sake. One earns respect by performing dutifully.

At the postconventional level, we have:

Stage 5: A social-contract orientation, generally with legalistic and utilitarian overtones. Right action tends to be defined in terms of general rights and in terms of standards which have been critically examined and agreed upon by the whole society. There is a clear awareness of the relativism of personal values and opinions and a corresponding emphasis upon procedural rules for reaching consensus. Aside from what is constitutionally and democratically agreed upon, right or wrong is a matter of personal "values" and "opinion." The result is an emphasis upon the "legal point of view," but with an emphasis upon the possibility of *changing* law in terms of rational considerations of social utility, rather than freezing it in the terms of Stage 4 "law and order." Outside the legal realm, free agreement and contract are the binding elements of obligation. This is the "official" morality of American government, and finds its ground in the thought of the writers of the Constitution.

Stage 6: Orientation toward the decisions of conscience and toward self-chosen *ethical principles* appealing to logical comprehensiveness, universality and consistency. These principles are abstract and ethical (the Golden Rule, the categorical imperative); they are not concrete moral rules like the Ten Commandments. Instead, they are universal principles of *justice,* of the *reciprocity* and *equality*

"Virtue-words like honesty point approvingly to certain behaviors but give us no guide to understanding them."

of human rights, and of respect for the dignity of human beings as *individual persons.*

Up to Now

In the past, when psychologists tried to answer the question asked of Socrates by Meno "Is virtue something that can be taught (by rational discussion), or does it come by practice, or is it a natural inborn attitude?" their answers usually have been dictated, not by research findings on children's moral character, but by their general theoretical convictions.

Behavior theorists have said that virtue is behavior acquired according to their favorite general principles of learning. Freudians have claimed that virtue is superego-identification with parents generated by a proper balance of love and authority in family relations.

The American psychologists who have actually studied children's morality have tried to start with a set of labels—the "virtues" and "vices," the "traits" of good and bad character found in ordinary language. The earliest major psychological study of moral character, that of Hugh Hartshorne and Mark May in 1928-1930, focused on a bag of virtues including honesty, service (altruism or generosity), and self-control. To their dismay, they found that there were *no* character traits, psychological dispositions or entities which corresponded to words like honesty, service or self-control.

Regarding honesty, for instance, they found that almost everyone cheats some of the time, and that if a person cheats in one situation, it doesn't mean that he *will* or *won't* in another. In other words, it is not an identifiable character trait, *dis*honesty, that makes a child cheat in a given situation. These early researchers also found that people who cheat express as much or even more moral disapproval of cheating as those who do not cheat.

What Hartshorne and May found out about their bag of virtues is equally upsetting to the somewhat more psychological-sounding names introduced by psychoanalytic psychology: "superego-strength," "resistance to temptation," "strength of conscience," and the like. When recent researchers attempt to measure such traits in individuals, they have been forced to use Hartshorne and May's old tests of honesty and self-con-

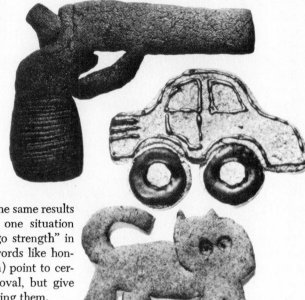

trol and they get exactly the same results —"superego strength" in one situation predicts little to "superego strength" in another. That is, virtue-words like honesty (or superego-strength) point to certain behaviors with approval, but give us no guide to understanding them.

So far as one can extract some generalized personality factor from children's performance on tests of honesty or resistance to temptation, it is a factor of ego-strength or ego-control, which always involves non-moral capacities like the capacity to maintain attention, intelligent-task performance, and the ability to delay response. "Ego-strength" (called "will" in earlier days) has something to do with moral action, but it does not take us to the core of morality or to the definition of virtue. Obviously enough, many of the greatest evil-doers in history have been men of strong wills, men strongly pursuing immoral goals.

Moral Reasons

In our research, we have found definite and universal levels of development in moral thought. In our study of 75 American boys from early adolescence on, these youths were presented with hypothetical moral dilemmas, all deliberately philosophical, some of them found in medieval works of casuistry.

On the basis of their reasoning about these dilemmas at a given age, each boy's stage of thought could be determined for each of 25 basic moral concepts or aspects. One such aspect, for instance, is "Motive Given for Rule Obedience or Moral Action." In this instance, the six stages look like this:

1. Obey rules to avoid punishment.
2. Conform to obtain rewards, have favors returned, and so on.
3. Conform to avoid disapproval, dislike by others.
4. Conform to avoid censure by legitimate authorities and resultant guilt.
5. Conform to maintain the respect of the impartial spectator judging in terms of community welfare.
6. Conform to avoid self-condemnation.

In another of these 25 moral aspects, the value of human life, the six stages can be defined thus:

1. The value of a human life is confused with the value of physical objects and is based on the social status or physical attributes of its possessor.
2. The value of a human life is seen as instrumental to the satisfaction of the needs of its possessor or of other persons.
3. The value of a human life is based on the empathy and affection of family members and others toward its possessor.
4. Life is conceived as sacred in terms of its place in a categorical moral or religious order of rights and duties.
5. Life is valued both in terms of its relation to community welfare and in terms of life being a universal human right.
6. Belief in the sacredness of human life as representing a universal human value of respect for the individual.

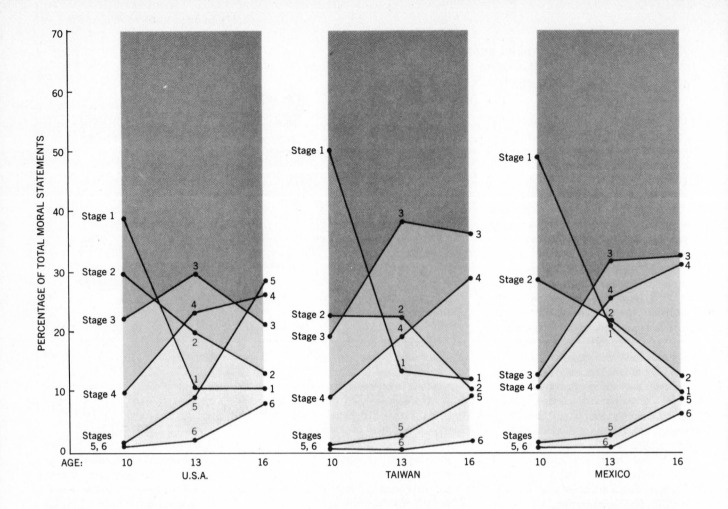

1. Middle-class urban boys in the U.S., Taiwan and Mexico (*above*). At age 10 the stages are used according to difficulty. At age 13, Stage 3 is most used by all three groups. At age 16 U.S. boys have reversed the order of age 10 stages (with the exception of 6). In Taiwan and Mexico, conventional (3-4) stages prevail at age 16, with Stage 5 also little used.

2. Two isolated villages, one in Turkey, the other in Yucatan, show similar patterns in moral thinking. There is no reversal of order, and preconventional (1-2) thought does does not gain a clear ascendancy over conventional stages at age 16.

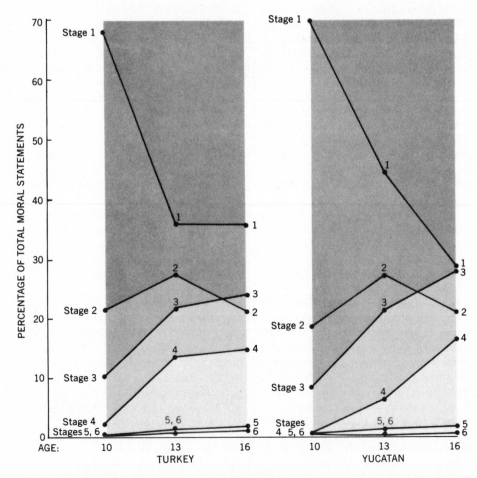

"Children have many ways of making judgments which do *not* come in any direct way from parents, teachers or other children."

I have called this scheme a typology. This is because about 50 per cent of most people's thinking will be at a single stage, regardless of the moral dilemma involved. We call our types *stages* because they seem to represent an *invariant developmental sequence.* "True" stages come one at a time and always in the same order.

All movement is forward in sequence, and does not skip steps. Children may move through these stages at varying speeds, of course, and may be found half in and half out of a particular stage. An individual may stop at any given stage and at any age, but if he continues to move, he must move in accord with these steps. Moral reasoning of the conventional or Stage 3-4 kind never occurs before the preconventional Stage-1 and Stage-2 thought has taken place. No adult in Stage 4 has gone through Stage 6, but all Stage-6 adults have gone at least through 4.

While the evidence is not complete, my study strongly suggests that moral change fits the stage pattern just described. (The major uncertainty is whether all Stage 6s go through Stage 5 or whether these are two alternate mature orientations.)

How Values Change

As a single example of our findings of stage-sequence, take the progress of two boys on the aspect "The Value of Human Life." The first boy Tommy, is asked "Is it better to save the life of one important person or a lot of unimportant people?". At age 10, he answers "all the people that aren't important because one man just has one house, maybe a lot of furniture, but a whole bunch of people have an awful lot of furniture and some of these poor people might have a lot of money and it doesn't look it."

Clearly Tommy is Stage 1: he confuses the value of a human being with the value of the property he possesses. Three years later (age 13) Tommy's conceptions of life's value are most clearly elicited by the question, "Should the doctor 'mercy kill' a fatally ill woman requesting death because of her pain?". He answers, "Maybe it would be good to put her out of her pain, she'd be better off that way. But the husband wouldn't want it, it's not like an animal.

If a pet dies you can get along without it—it isn't something you really need. Well, you can get a new wife, but it's not really the same."

Here his answer is Stage 2: the value of the woman's life is partly contingent on its hedonistic value to the wife herself but even more contingent on its instrumental value to her husband, who can't replace her as easily as he can a pet.

Three years later still (age 16) Tommy's conception of life's value is elicited by the same question, to which he replies: "It might be best for her, but her husband—it's a human life—not like an animal; it just doesn't have the same relationship that a human being does to a family. You can become attached to a dog, but nothing like a human you know."

Now Tommy has moved from a Stage 2 instrumental view of the woman's value to a Stage-3 view based on the husband's distinctively human empathy and love for someone in his family. Equally clearly, it lacks any basis for a universal human value of the woman's life, which would hold if she had no husband or if her husband didn't love her. Tommy, then, has moved step by step through three stages during the age 10-16. Tommy, though bright (I.Q 120), is a slow developer in moral judgment. Let us take another boy, Richard, to show us sequential movement through the remaining three steps.

At age 13, Richard said about the mercy-killing, "If she requests it, it's really up to her. She is in such terrible pain, just the same as people are always putting animals out of their pain," and in general showed a mixture of Stage-2 and Stage-3 responses concerning the value of life. At 16, he said, "I don't know. In one way, it's murder, it's not a right or privilege of man to decide who shall live and who should die. God put life into everybody on earth and you're taking away something from that person that came directly from God, and you're destroying something that is very sacred, it's in a way part of God and it's almost destroying a part of God when you kill a person. There's something of God in everyone."

Here Richard clearly displays a Stage-4 concept of life as sacred in terms of its

place in a categorical moral or religious order. The value of human life is universal, it is true for all humans. It is still, however, dependent on something else, upon respect for God and God's authority; it is not an autonomous human value. Presumably if God told Richard to murder, as God commanded Abraham to murder Isaac, he would do so.

At age 20, Richard said to the same question: "There are more and more people in the medical profession who think it is a hardship on everyone, the person, the family, when you know they are going to die. When a person is kept alive by an artificial lung or kidney it's more like being a vegetable than being a human. If it's her own choice, I think there are certain rights and privileges that go along with being a human being. I am a human being and have certain desires for life and I think everybody else does too. You have a world of which you are the center, and everybody else does too and in that sense we're all equal."

Richard's response is clearly Stage 5, in that the value of life is defined in terms of equal and universal human rights in a context of relativity ("You have a world of which you are the center and in that sense we're all equal"), and of concern for utility or welfare consequences.

The Final Step

At 24, Richard says: "A human life takes precedence over any other moral or legal value, whoever it is. A human life has inherent value whether or not it is valued by a particular individual. The worth of the individual human being is central where the principles of justice and love are normative for all human relationships."

This young man is at Stage 6 in seeing the value of human life as absolute in representing a universal and equal respect for the human as an individual. He has moved step by step through a sequence culminating in a definition of human life as centrally valuable rather than derived from or dependent on social or divine authority.

In a genuine and culturally universal sense, these steps lead toward an increased *morality* of value judgment, where morality is considered as a form of judging, as it has been in a philosophic tradition running from the analyses of Kant to those of the modern analytic or "ordinary language" philosophers. The person at Stage 6 has disentangled his judgments of—or language about—hu-

"Socrates, Lincoln, Thoreau and Martin Luther King tend to speak without confusion of tongues."

man life from status and property values (Stage 1), from its uses to others (Stage 2), from interpersonal affection (Stage 3), and so on; he has a means of moral judgment that is universal and impersonal. The Stage-6 person's answers use moral words like "duty" or "morally right," and he uses them in a way implying universality, ideals, impersonality: He thinks and speaks in phrases like "regardless of who it was," or ". . . I would do it in spite of punishment."

Across Cultures

When I first decided to explore moral development in other cultures, I was told by anthropologist friends that I would have to throw away my culture-bound moral concepts and stories and start from scratch learning a whole new set of values for each new culture. My first try consisted of a brace of villages, one Atayal (Malaysian aboriginal) and the other Taiwanese.

My guide was a young Chinese ethnographer who had written an account of the moral and religious patterns of the Atayal and Taiwanese villages. Taiwanese boys in the 10-13 age group were asked about a story involving theft of food. A man's wife is starving to death but the store owner won't give the man any food unless he can pay, which he can't. Should he break in and steal some food? Why? Many of the boys said, "He should steal the food for his wife because if she dies he'll have to pay for her funeral and that costs a lot."

My guide was amused by these responses, but I was relieved: they were of course "classic" Stage-2 responses. In the Atayal village, funerals weren't such a big thing, so the Stage 2-boys would say, "He should steal the food because he needs his wife to cook for him."

This means that we need to consult our anthropologists to know what content a Stage-2 child will include in his instrumental exchange calculations, or what a Stage-4 adult will identify as the proper social order. But one certainly doesn't have to start from scratch. What made my guide laugh was the difference in form between the children's Stage-2 thought and his own, a difference definable independently of particular cultures.

Illustrations number 1 and number 2 indicate the cultural universality of the sequence of stages which we have found. Illustration number 1 presents the age trends for middle-class urban boys in the U.S., Taiwan and Mexico. At age 10 in each country, the order of use of each stage is the same as the order of its difficulty or maturity.

In the United States, by age 16 the order is the reverse, from the highest to the lowest, except that Stage 6 is still little-used. At age 13, the good-boy, middle stage (Stage 3), is not used.

The results in Mexico and Taiwan are the same, except that development is a little slower. The most conspicuous feature is that at the age of 16, Stage-5 thinking is much more salient in the United States than in Mexico or Taiwan. Nevertheless, it *is* present in the other countries, so we know that this is not purely an American democratic construct.

Illustration 2 shows strikingly similar results from two isolated villages, one in Yucatan, one in Turkey. While conventional moral thought increases steadily from ages 10 to 16 it still has not achieved a clear ascendency over preconventional thought.

Trends for lower-class urban groups are intermediate in the rate of development between those for the middle-class and for the village boys. In the three divergent cultures that I studied, middle-class children were found to be more advanced in moral judgment than matched lower-class children. This was not due to the fact that the middle-class children heavily favored some one type of thought which could be seen as corresponding to the prevailing middle-class pattern. Instead, middle-class and working-class children move through the same sequences, but the middle-class children move faster and farther.

This sequence is not dependent upon a particular religion, or any religion at all in the usual sense. I found no important differences in the development of moral thinking among Catholics, Protestants, Jews, Buddhists, Moslems and atheists. Religious values seem to go through the same stages as all other values.

Trading Up

In summary, the nature of our sequence is not significantly affected by widely varying social, cultural or religious conditions. The only thing that is affected is the *rate* at which individuals progress through this sequence.

Why should there be such a universal invariant sequence of development? In answering this question, we need first to analyze these developing social concepts in terms of their internal logical structure. At each stage, the same basic moral concept or aspect is defined, but at each higher stage this definition is more differentiated, more integrated and more general or universal. When one's concept of human life moves from Stage 1 to Stage 2 the value of life becomes more differentiated from the value of property, more integrated (the value of life enters an organizational hierarchy where it is "higher" than property so that one steals property in order to save life) and more universalized (the life of any sentient being is valuable regardless of status or property). The same advance is true at each stage in the hierarchy. Each step of development then is a better cognitive organization than the one before it, one which takes account of everything present in the previous stage, but making new distinctions and organizing them into a more comprehensive or more equilibrated structure. The fact that this is the case has been demonstrated by a series of studies indicating that children and adolescents comprehend all stages up to their own, but not more than one stage beyond their own. And importantly, *they prefer this next stage.*

We have conducted experimental moral discussion classes which show that the child at an earlier stage of development tends to move forward when confronted by the views of a child one stage further along. In an argument between a Stage-3 and Stage-4 child, the child in the third stage tends to move toward or into Stage 4, while the Stage-4 child understands but does not accept the arguments of the Stage-3 child.

Moral thought, then, seems to behave like all other kinds of thought. Progress through the moral levels and stages is characterized by increasing differentiation and increasing integration, and hence is the same kind of progress that scientific theory represents. Like acceptable scientific theory—or like *any* theory or structure of knowledge—moral thought may be considered partially to generate its own data as it goes along, or at least to expand so as to contain in a balanced, self-consistent way a wider and wider experiential field. The raw data in the case of our ethical philosophies may be considered as conflicts between roles, or values, or as the social order in which men live.

The Role of Society

The social worlds of all men seem to contain the same basic structures. All the societies we have studied have the same basic institutions—family, economy, law, government. In addition, however, all societies are alike because they *are* societies—systems of defined complementary roles. In order to *play* a social role in the family, school or society, the child must implicitly take the role of others toward himself and toward others in the group. These role-taking tendencies form the basis of all social institutions. They represent various patternings of shared or complementary expectations.

In the preconventional and conventional levels (Stages 1-4), moral content or value is largely accidental or culture-bound. Anything from "honesty" to "courage in battle" can be the central value. But in the higher postconventional levels, Socrates, Lincoln, Thoreau and Martin Luther King tend to speak without confusion of tongues, as it were. This is because the ideal principles of any social structure are basically alike, if only because there simply aren't that many principles which are articulate, comprehensive and integrated enough to be satisfying to the human intellect. And most of these principles have gone by the name of justice.

Behavioristic psychology and psychoanalysis have always upheld the Philistine view that fine moral words are one thing and moral deeds another. Morally mature reasoning is quite a different matter, and does not really depend on "fine words." The man who understands justice is more likely to practice it.

In our studies, we have found that youths who understand justice act more justly, and the man who understands justice helps create a moral climate which goes far beyond his immediate and personal acts. The universal society is the beneficiary.

Joseph Junell

THE LIMITS OF SOCIAL EDUCATION

New life-styles result from cruelty unwittingly inflicted
upon the learner. How should the schools respond?

Ever since the discovery of the "affective domain" several decades ago, educators have been enamored with the possibility of a new role which they believe parents have largely abdicated in favor of the school, namely, the socialization of America's children. Their main interest to date has been focused on citizenship or the inculcation of values associated with a democratic way of life; however, they have not failed to include certain moral values as well. While recent Supreme Court rulings have introduced anomalies into this role, it continues as one of the dominant themes in American education.

The condition is a curious one, since it has led to all sorts of conclusions, some muddled, others extravagant, as to the objectives American schools should pursue, their manner of pursuing them, and the degree to which they believe these objectives may be achieved. Few educators, however, are fully aware of the vast and complex forces, many of them rigidly deterministic in nature, which have not only placed severe limitations upon the school's influence over children, but have ironically produced results that were opposite from those intended. I shall attempt to deal only with those few which seem to me most prominent in their impact on school children's lives and suggest some approaches which lie within what appears to be a narrow but extremely important margin of opportunity.

Representative of the kinds of influences which have created enormous difficulties for schools as they are now constituted, but which we now accept as eminently humane, are the early laws designed to protect children from industrial exploitation. The discovery, for example, that the aptitudes and aspira-

JOSEPH S. JUNELL (2248, University of Washington Chapter) is a college supervisor, Central Washington State College, Ellensburg.

tions of many youth do not flourish within the present academic system designed for school children is certainly not new. Yet, for years now we have wittingly or unwittingly inflicted on this learner a kind of refined cruelty upon which it would be exceedingly difficult to improve. Where it was once a relatively simple matter for him to put an end to an intolerable situation by leaving school for the factory or farm, today's social pressures and stringent laws regarding compulsory attendance and child labor allow him no such avenue of escape. In large measure his response to grinding frustration cannot but take the form of compensatory life-styles which are on occasion unseemly, frequently disruptive, and sometimes seriously threatening to life and health. If much of this behavior has found sanctuary under threat of litigation, the bane of teacher and administrator alike, I cannot believe that it was brought about by any mere shift in school or parental authority. I am convinced it would have appeared in any case, as one of the many reflections of vast social change. Moreover, it will likely run its course for good or evil, in spite of all efforts to stop it.

An example of such change is what many critics view as a most sinister shift in allegiance among youth from the values of an adult society to those of the peer group. So significant is this change in social behavior, so foreboding of social disintegration and demise, that brief consideration must be given to the socializing process, for it is central to all problems regarding value and value change and largely determines the conditions under which values are internalized. Let us begin with the child. He enters the world, in the words of Shakespeare, "an infant, mewling and puking in the nurse's arms," with very little to recommend him at this stage of life or in the weeks which immediately follow. Only by the most deliberate exercise of our romantic sensibilities could we attri-

bute to this behavior any of the virtues which set him apart as a human. And yet, if we may accept Erikson's assessment of this phase of his development, it is, in a social sense, the most crucial one he will ever pass through. For upon the quality of his oral and other physical experiences will be established his fundamental trust or mistrust of the world – a factor, Erikson goes on to say, which in no small part determines not only the success of his future interpersonal relationships but the kinds of values he will choose to live by.[1] If this sounds like a highly deterministic view of what happens to all of us, it is one which authorities such as Piaget and Sears, in addition to Erikson, tend by and large to corroborate.[2]

The primary mechanism by which socialization takes place, however, is known as identification, a learning principle to which educators must begin paying closer attention than they ever have in the past. There is yet a great deal to be learned about this principle and its effects on cognition; however, one of its key functions, under ideal conditions, appears to be that of enabling very young children to internalize smoothly and effortlessly the stabilizing behaviors of the preceding generation that are deemed imperative to the survival of the species.

The concept was first advanced by Freud and later amplified by Anna Freud, Erikson, Horney, Adler, and others. It is commonly described as a dependency relationship with some significant figure, generally a parent, whose functions are, among other things, nurturant and supportive; but crucial to the condition is that it be based on the child's "emotional tie with the object."[3] Moreover, it is unique, according to Sears, in that it is entirely self-motivated, operating without need of reinforcement or special training.[4]

As we read some of the recent and fascinating literature on imprinting among animals, we find a strange parallel in which a specific kind of experience must match a particular phase in the animal's maturation, if normal development is to occur. Bettelheim, for one, views this phenomenon, or something similar to it, as one of the key factors in the relationship between emotional and cognitive development and in his own studies has found that when children have been deprived of this crucial experience, both socialization and cognitive ability are often seriously impaired.[5] The timing, to be sure, is far less critical in humans; but the most sensitive period appears to begin at about the age of two and a half or three and continues at a decelerating rate until puberty, when it is largely, though not entirely, extinguished.[6]

Two factors seem most predictive of the success or failure of this learning principle: the quality of human contact and the length of time in which the principle is allowed to operate. Any extraneous forces altering these two factors are very likely to bring about parallel changes in social behavior.

One of the better accounts of how this socializing principle has been profoundly affected by the impact of technology and the consequent altered styles in family life may be found in Bronfenbrenner's comparative studies of American and Russian patterns of child rearing and education (*Two Worlds of Childhood*). In his analysis of the two cultures, he carefully pinpoints the various influences within each society — mass media, modified family habits, enforced peer relations — as they impinge upon the child. From these he extrapolates the probable effects on the child's behavior. All lead up to a startling, carefully documented conclusion: Russian children make significantly more choices favoring adult values than do American children. This in itself would not merit critical attention were it not for his further well-established observation that such choices are far more consistent with acceptable behavior than are those of peer-value oriented children who are more prone to engage in misdemeanors, violence, and other acts of an antisocial nature.[7]

At first Bronfenbrenner had reason to interpret his findings in terms of a growing tendency in American families toward greater permissiveness in the rearing of children. Later, in the light of new data, he was forced to reassess his position. Although still "consistent with the trend toward permissiveness," it now probed more deeply into the heart of the matter. Of greater significance

was the discovery of a "progressive decrease, especially in recent decades, in the amount of contact between American parents and their children." Along with this, moreover, he noted a relative lack of emotional tone and intensity in the relationship. To summarize, "whether in comparison to other contemporary cultures, or to itself over time, American society emerges as one that gives decreasing prominence to the family as a socializing agent...."[8] From this, one may logically infer that, apart from the quality of the child's contact with adults, the degree of the child's allegiance to adult values is directly related to the amount of time in which the identification principle is allowed to operate.

In what exact way this affects student behavior is hard to determine; however, one logical assumption is that enforced and prolonged peer relations must ultimately lead to a serious questioning of much that is commonplace and ritualized in adult behavior to which time has given an aura of veneration and acceptance. Such questioning can be both good and bad. Where it exposes moral phoniness and appearance, it is to be lauded. Where its energies are directed toward forms of withdrawal, irrational violence, and destruction, it is most dangerous, particularly when its manifestations show increasing brutality and can no longer be accepted as youthful larks.

Also seriously affecting the identification principle is the limitation inherent in the philosophy to which schoolmen by and large adhere. In America, no less than in other nations, schools are regarded, among other things, as instruments for perpetuating the prevailing form of government. In the United States, one might say, the objective is to discover means of relating the ideals of democracy to the amount of social cohesion that is necessary to realize their fulfillment.

With this objective I am in full agreement. It is when we examine what social cohesion means in terms of these ideals that I am in doubt. I question, in particular, the heavy emphasis placed on the teaching of "rational processes" as a means of achieving these ideals. The format, as we know, is usually one in which students, through the application of inquiry techniques, are encouraged to "make up their own minds" on matters involving social and moral issues. As a technique for teaching values, I find it difficult to accept on two counts. First, I question its effectiveness from a logi-

cal point of view. Second I view with considerable trepidation its implied dictum: *To follow wherever scientific intelligence may lead us.* I shall take up these matters point by point.

My first point involves the relationship of truth to behavior, or, more precisely, the demonstrated proof of a belief as a basis for behavior. Obviously, some beliefs are easy to prove; others are not. Let us take the democratic ideal, *the right of equality,* as an example of the latter. Now, it must be admitted that whatever value we attach to this ideal, it will stem primarily from our feelings regarding it rather than from any demonstrated proof that all men do in fact have this right. In point of fact, in any kind of moral reasoning, as in the making of moral judgments or decisions, the one question which must take precedence over all others is the ultimate question of our feelings about good or evil — whether a thing is right or wrong, good or bad. But many statements such as *the right of equality,* as one distinguished philosopher of logical analysis points out, are linguistic utterances having only an expressive function, not a representative one. They have no theoretical sense; they contain no knowledge; they can be proven neither true nor false.[9] This is what Joseph Wood Krutch meant when he said that science cannot prove that compassion is better than cruelty.[10] It is also what Bertrand Russell meant when he talked about "things which are legitimately matters of feeling" whose investigations lie outside the province of scientific method.[11] As feeling states (intellectualized to be sure) they cannot be rationally tested, except in relationship to other feeling states, which suffer from the same limitations.

Our feelings, in short, are central to the issue. Thus when hearing statements which attempt to equate moral reasoning ability with moral character, one doesn't know whether to laugh or cry. It is like saying that benevolent simpletons make wiser observations about moral principles than intelligent scoundrels.[12] I recommend that anyone suffering this delusion observe the psychopathic ward of any mental hospital.

The condition is a slippery one for the proponent of scientific methods, for there is nothing in his repertoire of techniques which enables him to cope with the central issue of value, which is feeling. Since he can only deal with data that can be proved or disproved, he must of necessity put all beliefs, either moral or intellectual, to the same test, without regard for the distinction that may greatly separate them. Finally, he must assume that children will automatically select what is demonstrably true over what is demonstrably false as a valid basis for behavior. Surely the most naive of all assumptions, it is tantamount to saying that when youth at last learns the truth about drugs, the problem will cease to exist.

Let us not delude ourselves. It is feeling, not reasoning, that keeps alive many of our most widely held moral beliefs and provides us with the motivation for following their precepts. An investigation may well reveal one of them as being deleterious in relationship to some other more fundamentally held value or social norm, but once this determination has been made, any attempt to induce new modes of behavior that does not utilize the emotional component as the primary anchor point in the learner's experience is by and large doomed to failure.

My second point concerns the grave danger I believe to be couched in a method of teaching that holds scientific intelligence as the chief arbiter of the decision-making process. Paradoxically, the sentiment expressed in the statement, *"to follow wherever scientific intelligence may lead us,"* is typically identified with many men who combine great powers of thought with deep moral insight. When we examine carefully the lives of such men, however, we often find a strange contradiction. Almost invariably their intellectual powers have been employed in the interests of promoting some profound moral outlook that suspiciously resembles an absolute. This assertion could be made of John Dewey no less than of Bertrand Russell. While such men would argue that action based on intelligence is better than action derived from simple moral conviction, they readily admit that unscrupulous men are often very intelligent. As leading advocates of scientific intelligence, they are in fact guilty of practicing what their formal systems of thought strongly disapprove: advancing arguments in terms of abiding moral reference points.

In the classroom, however, such practices by the teacher are viewed with reservation. Moral reference points are, after all, what they are – fixed beliefs strongly tinged with emotion – and therefore highly suspect. Thus, one day, after watching a fourth-grade teacher listen proudly while her youngsters ticked off documented reasons for our

Vietnam involvement, I inquired:

"What do you think of the decimation of whole villages, the mutilation of bodies, and mass killings?"

She was surprised. "I think it's horrible."

"Then why don't you tell them so, with all the passion you can muster? If they think well enough of you, they just might start believing as you do."

She still hesitated. "Yes, but you see, that's not the way inquiry is taught. . . ."

No, that was not the way inquiry is taught. The ideal teacher is one who never persuades but rather guides his students to sources of information that will substantiate or refute their own beliefs. The term currently used, I believe, is value clarification, a process by which students, using all sorts of knowledge for testing their values, are supposed to arrive at a new moral synthesis.

Whatever reservations I may hold regarding the possibility of such an occurrence, this is not intended as a condemnation of value clarification, which has its own purpose and need. On the contrary, I consider it a matter of utmost importance for a person to discover if his values are those of a scoundrel, a saint, or a homicide.

The question of who is or who isn't a homicide, for example, deserves a moment's comment, since it bears distinctly on the average teacher's ability to use the "process of reasoning" in his own private judgments on important moral issues. Within the meaning of the term I would include a majority of the public at large. My feelings that this might be true were first formed in the early years of the Vietnam war when any number of people I talked to assumed a strongly belligerent stance on policy questions about which they had only the foggiest information. I was dismayed, but not without hope. There were still the teachers, in whose hands the prospects of a more humane world were safely ensconced. Armed with the new techniques for discovering truth, they were the largest and best educated teacher group in the world.

Alas, I had reckoned without checking my facts. As I entered into conversations with these persons, I found many of them amazingly truculent and warlike. It was a great disappointment to learn that, in spite of their sophisticated arguments, they were no different from the others. In vain did I try to point out how incompatible was our moral position with the facts of our own historical development – arguments that were being brilliantly and movingly advanced

by Norman Cousins in the editorial pages of the *Saturday Review*. I had discovered a bitter truth: Teachers, like the rest of the people, are far more interested in exterminating their enemies than they are in the possibility of planetary extinction or of finding means of peaceful coexistence.

Even so, I should have been reluctant to take a public stand on this were it not for an incident that occurred several years later in which a large local branch of the National Education Association was asked to respond to the following resolution:

> Whereas the United States has been involved in Indochina for more than 20 years and whereas professional educators have a duty to voice their consciences concerning a terrible and unjust war, we . . . call for an immediate withdrawal of all United States personnel from Indochina. . . .

The resolution was turned down by a vote of five to two.[13]

Nowadays, of course, it has become fashionable to condemn the war on the ground that it was a gross blunder on the part of someone else. But whether or not this new outlook reflects any fundamental change of heart is a matter upon which I look with the greatest suspicion.*

I suppose my morality and the way I think morality ought to be taught in school is terribly old-fashioned, but it is difficult to have lived nearly 60 years without gaining some awareness of the cunning and rapacity of which men are capable in their determination to promote the good of mankind. Hence I tend to view civilization as a fragile veneer constantly in danger of being ripped away by the most carefully reasoned acts of violence. It is for these reasons that I find myself returning again and again to a consideration of the need for an inner discipline based on a few moral beliefs held in common by a great many men. Thus, in the interests of perpetuating democracy and its ideals, I see the school's major objective as one of combining children's need for a life of freedom with the amount of emotional conditioning that seems to me imperative to the maintenance of social stability.

I recognize that the word condi-

---

*Actually, I believe people become bored with an enemy whose lack of capability for retaliation ceases to arouse their desire to eliminate him.

tioning strikes terror in some hearts, for it smacks ominously of indoctrination. And there is indeed a sense in which conditioned allegiance to value is predominately absolute and irreversible. If the ego is involved, thus giving to allegiance a strong emotional component, it is especially imperious and demanding, a jealous mistress who brooks no trifling with the claims of rival beliefs. Even more unfortunate, the condition often poses at one and the same time the alternate paths of survival or annihilation. Few have pointed out more dramatically than Malinowski the survival value of taboo in primitive cultures where the social and economic life of the populace is reasonably stabilized. When stability is threatened, however, powerfully induced modes of behavior become virtual deathtraps which have rung the curtain down on more than one society, including many among our own Indian tribes.

I suppose that considerations like these have to some degree caused educators to look askance at all educational systems leading to rigid belief. Any system, however, that attempts to strike a compromise between the philosophies of unbridled freedom and totalitarianism must take a calculated risk, and I, for one, would rather see that risk taken on the side of what appears to me to be man's predominant genetic tendencies to behavior, namely, that he is primarily a creature of emotion, that his adherence to reason in the role of decision making is more figment than fact, and that his philosophies are far more the product of his ego needs than his ego needs are the image of his philosophies. What powers of reason he does possess, however, are among his most unique attributes and are not to be underestimated. But unless he is taught early in life to use these powers in support of a few strongly conditioned attitudes and beliefs to which all men can accede, his presence on earth will continue to grow steadily more uncertain.

Educationally speaking, the one — and perhaps only — avenue left open to him is narrow but fairly well defined. It must incorporate the primary socializing principle by which all humans are made more humane. In previous articles* I have tried to show how this may be in part achieved when teachers adopt the role of social critic and become adept in the art of dramatizing materials in

terms of social and moral conflict. Now I should like to consider briefly what Rosenthal (*Pygmalion in the Classroom*) has called the "untrained educational style" and its possible effect on the lives of very young children.

The notion deserves a moment's comment. Surely one of the grim aspects in American society, which we have already noted and to which we may no longer close our eyes, is the frightening list of deviant adolescent behaviors reflected by a growing alienation between adult and child. While rebellion against adult standards has always characterized youth, it is also true that there must be maintained between generations a baseline of mutual respect, communication, and agreement on some very fundamental ways of thinking and acting if social stability is not to be seriously impaired.

Are some teachers in fact instrumental in maintaining and perpetuating this baseline? The pre-school environment is unquestionably the single most influential factor in developing it. Nevertheless, there is good reason to believe that certain teachers also may be affecting it constructively, at least in part. Evidence of this is logically implied in Bronfenbrenner's analysis of the Soviet child's upbringing[14] and in Bandura's extensive explorations into modeling.[15] An experimental search for this teacher seems to me one among several of the highest priorities to which educators may address themselves.

The concept of single and multiple modeling itself demands equal attention, for it utilizes identification as its key operating principle. Bronfenbrenner, in particular, is convinced that modeling carries provocative implications for educational and social programs. In the relationship between teacher and child, he rates *teacher status* as the most essential quality. Indeed, in order for the "teacher . . . to function as an effective model and reinforcer, she must possess the characteristics which we have identified as enhancing inductive power; that is, she must be perceived by pupils as a person of status who has control over resources. . . ."[16]

Whether or not Bronfenbrenner's choice of catalyst (teacher status) is the correct one remains to be seen. However, in the current frantic search for expertise in behavioral objectives, performance criteria, and other related materials, the concept of modeling strikes me as the most fruitful and significant approach to make its appearance within the past decade. Apart

from experimentation with drugs, sleep therapy, hypnosis, or forms of medical and biological intervention, I can envision little else that would make a real difference.

The fact remains that in the realm of attitudes and values we find ourselves in a quicksand world where good or evil so often hinges on mere impulse, right or wrong on simple conviction, and truth or falsehood on the heart's desire. As inadequate for making judgments as these criteria may be, we cannot entirely escape them. Because so much of our "rational thought" is dominated by our past emotional conditioning, our only hope, as I see it, is that we learn to reverse this blind process by deliberately inculcating our very young children with a few attitudes calculated to ensure a more humane utilization of reason in the pursuit of ideals consistent with happiness and survival. The greatest of all ironies might well turn out to be simply this: The *modus operandi* which at one time or another enslaved so much of the world is the only one that can free it.

1. Erik H. Erikson, *Childhood and Society*. New York: W. W. Norton, 1963, pp. 247-51.
2. Henry W. Maier, *Three Theories of Child Development*. New York: Harper & Row, 1969, pp. 212-24.
3. Urie Bronfenbrenner, "Freudian Theories of Identification and Their Derivatives," *Child Development*, 1960, pp. 15-40.
4. Robert R. Sears, "Identification as a Form of Behavior Development," in *The Concept of Development*, D. B. Harris, editor. Minneapolis: University of Minnesota Press, 1957, pp. 149-61.
5. Bruno Bettelheim, *The Empty Fortress*. New York: The Free Press, 1967, p. 231.
6. Maier, *op. cit.*, pp. 188-226.
7. Urie Bronfenbrenner, *Two Worlds of Childhood*. New York: Russell Sage Foundation, 1970, pp. 95-119.
8. *Ibid.*, pp. 95-99.
9. Rudolph Carnap in *The Age of Analysis*, Morton White, editor. New York: Mentor Books, 1961, pp. 203-25.
10. Joseph Wood Krutch, "A Humanist's Approach," *Phi Delta Kappan*, March, 1970, p. 378.
11. Bertrand Russell, *A History of Western Philosophy*. New York: Simon and Schuster, 1945, p. 834.
12. This is in large part the major argument of the Committee on Religious Education in the Public Schools of the Province of Ontario, Canada. See pp. 41-70 in their publication titled *Religious Information and Moral Development*, 1969.
13. *Bellevue American*, Bellevue, Wash., p. 1.
14. Bronfenbrenner, *op. cit.*, pp. 70-91.
15. Albert Bandura, in *The Young Child: Reviews of Research*, Willard W. Hartup and Nancy L. Smothergill, editors. Washington, D.C.: National Association for the Education of Young Children, 1970, pp. 42-59.
16. Bronfenbrenner, *op. cit.*, p. 154. □

---

*See Joseph Junell, "Can Our Schools Teach Moral Commitment?," *Phi Delta Kappan*, April, 1969, pp. 446-51; "Is Rational Man Our First Priority?," *Phi Delta Kappan*, November, 1970; and others.

Emotional Barriers to Education

By Richard E. Farson

TOMORROW'S WORLD, with the push-button machine replacing the button-down mind, will be automated, calibrated, and cybernated—and yet I believe that the ultimate in mechanization will make us more human. The lines will be clear—what man is for and what machines are for—and we will value each other for our humanness rather than because we are "useful" and "productive."

We all know that the 21st century will be technologically different from this one. We have been told about space exploration and sea-farming, about computerized kitchens and waterless bathing. What we do *not* know is that people themselves will change, too. Their goals will be to develop uniquely human capacities to the fullest—capacities for love, creativity, joy, sensory and esthetic appreciation, and interpersonal skills, for continuing growth along every dimension, not only the cognitive.

Our educational system, then, will face a new set of human values as well as a new technology. If it is to be ready, we must change not only our educational *methods*—that is hard enough—but our basic *concepts* of education. That is far more difficult.

Neither the goals of education, the curriculum, nor classroom instructional methods have changed in any fundamental way for generations. Yet there are, in abundance, fresh, creative, and workable ideas that could revolutionize education almost overnight. Educators, behavioral scientists, teachers, and students already know a lot about how to create a favorable climate for learning. In part, we have been prevented by political, social, and economic obstacles from putting our knowledge to use. Equally frustrating are psychological barriers to change, which too often go unrecognized. Fortunately, though, psychological barriers sometimes topple when we do no more than point a finger at them. So I want first to discuss some of these psychological barriers, and then to talk about new ways for bringing about change.

Pointing The Finger

One of the most difficult barriers to overcome is the notion that education should be irksome. "You can't get something for nothing" is the motto which governs our view of learning. Somehow, we feel that if learning is exciting, fun, easy, then it can't be "educational."

Another barrier is what might be called our allegiance to the accustomed. We try to create conditions which are familiar to us, to change a strange situation until it resembles what we are used to. So no matter how wretched our school experience may have been, when we set about designing a learning environment for our children, we make it as similar as possible to what we knew. We may accept a new idea, but then we proceed to take the newness out of it. For example, we accept the idea that letter grades are bad, but we replace them with nothing more radical than their verbal equivalents—"satisfactory for grade level," "above grade level."

We feel the same way about the content of education. Education as we knew it was a dignified and formal process of transmitting information, imparting facts, stimulating the higher mental processes, and providing techniques for analyzing and solving intellectual puzzles. So today we apply the term "education" only to those activities which seem to involve "thinking." Developing the other dimensions of humanness—awakening the senses, recognizing feelings and emotions, deepening esthetic sensitivity, acquiring taste and judgment, and expanding skills in the vast area of human relations—this seems to us only to be "doing what comes naturally" and therefore not within the province of education.

Pandora's Box

At present noncognitive and nonverbal skills just aren't considered academically respectable. They have not yet been formulated into a conceptual structure; and they seem imprecise, fuzzy, vague, and even threatening. We feel we must keep the lid tightly closed on Pandora's box, for we fear that it contains the irrational, the potentially explosive elements of human nature.

When emotionality or interpersonal relationships escape from the box, we flinch and take refuge in the dictum that only the qualified professional is capable of dealing with the layers of humanness below the rational. Old-fashioned psychiatry is largely responsible for the prevailing attitude that teachers should avoid tampering with children's psyches. This nonsense has so frightened teachers that they shun almost any engagement with the student as a person.

We treat each other as if we were very fragile, as if any hurt or penetration of our defenses would lead to a crumbling of the entire person; or we regard each other as a tenuously contrived set of social roles which serves to cover what might be the frightening reality—a vicious beast, or at best man's "animal nature."

There is no doubt that educating for humanness will call upon teachers and students to encounter each other in their totality as human beings, with all of the problems and possibilities, the hopes and fears, the angers and joys, that make up a person. To relate to each other in this way, we will have to learn to be less afraid of what people are like and to recognize that they are not likely to shatter the moment anyone engages them on an emotional level.

This fear of emotionality is in part, I think, responsible for our widespread fear of intimacy. We dare not reveal ourselves, share our feelings. We have developed an elaborate set of social devices which allows us to put distance between ourselves and others, which lubricates our relationships, and which gives us privacy in a crowded and complex society. Even to use such terms as "intimate" or "loving" disturbs most people. Popular belief and much professional opinion hold that the machinery of any social organization, and certainly of a school, will become clogged if people are concerned with each other instead of tending to business. Nevertheless, we have a deep need for moments of shared feeling, for they give us a sense of community and remind us of our membership in the human race.

"Don't Rock The Boat"

Increasingly in the last few years, most of us who are concerned with education have discoursed on ways of fostering creativity in the classroom. We talk as if it were difficult to identify creativity in people and even more difficult to liberate it. But it is just the other way around. The potential for creativity exists in almost everyone, and it is easy to liberate. The trouble is that, although we want creativity, we want it only in manageable amounts—because its offspring, innovation, rocks the boat. So the only creativity we tolerate in school is the kind which follows the rules, pleases teachers and parents, and isn't noisy.

Another barrier to change is that many of us secretly enjoy viewing with alarm. We *like* to be mad at something or somebody; it is exhilarating, a safety valve for our frustrations, perhaps. But unfortunately the expression of outrage is often sufficient. We don't really care whether the situation is rectified—indeed, we often are disappointed if it is.

One of the great paradoxes of change —and perhaps one of the most important reasons that organizations and institutions resist change—is that the inevitable consequence of improvement is discontent. When things get better, we ask "Why stop here?" The higher we climb, the wider the vista before us; we see the discrepancy between what we have and what we now see it might be possible to have. The urgent need for educational change is itself an illustration of this paradox. The enormous advances in technology, which so radically have improved the material aspects of American life, demand that the methods and goals of education be changed to meet newer and higher needs. As Abraham Maslow, the president of The American Psychological Association, has put it, when our grumbles result in improved conditions, we get "meta-grumbles."

But social institutions do change, even if they fail to keep up with the changes in science and technology. How are the barriers overcome? In education, as in other fields, most innovation will be brought about by invasion from without and by rebellion from within.

Technology—Hardware

One wave of invasion already has begun: an overwhelming technological revolution is under way in the education industry. Its impact will be monumental, and I say this with all due respect for the ability of the educational enterprise to resist technological changes. It is significant that the greatest resistance comes less from parents than from teachers. One might suppose that teachers would welcome relief from routine tasks which better can be accomplished by machines, but this does not seem to be the case. No matter how serious the shortage of personnel, no teacher is immune to fear of being replaced by a machine. Seldom do teachers see the machine as an assistant, and perhaps they are right.

For although machines can relieve the teacher of burdensome detail, they will change enormously the teacher's role vis-a-vis the students. And very likely this new role will at first seem far more complex and demanding, though actually it may turn out to be simpler and far more joyful. Teachers have chafed under the record-keeping, evaluation-oriented tasks of present day schools, but I suspect that most teachers would have mixed feelings about interacting with their students in real person-to-person relationships, unprotected by the buffer of these tasks and roles.

In the last few years, scores of major American business firms have moved into the great new "people" industries— health, education, welfare, recreation, and entertainment. This shift from the production of goods to the provision of services is significant for both public and private educational systems because it is these systems that will have to furnish the manpower for the people industry. The schools will have to educate for new qualities—they will have to produce people who are suited for human service. The task will be as different from the present one as educating graduates for the automobile industry is different from preparing people for the Peace Corps.

The human service industries are already big business; well over 150 major American firms recently have moved into the educational business. They and other organizations will invent, produce, and sell more sophisticated, effective devices for teaching that inevitably will transform education. They plan only to *service* education. It may be that soon they will try to *replace* the present educational system with something quite different.

At present, only about half a billion dollars are spent by educational systems for discretionary purchases, so the market for educational services that might be provided by American industry is not very large. Industry might try to enlarge it by developing demand outside the schools—or by moving into school systems in somewhat the same way that certain large firms have taken over the organization, management, and operation of some Job Corps centers.

Technology—Social

The new technology does not consist solely of audio-visual aids, computers, and programmed instruction. One of the most important resources for change— perhaps the most important of all—is the new social technology, which enables us to use social processes to change a social system so that it becomes freer, more flexible, and more responsive to the needs and goals of all its members.

One of these new social technologies is known as "systems engineering." The most popular new word in education—as in almost every other field—is "systems." Its wide and often inappropriate usage may obscure the subtle revolution that is being put in motion by the application of systems engineering to education.

In its simplest terms, systems engineering is the application of common-sense analysis to a large and complex organization. It means looking at the overall picture, trying to understand the informal as well as the formal ways the organization functions, its implicit as well as its explicit goals. To understand the operation of an educational system, assessment of the physical facilities would be only the first step; one would need to analyze not only the activities and goals of students, teachers, administrators, parents, and school-board members, but the activities and goals of all the systems that articulate with the educational system, to see what bearing they have on its operation.

Systems analysis forces an organization to clarify its real goals; it studies what people really do and really need; and it provides the means for confronting people with rapid feedback on the effects of their action. Finally, it capitalizes on the fact that almost any well-intended disruption of a given system seems to produce a reintegration of the system at a somewhat higher level. Apparently, there are reliable forces toward growth and integration in any organization if some means can be found for releasing them.

Another social technology which is becoming increasingly familiar under a variety of names, is the "intensive small group," "T-group," "sensitivity-training group" or "human-relation group." After a slow start, the use of the small group now is spreading with astonishing rapidity through all the institutions of society —schools, churches, industries, business organizations—to promote personal growth and organizational effectiveness.

At the Western Behavioral Sciences Institute, we have done research on such groups in a variety of settings. Currently, a parochial school system which embraces all levels of education from kindergarten through college is cooperating with Carl Rogers of WBSI, who explains that he wants to learn whether involving all members of the system in the intensive group experience will "create a climate conducive to personal growth in which innovation is not frightening, in which the creative capacities of administrators, teachers, and students are nourished and expressed rather than stifled. (For) educators themselves must be open and flexible, effectively involved in the processes of change. They must be able both to conserve and convey the essential knowledge and values of the past, and to welcome eagerly the innovations which are necessary to prepare for the unknown future."

Still a third new social technology, which has been co-opted from the re-search laboratory to the classroom, is the simulation exercise, or "educational game." Classroom use of simulations has received a great deal of attention recently, not because simulations offer a better way of teaching subject matter—they may not—but because they alter the social structure of the classroom—that is, the relation between teachers and students. The teacher who uses simulations is released from his traditional role as evaluator, content specialist, disciplinarian, and record keeper because the rules of the simulation require that the students themselves perform those functions. Freed of routine chores, the teacher can deal with deeper, more interesting individual learning problems arising during and after the simulation exercise.

At WBSI, Hall Sprague has developed and tested a variety of simulation games in which students represent decision-makers in business and in national and international politics. On the basis of his experiences, Sprague says that simulations "may lead students to more sophisticated and relevant inquiry, may help them learn such nonacademic skills as decision-making, communication, and influence-resisting, and may integrate the subject matter and make it seem more realistic and relevant. They also may produce a more relaxed atmosphere between teacher and students later on."

Educational games now are being used to teach concepts of international relations, national politics, community leadership, business decision-making, home management, career planning, and the like, but there is no limit to the subjects that might be learned through simulation. We presently are developing a game which will confront a school system with probable changes in its future so that all the members of the system may simulate responses to these events. As a result of playing the game, they will be developing a long-range plan—inventing their future, if you will.

Rebellion From Within

It is almost impossible nowadays to pick up a magazine or a newspaper without encountering some reference to the "student revolt" or the revolt of youth embodied in the Hippie movement, the New Left, or the war- and draft-resisters. These rebellious young people are telling us, in the words of their own poet, Bob Dylan, that "The times, they are a-changin'." And these youths are, in effect, joining forces in an attempt to create a new kind of society which will fulfill a new set of demands—their right to be fully human, to be honest, to be themselves, to create their own experiences and to discover new experiences, and to control their own lives.

Perhaps on the whole, these young people know more than we adults do about what life in the 21st century will be like, because I think they are shaping it now. They are demanding the right to have a voice in the decisions which affect them. They take education more seriously than we do, for they are saying in countless ways, "We refuse an education that merely prepares us for a place in this impersonal machine which our society has become. We refuse to be 'taught' only what you think we ought or need to know; we demand the right to learn everything we can about the things that really matter."

In "New Schools" and "Free Universities," on and off the campus, they are re-creating, in a sense, the medieval university, in which the students decided what they wanted to learn, and hired and fired the scholars who taught them. And the young rebels are being joined by a few professors, teachers, parents, counselors, and even administrators who equally constitute a powerful force for change from within. We already are beginning to see major shifts in educational practices at the college and university level, where revolutionary experiments in student-oriented and student-determined education are being permitted.

"Underground" newspapers, published by bright young high-school and even junior high-school students are causing ripples in supervisory circles. One high-school "underground" editor reports spending half his time in the Vice Principal's office: "He wants to explain to me all the reasons for his decisions, before they are announced to the students." This is hopeful. Last year, author Lyn Tornabene posed as a high-school student to research what she planned as a funny book. She got by successfully with her masquerade, but she found only miserable students in boring courses. Her book was *not* funny.

Education in the 21st century will be a lifelong, richly rewarding experience, engaged in because it is fun, joyful, deeply involving. It will be designed to expand and enrich all aspects of human experience—sensory, emotional, and esthetic, as well as intellectual—and to liberate creativity in all these realms.

And people will be declaring, as they are today, that education isn't nearly as good as it could be, and that something will have to be done about it. ∎

AFFECT AND COGNITION:

A Reciprocal Relationship

IRA J. GORDON

COGNITIVE psychologists have been fond of quoting Piaget as a major source of our ideas about how intellectual development occurs. We have been busy attempting to engineer this profound developmental theory into an instructional theory. We have, however, focused on only some aspects of the theory, and have usually singled out the classes of behaviors, such as conservation, which mark transitions from stage to stage, as the basis for curriculum innovation.

Piaget's new book (Piaget and Inhelder, 1969) may come as a surprise to those of us who have had such tunnel vision. The dichotomy between cognition and affect is destroyed in such statements as, "There is no behavior pattern, however intellectual, which does not involve affective factors as motives. . . . Behavior is therefore of a piece. . . . The two aspects, affective and cognitive, are at the same time inseparable and irreducible" (p. 158). I see (with the affective components of joy, excitement, and relief) that Piaget depicts a fully integrated developing child. He helps us get out of our trap of cognition versus affect, and gives us the subject of this paper, affect implies cognition, cognition implies affect.

Many who were involved in education reform treated affect and cognition as though they were mutually exclusive territories of human behavior. The "new curricula" were seen by friend and foe as stressing cognition. The recommendations emerging from developmental psychologists and others concerned with the young child were assailed by early childhood educators because they were "cognitive."

Somehow cognition was viewed as cold, distant, mechanistic, and therefore "bad" by those who saw themselves as warm, loving, and accepting.

Correspondingly, "cognitive" people made equally nasty comments about those whom they saw as concerned "only" with the self-esteem and personal-social development of the child. In effect, this split destroyed what used to be a central notion in progressive education, the concept of the "whole" child. I should like to put the body back together again.

The Synthesis

The synthesis of affect and cognition is first demonstrated in the infancy period in the way the child relates to the objects and people in his environment. There is a very close connection between the discovery by the infant of the cognitive principle that objects have permanence and his affective ties to people who now begin to take on a life of their own (Guin-Decarie, 1965). The mother, for example, is an object who attains some permanence, is assigned a host of meanings, and influences the emergence of further object relations.

A special tie between affect and cognition exists in the development of language and symbolism. The years from two to six are the time in which the child, through fantasy, imagery, and the acquisition of language, all of which are cognitive tasks, learns to see himself as separate and unique and finds ways to cope with the conflicts that exist between his needs and the demands of the environment. In this effort, affect and cognition serve each other. The child uses language not only to communicate with those around him but also to enable him to comprehend what is happening, to role-play, to talk to himself, to think out loud. Language and thought processes develop from these efforts to assimilate and accommodate; the growth in turn creates new tensions which require further cognitive development.

The human being is a meaning-seeking animal and has strong needs to order and organize the environment so as to deal effectively with it. The child is constantly engaged in ordering and reordering his experience (Gordon, 1969). The existence of disequilibrium created from the transactional relationship between internal growth and external social pressures acts as a motivating force for development. "The formation of personality is dominated by the search for coherence" (Piaget and Inhelder, 1969, p. 158).

A product of this transactional process of inner ⟷ outer and, within the inner, affect ⟷ cognition, is the emergence of concepts of self, which are inseparable syntheses of cognition and affect, subject and object, actor and evaluator, internal and external. The child moves along the egocentric → decentered dimension as he grows in ability to reconcile the inner and external worlds. The growth of intelligence proceeds along this transactional exchange point. As the child incorporates aspects of the external world to fit his views, and as he changes some of his ideas and patterns because of his contacts with reality, he grows in competence and in self-esteem. He becomes more able to search for (and build) coherence.

This search goes on not only in the infancy and childhood periods, but also during adolescence when youngsters are able, because of their cognitive development, to examine their world through language and logical systems but are faced with the discrepancy between neat, intellectual propositions and disorderly patterns of social action which surround and overwhelm them. Their search for coherence is an affective search, which provides the motive power which can be used in schools for cognitive growth, provided the cognitive demands and tasks are so organized and instituted that they are seen by youth as relevant to their affective strivings.

At all ages, from birth to death, cognitive organization, development, and change are inspired and fed by a search for meaning which is affective. As cognitive development takes place, the person moves toward resolutions of states of disequilibrium, but each resolution, because of the cognitive element, is at a higher and more complex level of organization. Each resolution is thus both inseparably affective and cognitive.

Application to Education

So what? What does this contribute to school organization or teacher behavior? It means that a good classroom cannot be understood if we take apart these two elements and focus only on one. It means that any teaching act or learning behavior is an inextricable mix. It means that the child or learner is an active agent who will seek out, master, and devour intellectual activities when they are matched to his present resolution and so challenge him because they create some disequilibrium in his present system. As Don Snygg (1966) indicated, "The optimum level of difficulty is one which allows a student to win success after difficulty" (1966, p. 93).

What do we know about the "mix" in the classroom? *First*, data show relationships between affective climate and cognitive development. Soar (1967) showed that various patterns of teacher affective behaviors related differentially to pupil growth in reading and vocabulary. Schaefer's (1969) analysis revealed that maternal affective behavior at home was predictive of intellectual performance on the Stanford-Binet at age three. Children whose mothers were classified as "hostile—noninvolved" did poorest. What is striking is the close relationship between Soar's teacher dimensions and Shaefer's maternal dimensions. Adult behavior which was both aloof and hostile produced deleterious effects on cognitive learning in both home and classroom. If these studies had focused only on cognitive elements, they would not have yielded the information on adult affective behavior which relates highly to intellectual growth.

Second, data show the predictive relationship between self-esteem and attitudes toward self in relation to school (affective) and academic performance (cognitive). Wattenberg and Clifford (1962) and Lamy (1965) report that the best single predictor of beginning reading achievement in first grade was children's perceptions of self in kindergarten. The best single predictor of freshman grade point averages of black male junior college students was their perceptions of self in relation to teachers and school. Those favorably disposed to teachers and school tended to have higher grade point averages, regardless of achievement test scores, than those who did not have this view (Clarke, 1968).

Third, Sears and Sherman (1964) present a model depicting the linkages between affective and cognitive variables and demonstrate, through case studies, how these function in both directions.

Any way in which children learn a skill,

can demonstrate adequacy, or are treated as adequate in real-life settings has both affective as well as cognitive payoff. The entry point can be along either the affective or the cognitive dimension. Children are not easily fooled by phony situations. They learn best when learning is "real" and respects their integrity. Heightened arousal and affective drive for learning are most likely to occur when what is to be learned is interesting, exciting, worthwhile, and real, and provides the child with some measuring rods against which he can assess himself. Watch the concentration of a kindergartner doing a difficult jigsaw puzzle. Note his facial expression, note his body movements, and especially note the smile, the glee, the hand-clapping, the reward he gives his own performance when he succeeds. This is the mix.

If we can provide the high schooler with that intensity of experience in facing the social problems of his day, if we can approach the beginning reader in ways that create the same excitement, then the reciprocal relationship of affect and cognition will lead to effective learning. In these examples the learner is faced with something real outside himself to which he must accommodate, with which he must cope. This type of challenge stretches him and relates to Syngg's optimum level of difficulty. In this type of setting, possibilities and goals are unlimited and cognitive power enhanced. It does not stress affect as precursor of cognition nor does it stress a dry, intellectual, flat affect exercise. It is a far cry from turning inward or turning off; it capitalizes instead on the motive power of the learner's presently developed intellectual organization and his urge to comprehend his world.

The reciprocal relationship of affect and cognition requires the types of learning tasks in school which turn youngsters on and outward. Their minds can then expand from contact with the world, not from drugs. They go forward to the world; they do not retreat into themselves. To be competent is motive to behave competently. Knowing self and world heightens affect and creates that measure of discontent which, in turn, can spur us on to achieve our human potentialities.

References

J. R. Clarke. *Identification of Disadvantaged Junior College Students and Diagnosis of Their Disabilities.* Final Report, July 1968, St. Petersburg Junior College, Grant No. OEG-1-7-070020-3905, Project No. 7-D-020, U.S. Office of Education.

I. J. Gordon. *Human Development: From Birth Through Adolescence.* Second edition. New York: Harper & Row, Publishers, 1969.

T. Guin-Decarie. *Intelligence and Affectivity in Early Childhood.* Translated by Elizabeth and Lewis Brandt. New York: International Universities Press, Inc., 1965.

M. W. Lamy. "Relationship of Self-Perceptions of Early Primary Children to Achievement in Reading." In: I. J. Gordon, editor. *Human Development: Readings in Research.* Chicago: Scott, Foresman and Company, 1965. pp. 251-52.

J. Piaget and B. Inhelder. *The Psychology of the Child.* Translated by Helen Weaver. New York: Basic Books, Inc., Publishers, 1969.

E. Schaefer. "Home Tutoring, Maternal Behavior and Infant Intellectual Development." Paper presented at the meeting of the American Psychological Association, Washington, D.C., September 4, 1969.

P. Sears and V. Sherman. *In Pursuit of Self-Esteem.* Belmont, California: Wadsworth Publishing Company, Inc., 1964.

D. Snygg. "A Cognitive Field Theory of Learning." In: Walter Waetjen, editor. *Learning and Mental Health in the School.* 1966 Yearbook. Washington, D.C.: Association for Supervision and Curriculum Development, 1966. pp. 77-98.

R. S. Soar. "Optimum Teacher-Pupil Interaction for Pupil Growth." *Educational Leadership* 26 (3): 275-80; December 1967.

W. Wattenberg and C. Clifford. *Relationships of Self-Concept to Beginning Achievement in Reading.* Final Report, 1962, Wayne State University, C.R.P. No. 377, U.S. Office of Education. □

VII. TEACHER INFLUENCE

One longstanding concern of educational psychologists has been to measure the influence of teachers and their teaching behavior upon learners and their learning. The common sense of popular mass culture provides ambivalent and highly subjective answers to this question. Adult Americans often reminisce about their own recollected experiences in school. They tend to conclude that a few teachers influenced them significantly, while most had a negligible effect; nevertheless, they conclude that the overall experience of being taught was of great importance and they continue to prescribe it for their children. The task before educational psychologists has been to attempt to surmount the distortions of memory and subjective hindsight in an effort to gauge the effects of teaching upon learning.

A half century of inquiry culminated in the decade of the 1960's in a great debate over the issue which will very likely continue to rage for at least another ten years, if not longer. The cumulative empirical evidence obtained by educational and behavioral research has produced the generalization that, relative to other influences, classroom teaching has minor, often negligible effects upon learning. While schoolteaching is more influential than facilities, materials, or curricular methods, it is far less influential than family socialization, peer group relations, mass media communications, and work experiences. The influence varies, obviously, with *what* is being taught, and by whom.

The same half century of research evidence suggests with considerable consistency that what the learner brings with him or her into the learning situation is more influential than the effect of any type of teaching upon the learning outcome. Socioeconomic status, ethnicity, pre-school learning opportunities, and the combined effects of these factors upon the learner's view of self and his or her aspirations, tend to outweigh all classroom teaching influences of all twelve years of elementary and secondary schooling. A review of the famous study, *The Equality of Educational Opportunity*, is included in this section because it amplifies this point.

In addition, as Paul Kohn's article indicates, the research literature in educational psychology suggests that the teaching-learning *situation* itself is more influential than the formal and didactic content of instruction. The attitudinal expectations of teachers contribute to defining the situation in which learners learn. Teacher estimates of how well students should perform thus affect the conditions under which learning takes place.

The great debate about the implications of the findings of thousands of empirical studies centers on what to do next. Many teachers argue that the studies are theoretically misguided and methodologically invalid, that teacher influences are considerable but very hard to isolate for analysis. Some philosophers of education such as Ivan Illich, at the opposite extreme, have called for the abolition of schools and classroom teaching as we know them.

Others, as Howard Spicker's article in this section makes plain, have argued that effective teaching should be aimed at children between birth and age three, when more learning and cognitive development take place than in all other periods of the life cycle combined. By this logic, a society's ablest teachers would come to concentrate on infants, and the reward structure which today pays an infant educator in American $6,000 and a college educator $18,000 might have to be reversed. And others, represented in this section by Kim Marshall's article, would argue that educational psychologists have held a mirror up to the *status quo* in education; that what is needed are teaching behaviors that are not conventional but are designed to be influential—to have an impact upon learning. Here, the emphasis is upon inventing alternative strategies for teaching.

The great debate is far from concluded. All lines of inquiry and argument are still open, for the very idea of testing such a question about teaching is novel and wanting for public support. The United States government, for example, spends about five percent of its defense budget each year for weapons system research and development, while it spends about one half of one percent of its education budget on educational research and development.

While the debate rages, the impact of inconclusive knowledge is profound, however. Schoolteachers act daily from the premise that their influence is relatively influential. They expect to be able to control the learning situations they occupy. Yet, evidence to the contrary has become so widespread as to erode their authority. David Hawkins' article in this section, finally, suggests that we have yet to fathom the nature of the teaching act, and that when we do, we can begin to make it effective.

157

Equality of Educational Opportunity

by Robert A. Dentler

Science is more than a method and body of knowledge. It is also a way of asking questions, and the hallmark of good scientific inquiry is a substantial contribution to the economy of further research. *Equality of Educational Opportunity**, by James S. Coleman and associates, when judged by this standard, makes a contribution to the study of American intergroup relations second only to Myrdal's *American Dilemma*. More than this, though, when its full implications have been mined, *Equality of Educational Opportunity* will very likely become the single best empirical work in the American sociology of education.

Social scientists and educators who are heavily invested in the study and designing of school desegregation in Northern cities should be especially delighted with the *reductive* power of this monumental survey analysis. Certain important questions which are expensive to answer, in terms of ingenuity as well as money or time, have been answered here authoritatively. And among the essential researchable questions that remain, this study has reduced their scope considerably.

Several aspects of the Coleman Report seem to have obfuscated rapid reception of its message. The survey team's early difficulties in securing a representative sample were over-advertised among researchers: the fact that 30 percent of the schools selected for the survey did not participate became widely known. Somewhat neglected, however, was the fact that all district superintendents, principals, teachers and third, sixth, ninth, and twelfth-grade pupils in 4,000 schools, along with first graders in about 2,000 schools, did take part, and the fact that the estimates of both sampling and measurement reliability were extremely impressive. Then, too, the little summary of the analysis, which was separately printed as well as included in the chief publication, has been much more widely distributed and read, yet it contains only a handful of the essential implications to be found in the full monograph.

More crucially, many of the findings run contrary to the favorite assumptions of three of the most concerned audiences: militant school integrationists, militant school segregationists (along with their camp-following, the militant proponents of the neighborhood school), and the many professional educators who focus their efforts too exclusively upon school facilities, curriculum reform, and teacher training.

Many schoolmen and elective as well as appointed local, state, and federal officials have said that the statistical density of the report has prevented their understanding the findings. This will be remedied partly by time, as various reviewers and education writers translate the results, and partly by the discovery of readers who take the trouble to look between the tables and figures to discover that the verbal exposition is plain and stripped of educational or sociological jargon.

The aim of this review is to identify some of the questions I believe have been answered well enough to be set aside, and to suggest the lines of inquiry that ought to be emphasized strongly in all future research and planning on Northern urban school desegregation issues. I would emphasize, however, that

---

*Supt. of Documents, U.S. Government Printing Office, Washington, D.C., 20402. Catalogue No. FS 5.238:38001, 1966. $4.25. Correlations separately bound.

this is not a *technical* review.‡ Here, instead, let us accept the over-all relia-bility and validity of the research in a willing suspension of disbelief. Further, this discussion shall concentrate on findings concerning the metropolitan North.

The basic findings of the Coleman Report in this regard are these: in the metropolitan North Negro and Puerto Rican pupils, as compared to white pupils, attend school in older, larger, more crowded buildings. They have access to fewer laboratories and library books, auditoriums and gymnasiums. Their elementary teachers show a slightly lower score on a short vocabulary test. Even their cafeterias and athletic playing fields are in shorter supply.

Accelerated programs for rapid learners are typically more available to white than to Negro or Puerto Rican pupils, as are course opportunities for 12th graders to obtain advanced placement or college credit. Negro pupils on the average enjoy a greater advantage in but three respects: more of their teachers are Negroes, and more remedial and correctional programs and services are available in their schools.

What awaits the Northern metropolitan Negro or Puerto Rican learner, of course, complements what he brings with him to school as a burden of back-ground disadvantages. When this burden is joined with those of his peers, he *attends a school where his fellow students generally come from econom-ically poorer, less stable homes, which are more poorly equipped to give stimulation to the educational pursuits of the children. The families are larger, and less frequently have both real parents living at home; the par-ents' level of education is lower, and the homes more frequently lack modern conveniences and reading materials such as daily newspapers, encyclopedias and home libraries.* Of all the characteristics of schools which distinguish the education being provided the average white and Negro students, it is the environment provided by the fellow students where the differences are most dramatic [emphasis mine].

These findings confirm authoritatively dozens of much smaller studies con-ducted during the late nineteen fifties and early sixties in dozens of individual cities and suburbs throughout the Northeast. Here, however, the Coleman Report clears the deck and allows the research to get on with what is less obvious. The Coleman data are comprehensive enough and the findings dis-tinct enough to release us from endless cycling on questions of equality of public educational services. *Facilities, staffs, and services are distributed un-equally.* Without exception, on the factors catalogued, the pattern of the in-equality uniformly reinforces handicaps brought to the school by the low-income, minority-group learner. If further studies must be carried out on these surface factors, let them be done against norms struck in the Coleman Report: how much, and in what particulars, does a school district depart from the unequal distribution common to the northeastern metropolitan re-gion as a whole? How much better are the facilities and services provided for the whites within a given city or suburban district, when contrasted with those of the region as a whole? The basis for settling this general question or for enlarging its meaning through comparison is now at hand.

‡*There are significant innovations as well as difficulties in the techniques of analysis used in the Coleman Report. The URBAN REVIEW will carry a technical review in a subsequent issue.*

The same economy of future effort is made possible by the definitiveness of the Coleman Report on the over-all differences in achievement between white, Puerto Rican, and Negro students in the metropolitan Northeast. The mean grade levels on three tests of each of these groups can be summarized as follows:

Test	Group	6th Grade	9th Grade	12th Grade
Verbal Ability	White	6	9	12
	Puerto Rican*	3.3	6.1	8.4
	Negro	4.4	6.6	8.7
Reading Comprehension	White	6	9	12
	Puerto Rican	2.9	5.7	8.3
	Negro	4.2	6.4	9.1
Mathematics	White	6	9	12
	Puerto Rican	3.2	5.6	7.2
	Negro	4	6.2	6.8

Obviously, the achievement differences between whites, on the one hand, and Negroes and Puerto Ricans, on the other, are very great. At grade 6, the average Negro in this region is more than 1¾ years behind the average white in reading comprehension. At grade 9, he is more than 2½ years behind that of the average white. And, at grade 12, he is nearly 3 years behind. The record of Puerto Rican performance is even poorer than that of Negroes, except at one point: 12th grade mathematics.

Obviously, too, something happens over the school years that widens the gap in achievement between whites and the two minority groups. In no instance is the initial gap narrowed rather than widened as a result of intervening educational experiences. Thus, the disadvantage with which Negro and Puerto Rican students begin school remains with them when they finish high school. No doubt, certain students manage to overcome initial handicaps, but their gains are swamped statistically by the cumulative retardation of the great majority.

Similarities and differences between the three groups in the Northeast metropolitan region on attitudes, aspirations, and future plans are also portrayed in the Coleman Report. Below is a summary of the principal findings:

Puerto Rican means are for entire sample, which includes other regions. But the sample, like the population itself, is heavily concentrated in the metropolitan Northeast.

Question and Response	12th-Grade Percentage Distribution		
	White	Negro	Puerto Rican*
If something happened and you had to stop school now, how would you feel? "Would do almost anything to stay."	47	47	35
How good a student do you want to be? "One of the best students."	36	48	36
How much time do you spend on an average school day studying outside of school? (Sum of 2 hour & 3 hour replies.)	44	45	32
About how many days did you stay away from school last year just because you did not want to come? "None."	61	68	53

How many books did you read during the Summer of 1965? *"One to five books."*	50	47	39
How far do you want to go in school? *All responses for beyond high school.*	86	86	67
Do you plan to go to college next year? *"Definitely yes."*	46	31	26
Have you ever read a college catalog? *"Yes."*	73	59	45
Have you ever written to or talked to a college official about going to college? *"Yes."*	46	32	25
What type of job do you think you will have when you finish your education? *"Professional or technical."*	53	39	28

Puerto Ricans not restricted to Northeast.

On attitudes toward school and academic work generally, differences between whites and Negroes in this region are negligible. Only when it comes to matters of firm steps toward college do the proportions of Negro students fall notably below the characteristics common to whites. Puerto Rican students, in contrast, present differences in all areas. They display lower aspirations, do less reading, and are much less likely to be taking steps to continue their schooling beyond high school.

Both minority groups, however, depart substantially from the favored white group on Coleman's three indicators of the student's sense of control over his environment. This is a central point.

	Northeastern Metropolitan		
Percent Who Agree That:	*White*	*Negro*	*Puerto Rican**
Good luck is more important than hard work for success.	4	9	19
Every time I try to get ahead, something or somebody stops me.	13	21	30
People like me don't have much of a chance to be successful in life.	5	12	19

Puerto Ricans not restricted to Northeast.

There is an objective basis for these differences, Coleman asserts: "Minority children have less chance to control their environment than do the majority whites." Coleman goes on to demonstrate the relation between feelings of control and individual achievement, when other background differences have been held constant and concludes: "Of all the variables measured in the survey, including all measures of family background and all school variables, these attitudes showed the strongest relation to achievement, at all three grade levels (6th, 9th, and 12th)....These attitudinal variables account for more of the variation in achievement than any other set of variables (all family background variables together, or all school variables together). When added to any other set of variables, they increase the accounted for variation more than does any other set of variables." Further, among the attitude items used in the correlation analyses, none was more firmly associated with achievement than the three indicators of a sense of control over one's environment.

This association is *not*, at least for minority groups, a by-product of the natural relation between achievement and a student's subjective assessment of his school abilities, or his feelings about his life chances. It is rather that "for children from disadvantaged groups, achievement...appears closely related to what they believe about their environment: whether they believe the environment will respond to reasonable efforts, or whether they believe it is instead merely random or immovable."

Very little educational research and development work is currently aimed specifically at these student attitudes, although they are generally well understood by teachers. But, when one considers the range of factors that matter *very little* by comparison, and on which most of our efforts at reconstruction in the research and development tradition are based, the ironies are noteworthy.

For instance, the Coleman Report documents a long-respected generalization in the sociology of education as it has never been so solidly documented before:

"School to school variations in achievement, from whatever source (community differences, variations in the average home background of the student body, or variations in school factors), are much smaller than individual variations within the school, at all grade levels, for all racial and ethnic groups....Over 70 percent of the variation in achievement...is variation within the same student body." Indeed, when the analysis is restricted to differences in achievement between Negroes and whites, "Only about 10 to 20 percent of the total variation in achievement for the groups that are numerically most important lies between different schools."

In case the point is not as clear as it ought to be: "Our schools have great uniformity insofar as their effect on the learning of pupils is concerned....Variations in school quality are not highly related to variations in achievement of pupils."

This principle is counterbalanced solely by the qualification that Negro and Puerto Rican students in the North are more sensitive (that is, more responsive) to differences in quality from school to school than are whites. The percentage of the difference in individual verbal achievement scores that can be accounted for by differences between schools is summarized below as evidence of this qualification:

Verbal Achievements: Group	Percent of Total Variance by Grade Level				
	1st	3rd	6th	9th	12th
Whites, North	11.1	11.4	10.3	8.7	7.8
Negroes, North	10.6	19.5	13.9	12.7	10.9
Puerto Ricans	16.7	26.6	31.3	21.0	22.3

Let us explore in more detail what factors *do* affect achievement before summarizing what Coleman reveals as being of little or no significance. We have emphasized the importance of student attitudes, particularly the part played by the learner's sense of control over his environment. Two other rather classic sociological variables—family socioeconomic status and aggregate socioeconomic status of the student's classroom peers—are also shown to be critically related to academic ability.

The Coleman Report, it should be said, nowhere discusses social status with the forthrightness that it uses in the analysis of ethnic groups. But its indicators of "family background" are impressively comprehensive. Objective items include urbanism of background, migration, parents' educational attainment, structural integrity of the home, size of family, the presence of selected items in the home (e.g., TV, telephone, record player, refrigerator, automobile, vacuum cleaner), and reading material in the home. Subjective items include parents' interest in the child's schooling and parents' educational desires for their children.

When between-school and within-school differences are considered together, the family background and attitudes account for 35.7 per cent of these differences among sixth grade Northern whites, 26.4 per cent among sixth grade Northern Negroes, and 40.3 per cent among sixth grade Puerto Ricans. Because the accounted for differences decline from the sixth to 12th grade, Coleman concludes that "the family's impact on the child has its greatest effect in earliest years, so that family-to-family differences in achievement...decline after the beginning of school." The impact of differences in the socioeconomic status of the family on the school performance of children is, if anything, *understated* in the Coleman Report. For the influence of this variable is exceeded only by students' own attitudes toward their life chances, attitudes which are themselves highly associated with background differences. In other words, the degree to which a learner believes himself to be in control of his fate is very likely to be a function of his understanding—conscious or unconscious, realistic or unrealistic—of his socioeconomic place in life.

The backgrounds and attitudes of peers also strongly affect school achievement. Coleman notes: "Attributes of other students account for far more variation in the achievement of minority group children than do any attributes of school facilities and slightly more than do attributes of staff." Individual achievement is facilitated when a student attends school with peers who are socioeconomically advantaged, whose parents are more interested in school success, and whose mobility is low. Achievement is dampened for students whose classmates are relatively more disadvantaged, whose parents are less interested, and whose movement from school to school or community to community is high. Moreover, Negro and Puerto Rican students are more affected than Northern whites by this peer influence.

Of equal interest are factors that contribute only negligibly to explaining achievement differences. For example: "Contrary to much that has been written, the structural integrity of the home (principally the father's presence or absence) shows very little relation to achievement for Negroes." In grades one and three, neither school characteristics nor student body composition contributes much to explaining variations in achievement. Also intriguing is the fact that Coleman dropped class size or pupil/teacher ratio from the multivariate analysis because "it showed a consistent lack of relation to achievement among all groups under all conditions." Thus, while class size is important to the well being of the teacher, its direct significance for student achievement remains questionable.

But then questions which rage most enduringly among schoolmen and women fare rather poorly at all points in the Coleman Report. The following table summarizes the differences in verbal achievement accounted for by teacher characteristics, as against school variables and student environment or peer composition:

Group	Teacher	Grade 12 School	Students	Teacher	Grade 6 School	Students
Whites, North	1.9	3.2	3.8	1.7	2.0	4.8
Negroes, North	4.3	6.7	8.9	2.2	2.7	4.9
Puerto Ricans	18.4	20.0	26.4	8.1	10.8	13.9

The school factor includes per pupil expenditures on staff, volumes per student in library, science laboratory facilities, extracurricular activities, size, school location, and several indicators of quality of curriculum. The relative *unimportance* of these factors can be shown when the total variance accounted for by facilities and curricular measures for 12th grade Northern Negroes is shown as 3.1 per cent, if student background is held constant. For sixth grade Northern Negroes, it is .77 per cent, and for sixth grade Northern whites, .32 per cent.

Teacher characteristics were more influential in explaining variations in verbal achievement than were factors of facilities and curriculum. But when considered alone they were discouragingly limited in effect. Even when background factors were controlled (as in the summary table above), teacher characteristics were second in strength of influence to student peer characteristics. Teacher differences made about a 2 per cent contribution for sixth grade Northern whites and Negroes, but contributed more for Puerto Ricans (8.1 per cent).

Among the teacher characteristics that showed most marked association with pupil verbal achievement, and which became part of the Coleman index, were educational attainment of the teacher's mother (and her socioeconomic status), years of teaching experience, localism of the teacher, educational attainment of the teachers themselves, vocabulary test scores, teacher's preference for teaching middle class and white collar students, and proportion of teachers who were white. The index is an aggregate and so does not allow for analysis below the level of school-to-school differences.

Teachers, then, do influence achievement, but slightly. Moreover, "Good teachers matter more for children from minority groups." For children who enter school with background advantages or who attend schools filled with advantaged peers, teacher quality is of much less importance in predicting pupil achievement. And limited as is the overall influence of teacher characteristics, the influence is cumulative in effect over the years in school. It appears to be very small initially and then expands notably between ninth and 12th grade.

One of the central implications for Northern urban school desegregation that arises from the Coleman Report may now be understood in its full complexity: What the child brings with him to school as strengths or weaknesses determined by his social class is the prime correlate of school achievement. It is influenced—offset or reinforced—most substantially not by facilities, curriculum, or teachers but by what other pupils bring with *them* as class-shaped interests and abilities. In practical terms, as the proportion of white pupils increases in a school, achievement among Negroes and Puerto Ricans increases because of the association between white ethnicity and socioeconomic advantage.

It should be said that while the peer influence *may* increase the minority child's sense of control over his environment, it *may* also decrease his self-concept. There likely are probable costs as well as benefits for achievement involved in desegregation. But the Coleman Report makes crystal clear that *desegregation does affect factors of immediate relevance to student achievement*. These factors are: individual academic motivation and peer environment.

Further implications may include the suggestion that changes in student composition have little direct bearing upon the achievement of Northern urban *white* students (save that through intergroup contact, if properly treated by the school and community, they may become better citizens, matters that are not dealt with in the Coleman Report). These majority group students achieve more or less well because of what they bring with them to school from their homes. Negro and Puerto Rican students, however, can gain from positive changes at nearly all points: improved peer environment, improved levels of interest that spring from peer influences, better teaching, facilities, and curricula. As the case studies in the Coleman Report suggest, minority group children can gain in achievement to the extent that the desegregation plan is deliberately executed to accomplish that objective.

What are we left with, then, as important unanswered questions? We are more certain than ever that the peer environment, including racial mix, is a social determinant of school achievement, but we know very little about the particulars of this environment in the elementary or junior high school. What blend of social heterogeneity is optimal under what conditions of age, past school experience, and so forth? If we can answer this through field research, how can the results be translated into school districting, zoning, and grouping practices? Schoolmen have long given detailed attention to arranging peer environments. When some of their traditional practices, e.g., in segregating pupils racially or economically, are called sharply into question through research, what feasible alternatives can we suggest? Desegregation procedures can prove as indiscriminate and thus unhelpful for learners as segregation has proved to be harmful for learning. Mere gross ethnic balancing will hardly speak to this question, vital as it may be as a start.

We need to know much more, as well, about the nature of changes in achievement on the one hand and attitudes and peer relations on the other *over time*. What handful of pupils exhibit achievement gains somewhat independent of social context? At what strategic points in the process of cumulative retardation among urban Negro and Puerto Rican learners would intervention or school reform prove truly influential? Panel surveys and longitudinal studies of whole school districts and communities are among the inquiries that are needed most if processes of change are to be identified.

In connection with both peer environments and changes in school achievement over time, we need to confront the fact that the greatest variance in school learning occurs under what Coleman calls "within-school" conditions. His survey, however, offers little illumination of the internal reward structure of the neighborhood school which helps to produce student differentiation. What is the nature of the "within-school" stratification system? How do principals and teachers sustain it and thus reinforce selectively the achievement of some students, perhaps at the expense of the retardation of others? Could one redesign this reward structure? How far can one depart from the stratification system of the larger community and still operate a neighborhood public school?

Finally, professional leadership is so important a factor, I believe, that the Coleman Report needs supplementing through analysis of the relation between the quality of school administration and the variations in student achievement between school districts and within them. Superintendents and principals were questioned but by and large they were not questioned about themselves or their professional behavior. Rather, they reported upon the schools, staffs, and students for whom they have legal responsibility.

My own hypothesis is that differences in the quality of school administrations—holding pupil backgrounds constant—should account for as much of the difference in student achievement as does peer environment. The validity of the argument hinges strongly, of course, upon measures of leadership.

This review has ignored not only the technical aspects of the Coleman Report. It has also neglected its contributions to the survey analysis of future teachers, to higher education, school withdrawal, case studies of integration planning, pre-school education, and vocational education. By mentioning these oversights, it is hoped to stimulate even wider reading than this appreciation of the heart of the report may accomplish.

RELATIONSHIPS BETWEEN EXPECTATIONS
OF TEACHERS AND PERFORMANCE OF STUDENTS
(Pygmalion in the Classroom)

PAUL M. KOHN, PH.D

There is a story, probably apocryphal, about a late-blooming graduate student who was widely regarded as one of the top students in his department, although his promise had evidently not always been great. In fact, his principal in elementary school, noting his unimpressive record, urged him not to enter the academic stream in high school as it would be "a bloody wonder" if he made it past his sophomore year.

However, he was a defiant fellow and persevered, eventually with great success. When he earned his doctorate, he recalled the principal's prognosis and decided to write him a letter. It went somewhat as follows (any resemblance to the names of real persons is unintentional):

> Dear Mr. Wilson:
> My name is Fenwick F. Fenwick. I was one of your pupils, and, before I graduated in 1956, you told me it would be "a bloody wonder" if I made it past sophomore year in the academic stream at high school.
> This is to inform you that on June 15 shortly after 2:30 P.M. I shall be receiving my Ph.D. in astrophysics from Ivy University.
>
> Yours sincerely,
> Fenwick F. Fenwick

Shortly before the commencement ceremonies. Fenwick received the following telegram:

> It *is* a bloody wonder.
>
> Yours sincerely,
> Wilson W. Wilson

This kind of communication between teacher and pupil is what diplomats would call a "frank expression of views." Usually teachers are not quite that frank, perhaps because it is considered bad pedagogy and also invites trouble from parents. Teachers, however, do have preconceptions about the abilities of many of their pupils, and probably communicate them — subtly, covertly, and inexplicitly, but communicate them

nonetheless. The purpose of this paper is to review research on the possible effects such preconceptions and their communication have on the actual intellectual development and school performance of pupils.

The best known study in this area is that of Rosenthal and Jacobson.[1] They administered to all the children in a San Francisco area school a little known nonlanguage intelligence test. This measure has a verbal subtest to assess information, vocabulary, and linguistic concepts (*eg,* food *vs* nonfood), and a reasoning subtest to assess the ability to understand relationships and abstract concepts (*eg,* angular *vs* rounded figures). The test was misrepresented to the classroom teachers as "The Harvard Test of Inflected Acquisition," an intelligence measure designed, not just to assess immediate IQ, but also to predict spurts, gains, and upward inflections in the fairly near future. The investigators arbitrarily designated a randomly selected 20 per cent of the pupils in each classroom as being intellectually "about to bloom." Subsequent testings took place four, eight, and 20 months later.

The question being investigated was this: Would the manipulation of teachers' expectations become a self-fulfilling prophecy? Would those children to whom a sudden growth of intellect was ascribed by the grace of the table of random numbers, in fact, show such growth? The question is important because it may bear on the interests not just of individual pupils, as in the anecdote, but also of entire social groups such as ethnic minorities and the poor. Insofar as there are stereotypical preconceptions of the abilities of such groups, might not such conceptions also become self-fulfilling prophecies?

The answer suggested by Rosenthal and Jacobson's data is complicated. It all depends on what combinations of grade, testing time (four, eight, or 20 months after the manipulation), sex, ability grouping, and intelligence subtest you look at. The test scores of children designated as bloomers were compared to those of their classroom peers. At four months, bloomers in Grades 3-6 showed a significant advantage over their peers, while bloomers in Grades 1 and 2 did not; at eight months, only the younger bloomers outshone their peers — very substantially; and, at 20 months, again only the older bloomers seemed to benefit. Blooming girls outshone their control-group peers in reasoning IQ (but not verbal IQ) at all three points in time. Blooming boys only showed an expectancy advantage in verbal IQ at 20 months. Medium track bloomers benefited significantly in reasoning IQ at all three post-tests while their slower and faster colleagues did not. Mexican children showed an expectancy advantage in verbal IQ at 20 months only, and in reasoning IQ at eight months only. However, Mexican boys (but not girls) benefited more from the manipulation in full-scale IQ and both subscales at eight and 20 months, the more Mexican they looked.

In terms of academic performance, the one area where the bloomers, in fact, bloomed more conspicuously than their peers was reading. Again, younger and middle-track bloomers benefited most.

About a decade earlier, Pitt[2] had conducted similar experiments with Grades 5 and 6 boys in Toronto, Canada. One experiment compared pupils whose IQ's were known by teachers with pupils whose IQ's were unknown by teachers as to their achievement-test performance; classroom marks; perceptions of self, school, and teacher; and teacher's perceptions of them. The second experiment made the same comparisons on three group of boys: ones whose IQ's were correctly represented to teachers; ones whose IQ's were underrepresented by ten points; and ones whose IQ's were overrepresented by ten points. There were very few significant effects in either experiment despite the extensive analyses conducted. One finding was that boys about whose IQ's teachers had accurate knowledge tended to get higher spelling marks than boys about whose performance teachers were misinformed (either way). In the case of the underrepresented boys, the inferior spelling performance was peculiar to the (objectively) less bright ones (IQ< 115) with low spelling marks prior to the experimental manipulation.

The underrepresented boys reported seeing themselves as less hard-working than others did,
but paradoxically also saw schoolwork as being more difficult for them than did the others. They also seemed to see the teacher as more unfair to them than their peers reported for themselves. Both misrepresented groups tended to think that the teacher considered them lazy in comparison to the perceptions of the accurately represented group.

The relationship of test information to teachers' reported preconceptions seemed more important than the preconceptions themselves. Over the course of the year, the school performance of pupils whose intelligence teachers reported underestimating in relation to test information improved, while that of overestimated pupils declined. There were no corresponding effects on achievement test scores. This improved school performance may have been related to the teachers' self-reported tendencies to increase their demands on previously underestimated pupils, and decrease their demands on previously overestimated ones. It should again be noted that the few positive results reported here represent a sparse yield from a very large number of analyses.

The results of the two pioneering studies on teacher expectancies are fairly complex. The following subsequently conducted studies do not necessarily simplify matters.

Evans and Rosenthal[3] conducted a study like Rosenthal and Jacobson's at two urban Midwestern schools. At the end of one year, they found a significant expectancy gain in reasoning IQ for boys, and a significant expectancy loss in verbal IQ for girls. These results are substantially different from those of Rosenthal and Jacobson.

Another replicational study, this by Conn, Edwards, Rosenthal, and Crowne,[4] yielded very complex results. After one semester, males (only) in the blooming group showed almost significantly greater gains in verbal IQ than their control group peers ($p<0.10$). With the further passage of one year all apparent benefits of the expectancy manipulation disappeared except in certain special subgroups. Conn et al also had measures of their S's accuracy in detecting the emotional quality of adult male and female voices. (Sensitivity to the vocal expression of emotion by males *vs* females turned out to be fairly independent of one another ($r=0.23$, $p<0.01$).

For males, sensitivity to the female voice was associated with expectancy gains in reasoning IQ after one semester. This suggests that it serves a fellow well to be responsive to the subtle nuances of the adult female voice! However, the short-term expectancy advantage of this group appeared to have dissipated a year later. For female pupils too, a short-term expectancy advantage (but no long-term advantage) was associated with sensitivity to the adult female voice; however, for girls, the fleeting advantage was on the verbal rather than the reasoning subscale.

It is interesting that after one semester, males who were more accurate in detecting the emotional qualities of the adult male voice tended to benefit *less* from the expectancy manipulation in reasoning IQ than their less male-sensitive male peers ($p < 0.10$). After another year, the male-sensitive males showed *more* expectancy advantage in both verbal and reasoning IQ (p's < 0.05 and < 0.01, respectively). Conn et al claimed that available research indicates that male sensitivity to male vocal emotion is associated with self-confidence and emotional maturity. Consequently, they argued, male-sensitive males, being less dependent, should be less influenced by teachers' preconceptions in the short term; however, in the long run, their self-confidence and general maturity result in greater benefit from positive teacher expectations. (Presumably, the same characteristics should confer both short- and long-term immunity to negative expectations.)

Claiborn [5] also conducted an experiment to replicate and extend that of Rosenthal and Jacobson. Although he found a massive overall increase in IQ, about 11 points, across treatment conditions, he obtained no significant differential change between bloomers and controls. Interestingly, unlike both Rosenthal and Jacobson, and Evans and Rosenthal, Claiborn did find that teachers showed quite good recall for the names of bloomers in their classes. Possibly, the much shorter recall interval in his experiment (two months) is responsible for the discrepancy.

As to the more serious discrepancy of finding *vs* not finding some expectancy effect, Claiborn expressed skepticism about the reality of the so-called Pygmalion effect. Although he noted differences between his and the Rosenthal-Jacobson designs, notably the late introduction of the expectancy manipulation and the short test-retest interval in his own study, he argued that these were probably irrelevant by pointing out that they did not prevent expectancy effects from emerging in two other experiments.

A study with more positive results was reported by Palardy.[6] He compared the male and female pupils of five Grade 1 teachers who believed that girls learned reading more easily than boys with those of five teachers who did not share that belief as to their actual subsequent reading performance. The teachers' preconceptions did seem to constitute a self-fulfilling prophecy: girls were superior in the classrooms of teachers who expected it, but not in those of teachers who did not. The discrepancy in apparent reading superiority of the girls was primarily attributable to differences in the performance of the two groups of boys, differences which approached significance ($p < 0.08$). The boys did better when they were not expected to do worse than the girls than when they were.

Beez [7] also reported an experiment with positive results. He had each of 60 graduate students in education administer a symbol-learning task and crossword puzzles to a child in Project Headstart. Each experimenter-teacher had received a psychological evaluation which gave either a positive or a negative prognosis on the child's probable future adjustment in school. The two prognoses were, of course, randomly assigned. The results on the symbol-learning task were quite dramatic! The positive-prognosis group learned about twice as many symbols as the negative-prognosis group. However, there were no reliable differences in crossword puzzle performance.

There were strong effects on the attitudes and behaviours of the teachers. Substantially more teachers of negative-prognosis pupils (63 per cent) saw the symbol learning task as too difficult for their charges than did teachers of positive-prognosis pupils (3.3 per cent). The former teachers also rated their pupils lower on achievement, social competition, and intellectual ability. Correspondingly, these teachers of negative-prognosis pupils spent more time per problem, taught more repetitively, and spent more time on non-task-oriented interaction with their pupils.

Anderson and Rosenthal [8] conducted an expectancy-manipulation experiment with 28 boys in a New England school for the retarded as their pupil-subjects. Quite apart from the positive expectancy manipulation, some of the boys were having intensive one-to-one contact and reading instruction with volunteer tutors from area high schools. Boys who were both designated as about to bloom and being tutored showed a significant *decline* in reasoning IQ both absolutely and in relation to the other three treatment-groups. On the other hand, the intended bloomers were rated as showing significantly more improvement in practical self-management than their peers.

Rosenthal [9] later reported follow-up data on the Anderson-Rosenthal study, data collected nine months after the original manipulation (and seven months after the first post-test). The specific expectancy disadvantage of the "tutored bloomers" disappeared by this time. However, the boys who received either one of these two treatments did better on reasoning IQ and total IQ than boys who received both or neither. Furthermore, the data suggested that the bloomers had been receiving less attention from their counselors, and they had developed a greater degree of independence than their peers.

Meichenbaum, Bowers, and Ross [10] did an expectancy-manipulation experiment in an Ontario training school for adolescent female offenders. Their study was distinctive in a number of ways:

1. They took greater care than heretofore to ensure the success of their manipulation through intensive discussion with the teachers as a group. The result apparently was an acceptance of even the less plausible nominations of bloomers which the teachers rationalized through hindsight wisdom.
2. They had only four teachers who had intensive contact with each of the six experimental and eight control subjects.
3. They made systematic observations via one-way mirrors of both teachers' and pupils' classroom behaviours.

The bloomers showed more improvement than controls in objectively graded (but not subjectively graded) academic performance and rated appropriateness of classroom conduct. The three teachers in whose classrooms the bloomers did excel their peers either increased their positive interaction or decreased their negative interaction with the bloomers.

What is notable about the empirical literature reviewed here is its inconsistency. Sometimes, expectancy manipulations work; sometimes not; and other times they seem to backfire. The data on expectancy benefits for various subgroups (*eg,* boys *vs* girls) are no less contradictory. In general, these studies do not lend themselves to facile summarization.

In a way, this should not be surprising as research in this very complex area has proceeded in the virtual absence of any conceptual framework. It is the absence of theory which is surprising because teachers' communication of their preconceptions about pupils to the pupils would seem to be a special case of communication and persuasion. Moreover, the latter area is rich in theoretical resources. Accordingly, let us consider some possible applications.

The first question has to be whether or not a teacher even has preconceptions about the abilities of given pupils. In correlational research and everyday life, this is a problem of assessment; however, in experiments which the bulk of studies in this area have been, the problem is whether or not the expectancy manipulation *registers*. If it does register, there then arises the question of how long it is retained. Studies have varied in the care given to establishing the manipulation, with that of Meichenbaum et al being exemplary. With respect to retention, it seems that teachers are incapable of accurately recalling the names of bloomers after such long intervals as an academic year (Evans and Rosenthal) or 20 months (Rosenthal and Jacobson) but not intervals as brief as two months (Claiborn).

Insofar as who the bloomers are fails to register consistently or misregisters in the case of some nonbloomers, one should expect rather confused effects, if any. Retention, however, is another matter. If teachers treat bloomers and nonbloomers differently early on, but later forget who's who, the early treatment differences could have an effect which is sustained subsequently for other reasons (*eg,* improved self-confidence in the bloomers, enhanced intrinsic enjoyment in using one's intellectual skills).

Insofar as an expectancy manipulation is successful, its primary behavioural effects must be on the teacher. Studies of small groups,[11] parent-child relationships,[12,13] and even the modes of second-person address [14] all suggest two important dimensions of interpersonal behaviour: an affectional or solidary dimension, and an authoritative or power-status dimension. How do teachers' expectations about a pupil's abilities affect his behaviour on these dimensions? One likely effect is that teachers' expressed *demands* and standards vary according to the perceived ability of the pupil; indeed, some of the findings by Pitt, by Rosenthal and Jacobson, by Anderson and Rosenthal, and by Beez support such a presupposition. (See also Brophy and Good,[15] and Rubovits and Maehr.[16]) It may be that the quality of a student's work will improve as the demands of his teacher increase, provided the demands are within the student's capabilities.

In addition, teachers' attitude, evaluation, or attraction to pupils and their expression of this could vary with their preconceptions about pupils' abilities. Teachers may generally find seemingly brighter children more attractive and could act accordingly, either implicitly, or explicitly, or both. The results of Meichenbaum et al are an example. (See also Rubovits and Maehr. These authors reported that students arbitrarily designated as gifted were praised more for their contributions to a discussion than students of equivalent ability identified as nongifted. In a later study,[17] they found that such differential praise as well as differential soliciting of "gifted" and "nongifted" students' opinions occurred with white, but not black, students. The teachers were white undergraduate females in teacher-training courses who generally solicited blacks' opinions less, praised them less, and ignored and criticized them more).

However, teachers' preconceptions should affect their expressed attitudes less consistently than their expressed demands, for it is normatively acceptable for teachers to demand more from abler pupils, but not to prefer them. Also, there are other bases for interpersonal attraction than ability (even for teachers!). Thus, teachers should vary in how much they discriminate affectionally. Insofar as teachers' affectional behaviour contributes to expectancy effects, these should be less apparent with more impersonal teachers. Paradoxically, such teachers might be less effective generally. Rosenthal and Jacobson found a significant and substantial positive correlation between bloomers' and nonbloomers' gains for the same classrooms.

Next, insofar as an expectancy manipulation has been successful and has become translated into the expression of corresponding demands and/or affect, the question of pupil response arises. There is a distinction in the persuasion-and-communication literature between comprehending the position of a persuasive communicator, and yielding to it. This distinction should apply to the teacher-pupil case. Furthermore, children should differ in their predispositions for both comprehension and yielding.

First, some pupils may be more accurately sensitive than others to a teacher's like or dislike of them and the level of work demanded of them. Sensitivity to the emotional timbre of the adult voice of the teacher's sex, as investigated by Conn et al, seems relevant here. It may well be more relevant to the expression of affect which is usually implicit than to the expression of demands

which is usually more explicit. In this case, simple intelligence (and possibly defensiveness) may be more important.

Secondly, if a pupil accurately comprehends a teacher's attitude and aspiration level for him, he can yield or resist the behavioural implications to varying degrees. Such differences should generally be more evident for negative than positive preconceptions. Most pupils would be expected to react positively to the latter. With respect to negative preconceptions, the degree of pupil yielding and hence self-fulfillment of teacher prophecy would probably vary with the pupils' self-esteem and self-conception of his abilities. Students with positive self-evaluations generally and/or specific to their abilities should be less influenced by negative teacher preconceptions than their less positively self-evaluating peers.

The present type of analysis has the advantage of generality. It should apply to any dyadic relationship where one party has preconceptions about the other, and, indeed, it is largely derivative from a general approach to the broader area of persuasion and communication. There is no intrinsic reason why the same principles should not apply and similar phenomena occur in the case of pupils' preconceptions about teachers.

Kelley[18] long ago established that students' preconceptions about a teacher at the university level, specifically with respect to his interpersonal warmth *vs* coldness, affect students' perceptions of and behaviour toward the teacher. Teachers who met a discussion class only once were perceived as more sociable, more popular, better natured, more humorous, and more humane by those students to whom they were described in advance as warm rather than cold persons. Furthermore, the students whose prior information about the teacher described him as warm participated more in the classroom discussion.

Furthermore, a study by Jenkins and Deno[19] suggests that teachers are not necessarily unaffected by such reactions. They had undergraduate confederates respond in a predeterminedly positive and interested, or negative and bored manner to lectures by senior education students. The novice lecturers' self-evaluations were predictably affected.

Very recently, Herrell[20] took Kelley's work another step further. He demonstrated that teachers represented prior to a guest lecture as warm actually taught with a warmer, more relaxed, and generally better teaching style than the same teachers represented as cold.

Furthermore, this judgment is based not on the reactions of the immediate audience, but rather on the ratings by neutral and treatment-blind judges of tape-recorded lecture-segments. Judges' ratings did not distinguish the early segments of warm and cold presentations, presumably recorded before the audience's preconceptions could have had any impact on the speaker; however, the judges rated the later segments of warm lectures as superior to those of cold lectures. Teachers may be no less susceptible to self-fulfilling prophecies than their pupils.

To conclude, it is hoped that this paper achieves its intended objectives. First, it should make the reader appreciate the complexity and contradictory nature of the empirical findings on teacher expectancy effects. Second, it offers a conceptual framework intended to reduce some of the complexity and resolve some of the apparent contradictions. Third, it is hoped that the conceptual framework illuminates some of the steps intervening between an expectancy manipulation and whatever effects it has, if any. It may well be the many possible slips 'twixt cup and lip which account for contradictory findings. If such variables are accurately identified, they can be controlled, measured, or manipulated rather than continuing their massive contributions to error variance. Finally, we should all realize that self-fulfilling prophecies probably occur irrespective of such status distinctions as that between teacher and pupil.

REFERENCES

1. Rosenthal R, Jacobson L: Pygmalion in the Classroom. New York, Holt, Rinehart and Winston, 1968.
2. Pitt CCV: An experimental study of the effects of teachers' knowledge or incorrect knowledge of IQ on teachers' attitudes and practices; and pupils' attitudes and achievement. Unpublished doctoral dissertation, Columbia University, 1956.
3. Evans JT, and Rosenthal R: Interpersonal self-fulfilling prophecies: further extrapolations from laboratory to classroom. Proc Ann Conv Am Psych Assoc 77:371, 1969.
4. Conn LK, Edwards CN, Rosenthal R et al: Perception of emotion and response to teachers' expectancy by elementary school children. Psychol Reps 22:27, 1968.
5. Claiborn WL: Expectancy effects in the classroom: a failure to replicate. J Educ Psychol 60:377, 1969.
6. Palardy JM: What teachers believe—what children achieve. Elem Sch J 69:370, 1969.
7. Beez WV: Influence of biased psychological reports on teacher behaviour and pupil performance. Pro Ann Conv Am Psych Assoc 76:605, 1968.
8. Anderson DF, Rosenthal R: Some effects of interpersonal expectancy and social interaction on institutionalized retarded children. Proc Ann Conv Am Psych Assoc 76:479, 1968.
9. Rosenthal R: Teacher expectation and student learning. *In* Strom RD (ed): Teachers and the Learning Process. Englewood Cliffs, N.J., Prentice-Hall, 1971.
10. Meichenbaum DH, Bowers KS, Ross RR: A behavioural analysis of teacher expectancy effect. J Person Soc Psychol 13:306, 1969.
11. Bales RF, Slater PE: Role differentiation in small groups. *In* Parsons T, Bales RF, Shils EA: Working Papers in the Theory of Action. Glencoe, Illinois, Free Press, 1953.
12. Schaefer ES, Bell RQ: Patterns of attitudes to child-rearing and the family. J Abnorm Soc Psychol 54:391, 1957.
13. Siegelman M: Evaluation of Bronfenbrenner's questionnaire for children concerning parental behaviour. Child Devel 36:164, 1965.
14. Brown RW: Social Psychology. New York, Free Press, 1965.
15. Brophy JE, Good TL: Teachers' communication of differential expectations for children's classroom performance: some behavioural data. J Educ Psychol 61:356, 1970.
16. Rubovits PC, Maehr ML: Pygmalion analyzed: toward an explanation of the Rosenthal-Jacobson findings. J Person Soc Psychol 19:197, 1971.
17. Rubovits PC, Maehr ML: Pygmalion black and white. J Person Soc Psychol 25:210, 1973.
18. Kelley H: The warm-cold variable in first impressions of persons. J Pers 18:431, 1950.
19. Jenkins JR, Deno SL: Influence of student behaviour on teachers' self-evaluation. J Educ Psychol 60:439, 1969.
20. Herrell JM: Galatea in the classroom: student expectations affect teachers' behaviour. Proc Ann Conv Am Psych Assoc 79:521, 1971.

HOWARD H. SPICKER

Intellectual Development Through Early Childhood Education

AFTER 4 years of public acclaim the honeymoon for Project Head Start ended abruptly. The opening shot was fired by Jensen (1969) and was followed by an even more devastating barrage by Cicirelli (1969) reporting for the government sponsored Westinghouse study. Both critics concluded that Project Head Start in general had been unsuccessful in increasing the intellectual abilities of disadvantaged or culturally different children. In those instances where significant IQ increases had been demonstrated they were seldom maintained beyond the second grade. Even more devastating was the finding that Head Start experiences had done little to prevent scholastic failure in the elementary school grades.

The bulk of the evidence indeed supports these conclusions. However, there is great danger in applying these findings to all early childhood intervention programs. Such a conclusion assumes that all preschool programs are the same. A brief visit to a few Head Start classes will quickly demonstrate the errors inherent in generalizing on the basis of these reports alone. There are in fact almost as many differences in content and quality among preschool programs as there are programs.

> There are in fact almost as many differences in content and quality among preschool programs as there are programs.

This article identifies some of the critical variations among preschool programs and discusses the manner in which such variations seem to affect the intellectual development of disadvantaged or culturally different children. For this purpose an in depth analysis will be made of a select group of carefully designed experimental preschool studies. Attention will be given to the effectiveness of different curriculum models, the effectiveness of home interventions, the optimum age for intervention, and the effect of differing lengths of intervention programs.

> Attention will be given to different curriculum models, home interventions, age for interventions, and program length.

Curriculum Models

Prior to the advent of Project Head Start in the summer of 1965, there were few programs for disadvantaged or culturally different children. There were even fewer curriculum models specifically designed to remedy the specific learning, language, motoric, and affective deficits and/or differences often exhibited by such children. It is, therefore, not too surprising that many Head Start programs adopted the available traditional nursery school curriculum models developed for middle class children. These "traditional" models emphasize social and emotional development through the media of unstructured free play, field trips, music, dramatics, arts and crafts, storytelling, and games. Intellectual and language development is fostered indirectly by providing the children with incidental rather than specifically designed learning experiences. Convinced that a more direct approach was needed to ameliorate the specific learning deficits exhibited by many disadvantaged children, the majority of early childhood investigations in the 1960's concentrated on developing new or modifying old curriculum models. These efforts resulted in the formulation of at least three major types of curriculum models: The first places emphasis on intellectual or cognitive development, the second on perceptual-motor development, the third on academic skill development.

> It is not too surprising that many Head Start programs adopted traditional nursery school curriculum models.

*Cognitive Development
Models*

These models attempt to improve aptitudes for and attitudes toward school by improving oral language abilities, memory, discrimination learning, problem solving ability, concept formation, general information, and comprehension. The major features that differentiate the various cognitive development programs (e.g., Gray & Klaus, 1968; Hodges, McCandless, & Spicker, 1971; Karnes, 1969; Weikart, 1967) are the specific strategies each uses to achieve the above goals.

*Perceptual Motor
Development Model*

This model is exemplified by the classic Montessori curriculum (Montessori, 1964). Visual discrimination and visual motor integration are the key elements. The Montessori program in particular stresses sensory training and psychomotor learning through independent manipulation of didactic materials. The approach is thought to teach independence, self control, and concentration which in turn provide the child with greater self confidence, maturity, and readiness for school learning.

*Academic Skills
Development Model*

This model is the most direct of the three intervention approaches. It is best illustrated by the Bereiter and Engelmann (1966) curriculum. The model assumes that disadvantaged children fail in school because they receive ineffective instruction. The approach, therefore, attempts to provide systematic direct instruction in oral language, reading, and arithmetic prior to first grade school entrance.

The approach attempts to provide systematic, direct instruction in oral language, reading, and arithmetic.

Comparative effects of these curriculum models are just beginning to emerge.

Because the majority of these curricula were only recently developed, studies on comparative effects of these curriculum models are just beginning to emerge. Weikart (1969) compared a traditional model to a cognitive and an academic skills development model. Referring to the traditional model, Weikart states,

> The hallmarks of this curriculum are introduction of themes and material to acquaint the child with the wider environment, close attention to the individual social and emotional needs of each child, and a considerable degree of permissiveness in classroom operation [p. 4].

The cognitive model developed by Weikart "was based on methods of 'verbal bombardment,' socio-dramatic play, and certain principles derived from Piaget's theory of intellectual development [p. 4]." The academic skills model is the one developed by Bereiter and Engelmann. Each curriculum model was presented to a group of approximately eight functionally retarded disadvantaged 3 and 4 year old children on a half-day basis. This presentation was supplemented by a 90 minute home teaching session every other week.

The most surprising aspect was that the traditional approach proved as effective as the two specifically developed for disadvantaged children.

After one year of instruction all three groups had made large IQ score increases and substantial social-emotional and general development improvements. However the improvements made by the three groups were not significantly different from one another. The most surprising aspect of the study was the finding that the traditional approach proved to be as effective as the two approaches that had been specifically developed for disadvantaged children. Similar success with a traditional curriculum approach has recently been reported by Karnes (1969) and by Kraft, Fuschillo, and Herzog (1968). It is important to note that these studies had one major element in common—the traditional preschool classes under investigation were directly controlled by the investigators. This meant that teachers were assisted by a research staff in planning the details of the curriculum. Short- and longterm goals were established; daily lesson plans were constructed; teachers were convinced that their approach would produce positive results. In addition, the teachers often worked in teams with experienced teachers providing constant consultation and supervision. Traditional programs in experimental settings like these are much more structured than nonexperimental traditional preschool programs. In fact whenever the traditional curriculum model has been evaluated in the absence of such an experimental structure, it has been found to be significantly less effective with disadvantaged children than curriculum models that were designed specifically for such children (Cicirelli, 1969; DiLorenzo, Salter, & Brady, 1969; Karnes, 1969).

To determine the extent to which curriculum structure affects program effectiveness, Karnes (1969) compared five preschool intervention programs which had different degrees of structure. Structure was defined as the intensity of formal teacher-child instruction. Table 1 describes each of the programs in ascending order of structure as seen by the major investigator.

All groups received their specific treatment for one year starting at chronological age (CA) 4. The Traditional, Community Integrated, and Montessori groups entered a regular kindergarten for 5 year olds. The Ameliorative

TABLE 1

Illinois Project Program Descriptions

Group[a]	N	Program Description
Traditional	25	Project-operated, self contained class of disadvantaged children. Emphasis on personal, social, motor, and general language development through incidental and informal learning opportunities.
Community Integrated	16	Same as above except disadvantaged children were integrated into community operated traditional preschool classes of predominantly middle class children.
Montessori	13	Under Montessori society control; emphasis on sensory training and psychomotor learning through independent manipulation of didactic materials.
Ameliorative	24	Cognitive approach emphasizing language development through manipulation of concrete materials, the teaching of mathematical concepts, language arts, reading readiness, and science-social studies.
Direct Verbal	23	Bereiter-Engelmann academic skills approach which uses pattern drills for teaching language and arithmetic and a modified initial teaching alphabet (i/t/a) approach for teaching reading.

[a] Programs are listed in order from the least structured to the most structured.

group received one hour of special instruction in addition to regular kindergarten participation. The Direct Verbal group continued to receive the Bereiter-Engelmann program in a special kindergarten. In the third year all children entered regular first grade without further special treatment.

After one year of preschool intervention the findings indicated that the Ameliorative, the Direct Verbal, and the Traditional groups had made significantly greater IQ and language gains than had the Community Integrated and Montessori groups. As has already been indicated it is quite possible that an experimentally controlled traditional preschool class probably has more structure than a nonexperimental, traditional preschool class. Structure alone, however, cannot account for the greater IQ gains that are made in certain preschool programs. It must be remembered that the Montessori curriculum is considerably more structured than most traditional programs. Yet

Structure alone cannot account for the greater IQ gains that are made in certain preschool programs.

Montessori-trained disadvantaged children consistently make few IQ gains and, when compared to children educated by other preschool curricula, often show the least oral language progress (Berger, 1969, and Miller, 1970). Such poor language performance should come as no surprise since the curriculum provides little formal teacher-pupil verbal interaction or other specific procedures designed to stimulate pupil verbalizations. Whereas intelligence tests such as the Stanford-Binet are highly verbal in nature, preschool programs that do not stress language development are less likely to produce significant verbal IQ gains.

What about differences in effectiveness between a cognitive development and an academic skills development approach? According to the Weikart and Karnes comparative studies, cognitive approaches produce essentially the same improvement in IQ, language, and social development as an academic skills approach such as that of Bereiter and Engelmann.

A separate study by Bereiter and Engelmann (1967) reported that in addition to having made highly significant IQ, language, and social adjustment improvements after 2 years of instruction (preschool plus kindergarten), their 6 year old children prior to first grade entrance were scoring at grade levels of 2.6 in reading, 2.5 in arithmetic, and 1.9 in spelling on the *Wide Range Achievement Test* (WRAT).

The crucial question however, is whether the achievement test score advantages of these children will be maintained when children educated by other preschool approaches are exposed to reading, writing, and arithmetic instruction. When a cognitively trained group of children finished first grade, Karnes (1969) found that their reading and arithmetic achievement test scores did not differ significantly from those scores made by the group trained through the academic skills (Bereiter-Engelmann) model. In fact children taught by the Bereiter-Engelmann approach had scored one half-year lower in reading comprehension (1.7) than in reading vocabulary (2.24) on the *California Achievement Test*. This suggests that the academic skills approach teaches the mechanical skills of reading instead of reading comprehension. This may also account for the unusually high *Wide Range Achievement Test* (WRAT) scores reported for Bereiter-Engelmann trained children. The WRAT measures word recognition ability rather than reading comprehension, and arithmetic computation rather than arithmetic reasoning.

Additional insights about the effects of preschool and kindergarten instruction on later school achievement can be obtained from the followup data in the Indiana Project (Hodges, McCandless, & Spicker, 1971). In each of 3 years an experimental group received a one year cognitively structured kindergarten curriculum designed to remedy specific, diagnosed deficits of individual children in language development, fine motor coordination, concept formation, and socialization.

Despite similar IQ increases (approximately 20 points on the Binet and 30 points on the *Peabody Picture Vocabulary Test*) as well as similar language increases made by both groups (approximately 19 months on the ITPA), the followup data through second grade for first year and second year experimental groups were radically different. First year experimental children were achieving almost a year behind their middle class CA peers; second year experimental children were achieving at or near the grade

The crucial question is whether the achievement test score advantages will be maintained.

This suggests that the academic skills approach teaches the mechanical skills of reading instead of reading comprehension.

level of their CA peer group. The achievement differences appear to be directly related to major curriculum changes implemented during the second year of the project. Language lessons were developed around traditional school themes such as the farm, home, foods, transportation, and community helpers; these themes were continued throughout the day in such activities as the story of the week, adaptive art, music, and physical education. In addition a series of lessons designed to improve fine motor abilities was introduced. A comparison of the Stanford-Binet test protocols of the two groups upon completion of kindergarten indicated that second year children had acquired school related skills to a greater extent than had first year children. They were able to remember instructions and execute them; they excelled in behavior requiring motor skills; they were superior in expressive vocabulary and number concepts. In short, the group had acquired the techniques for attacking the formalized, rote memory types of tasks frequently demanded in the elementary schools they later attended.

It thus appears that if one has no control over the subsequent elementary grade curriculum, a preschool intervention must provide the child with experiences that will prepare him for the existing school situation. Hopefully the government sponsored Project Follow Through program will offer investigators an opportunity to develop experimental primary grade curricula which will be more effective than most traditional ones in building upon what has been learned in some of the more innovative preschool programs.

The following conclusions regarding the role of preschool curriculum approaches for increasing intellectual development and school achievment seem appropriate at this time.

1. Curriculum models which stress cognitive or academic skill development produce the largest IQ score increases.
2. "Traditional" curriculum approaches produce significant intellectual growth only when the programs contain specific short- and longterm goals including language development and are highly structured and well supervised.
3. Structured programs other than cognitively or academically oriented ones produce intellectual gains only when they incorporate strong oral language development components.
4. A preschool academic skill oriented program such as that developed by Bereiter and Engelmann tends to produce rote reading and arithmetic computation skills rather than improved reading comprehension and arithmetic reasoning skills.
5. Unless the primary grade curriculum can be modified, preschool programs must develop the fine motor, memory, and general language abilities of disadvantaged children. These skills, rather than abstract reasoning, critical thinking, and creative thinking, appear to be needed to succeed in the primary grades of many existing elementary schools located in inner city ghettos and rural communities.

Home Intervention

The specific contribution of a home intervention program to the intellectual development of disadvantaged 4 year old children was recently reported by Karnes (1969). Mothers of children not attending a preschool program were provided 11 weekly 2 hour sessions at a neighborhood elementary school. These sessions taught mothers procedures for increasing the language abilities of their children with opportunities to prepare inexpensive instructional materials for home use. The 3 month program resulted in a 7 point Binet IQ increase for the experimental children and no IQ gain for the control children.

On the basis of the positive effects of the shortterm home intervention on intellectual development, Karnes added a home intervention program to her cognitively oriented Ameliorative curriculum. At the end of the 7 month intervention period, scores achieved on the Stanford-Binet, *Frostig Development Test of Visual Perception,* and the *Metropolitan Reading Readiness* tests showed the performance of both cognitively oriented groups to be almost identical, with or without home participation by the mothers. These two investigations seem to indicate that a home intervention contributes to intellectual development when no preschool program is available to the child; however it apparently adds little to the benefits the child derives from a fulltime preschool curriculum intervention alone.

A home intervention contributes to intellectual development when no preschool program is available. However, it adds little to the benefits the child derives from a fulltime preschool curriculum intervention.

Although home interventions seem to contribute minimally to the IQ increases of children in a fulltime preschool program, family involvement does appear to contribute in other ways. For example, let us look at the benefits of a home intervention that is coupled with a shortterm school program. As indicated by the Westinghouse study (Cicirelli, 1969), shortterm curriculum intervention programs like summer Head Start have been highly unsuccessful. Yet one notable exception has been the Klaus and Gray (1968) Early Training Project. With only a two to three summer curriculum intervention program lasting 10 weeks for a period of 4 hours a day, significant IQ and language gains were made by experimental groups of 4 and 5 year old black children. It should be noted, however, that children in the experimental group and their mothers received weekly home visits for a minimum of 2 school years from teachers who provided instruction to the children in the presence of their mothers. This was in addition to the shortterm summer preschool intervention.

Communities that can only provide shortterm preschool programs to disadvantaged children should supplement them with a home intervention.

Although the extremely innovative curriculum developed by Klaus and Gray for the project should not be ignored as a contribution to the positive results of the study, it is highly unlikely that the program would have been as successful without the home intervention component. It seems safe to conclude that communities that can only provide shortterm preschool programs to disadvantaged children should supplement them with a home intervention.

There appear to be still other benefits accruing from home intervention programs. In urban communities where families tend to live close together, there is a high probability of a positive spillover effect from experimental group children and their families to other children and families living in close proximity—a phenomenon called "horizontal diffusion" (Gray, 1969). An even more intriguing side effect of a home intervention is what Gray calls "vertical diffusion," the spread of effect from older to younger siblings. It was found that younger siblings closest in age to the experimental group children scored significantly higher on the Binet than the younger siblings from the control groups. Furthermore the effects of teaching intervention techniques to mothers seem to spread to the children closest in age to those for whom the technique was designed. It is quite possible that the indirect positive effects of home and preschool interventions on neighborhood children and younger siblings may be even greater than the direct effects of the interventions on the children receiving them.

It is quite possible that the indirect positive effects of home and preschool interventions on neighborhood children and younger siblings may be even greater than the direct effects of the interventions on the children receiving them.

Age at Intervention

It is generally assumed that the earlier one intervenes with disadvantaged children the better will be the result.

It is generally assumed that the earlier one intervenes with disadvantaged children the better will be the result. Until some of the ongoing infant intervention projects are completed, however, this assumption can only be examined partially by comparing existing intervention studies that began with either 3 or 4 year old children.

Many ask if an intervention initiated with 3 year old children is more effective than one initiated with 4 year olds. Comparing the effects of her cognitive (Ameliorative) program initiated with 3 year old disadvantaged children to the effects of that program initiated with 4 year olds, Karnes (1969) found no significant differences between the progress made by the 3 year old children and that of the 4 year olds after a one year intervention. Both groups had gained an average of 15 IQ points on the Binet, 11 points on the *Peabody Picture Vocabulary Test*, and 7 months in total language age on the ITPA. During the early phases of his intervention work (Waves 0 and 1), Weikart (1967) also failed to find any advantages in an intervention begun at age 3 when compared with one begun at age 4. However after the experimental curriculum had been strengthened by applying the concepts of intellectual development devised by Piaget, subsequent interventions (Weikart, 1969) produced substantially higher overall IQ and language gains when initiated with 3 rather than 4 year old children. It may be that the cognitive stages identified by Piaget more adequately specify the progressive learnings that distinguish the needs of 3 year old children from those of 4 year old children. Those who are familiar with preschool programs for 3 and 4 year old children would probably agree that such programs are more alike than different. In addition to cognitive differences it is possible that the interest levels of 3 and 4 year old children are also sufficiently different to require major curriculum variations for the two groups.

Duration of Intervention

The discussion thus far has been limited to the effects of preschool interventions that were either extremely short in duration, similar to summer programs, or only a year in duration. What about the effects of longer periods of preschool intervention? Because of extremely high classroom attrition in most inner city schools, it is very difficult to keep an experimental group together for more than one year. As a result there are very few studies to draw upon for an analysis of longterm intervention effects. Two of the investigators who were able to maintain their groups over a 2 year period experimented with the Bereiter-Engelmann approach. The first study was conducted by Bereiter and Engelmann (1967) themselves. The investigators chose Head Start-eligible 4 year old disadvantaged children with mean Binet IQ's of 95; the experimental group children who daily received 2 hours of Bereiter-Engelmann curriculum showed a 17 point gain during the first year and an additional 9 point gain during the second year. The comparison group which daily received 2 hours of traditional curriculum made an 8 point gain the first year and lost 3 points the second year. In the Karnes (1969) curriculum comparison study reported earlier, the Bereiter-Engelmann trained group made Binet IQ gains of 13 points during the first year and 6 additional points during the second year. Although the Karnes group IQ gains were slightly lower in both the first and second years than those reported in the Bereiter-Engelmann study, the findings of the two studies are similar. Both studies appear to indicate that intelligence test scores can indeed be increased by adding a second year of intervention; however it would seem that the second year increases tend to be one-half as large as those produced during the first year.

Both studies indicate intelligence test scores can be increased by adding a second year of intervention.

Not all 2 year programs have produced cumulative IQ gains.

Not all 2 year programs have produced cumulative IQ gains. After an initial Binet IQ gain of 12.8 points (at age 4) and 11.5 points (at age 3) during the first year of intervention (Wave 0 and Wave 1 groups), children in Weikart's (1967) study demonstrated a slight mean loss of 2.1 and 1.5 points respectively during the second year of preschool. Similar disappointing second year results were obtained by Karnes (1969) with her Ameliorative program. After a Binet IQ increase of 12 points the first year (at age 3), no further increase was made during the second year (at age 4). One might conclude that the second year of intervention was effective because it helped maintain the IQ increases made during the first year. On the other hand one might just as easily conclude that the second year curriculum was inadequately designed to further the cognitive gains produced during the first year. The latter hypothesis receives additional credence when one considers that the successful cumulative effects were obtained by the Bereiter-Engelmann approach—a program carefully sequenced to produce increasingly higher levels of proficiency in language, reading, and mathematics over a 2 year period.

Other Related Variables

There are several other variables which appear to affect the outcome of preschool interventions. Unfortunately there is at present little available specific data from which one can analyze these variables in depth. A few general observations and speculations about some of these variables, however, may be helpful in planning future programs.

A common feature to all successful intervention studies was the large proportion of adults to children in each of the experimental classrooms.

A common feature to all of the successful intervention studies was the large proportion of adults to children in each of the experimental classrooms; in no case was the ratio lower than 2 adults to every 15 children. Generally, there was one teacher and one aide. In every instance the aide, with daily inservice instruction from the head teacher, was expected to teach and interact with individual as well as groups of children. This is a significant departure from the kinds of nonacademic chores usually delegated to aides (e.g., setting out materials, cleaning up messes, preparing snacks, serving lunches, supervising free play); this change in aide role constitutes a practical procedure for providing the more individualized instruction that disadvantaged children require.

A variable inadequately researched but often mentioned as a major factor affecting the longterm outcomes of preschool programs is the school environment to which the child is exposed following the preschool intervention. "School environment" here refers to such factors as appropriateness of curriculum, teacher competence, and teacher attitudes toward disadvantaged children. Some of the recently sponsored government experimental Follow Through projects should provide data on what constitutes an appropriate follow through curriculum for disadvantaged children. Perhaps they may even identify specific competencies and attitudes specifically needed by teachers to effectively teach disadvantaged children.

Follow Through projects should provide data on appropriate follow through curriculum for disadvantaged children.

These, then, are some of the major variables which appear to influence preschool experimental intervention outcomes. The time is long overdue to apply these experimental findings to general preschool programs such as Head Start to determine whether such modifications will improve preschool intervention results with disadvantaged children.

References

Bereiter, C., & Engelmann, S. *Teaching disadvantaged children in the preschool.* Englewood Cliffs, N.J.: Prentice-Hall, 1966.

Bereiter, C., & Engelmann, S. The effectiveness of direct verbal instruction on I.Q. performance and achievement in reading and arithmetic. Unpublished manuscript, University of Illinois, Urbana, 1967.

Berger, B. *A longitudinal investigation of Montessori and traditional prekindergarten training with inner city children.* New York: Center for Urban Education, 1969.

Cicirelli, V. *The impact of Head Start: An evaluation of the effects of Head Start on children's cognitive and affective development.* Springfield, Va.: US Department of Commerce Clearinghouse, PB 184 328, 1969.

Di Lorenzo, L. T., Salter, R., & Brady, J. J. Prekindergarten programs for educationally disadvantaged children. Final report, N.Y. State Education Department, Grant No. OE 6-10-040, US Office of Education, 1969.

Gray, S. W. Selected longitudinal studies of compensatory education—A look from the inside. Paper presented at the annual meeting of the American Psychological Association, Washington, D.C., Sept., 1969.

Gray, S. W., & Klaus, R. A. *The early training project: A seventh year report.* Nashville, Tenn.: Demonstration and Research Center in Early Education, George Peabody College, 1969.

Hodges, W. L., McCandless, B. R., & Spicker, H. H. *Diagnostic teaching for preschool children.* Arlington, Va.: The Council for Exceptional Children, 1971.

Jensen, A. R. How much can we boost I.Q. and scholastic achievement? *Harvard Educational Review,* 1969, **39** (1), 1–123.

Karnes, M. B. Research and development program on preschool disadvantaged children. Final Report, Vol. 1, University of Illinois, Contract No. OE–6–10–235, US Office of Education, 1969.

Klaus, R. A., & Gray, S. W. The early training project for disadvantaged children: A report after five years. *Monographs of the Society for Research in Child Development,* 1968, **33** (4, Whole No. 120) .

Kraft, I., Fuschillo, J., & Herzog, E. Prelude to school: An evaluation of an inner-city preschool program. *Children's Bureau Research Reports,* No. 3, 1968.

Miller, L. B. Experimental variation of Head Start curricula: A comparison of current approaches. Progress Report #7, University of Louisville, Grant No. CG 8199, Office of Economic Opportunity, 1970.

Montessori, M. *The Montessori method.* New York: Schocken Books, 1964.

Weikart, D. P. (Ed.) *Preschool intervention: A preliminary report of the Perry Preschool Project.* Ann Arbor, Mich.: Campus Publishers, 1967.

Weikart, D. P. Comparative study of three preschool curricula. Paper presented at the biennial meeting of the Society for Research in Child Development, Santa Monica, California, March, 1969.

HOWARD H. SPICKER *is Professor and Chairman, Department of Special Education, Indiana University, Bloomington. The research reported herein was performed in part pursuant to Grant No. OEG 9–242178–4149–032, US Office of Education, Bureau of Education for the Handicapped, awarded to Indiana Center for Research and Development on Handicapped Children.*

What it Means to Teach

David Hawkins

A teacher I know commented recently that what held her to the profession, after thirty-five years, was that there was still so much to be learned. A young student reacted in amazement. She supposed it could all be learned in two or three years.

It may be possible to learn in two or three years the kind of practice which then leads to another twenty or forty years of learning. Whether many of our colleges get many of their students on to that fascinating track, or whether the schools are geared to a thoughtful support of such endless learning by their teachers, is another matter.

To understand the dimensions of the teaching art, complex and inexhaustible though it be, is an equally endless commitment and one which needs constant renewal. In this essay I shall try to uncover part of the topic, a part which has fascinated me and one which needs much further investigation. What we mostly know already comes from two sources, one rather diffuse and one rather focused.

The diffuse source is our common sense, where all knowledge begins. By this I do not mean what at any given moment we happen to believe. Honorifically understood, common sense is what we can be led to see and acknowledge when our thoughtful attention is directed to it; knowledge is already there, implicitly, and only needs elucidation and coherent form. It is the kind of knowledge which Plato illustrated in the story of the slave-boy, who, it turned out, knew a lot of geometry though he had never studied the subject and didn't know what he knew. Needless to add, the philosophers are the traditional custodians of this art of teasing out and codifying the things we already somehow know. Though, I hasten to add, they often go off on other tacks, and surely they have no exclusive rights in this domain.

The more focused source is what teachers have learned when they have had cumulatively successful experiences and are able to bring sharp critical attention to the nature of the art they practice.

It might be thought, I should add, that there exists a third source to our knowledge about teaching, that of professional scientific research. But when we ask what notable developments there are in our understanding or control of educationally significant learning, I think the verdict must be that we have very little from formal research. A parallel in the history of science might be nineteenth-century medicine, when most advances came from thoughtful practitioners, and when such novelties as the germ theory had not yet reached beyond the laboratory.

I should like to begin by observing that the teacher-learner relationship is at least as old as our human species, and that its formal institutional framework, though much more recent in origin, is only a stylized and often stilted version of something which goes on all the time among us, especially between the older and the younger. I want to underline the antiquity of this honorable relationship if only to remind you of the obvious, that it is a key link in the chain of human history and culture, and that without it we would perish immediately. Also, to remind you that it is not something on which anyone has a patent.

We in America are sometimes inclined to the view that nothing is known which is not known to a group of people campaigning to have it decided that they are the official knowers. In the past, this kind of claim was often buttressed with special credentials, and it was sometimes justified. In our own milieu it is likely to require certificates of proficiency in something called the scientific method. But the scientific method is also at least as old as our species, and we should remember that the uncertificated may possess a good deal of it. We have indeed seen a number of recent attempts to patent the idea of teaching. The way this is done is typical patent office procedure. You design something called a model, get a grant from a suitable public authority, "train" a group of people to operate it, invent a scale of evaluation, and then show that your model ranks higher on this scale than something else does. In this way, we have discovered the carrot, the stick, the blinder, the shoe, the collar, the bit, the curb, and many other refinements. Most characteristically, we have shown that a programmed computer works a little less badly than a programmed adult, and at least could be cheaper. We need to remind ourselves that all these kinds of things, including the program, if not the machine, have been in the public domain for a long time, and that we should replace the patent office with an institute for the study of educational antiquities.

Having suggested the antiquity of the teacher-learner relationship, and its necessary centrality in all the transmission and evolution of culture, I want also to characterize it in another way. It is a moral relationship; teaching lies inescapably in the moral domain and is subject to moral scrutiny and judgment. If teaching is good or bad, it is morally good or bad. This claim, as I intend it, is not a recommendation or a hoped-for view of the case, but is a claim of fact. The relationship, by its very nature, involves an offer of control by one individual over the functioning of another, who in accepting this offer, is tacitly assured that control will not be exploitative but will be used to enhance the competence and extend the independence of the one controlled, and in due course will be seen to do so.

Of course, all distinctively human relations are moral in this sense, and perhaps also in the sense related to teaching and learning. John Dewey suggested, very profoundly, that the worth of any association and any institution could be measured by its educative value.

Master and Slave   The simplest parody of the teacher-learner relationship is that of the master and the slave, into which the former relation sometimes degenerates. This is particularly easy in the relation of adults to children, and almost inevitable in performance-oriented schools and curricula which try to prespecify the control of children's behavior in a detailed timetable. The classic exposition of the dialectic of the master-slave relation is that of Hegel. What develops hinges on the fact that the slave, deprived of the opportunity to exercise his own powers of self-direction, and accepting his lot, finds himself idle in spirit, however busy in the flesh. In school we used to call this busywork, and its contemporary symbol is the workbook, designed to relieve the master of the tedium of detailed incessant instruction.

But idleness of spirit is a call to rumination and reflection. So the slave becomes reflective; the master, however, is too busy for reflection. The master thinks he is the master because the slave is a slave, while the slave, starting from the opposite premise, realizes that the master's role is itself an enslaving one and learns to manipulate it to his own ends, very much the way in which the cat is sometimes rumored to outwit the inventor of the Skinner box.

If we ask how the teacher-learner roles differ from those of master and slave, the answer is that the proper aim of teaching is precisely to affect those inner processes which, as Hegel (and the stoic philosophers before him) made clear, cannot in principle be made subject to external control, for they are just, in essence, the processes germane to independence, to autonomy, to self-control.

A reasonable general account of the relationship is, therefore, that the teacher is one who acquires authority through a compact of trust, in which the teacher seeks to extend the powers of the learner and promises to abridge them only transiently and to the end of extending them. The teacher offers the learner a kind of loan of himself or herself, some kind of auxiliary equipment which will enable the learner to make transtions and consolidations he could not otherwise have made. And if this equipment is of a kind to be itself internalized, the learner not only learns but begins, in the process, to be his own teacher—and that is how the loan is repaid.

If you like the imagery of feedback loops and information pathways, you can describe the loan in those terms, though I think the human situation is inherently richer than such an analogy can easily suggest, and infinitely richer than the world of our present-day automata. For the enhancement of powers which a teacher offers has to be across the full range of experience—that of goal setting and goal seeking; that of thought and action; that of recapitulation and enjoyment. One of the extraordinary jargons of our time is that which separates education into "cognitive" and "affective," as though feeling were not the monitor of thought, or thought the vehicle of feeling. Pretty soon we will discover the faculty still untouched, and come back around the circuit of antiquities to conative education, the training of the will. God help us. In the old faculty psychology, the cognitive, the affective and the conative were at least seen as inseparable dimensions of any human activity, and not reduced to separate and mutually irrelevant bundles of process.

So it is clear that a teacher does many kinds of things, and of course, the next thing is to say that these all involve communication, two-way interchange. However one studies typical school situations, one finds very little of that. What is found mostly is unidirectional flow, a truncated communication of "instruction" punctuated by fixed alternative responses. Hans Furth has directed all of Piaget's big guns against this dominance of verbally codified unidirectional flow in our schools, but in the process he has managed not to re-emphasize the importance of a different kind of communication, more properly so called, which is two-way and not predictable in its outcome from a perusal of the teacher's notebook.

I think the trouble here, as with much present-day talk about communication and so-called communication skills, is the truncation of an essentially three-term relation so that it is thought of as a two-term relation and, finally, I am tempted to use the absurd expression, a one-term relation. The three-term relation is that of teacher, learner, and subject matter.

Human beings are always engaged in something which William James called flights and perchings. Sometimes, though less often, they are not only momentarily engaged, but are engrossed, concentratedly. John Dewey celebrated the continuity and culmination of this sort of engagement with his famous distinction between experience and *an* experience, that which orders and unifies, which is consummatory, which brings enhancement in its wake. Dewey elsewhere saw this kind of phase as a precondition both of artistic expression and scientific achievement, coming only, as he said, after long absorption in a subject matter which is fresh. Subject matter, then, does not mean, primarily or essentially, what is in books or lectures—and surely not what is in workbooks. Books and lectures have their place—even workbooks on some rare occasions have a place —but subject matter is not what is in them; it is that which they are or try to be about. Subject matter belongs to the universe, and books and lectures are only a small part of the discipline of being engrossed in subject matter. Have you ever though about alternative demonstrations to the one in Euclid, that the area of a triangle is the product of any base times half the corresponding altitude? Two scissor cuts will do it, and I would not dare to guess how many other demonstrations might be found. They all belong to the subject matter, though only one to Euclid.

So communication is a relation between persons whose time tracks of involvement in subject matter are sufficiently parallel to have that subject matter before them jointly, or between them, or sustaining them; then they can both teach and learn. The truncation occurs when codified knowledge takes the place of subject matter in this basic sense. Such truncation is sometimes a component of good teaching, but only when the learner's involvement in primary subject matter has preceded and is temporarily suspended. You can only understand a textbook when you are at the point where you almost don't need to read it, where it helps you comprehend (if it is any good) some higher-order connections among things which you separately have already worked your way through or around. A young child can delight in a story about an elephant family because he can bring to this narrative a wealth of unorganized perceptions and insights which it enables him to recollect, as the poet said, in tranquility. The subject matter is not supplied by the novelist; he must rely all along the way on his many readers' unequal mastery of the implicit order within human affairs; he must design his tale so as to enlist their trust, their surrender of control over their own imaginations, and their ability to bring alive, at his subtly organized command, the inwardness of lives they have never lived.

The presence of subject matter, real or vicariously animated, is the *sine qua non*, the It without which I can know Thee not. People know each other through their common involvements and commitments. To be uninvolved and uncommitted is to have nothing to give and nothing to receive. Billing and cooing have their place, of course, but when you look at that place you see it to be full of complexities which you can only sort out when they take you back to the real world of man and nature. We are so constituted that we amount to nothing without it.

Asymmetry   So I come back to the teacher and learner and the nature of their communication, which has a certain asymmetry required of it. This asymmetry is not the obvious kind, as though the roles could never be reversed. Indeed, the desired outcome is that full symmetry be established, and learners turn into teachers. Part of what a teacher learns along that thirty-five year pathway is quite literally taught by his students. Nevertheless, the asymmetry, if transient, is still there, and we must try to analyze it in more detail.

Let me focus now on what might be called the differential aspect of teaching. This is a sort of short-term cycle which a teacher constantly re-enacts. How does a teacher manage to "lend" resources which a learner will appropriate?

The most obvious metaphor is that of mind-reading. In our philosophical traditions, the idea was dominant for a long time that mind was something private, inner, unobservable, and therefore mind-reading implied some occult faculty, some telepathic invasion. What was available for observation of the ordinary kind was body, behavior. We might try to interpret from behavior what was going on in another's mind.

Now we must not object to this way of talking in everyday life, for the problem of discerning others' thoughts and intentions is often real enough. But the philosophers took it farther. Their analysis seemed to make a total and permanent mystery of what came to be called "the problem of our knowledge of other minds." What we observe is behavior, not mind or conscious existence. For all you know I may be an unthinking automaton, and for all I know you may be. But we can't all be, because I know I am a thinking reed; I also know you say you are as well, but of course you may only be programmed to say this. I hear your retort, and the symmetry of our dilemmas, each saying he knows, is a bit nerve-wracking.

Out of this marvelous philosophical stalemate—the idea that minds are unobservable and unknowable except by a question-begging analogy—came a number of other oddities, like the subjective idealism usually attributed to Berkeley, and like its alter ego, "behaviorism." Psychology wants to be a science, and if we decide that psyche is intrinsically unobservable except by something called introspection, then although we can be polite and admit each other's psyches, we cannot observe them and, therefore, cannot be scientific about it. Behaviorism said let's do away with mind altogether and just study behavior, calling the rest metaphysics. What the behaviorists failed to realize was that it was their own metaphysics they were attacking, and they have persisted in this unenlightened state ever since, in the remarkable belief that their own structure of categories is not metaphysics because it is something they call science. In fact, the word "metaphysics" tends to suffer from a trouble opposite to that of the word "mind" —it is something which only other people suffer from.

Once you reject the conception that minds are things concealed by and within bodies, the whole basis of behaviorism evaporates. It is not even a debatable assertion that human beings have been learning about each other's minds for as long as history, and they have been learning these things in the full context of their own and each other's behavior. Otherwise, we would never have the public concept of mind in the first place to get into philosophical troubles over, when reflection brought us to the point of serious philosophical gambitry.

The trouble with behaviorism is not that it threw out a useless metaphysical notion, but that it did not throw out the gambit that led to that useless notion. Thought words, mind words, words like "concept," "idea," "hope," "intend," "wish," "feel," "fear," "see," etc.—a very big part of the total vocabulary in all languages—do not refer to things which we know in subjective experience and can only (unscientifically) impute to others. They are complex dispositional nouns and verbs, which have evolved over a long history of human communication as being precisely a way of making sense out of human behavior, our own included. Anger is at least as observable as magnetism. The inner subjective feeling, which I feel when I am angry, and you need not, is not the state we call "being angry." My anger is a complex, charged-up state of me which you and I both apprehend —so far as we apprehend it—in the same way. I recognize my state as angry because I am behaving in a way which is properly called angry, and this is true even when I am concealing part of the usual symptoms. If I could conceal them all from you, granted that you are a subtle observer, I would be concealing them from myself as well, and I might then not even know I was angry. And often, as we know, we can understand each other better than we understand ourselves.

So the behaviorists are not wrong in thinking that their subject matter is behavior. The error lies in thinking that the only way, or the only scientifically useful way, of describing behavior is in a version of part of the language of nineteenth-century physics.

Let me illustrate by coming back to mind-reading. Let the learner be a young child not much given to long discourses, but present and operative in a material environment which the school and the teacher have provided, and let the child be singled out for attention because of any one of a variety of circumstances— manner of association with others in a specific activity, manner of involvement or non-involvement with materials, content and style of communication, etc., etc. The teacher begins to assemble such information over a variety of children, although for thirty the task is enormous, and even the best teachers will confess many omissions. Then there is a trial-and-error of communication, further observation, a gradual and still tentative sort of portraiture involving the child's style—strengths, weaknesses, skills, fears, and the like. I single out one aspect of this complex, the way a child comes to grips with some subject matter, matter originally provided because it matches the general level of interest and ability of a still individually unknown group—building blocks, clay, paint, batteries and bulbs. If this subject matter represents something which the teacher has valued and learned from, and seen others learn from, then the teacher has a background for reading the behavior of that child. In a film from Cornell University, a series of kindergarteners come spontaneously to a table to play with an equal-arm balance and a large number of washers and other weights. In watching the film, the observer begins to recognize in himself—if he is personally familiar with the large variety of balance situations which are possible here, and with some of the underlying ideas—the ability to read the levels and the specializations of interest represented in these children, no two alike. What he finds himself doing (but only if he is acquainted with this kind of balance phenomenon and others related to it) is beginning to build what I would call a map of each child's mind and of the trajectory of his life. It is fragmentary, fallible, but it is subject always to correction. And next the observer thinks to himself, what could I do to steady, extend, deepen this engagement I have glimpsed?

The important thing is that, as in all self-instruction, the participant does something. The diagnostic hunch leads to some special provision for this child or that twosome, some intervention, some special protection for a delicate and perhaps fearful beginning, some withdrawal of old materials and insertion of new ones. With large groups, the teacher must be a manager of great skill, evolving a context in which most are involved and self-directing most of the time, so he can really focus for a period on one or a few—discussing, joining, enjoying, directing, or deferring to a child's direction.

In every case, the aim is to repeat this cycle of diagnosing, designing, responding, and then rediagnosing from failure or from a child's confirmation of success. That's the cycle, and with variations it recurs over and over again, never twice the same in detail but with an assurance that will grow by what it feeds on—the finding of match and mismatch between children as the teacher reads them and those kinds of order and organization this reading has helped them extract from their world. I think that is the way it is, every day.

Integral Teaching   But there is another level in teaching, which can be called integral rather than differential. A teacher knows and works with children over a period of time, which, from their perspective, is long. One swallow, or one fine day, as Aristotle observed, does not make a summer. If every day is the same, if there is no movement, no change of pace, and no cumulative history, the process has in some way failed. Many of us know teachers, know classrooms, where the cycle of a teacher's work comes to no apparent fruition in spite of good beginnings. What further conditions must be discussed? It is at this point that I would hesitate and turn the question over to those experienced and reflective teachers from whom, if we persist, we can learn much. But I venture two suggestions, two directions of further inquiry. The first concerns the relation between a curriculum and the teacher's repertoire, as I would call it. The second concerns the art of planning, an art which depends quite essentially on the nature of that repertoire.

The first suggestion is that the way in which a teacher needs to understand subject matter is much richer than that of the linear sequential order which we associate with outlines and syllabi and textbooks. These represent, at their ideal best, a stepwise organization of what has been learned. For a mathematician, it proceeds by steps of logic. For an historian, its steps are chronological, each narrative episode providing a context within which the next can be understood and interpreted. But no such formalized order should be supposed to represent the pathway along which learning does or can probably take place. The latter kind of order is determined by the antecedent learning and other resources of the learner. Very often this inductive order is the reverse of the logical or historical. In an overall sense, history starts in the here and now, a here and now sufficiently discordant with itself to awaken curiosity about how it came to be. Mathematical insight often develops first through involvement with a complexity of pattern and relationship intuitively grasped through practical experience. Aristotle remarked that what is first in the order of intelligibility is often last in the order of learning. In the mind of a good teacher that dictum has the status of a truism. Through practical experience such a teacher knows the diversity of such pathways of learning and is alert to discover new ones. In the mind of such a teacher the organization of subject matter is a network of multiple interconnections, not a single sequence of topical steps laid out in advance. In the first place, that formalized ordering is never unique, as I have already suggested. The history or the Euclidean geometry could be rewritten with equal (or greater) cogency in many different ways. The Pythagorean theorem could be an early simple consequence of the flatness of the plane, and the story of slavery could surely be a part, more problematic and central than it now is, of the bicentennial record.

But in the second place, the network of possible learning paths is more complex and looser in its connections than any text. A teacher's growing knowledge of it (not to be more than started in a college course) can only be coextensive with the constant search for and recognition of learning opportunities for individual children with their unique abilities, backgrounds, and budding interests.

Such a growing repertoire not only increases the target area for initially involving children in fresh subject matter, but facilitates that sort of transition and continuity out of which learning is deepened and extended, out of which education becomes more than a summation of unintegrated episodes.

In an early essay, "The Child and the Curriculum," John Dewey gave recognition to this need for constant re-examination and restructuring of subject matter, and called it, I think unfortunately, the "psychologizing" of knowledge. One aspect (but only one) of this task has been pursued in the traditions of child development, namely in relation to the concept of readiness as a developmental complex. Thus the educative value of young children's aptitude for play has gained recognition, at least in a good though small minority tradition. There, water and sand, clay and blocks, dolls and doll houses do not need to be argued for. But one has the uncomfortable impression that such things are often valued lopsidedly, for only one part of their true worth. Play with such materials is seen as therapeutic and as contributing to children's social maturation among their peers. But the intellectual values of such play, as an exploration of intrinsically worthy subject matter, appears to me to have been typically overlooked. One unfortunate result, I believe, is that in the majority of our schools (in this case nursery school and kindergarten) such materials have been cast out as unrelated to "pre-reading, pre-writing, and pre-arithmetic." In our own work, we have quite consciously and truthfully emphasized the value of play with such materials as encouraging the roots of early science and mathematics. But teachers will not know how to support such aspects of learning unless they themselves have been encouraged to explore and appreciate the manifold ways these simple materials of childhood play are related, as subject matter, to the style and character and history of the great world around us. Balance and flow, size and scale, number and form are all there to be enjoyed, wondered about, and put in place. Unfortunately, such subject matter, though enjoyed and appreciated by some of our best minds in research and scholarship, are not much valued in our college curricula; they are too "elementary."

It may be thought that this imbalance has been redressed through our increasing attention to the "cognitive" investigations of Piaget, and indeed that work is a valuable contribution to the need which Dewey defined. But just as Freudian glasses filter out much from one perspective, so those of the Piagetian schemes give us only a one-dimensional view of a potential repertoire which almost no one, as yet, has begun to build in its true proportions. And surely this repertoire, as skillful teachers will help evolve it, will provide in its network for all the human faculties, which it is the aim of education to cultivate. Such teachers need our respect, as they need our help.

VIII. TEACHER INTERACTION

In order to measure, let alone to modify, the effects of teaching upon learning, educational psychologists must strive constantly to clarify knowledge about the nature of the teacher-student relationship. Common sense metaphors that define this relationship are very ancient: The student has often been imagined to be an empty vessel into which the teacher pours knowledge, or an empty slate, waiting to be inscribed.

Each branch and each school of psychology approaches this issue differently. David Elkind's article in this section, for example, uses a combination of social and cultural psychology to characterize the contractual elements in a two-person interaction system. Robert L. Hamblin and associates applied the learning theory of B. F. Skinner to a process for modifying, through positive and negative reinforcements, the nature of teacher-student interactions. The task of the educational psychologist is to integrate the theories of many behavioral scientists and to design research that will test the integration.

Neo-Freudian studies of the issue, such as those conducted by the late Jules Henry, have made plain the proposition that teacher-student transactions *cannot* be understood through information gathered by interviewing teachers. Henry showed that teachers may express a philosophy of teaching that bears no discernible resemblance to their observed behavior with students. Video-taping classroom teachers, or what is called *micro-teaching*, verifies the proposition. Most teachers are shocked to witness themselves on the video screen. They are not accustomed to seeing themselves from without. And, since the classroom is usually one of the last visited of locations, from first grad to graduate school, teachers get little feedback on their performances.

Similarly, research that concentrates exclusively on categorizing or rating teaching behavior through the use of observers has been shown repeatedly to yield findings that have weak correlations with learning outcomes. What is required instead is systematic observation of the *interaction* between teacher and students and between students within a learning group.

Even then, where studies of elementary schoolchildren are concerned, little of value may result. One of the reasons is implied in the articles by Todd Risley and Sara H. Arnaud in this section. Risley's views complement those of Elkind. They imply that the student must be equipped with contractually appropriate behaviors—skills and attitudes—before the interaction within a classroom can prove efficacious. In this view, the quality of the interaction depends very heavily upon the presence of "inputs" from the learner.

Arnaud suggests that the cultural frame of reference of the classroom teacher should be expanded to include more than the readiness of the learner to *work*. Her emphasis upon the value of play and creative imagination as resources for cognitive development implies the presence of a teacher who is capable of imaginative utilization of these resources.

Beginning teachers often panic for want of directions about how to interact educatively. They know, for example, that they are supposed to be knowledgeable, to evaluate the needs and interests of their students, to plan instruction around these evaluations, to be fair and sensitive, yet in control of the classroom. But when all of this is said and done, what transactions with the students will turn out to make some observable difference? The panic subsides, usually, as beginners *model* their teaching after influential teachers they have known and as they take in clues from the veteran teachers they meet in the lounge and in the corridors. These sources may prove misleading, of course, for the beginner has no way of knowing whether her or his models or new associates have devised effective transactions.

As educational psychologists manage to generalize knowledge about the relative effectiveness of a typology of teacher-student interactions, teachers in the future will be prepared with greater precision to be able to shape their behavior efficaciously. The emergence of a true profession of teaching hinges upon the advent of such knowledge.

Teacher-Child Contracts[1]

David Elkind

Every historical period has a particular emphasis or focus that gives it a unique quality and character. In many ways we are perhaps too close to our own era to see it clearly and with perspective. Nonetheless, I shall venture to say that one theme of our era in history is the concern with creativity, with new and emergent phenomena and the processes that have brought them about. We are, I believe, moving rapidly away from the reductionist theories which dominated the physical, biological, and social sciences in the nineteenth and early twentieth centuries and which have been progressively challenged by the derivations of Einstein's theory of relativity.

Within psychology, the movement away from reductionism was hampered by the dominance of learning theory in academia and of psychoanalysis in the clinic. Although these two approaches to human behavior were and often are violently opposed to one another, they are alike in holding to the belief that complex human behavior can best be understood by reducing it either to its elementary components (learning theory) or to its historical and instinctual determinants (psychoanalysis). It is my belief that psychoanalysis and learning theory can coexist, despite their differences, because of their common belief that human behavior cannot be taken at face value but rather has to be seen as something else, something more simple, before it can be understood.

There are many evidences, however, that a new, *epigenetic* approach to human behavior is becoming increasingly prominent in modern psychology. The work of Jean Piaget, as an illustration, has emphasized the emergence, at successive age levels, of new mental structures that cannot be derived from or reduced to the preceding structures in any simple way. Likewise, the work of Erik Erikson has emphasized the emergent strengths and traits that occur at each stage of the life cycle and which, again, are not reducible to instincts or past history alone. The growing "human potentials" movement is still another illustration of the trends away from reductionism and toward an appreciation of creation and of emergent phenomena in human behavior.

The following discussion of teacher-child contracts stems from this new mode of thinking within psychology. It assumes that interpersonal relations are themselves creations or constructions which cannot be reduced to the personalities, or personal qualities, of those who participate in them. Just as crowd or mob behavior cannot be understood solely in terms of the personalities of the members of the crowd, so the interaction between even two persons cannot be understood solely in terms of their individual personalities. To understand their behavior we need, in addition, to know what emerges in the process of interaction. The present paper is concerned with one such emergent phenomenon.

Let us begin with the assumption that every human interaction presupposes some form of contractual relationship. Take, for example, the most casual encounter between acquaintances. After greetings have been exchanged and polite conversation begins, certain contractual obligations come into play. Each participant agrees to listen to the other and to respond with appropriate signs of interest and concern. That such contracts do exist is immediately obvious when the contract is broken. For example, if participant A is inattentive, looks at the girls passing by, calls participant B by the wrong name, and in other ways gives evidence of not having listened to a word that was said, participant B will become angry. He becomes angry because participant A has broken the implicit contract that exists between any two people holding a conversation.

I could give many more examples, but perhaps this one will suffice to suggest the generality of interpersonal contracts. There are certain advantages to looking at human interactions in terms of contracts. One of the most important of these advantages is that it takes us away from looking at interpersonal problems in terms of personality. To illustrate, anyone can be sufficiently preoccupied at some point in his life to violate the conversational contract in the manner of participant A in the example. To attribute A's difficulty with participant B to A's personality would thus miss the crux of the problem, which has to do primarily with a breach of contract and its consequences.

The same (or so it seems to me) holds true in education. Too often, the academic failure of students is attributed to personal qualities such as low intelligence or "laziness" when in fact the problem lies in the relationship between pupil and teacher or child and parents. Likewise, the failure of many teachers in the inner city is often attributed, directly or indirectly, to the evilness of their personalities. In fact, however, the culprit is more often a real or imagined breach in the implicit contractual arrangements between teacher and child. As long as we search for "the personality" of the school dropout or of the unsuccessful teacher we will be seeking something as ephemeral as a will-o'-the-wisp. A more productive approach, in my view,[2] is to look at both school failure and success from the standpoint of the extent to which teachers and children fail to meet their unspoken contractual obligations.

As a general rule, a contract consists of mutual expectations of the contracting parties. In the case of children, these expectations arise in the context of the child's earliest interpersonal relations with his parents and are then generalized and modified as the child's social world expands and he begins to interact with other children and adults. Most economically advantaged children have, by the time they enter school, come to operate on the basis of three, more or less general, contractual arrangements. These parent-child contracts dictate the initial contractual expectations children have with respect to their teachers.

First of all, the economically advantaged child has come to expect that he will be given new freedoms according to his willingness to accept new responsibilities. The basis for these expectations is laid early in childhood, when parents allow the child to do such things as pour his own drinks and handle his own food if he demonstrates he will not spill the drink or throw the food on the floor. As the child grows older the freedoms and responsibilities change as the child's capacities and skills mature. To illustrate, a preschool child may be allowed to cross the street if he demonstrates that he looks both ways and does not cross until it is safe. In adolescence the same contract holds, but with different content. The adolescent boy may be allowed to use the car if he demonstrates skill and care in driving. The young person thus comes to expect that he will be granted freedom when he demonstrates a reciprocal willingness to assume responsibility.

A second expectation held by the economically advantaged child is that his achievements will be rewarded with emotional, intellectual, and material support. Again, the character of the achievements and supports changes as the child matures, but the nature of the contract remains the same. The young child expects to be rewarded for going to the toilet by himself, putting on his own clothes, learning the alphabet, and being able to count to ten.

He is rewarded with hugs and kisses, verbal approval, toys, and sweets. At a more advanced age level, the child's achievements are, again, supported in multiple ways. The child who does well in school is rewarded materially, verbally, and affectively by his parents. Likewise, the child's extracurricular activities, such as participating in drama or in sports or playing a musical instrument, are supported by the parents' financial investment in coaching and lessons and by parental attendance at plays and recitals. At all age levels, the economically advantaged child comes to expect that his achievements will be rewarded by support from his parents.

Still a third expectation the economically advantaged child brings to school has to do with loyalty and commitment. Generally a child is loyal to his parents, in part at least, because the parents are the basic providers. As the child grows older and more independent, he begins to assess parental commitment in terms of the time his parents spend with him. The child tends to apportion his loyalty to parental values and activities according to how much he regards his parents as committed to him. This particular contract, and this is true somewhat for the others as well, has something of a sleeper clause. The child who feels he has not received sufficient freedom, support, or commitment may not express his dissatisfaction until adolescence. In part, the intensity of the adolescent rebellion derives from the fact that it is a reaction to real or imagined wrongs that have accumulated during the whole era of childhood. However that may be, even the kindergarten child from an economically advantaged home comes to school with expectations that he will be given freedom in return for taking responsibility, that he will be given support for his achievements, and that the teacher will be committed to his education to the extent that he is loyal to the values and activities she represents.

Let us look now at the expectancies held by the teacher as she enters the classroom. In a majority of cases, she herself comes from an economically advantaged family and is therefore aware of the contractual expectancies of her pupils and is ready to reciprocate. The relative "easiness" of teaching in suburban schools derives from the fact that teachers and children come into the classroom with reciprocal and matching contractual expectations. The teacher perpetuates the contracts of the parents when she, for example, allows a child the freedom to go to the library on his own when he demonstrates that he will not abuse this privilege. Likewise, she rewards academic success with verbal praise and high grades. Finally, she reciprocates the loyalty shown her by her pupils, usually in the form of demonstrations of respect and obedience, with the commitment of much time and energy to her children.

Over and above these contractual expectancies, which both teachers and children carry over from their experiences at home, are additional contracts unique to the school situation. The individual classroom, where the child is among a large group of his peers with a single adult present, engenders three new contractual expectancies. That is, some teacher-child contracts merely perpetuate expectancies originating in the home, others are new and emerge out of the uniqueness of the classroom situation.

The first and perhaps the most important teacher-child contract has to do with fairness and cooperation. Children, individually and as a group, expect that teachers will not show favoritism among their charges. They expect that special privileges and desired chores and grades will be distributed to all children on the basis of equality and merit rather than on the basis of personal attributes. In return for their teacher's fairness, the children are willing to grant her the *sine qua non* for sanity in the classroom, namely, cooperation. (Obviously this contract holds in families, too, but age differences confound the picture, since such differences make inequality of treatment—such as the setting of different bedtimes—fair because of inequality of age.)

A second contract that comes to play in the classroom situation has to do with competence and respect. Children think of the teacher as a professional, an expert like a doctor or a dentist, who knows her job. When the teacher comes to class prepared, when she shows she can handle the group, the children feel they are learning and growing and extend her that lovely attitude, respect. Contrariwise, the teacher who does not come prepared with the appropriate educational materials or who does not have the ability to handle her pupils loses their respect because of her incompetence.

A final contract, which is a little harder to observe and quantify, involves the teacher's warmth on the one hand and the children's affection on the other. The warm teacher is one who likes and enjoys children. Such a teacher makes the classroom a happy place by her laughter, her willingness to play as well as to work, and her tolerance of childish frailties. A warm teacher is not necessarily an overpermissive teacher; she can set limits with firmness but without harshness. Such teachers readily win the affection of their children.

These, then, are three of the contractual arrangements that emerge in the classroom situation between teachers and children. The teacher who is fair in her treatment of children wins their cooperation, and their cooperation strengthens her willingness to be fair. Likewise, the teacher who is prepared, who demonstrates that she is competent to teach, wins the respect of her children, and this respect strengthens her sense of being prepared and in control. Finally, the teacher who displays warmth toward her charges wins affection in return. Obviously, to the extent that the teacher is unfair, incompetent, or cold, to that extent will the children be uncooperative, disrespectful, or hostile. However, it is also true that uncooperative, disrespectful, and hostile children can force a teacher to be unfair, incompetent, and cold. In other words, children as well as teachers can initiate the breach of contract. Let us now look at some familiar classroom offenses from the standpoint of the contracts outlined above.

Consider, for example, the undisciplined child. Such a child often takes liberties such as leaving his seat or the room without taking corresponding responsibility. That is, he not only leaves his seat but also bothers other children. Clearly the undisciplined child has violated the freedoms-responsibility contract. What often follows is that the teacher in effect rewrites the contract, which now becomes a freedoms-punishment arrangement. The child is told, and now the teacher verbalizes the new contract because the implicit verbal contract was not honored, that if he takes unearned freedoms he will be punished.

Another way of handling the situation is to verbalize the freedoms-responsibility contract and hence to offer the undisciplined child freedoms for taking responsibility. Here, contract theory touches upon behavior-modification procedures. Behavior modification involves rewarding desired behaviors and ignoring undesired ones, just what the contract theory urges. In addition, however, contract theory suggests that what is being modified is not simply behavior but rather the expectations of what that behavior will bring. Contract theory also dictates what *kinds* of rewards should be used to reaffirm the interpersonal contracts that underlie successful human interactions at home, at school, and elsewhere.

Children are not, however, the only ones in the classroom who break contracts; teachers can violate them as well. Consider the uncommitted teacher who is chronically unprepared and unwilling to do more than the absolute minimum amount of work for her children. This lack of commitment is immediately sensed by the children, who feel, correspondingly, that they owe her no loyalty and that her poor teaching warrants no respect. As a result the children may, among other things, talk and complain about her to their parents and to other teachers. Such a teacher can often be helped by a sympathetic supervisor or principal who sees the problem in contractual terms. Often, the teacher in question is unaware of the relationship between her behavior and the pupil reaction. When the matter is discussed in terms of contracts rather than in terms of her character, the teacher feels less threatened and more willing to change than if her personality were brought into question.

Many more examples of classroom difficulties could be discussed from the standpoint of contract theory, but the examples cited above may help to suggest how it can be applied in practical situations where teachers and children come with the same general contractual expectations. Before we turn to the situation where there is a marked discrepancy between the expectations of the teacher and the majority of her pupils, a few general comments about teacher-child contracts are in order so that misunderstanding will be avoided.

First of all, both teachers and children necessarily break their contracts on one occasion or another. By and large this does no permanent damage, and the work of the classroom is only temporarily disrupted. When, however, the child or the teacher continually violates the contractual agreements, severe ruptures are bound to occur in the relationships in question. Children who are perpetually disruptive and teachers who are chronically unprepared, for example, force a rewriting of the teacher-child contract. In other words, it is only long-standing violations of the contractual obligations between teacher and child that severely disrupt the educational process.

A second aspect of contractual lapses is that ruptures in one contract can be remedied by close adherence to obligations under a different contract. For example, the undisciplined child who is also very loyal and is a high achiever will be given more consideration than a child who is both a nuisance and a poor performer in school. Likewise, children will tolerate a humorless, overstrict teacher if she is committed to her teaching activities and is assiduously fair with her students. Violations of one aspect of a teacher-child contract can, then, be softened by better-than-average fulfillment of obligations in other domains.

So far we have spoken of economically advantaged teachers and children, and we now need to consider the situation where the economically advantaged teacher is confronted with a roomful of economically disadvantaged children. Such confrontations are dangerous for two different but related reasons. One reason is that teacher and children come into the classroom with quite different contractual expectations. The second and more significant reason is that both teacher and children are usually unaware that their expectancies are not in agreement. In these circumstances what often happens is that both teacher and children feel that the contract has been violated. But the blame is not laid to a mutual misunderstanding but rather to the prejudice of the teacher (by the children) and to the stupidity and poor upbringing of the children (by the teacher). It is my belief that much of the difficulty in urban schools lies in the contractual violations unwittingly perpetuated by teachers and children in the ghetto school.

By and large, the economically disadvantaged child has had experience wth responsibility, achievement, and loyalty contracts, but his contractual expectations are likely to be different from those of the child from an economically more advantaged home. While it is dangerous to generalize because of the many exceptions, it is probably fair to say that, on the average, children from economically distressed homes are more likely than children from affluent families to have experienced negative rather than positive contractual arrangements. That is, economically limited parents are more likely than affluent parents to threaten punishment for lack of responsibility, achievement, and loyalty. In such families the mothers often work, and the fathers may be absent or holding two or more jobs. Achievement, responsibility, and loyalty on the part of the children are seen as necessities for survival and for moving out of economic distress. It is because the economically pressured parent views achievement, responsibility, and loyalty as essential to the survival of his children that he punishes them

if they fail to perform appropriately.

When children with a punishment-avoidance orientation toward interpersonal contracts come into a room with a teacher who has a reward-gaining orientation toward contracts, difficulties are bound to ensue. What often happens is that the children want to clarify the contract—to discover the nature of the punishments they will receive for any lack of achievement, responsibility, loyalty, or cooperation. They may, as a consequence, defy the teacher and refuse to work or to cooperate in any other way. If the teacher does not understand this behavior as an attempt to clarify the contractual arrangement, she will interpret it as a flagrant example of uncooperativeness, disrespect, and hostility. In these circumstances she feels no obligation to fulfill her part of the bargain—to be fair, warm, and prepared—and sees her role as one of merely meting out punishment.

What happens, then, is that the children are reinforced in their belief that the major reason for achievement, responsibility, loyalty, and cooperation is the avoidance of punishment. School then becomes a game wherein the children try to be as unachieving, irresponsible, disloyal, and uncooperative as possible without incurring punishment. The teacher, for her part, gives up her intention to teach and becomes, in many ways, the same kind of adult the children have already experienced, namely, one who urges them to achieve, to be responsible and cooperative, not for positive rewards but rather to avoid punishment. The avoidance of punishment is, of course, the least effective of all educational motivations.

How can this vicious cycle be broken? It can be broken, it seems to me, if the teacher is cognizant of the expectations her children bring to class. In the case of economically disadvantaged children, the teacher's first task is to teach them the terms of the contractual relationship. She needs to emphasize the positive rewards of achievement, responsibility, and cooperation. Instead of punishing children for their misbehavior she must reward their positive achievements. Again, the aim is not simply to modify behavior but rather to modify the child's understanding of the contractual arrangements.

Let me give a concrete example. Several years ago I taught second-grade children for one full semester. Most of the children were black and from the ghetto. In the beginning the children did a great deal of testing to see what kind of punishment I would mete out. While I indicated that I did not approve of misbehavior, I took an accepting, somewhat joking attitude toward it. Moreover, I tried to introduce the positive system of giving rewards for cooperation and achievement.

During reading, for example, everyone was given some special function. Two children, a boy and a girl, were "choosers" who chose the children who were to read next. Another child was the "keeper of the place" and helped the other children who had lost their place in the story. Another child was "keeper of the page" and wrote on the board the number of the page we were reading. A rather big, husky boy was chosen as the "shusher" to keep the whispering children from disrupting the reading. A good reader was chosen as the "helper" who helped children who were having difficulty reading particular words. Other children were chosen as "keepers of the books," and they distributed and collected the books. Still other children were chosen to erase the board and to straighten the desks. Not only were the children kept busy; they were learning that rewards, in the form of special recognition, could be the result of achievement and cooperation.

While I do not suggest that my practice be adopted as a model, I do think the general principle is valid. The teacher's first task is to clarify the contractual expectations between herself and her children. If there is a discrepancy she must try to teach the children, or the child, what the nature of the contract is. And, since positive attitudes are much more effective than negative ones, teacher-child contracts based on rewards are likely to be more effective in furthering the educational process than contracts based on punishments.

To be sure, the clarification of teacher-child contracts will not resolve all educational ills, many of which derive from other sources. What contract theory can do is give the teacher another way of looking at and conceptualizing her relationships with her pupils and a new direction for handling interpersonal difficulties. The advantage of the contractual model for looking at the teacher-child relationship is that it gets away from the idea of "blaming" anyone for the difficulty and hence away from arousing defensive and educationally nonproductive attitudes and behaviors.

It should be said, in closing, that this way of looking at classroom interaction is a schema derived from my own experience in working with children and teachers. It would, however, be relatively easy to test in an experimental way. For example, the schema suggests that teachers who were rated highest in competence, fairness, and warmth by their pupils or by independent observers in the classroom would have the most cooperative, respectful, and affectionate pupils. Likewise, one would predict that an extremely competent but unfair teacher would be rated less highly in respect than an equally competent teacher who was fair. These are but some of the predictions which the contract approach to teacher-child contracts suggests. Regardless of whether this particular schema wins research support, however, I believe we need a theory which will look at teacher-child interactions as a new phenomenon not entirely reducible to the personalities and backgrounds of the participants.

1. Commencement address delivered at Bank Street College of Education, June 5, 1970.
2. Contract or "exchange" theory is widely applied in economics and sociology, but to my knowledge it has not yet been employed in the discussion of educational issues. This type of theory bears no relation to the currently popular "performance contracting."

JENNY LEE

Learning & Lollipops

By Todd Risley

Play with a play car.
Play with a truck, play with a play car, get on a seesaw and play with a train.
My mama bought them last night when Dan's daddy took her to the Salvation Army.
The Salvation Army is uptown, uptown.
All the way up there in the projects, Dan lives in the projects.
Dan lives across the street from Edward's house.
Me and Dan. Me and Dan went to the store and bought some candy.
Here's one that was on the floor.
We found it on the ground.
Some money.
We found it; we found it on the ground. One penny, two penny.
We found it.
A penny.
And we ride the play cars to the store.
Some sugar and a sucker for to eat.
We eat a candy sucker.

These lines are not blank verse, or at least they were not intended as such. They were spoken by a four-year-old boy receiving narration training at a preschool for culturally deprived children. His teacher has asked, "What do you do when you go home from school? . . . And what else . . . and what else . . . and what else?" This boy is an inarticulate child from an inarticulate family, the kind of child who grows up in our society to be Stanley Kowalski.

As a child grows up, he acquires "culture" chiefly from three sources: from his parents, from his peers, and from the public schools. In view of that fact, it is hardly surprising that those who are culturally deprived as infants usually become culturally deprived adults. Parents and peers cannot easily transmit what they themselves lack, and the public schools apparently offer too little too late —or, to put it another way, too much too soon.

When the culturally deprived child enters kindergarten, he lacks the social and language skills that the schools assume a child of five will possess. Since his parents do not stress the importance of school achievement, he also lacks motivation. In addition, the situation at home may be such that he is not particularly sensitive to the smiles and frowns with which his teacher will attempt to shape his behavior.

One way to attack this problem is to find a way to modify the behavior of the deprived preschool child so that when he enters school, he will be in a better position to learn what is being taught there. This is the purpose of the Juniper Gardens Children's Project.

The residents of Juniper Gardens, an area located in northeastern Kansas City, Kansas, have the lowest median annual income in the city. 90 per cent of them belong to the poverty class; 99.5 per cent are Negro; and about 70 per cent of those over 25 have not graduated from high school.

Under the auspices of the University of Kansas, my colleagues and I are conducting two preschool programs with the children and parents from Juniper Gardens. One is for members of the "hard-core" poverty class, the other for members of the "upwardly mobile" poverty class. The chief difference between the two programs is that the first is for children only, whereas the second is for children and their mothers, and especially for the mothers.

In the program for the hard-core group, the Turner House program, we teach the children skills that we hope will be useful to them in public school— to follow directions, to describe objects and events, and so forth. In the program for the upwardly mobile group, the Parent-Teacher Cooperative Preschool, we teach mothers how, in general, to communicate more effectively with their children and how, specifically, to teach them skills they will need in school. That is, the Turner House program supplements, while the Parent-Teacher Pre-school attempts to modify, the home environment of the child.

For Turner House, we recruited four-year-olds from families characterized by multiple problems: absence of a father, many children, extreme poverty, ramshackle housing, child neglect, and histories of unemployment, poor health, criminal and deviant behavior, alcoholism, and the like. In some cases, it proved necessary to offer the mother a weekly cash fee for her "trouble" in getting the child ready for preschool; thus some of the twelve children in the program were, in effect, rented.

Most children arrived at school without breakfast. We therefore fed them supplementary meals, and we also experimented, very successfully, with the use of food as a reinforcement for behavior we wanted maintained. This is quite a departure from the usual teaching techniques of both public and nursery schools, which are based chiefly on positive social reinforcement. But with these children, warm praise rarely proved powerful enough rapidly to effect extensive changes in behavior.

The teachers carried about, in baskets and in their plastic-lined jumper pockets, sugar-coated cereals, grapes and pieces of apple, tiny sandwiches, M&M candies, and cookies. When the children worked at tables, teachers carried pitchers and poured small quantities of milk, juice, or warm soup into mugs for each child. These snacks invariably were accompanied by smiling, warm-voiced statements of approval, appreciation, or affection, and these statements very often were offered without food. We hoped in this way to increase the effectiveness of social reinforcement with the children, and thus prepare them for the public-school classroom.

Some of the behavior we tried to teach the children at first may seem trivial. For example, we spent considerable time teaching them to say "good morning" to their teachers. This may not seem the stuff from which successful scholars are made. However, the child who says "good morning" cheerfully and consistently when he arrives at school will dispose most teachers quite favorably toward him—our own teachers testified to this during the experiment—and the credit he gains may survive a good deal of academic bumbling later in the day. This credit is useful, because it may make the teacher more likely to praise approximations of learning in the child.

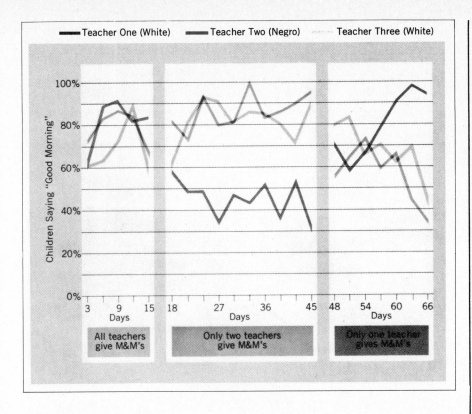

Teacher One (White) Teacher Two (Negro) Teacher Three (White)

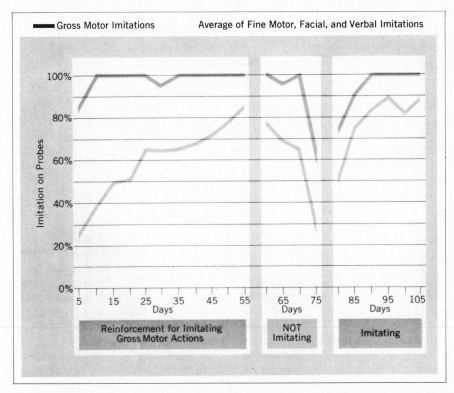

Gross Motor Imitations   Average of Fine Motor, Facial, and Verbal Imitations

A similar rationale lay behind several other "social" projects, such as teaching the child to be quiet in some work situations and to converse in others, and to raise his hand and wait to be recognized before speaking in group discussions.

Rightly or wrongly, formal schooling is chiefly an exercise in language, so we gave considerable attention to developing the language skills of the children.

We tried to improve their skill at imitation, so that they might make linguistic gains from any language community in which they found themselves. We also picked one especially inarticulate child —the author of the "poem" that opens this article—and taught him to describe, in logically connected, meaningfully elaborated, and even factually correct narratives, his own experiences.

These projects will serve to illustrate the kind of thing we tried to do and the way we tried to do it, but there were others, of course. For example, we trained the children in the use of color and number adjectives and studied the effect the training had on their spontaneous conversation. And we experimented with various different kinds of reinforcement and reinforcement conditions. One, in addition to food, that proved especially powerful was the materials and equipment of the schoolroom. It seemed that, when a child wanted to ride a tricycle, nothing in his environment was as important to him as that tricycle. Teachers therefore made it available to the child only after he had performed some task, such as naming or describing it.

As each child entered the preschool in the morning, removed his coat, and proceeded to his seat, each of the three teachers smiled at him and said, "Good morning." At the beginning of the school year, only about 20 per cent of the children answered any teacher appropriately. These the teachers would reinforce with social approval. Over the next three months, the average number of children answering the teachers' greetings rose from 20 per cent to between 70 and 80 per cent.

By mid-December, it was clear that no further improvement was likely. So, as a test of the durability of this new skill, the teachers discontinued the stimulus to which the children had responded. They stood at the door as usual, but they did not speak to the children as they entered. Although the children who continued to say "good morning" were answered and praised as usual, the number who did so fell immediately to 20 per cent and fluctuated from 15 to 45 per cent for six days. Then it collapsed to zero.

It appeared that behavior with social consequences would not be maintained unless supported at both ends, by a preceding stimulus as well as by subsequent approval. When the teachers began greeting the children with a smiling "good morning" again, 80 per cent of the children promptly began replying.

However, our aim was to teach the children to say "good morning" whether greeted first by the teacher or not. Therefore we brought a more powerful reinforce into play. Each teacher gave an M & M to each child who answered her greeting appropriately. The number of children replying rose at once to 100 per cent and remained there for the last five days of this condition. Then the teachers again discontinued their initial greetings. As before, some children stopped saying "good morning" as they entered, but far fewer stopped than before. As long as the M & M's were used, about 95 per cent continued to greet the teachers despite their silence.

To make sure it was the candy that made the difference, we stationed all three preschool teachers at the door but supplied only one of them with M & M's. We thought that over the weeks, when first one teacher and then another had the M & M's, the children would speak most often to the teacher who distributed the candy. This turned out to be true [*see illustration, page 30*]. However, we also expected the children to behave with a modicum of consistency toward the third teacher, who throughout the whole ten weeks of the experiment offered social reinforcement only, no M & M's.

Instead, most children spoke to the third teacher whenever they spoke to the first teacher. During the first seven weeks of the experiment, when the first teacher had M & M's and the third did not, the most children said "good morning" to both of them; during the last three weeks, when the first teacher had no candy, greetings to the third teacher fell off as well. I am sorry to report that this seemed to indicate racial discrimination in our children: the first and third teachers were white, and the second was Negro.

The public school, of course, does not offer M & M's for desirable behavior. However, our results indicate the need for something more powerful than friendly approval to establish durable behavior in the children, especially if the behavior is to remain despite minimal stimulus support. Had we not run out of time, we would have begun shifting the behavior maintained by candy to the control of social approval only, a process that requires consistent social reinforcement combined with a gradual cutback on the distribution of M & M's.

An ability to imitate the teacher, especially her use of language, is particularly valuable for the child from a culturally deprived background. Most culturally deprived children learn a different dialect at home from the one they will hear in school. Consequently they will have trouble understanding what they hear and being understood when they speak. It is unlikely that the child's dialect will be modified in school unless he under-

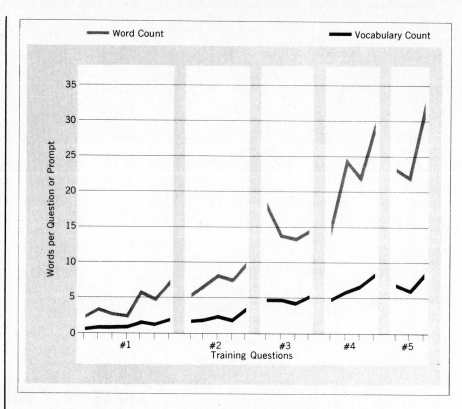

takes the modification himself, a possible task—many a Midwesterner has done it at Harvard—but one that requires what is called a "good ear."

Therefore we set out to develop the children's ability to imitate. We did not begin by asking them to imitate verbal statements. We started with gross motor imitations, progressed to fine motor imitations, and then to facial responses, and only at the end added

verbalizations. The program had two parts: training sessions that stressed each kind of imitation in turn, and nontraining sessions, or probes, that tested the effects of the training.

In the training sessions, three children worked with a model teacher. At first, the teacher did nothing more than sit down on a rug and take a bit of snack for herself from a bowl. The children were prompted by another teacher to

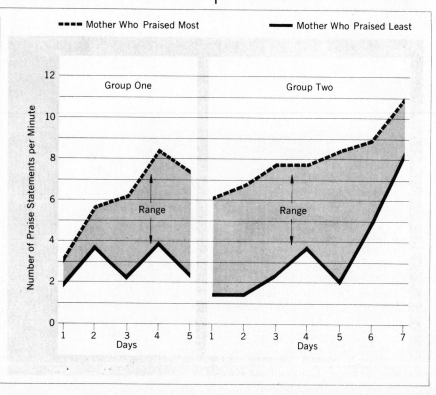

do as the model teacher had done, including taking a bit of snack in their own cups.

Then the second teacher took charge of the snack bowl, and she provided food only when the child imitated the part of the model teacher's behavior that was the subject of training. In early sessions, the child was given a snack whenever he imitated the model teacher's gross motor behavior—raising the arms, leaning to one side, and the like. Later, training passed to more detailed motor imitations and finally to speech.

Periodically, the model teacher tested each child's ability to imitate a complex performance. The tests consisted of four acts performed simultaneously: a gross motor act, a fine motor act, a facial expression, and a verbal statement. For example:

Probe I. Arms out to the side, palms of hands turned back, face frowning, statement: "This too shall pass away." During the test each child was reinforced if he imitated the teacher's gross motor act, whether he imitated the other components of her performance or not.

As it turned out, the children imitated all the teacher's actions with increasing accuracy. They imitated best the act that was the subject of training at the time, but they did not lose the skills they had learned earlier. So, when speech finally was added to the training, the children began to imitate it reliably, and they continued at the same time to imitate gross, fine motor, and facial acts. This apparently represented a growing ability to observe and imitate a complex performance, even when unreinforced, which was exactly the result we wanted.

It is always important in studies like this one to demonstrate that the outcome was indeed the result of the conditions applied. Otherwise one finds oneself clinging superstitiously to useless procedures. So, after the children were far into the program, we began giving bits of food to one child in each group of three when he did *not* imitate the model teacher. The procedure did greatly reduce that child's tendency to imitate. When snacks again were given for imitation, the child also began to imitate again, as well as or better than he had before. [*See illustration, page 31.*]

The ultimate intent of imitation training was to give the children the ability to listen to novel language performances and to repeat them. In one year, it was possible only to develop training to the point where the children consistently imitated fairly short sentences. To be useful, the program would have to increase the children's skill with longer and longer verbal performances. Whether that can be done remains to be seen; it is one subject of the current year's research. But the success of the program so far suggests that the extension of verbal imitative skills to complex statements is probably a practical goal.

Any child may have a much more elaborate verbal repertoire than he demonstrates in a spontaneous account of some happening. To find out whether we could bring that repertoire into use, and perhaps add to it as well, we chose a child who was probably the least articulate in the group.

We began by finding out just how inarticulate he was. The teacher asked, repeatedly over a period of 13 days, five questions such as "Who do you like to play with?" In answer to these questions, the child usually answered with one word or two, yielding a grand average over repeated inquiries of one-and-one-half words per answer.

Then the teacher began training. She asked, "What did you see on the way to school?" When she prompted the boy's answers with "What else," he simply repeated one- and two-word answers, alternating between the two responses, "A doggie" and "TV," and repeating the pair over and over.

When it had become clear that this pattern was not likely to change by itself, the teacher provided a more logical prompt: "What kind of doggie?" The boy replied that it was a German shepherd, and the teacher praised him and gave him a bit of snack. Then she asked again what he saw on the way to school. He answered, "A doggie." At this point, the teacher raised her eyebrows, cocked her head, and waited. Presently the child amended his answer: "A German shepherd doggie," and was praised and fed.

When the original question was asked again, with the reply "A German shepherd doggie," the child was given a second prompt: the teacher asked what the doggie was doing. In this way the training proceeded, with the teacher prompting each logical step, waiting for all previous steps to be chained together in reasonable sequence, and reinforcing only increasingly long and meaningfully connected sequences. The child's average answer to this first question eventually rose to about 200 words per ten-minute session, which amounted to about 50 words per session if duplications were eliminated.

Then the teacher asked a new question, "What do you do when you go home from school?" The child's answer showed that he had profited from the training on the first question; therefore the teacher reduced her logical prompts and asked simply, "what else" or "what then," while continuing to dispense praise and snacks only for more and more elaborate phrases.

The child was trained on five questions in all. [*See illustration, page 62.*] After each of them, the teacher asked five other questions on which he had not been trained. The child answered them at length, in a meaningfully connected and understandable way. The average length of his answers to these questions was over five times greater than that of his answers to the questions that preceded training.

Although the boy's narrative skill developed admirably as the program progressed, it was thought that the accuracy of his stories was perhaps questionable. So the last training question was one that the teacher could check: "What have you been doing at school today?" The boy was reinforced only for accurate elaborations, and his answers to the question were not only longer and longer but more and more accurate.

We do not know yet whether this technique will work with other children, or whether it can be used with groups. But it is encouraging to discover that narrative ability can grow without step-by-step and word-by-word training. In many cases, the child seems to know the words and how to use them, so that virtually all he needs is an invitation.

Visitors to Turner House are sometimes surprised to find that it looks very much like any other nursery school, except that the children are somewhat better behaved. They enjoy the usual activities—playing house, painting pictures, "dancing" to piano music—and get along well with each other and with their teachers. It is true that every now and then a child receives a bit of food, and that observers with clipboards and stopwatches are scattered about the room, but the general atmosphere is warm, cheerful, and distinctly unmechanical.

Despite appearances, Turner House is in fact quite different from the traditional nursery school and from its stepchild, the "enrichment" preschool for the culturally deprived. It is unfortunate that enrichment nursery schools tend to be modeled on middle-class nursery schools, because middle-class nursery schools are for middle-class children. For example, they attempt to develop the child's ability to get along with other children, but skill at social interaction rarely is lacking in a child with a large family and many siblings near his own age. They try to enhance motor skills, and uninhibited activity, but those skills are usually well developed in a child whose playground is the street. They try to stimulate intellectual development with puzzles, books, and manipulative toys, but the content of these items is as meaningless to the culturally deprived preschool child as to the culturally deprived kindergartner.

In addition, the methodology of the middle-class nursery school is inappropriate for the culturally deprived child. For example, fighting and "making trouble" are likely to be regarded as symptoms of insecurity, and therefore to be met by the teacher with understanding, acceptance, and love. In the culturally deprived child (and, indeed, in the middle-class child), aggressive and disruptive behavior may be nothing more sinister than a useful social tool—a tool which the child must replace if he is to get along well in public school. It is therefore more suitable to ignore the child when he behaves badly, and to reserve attention for behavior that one wants him to maintain.

Finally, though an atmosphere of warmth and approval is certainly helpful, its chances of success in effecting radical changes in the child's behavior are slim. For one thing, since responses to social reinforcement are usually weak and deficiencies in skills are unusually large in culturally deprived children, it may be necessary to begin with something to which they *do* respond, like food, in order to establish new skills rapidly. For another, if social reinforcement is to be effective at all, it must be specific. It must *immediately follow* the behavior to which it relates. Teachers who are not trained to praise a child's small achievements at once often fail to do so, because without close attention and also considerable patience, it is easy to miss the brief and infrequent moments of desirable behavior that occur at first.

It would be better, in the long run, to modify the home environment of the culturally deprived child than to try to make up for its deficiencies through a supplementary program. As a small step in this direction, the Juniper Gardens Parent-Teacher Cooperative Preschool provides daily lessons for mothers on how to teach their preschool children the skills that they will need for elementary school work.

For this project we chose 30 four-year-olds and their mothers from upwardly mobile poverty families. The parents had a considerable amount of ambition for their children, and our aim was to channel that ambition into constructive behavior.

Compared to the children in the hard-core group, the upwardly mobile children had somewhat more motivation to achieve in school and somewhat stronger responses to social reinforcement. In addition, their mothers were willing to participate in the program. We did find, however, that it was useful to provide a bonus for attendance: we gave each mother a place setting of inexpensive china each week, at the rate of a dish a day, for coming to the preschool with her child.

The Parent-Teacher Preschool included many traditional preschool group activities, plus a carefully graded sequence of 150 daily lessons. The lesson series trained the mothers in teaching techniques and also showed them what their children should be learning—colors, numbers, rhymes, and so forth.

For the first six months of the program, each mother taught lessons to her own child. At a certain time during the day, she and the child would retire to one of several booths, each containing two chairs, a TV tray, and a shoebox of lesson materials such as crayons, toys, and pictures of various objects.

At first, the mothers were poor teachers. They used almost no praise or approval, and they showed very little grasp of the technique of attacking a complex problem by starting with its simplest form. Their usual pattern was to present a difficult problem and then to punish errors or silence with nagging or threats. They told the child to sit up, to pay attention; they informed him that they knew he knew the answer, so he had better say it.

Therefore we devised written instructions for the mothers to read before each lesson. Early instructions were very detailed. For example, Lesson One on naming objects began: "Hold up an object in front of the child. Say 'Can you tell me what this is?' Praise him by saying 'Good for you!' if he names it right." The same lesson ended with a general plea: "When he names something right, praise him."

Later in the lesson series, unless radically different materials or procedures were called for, the instructions were simple statements of what the child was to learn from the lesson.

Using these instructions, and with help from preschool teachers, the mothers' skill increased rapidly. But by the end of the year, though they praised their children's appropriate behavior much more often, they still did not praise it often enough. And the tendency to nag and threaten persisted.

So, at the start of the next school year, we made two changes in the program. First, we had each mother begin not with her own child, but with someone else's. Second, we had the preschool teacher keep track of how often the mother dispensed praise, and flash a red light, mounted where the mother could see it, each time praise was recorded. We explained the purpose of the record and the light to the mothers, and we encouraged them to inspect the record after each lesson.

Under these revised conditions, all the mothers began to be much more liberal with praise [*see illustration, page 63*]. At the same time, nagging and threats almost disappeared. Then we asked the mother to press a foot pedal whenever the child answered a question right. Her record of correct answers eventually corresponded to the preschool teacher's record of the mother's praise. At this point, except for covert reliability checks, we allowed each mother to record her own praise rate under the guise of recording the child's right answers.

After the mothers had learned to praise other people's children, we allowed them to begin teaching their own. In general, they continued to praise and to refrain from nagging. However, they did not teach their own children in quite the same way that they taught other children. When a mother taught her own child a lesson she already had taught to other children, she tended to praise him more than she had the others. When she taught him a lesson she had not taught before, she praised her child less than she later praised other children.

During the part of the day that was not taken up with lessons, the mothers supervised the children's group activities. As the rate at which they dispensed praise during the lessons rose, it also rose during play periods. However, it quickly became apparent that the mothers had little skill in maintaining order. They responded to shouting and fighting by shouting back, shaking the children, and so forth. This was not only ineffective but directly contrary to the guiding principle of the program, which was to reinforce with attention only the behavior that they wanted the children to continue.

To remedy this situation, we developed a system for structuring the activities of the playroom. We defined the boundaries of each area—doll corner, block corner, and so forth—and then required the children to complete a "switching requirement" before moving from one area to another.

The switching requirement was a simple matching problem involving pegs on a pegboard. The child was told to go to the board, complete the problem, and raise his hand. At that point a mother would come over, approve of his work, and allow him to choose a ticket to a new play area.

We imposed the requirement more for immediate, practical reasons than for training in skills that mothers or children could use outside the preschool. It did, however, have some interesting results. Noting that a one-row problem increased the average time a child spent in one activity area from ten minutes to 26, we decided to see what effect a four-row problem would have. In addition to reducing the switching rate still further,

the four-row problem taught the children a good deal about matching. The first time one boy tried the problem, it took him half an hour; his eighth attempt took a mere nine minutes. In other words, moving from area to area served as an effective reinforcement for learning, just as did the use of equipment and materials at Turner House.

The Parent-Teacher Preschool was primarily a training program for mothers, but it did, of course, affect the children as well. Its benefits can be inferred from the marked change in their IQ scores. At the beginning of the program, the average child's score on the Peabody Picture Vocabulary Test was 69 and the range was from 48 to 81. At the end of the program, the average child's score on the same test was 87 and the range was 67 to 117.

As for the mothers, we found that they can learn to become fairly good teachers. However, they tend to teach other children better than they do their own, and they have trouble putting principles of positive reinforcement into practice in unstructured situations. These are problems that we are working on this year.

An important by-product of the project is that the mothers have participated

in a community project, many of them for the first time. Indeed, we have tried to involve the community as closely as possible both at Turner House and at the Parent-Teacher Preschool. For example, one of the three full-time teachers at Turner House is a girl of 19 from Juniper Gardens, who came to us from the neighborhood Youth Corps. The Parent-Teacher Preschool is supervised this year by one professional teacher instead of three; now the two assistant teachers are mothers who participated in the program last year.

In summary, it seems best simply to repeat the logic that led us to develop the Turner House program and the Parent-Teacher Preschool. One characteristic of culturally deprived children is that they have trouble in school, and in the United States we rely on the public schools to teach children the behavior that our society considers useful. The right kind of preschool might make it possible for culturally deprived children to learn what the public schools set out to teach.

Ideally, the schools will be teaching something meaningful, and teachers will see these particular children as valuable people for whom it is worth opening the doors to knowledge.

Some Functions of Play in the Educative Process*

Sara H. Arnaud

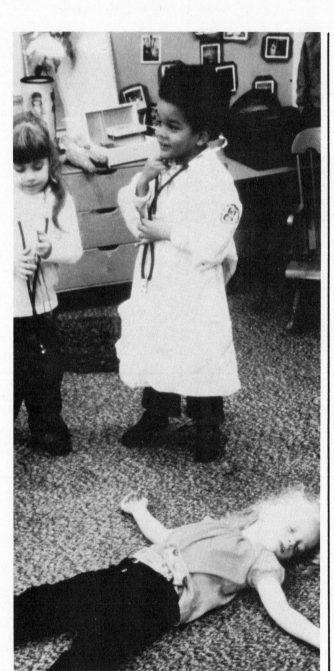

THE PREVAILING TENDENCY to regard children's play as enjoyable and natural for children *outside of school* when they have nothing more important to do and to value play in the preschool chiefly for its contribution to socialization and peer relations has come under renewed examination in the last five years or so. This recent greatly heightened interest in children's play as a phenomenon in its own right has generated a series of interlocking questions, some of which are being subjected to experimental analysis and others more closely examined in descriptive studies, videotapes, films, etc.

What functions does play serve? How much does play follow universal human developmental lines? What about the influence of the social, cultural context in which the child lives —his neighborhood, his family, his physical environment? In what ways, for instance, does the play of children being brought up on the great rolling plains of the Midwest differ from that of children growing up in hilly, crowded, highly industrialized Pittsburgh? How does the play of American Indian children in a reservation compare with that of Appalachian mountain children? And does it serve the same functions for both groups of children?

REASONS FOR RENEWED INTEREST IN PLAY

Children's play has become not only respectable, but deemed worthy of intense, rigorous scientific study (Singer, 1973). This shift in attitude reflects the confluence of several independent trends.

* Based on a paper presented at the annual conference of the Manitoba Association for the Education of Young Children, Winnipeg, December 1, 1973.

200

(1) First, we must credit the ethologists, those naturalists who study animals in their natural habitats rather than under the unavoidable constraints and artificialities of the laboratory or the zoo. There is now abundant evidence that, in the wild or feral state, animals show a much wider range of behaviors and much more cleverness and ingenuity than their cousins in captivity. Ethological studies of diverse mammalian species reveal that the young (and sometimes the not-so-young) of many species engage in playful and even game-like activities. Raccoons do, otters do, apes and monkeys do—kittens and puppies notoriously do.

Moreover, the more complex the nervous system of the species, the more playful are their young. Inevitable questions arise: What function does play serve in the survival of the species? Is it exploration? Mastery? Development of physical skills? Is it perhaps the way the young learn the fundamental social skills of their own species' social order? Here one might consider, for instance, Jane van Lawick-Goodall's observations of the social play of chimpanzees or Irven DeVore's studies of baboons, and Harlow's work with rhesus monkeys on the socialization that comes from play.

Still open is the question of *why* the apparent association between nervous-system complexity and variety in play. It is as though the more intelligent the animal, the more playful.

Given these observations, can it be maintained that play is only a trivial energy release, or only a secondary support to other primary functions of mankind, such as cognition and muscular coordination (Sutton-Smith, 1970)?

(2) Second, at a more pragmatic level, we find growing disenchantment in education circles with the strictly cognitive curriculum devised to hasten three- and four-year-olds into reading and number mastery by focusing them quite narrowly on restricted sets of activity. These "cognitive" curricula have usually been set up on the basis of *adults' notions of what children need to learn*—with little regard for how children at different ages learn most naturally and effectively. (Indeed, what a tremendous amount they have to learn about the world in these early years that has nothing to do with reading or arithmetic.)

(3) A third, somewhat indirect, influence has been Piaget's monumental work, which has shown us that children come to learn, understand and achieve intellectual mastery through their intense interactions with their own environments; that the mode of children's interaction with environments varies with age; and that, though these stages can be enriched, they cannot be hurried or accelerated. Piaget's findings have encouraged growing respect for what the child himself brings to the situation. In addition, Piaget's study of play (1962) has itself become a classic.

(4) Fourth, certain cultural attitudes have come under scrutiny, in particular those attitudes in the Puritan work ethic that look with suspicion on things that are pleasurable and fun—when there's work to be done. Some writers set this new scrutiny of values against the broader social context of the current soul-alienating experiences of workers in giant industries and what they consider the approaching "post-industrial era" of much greater leisure. I will try to link this idea up later with the ideas of self-realization and self-actualization, as these may be promoted by playfulness and art.

SOME FUNCTIONS OF PLAY[1]

I would like to start this section on the functions of play with three postulates adapted from an earlier paper (Arnaud, 1971).

Play and Cognition

(1) Play, by virtue of its spontaneous, highly enjoyable qualities for children, acts as an energizer and organizer of cognitive learning. The variation and scope of play bring deeper and more extended cognitive or intellectual gains than single-channel or narrow-channel teaching does.

Play and Anxiety

(2) The power of play in helping children master anxiety and normal developmental conflicts, as well as individual traumatic experiences, has been exceedingly well documented in the psychodynamic literature. In this capacity, play provides both a humanitarian service in lessening the child's pain and a cognitive service in lessening emotional turmoil disruptive to learning.

Play and Egocentrism

(3) When shared with other children, play is a major vehicle for lessening naive egocentrism, for deepening children's empathy for others, and for developing the skills involved in constructive socialization with other human beings. Piaget has demonstrated the powerful influence of peers on the lessening of egocentrism.

Other functional aspects of play deserve further study, such as:

Play and Symbolization

(4) The notion that play leads into the mastery of abstract symbolization; that the mental set involved in temporarily suspending attention to concrete, immediate reality in order to adopt a stance of "let's pretend," "let's act as if . . ." may underlie the ability to grasp situations that the child has never directly experienced. Examples are readily evident in the study of history, geography and literature, as Smilansky has pointed out in several of her

[1] In what follows about the functions of play in promoting children's growth toward optimal self-actualization, I have no intent to claim that play is the *only* way to achieve these human goals. Rather, I would like to point out that play can be useful in the educative process, as well as in fostering healthy personality development; that play is a natural mode for children and easily becomes absorbing and highly satisfying to them. Play is not enough, however; many other experiences and tasks are necessary for the growing child. Yet, in play, children can often bring together, in an organizing, integrating way, disparate aspects of their experiences and enrich their understanding of those experiences.

papers (Smilansky, 1968, 1971). These school subjects require a willingness to toy with the idea that other people whom you never knew may truly have lived in other times and other places and that maybe they even did interesting things. Brian Sutton-Smith, a leading theorist in play today, has cited experimental evidence that certain poor readers who were quite concrete and even wary of flights of imagination made notable gains in reading comprehension after they had joined an informal group where the leader actively stimulated the children to playful use of their own imaginations. Sutton-Smith (1970, 1971), Curry (1971) and others have explicated the theory that children are greatly aided in accepting the arbitrariness of the symbols of our alphabet and arabic numerals, if in their play they have already discovered the convenience of using one object to represent another (for instance, boys playing firemen and using long blocks to represent fire hoses).

Play and Physical Development

(5) The contribution of play to physical development, muscle skills and coordination is striking in children's ritualized games, such as tag or hide-and-seek and, later on, football or soccer. The development of physical skills is very obvious in these games; but it may also occur in other activities that involve covert role-enactment not evident to the observer unless the child tells him (for instance, the boy who climbs a tree, peers around, then climbs down and stalks through the woods, deep in the role of an heroic Indian chieftain).

Play and Innovation

(6) When faced with novel situations and materials, children may first approach them in an exploratory, curiosity-driven way. Once the novel thing is mastered, however, children tend to become playful and try many playful variations, thereby occasionally stumbling onto innovative, creative uses of the material (Hutt, 1966).

In other words, where does innovation come from? It comes when you are comfortable enough with something new to really try different variations, and this exploration is often done in a playful manner. Blockbuilding would provide a familiar example. At first the young child indulges in a sort of pell-mell stacking up and knocking down of blocks; but with experience the child gradually builds highly elaborate structures, which serve many purposes and require mastery of some basic engineering principles. Creative scientists, inventors and artists have often described the playful tossing around of ideas and possibilities as an underlying process in their most creative and innovative work.

Play and Problem-Solving

(7) In play there is no pre-set, prescribed way of working through a problem. The initiation of the situation comes from the child, as does the resolution, whether he is playing by himself or in cooperation with other children—take, for instance, the common play-theme of how to deal with wild aggressive

things. Children play out various solutions as though experimenting with them: Do you fight the aggressor, do you escape from it, do you trick it?

In a film on role-enactment in children's spontaneous play, which we recently made (Arnaud and Curry, 1973a), there is a small episode concerned with a "moat monster"—based on a creature one of the children saw on television, we assume, since the children around Pittsburgh do not have any experience with oceans and moats. As the play episode develops, it turns out that this moat monster can be both fought and escaped from if you have a car, because the car goes faster than the moat monster and can also be driven into the monster—so the way to escape is to attack him with a car and then speed away. Such strategies developed in play may seem like very trivial things, but they are really quite profound symbolic experimentations in how to deal with the aggressive, frightening things everybody meets at every stage of life.

Children's gradual realization that there are *many* ways to solve problems probably comes chiefly from reality experiences with real-life tasks and also in games of strategy; but sociodramatic play may reinforce these notions at another level of experience. If one method doesn't work, let's try another, or let's try a combination of approaches.

Play and Expression

(8) Susan Isaacs and Ruth Griffiths in the 1930s and Brian Sutton-Smith in the 1970s (Sutton-Smith, 1971a) have argued in forceful and convincing ways that an individual may most fully realize his own uniqueness and his own sense of self through subjective experiences that include play and art—these add dimensions to his life obtainable in no other way. Sutton-Smith proposes that both play and art may spring from the same internal source and that they serve as an antidote to feelings of alienation and identity confusion purported to be so prevalent in society today, at least in the United States.

Certainly play permits children to express and explore, without penalty, both approved and forbidden feelings (such as hatred and envy) by symbolic displacement onto toys and make-believe. In play one can act out various options and solutions that might be disastrous if carried out in real life—for instance, beating up your sister. It is all pretend. There are no final, irreversible consequences. Yet the child has had the freedom to explore these ideas and feelings and sometimes to come to at least a temporarily satisfying resolution through play —the same boy bothered by his small sister might arrive at the notion, "Maybe my sister's not so bad after all. It's fun when we play Robin and Bat-girl."

Play and Integration of Experience

(9) Another mind-teasing possibility has occurred to me lately. If we consider dramatic play to be an acting out or externalization of internal fantasy, what relation might it have to that other great internal fantasy, the sleep-

ing dream? The highly sophisticated advances in dream research in the last decade, made possible by polygraph monitoring of sleep, have offered considerable support for Freud's theory that dreams, as the "guardians of sleep," provide both emotional catharsis and wish fulfillment. But the same research has also engendered intriguing new theories about additional functions of the dream—particularly the theory that the dream serves to review the day's happenings and to organize and encode these happenings in relation to previous experience (Breger, 1967).

So, does play—particularly highly invested, absorbing play—help the child make sense out of his experiences, his thoughts and his reactions? Does it help the child to order and organize these experiences, integrate them, and in memory code them for future reference?

The nine functions of play just outlined, while sometimes overlapping, are exceedingly complex and varied. You might very well ask, "Isn't that a ridiculous burden to place on the simple, natural phenomenon of children's play?" To which, all one could plead is that the genius of the human species is to use the same pattern of activities to serve many, many functions at the same time.

UNIFORMITIES AND DIFFERENCES IN CHILDREN'S PLAY

As in all human development, there is a lawfulness and predictability about the development of children's play from infancy to adolescence.

In a film we have just made under a grant from the U.S. Office of Education, the focus is the developmental regularities of one aspect of children's play: the enactment of a role other than self (Arnaud and Curry, 1973b). Across the ages of two years to ten years, the film illustrates changes with age in the children's cognitive processes as revealed in play, in their perceptual organization, and in the sorts of social interactions that take place, all of which feed into the increasing complexity of role-enactment with advancing age. In a way the film served as a quasi-experimental verification of such developmental regularities, in that the "predictions" about age changes written in the pre-filming scripts were substantiated in the children's play during filming. The filming itself was based on a strictly time-limited sampling of children's ongoing, spontaneous play at Arsenal Family and Children's Center.

The assumption of lawfulness and predictability in how play is expressed at different ages raises the extremely important issues of universality in human behavior versus crosscultural differences. Our working hypotheses have been that the props and manifest content of play (for example, space play, monster play) would differ from one social-cultural context to another—here, for instance, you might think of the influence of TV on what is played—and so might the amount of adult influence and intervention into children's play differ from one social-cultural context to another. According to Brian Sutton-Smith (1971b), testing-

contesting play abounds where conditions are rough and highly competitive, as in the ghetto streets and among Australian aborigines in the outback. This sort of play is highly adaptive to the life these children lead and will continue to lead (though it may be argued that they can be introduced to new forms of play, as well, in order to expand their horizons and coping strategies).

On the other hand, we speculated (and intend to examine in further filming) that some common stylistic elements and thematic content might be discernible across several different social-cultural contexts; that, for instance, there might be stylistic similarities in such things as the use of miniature objects and symbolic representations of emotionally meaningful objects and figures—i.e., toys and toy-like objects. There might also be certain common themes expressing significant human experiences, such as interest in family relationships and playing out of scary things—although the scary thing itself might be quite different depending upon the children's experiences. For example, it has been reported that, following the 1971 California earthquakes, preschool children who experienced the jolting tremors and collapsing buildings that accompanied the quakes for days later in school rocked wildly in their chairs and perseveratively constructed block buildings which they shook and then knocked down (Curry, 1971).

Role of Adult

Here the role of the adult—teacher or parent or caretaker—is extremely influential. He or she is the representative of cultural values and conveys them to the children, whether or not they wish it. ("Boys don't cry." "Only girls play sissy games.") The adult also conveys his/her own personally arrived at attitudes and values. ("There should be no housekeeping corners in any preschool—that's sexist!") Of prime significance for the child is *what* the teacher attends to, approves and encourages; *what* the teacher ignores, suppresses, avoids (the teacher who will permit no play that he/she terms as "morbid," such as play around death, nightmares, monsters—all of which are very vital concerns of the young growing child, in addition to the joyous, zestful things of life).[2]

EDUCATIONAL SIGNIFICANCE OF PLAY

Solidly based experimental and experiential evidence indicates that play can serve as a powerful support and energizer to some basic goals of education:

---

[2] As an aside, it should be added that the teacher facilitates or hinders play in a number of ways. One extremely important task is to keep track of the play sufficiently to redirect it if it becomes too anxiety-provoking for the children, or overstimulating, or potentially guilt-producing, or harmful to other children. By verbalizing what is going on the teacher can clarify matters for the children and can reassure them by reminding them that after all it is just pretend.

□ Play is a lawful phenomenon, showing clear developmental trends and serving profound and intermixed human needs.

□ The "as if" attitude of play is related to abstraction, symbolization and creative cognitive processes.

□ Play integrates cognitive, emotional and social elements in the child's thinking and behavior. It helps him or her understand and integrate disparate experiences and aspects of his own behavior.

□ Insofar as the child is the initiator and doer in his play, it gives him a feeling of having some control over his destiny; it fosters initiative and diversified problem-solving.

□ Play permits the child to experiment with possible options and solutions and to get others' reactions to these, without committing himself to the consequences of having tried out these alternatives in real life—e.g., spanking the doll that represents a pesky little sister.

The role of spontaneous play in the curriculum in early childhood education must be determined by the individual teacher, who can facilitate it, integrate it with other cognitive and curricular materials, or inhibit it.

References

Arnaud, Sara H. "Polish for Play's Tarnished Reputation." In *Play: The Child Strives Toward Self-Realization*. Washington, DC: National Association for the Education of Young Children, 1971.

Arnaud, Sara H., and Nancy Curry. *The Moat Monster*. 16mm color-sound film, 13 min. New York: Campus Film Distributors, 1973a.

———— and ————. *Role-Enactment in Children's Play: A Developmental Overview*. 16mm color-sound film, 29 min. New York: Campus Film Distributors, 1973b.

Breger, L. "Function of Dreams." *Journal of Abnormal Psychology Monograph* 72, 5 (1967), Whole No. 641.

Curry, Nancy E. "Consideration of Current Basic Issues on Play." In *Play: The Child Strives Toward Self-Realization*. Washington, DC: National Association for the Education of Young Children, 1971.

DeVore, I. "Mother-Infant Relations in Free-Ranging Baboons." In *Maternal Behavior in Mammals*, H. Rheingold, ed. New York: Wiley, 1963.

Griffiths, Ruth. *Imagination in Early Childhood*. London: Kegan Paul, Trench & Trubner, 1935.

Harlow, H., and M. Harlow. "Social Deprivation in Monkeys." *Scientific American*, 1962.

Herron, R. E., and B. Sutton-Smith. *Child's Play*. New York: Wiley, 1971.

Hutt, Corinne. "Exploration and Play in Children" (1966). Reprinted in *Child's Play*, R. E. Herron and B. Sutton-Smith, eds. New York: Wiley, 1971.

Isaacs, Susan. *Social Development in Young Children*. London: Routledge & Kegan Paul, 1933.

Piaget, J. *Play, Dreams and Imitation in Childhood* (1951). New York: Norton, 1962.

Singer, Jerome L. *The Child's World of Make-Believe: Experimental Studies of Imaginative Play*. New York: Academic Press, 1973.

Smilansky, Sara. "Can Adults Facilitate Play in Children? Theoretical and Practical Considerations." In *Play: The Child Strives Toward Self-Realization*. Washington, DC: National Association for the Education of Young Children, 1971.

————. *The Effects of Sociodramatic Play on Disadvantaged Preschool Children*. New York: Wiley, 1968.

Sutton-Smith, B. "Child's Play—Very Serious Business." *Psychology Today* 5 (1971a): 67-69, 87.

————. "The Playful Modes of Knowing." In *Play: The Child Strives Toward Self-Realization*. Washington, DC: National Association for the Education of Young Children, 1971b.

————. "The Psychology of Childlore: The Triviality Barrier." *Western Folklore* 21 (1970): 1-8.

van Lawick-Goodall, Jane. *In the Shadow of Man*. Boston: Houghton-Mifflin, 1971.

See also:

ACEI. *Play: Children's Business*. Washington, DC: The Association, 1974. 64 pp. $2.95. This revision of an ACEI classic, just off the press, re-evaluates play and its impact at various developmental levels. Listed are suitable play materials for children, infancy through later childhood. Extensive bibliography.

Frank, Lawrence K. *Play Is Valid*, ACEI Position Paper. Washington, DC: The Association, 1968. 8 pp. 35¢, 10 copies $3.

Changing the Game from "Get the Teacher" to "Learn"

New reinforcement techniques have made good students of the
"too aggressive," "too young," and the autistic.

ROBERT L. HAMBLIN, DAVID BUCKHOLDT, DONALD BUSHELL, DESMOND ELLIS & DANIEL FERRITOR

Almost any educator of experience will assure you that it is next to impossible—and often actually impossible—to teach normal classroom subjects to children who have extreme behavior problems, or who are "too young." Yet at four experimental classrooms of the Central Midwestern Regional Educational Laboratories (CEMREL), we have been bringing about striking changes in the behavior and learning progress of just such children.

In the 18 months of using new exchange systems and working with different types of problem children, we have seen these results:

■ Extraordinarily aggressive boys, who had not previously responded to therapy, have been tamed.

■ Two-year-olds have learned to read about as fast and as well as their 5-year-old classmates.

■ Four ghetto children, too shy, too withdrawn to talk, have become better than average talkers.

■ Several autistic children, who were either mute or could only parrot sounds, have developed functional speech, have lost their bizarre and disruptive behavior patterns, and

their relationships with parents and other children have improved. All of these children are on the road to normality.

Our system is deceptively simple. Superficially, in fact, it may not even seem new—though, in detail, it has never been tried in precisely this form in the classroom before. In essence, we simply reinforce "good" behavior and non-punitively discourage "bad" behavior. We structure a social exchange so that as the child progresses, we reinforce this behavior—give him something that he values, something that shows our approval. Therefore, he becomes strongly motivated to continue his progress. To terminate bizarre, disruptive or explosive patterns, we stop whatever has been reinforcing that undesirable behavior—actions or attention that teachers or parents have unwittingly been giving him in exchange, often in the belief that they were punishing and thus discouraging him. Study after study has shown that whenever a child persists in behaving badly, some adult has, perhaps inadvertently, been rewarding him for it.

"Socialization" is the term that sociologists use to describe the process of transforming babies—who can do little but cry, eat, and sleep—into adults who can communicate and function rather effectively in their society. Socialization varies from culture to culture, and, while it is going on all around us, we are seldom aware of it. But when normal socialization breaks down, "problems" occur—autism, nonverbal or hyperaggressive behavior, retardation, delinquency, crime, and so on.

The authors, after years of often interesting but by and large frustrating research, realized that the more common theories of child development (Freudian, neo-Freudian, the developmental theories of Gesell and Piaget, and a number of others) simply do not satisfactorily explain the socialization process in children. Consequently in desperation we began to move toward the learning theories and then toward the related exchange theories of social structure. Since then, working with problem children, our view has gradually been amplified and refined. Each experimental classroom has given us a different looking glass. In each we can see the child in different conditions, and can alter the conditions which hinder his socialization into a civilized, productive adult capable of happiness.

By the time they become students, most children love to play with one another, to do art work, to cut and paste, to play with Playdoh, to climb and swing on the playground, and so on. Most pre-schools also serve juice and cookie snacks, and some have television sets or movies. There is, consequently, no dearth of prizes for us to reward the children for good behavior. The problem is not in finding reinforcers, but in managing them.

The Basic System: Token Exchange

One of the simpler and most effective ways, we found, was to develop a token-exchange system. The tokens we use are plastic discs that children can earn. A child who completes his arithmetic or reading may earn a dozen tokens, given one by one as he proceeds through the lessons. And at the end of the lesson period comes the reward.

Often it is a movie. The price varies. For four tokens, a student can watch while sitting on the floor; for eight, he gets a chair; for 12, he can watch while sitting on the table. Perhaps the view is better from the table—anyway, the children almost always buy it if they have enough tokens. But if they dawdled so much that they earned fewer than four, they are "timed out" into the hall while the others see the movie. Throughout the morning, therefore, the children earn, then spend, then earn, then spend.

This token-exchange system is very powerful. It can create beneficial changes in a child's behavior, his emotional reactions, and ultimately even his approach to life. But it is not easy to set up, nor simple to maintain.

At the beginning the tokens are meaningless to the children; so to make them meaningful, we pair them with M&M candies, or something similar. As the child engages in the desired behavior (or a reasonable facsimile), the teacher gives him a "Thank you," an M&M, and a token. At first the children are motivated by the M&Ms and have to be urged to hold on to the tokens; but then they find that the tokens can be used to buy admission to the movie, Playdoh, or other good things. The teacher tells them the price and asks them to count out the tokens. Increasingly, the teacher "forgets" the M&Ms. In two or three days the children get no candy, just the approval and the tokens. By then, they have learned.

There are problems in maintaining a token exchange. Children become disinterested in certain reinforcers if they are used too frequently, and therefore in the tokens that buy them. For instance, young children will work very hard to save up tokens to play with Playdoh once a week; if they are offered Playdoh every day, the charm quickly fades. Some activities—snacks, movies, walks outdoors—are powerful enough to be used every day.

As noted, the children we worked with had different behavior problems, reflecting various kinds of breakdowns in the socialization process. Each experiment we conducted concentrated on a particular type of maladjustment or a particular group of maladjusted children to see how a properly structured exchange system might help them. Let us look at each experiment, to see how each problem was affected.

Aggression

Unfortunately, our world reinforces and rewards aggressive behavior. Some cultures and some families are open and brazen about it—they systematically and consciously teach their young that it is desirable, and even virtuous, to attack certain other individuals or groups. The child who can beat up the other kids on the playground is sometimes respected by his peers, and perhaps by his parents; the soldier achieves glory in combat. The status, the booty, or the bargaining advantages that come to the aggressor can become reinforcement to continue and escalate his aggressions.

In more civilized cultures the young are taught not to use aggression, and we try to substitute less harmful patterns. But even so, aggression is sometimes reinforced unintentionally—and the consequences, predictably, are the same as if the teaching was deliberate.

In the long run civilized cultures are not kind to hyperaggressive children. A recent survey in England, for instance, found that the great majority of teachers felt that aggressive behavior by students disturbed more classrooms than anything else and caused the most anxiety among teachers. At least partly as a result, the dropout rates for the hyperaggressives was $2\frac{1}{2}$ times as great as for "normals," and disproportionate numbers of hyperaggressives turned up in mental clinics.

The traditional treatment for aggressive juveniles is punishment—often harsh punishment. This is not only of dubious moral value, but generally it does not work.

We took seriously—perhaps for the first time—the theory that aggression is a type of exchange behavior. Boys become aggressive because they get something for it; they continue to be aggressive because the rewards are continuing. To change an aggressive pattern in our experimental class at Washington University, therefore, we had to restructure appropriately the exchange system in which the boys were involved.

As subjects we (Ellis and Hamblin) found five extraordinarily aggressive 4-year-old boys, all referred to us by local psychiatrists and social workers who had been able to do very little with them. Next, we hired a trained teacher. We told her about the boys and the general nature of the experiment—then gave her her head. That is, she was allowed to use her previous training during the first period—and this would provide a baseline comparison with what followed after. We hoped she would act like the "typical teacher." We suspect that she did.

Let's Play "Get the Teacher"

The teacher was, variously, a strict disciplinarian, wise counselor, clever arbitrator, and sweet peacemaker. Each role failed miserably. After the eighth day, the average of the children was 150 sequences of aggression per day! Here is what a mere four minutes of those sequences were like:

Mike, John, and Dan are seated together playing with pieces of Playdoh. Barry, some distance from the others, is seated and also is playing with Playdoh. The children, except Barry, are talking about what they are making. Time is 9:10 A.M. Miss Sally, the teacher, turns toward the children and says, "It's time for a lesson. Put your Playdoh away." Mike says, "Not me." John says, "Not me." Dan says, "Not me." Miss Sally moves toward Mike. Mike throws some Playdoh in Miss Sally's face. Miss Sally jerks back, then moves forward rapidly and snatches Playdoh from Mike. Puts Playdoh in her pocket. Mike screams for Playdoh, says he wants to play with it. Mike moves toward Miss Sally and attempts to snatch the Playdoh from Miss Sally's pocket. Miss Sally pushes him away. Mike kicks Miss Sally on the leg. Kicks her again, and demands the return of his Playdoh. Kicks Miss Sally again. Picks up a small steel chair and throws it at Miss Sally. Miss Sally jumps out of the way. Mike picks up another chair and throws it more violently. Miss Sally cannot move in time. Chair strikes her foot. Miss Sally pushes Mike down on the floor. Mike starts up. Pulls over one chair. Now another, another. Stops a moment. Miss Sally is picking up chairs, Mike looks at Miss Sally. Miss Sally moves toward Mike. Mike runs away.

John wants his Playdoh. Miss Sally says "No." He joins Mike in pulling over chairs and attempts to grab Playdoh from Miss Sally's pocket. Miss Sally pushes him away roughly. John is screaming that he wants to play with his Playdoh. Moves toward phonograph. Pulls it off the table; lets it crash onto the floor. Mike has his coat on. Says he is going home. Miss Sally asks Dan to bolt the door. Dan gets to the door at the same time as Mike. Mike hits Dan in the face. Dan's nose is bleeding. Miss Sally walks over to Dan, turns to the others, and says that she is taking Dan to the washroom and that while she is away, they may play with the Playdoh. Returns Playdoh from pocket to Mike and John. Time: 9:14 A.M.

Wild? Very. These were barbarous little boys who enjoyed battle. Miss Sally did her best but they were just more clever than she, and they *always* won. Whether Miss Sally wanted to or not, they could always drag her into the fray, and just go at it harder and harder until she

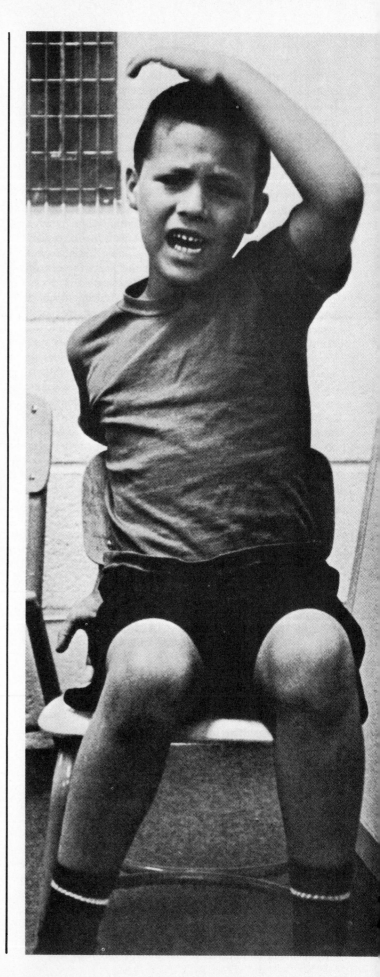

capitulated. She was finally driven to their level, trading a kick for a kick and a spit in the face for a spit in the face.

What Miss Sally did not realize is that she had inadvertently structured an exchange where she consistently reinforced aggression. First, as noted, whenever she fought with them, she *always lost.* Second, more subtly, she reinforced their aggressive pattern by giving it serious attention —by looking, talking, scolding, cajoling, becoming angry, even striking back. These boys were playing a teasing game called "Get the Teacher." The more she showed that she was bothered by their behavior, the better they liked it, and the further they went.

These interpretations may seem far-fetched, but they are borne out dramatically by what happened later. On the twelfth day we changed the conditions, beginning with B1 (see Figure 1). First, we set up the usual token exchange to reinforce cooperative behavior. This was to develop or strengthen behavior that would replace aggression. Any strong pattern of behavior serves some function for the individual, so the first step in getting rid of a strong, disruptive pattern is substituting another one that is more useful and causes fewer problems. Not only therapy, but simple humanity dictates this.

First, the teacher had to be instructed in how *not to reinforce* aggression. Contrary to all her experience, she was asked to turn her back on the aggressor, and at the same time to reinforce others' cooperation with tokens. Once we were able to coach her and give her immediate feedback over a wireless-communication system, she structured the exchanges almost perfectly. The data in Figures 1 and 2 show the crucial changes: a gradual increase in cooperation—from about 56 to about 115 sequences per day, and a corresponding decrease in aggression from 150 to about 60 sequences!

These results should have been satisfactory, but we were new at this kind of experimentation, and nervous. We

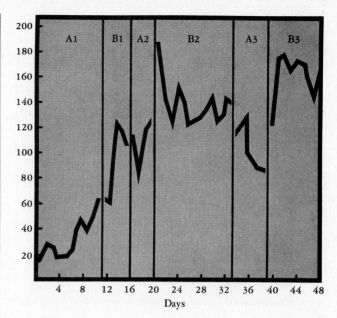

Figure 2. Frequency of cooperative sequences. In A1, A2 and A3 the teacher structured a weak approval exchange for cooperation and a disapproval exchange for noncooperation. In B1, A2, B2 and B3, she structured a token exchange for cooperation.

wanted to reduce the frequency of aggression to a "normal" level, to about 15 sequences a day. So we restructured the exchange system and thus launched A2.

In A2, we simply made sure that aggression would always be punished. The teacher was told to *charge* tokens for any aggression.

To our surprise, the frequency of cooperation remained stable, about 115 sequences per day; but aggression *increased* to about 110 sequences per day! Evidently the boys were still playing "Get the Teacher," and the fines were enough reinforcement to increase aggression.

So, instead of fining the children, the teacher was again told to ignore aggression by turning her back and giving attention and tokens only for cooperation. The frequency of aggression went down to a near "normal" level, about 16 sequences per day (B2), and cooperation increased to about 140 sequences.

Then, as originally planned, the conditions were again reversed. The boys were given enough tokens at the beginning of the morning to buy their usual supply of movies, toys, and snacks, and these were not used as reinforcers. The teacher was told to do the best she could. She was not instructed to return to her old pattern, but without the tokens and without our coaching she did— and with the same results. Note A3 in Figures 1 and 2. Aggression increased to about 120 sequences per day, and cooperation decreased to about 90. While this was an improvement over A1, before the boys had ever been exposed to the token exchange, it was not good. The mixture of aggression and cooperation was strange, even weird, to watch.

When the token exchange was restructured (B3) and the aggression no longer reinforced, the expected changes recurred—with a bang. Aggression decreased to seven sequences on the last day, and cooperation rose to about 181 sequences. In "normal" nursery schools, our observations have shown that five boys can be expected to have

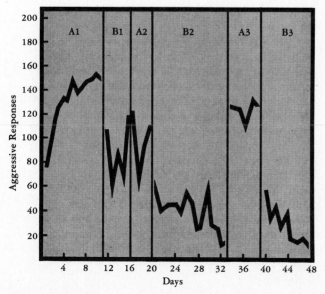

Figure 1. Frequency of aggressive sequences by days for five 4-year-old boys. In A1, A2 and A3 the teacher attempted to punish aggression but inadvertently reinforced it. In B1, B2 and B3 she turned her back or otherwise ignored aggression and thus did not reinforce it.

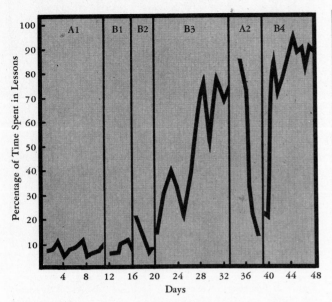

Figure 3. Percentage of scheduled time spent in lessons by days for five hyperaggressive boys. In A1 and A2, teacher structured approval exchange for attendance, disapproval for non-attendance. In B1 and B2, a token exchange for attendance was structured, but not effectively until B2 and B4.

15 aggression sequences and 60 cooperation sequences per day. Thus, from extremely aggressive and uncooperative, our boys had become less aggressive and far more cooperative than "normal" boys.

Here is an example of their new behavior patterns, taken from a rest period—precisely the time when the most aggressive acts had occurred in the past:

All of the children are sitting around the table drinking their milk; John, as usual, has finished first. Takes his plastic mug and returns it to the table. Miss Martha, the assistant teacher, gives him a token. John goes to cupboard, takes out his mat, spreads it out by the blackboard, and lies down. Miss Martha gives him a token. Meanwhile, Mike, Barry, and Jack have spread their mats on the carpet. Dan is lying on the carpet itself since he hasn't a mat. Each of them gets a token. Mike asks if he can sleep by the wall. Miss Sally says "Yes." John asks if he can put out the light. Miss Sally says to wait until Barry has his mat spread properly. Dan asks Mike if he can share his mat with him. Mike says "No." Dan then asks Jack. Jack says, "Yes," but before he can move over, Mike says "Yes." Dan joins Mike. Both Jack and Mike get tokens. Mike and Jack get up to put their tokens in their cans. Return to their mats. Miss Sally asks John to put out the light. John does so. Miss Martha gives him a token. All quiet now. Four minutes later—all quiet. Quiet still, three minutes later. Time: 10:23 A.M. Rest period ends.

The hyperaggressive boys actually had, and were, double problems; they were not only extremely disruptive, but they were also washouts as students. Before the token system (A1), they paid attention to their teacher only about 8 percent of the lesson time (see Figure 3). The teacher's system of scolding the youngsters for inattention and taking their attention for granted with faint approval,

if any, did not work at all. To the pupils, the "Get the Teacher" game was much more satisfying.

After the token exchange was started, in B1, B2, B3, and B4, it took a long, long time before there was any appreciable effect. The teacher was being trained from scratch, and our methods were, then, not very good. However, after we set up a wireless-communication system that allowed us to coach the teacher from behind a one-way mirror and to give her immediate feedback, the children's attention began to increase. Toward the end of B3, it leveled off at about 75 percent—from 8 percent! After the token exchange was taken out during A2, attention went down to level off at 23 percent; put back in at B4, it shot back up to a plateau of about 93 percent. Like a roller coaster: 8 percent without, to 75 with, to 23 without, to 93 with.

Normal Children

These results occurred with chronic, apparently hopeless hyperaggressive boys. Would token exchange also help "normal," relatively bright upper-middle-class children? Sixteen youngsters of that description—nine boys and seven girls, ranging from 2 years 9 months to 4 years 9 months—were put through an experimental series by Bushell, Hamblin, and Denis Stoddard in an experimental pre-school at Webster College. All had about a month's earlier experience with the token-exchange system. The results are shown in Figure 4.

Study in 15-Minute Periods

At first, the study hour was broken up into 15-minute periods, alternating between the work that received tokens, and the play or reward that the tokens could be used for. Probably because the children were already familiar with token exchange, no great increase in learning took place. On the 22nd day, we decided to try to increase the learning period, perhaps for the whole hour. In A2 (Figure 4), note that the time spent in studying went up rapidly and dramatically—almost doubling—from 27 to level off at 42 minutes.

During B, the token exchange was taken out completely. The teachers still gave encouragement and prepared interesting lessons as before. The rewards—the nature walks, snacks, movies, and so on—were retained. But, as in a usual classroom, they were given to the children free instead of being sold. The children continued at about the same rate as before for a few days. But after a week, attention dropped off slowly, then sharply. On the last day it was down to about 15 minutes—one-third the level of the end of the token period.

In A3, the token exchange was reinstituted. In only three days, attention snapped back from an average of 15 minutes to 45 minutes. However, by the end of A3, the students paid attention an average of 50 of the available 60 minutes.

A comparison of the record of these normals with the record of the hyperaggressive boys is interesting. The increase in attention brought by the token exchange, from about 15 minutes to 50, is approximately threefold for the normal children; but for the hyperaggressive boys

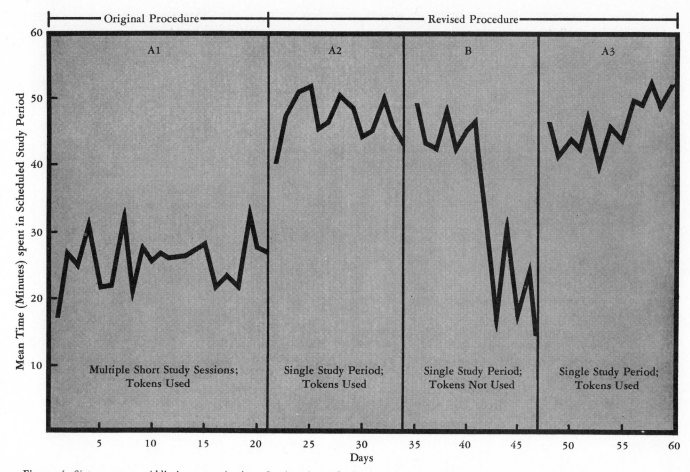

Figure 4. Sixteen upper-middleclass pre-schoolers. In A1, A2 and A3 the token exchange was used; in B, only approval.

—who are disobedient and easily distracted—it is about eleven-fold, from 8 percent to 93 percent of the time. The increase was not only greater, but the absolute level achieved was higher. This indicates strongly, therefore, that the more problematic the child, the greater may be the effect of token exchange on his behavior.

The high rates of attention were not due to the fact that each teacher had fewer children to work with. Individualized lessons were not enough. Without the token exchange, even three teachers could not hold the interest of 16 children 2 to 4 years old—at least not in reading, writing, and arithmetic.

Praise and approval were not enough as rewards. The teachers, throughout the experiment, used praise and approval to encourage attention; they patted heads and said things like "Good," "You're doing fine," and "Keep it up"; yet, in B, when the token exchange was removed, this attention nevertheless ultimately declined by two-thirds. Social approval is important, but not nearly so powerful as material reinforcers.

Finally, it is obvious that if the reinforcers (movies, snacks, toys, or whatever) do not seem directly connected to the work, they will not sustain a high level of study. To be effective with young children, rewards must occur in a structured exchange in which they are given promptly as recompense and thus are directly connected to the work performed.

The Very Young Child

According to accepted educational theory, a child must be about six and a half before he can comfortably learn to read. But is this really true, or is it merely a convenience for the traditional educational system? After all, by the time a normal child is two and a half he has learned a foreign language—the one spoken by his parents and family; and he has learned it without special instruction or coaching. He has even developed a feel for the rules of grammar, which, by and large, he uses correctly. It is a rare college student who becomes fluent in a foreign language with only two and a half years of formal training—and our college students are supposed to be the brightest of our breed. Paul Goodman has suggested that if children learn to *speak* by the same methods that they learn to *read,* there might well be as many non-speakers now as illiterates.

What if the problem is really one of motivation? If we structured an exchange that rewarded them, in ways they could appreciate, for learning to read, couldn't they learn as readily as 5-year-olds?

We decided that for beginners, the number of words a child can read is the best test of reading ability. In an experiment designed by Hamblin, Carol Pfeiffer, Dennis Shea, and June Hamblin, and administered at our Washington University pre-school, the token-exchange system

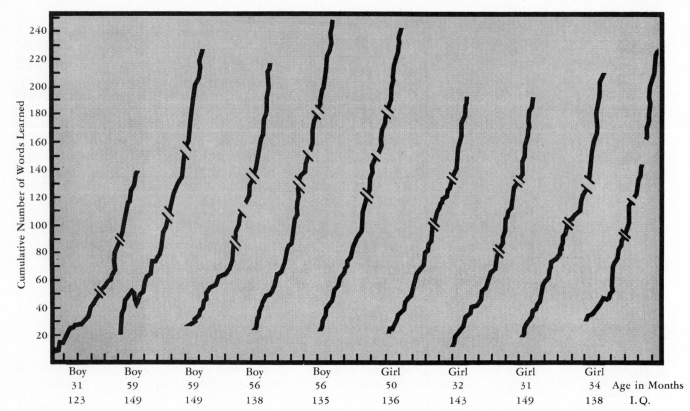

Figure 5. Number of sight-words learned through time by five 4- and 5-year-olds, and four 2- and 3-year-olds. Note that the younger children did about as well as the older ones—except for one boy whose I.Q. was somewhat lower than the others in the group. (Gaps indicate absences.)

was used to reward children for the number of words each learned. The results are given in Figure 5. Note that the 2-year-olds did about as well as the 5-year-olds; their sight vocabularies were almost as large.

There was an interesting side effect: at the end of the school year, all but one of these children tested at the "genius" level. On Stanford-Binet individual tests, their I.Q. scores increased as much as 36 points. It was impossible to compute an average gain only because three of the children "topped out"—made something in excess of 149, the maximum score possible.

In general, the lower the measured I.Q. at the start, the greater the gain—apparently as a result of the educational experience.

The Non-Verbal Child

What happens when ghetto children are introduced into a token-exchange system? At our Mullanphy Street pre-school, 22 Afro-American children—age 3 to 5—attend regularly. All live in or near the notorious Pruitt-Igoe Housing Project, and most come from broken homes. When the school began, the teachers were unenthusiastic about a token exchange, so we let them proceed as they wished. The result was pandemonium. About half of the children chased one another around the room, engaged in violent arguments, and fought. The others withdrew; some would not even communicate.

After the third day, the teachers asked for help. As in the other experimental schools, we (Buchholdt and Hamb-

lin) instructed them to ignore aggressive-disruptive behavior and to reward attention and cooperation with social approval and the plastic tokens, later to be exchanged for such things as milk, cookies, admission to the movies, and toys. The children quickly caught on, the disruptions diminished, and cooperation increased. Within three weeks of such consistent treatment, most of the children took part in the lessons, and disruptive behavior had become only an occasional problem. All of this, remember, without punishment.

Our attention was then focused upon the children with verbal problems. These children seldom started conversations with teachers or other students, but they would sometimes answer questions with a word or perhaps two. This pattern may be unusual in the middle classes, but is quite common among ghetto children. Our research has shown that children so afflicted are usually uneducable.

As we investigated, we became convinced that their problem was not that they were unable to talk as much as that they were too shy to talk to strangers—that is, to non-family. In their homes we overheard most of them talking brokenly, but in sentences. Consequently, we set up a token exchange for them designed specifically to develop a pattern of talking with outsiders, especially teachers and school children.

As it happened, we were able to complete the experiment with only four children (see Figure 6). During A1, the baseline period (before the tokens were used), the four children spoke only in about 8 percent of the 15-second sampling periods. In B1, the teachers gave social approval and tokens *only* for speaking; non-verbalisms, like pointing or headshaking, would not be recognized or reinforced. Note the increase in verbalization, leveling out at approximately 48 percent.

In A2 we reversed the conditions by using a teacher new to the school. The rate of talking dropped off immediately, then increased unevenly until it occurred in about 23 percent of the sample periods.

In B2 the new teacher reintroduced the token exchange for talking, and once more there was a dramatic rise: The speaking increased much more rapidly than the first time, ending up at about 60 percent. (This more rapid increase in known as the Contrast Effect. It occurs in part, perhaps, because the children value the token exchange more after it has been taken away.)

In the final test, we again took out the token exchange, and introduced yet another new teacher. This time the drop was small, to 47 percent.

We followed the children for three months after the end of the experiment. Their speech level remained at 48 percent, with little dropoff. This compares with the 40 percent talking rate for our other ghetto children, and the 42 percent rate for upper-middle-class children at the Washington University pre-school.

Frequency of speech, however, was not the only important finding. At the end of B1, the children spoke more often but still in a hesitant and broken way. By the end of B2, they spoke in sentences, used better syntax, and frequently started conversations.

Mothers, teachers, and neighbors all reported that the children were much more friendly and assertive. But some claimed that the children now talked too much! This could reflect individual bias; but there was little doubt that at least one child, Ben, had become an almost compulsive talker. He was given to saying hello to everyone he met and shaking their hands. So we terminated the experiment—what would have happened to Ben had we started *another* exchange?

This experiment shows that token exchange can bring on permanent behavior change, but that the culture must reinforce the new behavior. Talking is important in our culture, and so is reading; therefore they are reinforced. But other subjects—such as mathematics beyond simple arithmetic—are not for most people. For behavior to change permanently it must be reinforced at least intermittently.

Autism

The problems of autistic children usually dwarf those of all other children. To the casual observer, autistic children never sustain eye contact with others but appear to be self-contained—sealed off in a world of their own. The most severe cases never learn how to talk, though they sometimes echo or parrot. They remain dependent upon Mother and become more and more demanding. They develop increasingly destructive and bizarre behavior problems. Finally, between 5 and 10 years old, autistic children ordinarily become unbearable to their families and at that point they are almost invariably institutionalized. Until

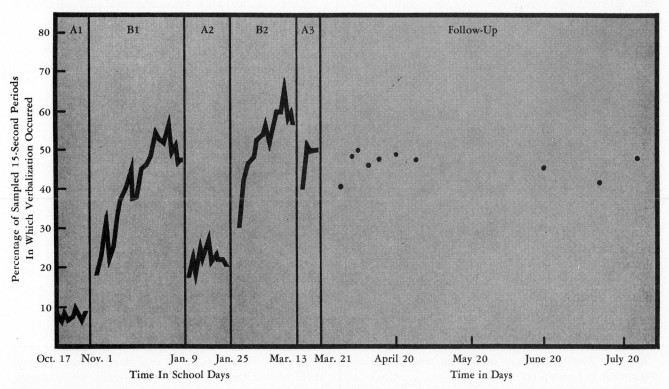

Figure 6. Percentage of sampled periods in which talking occurred through time for four non-verbal "culturally deprived" children, and through five experimental conditions. In each of the A conditions a new teacher was introduced, and she structured a token exchange for participation in lessons. In the B conditions, the teacher then structured a token exchange for talking. The follow-up was similar to the A conditions.

recently, at least, this meant a rear ward to vegetate in until they died.

The breakthrough in therapy from autism came in 1964 when Dr. Ivar Lovaas and Dr. Montrose Wolfe and a graduate student, now Dr. Todd Risley, simultaneously developed therapy systems using well-established principles of operant conditioning. They were particularly successful with those children who randomly echoed or imitated words or sentences (this is called echolalia).

The therapy systems we have designed, developed, and tested, though similar in some ways to those developed by Lovaas, Wolfe and Risley, are quite different in others. First, we do not use punishment, or other negative stimuli. We simply terminate exchanges that reinforce the autistic patterns, and set up exchanges that reinforce normal patterns. Second, our children are not institutionalized; they live at home, and are brought to the laboratory for twenty minutes to three hours of therapy per day. Third, as soon as possible—usually within months—we get the children into classrooms where a therapist works with four or five at a time. Fourth, we train the mother to be an assistant therapist—mostly in the home, but also in the laboratory. These changes were introduced for several reasons, but primarily in the hope of getting a better, more permanent cure for autism.

The Etiology of Autism

Is autism hereditary, as many believe? Our studies indicate that this is not the important question. Many mental faculties, including I.Q., have some physiological base. But the real issue is how much physiologically based potential is socially realized, for good or bad. As far as we can tell, the exchanges that intensify autism get structured inadvertently, often by accident; but once started, a vicious cycle develops that relentlessly drives the child further into autism.

When autism starts, the mother often reacts by babying the child, trying to anticipate his every need before he signals. Thus normal communication is not reinforced, and the child never learns to work his environment properly. But even if he doesn't know how to get what he wants through talking, he does learn, through association, that his oversolicitous and anxious mother will always respond if he acts up violently or bizarrely enough. And she must, if only to punish. He thus learns to play "Get mother's attention"; and this soon develops into "Get mother exasperated, but stop just short of the point where she punishes and really hurts." Here is an example (observed by Ferritor in the first of a series of experiments by the Laboratory's staff, not reported here):

Larry is allowed to pick out his favorite book. His mother then attempts to read it to him, but he keeps turning the pages so she can't. He gets up and walks away from the table. The mother then yells at him to come back. He *smiles* (a sign of pleasure usually but not always accompanies reinforcement). Mother continues to talk to the child to try to get him back for the story. Finally, he comes over to the table and takes the book away from her. She lets him and goes back to the bookcase for another book. He then sits down and

she begins to read. He tries to get up, but his mother pulls him back. Again. Again. She holds him there. He gets away and starts walking around the room. Goes to the toy cabinet. Mother gets up to go over and take a toy away from him. He sits on the floor. The mother comes over and sits down by him. He gets up and goes over by the door and opens it and tries to run out. She tells him he has to stay. He *smiles*. She resumes reading. He gets up and starts walking around the table. She grabs him as he comes by. He *smiles*.

A clinical psychologist who had tested Larry did not diagnose him as autistic, but as an educable mental retardate with an I.Q. of perhaps 30. Yet he had gaze aversion and we suspected that Larry, like other autistics, was feigning inability as a way of getting what he wanted from his mother, and then from other adults. He began to respond to the attractive exchanges that we structured for him, and as we did, he began to tip his hand. For example, at one point when his mother was being trained to be an assistant therapist, the following incident occurred:

Mrs. C. told Larry that as soon as he strung some beads he could have gum from the gum machine that was across the room. For about 10 minutes he fumbled, he whined, all the time crying, saying "I can't." Finally, he threw the beads at his mother. Eventually, the mother had the good sense to leave the room, saying, "As soon as you string those beads, you can have your gum." With his mother out of the room, according to our observers he sat right down and, in less than 30 seconds, filled a string with beads with no apparent trouble.

Just two weeks later, after the mother had been through our 10-day training program, they again had a "story time."

The mother begins by immediately asking Larry questions about this book (the same book used a few weeks before). He responds to every question. She gives approval for every correct answer. Then she tries to get him to say, "That is a duck." He will not say it intelligibly, but wants to turn the page. Mother says, "As soon as you say 'duck,' you may turn the page. Larry says "Duck" and turns the page. He *smiles*.

After seven minutes, Larry is still sitting down. They have finished one book and are beginning a second.

Most autistic children play the game "Look at me, I'm stupid," or "Look at me, I'm bizarre." These are simply attention-getting games that most adults repeatedly reinforce. Man is not a simple machine; he learns, and as he develops his abilities, he develops stronger and stronger habits. Thus, once these inadvertent exchanges get established, the child becomes more and more dependent, more and more disruptive, more and more bizarre, more and more alienated from the positive exchanges that are structured in his environment. What is sad is that the parents and the others in the child's life sense that something is terribly wrong, but the more they do, the worse the situation becomes.

It seems to those of us who have been involved in these experiments from the beginning that the exchange techniques and theories we have used have without question demonstrated their effectiveness in treating and educating problem children. Watching these children as they go peacefully and productively about their lessons toward the end of each experimental series is both an exhilarating and humbling experience. It is almost impossible to believe that so many had been written off as "uneducable" by professionals, that without this therapy and training—or something similar—most would have had dark and hopeless futures.

But it is not inevitable that so many hyperaggressive or environmentally retarded ghetto children become dropouts or delinquents; it is not inevitable that so many autistic children, saddest of all, must vegetate and die mutely in the back wards of mental hospitals.

FURTHER READING SUGGESTED BY THE AUTHORS:

The Analysis of Human Operant Behavior by Ellen P. Reese (Dubuque, Iowa: William C. Brown Company, 1966).

The Emotionally Disturbed Child in the Classroom by Frank Hewett (Boston: Allyn and Bacon, Inc., 1968).

Early Childhood Autism edited by J.K. Wing (London: Pergamon Press, Ltd., 1966).

Case Studies in Behavior Modification by Leonard P. Ullman and Leonard Krasner (New York: Holt, Rinehart and Winston, Inc., 1965).

IX. TEACHER ALTERNATIVES

With few exceptions, academic and professional learning in western societies has proceeded along three main pathways for centuries. One pathway has been self-study, aided mainly by books, travel, and individual experimentation. Another has been apprenticeship, in which work is exchanged for guidance from a seasoned practitioner. The third leads into and through the schoolroom, where the teacher defines what is to be learned and is aided at most by the technology of books, slates or paper, and pencils. Not until the twentieth century did these pathways of learning begin to intersect and to multiply in many ways.

By 1960, alternative ways of learning were so abundant as to raise fundamental questions about the adequacy of the pathway through the schoolroom door.

The sharpest challenges to the adequacy of classroom-based, teacher-led, group instruction grew out of the inventions born of necessity during World War II. When thousands of soldiers had to become proficient almost overnight in foreign languages, for example, linguists and engineers were commissioned to develop an Army Language School. There, students could become bilingual within a few months of training. Pilots had to be taught to fly and navigators to navigate, and to do so accurately and reliably, on a mass basis and in a very short period of time. Educational psychologists joined with engineers and scientists to revolutionize the methods of instruction between 1940 and 1945, but the revolution did not reach the classroom door until the 1960's.

Old customs persist. The most universal mode of teaching continues to be the single teacher classroom in the school, aided by very little technology. Alongside the school, however, the military, and business and industry have proliferated content and skill training systems that dwarf the scope of schools and colleges. In addition, self-instruction — through programmed materials, television and radio and the recording industry, and non-school-based programs of study — has flourished. Work-study, cooperative education, and flexible campus or field-based education, moreover, have begun to complete with the classroom. The apprenticeship pathway is now incorporated into systems of instruction everywhere.

"The Talking Typewriter" essay in this section expresses the ways in which the role of the teacher has been changed by these developments. Omar Khayyam Moore synthesized the principles of self-instruction within what he called an auto-telic environment, the products of engineering hardware, and the principle of early learning, to design a process in which pre-school children learned to type-write, read, and even to take dictation, with an absolute minimum of teacher intervention.

Hardware will *not* replace educators, although it may change their roles significantly. Nor will machines produce miracles in academic learning. Hardware does tend to change the teacher from a figure lecturing or leading group discussion in front of rows of desks into a learning materials gatherer, a designer of instruction, a facilitator of study, and an evaluator, however. In these alternative roles, the teacher becomes something she or he was not before, at least not in as full a sense.

One of the tasks of the educational psychologist has become that of *evaluating* the effects and implications of these changes. Are the new designs, modes, and technologies productive of faster and better learning? Are the costs of these changes too great for the results? What is gained and what is lost in the transformation of teaching? Educational psychologists try to obtain systematic, empirical answers to these questions, at the same time their colleagues help research and invent the new technologies. Their dream is of a time when the abilities of the teacher will be matched with the instructional technology best suited to the needs and interests of students. This vision of ideal teaching-learning situations transcends the classroom and its customs.

The Talking Typewriter

by Maya Pines

Should early education push young children—or is there a low-pressure way to develop competence? Omar Khayyam Moore, the University of Pittsburgh professor who invented the talking typewriter on which children as young as three and four have learned to read, write, and compose poetry, firmly believes in the low-pressure way. He also wishes that people would pay less attention to the "hardware" and more to his responsive environments method.

This method consists of letting the child teach himself skills in his own way, without adult interference. In principle, at least, the child always takes the initiative. The environment—both man and machine—simply responds in certain ways, depending on what the child has done. This means that no two programs are alike— each child faces puzzles that are programmed just for him, and that keep changing as he goes along. He never needs to please an adult, or to achieve anything. But if he keeps at it, he gradually makes a series of interlocking discoveries about sounds, words, and sentences, much in the way that young children learn to talk.

Moore has found that children not only learn rapidly in this fashion, but also like it enough to keep coming back for more. Particularly between the ages of two and five, he believes, children are capable of extraordinary feats of inductive reasoning if left to themselves in a properly responsive environment. Unlike most adults, he says, children can and do enjoy learning.

Although he uses a machine, his approach thus seems much less mechanical than Bereiter and Engelmann's. They depend on praise and pressure from the teacher; Moore tries to eliminate all extrinsic rewards. They use predetermined sequences, making every child follow exactly the same path; Moore emphasizes that the coming revolution is individualized instruction— "and I don't mean just individual pace."

His own work, he feels, stems from the American progressive and pragmatic movements, as expressed by John Dewey and George Herbert Mead, and represents, for better or for worse, the lively part of the progressive tradition. "Now, for the first time in human history," he says, "you can have an educational scheme truly tailored to the individual person, even if persons occur by the millions. In the Dewey progressive scheme, the whole idea was just that; but it was merely a pious hope until technology made it possible."

On the technological side, Moore's system involves the talking typewriter—a loose term which may mean a slightly modified electric typewriter, plus dictation equipment, an exhibitor, and a human instructor (its original version), or a fancy, $35,000 automated machine called the E.R.E. (Edison Responsive Environ-

216

ment). Highly complex and subtle, the E.R.E. can be programmed to talk, play games, read aloud, take dictation, and show pictures. It boasts an electric typewriter with keys that cannot jam; a narrow window, through which letters, words, or sentences may be exhibited; a slide projector; a microphone; and a speaker —all connected to a small computer and weighing about 500 pounds.

Naturally, in a gadget-loving society, the E.R.E. has caught the spotlight of attention. But most of Moore's work was done with the earlier, inexpensive version of the talking typewriter, or with semiautomated models, in the use of which human teachers still played essential roles. He never tried to rely entirely on automated instruments. And since a separate program must be worked out for each child, the presence of a human being will continue to be necessary—at least with the younger children, and at least some of the time.

Yet people persist in seeing only a fabulously expensive machine which, they believe, does all the work of teaching by itself. And when educators see any machine that is supposed to help children learn something, they generally react either with contempt ("It's just another gimmick") or with fear that it will replace the teacher. Both these extremes ignore the fact that a machine— like a book—is only as exciting, rigid, provocative, or dogmatic as the ideas of the person who devises its program.

Like most inventors, Moore defies classification. A man of medium height and a quiet but intense manner, he comes from outside the world of teachers' colleges or even conventional psychology. Born in the small town of Helper, Utah (Omar Khayyám was his father's favorite poet), raised in Nebraska, he took his Ph.D. in sociology at Washington University in St. Louis, Missouri, and taught experimental sociology—a rare field— at Yale. Crossing into another discipline, he then became professor of psychology at Rutgers. Now, at the age of forty-six, he is professor of social psychology at the University of Pittsburgh, but on leave to do a large-scale study of his method for the Office of Economic Opportunity. Through it all, his main interest has been human higher-order problem solving—he turned to children only to investigate how they solve certain problems.

He began by studying how adults learn symbolic languages. He taught symbolic logic to Navy recruits by means of cubes with logical symbols, a record, a projector, and a program that ranks among the first examples of effective programming—the technique of presenting materials in sequences so precise that they can be used either within teaching machines or in self-teaching textbooks. But after a while he shifted his emphasis from deductive to inductive processes. His research with adults then became more and more difficult. What he needed was a lab in which an entirely new order of things had to be discovered—as if on the moon. Rather than create a whole new environment that was strange enough, Moore decided to go in for ignorant subjects. The most ignorant subjects, of course, were newborns. And the most practical time to start experimenting was when these children were walking and talking, at two or three.

This led to the Responsive Environments Project, a long-term research program which Moore began at Yale in 1959. One of the movies he made then, showing youngsters of two and three learning to read and write on an electric typewriter, caught the eye of a private-school headmaster, Edward I. McDowell, Jr., who invited him to set up a demonstration project at his school. Accordingly, with help from the Carnegie Corporation of New York, Moore opened a Responsive Environments Laboratory on the campus of the Hamden Hall Country Day School, a coeducational school for 340 children from nursery to twelfth grade.

The lab was a green prefabricated structure, with six soundproofed booths, which some sixty of the youngest children visited voluntarily every day. Its rules were simple: No child could stay longer than half an hour a day, though he could leave sooner if he wished. Since there was room for only six children at a time, they took turns coming, but were always free to pass up their turns.

On their first visit to the lab, the children were shown around by another child—part of Moore's plan to make them feel that the lab belonged to them. Parents were never permitted to see their own child in the lab. Even the regular teachers, whom the children might have wanted to impress or defy, were kept in the dark about their pupils' progress. A separate staff, made up largely of Yale graduate students' wives, was carefully instructed never to praise or blame any child. In Moore's words, "The lab represents thirty minutes away from the significant persons in the child's life—he is on his own, in a new environment, where all activity is carried on strictly for its own sake."

Sitting before a talking typewriter for the first time, the child was given no instructions at all. He soon discovered that this interesting, adult-looking machine was all his to play with. Whatever key he struck, the machine responded by typing the corresponding symbol in jumbo type, while a voice named the letter. Four days out of five, the voice was simply that of the human monitor sitting beside him, but if he was in the fully automated booth the machine spoke in the voice of whoever had programmed it. The typewriter's responses came as frequently as he desired. Especially for the youngest children, this sometimes proved irresistible: To test his new-found powers, one three-year-old gleefully struck the asterisk key seventy-five times in suc-

cession, while the poor human monitor repeated doggedly, "Asterisk, asterisk, asterisk, asterisk. . . ."

No two children proceeded in exactly the same way. Some tried each letter in a row, methodically; some played with numbers; others seemed to peck anywhere, at random. When their interest in this free exploration waned, the monitor switched a control dial and changed the game to a puzzle.

Without warning, a letter would appear on the exhibitor facing the child. The machine—or the monitor—would name the letter. And to the child's amazement, all the keys would be blocked, except the one that had been named. It was now a game of try-and-find-me. Eventually the child would hit the right key. Bingo! The key would go down, the machine would type the letter, which would be named again, and after a short interval another letter would appear on the exhibitor.

Urged on by curiosity and a desire to hit the jackpot, the children soon learned to find any letter, number, or punctuation mark that appeared and was named. Sometimes they tried to beat the machine—in fact, the voice could be slowed down or speeded up, according to the child, to make sure each one succeeded in naming some letters ahead of the machine. The children became familiar with various styles and sizes of type—upper-case, lower-case, cursive—as well as with handwritten letters, which could be flashed on the projector's screen. And they learned the sounds of the letters as well as their names.

At the same time, the children effortlessly learned to touch-type. One of the details they liked best about the lab was the chance to get their fingernails painted eight different colors, to match the colors on the typewriter keys. Each set of keys to be struck by a particular finger had its own color. Furthermore, the whole group of keys meant for the right hand responded to a slightly different pressure from that meant for the left. In this way they picked up the correct fingering technique without actually noticing it.

As soon as a child became expert at this game and the challenge diminished—this could be seen when his stroke count for the day decreased—the rules were changed once again. Instead of a single letter, a word would appear on the exhibitor. The word came from the child's own vocabulary, since one of the monitors had previously had him talk into a tape recorder for this very purpose. This ensured that the child was interested in this particular word, and also that he understood it.

Suppose a little girl had talked about her new baby brother. During her next session with the talking typewriter, after a little free-typing of letters and some try-and-find-me, she would suddenly see four letters on the exhibitor, with a red arrow pointing to the first one—B. The voice would say, "B-A-B-Y, baby." If she tried to type Y first, the key would refuse to go down. A would be blocked too. Only when she typed the letters in the right sequence would the keys respond, and then the voice would repeat "B-A-B-Y, baby," before going on to another word.

At no time was the child actually "taught" anything. For many children, this phase proved somewhat annoying; they would frequently ask, and get, a chance to go back to free-typing of letters. But after periods of varying lengths—days, weeks, or sometimes months—the child would suddenly realize that the letters he knew actually made up words that had a meaning, and that he himself could now write such words. This discovery is so elating that when it happens, children have been known to jump up and down in excitement, or run out of the booth to talk about it.

In Moore's opinion, this is the way to introduce learning to children—to make it so exciting that they are hooked for life. "It's an affront to your intelligence to be always told, always presented with everything," he says. Most systems in school alienate children for this reason. The children who are very able will learn anyway, but they won't like the learning part because it is too didactic.

Many details must be planned ahead to make the responsive environments system work. Every afternoon, the lab staff met to discuss the children's progress—an essential step, since the monitors took the children at random and had to know their idiosyncrasies, as well as the stage each had reached. Much depended on the sensitivity and intelligence of the lab supervisor. An experienced teacher, she decided when to shift the children from one phase to the next, on the basis of their performance and the monitors' reports.

The role of the monitor during lab sessions varied with the degree of automation in the booth. Sometimes she took over the voice part, speaking as gently and patiently as the E.R.E. Sometimes she operated the exhibitor by hand. When the child in her care used the fully automated booth, she watched through a one-way mirror, listening through a headphone, so she could come to his rescue if he needed help. A child was never simply left alone with the machine—he might need a handkerchief, or a change of program, or, depending on his mood, some human company. There was also the possibility, with the early models, of some mechanical malfunction which would have to be corrected immediately.

About once a week, each child at the lab played with chalk and a blackboard in the booth which had the least-automated equipment. Since the child had formed a mental image of various letters, sooner or later he would try to trace them on the blackboard's horizontal lines. At this point, the monitor would put the appropriate letter on the projector and suggest that he draw one like it. Thus, the child would learn to print as painlessly as he had learned to touch-type.

The dictation equipment in the talking typewriter was used nearly every day. Moore's plan was to give equal weight to all forms of language—reading, writing, speaking, and listening—so as not to produce speakers who have difficulty in writing, or tongue-tied writers. In many schools the curriculum for the first six grades tends to treat reading and writing as separate subjects, he says. Writing, in the sense of composing original stories, is yet another subject. Spelling and particularly punctuation are handled as special topics. The lab curriculum represents an attempt to deal with these skills and topics as part of an integrated complex. The child alternates between seeing words on the exhibitor, with the voice spelling them out, and hearing them on the tape recorder, as he himself had spoken them. He learns to write both kinds.

At first, the lab introduced the names of letters, so the children could know what to call them. Then it exposed them to the variety of sounds that went with these names. One of the many things a child induced, for example, was that "g" takes on different sound values in "gem" and in "game." He was provided with clean-cut cases, out of his own vocabulary. This led him to learn such letter combinations as "ea" in "ear" and "th" in "mother."

A further variation was to include words collected from stories that had proved interesting to children at the lab, so as to prepare them for actually reading these stories by themselves. Such word lists kept changing along with the children's interests, but nearly all of them included such necessities as "an, are, could, where, what, they." Occasionally some families of words were thrown in: "mat, pat, hat, rat." The words appeared in various forms: filmstrips, typed paper, handwritten cards.

Once over the hump of making and reading words, the children slid into whole sentences and paragraphs. Again they alternated between composing their own sentences and reading those taken from stories. Soon they became voracious consumers of written material. Seeing the rapid turnover of children at the lab—five every half hour, for about six hours a day—I asked how the lab kept up with all this. Where did most of the material come from?

"You get it from the kid," answered Moore firmly. "We've been telling people the same thing for years, but they just don't believe it! Of course, you must have some time with the child first, to listen to him. So one of our people will sit and listen to him, and record what he says on tape. Then his conversation will be broken down into its component words, sentences, and paragraphs."

Under the usual school system, Moore points out, a

wave of children comes in in September, is treated impersonally, and many of them fall behind. By the fourth grade, when the failures become too obvious to ignore, the school begins its remedial steps. At that point, it takes its first close look at the child. The more deviant he is, the more attention he gets. The only way he can be treated as a person is to fail, says Moore, "and that's a strong motive to keep lousing up!"

It is one of the delights of this method that it shows clearly the infinite variety of things about which children care. A four-year-old boy who comes in with a bad cold eagerly confides his symptoms to the tape recorder and then flips a switch to hear himself played back: ". . . coughing and spitting the mucus." When the booth monitor writes some of the key phrases for him on a pad, he types them up with great self-absorption. Another child wants to compose endless shopping lists, mixing in bits of recipes. Another one free-associates: "mouse, letter, dog, octopus."

One spring morning, at Hamden Hall, I watched some of the youngest children, the nursery group, as they walked, skipped, or ran into the lab. First they went to a long table where a teacher painted their fingernails, dipping little brushes into open jars of bright-colored paints. Then they scattered to the six booths, to which they had been assigned at random.

An attractive little girl of four, who had been in the program nearly a year, sat next to a monitor and wrote her own sentences. She spelled the words out loud as she wrote: "After my nap I am going to the circus with my daddy. We s— I don't know how to spell 'saw'——[the monitor quietly said, "a," "w"] saw the parad ["Silent 'e,' " prompted the monitor] e yesterday. . . ." "Do you want to read it?" asked the monitor when the story was finished. The little girl shook her head. "I want to read a book!" she said. The monitor handed her *Time to Play*, a book labeled "Second Preprimer." The child picked it up and began to read quite fluently, chuckling in a satisfied way as she turned the page, "Look here, here we come, look at Pepper and Sue."

Meanwhile, in the automated booth, another child typed away and the machine sounded out each letter that she struck. She wrote her brother's name, her own, several numbers and punctuation marks, then suddenly raised her hand. The monitor came in. "I want a book," the child demanded. "I want to read it by myself." She opened to a page and started reading into the mike: "We are all small. . . ."

Nearby, a boy was slowly making up some words on the typewriter, in capital letters. "You've got 'MON'; now let's finish it," said the monitor, pronouncing "th." The boy wrote "F." "No," said the monitor, "but you're close."

I glanced into the booth where children usually spent some time at the blackboard. Two little girls were taking turns reading into the mike. The words they read had been culled from one of their books: "Bat, bait, mat." They giggled and fooled around. "Okay, listen to yourselves," said the monitor, flipping some switches. The girls listened raptly. When it was over, they giggled again. Then they talked into the mike, telling each other stories about how their daddies mowed the lawn.

Obviously the nursery-group children were at many different levels. Some of them had started reading sentences early in the year, after only three or four months in the program, while others still struggled with simple words. These individual differences became ever more pronounced as time went on. In the next group, kindergarteners who had been there nearly two years, there were also some children who still worked with the easiest words.

In each case, the child's mood on a particular day had much to do with his performance. For example, a five-year-old boy from the kindergarten group came in morosely and typed, first his own name, then his sister's, then his brother's. Then he hesitated and did nothing for quite a long time. "Do you want to type your father's name?" suggested the monitor. "No!" shouted the boy, turning away from the typewriter altogether. The monitor then switched on the projector, with the beginning of a story that the boy could read. "I don't want to!" said the boy angrily. He glanced at a pile of books. The monitor picked up a few, suggesting *Curious George*. "I don't want to!" the boy said again, but less vehemently. He finally picked out another book by himself, and began to read *The Cat in the Hat Comes Back*.

Another kindergartener bounced in and asked for a book she had started the day before, C. N. Bonsall's *Who's a Pest?* She read with obvious enjoyment, stopping only to laugh at the story itself. Only a few words stumped her; at such times the monitor gave helpful hints. Then the child settled herself in front of the typewriter, picked out a word from the book—"extra" —and typed it. Next she selected another word—"and." Then, in a row, "dismay, yes, simple, even, noise, electric." There seemed to be some method to her selection, so after the session was over I asked the monitor about it. "Oh, it's a game," explained the monitor. "She likes to pick out words which start with the last letter of the word she has just finished typing."

Many of the kindergarteners read at first- or second-grade level, I was told. I watched one little girl as she read into a tape recorder from a standard second-grade filmstrip prepared by the Educational Development Laboratory of Huntington, Long Island. She read fluently: "Spot didn't like it because the ball would not roll where he wanted it to," then stopped abruptly and said, "I want to listen to it!" and had it played back.

The filmstrips were used for testing purposes. They showed that the first-graders read up to sixth-grade level, with the average around third-grade level, whereas the second-graders, who had been in the program two years, read up to ninth-grade level, with the average about sixth grade.

Far more impressive than these figures was the free use of language—spoken, written, typed, or dictated—by many children at the lab. The first-graders actually put out their own newspaper, *The Lab Record*, written and edited entirely by the children themselves. They dictated their stories into the tape recorder, typed them up, edited them, and typed the final copy. Those who could not yet read or write fluently enough stopped after the dictation phase. The newspaper contained drawings, riddles, and poems, as well as stories. One poem by a girl not quite six years old was entitled "A Duck," and read as follows:

> There was a duck,
> Who could kick.
> He had good luck,
> Because he was quick.
> He could run in a race,
> He would win.
> He would get some lace
> And a magic pin.

When I met the pint-sized poet she was engrossed in her daily session with the talking typewriter. A pretty little girl with long brown hair, she read fluently from the projector: "Once upon a time the African magician came to China to find a wonderful lamp . . ." and with dramatic flair continued, "Give me the lamp, and I will help you out." She then questioned the monitor about the story's plot, and answered the monitor's questions about the meaning of certain words. When she came out of the booth, she sat down with me in an empty office. I asked her if she wanted to be a poet when she grew up. "No," she replied without hesitation, "I want to be a housewife." Writing poetry was fun, she said, but the really nice part was being able to work on the newspaper "with Jeff," one of the editors. Did she prefer the lab when a monitor was in the booth with her, as today? She liked it best when she was alone in it, she replied emphatically, "so I can do *exactly* what I like."

Riddles were constant favorites: "Why does the firemen [sic] wear suspenders? *Answer:* To keep their pants up." "Why is grass like a mouse? *Answer:* Because the cat'll eat it."

Besides the newspaper, the children sometimes found special uses for their access to the lab. On one of my visits, a five-year-old boy whose mother was critically ill requested a specific typewriter, sat down before it and, in silent concentration, composed the following letter:

> Dear Mother,
>   Get better soon!
>   I love you very much and want you better very fast.
>   I wanted to surprise you by typing you my
> first letter. Are you proud of me? I did it just
> for you Mother.
>   I pray for you every night.
>   Love and a big kiss from

After signing his name, he added: "I typed all of this letter by myself on the big grown up script typewriter."

Many reasons can be offered for these children's extraordinary facility with reading and writing: their high socioeconomic level (which may be necessary, but not sufficient); their innate ability (of the eleven children in the Lab's oldest group, two had IQ's in the genius range; however, the others were only slightly above the average for middle-class children); their freedom of action (similar to that of children in progressive nursery schools and kindergartens where they do not learn to read or write). But one factor cannot be ignored: the cumulative effect of exposure.

Because typing on an electric typewriter is so much easier for little fingers than making letters by hand, the children who came to the lab produced—and were exposed to—many more symbols than would be possible elsewhere. Even in ten minutes they could chalk up an impressively large stroke count. Those who stayed in the booth longer typed an average of 2,000 strokes a week, counting punctuation and spaces. They were surrounded by symbols, just as toddlers must be surrounded by words before they can learn to speak.

I visited the lab some three months after the beginning of the school year, and watched a boy of four and a half as he started banging on his talking typewriter energetically. He tried upper case and lower case; he ranged all over the keyboard; he typed the numbers from 16 to 20 in proper sequence; he played with the quotation marks; he wrote several nonsense words; then he typed carefully: "Barry is a RAT." The next few minutes were spent playing with the carriage return. He banged, and the machine's voice responded, "Carriage return" every time. Suddenly he added "and a cat." He was using correct fingering technique. During his twenty-seven minutes in the booth, he hardly stopped typing *something*. Later on, checking his records, Moore told me that the number of minutes the boy had stayed in the booth, and his stroke count, had gone up steadily since the beginning of the year. In his twelve weeks at the lab, he had struck a total of approximately 25,000 symbols—and by now he could read and write any simple sentence. Though he was bright, he did not test in the "gifted" range, which begins above an IQ of 140. He did have one incalculable advantage: permissive parents who laid great emphasis on intellectual skills, thus giving him much to relate to what he learned in the lab.

An even younger child, who did not attend the nursery school—the headmaster's little daughter, aged 2 years and 8 months—had taught herself on the typewriter all the letters in the alphabet, both upper- and lower-case, in about two months. She could also write some of them on the blackboard. I watched as she went into the automated booth and, with help because she was so small, hoisted herself on the chair facing the keyboard. First she pressed the carriage-return key a couple of times, then she banged on "c" and listened to the machine's voice. For awhile she hummed a tune. Next, she fiddled with a side lever. Finally she began to type a few letters rapidly, glancing up at the characters she produced and alert to the voice that came from the machine's speaker. After eighteen minutes in the booth, she raised her hand. A monitor came in to help her off the chair. "By-by," said the little girl, and walked out.

In general, those who start younger do better, says Moore. They have an easy, natural swing to their behavior. The older ones are more careful and deliberate. But a three-year-old will act as if he weren't paying attention. It's *really* free exploration, in a relaxed, fluid way.

At that age they can also tolerate a great many more errors than older children—or adults—will accept. Older, in this case, means children who have reached the ripe age of 6. One such newcomer to the lab was so afraid of making a mistake that he would hesitantly press a few keys and then run out to ask the monitor, "Am I doing it right?" He needed constant reassurance from an adult.

Moore's own daughter, Venn, started playing with the talking typewriter when she was 2 years and 7 months old. She could read first-grade stories before she was three. A very gifted child, she took part in Moore's first experiments with his method at Yale University, and starred in the short documentary movie that was made at that time. The movie shows her reading in a babyish voice, at two years, eleven months, typing sentences while singing out the names of the letters, and laughing or clapping her hands when she succeeds in finding the right symbol.

When I first met her, Venn was in Hamden Hall's first grade and acted as one of *The Lab Record*'s editors. The other editor, Jeffrey, had also started using the talking typewriter during Moore's experiments at Yale. By then, both 6-year-olds could read seventh-grade books with pleasure. To test their skill, I opened a copy of

Scientific American at random and asked them whether they could read it. They did so exuberantly, taking turns. Although they stumbled over some words which they did not understand, they could clearly handle anything phonetically.

Moore's respect for three-year-olds knows no bounds. "I wouldn't pit myself against a three-year-old any day, in meeting an utterly new problem or a radically new environment," he declares. "You've got your top problem-solvers there. By the time a child is three, he has achieved what is probably the most complex and difficult task of his lifetime—he has learned to speak. Nobody has instructed him in this skill; he has had to develop it unaided. In bilingual or multilingual communities, children pick up several languages, without accent, at a very early age. There's plenty of information-processing ability in a mind that can do that."

Unlike parrots, young children don't learn item by item, but by over-all search—they absorb whole patterns, Moore believes. Some of civilization's most important patterns are those which he calls "autotelic folk models." (Autotelic means that they contain their own goals and do not relate to immediate survival or welfare.) Through such models, children learn skills that will enable them to deal with the recurring problems of chance and strategy, with the puzzles posed by nature, and with various forms of art. Every society known to anthropologists has generated models of this sort. Simple forms of these models are internalized in childhood, says Moore, and more complex versions of them sustain us in adulthood. Without these abstractions, men would have been imprisoned in small groups, not unlike bands of especially intelligent baboons.

It is only recently that mathematicians have analyzed games of chance and of strategy, he points out. The mathematical theory of puzzles has not been very well worked out yet, and for esthetics there is no theory at all. But, so far, none of these four classes of models has required any technological expertise; for example, bits of wood will do for checker pieces. The models themselves are essentially static entities, in which the rules remain constant. They mirror the static quality of unchanging or imperceptibly changing societies, says Moore. In the past they have generally proved so successful that people had to be prohibited from playing too much. They have also served as a school for emotional expressions—the kind of school in which boredom is unlikely and uncontrolled emotional frenzy is forbidden. All in all, they have served man well—as did the Newtonian conceptions of space and time.

Today, Moore believes, dynamic models are needed. The rules of the game must keep changing, though not arbitrarily or irrelevantly. This will require extensive use of technology, since the players cannot be interrupted to explain each change.

From this standpoint, Moore comments that IQ tests measure only one aspect of people's abilities: the ability to solve short, static puzzles. They do not measure the ability to handle dynamic puzzles, or games of strategy, or esthetic objects. Better tests, like better models, would require a full use of modern technology.

Drawing on existing folk models, Moore tries to create as closely as he can the conditions of play: It has to be fun, and it must be fixed so there are no serious consequences. He also emphasizes inductive reasoning, "because in our world we can't stand pat. We have more new problems today than we can even name, and we must turn out larger and larger numbers of youngsters who can make fresh inductions about them, not just follow rules. This is our chief trouble today: technological change but intransigent behavior. It's too late for us—our generation can't make it. At best, we are just the transition group."

Creating the conditions of play is not so easy. As a hideous example of autotelic activities turned sour, Moore points to Little League play, which isn't play at all. Some parents can ruin almost any play situation, he says.

Children often seem to forget something they knew well before; at such times, it is particularly difficult for adult human beings to refrain from "helping" them. One of Moore's recent movies shows a little girl who suddenly forgot how to switch the keyboard to lower case. Until then, she had operated all the keys with ease, but now, after writing an upper-case "T," she did not know what to do. "Lower case," said the E.R.E. machine. The little girl explored the keyboard at random, but to no avail—all the keys seemed locked. About every fifteen seconds, the machine quietly repeated "Lower case," as a reminder. To an adult observer, the situation was almost intolerable. One wanted to run into the booth and show the child what to do. But the little girl did not seem at all concerned. After a moment's hesitation, she calmly began to try out all the keys systematically, column by column, until at last she hit the right one. At once, the machine responded, the pointer moved to the next letter on the exhibitor, and the voice simply sounded it, "o," as if nothing had happened.

In the privacy of a booth, children who don't understand very quickly need not be embarrassed or suffer from constant comparisons with the fast learners. The talking typewriter has infinite patience. It plays no favorites. It never tires of repeating things. It never gets angry, and no child need feel anxious about losing its love. Thus, the slower children are not deprived of the chance to make their own discoveries, and the brighter ones can proceed without boredom.

So far, only a handful of mentally retarded children have tried out Moore's method. The results have been encouraging. A boy with an IQ of 65, for example, took nine months to learn what the brightest children had learned in three weeks—but eventually he got there, without any pressure, and learned to copy simple words, sentences, and stories. Moore's method thus holds hope for many kinds of retarded or handicapped youngsters—not just normal preschoolers. It can also be used to present foreign languages to students of all ages.

As a lesson in patience, all the monitors in the Hamden Hall Lab spent some time observing the fully automated E.R.E., so as to model their behavior on it. Nevertheless, there are certain limitations to human beings in this situation. Especially at the beginning, when a child is actively exploring the keyboard, a human instructor has a hard time keeping up with him. The faster a child goes, the more difficult for the monitor to keep up—or to remain calm and impersonal about it. Sometimes the child spends weeks testing the monitor's patience in this way.

It was to get around this problem that Moore and Richard Kobler, an engineer who is now manager of the Thomas A. Edison Laboratory of West Orange, New Jersey (a part of the McGraw-Edison Company), together invented the E.R.E. machine. The first prototype became available in 1961.

As Kobler puts it, the child who faces an E.R.E. is "in a monastic condition, in which nothing counts but the interplay between him and the machine. . . . He can attempt many errors during the phase with blocked keys, but he is not allowed to execute these errors. And so it becomes something very private: Nobody knows whether he made a mistake. He can only execute successes—but maybe after intensive inner battles, of the kind that belong to man's greatest experiences."

However, the E.R.E. could be programmed in countless different ways—even ·with electric shock or with pellets, Moore points out. It can be made rude, impatient, insulting, or even cruel. People who buy the machine sometimes do not realize they are merely buying a blank page—Moore's program does not come with it. The machine is easy to program from the technical point of view: The teacher or monitor simply puts one of the blank program cards into the typewriter, sets a few dials, and types out what he wishes, up to 120 words per card; these will then appear in any desired sequence on the exhibitor, and will also control the operation of the typewriter keys. The audio part is encoded by speaking into a microphone. The real problem is deciding what to program. To many teachers, the temptation is nearly irresistible to use the machine merely to present traditional, formal instruction in a more efficient form. Because of the time and labor consumed in programming, they would dearly like to have a program that could be applied indiscriminately to all children.

This is precisely where Moore's method differs from other forms of programmed instruction or teaching machines. It differs so much, in fact, that according to P. Kenneth Komoski, who evaluated such methods as president of the nonprofit Center for Programed Instruction at Columbia University's Teachers College, Moore does not have a "teaching" machine at all; he has a "learning" machine. While teaching machines generally make students come up with the right answer by leading them in a straight line from one little piece of information to the next, Moore's system gives children the opportunity to preserve a natural, inquisitive attitude.

Moore himself says that the other types of programming are too didactic. They inculcate a method of search that is prejudicial to finding a creative solution. The programmer takes a godlike position with relation to his subjects: He plans in advance, not the general environment, but the detailed steps they must take. This makes no provision for the students' possible contribution—for the possibility that they may come up with a solution he hasn't thought of. "It also presupposes," says Moore, "that we have some theory about human learning that is adequate—well, we don't."

He compares his system to a matrix, or a spider web. The others, he says, do not allow browsing; they are really a return to the scroll, over which books were an improvement. Why have an electronic scroll? asks. Moore.

Moore's goal, then, is to produce independent thinkers—not to stuff any child with rules or facts. This has been widely misunderstood. Frequently it is the disciplinarians, those who want skills taught in a hard, didactic way, who are most attracted to the idea of using a machine. The progressives, who should favor whatever increases the child's individuality, tend to like programs that postpone intellectual activity. "Everyone's on the wrong side," complains Moore. "This is really an ultra-progressive program. It's too bad people can't rationalize their positions better."

Since the lab took up no more than half an hour a day, the children still had their sandbox, paints, and other time-honored preschool activities. In fact, the lab actually allowed the prolonging of some of these things. As traditionally handled now in the nursery schools, at least the children are free, though they receive little intellectual stimulation. But in the first grade the game is over. At the very time when the child is becoming interested in the wider world around him, he must divorce himself from such matters and confine himself to squiggles. He must learn the alphabet, learn to print, and because of his low skill, read baby stories that are not appropriate for him. All of this takes so long that many important things are dropped as frills—painting

and music, for instance. No wonder so many children develop a hatred for intellectual work early in school, says Moore.

By contrast, the first-graders who went to the lab had plenty of time for what is normally called enrichment, since their teacher did not have to drill them in reading and writing. The children read fourth-grade geography books, listened to music and poetry, played games, and went on field trips. Each one also read up on specific subjects that interested him particularly—boats, rockets, the moon.

"People used to ask me, What in the world will they do in first grade?" recalls Moore. "A year later, they asked, What in the world will they do in second grade?"

The second grade that evolved for the lead group from the lab was, in fact, so unusual that it nearly split Hamden Hall into two warring factions. Since the regular second-grade curriculum was obviously unsuited to them, a special class for only nine children had to be conducted in a separate building, with a separate teacher who had formerly been a booth monitor.

When I first visited this class, the children were listening to a record of Robert Frost reading his own poetry—"Stopping by Woods on a Snowy Evening." "It will take a little time to get used to his voice," said the young teacher, "so I'll read it, and then we'll listen again." Meanwhile, she passed around the record cover, with a picture of Frost. After the second hearing, she began to ask questions. "Miles to go before I sleep—what would you say this means?" she asked the class. Some children suggested "before night" and "before he falls asleep." One girl gasped, "Oh, I know! Before he dies." "Right," said the teacher, "and what do you call that?" A bucktoothed little blonde with a high-pitched voice piped up. "It's a euphemism!" she said. The children were all seven years old, except one girl who had just turned eight. They launched into a lively discussion of "why he said that when he's so old," as one boy put it. After a few more questions, the teacher asked, "Now, do you want to hear it again?" "Yes!" shouted the class. And in utter silence they listened: "The woods are lovely, dark and deep. But I have promises to keep, And miles to go before I sleep,/ And miles to go before I sleep."

In general, she tried to steer away from themes of death or growing old, the teacher later explained. But she did pick interpretive, rather than just descriptive, poetry, and by now the children understood the meaning of such terms as onomatopoeia and alliteration. She had read them some Tennyson, Shelley, Byron, and Wordsworth; many questions had been asked back and forth. It was Moore's idea to read them adult poetry, not just childish, sing-song verses.

"Ancient Chinese proverbs are particularly useful," added the teacher, Mrs. Anne Schrader. "They're excellent to make the children find their own interpretations. Then they invent their own proverbs." At times the children solved crossword puzzles which she made up for them, using words they had just come across.

Their day started with their least-liked subjects: penmanship and arithmetic. To make this more pleasant, Mrs. Schrader always played music for them while they worked—"Carmen," "Victory at Sea," "The Sorcerer's Apprentice," and other favorites. Each child worked on his own, generally with third- or fourth-grade workbooks. After that came vocabulary or poetry, and then recess.

I went down to the basement, drawn by the noise of children at play. "Here we go Loopy Loo! Here we go Loopy La!" sang the kids at the top of their lungs, trying to outdo the record player and swinging each other about.

Exhausted, yet refreshed, the children trooped back to their classroom, still full of fun. After some shuffling of chairs, they formed into three small groups; in each group a child began to read aloud—not too loud, so as not to disturb the other groups—from a book. A boy started reading from The Brave and the Free, a book of stories designed for sixth-grade reading programs. He read very fluently to the last paragraph on the page, as three little girls listened. When he stopped, the little girl to his left picked up the book and continued much more slowly, in a high-pitched voice. "All right, go ahead!" impatiently muttered another girl, who was interested in the story. The child tried to read faster, but stumbled over some words, so the first boy complained that he couldn't catch what she was saying. She finally settled down to a comfortable pace, and read to the end of the page. The other children took their turns. Occasionally they corrected each other's pronunciation ("Not pro-fit -able, pro'-fit-able!"), but without animosity. At the end of the story the children took turns asking each other questions about what they had read. "What does 'Zowie' mean?" asked the boy. "It's something you say when you don't know what to say," replied the high-pitched girl. The boy was not satisfied. "There are many other words you could say instead," he argued. They went and looked it up in the big Unabridged Webster's which lay on its stand in the front of the room, next to a relief globe of the world.

After lunch, the children had music or art with the regular teachers, then gym, French, and their daily session at the lab. They no longer needed the automated typewriter—in fact, this would slow down their typing, since the keys were set to give the voice enough time to respond. But they did read books on subjects they found particularly interesting; they did use the recording and dictation equipment, and they worked on their newspaper. (By then, the new first grade had a newspaper of

its own.) One child wrote: "Haiku is Japanese poetry. The form of it is, the first line has to have five syllables, the second line has seven syllables, the last or third line has five syllables like the first line. It has to have three lines, but it isn't supposed to rhyme." And then she composed her own haiku:

Ivy on a wall
Like wee little animals
Climbing to their homes.

The regular teachers at Hamden Hall, meanwhile, watched these goings-on with dismay—and often a good deal of hostility. To them, the lab was an intrusion: Some of them had been at the school as long as twenty-seven years. They complained that the children who went to the lab were hard to handle as a group. "They all want individual attention because they're used to this one-to-one relationship," said one teacher. "They can't wait—they all want their table to be the first to get books."

"It's all too permissive," grumbled another teacher. "The children are less mature. When I was in public school, you had to finish one level first before going on to the next. Here they read one page of a second-grade workbook, and they say it's too easy, they want to go on to a higher level! They never finish anything—they just claim they've done that level!"

One teacher who taught the traditional first grade said, "They're reading at third-grade level in my class too, without the lab!" A science teacher commented that the lab group couldn't add or subtract properly; all they knew was how to work with Cuisenaire rods.

"I had to slap Jimmy once because he wanted to push all the buttons in the French-language lab," recalled the French teacher.

The school was soon so split on the issue of the lab that it became a political act for a teacher merely to visit the place—and during the three years of the demonstration program very few teachers did visit. Then the money ran out. The board of trustees decided it could not afford to continue the program, which cost between $25,000 and $30,000 a year (about $500 per child), all by itself. The parents of children in the top elementary and high-school grades were totally uninterested in the lab. The parents whose children did attend the lab volunteered to raise most of the money for the program, but the trustees rejected their offer. "There were no long-range plans for interweaving these children with the school," the board's president, G. Harold Welch, Jr., told me later. "There comes a point—about the third grade—when we wouldn't have enough students for two different third grades, because of the high mobility of parents. We have to have a single track."

Meanwhile, the school's headmaster, who had been closely associated with the lab, was forced out. Mc-

Dowell had invited Moore in the first place and had two of his own daughters in the program. He described the lab as a gentle, humane environment in which young minds and emotions could and did flower. He believed that the kind of individualized instruction provided by the lab would lead to an ungraded school system all the way up the line. Educationally this is nothing new, but administratively it's quite a problem. Together with Moore, he formed an independent foundation, the Responsive Environments Foundation, Inc., in Hamden, Connecticut, to continue the work with different groups of children. And although the two men later parted company, McDowell remains convinced that the responsive environments method is "the soundest thing I've heard of in education. I've seen nothing since that comes close to it."

Toward the end of Moore's three-year demonstration at Hamden Hall, he asked the Educational Testing Service of Princeton, New Jersey, to come and test the lab children, because he wanted some outside confirmation of how well they were doing. Dr. Scarvia Anderson, E.T.S.'s director of curriculum studies, selected two standard achievement tests that are normally given to children in the fourth, fifth, and sixth grades. She then administered these tests to the second-graders who had attended the lab. One test—the Sequential Test of Educational Progress (STEP)—required the children to read a paragraph, read some questions referring to it, and select the correct answers to these questions. Six of the eight children she tested with it scored in the 80th to 99th percentile, far above the median for a national sample of fourth-graders, and two of them were above the median for eighth-graders. In another form of the STEP, the listening form, the examiner read both the text and the questions; the children were required to select one of four written answers. The entire class scored well above the median for fourth-graders on this test, and half the class scored above the median for eighth-graders.

From another point of view, Dr. Edith Lisansky, a clinical psychologist who tested the children at regular intervals, found that their Rorschach tests tended to show greater richness and better balance as they advanced in the program.

Moore collected much data on the children in the lab, but since it was a pilot project rather than an experiment comparing two groups of youngsters, he used this information only to change his procedures and equipment as he went along. He never published any detailed description of his method or its results. Though hundreds of educators visited the Hamden Hall lab, there are no written guides for teachers who may wish to duplicate what he did there.

This has produced enormous confusion among teachers, administrators, and prospective buyers of the E.R.E., who are led to believe that the machine alone can perform miracles. Educators who want to watch Moore's techniques in action can go to his foundation in Hamden, where a reduced staff works with some twenty to thirty children a day, using both automated and nonautomated equipment. But most people find it easier to attend one of the demonstrations and sales talks offered by the distributors of the E.R.E. in New York City.

The greatest source of confusion has been the matter of automation. Moore's position is that nobody has yet found the optimal mix of automated and nonautomated equipment. This may actually vary with each child. At Hamden Hall he had at most a ratio of 1 to 4—and much of the time the machine, a prototype, was not working at all. At his foundation, the ratio is now 1 to 2—one automated booth for two that are nonautomated. Under his present plans the fully automated equipment will not be used more than half the time.

The E.R.E. was designed as a research instrument, Moore adds. Its cost makes it prohibitive as standard equipment in schools. Together with the engineer, Richard Kobler, he has been working on much cheaper devices that will perform some of the E.R.E.'s functions. One of these, about to be released, consists of a special surface on which a child could trace letters or write words with a stylus, and get a spoken response. Moore visualizes it as a classroom aid in a variety of kindergartens.

As to the responsive environments method itself, the question remains whether it is well suited to mass use. An experiment now in progress in Chicago should furnish some answers. In a desperately poor neighborhood called the Marillac area, 120 youngsters of three and a half and four have started using both automated and nonautomated talking typewriters under a program sponsored by the Cook County Department of Public Aid, with funds from the OEO. Their parents are either functionally or totally illiterate. The children's progress will be compared with that of a matched control group. During the late afternoon and evening, the Chicago Board of Education uses the same equipment to teach reading to school dropouts and illiterate adults. Each person's program is tailored individually. Moore is chief adviser for this experiment, which is expected to provide detailed statistics from various kinds of tests.

Moore's work thus represents a gallant effort to tame the products of modern technology, and make them serve the interests of each individual child. Throughout the country, big business is preparing to enter the field of education with computers and automated equipment. Most of these plans call for fitting strict programs onto whatever machine the company wants to sell—thus locking the student into a rigid system that demands total conformity. Going against this powerful tide, Moore remains concerned above all with the uniqueness of the learner.

The Open School: A Way of Thinking About Children, Learning, Knowledge

by Roland S. Barth and Charles H. Rathbone

Education, from preschool to post graduate, like so many other established institutions today, is under attack. We are in for a long period of critical, albeit reluctant, self-examination as traditional assumptions about how teachers teach and how students learn and what knowledge is appropriate are debated.

It is in this forum of flux that "open education" is finding an increasingly important place. Interest in this movement is no doublt, in part, a reaction to the wave of technology and behaviorism which is so rapidly swamping the educational system. But more important, interest is motivated by a growing recognition that traditional practices and theories have failed and that a search for fresh alternatives must begin.

What is open education? Some of the phrases used to describe the notion include "free day," "integrated day," "integrated curriculum," "informal classroom," "developmental classroom," "Leicestershire model." Whichever, open education has its most immediate roots in England. It is a way of thinking about children, learning and knowledge.

It is characterized by openness and trust, and by a spatial openness of schools: doors are ajar and children are free to come and go, bringing objects of interest in and taking objects of interest out. The organization of each room is open, subject to change with changing needs. Children move comfortably in this openness from place to place and from activity to activity.

Time is open . . . open to permit and release and serve children rather than to constrain and prescribe and master. The curriculum is open to significant choice by adults and by children as a function of the needs and interest of each child at each moment.

Perhaps most fundamental, open education is characterized by an openness of self. Persons are openly sensitive to and supportive of other persons, not closed off by anxiety, threat, custom and role. Feelings are exposed, acknowledged and respected, not withheld in fear and defensiveness. Administrators are open to initiatives on the part of teachers; teachers are open to the possibilities inherent in children; children are open to the possibilities inherent in other children, in materials, in themselves.

In short, open education implies an environment in which the possibility for exploration and learning of self and of the world are unobstructed.

But open education is not a romantic ideology finding substance only in theory. It exists in fact not only in England but in this country as a growing number of films attest. Despite the fact that American education is hardly an institution built upon trust, public schools in Boston New York, Philadelphia, Los Angeles, Grand Forks, N. D. and Washington are currently exploring this kind of learning environment. Independent schools in places as varied as Cambridge, Bennington and Atlanta are doing the same. Even more important, individuals all over the country are beginning to translate their interest in the idea of open education into various kinds of personal actions. The work of Lillian Weber *(Center Forum,* May 15, 1969) is a notable example.

A few teacher training institutions are beginning to reorient themselves towards open education and are now struggling with the problem of preparing teachers for this kind of setting. Wheelock College in Boston, the City College of New York, and the University of North Dakota are three examples. State departments of education, such as Vermont, New York, and New Jersey are showing an interest in this movement and federal programs which are concerned with early childhood education, such as the Follow Through Program, are already reflecting a considerable influence.

Open education is thus facing the possibility of rapid growth. Consequently it faces serious perils as well as opportunities: with its emphasis on student choice and initiative, open education can easily become a cover for those who don't know how to relate to children and who are unsure of what is best for children. Like a similar groundswell in the '30s, open education when employed by those who little understand it, can easily degenerate into sloppy permissiveness and wistful romanticism. For open education, if anything, demands of teachers the deepest thinking through of what learning is, what knowledge is, and what their craft is.

The movement toward open education has been evolving in England for more than 50 years, a fact that does not seem to deter those, who in the American tradition, would stimulate a fad or mount a crash program. Change which is too rapid, however, accompanied by little understanding or acceptance of underlying rationale and assumptions, can only have the effect of adopted terminology, modified appearance, and a confused and inconsistent experience for children. Superintendents have never been and will never be able to change teachers' attitudes and practices by fiat. Therefore, should an attempt at this kind of change be made again, it's a good bet that open education would follow team teaching, programmed instruction, and educational television to the graveyard of educational panaceas.

Also dangerous is the possibility that, because of the desperate need for significant and immediate changes in American education, open education will be adopted without a critical examination, without research, or without sufficient evidence that these ideas and practices do in fact bring about more desirable changes in children than other traditional means. It is toward the start of that kind of national discussion that the annotated bibliography that follows is offered.

One thing is certain; open education, whether widely accepted or not, will have served a valuable purpose if it encourages and fosters a fresh examination of what we are currently doing; if it helps provoke each educator to make more conscious, to examine, and to develop his *own* assumptions about children, learning, and knowledge. This could only serve to stimulate and legitimize the development of alternative kinds of teaching, learning, and school experiences, and it is the existence of alternatives which is so badly needed today. When each educator can become sure of that in which he believes, all will profit.

READINGS ON BRITISH PRIMARY EDUCATION AND ITS AMERICAN COUNTERPARTS: A SELECTED BIBLIOGRAPHY:

Advisory Centre for Education, *Where.* Advisory Centre for Education, 57 Russell Street, Cambridge, England.
A magazine published by the Advisory Centre, containing articles on a variety of topics in British education. Occasional "supplements" on special topics are also published, such as #13 (on Nuffield math and science projects) and #12 (on unstreaming the comprehensive schools).

Allen, Gwen, et al., *Scientific Interests in the Primary School.* National Froebel Foundation, 2 Manchester Square, London W.I., 1966. @ 3/6d.
A practical guide for teachers, including extensive bibliographies and addresses of curriculum publishers.

Armstrong, Michael, "New Trends in Secondary Education," *Arena.* London: The Architectural Association, July 1967.
A relatively theoretical consideration of the implications of open education for the secondary school.

Alschuler, Alfred and **Terry Borton,** *A bibliography on Affective Education,* Albany, N. Y.: New York Educational Opportunities Forum, State Board of Education, 1969.
"A bibliography on Affective Education, Psychological Education, the Eupsychian Network, Curriculum of Concerns, Personological Education, Synoetics, Personal Learning, etc." including names of organizations and individuals concerned with these matters. Although not necessarily concerned with open education, this view offers an important perspective on what happens in open education classrooms.

Barth, Roland S., "Open Education: Assumptions About Learning and Knowledge," *Educational Philosophy and Theory.* Oxford: Pergamon Press, 1969.
A thorough attempt to identify and classify the assumptions held by British and American open educators concerning children's learning and the nature of knowledge.

Barth, Roland S., "Science: Learning Through Failure," *Elementary School Journal,* Vol. 66, No. 4, January 1966.
The author describes how a fifth grade class became aware of the power of scientific techniques by trying to investigate and explore without them. The resulting failures had a profound effect upon subsequent activities. He concludes that it is possible for teachers to not only tolerate failure in children but to deliberately mold failure, taking advantage of it as a powerful aid to learning.

Barth, Roland S. and **Charles H. Rathbone,** *Open Education: An Annotated Bibliography.* Newton: Education Development Center, September 1969. Available (free) as *Occasional Paper 3,* Early Childhood Education Study, 55 Chapel Street, Newton, Mass. 02160.
The entire, comprehensive bibliography of which this present selection represents a little more than one-half.

Bernstein, Basil, "The Open School," *Where.* (Supplement #12). Advisory Centre for Education, 57 Russell Street, Cambridge, England, 1967.
Viewing schools as complex social organizations, Professor Bernstein applying Durkheim, posits two classifications: open (or organic) and closed (mechanical). The open school, emphasizing differences among children, educates for breadth not depth. It sees knowledge as uncompartmentalized, and teachers as problem posers rather than solution givers. Its pedagogy classes for exploration of principles (not merely the memorization of standard operations); hence its boundaries seem ever flexible. This article offers an interesting point from which to view open education.

Vermont State Department of Education, *Vermont Design for Education.* Montpelier: State Department of Education, May 1968. Single copies available (free) from: Office of the Commissioner of Education, Montpelier, Vermont 05602.
The articulation of 17 premises which taken in summation "constitute a goal, an ideal, a student-centered philosophy for the process of education in Vermont," followed by a consideration of several suggested strategies for implementation of those ideals. In all, an unusual expression of commitment by a state agency to the principles of open education.

Walters, Elsa H., *Activity and Experience in the Infant School.* National Froebel Foundation, 2 Manchester Square, London W. 1.
An examination of the principles behind the so-called "activity method" including consideration of how children learn ("each stage of development must be lived fully if the child is to be prepared to pass on to the next"), the development of a "work attitude," the role of a teacher in maintaining an "atmosphere of security," some ways of making the change from formal to free classrooms.

Walters, Elsa H., *Activity and Experience in the Junior School.* National Froebel Foundation, 2 Manchester Square, London W. I.
A continuation of her infant school pamphlet, with emphasis on the necessary differences between junior and infant schools. Freedom and respect, she warns, are also due to teachers who, given them, will continue to grow. How to help teachers change is a central concern.

Weber, Lillian, *The English Infant School: A Model for Informal Education.* New York: Agathon Press, 1969.
A comprehensive study by a CCNY Professor of Early Childhood Education who recently spent 18 months in England studying the organization and program of British infant schools.

Weber, Lillian, *Infants School* (film). Education Development Center, 55 Chapel Street, Newton, Mass. 02160, 1966.
Thirty nearly unedited minutes of activity in London's Gordonbrock Infant School, with concentration on children's movement in the classroom. For a transcription of an interview with Miss Susan Williams, headmistress of this school, see Cazden's "Infant School" pamphlet.

Yeomans, Edward, *Education for Initiative and Responsibility.* Boston: National Association of Independent Schools, November 1967. Available @ $1.00 from: NAIS, 4 Liberty Square, Boston, Mass. 02109.
Thoughtful comments on a visit to the schools of Leicestershire County in April 1967, with special attention to describing and analyzing "Integrated Day" and "Vertical Grouping." Appendix III of this pamphlet lists curriculum materials and equipment recommended for an open education classroom, including addresses of manufacturers.

Yeomans, Edward, *The Wellsprings of Teaching.* Boston: National Association of Independent Schools, 1969. Available @ $1.00 from NAIS, 4 Liberty Square, Boston, Mass. 02109.
Subtitled, "A discursive report of a teachers' workshop on the philosophy and techniques of the Integrated Day," this pamphlet describes a one-month summer program designed to help teachers not so mush prepare directly for work in school as to explore and think about their own learning.

Young, Michael and **Michael Armstrong,** "The Flexible School," *Where.* Supplement #5 (Autumn 1965). Entire issue available @ 5/6d. from: Advisory Centre for Education, 57 Russell Street, Cambridge, England.
A thorough, carefully reasoned monograph which, in advocating the abolition of "streaming" in British Comprehensives, proposes the flexible school as a viable alternative. Such attempts at individualization as team teaching, programed instruction, the 6th Form model, correspondence courses, the university tutorial and broadcasting are all considered in this wide ranging discussion of practical as well as theoretical matters pertaining to the intellectual segregation of children in schools and its disadvantages.

English Infant Schools

by Lillian Weber

In the general revision of all primary education towards "informality," much of the training and retraining was (and is) conducted outside the colleges. The heads [the equivalent in rank of an American school principal] were interested and had need to experiment and to consider ideas more quickly than could be serviced by the colleges. Thus they came to depend for their growth on the many in-service courses offered, some of them organized directly by the inspectors.

The H.M.I.'s and local inspectorate, of course, conducted in-service training all the time, just by their advice and by sharing the good programs they had seen. In-service courses by local education authorities, by the Ministry or Department of Education, by the Nursery Association, by the Froebel Institute, by the institutes of education and teachers colleges, and more recently by the Nuffield Foundation,* were always oversubscribed even though no increment was given for attendance. Even educational magazines and unions (National Union of Teachers) ran courses.

*The Nuffield Foundation in England has functioned very much as the Ford Foundation in the United States which with local boards of education, sponsored preschools prior to Operation Head Start and also sponsored trials of particular experimental approaches in education.

In almost every school I visited during my stay in England the headmistress told of conferences, special weekend courses, special leaves granted teachers to take advanced courses at the institutes of education of the universities. Some authorities owned old mansions set very pleasantly in the country where weekend or longer courses were in constant session. In addition, the Nuffield Foundation operated week-long, or weekend residential courses at teachers centers or residence halls of colleges all over the country demonstrating its approach to science and math by involving teachers in working with the materials as would the children.

The Plowden Report, which has much to say about in-service courses, itself stimulated much study before and after publication. Statements made to the Plowden Committee prior to formulation of its report were often the *result* of study groups. And then after publication many local authori-

ties set up and issued the report to working study groups.

Teachers colleges have used the report similarly. In addition, teachers centers sponsored by the New Schools Council and the Nuffield Project have proliferated since the Plowden Report, serving to bring together learning materials, publications, and reports of current research. The centers are often Laboratories, giving teachers a chance to become directly acquainted with learning materials, immersing them workshop-fashion in direct trials of new methods.

The Bristol Teachers' Center, as an example (there were 45 such centers set up through the Nuffield Foundation before I left England), staffed with personnel from the Nuffield Junior Science and Mathematics Project, was a center of several rooms fitted out as environmental workshops for exploration of almost *anything*. Teachers came in groups on certain afternoons for a total of 20 sessions and the plan was to reach all the teachers in Bristol primary schools. From what I saw and heard during several visits in Bristol this kind of exchange was significant in accounting for the spread of a "way," even without a syllabus or legal compulsion, and within an atmosphere of freedom.

Any new ideas gained by the head through attendance at institutes or courses were very easily spread to the teachers in her school. The spread followed from the very nature of the head's function in the school. She was the nexus, shaped and influenced by any factors, and influencing in turn through the sharing of her own special variation of practice. She shared and taught teachers by the example of her teaching all the time. And the open school — where teachers were influenced by contact with the other teachers and the head, and where they saw what was going on beyond their own classroom — fostered this sharing and this dissemination through example. The Plowden Report, describing the prevalence of such teaching, *strongly* recommended that heads *continue* to teach:

The fact that the head continues to teach raises the whole status of teaching.

Headmistress and the History

Certainly some of the credit for the

astonishing performance of the English heads and for the widespread acceptance of the *idea* behind the performance must accrue to the relationship of the heads and the inspectorate.

The work of the local inspectors and H.M.I.'s is, in effect, a significant force creating similarities within the freedom of practice. Their task *after* appointment of the head — which is made in the first place with obvious care and against high standards — is to make sure that communication remains open so that information and ideas can circulate. Sometimes they accomplish this by getting heads released for courses, for visits, or for the conferences described above. More often and more important, they have stimulated new ways of implementing "informal" ideas by *sharing* the good examples they've seen.

The professional background of the inspectorate is at least that of the heads and the teacher trainers. They may, prior to appointment, have been heads and then lecturers at colleges. Those I met impressed me with their deep commitment. Their influence seemed incomparable. They encouraged the work of the headmistress, supporting experiments in further clarification and implementation of the basic idea. They fostered the trying-out of interesting variations of the idea, carrying news of all this work in their reports and in conversations with heads. The experiments themselves served as models which inspectors then suggested to others for visits and observation.

In this setting, which allowed heads the freedom of action and developed an encouraging but non-interfering relationship, experiments had time to become complete and achieve depth. News carried in this unprescribed way was more acceptable as suggestion than formally prescribed change and was tried out with new variations and further experimentation. The isolated experiments developed within this freedom became models for the spread of a concept that molded all infant education. The Plowden Committee described this process:

Advances in education or practice are often surprisingly local and often owe much to local inspectors and advisors. They can be made widely known by H.M. Inspectors.

229

The inspectorate was described as an institutional safeguard within freedom. But the inspectorial function was weighted very greatly towards this suggesting, advising, persuading role. The freedom was real even when inspectors had doubts, as certainly was sometimes the case in the early pioneering days.

If the provision for good living was clear and the life of the school was rich, the standards and inspection did not mean a narrower, restricted, defined usage, but a great encouragement of ingenuity and variation towards maximal development.

The principle of inspection (derived in the 19th century from the need to supervise the expenditure of public money) has not, however, been discarded. Thus, the Plowden Report says:

> Assessment of a school is a necessary preamble to giving relevant advice ... Very occasionally children and the public still need to be protected.... Yet we welcome the growing stress on the role of adviser rather than inspector ... The more informal the schools become in their organization and relationships, the more informal ought to be the routines of inspection.

Headmistress and the Inspectors

Each infant head I had met in the United States and again in England had spoken of great freedom and had regarded, almost with horror, the idea of a "fixed," "prescribed" syllabus, the idea of all schools functioning in the same way. The headmistress felt free of control and free even to interpret aims in her own way. It was not only a *feeling* of freedom but an actual freedom. I quote confirmation from the Plowden Report, but the same confirmation could have been taken from the Hadow Report of 1933 or from Primary Schools, H.M.S.O., 1959:

> " ... 'The only uniformity of practice that the Board of Education desire to see in the teaching of public elementary schools is that each teacher shall think for himself, and work out for himself such methods of teaching as may use his powers to the best advantage and be best suited to the particular needs and conditions of the school. Uniformity in detail of practice (except in the mere routine of school management) is not desirable, even if it were obtainable. But freedom implies a corresponding responsibility in its use.' (1918 Code) This passage was reprinted in the preface to the 1937 edition of the Handbook. In 1944 the Code, which had become increasingly permissive, finally disappeared, and in the 1944 Education Act the only statutory requirement that remained was that children should be educated according to 'their age, ability, and aptitude.' "

Yet there *was* an entity called infant school that could certainly be described. Each infant school separately had impressed me and had been separately analyzed but I ended with *the* infant school. Diverse as infant schools might be I had found many, many similarities, really more similarities than differences, even within the many original and special approaches to different things. There was a concept of informal education that meant something. An infant school was of a certain small size, had an architectural shape meant to create some communal living, or its architectual shape was bent to do this. It had a headmistress whose role as communications facilitator, master teacher, and master agent creating the entity, was, in some sense, understood by all. It had an agreed-on range of environment, an agreed-on aim to use this environment freely. In every way — in timetable, in group structure (age or family), in mode of relationship of teacher and child, it tried to foster the use of this environment to create a whole, full, rich setting in which each child could live and learn in his own individually different way.

Underlying all the factors that produced this similarity within this very real freedom of the head was a *concept* of desired result, a *standard* of evaluation for what was attained. This concept and standard was evolving and developing, but was already at least somewhat formulated. It was part of the culture of the educational world in which the headmistress was formed.

It is an old history going back to Robert Owen, the founder of the Infant School, and to Margaret McMillan, to whose campaign is owed the first permissive legislation and state grants for nursery education.

In the conditions of the Industrial Revolution in England there was always need to have concern for the three-, four-, and five-year olds in school because they *were* in school. Very simply, the ages of the infant school population produced an inevitable interlocking of educational ideas from the nursery and infant school levels. About 1870 the statutory age of education was set at age five, but poor children of two to seven *were* in the infant schools and were allowed to be in if there was sufficient accommodation. The reports of 1888 urged that ample accommodation be encouraged for infants under five. This fact of under fives being in school in such large numbers between 1870 and 1900 — 45 per cent of the population of that age — necessitated the concern with what was really happening with them in the schools. The infant schools were no longer the Robert Owen schools — with children developing in a natural way in a garden. They were full, bursting, and responding with a "minding" kind of care.

Concern began to guide towards new developments through a series of remarkable government reports. In 1893 a circular from the H.M.I.'s had urged spontaneous activity and harmonious and complete development of the whole of the child's development. The Code of 1902 spoke in just these terms.

In 1905, a report of the Committee of Inspectors had the effect of stemming the direct public interest in the under-fives in infant school even while it defined the necessities of life for under-fives as later organized in the nursery school. It urged that under-fives be excluded from infant school because routine activity was mind-dulling and restriction of movement was prejudiced to health. The 1907 and 1908 reports recommended nursery school and thus paved the way for acceptance of the McMillan experiments in 1914.

It was clearly realized by the Hadow Report that just getting the children out of the infant school was not the whole answer, and that the nursery schools were also needed. It urged the Local Education Authorities, even though they were not *obliged* to furnish nursery provision, to consider their responsibility to provide this if these seemed to be needed.

But the economic difficulties of the time (post-World War I) meant that this was done with great difficulty. The nursery schools were set up first with the idea of serving about 40 children in each school and then with the idea that they could properly be increased to from 150 to 200 children. The Hadow Report thought that 60 to 80 would be an ideal number and nursery school was discussed as an "aid and supplement to the natural growth of a normal child," and as a place for "the spontaneous unfolding of the child's natural powers."

Susan Isaacs stood in the tradition of concern for betterment. Her work at the Malting House School, her famous books — *Intellectual Growth in Young Children, Social Development in Young Children,* and *The Children*

We Teach — all almost simultaneous with the Hadow Report — her work and writing for the British Nursery Association, all exerted enormous influence. While head (1933-43) of the first research Department of Child Development at the Institute of Education, University of London, a whole generation of advanced and mature students — future heads — studied with her the emotional, social, and intellectual mesh that *is* the development of the child. In this way, and even in this post-World War I period of economic stress, the private and free Froebelian kindergartens, the nursery schools, the schools for two-to-seven year olds, the nursery classes, and the influence of the examples and discussion summarized in committee and inspectorate reports, *had* resulted and were resulting in experimentation by more and more heads and in revision of the infant school.

Revision of many sorts — all necessarily adaptations to the physical circumstances of size of class — was motivated by observations of individual differences in children and by observations of the patterns of learning. Within this setting of freedom, heads could act, influenced by their observations, their concern, the reports, and of course by all the current intellectual ideas they could use to bolster their convictions.

Thus, even *before* Susan Isaacs gave a fuller rationale for their action, Montessori ideas had affected revision, had led heads to acceptance of the principle of individual pace and the responsibility for organizing the environment to allow this. Individual and group methods were applied at *least* to reading, writing and arithmetic even within still formal structures in which child purposes were still unrecognized. Project methods deriving from Dewey led to still wider revisions beyond the individualizing of skills, led to integration of subject areas, through activity. Observation had led to the recognition that learning was at a peak when the child pursued it to further his own purposes. Project method, unifying a whole group, was modified to accept the offering of many "starting points." The modification was in the direction of stress on the child's "choosing" and finally to stress on the child's "own question."

Wartime evacuation, necessitating teachers' care of the child in a very whole way, brought to the teachers' very close attention the tremendous significance of the home to the child and brought out a very great feeling of sympathy and closeness for both the impatience that a parent might have, and the burdens that a parent might have, and the tremendous and necessary support given by parents, within any or all of their impatience. Dorothy Gardner speaks of the contribution to teachers' understanding made by Anna Freud's and Dorothy Burlingham's work and books, *Young Children in Wartime* and *Infants Without Families*.

The wartime experience, and the books, broadened not only the teacher's sympathetic understanding for the parents' role and for home life and her willingness to include parents closely in the working of the school, and to incorporate into school life aspects of home experience, but also broadened her conception of her own role, of what school life could and should be and of the inextricable wholeness of the child's life and his responses. Almost every one of the heads I met had, when they were young teachers or even as youngsters prior to training, lived with children in evacuation conditions.

This development — in the *state* schools — towards what I've described as the infant school entity, can be traced in a *continuous* line. This is true in spite of slow and uneven progress. Certainly, some teachers provided "the environment," with little conception of a *changed* role, or *any* role for the teacher, without the infusing of meaning and life that can only come from understanding. Nevertheless, it seems to have been rather clear in the work of the pioneers that the role of the teacher was not *just* providing but was:

" . . . providing for, following up and stimulating, the interests and purposes of young children . . . . "

The teacher had to have:

" . . . the art of organizing and planning an environment suited to children and a deep understanding of the needs of the children as individuals."

The history reveals *adaptation, development,* not breaks.

That the unity of concept underlying wide spread of an entity such as I've described is not a sudden revolution of 1944 and since, but rather an affirmation in 1944 of an idea already widely held, is confirmed, again, by Dorothy Gardner:

"The progressive movement in Infant Schools was well on its way in London, for example, in 1930 when I first went into many schools through becoming an Infant Education lecturer. Indeed when I was at college — 1918-1921 — pioneer schools using play under Froebel influence were in existence. Froebel-trained lecturers spread the gospel to the State Schools. People like J. P. Slight, local Inspector for Leeds, for example, exercised influence and when I went there in 1936 progressive Infant Schools were so many that I could put all my 64 first year students into one for a first school practice. The reason Susan Isaacs' *Intellectual Growth* (1931) had so much influence was that it gave the 'Why's' to the progressive movement and led others to feel confidence in joining the pioneers who were well at work before this book appeared and so ready to see its tremendous significance for their work. The War (1939) caused a temporary setback, owing to children and teachers being moved about so much and even after the war it was some years before schools were rebuilt and populations stable and rehoused. . . . Progress was not uniform all over the country."

Headmistress and the Reports

The reports have a very special place in what I have called the "mechanism of dissemination." Their unique role goes far beyond legislative acts or administrative rulings. They have been the texts, not to be separated from the major educational literature, for study of educational practice, studied not as prescription but as *suggested illustration*. They were the pivotal points of the evolving unity of concept. They were studied to buttress experimental action at the time of their issuance and are still studied in the teachers colleges. All succeeding literature from the Ministry (now Department of Education and Science) reflected this evolving unity of concept and in turn was the instrument of further unity.

A characteristic of this non-prescriptive literature was its derivation *from* the schools and the resulting interaction. Thus, case studies of experiments in particular schools were published as such, without trying to generalize or pronounce absolutes. The case was allowed to stand on its own and the generalizing and application was made independently and variously. New reports arose from these independent and various applications.

Three months of observation in schools preceded *any* reading on my part in English education literature. I had found, on observation, conditions I had not anticipated. I thought I had discovered them, that my outside stance had noticed things taken for granted by the English. In some small sense this was, perhaps, in part so, in the emphasis and significance

I gave to certain aspects within the whole. But the things I'd noticed were *all* in the Hadow Report, in *Primary Education* (H.M.S.O., 1959), and in other books. An overwhelming and respectful impression of the very specific and concrete knowledge of the schools in these reports was borne in on me. The reports summarized the current situations, described the best of what they had seen.

The Hadow Report, as well as reporting the best, influenced the spread into other schools of the best of such reporting. It was a support for acceptance of variation of level; it suggested that the limitations imposed by buildings could be broken down. Speaking for individual work, it pointed out that classroom organization was no longer appropriate.

"The primary school should not, therefore, be regarded merely as a preparatory department for the subsequent stage, and the courses should be planned and conditioned, not mainly by the supposed requirements of the secondary stage, nor by the exigencies of an examination at the age of eleven, but by the needs of the child at that particular phase in his physical and mental development."

Primary Education: Suggestions for the consideration of teachers and others concerned with the work of Primary Schools (H.M.S.O., 1959) is practically a handbook of suggestions, of course again basing itself on a description of the nature and needs of children as central to educational practice. The things I noted are in this handbook but not with the emphasis I gave them. It is an earlier version of practice. It reports:

"In many schools, the hall, the corridors and other spaces outside the classroom are used almost as fully as the rooms or playground and garden, and almost everywhere in the building children may be seen hard at work at their different employments."

It suggests that materials should be available throughout the day. It reports family grouping in some schools. The head as teacher and leader is discussed in just the way I had understood from my observation. Such handbooks had been published from 1905 on and represented a distillation of H.M.I.'s experience in the schools, shared in this way.

The Ministry published illustrative examples, such as *Story of a School,* as part of this way of supporting ideas that came from schools, not expecting heads to copy it in detail but rather to be stimulated to specific concrete solutions and thinking. *Science in the Primary Schools, Mathematics in Primary Schools, Slow Learners at School* (all H.M.S.O.) all describe new ideas and approaches from the schools, a distillation from the many, many good ways observed. All start with a base in child development, in the child's ways of learning. The H.M.S.O. publication, *Mathematics in Primary Schools,* summarizing new approaches for encouraging mathematical thinking in schools, is a type of publication that probably will appear more and more, to be sponsored possibly by the new Schools Council which is taking over the research of the Nuffield projects. The Plowden Report notes the need for such curriculum bulletins.

The Nuffield Junior Science Project, prior to final formulation, published a trial edition of *Case Histories,* which continued the tradition of publication of case histories, *specific* examples, without generalizing. And in the context of everything I've said about English education, such case histories seem most apt. Just as the child is allowed to ask his own questions, so the adult, presented with the case history, can ask *his* own questions, and can select what is pertinent.

Running through all reports as a thread, finally, are the Parliamentary Committee reports. These collect current practice as base for conclusions, spreading descriptions of the best of these. English recommendations on education have not changed quickly with each political pressure or election, or educational fad, for that matter. Thirty years or more (the Hadow Report of 1933 is the report on primary education directly prior to the new Plowden Report) may come between reports of a Parliamentary Committee. But a Parliamentary Committee, when it has reported, has really drawn on the experience of the whole current scene, from schools, from training colleges, from the University Institutes of Education, from H.M.I.'s, from local education bodies, from doctors, from psychologists, from teachers, from heads, from parents.

An examination of the list of those giving testimony to the Plowden Committee shows this widespread involvement and responsible engagement from all levels of those concerned with schools. The report embodied the most serious thought and aims of each period and served as a guide for their spread. The descriptions of best practice in the report influence, guide, and stimulate change for a long time.

It was not only official reports that collected experiences. Studies sponsored by the institutes also gathered and synthesized and evaluated the experience of the schools and described the ideas on which this experience was based.

In addition, perhaps primary, as distiller of good practice, as clear synthesizer of the common analysis on child development, as needed research on *results* of good practice, were Dorothy Gardner's books. These were both theoretical and practical, a sharing of all her experience and of the work and experience of the many heads she knew — as inspector, as lecturer, as head of the Child Development Department, Institute of Education, University of London. Her research on results bulwarked the defense of experimentation and gave needed encouragement to further experiment.

The process was, all told, a two-way one. Experience collected from schools and heads was given back by the reports to the heads. Reported experiences were tried, were extended, new variations tested. It becomes no wonder that the similarities are so great, even without prescription. Thus, the Plowden Report:

"A deliberate change in the curriculum has been brought about not by the issue of programmes by states or universities as is often done in the U.S.A., but by pioneer work by teachers, clarified and focused by advisory services to teachers, and diffused on a national scale by in-service training in which self-help has played a major and essential part."

"The willingness of teachers to experiment, to innovate and to change has been one of the mainsprings of progress in the primary schools."

Sept. 4,

Ahead of you stretch 36 weeks, 180 days of teaching. Of triumphs and failures, of highs and lows, of frustrations and opportunities.

How to maximize the triumphs and take advantage of the opportunities?

One of the routes to the golden land is simply change—creative, intelligent change. But it takes a lot of courage, energy and persistence to alter the habits and customs of decades. The distance from a conventional, lock-step classroom to a more child-centered classroom may therefore seem to many of us measurable only in light years.

It isn't really that far, and more important, there's no need to cover the whole distance in one desperate leap. There are numerous and comfortable stations along the way, as Kim Marshall discovered in his Boston classroom.

The Learning Station Way

BY KIM MARSHALL

After an almost totally disastrous first year at the King School in Boston, I discovered learning stations in summer school and decided to try them in my sixth grade class in the fall of 1970. So I took a deep breath, pushed the desks into groups, each one for a different subject, and wrote worksheets for each station—math, English, social studies, spelling, creative writing, general and reading. On the first day, the kids came in and found seven worksheets tucked into "pockets" taped to the side of a desk at each station. That arrangement led them to circulate around the room musical-chairs fashion, stopping at each station to do the worksheets

The system, such as it was, had an immediate and dramatic effect on my teaching. I found myself spending most of my time actually teaching and talking to kids individually or in small groups, and the struggle for control was superseded by a beehive of academic activities, conversations and flirtations, all going on at the same time, all legal. Yet the place didn't fall apart; and in retrospect, I think the most important thing holding it together was that I insisted that each student hand in seven finished worksheets by the end of the day. At first it seemed like a lot of work to some of the kids, but they soon realized that there would never be more than seven sheets, that the material was tailored to their interests and abilities, and was quite often fun to do. So they cheerfully accepted hard work in return for freedom, and I had very little trouble convincing them to get

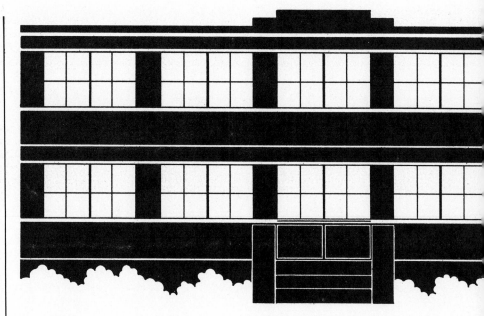

through their stations.

So things went well for a few weeks. Kids circulated happily from one station to another, and there was a kind of treasure-hunt quality to moving around the room. The worksheets at each station were always fresh and often contained incidents and names from the class or stories of recent events in the news (Arab hijackings and Angela Davis were big that September). Very quickly I began to feel like a good teacher and spent almost no time bellowing to the whole class or dealing with "discipline" problems.

I found it necessary to address the class as a group less and less; I did so only if there was something I wanted to discuss or go over, or if

things got too noisy or hectic. Even though there were seven different pieces of work being done simultaneously in the room, most of it was self-explanatory to most of the kids, and the remaining problems I could solve if I moved fast and succeeded in juggling jealous personalities. In the early weeks, the work time filled almost the entire day and kept the place surprisingly stable, to the point where there could be a small riot out in the corridor and the kids in my room wouldn't even notice it.

What kind of class was this I was running? There was a lot of freedom and movement and a constant hum of noise, which I suppressed only if it got too loud; there was a lot of work being done and a lot of nonacademic activities and conversations as well; and some of the work at the social studies and general and reading stations was quite unconventional. But while many people in the school regarded this kind of classroom as nothing less than revolutionary and subversive, it was hardly an open classroom.

The only real choice the kids were making was the *order* in which they did the seven worksheets. They still had to finish all the papers or I would keep them after school. The kids couldn't do other work or projects instead of a worksheet because they never asked and I never suggested any. They couldn't leave the room without a pass. They couldn't play cards or other games. There were no books or magazines in the room. And the worksheets in the four primary subjects were quite narrowly focused, the essential objective being to pre-

poisoned apple of conventional education. Yet in September of 1970, nobody could have convinced me that I hadn't made a real breakthrough in classroom techniques and successfully neutralized the pressures on the classroom from uptight parents, administrators, colleagues and kids who had a deeply ingrained notion of the way the class was "spozed to be."

I was wildly excited because I felt I had a system that satisfied the most conservative pressures (stiff work requirements, conventional curriculum, progress charts), yet gave the kids freedom to interact naturally, make some choices, do creative writing and topical reading and get truly individualized attention from me. I felt the system also liberated my own teaching talents by allowing me to write my own curriculum and teach kids in manageable groups or all alone. And last, it seemed to have ended the constant battle for order

tion you had left to visit and you couldn't sit with him? What if you were tired and just didn't feel like moving around? Moreover, why go all the way to the math station when all that was there was a jive worksheet that could be done at the North Pole as well as the math station? So the kids quickly modified my system by making a quick trip around the room to collect the seven papers, then staying put at one station with their friends.

At first I saw this as a grave threat and fought it. But one night I asked myself, why not? What intrinsic value was there in having them move around the room, unless I was going to put a great many props at the different stations—math games and puzzles at the math station, maps and globes and artifacts at the social studies station, dictionaries and word games at the spelling station—and wrote the worksheets so that they led

pare them for very conventional tests on Friday. Their grades on these tests went onto progress charts on the wall—full boxes for A's, half boxes for B's and C's, a diagonal line for a failing grade. (I did allow students to retake the tests and change their standing on the charts.) In each of the 36 weeks of the year, we covered a new skill in math and English, a new topic in social studies and a new list of 20 spelling words, most of which I gleaned from "official" sixth grade curricula.

A pretty uptight regime, no? Not a classroom that John Holt would think was groovy, nor one that would escape the charge of radical educators that it was mere sugar-coating on the

in the classroom by decentralizing activity and setting up the place so that it virtually ran itself. Learning stations also opened the door to one of the most delightful sets of personal relationships I have ever had, thus creating an atmosphere in which both the kids and I grew enormously.

I have used the learning-station system for three years now, but it hasn't stayed the same for more than a month at a time.

The first change came when the kids decided they didn't want to keep moving around the room to all those seven stations. What if you felt like doing creative writing and all the seats at that station were full? What if your friend was just finishing the one sta-

the kids to use these materials?

I didn't feel able to write that kind of worksheet and couldn't afford all that stuff, so the value of moving around the room was simply social, giving kids a chance to meet each other and make friends. Now that friendships had more or less formed for the rest of the year, I allowed the children to sit in groups all day, and began putting the worksheet pockets on the walls. It turned out not to be the end of the system—just an admission that it wasn't a learning-station system per se. (I admit that it's a misnomer, but I have continued to use it for sentimental reasons.)

The next crisis came when a lot of the kids got too fast and began fin-

Art by Michel Dattel & Greg Mock

ishing all the worksheets by lunch. Later, some of them were finishing by morning recess. This presented me with the problem of kids rattling around an otherwise empty room all afternoon with an "I've-done-my-work-so-why-should-I-do-anything?" attitude. It also tested my belief in the system I was using. I knew that seven worksheets were more than an honest day's work for sixth graders and certainly more than many conventional classes in the same school were plodding through in lock step in two days. So why did I have to put up with these noisy, empty afternoons? What was I doing wrong?

The problem was that I wasn't playing the game of stretching work throughout the day and chewing up spare time with little five- or ten-minute breaks, meaningless busywork and housekeeping activities. I wasn't controlling the pace at which the kids were doing their work, and I was giving them enough help both in

cipline problems and loud, obnoxious behavior in the second half of each day. My own sense of humor and ability to see crazy situations as funny tended to evaporate at around 1 p.m., and that only fed the flames.

My first counterstrategy was to try stalling at the start of the day, instigating discussions and going over papers from the day before and thus keeping from putting out the station worksheets until around 10 o'clock. The kids promptly complained that I was holding them back and spoiling their free time and retaliated by doing the work even faster or finding where I had hidden the worksheets and doing them secretly while I stalled. I tried making the worksheets longer and meatier, and I started typing them, which allowed me to squeeze more time-consuming material onto each page. This was fine but caused the kids to heave even noisier sighs of relief when they finished plowing through the work.

Slowly, as my pay increased and I got my personal spending under control, I bought some old typewriters, games, more and more paperback books and a rug for one corner. And the loose time began to take care of itself.

During the 1972–73 school year, I got together in a two-room team-teaching arrangement with a guy who had the energy and imagination to bring in decent art projects and movies on a regular basis. We also instituted a quiet reading time in the last 50 minutes of every day when kids would have to choose a book or magazine and read it in tomblike silence. This was a great success, providing welcome relief from a rising noise level and for frayed nerves in the last part of the afternoon. Moreover, it proved an excellent strategy for getting kids immersed in books. Our original hope was that just by having groovy books around we would get kids to read, but that proved somewhat naive. Nor had

person and in the content of the worksheets to enable them to zip through the day's labors quickly. The system also encouraged the kids to work very hard for two or three hours because there was a finite amount of work to do and a definite reward at the end. The freedom at the end of the work struck most kids as a fine deal, so they threw themselves into the work with real gusto, certain that I wasn't going to trick them by heaping more work on them as soon as they finished.

So I convinced myself that I wasn't doing anything wrong, that my class should simply be allowed to go home two hours before the rest of the school. When this proved impractical, I had to face increasingly ugly dis-

Not only did I lack a plan for the latter part of the day, but both the kids and I lacked the will to make proper use of that time because we thought we had already done a fine day's work. I prayed for a schedule that sent them out to their art, science, music, gym and shop classes in the last two periods of the day knowing full well as I did so that every other teacher in the school was praying for the same thing.

Eventually a number of obvious solutions emerged. I played songs on a tape recorder and had the kids read along with the lyrics. We played charades and other guessing games. We read plays. We occasionally had discussions, despite the fact I am the world's worst leader of discussions.

forcing students to do book reports accomplished anything, because the reports were easily faked by those who didn't want to read. The quiet reading time thus became the solution for two problems.

For my own part, I have found writing the worksheets one of the most stimulating parts of the whole system. At first it was time-consuming, but after a couple of months I developed a knack and cut the writing time for the seven worksheets down to about an hour and a half. Last year, I shared the writing with my colleague, Paul Casilli. That cut the work load even more and increased the input of different ideas because we constantly discussed the worksheets and compared notes on how they went over with our kids.

I still haven't reached what I think may be the ideal system—five or six teachers sitting down after school during free periods and tossing around ideas, then delegating the job of writing the sheets to various members of the group and sharing the output among the classes.

Paul Casilli and I learned that one problem with a sequential, unit-a-week approach to math, English and social studies is that kids forget what they learned a few weeks ago and usually don't get a chance to review it. So we got rid of the creative-writing station, incorporating it in the general station two days a week, and substituted a review station, which every day relentlessly harped on old skills. This was a real success in helping

kids retain basic skills. The review station also provided a way of teaching kids things they missed the first time around.

Another problem I ran into with my learning-station system back in 1970 was that there was an awful lot of correcting to do; with 25 kids, I had around 175 papers to do four days

a week. At first I plowed through all these to the tune of about one and a half hours a day, the theory being that this kept me in touch with how the worksheets were being received. But as I got better at writing the worksheets and assessing the kids' abilities, I began to wonder whether that one and a half hours was really worth it—

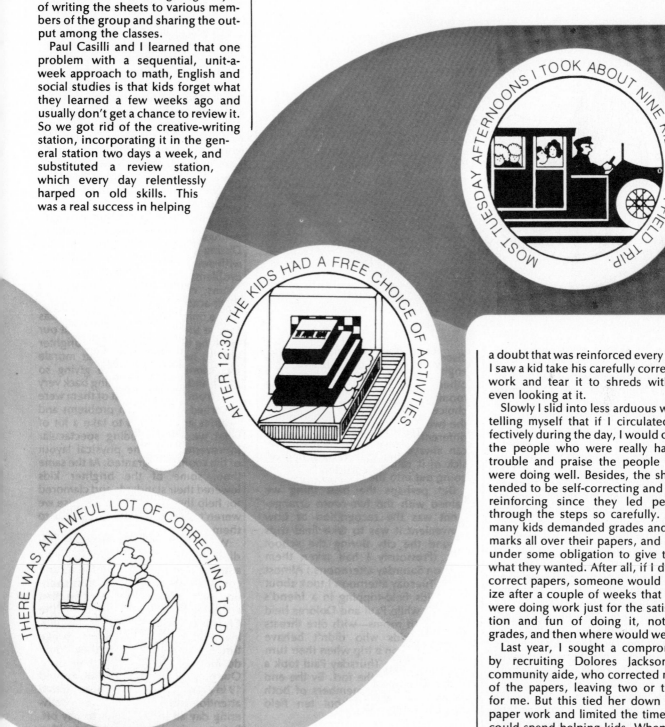

THERE WAS AN AWFUL LOT OF CORRECTING TO DO.

AFTER 12:30 THE KIDS HAD A FREE CHOICE OF ACTIVITIES.

MOST TUESDAY AFTERNOONS I TOOK ABOUT NINE KIDS ON A FIELD TRIP.

a doubt that was reinforced every time I saw a kid take his carefully corrected work and tear it to shreds without even looking at it.

Slowly I slid into less arduous ways, telling myself that if I circulated effectively during the day, I would catch the people who were really having trouble and praise the people who were doing well. Besides, the sheets tended to be self-correcting and self-reinforcing since they led people through the steps so carefully. Still, many kids demanded grades and red marks all over their papers, and I felt under some obligation to give them what they wanted. After all, if I didn't correct papers, someone would realize after a couple of weeks that they were doing work just for the satisfaction and fun of doing it, not for grades, and then where would we be?

Last year, I sought a compromise by recruiting Dolores Jackson, a community aide, who corrected most of the papers, leaving two or three for me. But this tied her down with paper work and limited the time she could spend helping kids. When she had to leave us briefly for a family emergency, we developed what seems the best method yet of dealing with all that correcting. During the quiet reading time, Paul and I both sat down and corrected like mad. We found that in 45 minutes we could get through most of the work, leaving only about 15 to 20 minutes of correcting for after school. Then the next morning we tried to go over the previous day's papers with each student.

The summer before we began our team-teaching project, Paul and I

spent a lot of time planning how we would use our adjoining rooms to best effect. We came up with what seemed to be a logical scheme. One room would be the "quiet room," with the seven learning-station worksheets and all the books; the other would be the "open room," with science experiments, games, animals, art projects and several typewriters. The kids would split the day between the two, my class having the quiet room for three hours and then trading places with Paul's class in the open room.

We abandoned this plan within a week, when Dolores pointed out that (1) three hours wasn't enough time for both finishing the worksheets and reading, and that (2) the kids who were assigned to the quiet room in the afternoon were in no mood to work at that point in the day—the first three hours of the day were the prime time for academic work. So we put seven pockets for station worksheets in both rooms and had the kids stay in their "home" room until about 12:30 doing the worksheets. Then we opened the door and allowed a free flow between the rooms and a free choice between books, games, typewriters and other attractions. Both rooms ended up having the same noise level at this stage, but we got our quiet in the

reading time at the end of the day.

The biggest advantage of the two-room format is the escape from isolation within one classroom that we had both felt in previous years; it is a real delight to be able to chat with another adult during the day. Other benefits include exposure to a greater number and variety of kids, the happy discovery that we can survive on one engine (when one of us is sick, the other stuffs all the kids into one room), and the greater range of choices provided for the kids, since the two rooms have developed quite different personalities. Thus the kids can always leave one when they're sick of it rather than raising hell or going out into the corridors.

But perhaps the best thing we gained with the two-room arrangement was the recognition of how convenient it was to take field trips around the city during the school day. (Previously I had taken them only on Saturday afternoons.) Almost every Tuesday afternoon I took about nine kids field-tripping in a friend's minibus while Paul and Dolores held down both rooms—with dire threats that the kids who didn't behave wouldn't go on a trip when their turn came. Then on Thursday Paul took a trip while I held the fort. By the end of the year, most members of both classes had taken about ten field trips around the area.

During my first two years with learning stations, my classes were in the middle of the tracking spectrum, 6-G and 6-D (the range is from 6-A to 6-K). The 6-G class had only two or

three kids with severe reading problems, and even they could read at about third grade level and do the worksheets with a certain amount of help from other kids and me during the day. The 6-D class was an academic section—part of the elite; the kids could read quite well. Consequently, the station worksheets I wrote for 6-D were considerably more meaty and difficult than those of the previous year.

Last year, Paul and I requested and were given 6-K and 6-J, the rock bottom of the sixth grade, the dumping ground for its academic and emotional problems. This both changed the way the learning-station system worked and hardened our attitudes toward the tracking system. The two classes had a number of repeaters, some of whom, purely for disciplinary reasons, were in the sixth grade for the third time. The average reading level in November was around third grade, with fully half the two classes reading below that level and seven or eight youngsters being virtual nonreaders. During the year, several more kids with severe emotional and academic problems were thrown into the rooms, complicating an already difficult academic situation.

The only solution we could see was to give the nonreaders almost all our teaching time and encourage brighter kids to help them, too. Our morale was often low; we were giving so much and seemingly getting back very little from the kids. Most of them were absorbed in their own problems and rivalries and seemed to take a lot of what we did, including spectacular inprovements in the physical layout of the rooms, for granted. At the same time, some of the brighter kids lowered their standards and clamored for help they didn't need because we weren't paying enough attention to them.

What really got us through this difficult period was the fact that Paul and I shared the same problems and could talk about them and thus shore up each other's morale. The first encouraging signs came after the Christmas break. Several of the original group of nonreaders broke through enough so that they could do most of the work on their own. Our numbers remained small, around 19 in each class, and the concentrated attention and help we had been delivering day after day began to pay off. Before spring had arrived, and with a lot of help from some of the brighter kids, we were able to get everyone through all the work. And a few of the "problem" kids began to warm up to us and give us the much-needed feeling that we were good people and good teachers.

Out of the experience came a deepening anger over the tracking systems that create the 6-K's and 6-J's of the world, an anger made deeper by the really brilliant kids we saw buried in the self-hate of these classes. We explained to the kids during the year why we refused to refer to the class by these labels. Then they would go to other classrooms in the school and be called just that by insensitive teachers. Outraged by this situation, I waxed demagogic one day: "Are we the dumb class?" I asked. "No," came back weakly, uncertainly. "Are we the dumb class?" I asked again. "No," a little stronger. "Are we the dumb class?" I asked once again. "*No!*" shaking the walls. This attitude and the hard, grade-level work and constant attention and praise we gave them increased their self-respect enormously. We got real rewards out of watching several cowering, uncertain kids blossom during the early months. But clearly our efforts were small and didn't attack the beast itself—the tracking system.

This year, I hope to have a genuinely heterogeneous class. Ideally, it will have only two or three nonreaders, a lot of kids in the middle, and three or four really bright ones. In a class like this, I could return to the more active and mobile role I had my first two years, giving attention more equally around the room; kids might be able to get more help from each other; and the nonreaders would be swept along by the momentum of the class rather than pulling their more literate peers down. My own ideal is to be able to spend at least 15 minutes each day alone with pairs of kids, listening to them read and talking to them, and thus giving everyone in the class a modicum of close personal attention and help on specific problems.

A really heterogeneous class in which most kids are self-sufficient would also allow me to handle more children. I concluded after dealing with last year's small class that open classrooms don't generate enough interaction and bustle with fewer than 20 kids. A perfect number would be 24 or 25, assuming that among them there were not more than three nonreaders.

This leads to a question that I have been asked frequently by other teachers: How can you teach kids of widely varying abilities with only one level of worksheets? How can you cater to individual differences when everyone in the class is doing the same seven worksheets? What about enrichment activities for the brighter kids, remediation for the slow kids?

My answer is that a choice can be made between having a multilevel curriculum that caters to every different ability level and allows the teacher to give similar amounts of time to each student, and a single-level curriculum in which the teacher gives widely different amounts and kinds of attention to students according to their individual needs. The crucial element in either approach is being able to recognize exactly where the kid is and taking him from there to where he can go. So far I haven't found any published books or materials that can communicate with my kids at several different levels. So my system has been to write a common set of materials geared to the general tone and interests of the class, then zero in on the individual differences in my conferences with kids. I have found that hard work and a willingness to devote large amounts of time to a few kids will make a single-level curriculum work, even with an ability range from nonreaders to grade-level students.

There are other reasons this is so. First, kids can derive different academic benefits from the same worksheet. An advanced student who does an entire reading worksheet by himself and gives sophisticated, original answers to the open-ended questions gets more out of it than a student who must read it with the teacher and then copy answers from the text. A spelling worksheet that asks kids to use words in sentences is a flexible tool because each kid will produce sentences at his or her own level of skill and originality. The same is true of creative writing and many of the social studies sheets. It is only the cut-and-dried worksheets that may be too easy for the bright students. But even then, many bright kids enjoy doing work at different levels and may gain additional confidence from exercises below their top potential.

Second, the same well-written worksheet serves different levels of competence if the teacher is sensitive and selective in the amounts of help he gives around the room. A reading worksheet written for a sixth grade level becomes manageable and instructive for a kid reading at the third grade level if the teacher reads along with the student, explaining hard words and encouraging him. Conversely, many kids on the lower rungs of the tracking system are very sensitive about doing separate, special work and insist on trying to do what the rest of the class is doing, even if it is too hard for them.

Third, it is the brighter students who finish early and have more time to use the books, games and typewriters in the room, all of which are in themselves an enrichment program. I think these kids get a good feeling from knowing that they have finished the day's work by lunch and can then structure their own program and not be harassed by a teacher anxiously trying to keep them out of trouble with busywork. Sure, they waste some time, but the activities they ultimately get involved in are freely chosen and therefore more meaningful to them.

Fourth, the brighter kids sometimes help explain worksheets to friends who are having trouble, and in teaching others they gain a deeper understanding of the material themselves. Besides, it is good for advanced kids to understand through experience the differences between other kids and themselves, and perhaps in the process see areas in which they are not the bees' knees.

So let's sum it up: The main advantage of the learning-station system is that it enables a class to plow through a good deal of academic work, trains kids in basic skills and reading, and defines a very concentrated, self-disciplined work period and a very free activity and reading period. The system has the additional advantage of presenting a regular, predictable and finite amount of work in a do-able and familiar format, and of giving equal weight to relevance and fun and basic skills.

The main disadvantage is the sometimes lethargic and uninvolved feeling kids have after they have finished the worksheets, which might prevent some of the creative departures found in a less structured class from occurring. There is also an insufficient allowance for individual differences, which puts the burden of individualizing the program on the shoulders of the teacher. I am happy to assume that burden; perhaps others aren't.

But then the stations system is not one you have to take or leave—rather it is my own personal compromise between freedom and structure. There must be lots of changes and improvements that others would want to make for themselves. The thing is to begin. ∎

Kim Marshall is a teacher at the Martin Luther King, Jr., Middle School in Boston and author of Law and Order in Grade 6–E—A Story of Chaos and Innovation in a Ghetto School *(Little, Brown), which goes into more detail on setting up a learning-station classroom and which was reviewed in* Learning's *December, 1972 issue.*

X. THE FAMILY

We do not agree with the most extreme advocates of early childhood education who argue that "it is all over by age three," but their basic argument, and the research that illuminates it, is compelling when it is qualified with vital exceptions. In his article in this section, Martin Cohen quotes Burton L. White as stating,

We believe that the critical period in child development begins at about the age of seven or eight months. By the age of three, children should have acquired the ability to understand most of the language they will use in ordinary conversation throughout their lives. They also have adapted their social styles, including the way they will relate to other children and to adults, such as future teachers. By age three, the basic shaping of the child is usually accomplished.

"Basic shaping" is a safe generalization because it does not place sharp limits around what has been left unshaped. Even Burton White agrees that, for everyone, it is worth going on beyond age three just to see what non-basics develop in later chapters of one's life story. Nevertheless, this generalization — supported by solid empirical evidence — carries the corollary that the most influential teaching in the life of a human is the teaching of parents or their surrogates.

The articles in this section by Robert Strom and Marion J. Rice take the primacy of parent teaching for granted. They move forward boldly to experiment with the question of how parents can be taught to be effective early childhood educators. Neither writer offers much evidence of the effects of their teaching strategies and stimulus materials, but both lead from the proposition that speaking and listening are the best educative tools available to the effective parent *qua* educator.

So, too, the prescriptions developed by the Harvard Study Group and reported by Martin Cohen are, in five out of nine instances, prescriptions for verbal communication that is abundant and precise. Bruce Peck and Thomas Stackhouse extend this emphasis upward in age to include older children whose reading problems, they think, are the result of faulty communications within the family.

With very few exceptions, educational psychologists concentrated their attention until the 1960's on the nature of teaching and learning among school-age children and youth. Similarly, with few exceptions, public schoolmen and women ignored infant and early preschool education in America, although they always stressed the importance of family influences upon student learning and conduct. Neither group — the researchers or the teachers — did very much about early learning or parent education. As a result, mothers and fathers were defined as important for *preparing* the child for success in school and as sources of support or blame for school success or failure. The influence of infant learning and parental shaping is at least as old as Freudian theory and the practice of psychoanalysis, of course, but its contemporary and revolutionary impact upon public education and educational psychology alike was delayed for roughly fifty years.

The new and restated knowledge about the primacy of early family influence has led educational psychologists and teachers to design new modes of collaboration between school and home. As Barbara Kaban and Bernice Shapiro note in their article in this section, "Mothering is a vastly underrated occupation." If schools of the future are to become more effective, they will include programs that restore and intensify the triangle of connections between the student, teacher, and the student's family. Much more that the conventional Parent Teacher Association or its equivalent will be required. Already, progressive public school districts are reaching out with parent education programs, just as communities are stretching to increase parent participation in designing the programs of schools.

Although our selections all stress infant and preschool family teaching and learning, educational psychology has also shown through empirical research that family socialization *persists* into adolescence as a primary influence over the learning of most youth. When the implications of this social fact are adequately absorbed into the profession of education, the structure and functioning of schools will be transformed.

Play and Family Development

by Robert Strom

She broke the bread into two fragments and gave them to the children who ate with avidity. "She has kept none for herself," grumbled the sargeant. "Because she is not hungry," said a soldier. "Because she is a mother," said the sargeant.

—Victor Hugo, *Les Miserables*

Each of us could describe memories of maternal sharing. That mothers give much of themselves to children is well known. Not so well known is the fact that the impression a mother has of herself can influence her child's achievement. As we enlarge the national effort to help mothers become more effective teachers at home, it seems appropriate to learn how mothers perceive the role of educator. What do mothers think of themselves as preschool teachers? How ready are they to change their concepts of themselves? Planning for parent education requires answers to these questions. The concerns deserve attention by individuals who would understand the place of play in family development.

Many studies have concluded that achievement and self-concept are closely related. Researchers generally agree that the way an individual views himself accounts to a large extent for his success. Indeed, for some children, aspiration and the drive to succeed are better predictors of achievement than scholastic measures (1). The child's first lessons on identity are learned at home and are influenced primarily by the mother's expectations (2). In these early lessons lie the beginnings of the child's opinion of himself. If boys and girls are to have a favorable self-concept, mothers will have to hold a favorable estimate of themselves. The recent Home Start movement broadens our educational task. We have to elevate the self-regard of school children, and we have to include the equally important goal of building mothers' confidence in their role of preschool teacher (3).

It is disappointing, but hardly a surprise, that many of today's mothers feel incompetent as teachers. After all, for years parents have been led to believe that they lack the ability to help children learn (4). The consequence of this perception is more devastating than one might suppose. Bear in mind the fact that the preschooler is especially reliant on his mother's impression of herself in the role of teacher. Her impression of herself in that role determines his self-estimate as a learner. The connection becomes clear when we recognize that the child's paramount motive is to enjoy his mother's affection. Because the loss of her approval is the child's greatest fear, a mother can inadvertently encourage or destroy healthy qualities like curiosity, experimentation, and imagination. It is also true that the mother who sees herself unfavorably is unable to consistently convey positive impressions to a child about himself.

Can a mother's concept of herself be changed? If so, under what conditions? Psychologists have written a great deal about the development of child personality and its susceptibility to influence. Mothers have been portrayed as representing certain child-rearing styles usually described more as fixed than flexible. To my mind, these interpretations of the parent's and the child's readiness for change are unwise. Perhaps if a mother had access to information about the differences between her view of herself and her child's view of her, she would be willing to make positive changes. The consequence would be an improvement in the child's model. Because the preschool child is in a stage of identification, it is imperative that we help the model he emulates if we expect him to adopt constructive behavior.

Until recently the relation between parent development and child development was slighted. Even Project Head Start was established in 1965 on the premise that some children need to be rescued from family influence. Since 1965 many studies have shown that parents are the greatest single influence on a child's self-concept and language development (5, 6). These research findings have brought about a shift in the federal position from the compensatory Head Start approach to the Home Start approach, which was introduced in 1971. The goal has changed from trying to overcome parents' influence to enlisting family support. This admission that parents are capable of teaching is overdue and has generated the current demand for large-scale parent-education programs (7, 8).

We know that self-concept develops through parent-child interaction, but the commercially available instruments do not lend themselves to ascertaining either the parent's assessment of herself in the role of teacher or the child's estimate of himself as a learner. Instead, most of the indices deal with phenomenological self-regard; few indicate clearly just what universe of self-concept the items represent; none assesses the interrelatedness of the parent and the child. Administration of self-concept measures is also a problem. The most popular instruments to measure self-concept are Q sort, semantic differential, and questionnaire. While all three types can be used with adults, the semantic differential and the Q sort present difficulties in comprehension and ranking for preschoolers. The best approach for young children seems to be an individually administered questionnaire that calls for the child to point his finger, or color, or draw.

Any rationale for parent education should regard mothers as individuals, not as a homogeneous group. Therefore, we sought to devise an inventory that could provide information about the kinds of help each mother needs to improve her influence on her child. It is our belief that individualized parent education will result in mother teachers who are less disposed to compare their children with peers than to educate them as individuals.

The instrument that we developed is based on a systematic review of measurement in early childhood education. The Parent As A Teacher Inventory includes fifty items, equally divided into five subsets, in which mothers express their feelings on a Likert-type scale. The items are designed to measure:

Mother's understanding of play as a source of learning

Mother's self-confidence as a teacher

Mother's need for child control

Mother's trend of frustration in child-rearing

Mother's support of the child's creative behavior

Because of the relationship between self-impressions of parent and child, the Child As A Learner Inventory was devised to parallel the Parent As A Teacher Inventory. In the two inventories the order of items and the content are identical. However, the Child As A Learner Inventory is designed to reveal the self-image that results from a child's percept of his mother's behavior.

By comparing subsets of the mother-child responses, we can help the parent understand her child-rearing strengths. Indeed, we can learn what practices she may safely continue and what behaviors she needs to modify. When a child perceives his mother differently than she intends, her awareness of the discrepancy can provide the motivation and the direction for change. The analysis is productive when mothers are helped to achieve the altered behavior they intend. Therefore, after administering the two inventories we engage mothers in a parent-education program for thirty clock hours over a period of several months. During their training, mothers acquire a common orientation to the possibilities of play education. The training emphasizes conditions unique to the family situation of each mother. While mothers attend the cost-free experimental program funded by the Rockefeller Foundation, their preschoolers join college student volunteers to participate in Toy Talk.

Toy Talk is a way of establishing a learning condition in which a child and an adult can each serve as teacher and share dominance. We use toys as the medium for adult-child conversation. This choice permits play, the child's favorite activity, to become his focus for learning. The choice also allows imagination to equal age as a source of authority. The child experiences respect for his ability to pretend, and the parent gets recognition for her superior verbal strength. A mother who is trained to use Toy Talk can increase desired affective behaviors, assess vocabulary comprehension, introduce new words in context, and immediately correct speech and misconceptions (9).

Each unit in the toy curriculum begins with an affective objective. Preschoolers, unlike older children, are influenced by every interpersonal encounter. Indeed four- and five-year-olds learn as much by observation as by listening. Adult feelings, moods, and attitudes become curriculum whether or not they are intended to be part of the curriculum. Therefore, we have written units that require grownups to manifest certain affective behaviors such as "the constructive use of power," "recognizing the needs and feelings of others," and "sharing fears and anxieties" (10).

To clarify the affective emphasis, consider how a goal like "sharing fears and anxieties" promotes mental health. It is well known that boys and girls live more with fear than adults do. The difference can be explained in part by the greater access children have to imagination. A child's day normally includes more fiction and his sleep more nightmares than adults'. Nevertheless, many parents are ashamed of fearful children and attempt to banish their fright by ridicule or denial. In homes where only the tangible is valued as real, imaginative experiences are described as "unreal." Yet whatever happens to a child is real for him; the fact that others do not share his experience does not nullify it.

Laughing at another's fears does not decrease their power over him. Instead the effect is to lower the individual's confidence in himself. Statements like "There is nothing to be afraid of in the dark" or "It's just a dream and not real," however well intended, inspire shame for having fears that grownups declare to be unwarranted. To laugh at a child's fears is to limit the relationship with him. Children—and adults—whose feelings are ridiculed soon stop sharing their experiences. The tragedy for parents is that they are reducing their chance to know their child better and forfeiting an opportunity to help him learn to cope with doubts, anxieties, and fears.

The first step in overcoming fear is to acknowledge it. Because preschoolers closely identify with parents, a sound way to reduce harmful consequences of children's fear is for parents to admit their own fears. A child who is afraid of the dark, of being alone, or of starting school should be assured by grownups that fear is a natural reaction and that to acknowledge fear does not make one a coward.

Although parents may contend that there is no danger in the dark, a child knows that Dad won't allow Mom out alone late at night. The doors are bolted only at night. A child should not be shamed for expressing his feelings of fear. After all, adults fear getting old, being alone, losing their hair, developing cancer, taking academic tests, and peer rejection. Fear is not limited to any one period in life. Unintentionally perhaps, the manufacturers of some monster toys have done us a service in exposing the need to express fear and anxiety.

Children should know someone who will hear their doubts and fears without judgment. They will have this experience if parents attach no contingency to acceptance. It should not be necessary for sons and daughters to repress fear or to feign bravery to gain their parents' esteem. Preschoolers are at a time in life when identification can encourage honesty. It is, therefore, inappropriate to urge preschoolers to deny their fears. On the contrary, early personality needs suggest that "sharing fears and anxieties" is a relevant and important affective goal (11, 12).

In Toy Talk, parents want to

reinforce affective objectives, and children want to repeat favorite play themes. The intentions of both parties can be honored in our curriculum. By observing children we have identified a variety of open-ended play themes: "The airplane is ready," "Let's play house," "It's cowboy time," "Someone wants the doctor," "Our boats can start," and "A monster is coming to town." For each theme parents are given a list of possible versions they might introduce during the play. If "A monster is coming to town," the parent who is interested in "sharing fears and anxieties" might introduce versions like these:

> He got lost on the way home.
> He needs to make noise, but it bothers people.
> He wants to go to school, but it's not allowed.
> He's sick but afraid to go to the doctor.
> He's friendly, but only the children know.
> He's told to stay out of town.

Some parents are reluctant to play the monster theme, for they regard monsters as unkind and destructive. By contrast, their tele-viewing children tend to assume that a monster is friendly and innocent unless he acts otherwise. It is disappointing to have grownups use appearances to prejudge others. The result is an undervaluing of the atypical. Many children seem ready to accept differences without evaluation.

To digress, I wonder if we unwittingly teach children prejudice in the name of classification. Grownups often ask preschoolers to decide: "Which one doesn't belong in the group?" Usually the choice is among objects, animals, or persons. The unintended lesson is that the different should be isolated because they do not belong. If integration is an American goal, the "unlikes" will have to go together. Maybe we can start by teaching the recognition of differences without insisting that the different be excluded.

Whatever play theme the child chooses, there are cognitive goals as well as affective goals. The child is expected to express his new knowledge in words as well as behavior. Accordingly, the lessons call for introducing vocabulary that is relevant to the play setting. When "A monster is coming to town," there are many appropriate words for "sharing fears and anxieties." A small sample is given here:

afraid	frighten	danger
sympathy	destroy	protect
stranger	enemy	different
gentle	peaceful	warn
lost	survivor	search
return	destination	escape

Before play begins, the parent chooses, from a vocabulary list, the words she wants her child to know. She then administers a vocabulary pretest to determine which of the words chosen need to be taught. Each item in the pretest has two parts. The first part requires a non-verbal response. The second part requires a verbal response. For the nonverbal component, a child is asked to select, by pointing, which of three pictures represents the word in question. To show his understanding of *afraid*, the child is shown pictures of a bird, a rabbit, and a lion. The child is asked:

"Which picture shows something that makes you afraid?" After his finger-point response, he is asked: "Why did you choose that one? What else makes you afraid?" To show his understanding of *sympathy,* the child is shown pictures of an obviously healthy ballet dancer, a happy clown, and a young child using crutches. The mother asks her child: "Which picture shows someone who needs sympathy?" After his nonverbal response, he is asked: "Why did you choose that one? What can you do to show sympathy?" Each parent is given a form on which to report the child's verbal and nonverbal responses as correct, incorrect, or not given. The pretest vocabulary that the child cannot define becomes his intended curriculum.

Toy Talk begins with the theme a child has chosen to focus the play. During the ensuing fiction, which the child dominates, the grownup tries to introduce theme variations and vocabulary whenever appropriate. She demonstrates the meaning of words by action if possible and repeats or defines the vocabulary in context. This procedure respects the child's imagination and assigns a supportive position to the adult, who offers possibilities but accepts the child's decisions without criticism.

In addition to the vocabulary assessments before and after Toy Talk, the suggested subthemes, and a vocabulary list, each play unit includes an annotated bibliography of children's books based on themes that correspond to the affective objective discussed during Toy Talk. The stories supplement the Toy Talk experience by providing a stimulus for parent and child to explore other related situations. The parent decides when to measure, by posttest, the cognitive effect of her teaching (13). If assessment indicates that a child still does not know a certain word or words at the verbal level, this vocabulary can be continued as curriculum.

To review, Toy Talk begins with the child's choice of a play theme. The parent then administers the vocabulary pretest, which is followed by play. During play the adult introduces variations of the theme and emphasizes the unknown vocabulary. Later, children's books are read to reinforce and further explore the affective goal. Finally, the parent gives the child a vocabulary posttest.

We have observed that adults have little difficulty in engaging in games like football and basketball, activities in which motor skill and judgment have a higher priority than imagination. These types of play please adults, and they can spend hours of involvement with older children. But most of us have trouble spending even a few minutes playing with a preschooler. In this situation, our attention span is short. We have stopclocked the play or the play observation of parents with four-year-olds. When we have asked parents to estimate how long they have played or watched, their estimates have generally been three to four times greater than the actual amount of time.

Since observation requires time, watching represents approval. In my judgment, giving a child time is a far more authentic reinforcement than praise. To give time requires an investment of self. No personal investment is required to say that a child's product is "good" or "wonderful." Observation seems to be a more effective form of reward than verbal reinforcement.

One of the best ways to show respect for someone is to watch him "do his thing." If we avoid spending time at play with our child, we lose a chance to share power and dominance; we lose an opportunity to acknowledge his strength and to respect him. By *respect* I mean letting another individual's power influence our relationship rather than keeping him in the position of subordinate.

Our research has involved about seventy mothers (Anglo, Mexican-American, Black) and a similar number of college students. The results of the research can best be seen in the case study reports. Because of the length of these reports, I shall offer group data. Consider two parallel studies, each concerned with a dozen mothers and preschool children (14, 15). The investigators sought to determine how Toy Talk training and experience influenced:

Self-concept of the mother as a teacher
Mother's perception of the teaching-learning process
Self-concept of the child
Verbal fluency of the child

The mothers in the experiment worked with toys donated by twenty-five companies who are members of the Toy Manufacturers of America. After eight weeks of training at home, the mothers demonstrated dramatic beneficial change.

A comparison of the mean difference in scores derived from the *t* ratios indicates that as a result of experience, a statistically significant change ($p < .005$) occurred in the mother's self-concept as a teacher. The gains could have occurred by chance in only five cases out of a thousand.

Mothers also made a significant gain ($p < .005$) in their knowledge of the teaching-learning process.

Toy Talk resulted in a significant change ($p < .005$) in the children's self-concept as learners.

Children's gains in word recognition, understanding, and elaboration were also significant ($p < .01$).

Our results were not obtained from an upper-income or intellectually elite group of parents. All the mothers live in inner-city Phoenix and qualify as poverty families. The data reported here represent the Black parents in the sample. Similar dramatic gains were achieved by the low-income white parent-child pairs. Mothers can be Toy Talk teachers. Older brothers and sisters can also engage in successful Toy Talk, as shown by our findings in Cleveland, Ohio, where college students worked with two dozen kindergarteners (16).

We have just concluded two experiments in the small agricultural community of Chandler, Arizona, where selected fourth-graders had two weeks of Toy Talk training and then became the child teachers of kindergarteners (17, 18). In these two studies, Black fourth-grade children taught Whites, and

Whites taught Blacks. Mexican-American Spanish speakers in the fourth-grade taught kindergarteners who spoke Spanish as well as kindergarteners who did not. Again, the preliminary data urge the same conclusion: Toy Talk is a natural medium for cognitive and affective growth, an important key to family development—in both the nuclear family and the larger family of man.

President Nixon recently vetoed a proposal that would have introduced public early childhood education on a national scale. His decision to oppose the legislation centered on its probable consequences for the family. Nixon's advisors felt that the family is weakened by reducing its responsibility. He was counseled to sponsor early childhood programs that will increase the ability of families to respond as an educational influence. This broad goal of family development has implications for our Toy Talk project.

We know that family development requires an individualized approach to parent education. To help insure this goal, we intend to do further empirical work on the parent-child inventories and improvement of the parent curriculum.

We know that family development requires a favorable self-impression for mothers and children. Increasing the vocabulary available for pretests and posttests will help mothers continue their motivation and guide their teaching. Children who are often observed at play conclude that imagination is important. Therefore, play observation skills are being added to the parent curriculum.

We know that family development requires a balanced emphasis on emotional growth and intellectual growth. A rationale is being prepared for each child-rearing goal parents may select. The intention to include fathers and grandparents in toy training should help enlarge the family faculty.

We know that family development requires that the home and the school combine their efforts. To discourage the notion that either the family or the school must be the sole agent for early childhood education, we will continue to disseminate our findings about the benefits of home-school collaboration.

We are learning how family development and child development can proceed together. Given access to play possibilities like Toy Talk, more preschoolers, mothers, fathers, siblings, grandmothers, and grandfathers will have the influence they desire and deserve.

References

1. Don Hamachek. *Encounters with the Self,* pp. 174-223. New York, New York: Holt, Rinehart and Winston, 1971.
2. Paul Bowman. "Family Role in the Mental Health of School Children," in *Education for Affective Achievement,* pp. 39-46. Edited by Robert Strom and E. Paul Torrance. Chicago: Rand McNally and Company, 1973.
3. Ruth O'Keefe. "Home Start: Partnership with Parents," *Children Today, 18* (January-February, 1973), 12-16.
4. Sara Stein and Carter Smith. "Return of Mom," in *Saturday Review— Education Supplement* (April, 1973), 37-43.

5. Sylvia Schwartz. "Parent-Child Interaction as It Relates to the Ego Functioning and Self-Concept of the Preschool Child," *Dissertation Abstracts* (1967), 27A, 2898A.

6. Phyllis Levenstein. "Cognitive Growth in Preschoolers through Verbal Interaction with Mothers," *American Journal of Orthopsychiatry, 40* (April, 1970), 426-32.

7. Ira Gordon. "Reaching the Young Child through Parent Education," *Childhood Education, 46* (February, 1970), 247-49.

8. A. Jones and Carolyn Stern. *Increasing the Effectiveness of Parents as Teachers,* pp. 1-14. Washington, D. C.: Educational Research Information Center, 1970.

9. Robert Strom. "Toy Talk: The New Conversation between Generations," *Elementary School Journal, 70* (May, 1970), 418-428.

10. Robert Strom and William Ray. "Communication in the Affective Domain," *Theory into Practice, 10* (October, 1971), 268-75.

11. Harriet Rheingold. "To Rear a Child," *American Psychologist, 28* (January, 1973), 42-46.

12. Ralph Tyler. "Assessing Educational Achievement in the Affective Domain," *Measurement in Education, 4* (Spring, 1973), 1-8.

13. Robert Rosenthal. "Teacher Expectation and Pupil Learning," in *Teachers and the Learning Process,* pp. 33-59. Edited by Robert D. Strom. Englewood Cliffs, New Jersey: Prentice-Hall, Inc., 1971.

14. Betty Greathouse. "The Effects of Toy Talk Training and Experience on Low Income Black Mothers and Their Preschool Children." Unpublished doctoral dissertation. Tempe, Arizona: Arizona State University, 1972.

15. Florence Sawicki. "The Effects of Toy Talk Training and Experience on Low Income Mothers and Their Preschool Children." Unpublished doctoral dissertation. Tempe, Arizona: Arizona State University, 1972.

16. Donna Brown. "Toward a Methodology for Improving Vocabulary Development of Low Income Children." Unpublished doctoral dissertation. Columbus, Ohio: The Ohio State University, 1970.

17. Guillermina Engelbrecht. "Formative Research in Peer Teaching Using Toys as a Medium for Instruction." Unpublished doctoral dissertation. Tempe, Arizona: Arizona State University, 1973.

18. Carol Kamin. "Formative Research in Black-White Peer Teaching Using Toys as a Medium for Instruction." Unpublished doctoral dissertation. Tempe, Arizona: Arizona State University, 1973.

How Parents May Use the Physical and Cultural Environments to Teach Others

by Marion J. Rice

All children are born into a speech community that has a definite code, a language for verbal communication. The speech community is located in a definite place which has a culture, an inventory of artifacts and behaviors. Language is specific to man. It is the nature of normal children to learn, and for adults, to transmit their language. Concepts are the names that men in a given speech community give to different phenomena to facilitate communication and environmental discrimination.

As a result of the previous factors, all parents teach concepts. They teach concepts intuitively, using a method rooted in applied psychology—a concrete associational method in which a label is identified with an object and repeated until the word becomes a symbol and can be used in place of the object. Anthropological observations indicate that parents in all cultures, preliterate as well as literate, teach in the above fashion. They teach so well that most normal children have learned at an unbelievable rate compared to what they will later learn. They have acquired an extensive vocabulary, mastered the syntax of their language and learned to make complete communicative statements using subject and predicate, and have acquired such skills as eating and dressing. The child has been taught by his parents, and taught well; otherwise, he could not have learned so much behavior, for behavior in the human is learned, not transmitted by genes.

But, all too frequently, this fantastic learning growth begins to slow. The child has made a satisfactory adjustment and teaching seems less important. Other children may arrive, and the parents become preoccupied with the new addition to the family. Systematic concept development, once emphasized unconsciously, becomes neglected. Teaching attrition also occurs in middle class homes, where teaching may very early be turned over first to the nursery school, then to the kindergarten, and finally the school. The child is transferred from the local environment, rich in sensory and personal experiences, to a school environment of manufactured artifacts for children—from the ingenious quacking duck on wheels to the slide and swing set. Gone are the rich aromas of the kitchen and the array of cooking tools; gone are hammer, saw, nails, and boards; and gone is the parent teacher to ask and answer that endless array of questions which stimulates the budding intellect.

This discussion does not open up new ground in the importance of home teaching. Historically, the antecedents are well documented in such neglected educational classics as *The School of Infancy* and the *Orbis Sensualium Pictus* of Comenius; Pestalozzi's *How Gertrude Teaches Her Children;* and Froebel's *Education of Man.* Neither will we attempt to review the psychological research on concept teaching, much of a preverbal nature which fits narrow laboratory experimentational needs rather than the practical needs of verbal concept teaching. We will primarily give a series of models for concept teaching, using both deductive and inductive procedures. Because such procedures inevitably use language, even when making use of concrete objects or props, we will begin with a discussion of the relationship of language and concepts.

CONCEPTS AND LANGUAGE

The effective teaching of concepts requires a practical and operational approach. The psychological literature, albeit extensive, provides little help. One reason is that experiments in concept formation with young learners by psychologists have concentrated on inferential, preverbal concept formation. Another is the preoccupation with personal concepts, rather than concepts which form, through language, the basis of meaningful communication.

There is, however, an easy solution. All concepts which are communicable without face to face contact requires the use of language. All concepts are given specific names in a language. These words and their public meanings hence become the operational base of concept teaching. To teach concepts is to teach language, which means to teach words and their meaning and to teach the grammatical arrangement of words into sentences.

A concept, therefore, may be defined as a word which stands for a general idea or thing, and is used meaningfully. The word is the symbol which gives to the concept

252

permanence and communicability. Words do not interfere with the learning of concepts. but become the means to see and differentiate among phenomena and to perceive relationships. The parent teacher may thus practically approach concept teaching as meaningful word teaching. In the early stages, the child acquires most readily the concepts of things, or nominative concepts. These are nouns, and much of early concept development consists of learning the names of things. After this differentiation, ideas of relationship may be developed in the form of specific and general statements. The easiest nouns to teach are nouns which have a concrete referent that the learner can experience with his senses. Concept learning, however, is not limited to concrete concepts; abstract concepts such as love and hate begin to be acquired at an early age.

The Richness of the Physical and Cultural Environment

The environment of the young child is a veritable storehouse of concrete concepts, but is rarely fully exploited. This results from the fact that parents and siblings adjust to their environment on a level of general, rather than specific, conceptual awareness. This economy of adjustment, however, often leads to the erroneous conclusion that there is little around the house to help a child learn. What is generally lacking is not the object, but a lack of terms to use in helping a child perceive and conceptualize.

For example, a common part of the architecture of most houses is the window. At the general concept level, young children learn the association of the word "window" with such a feature. However, the window is made up of many different parts, all of which have specific names. Learning the names of the parts of a larger object facilitates more careful observation and sub-concept development. It also leads to concept clustering, the organization of sub-concepts in a logical and systematic manner around a larger concept.

Instead of just learning the concept window, the normal double-hung sash window may be used to teach observation, discrimination, and related concepts, all with concrete referents, as follows:

General class name:
  Window
Sub-class names:

Window	box	Window	latch
	sash		lock
	pane		light
	screen		glass
	shutter		stile
	rail		dressing
	jamb		mullion
	frame		board
	crank		
Sash			
	weight		cord
	pulley		balance
Single hung		Double hung	
window		window	
Casement window		Bay window	
Putty			

Weather stripping (inside, outside)

Hinge	Lintel
Tension	Screw

Metal, aluminum, bronze, brass
Wood

In noun concept teaching, however, the teacher does not merely present labels as names of things. He also uses labels to clarify two other important ideas—how something is made and how it functions. For example, the concepts stile, rail, and mullion help to explain how wood pieces are used to make up a frame to hold the glass panes, with putty over the outside nails to make the panes watertight. The concepts double hung, jamb, moulding, cord, pulley, weight, and balance help to explain how an old-fashioned double hung sash worked. Today, in contrast, metal tension channels are used. But without these labels, these sub-concepts, the concept of window remains somewhat general and vague.

To prepare for concrete concept teaching, the parents should make an inventory of all the things in and about the house and in the yard which the growing child will encounter. If the mother does not know the name of an object, she should try to learn the name. If she does not know what it is made of, or how it functions, she should learn. By knowing, she is better able to help the child understand the meaning of the word labels.

The father as well as the mother has a role to play as a teacher. He is more likely to use household and yard tools. He is more likely to be responsible for household maintenance and the upkeep of the car, while the mother is more likely to cook, wash, sew, and perform similar domestic tasks. Much of parental teaching will take the form of incidental teaching, in which the learning of the child is incidental to the performance of the task by the parent. Many teaching occasions may be developed, in which the child is deliberately involved in a learning task.

Unless parents are science-oriented, it is not likely that they will be as conscious of the physical environment as they are of the cultural environment. All children live in a physical environment with the sun, the wind, the moon, and other celestial bodies and the phenomena of weather and seasonal change. There are trees and growing things. There are many simple science books written for elementary grades which parents can use to refresh their understanding of simple phenomena which they studied in school. They can also show a concern for how the environment is used, and combine affective concept learning with the learning of the names of concrete objects.

It is important to emphasize that every environment in which a child is reared offers many opportunities for concrete concept learning. In reality, there is no such thing as an impoverished environment. An environment may be deteriorated, dilapidated, disorderly and dirty, but these characteristics do not mean that objects are lacking with which to teach. What is really lacking is knowledge of the appropriate and specific nomenclature to give meaning and differentiation to the occurrence of phenomena. What is also lacking is a consciousness of the importance of concept formation, so that the parent does not try to explain and interpret the way things occur and function. To attribute learning deficiences to an environmental deficit when the deficiency is in the ability to teach is to give both a wrong diagnosis and prescribe a wrong remedy.

For purpose of illustration, let us imagine the picture of a rural tenant house, refrigerator and washing machine on the front porch, with an abandoned car in the yard in which children are playing. The caption might read "Poor children do not have a stimulating environment in which to play." In contrast, imagine a typical kindergarten picture, with many hands digging in a sandbox in the corner of the play yard. The caption might read "Creative expression is provided through varied kindergarten activities." The difference in the learning environment, however, is not in the objects. The "poor" environment is much richer in artifacts for teaching than the artificial environment of even the best equipped kindergarten or nursery school.

Sensory Experiences and Concrete Associational Learning

The normal child is born with the necessary sense organs to interact with his environment—he can see, hear, smell, touch, and taste. It is through these senses that he can have the experience of real things which are indispensable to the formation of intelligence.

In the human species, the most important senses are hearing and seeing. It is these senses in combination with the experience of a physical object that mainly permits him to develop concepts through language. Language is specific to man, and normal children acquire the language of their speech community through home rearing.

Sensory, concrete associational learning is the primary means of early concept learning. The procedures are known to parents, and need merely to be extended to a wider range of phenomena.

In the earliest phase, the procedure is reduced to the barest minimum. The child is given water to drink. The mother says "water." The child is bathed in "water;" he plays in "water." Eventually, the child tries to model the sound made by his mother. "Wa-wa." "No. water." In time, he will say "water." When he is able to use the word "water" to serve his needs, he has not only acquired the sound but he has acquired the concept. The word, "water", permits him to exercise not only environmental discrimination, but he can now control his environment. He can serve his personal needs by asking for "water."

In a second phase of concept learning, functional and descriptive terms may be added. "Ball." "Throw ball." "Rubber ball." "Spongy ball." "Catch ball." The addition of functional and descriptive terms help to enlarge the comprehension of the concept of ball, even though no formal definition by attributes is utilized.

Sensory, concrete associational learning may be schematized as follows:

(1) See ⟍
     ⟍⟶ Ball
     Hear ⟋

(2) Perception   Forms an Image of Ball
(3) Conception   Uses word "ball'

Concept learning is similar to the classical conditioning experiment, in which the meaningful word label serves to evoke appropriate conceptualization and behavior. Consequently, such commands as "Throw the ball," "Catch the ball," "Hit the ball," convey meaningful behaviors without the necesssity of any concrete behavior.

Because of the nature of language, children will progress further in powers of conceptualization and be able to use language to develop the meaning of abstract concepts. Extensive experience with concrete concepts, nevertheless, forms the necessary basis for abstract conceptualization. The tremendous advantage of concrete objects in early teaching is that some kind of mental image is apparently formed which permits conceptualization, without the need of elaborate verbal explanations which are beyond the capacity of the child. However, it is indispensable that the word label accompany the object in order that the child will not merely have an experience, but a means of holding and communicating the concept.

Picture Associational Learning

A variant of sensory, concrete associational learning is picture associational learning. Sight and sound are two senses utilized, as in concrete associational learning. But the picture lacks the sensory completeness that a concrete situation transmits.

Contrast, for example, the experience of taking a child to an Atlantic coastal marsh and out in a small rowboat on a tidal inlet. At high tide, the water fills the marsh; the world is a sea of water with green heads protruding. At low tide, the lake has shrunk to a mere ditch and the marsh grass stands high in an elevated field. The mud sighs with a thousand sounds; the water laps against the boat; the breeze brushes across the grass. And the smell—the pungent, odorous smell of salt, marsh mud, and decay. A picture cannot bring to mind this rich life and smell of the marsh.

However, pictures and similar substitutes also have great utility for teaching. From the logistic standpoint, they are more manageable. How much easier it is to look at pictures of rakes and men using rakes than to go through the steps described for the inductive teaching of the concept rake, or to explain the land food chain. How easily can these ideas be shown in a picture. Because picture associational learning does not require concrete objects, it can be introduced when concrete teaching is not possible—in a quiet time before nap or bedtime from his mother—even in the form of a lesson.

Unfortunately, there are not many good picture-learning books for young learners. Older children in the upper elementary grades have available many excellent books for parents to use with them, such as *The How and Why Wonder Book* of Grossett & Dunlap, the Silver Burdett Reading and Research Program simplifying the Life Nature Library, and the many individual titles issued by the Golden Press. Such books are excellent resources for parents as home teachers. The ideas are presented in an elementary manner, and thus help the parent to simplify the concepts for youngr learners. But specifically designed scientific books for preschool and primary children, which combine Twentieth Century technology and pedagogy, are generally lacking.

Parents may usefully maintain a picture file. Expensive mounting is not required and used file folders are excellent to separate and classify pictures by concept and concept clusters. Tearing out and saving pictures in this manner often provides a convenient picture resource from which to teach. If pictures are not saved and a file developed, it is sometimes impossible to find the needed pictures to develop a language concept.

Perhaps at some future date an enterprising publisher will decide to fill a need void and bring out a new and extended *Orbis Sensualium Pictus* (The World Sensed Through Pictures). In the meantime, pictures which are available may be used as concrete props in association with language to develop new concepts and language competency.

Models for Concept Teaching

There are two major models for concept learning—the deductive and the inductive. These models are sometimes called ruleg and egrule, because of differences in procedures. In the deductive, or ruleg, model, the meaning or rule is given after the word, followed by examples. In the inductive, or egrule, model, the examples are first given, attributes noted, a rule inferred, and finally, the approriate word supplied or given. With young children a concept which includes many different instances or examples, such as weapon, should probably be taught by ruleg methods. Egrule methods may be used when there is time for many questions and concrete observation, which a teacher may use as the basis for guiding toward an inference. In actual teaching situations, it is rare that the teacher, parent or school teacher, uses any one method exclusively. Generally, he uses a combination of methods according to the way the pupil responds to the learning task. Deductive methods are sometimes thought to be more rote methods of learning than are inductive methods, sometimes called discovery methods. The examples given of deductive methods emphasize understanding, not mere word learning. If a concept is not understood, the word that is used to name it is not a symbol—it is a mere sound, a noise without meaning.

In both procedures, however, the specific word must be given. Words are arbitrary symbols assigned by a speech community, and there is nothing in the particular attributes of an animal that he be called *horse, cheval,* or *caballo.* The following sections describe procedures for concept teaching all using concrete objects.

Inductive—specific object. Concept: rake.
Formal Definition: An implement with a handle and transverse attachment with tines or teeth for collecting leaves or trash or smoothing dirt.

Step	*Procedure*
1. Father assembles examples.	Get two different rakes, two different garden rakes, and potato rake, hoe, ax, hammer.
2. Ask lead question. (Encourage child to look at rakes and feel.)	"Here are three things. What do all have?"
3. Follow up question, with demonstration.	Possible answers: "Stick. Wood. Metal. They stick. They hurt." "What do we do with piece of wood?" Possible answer: "Hold it." "What we hold is called 'handle'." "Say 'handle'. Hold the 'handle'." "Does this thing have a handle, too?" Expected answer: "Yes."
4. Focusing question.	"Now look at what's on the handle." "Tell me what you see on this one (point to leaf rake). This one (garden rake). This one (potato rake) tool."
5. Demonstration.	"This is the way we use this tool" (leaf rake, rake up leaves or grass). "What am I doing?"
6. Application.	"You use this one." Child imitates father.
7. Repeat 5 and 6 with garden rake.	
8. Naming.	"These tools have a name. The name is rake. Say the name with me — rake." "What do we call these tools?" "Rake."
9. Specific naming.	"If we use this rake to rake up leaves and grass, what do we call it?" Establish label "leaf rake." "If we use this rake in the garden to smooth out dirt, what do we call it?" Establish label "garden rake."
10. Negative instances.	Present hammer. "Is this a rake?" Present ax. "Is this a rake?" Present hoe. "Is this a rake?" "What do we do with a rake?"
11. Infer rule. (Function) (Composition)	Possible answer: "Get up leaves and grass." "How is a rake made?" Possible answer: "Has a handle and something wide on end to rake with."

12. Evaluation: Positive but different instances.

Show garden rake: "What is this?"
Desired response: "Garden rake."
Show leaf rake: "What is this?"
Desired response: "Leaf rake."
Show all rakes: "What do we call these things?"
Desired response: "Rakes."

The preceding steps are highly formalized, and are characteristic of a deliberate attempt to teach the concept "rake." In home teaching, however, the child is most likely to learn the concept rake in the manner previously described for sensory, concrete associational learning incidental to some use of rakes. For example, father might say, "This old leaf rake is worn out." Or, "I need a new handle for the leaf rake." Or, "Hand me the leaf rake with the fingers."

The inductive procedure, however, forces the child to be more conscious of the distinguishing characteristics of the rakes, even when he lacks precise vocabulary to identify the attributes. As he encounters concepts in school, however, experience with inductive concept formation at home helps him learn concepts from example-rule through an inductive process in school.

Deductive—general class. Concept: tool. (Rule-Example)

Formal Definition: A tool is an implement used or worked by hand, as saw or hammer.

Step	*Procedure*
1. Assemble positive and negative examples.	Screwdriver, hammer, pliers, can opener, knife.
2. Give the concept (word).	"Here is a new word. Tool."
3. Define the concept (give attributes).	"A tool is something man holds to do work with."
4. Give examples and demonstrate.	"A screwdriver is a tool. We use a screwdriver to turn a screw into wood or metal. I hold it in my hand to do work. You try to turn the screw." "Here is a pair of pliers. I hold the handles in my hand. I squeeze hard. The teeth grip the nut with the pliers. Pliers are a tool." "Do you see another tool here? (Point to collection). What's that? A hammer. A hammer is what? A hammer is a tool. What do we do with a hammer?"
5. Ask for rule.	"Can you tell me what a tool is?" Expected response: "Something we work with by hand."
6. Negative instances. (Do not use with children who have difficulty in concept formation).	Show a ball. "Is this a tool?" Show a top. "Is this a tool?" Develop idea that a ball is not used to do work with.
7. Evaluation (Show knife).	"What's this?" "A knife." "What kind of thing is a knife?" "It's a tool." "Why is it a tool?" "Because we use it to cut with."

All concepts are general ideas or categories. A hammer, in general, merely has the attributes of a hammer—an object with a head attached to a handle to pound with. It can be small or big, a brick hammer or a nail hammer. Tool, however, is a much more inclusive concept, as are such concepts as implement, instrument, machine, animal, plant, weapon, furniture, and the like. In teaching inclusive concepts, it is necessary to have a variety of objects that demonstrate the class. Example-rule or inductive inclusive concept teaching appears less suitable with young children than deductive or rule teaching because the examples do not have enough common attributes from which to generalize.

The previous examples have emphasized concepts and their names. Young children can also be introduced to explanations of how objects function, using concrete objects.

The examples here involve the mechanical principle of the lever and the biological relationship of the land food chain. Both of these procedures use a combination of deductive-inductive methods.

Deductive—functional explanation. Concept: lever, fulcrum.
Formal Definition: A bar, resting on a fulcrum, which is used to do work.

Step	*Procedure*
1. Assemble exhibit of levers.	Crowbar, board, claw hammer, pliers, scissors, bat, brick or rock for fulcrum, heavy weight, nail in board, baseball bat.
2. Give the word (concept).	"Here is a new idea. Lever. Say lever."
3. Define the concept.	"A lever is a bar to do work with."
4. Demonstrate with examples.	"Can you lift this weight?" "No."
	"Put the weight on the end of the board. Rest the board over the rock. The board is our lever. The rock is our fulcrum, the thing we rest the lever against. Now stand on the board. See how the weight goes up. You can do work with a lever."
	"Can you pull the nail out? Use the claw hammer. Put the claws around the nail head. The head of the hammer is fulcrum. Now pull on the end of the handle. The handle is a lever. You can pull the nail out with a lever. You can do work with the lever."
	Demonstrate with other examples.
5. Application.	"Show me how you can use this crowbar as a lever. Can you show me the fulcrum of the crowbar?"
	"Here is a screwdriver. Show how you can use it as a kind of lever."
	"Is this baseball bat a kind of lever?"
	"Where would the fulcrum be?"
6. Ask for statement of rule?	"Can you tell me what a lever is?"
7. Evaluation.	Use other types of levers to do work.

If the concept lever is developed in conjunction with the concept of basic machines—plane, wedge, wheel and axle, pulley, screw, gear—the preschool learner can grasp a much better idea of the way mechanical things work. This type of simple science teaching appears especially suitable for boys, since so much of the preschool experience encouraged in the home—crayons, coloring book, scissors, paste, and the like—appears to have more appeal for girls. The involvement with machines also calls upon the exercise of more motor effort, a factor which makes machine teaching more interesting to the male learner. Such concepts should not be taught once and forgotten. Parents should have children practice the use of the terms and make practical applications until the concepts are comprehended in many different situations. After initial concept teaching, the parent may contrive ways for the learner to apply his knowledge, such as using a wedge to split a piece of small firewood or a plane to move a heavy object up a stairway. Pulleys can be utilized in a variety of ways for pleasure and entertainment—a chair lift up to the tree-house, a slide from a high tree or hill, a lift for hauling goods, or even signal display.

Deductive—explanatory. Concept: land food chain.
Antecedent concepts: sun, energy, food, plant, insect, plant eater, animal eater, decay, soil, nutrient.
Formal Definition: Dependence of animals on plants for food and cycle of plant growth and decay.

Step	*Procedure*
1. Assemble objects for demonstration.	Soil, fertilizer, plant, dead plant, grasshopper, bird, decayed bird on soil.

2. Presentation of concept.

We have a new idea today. It is land food chain. Say with me: land food chain.

3. Formal definition.

Land food chain tells us how things living on land—plants and animals—depend on each other.

4. Prior knowledge through focusing question.
   Expected response:

Do you know of any animals that live on plants? Those that eat other animals?

Cow, horse, rabbits eat grass. Cat eats a mouse; eagle, a bird or rabbit.

5. Arrange concepts in logical explanatory sequence.

The sun gives us energy. All living things get energy from the sun.

There are two kinds of living things—plants and animals. Plants use energy from the sun, nutrients from the soil, and water to make food. All food comes from plants. Some animals eat only plants, like the grasshopper or cow. They are plant eaters. Other animals live off smaller animals. Birds eat insects and seeds.

The insect is a plant eater. The bird is an animal eater and plant eater. The bird gets energy from the grasshopper. The grasshopper is food for the bird.

The bird dies. It decays. The flesh rots and goes back into the soil as nutrients. The dead flesh fertilizes the soil. The animal now serves as food for plants. This goes on over and over again. That is why it is called a land food chain. These animals and plants live on land.

6. Generalization, focusing question.

Do plants and animals live in water? Do you think this kind of chain is found in water? What might it be called?

7. Transfer.

Can you give me some examples of animals eating plants? Can you give me the names of some animal eaters? Why do animal eaters depend on plants? What kind of eater are you?

Here is a fruit fly. What kind of eater is it? Here is a spider. What would happen if we put the fruit fly in the spider's web? What kind of eater is a spider? How do animals get energy from the sun? What is a land food chain?

In the development of a process concept, such as land food chain, the parent must not expect to develop the idea in a meaningful fashion at one time. As noted, there are antecedent or prerequisite concepts which must be learned. Therefore, to develop the idea land food chain, the parent must have the idea as a major learning task, but approach the task through a series of minor learning tasks, based on the antecedent concepts. One learning task is, of course, "The sun gives us energy." Another is "Plants take the energy of the sun and make food." These ideas can be developed gradually over the course of a week. Finally, when the antecedent concepts have been learned, at least in part, they can be used to develop the explanation of land food chain.

Parents and other teachers of young children often think that such explanations are beyond the intellectual grasp of young children, especially those of preschool age. This results primarily from the failure to conceptualize the major outcome as a long term learning goal, and work on the parts as immediate learning tasks which help to achieve the learning outcome. This type of concept learning requires more deliberate teaching than concrete-associational learning, which primarily involves labelling. One of the major differences is that explanatory concepts, such as land food chain, also involves the use of many factual statements, e.g., "Energy comes from the sun." "Animals decay and nutrients go back into the soil." The synthesis of these ideas to explain a complex concept also requires more attention from the child and willingness to follow sequential ideas. For this reason, such explanations should not be strictly verbal, but also give the child an opportunity to perform, such as feeding the grasshopper to the bird. The intellectual development of the preschool child can be vastly expanded through such deliberate home teaching.

Naming by Television

Television brings to the young learner the sights and sounds of far-off places. It gives parents an opportunity to acquaint the child with a world beyond his immediate environment. There are few television programs designed to teach concepts to children, for most children's programs are designed primarily to entertain. Simply allowing children to watch television does not assure that they will learn. This is due to the absence of the appropriate language to help them see, fix, and recall the objects or behaviors described.

With young learners, it is not necessary to watch an entire program. As something occurs which might be used to teach, the adult can simply point it out to the child. "That big bridge is over the Golden Gate. The Golden Gate leads to the big bay at San Francisco. The bridge is a suspension bridge. See how those big suspension wires hold the bridge up. It suspends or hangs by those cables from the big towers. It is the Golden Gate Bridge." This is also a good time to get out an Atlas to show the child where San Francisco is located.

In the event of a ballet presentation, "Come see this pretty dance. See how the dancers stand on their toes. The lady dancers are called ballerinas."

Young children often wish to see certain programs. If they are suitable for a child to see, the mother might watch the program from time to time with the child, pointing out, naming, and having the child label and discriminate. In this way, total programs which have little meaning for a child can be used to extend the basis of concept learning.

The Short Trip and Journey

Trips away from the house offer chances to teach concepts that are not available at home—intersection, traffic signal, mailbox, shopping center, supermarket, to name a few. Often times, the need to pay attention to street or sidewalk traffic interferes with turning such experiences into a teaching-learning event. If one member of the family is driving, the other parent can be the teacher. Teaching in such situations may appear to be highly transient, but, repeated on many occasions, it helps the child to acquire appropriate labels to discriminate among phenomena which exist but are seldom seen as meaningful parts of the landscape.

The vacation journey is particularly fruitful for calling a child's attention to new phenomena. Traveling to a different place is itself stimulating. New scenery, new things appear more interesting than the same old scene of streets and shops, or woods and fields, that are seen day after day. The stimulating effect of a change in environment should be capitalized upon to teach new concepts, whether it is to an historic site, such as a fort, a national park, a house museum, or even just a family-fun vacation spot, such as the seashore.

Because so many different experiences occur so rapidly, it is often not possible for a child to learn and remember everything he sees and has been exposed to. Even adults remember little of the specific new things from their journey—perhaps an indication they have seen and not learned. Learning from an experience requires getting the labels to help fix and remember concepts.

If possible, parents should try to get advance information about where they are going and what they are going to see. They should note in particular the things which might be of most interest to their children and the simplest things which can be told about most clearly. It is better to teach a few things clearly.

One technique is to make the journey into an, "I find a ...." Stops are made as necessary to look and observe what is seen. During the trip, a game can be played, "I saw .... at ...." Finally, a story can be made up about what is seen.

This is the story that some children, with the help of their parents, made up about a journey. This type of experience, in which the child puts together different concepts, is a way-to help recreate the total experience of a journey. This synthesis is valuable for school transfer. One of the standard school compositions for returning children is, "My Vacation." Such verbal composition is a beginning stage for the more formal stage of writing down experiences. If children are first accustomed to speaking out what they have seen, it is much easier for them to cope with the stage of the written report.

THE DESERT

A desert is a dry place.

It is very hot.

Sometimes there are big sand dunes.

Sometimes there are lots of rocks.

There are funny plants with sticky leaves.

These are called cacti.

In Arizona, we saw a scary-looking cactus.

It was tall and had big arms. Its name is sauguaro.

Another kind was thin like a spider.

It is called ocotillo.

These plants can live in the dry desert.

The sky was always blue.

It did not rain.

It does not rain much in the desert.

We saw cotton growing, Also, lettuce.

It had to be watered, like our lawn.

Giving plants water is irrigation.

Irrigation helps men grow crops in the desert.

The hot sun and the water make the crops grow.

Once the wind blew hard.

There was much sand in the air.

It was a sandstorm.

Once I saw a rabbit.

Desert animals come out at night.

It is cooler at night.

We liked the desert.

We liked to play in the white sand.

There is a desert called White Sands.

But it is not really sand.

It is called gypsum.

THE PROBLEMS OF THE DISADVANTAGED HOME TEACHER

Thus far, nothing has been said about the special needs of the mother from a poor background who lacks both language and teaching skills. The emphasis on concept teaching by parents in the home environment has assumed such middle class competencies as high school education, interest in the role of the parent as a teacher, and a willingness to take time to teach. The primary teacher has been, and will be, the mother, and the emphasis has been on mother rather than father teaching. However, the principles are equally applicable.

The literature on using disadvantaged parents as home teachers is largely negative. The emphasis has been on the description of the lack of conceptualization, disordered approach, and authoritarian style of the parent in teaching tasks from a poor as compared to a more affluent background. Furthermore, the funding for working with parents has been very limited in comparison with the funding for traditional day care, nursery, and kindergarten programs. The premise of the past decade appears to be to get the child out of the home environment, rather than to work with parents in the home environment.

There are several reasons for this rationale. The child in a learning center is more pliable and amenable. Work with parents always involves a great number of conflicts which do not occur in formalized teaching. There is also the question of privacy. Involving parents as home teachers is a policy of intervention in the home, it does invade the home. It is extremely difficult to work out effective intervention strategies which do not imply that the parent is not doing a poor job of home rearing and teaching.

There is, nevertheless, a great challenge in the area of more effective home teaching. No matter how many teacher aides and programs are established, no day care situation can match the opportunities for learning in the home—if the parent tries to teach. Home teaching also avoids the complicated logistics of transportation and nutrition which pervades institutional instruction. Undoubtedly, more financial resources should be devoted to the development of ways and means to work effectively with poor parents. A small reallocation of resources from Headstart, Follow Through, and similar types of institutional intervention could greatly expand the resources to experiment with different types of home teaching intervention programs.

In the meantime, a few modest suggestions are in order. The first is that all girls, before they leave the ninth grade, have instruction in school concerning the importance of home teaching. A great deal of time is spent on ornamental subjects, but knowledge important to the health and safety of the race is ignored. Young people need to develop an early appreciation of the importance of home teaching. An effective sibling teacher can work the same miracle as an adult. But in the long run, it is important that prospective parents be socialized in the importance of teaching children in the home, a task which seems to be increasingly neglected.

A second suggestion is to experiment with the feasibility of a Home Demonstration Teacher. This is a position analogous to that of the Home Demonstration Agent. Instead of demonstrating how to can or cook, however, the Home Demonstration Teacher would visit with parents and teach them how to teach children. They would also, however, leave with the parents specific teaching suggestions, as simple and clear as possible, suitable for that particular locale. If a parent is to utilize the concrete environment for teaching, it is pointless to give a mother living in the South Georgia pine flats materials about high mountain lands.

Finally, most of the literature on home teaching with the disadvantaged seems to point to the need of actually providing the materials. Even when the materials are inexpensive, there is the problem that using such materials to teach children is not in the life-style of the family. It is, therefore, suggested that the Home Demonstration Teacher have "throw-away" types of materials which provide ideas for teaching, using the objects mothers are most likely to have in their home environments.

What is needed is not toy lending libraries. There are already materials to teach with in the home. What parents and siblings need are strategies to teach with. These strategies, if effective, of necessity must involve the use of language to develop concepts. What poor children lack are not objects with which to make associations, but the language to associate with the world in which all men live.

SUMMARY

We have defined concepts as words which are used meaningfully. The natural way for young children to learn the concepts of their speech community is to learn to associate the names of things with objects. The fundamental base of home learning is sensory, concrete associational learning. Both inductive and deductive strategies of conceptualization may be used with young learners, but a combination of deductive-inductive are generally more effective. While most home teaching is incidental, parents should systematically attempt to teach more concepts and relationships. Especially important are the concepts belonging to the world of science and technology; ideas which help a child to better understand the nature of the world in which he lives.

Most parents intuitively teach their children, and thus lay the foundation of success in formal school. Children of poor families are at a disadvantage not because their environments lack objects with which to associate language, but because their parents and other relatives lack the skills—linguistic and organizational—with which to teach. Institutional efforts to compensate for such a handicap have been encouraged. Money should be reallocated to the development of programs which focus on parents as home teachers, notwithstanding the fact that early childhood educators typically favor intervention away from the home. All parents, even the least skillful, teach. Certainly, there must be some means to help all parents become more effective home teachers. Concept learning, the foundation of intellectual development, begins in the home.

A WARNING TO CONSCIENTIOUS MOTHERS

The findings of an ongoing Harvard study offer surprising insights on the best ways to further a child's social and intellectual development.

By Martin Cohen

Two mothers—both with one-year-old infants—are trying to raise their children the right way. Each wants success and happiness for her offspring. But one will do a better job of helping her child achieve these goals. The Pre-School Project at the Harvard University Laboratory of Human Development, now entering its ninth year, is finding out what one mother is doing that seems more effective than what the other is doing.

The advantage would appear to be with the first, a woman we'll call Betty. She and her husband are college graduates with a comfortable income. The nursery is well stocked with educational toys for the second child, a son, and the home is always clean and orderly. Although the boy usually is in the playpen —with the television turned on so that he will be exposed to a great deal of language—Betty spends 30 minutes every day teaching him to recognize numbers, the alphabet, and objects in pictures.

The second mother, Jennifer, a high-school graduate, has three children and a home to care for. Her husband's salary doesn't allow for special toys for any of the children, and her schedule doesn't leave room for spending blocks of time with the youngest child. Instead, the boy is allowed free rein of the house, following his mother around while she does her chores, interrupting her work a few moments at a time when he wants her attention. Jennifer enjoys his chatter and doesn't mind his clutter. Her home, although clean, is seldom picture-perfect.

Surprisingly, perhaps, the Pre-School Project has found that Jennifer's child is likely to be more competent than Betty's.

"The mother is obviously the primary caretaker of young children," says Burton L. White, Ph.D., director of the project. "But we can go beyond that and state that during the critical period of development, it is she alone who usually is the single most important environmental factor influencing his developing competence.

"The child isn't only dependent on her for love and protection, but is completely fascinated by what she says and does —at least at first. She is responsible for the image that the child establishes of himself and how he will relate with others," explains Dr. White, a developmental psychologist and the father of four children. "She is his primary learning source."

The project, funded over the years by the United States Office of Education, the Carnegie Corporation of New York, and the Head Start Division of the Office of Economic Opportunity, has been in existence for nine years and is designed to establish how mothers can be the best primary caretakers possible. "The research is highly significant," says L. Joseph Stone, Ph.D., professor of psychology at Vassar College. "It has many strong practical and theoretical implications both for educators and parents."

The research that has come from the program thus far is challenging many traditional, previously accepted ideas about child development. Results have shown, for example, that:

• A child's development in preschool years is not totally dependent on his parents' marital status, income, education, or family size. Some low-income families with as many as eight closely spaced children were doing as well or better at raising children than families with fewer children and better incomes.

• Mothers of successful children neither harass nor hover over offspring, dispelling the myth that better mothers get their children off to a head start with lessons in reading, writing, and arithmetic. In fact, it is the children themselves who, through their own actions, initiate 80 percent of learning situations.

• A child's learning processes should be developed before he's of nursery or kindergarten age.

"In recent years, a lot of effort has been put into enrichment programs to bring the four- to five-year-old child up to a satisfactory level of competence, but generally these programs haven't succeeded," explains Dr. White. "We wanted to find out what it is that happens to preschool children at home that makes one child better able to cope with social and educational demands.

"We believe that the critical period in child development begins at about the age of seven or eight months," he says. "By the age of three, children should have acquired the ability to understand most of the language they will use in ordinary conversation throughout their lives. They also have adapted their social styles, including the way they will relate to other children and to adults, such as future teachers. By age three, the basic

shaping of the child is usually accomplished. If a child has fallen significantly behind his peers by then, it's hard to turn him around."

This three-year-old cutoff time, however, is not universally embraced by other researchers in the field. "When you understand that learning is cumulative, then the importance of early education is clear," says Vassar College's Dr. Stone, coauthor of *Childhood and Adolescence: A Psychology of the Growing Person* and of a new book, *The Competent Infant.* "If a child doesn't get this early education, I doubt that it's irreversible, but it's hard to make up."

"There are instances where children have been turned around," explains J. McVicker Hunt, Ph.D., professor of psychology and education at the University of Illinois, "but the truth of the matter is that we are not very good at turning a child around in school." According to Dr. Hunt, who was chairman of a White House task force on the role of the federal government in early education (1966-1967), "You really have to turn the family around. The family, the people who are closest to the child, are the most important."

The experts agree, however, that the earlier a child is reached, the better the chances of improving his competence.

When the Pre-School Project began, in 1965, some 400 families from eastern Massachusetts were initially screened. From this, a sampling of about 100 children—three, four, and five years old—was rated for competence in a wide range of social and nonsocial skills and studied during a two-year period. The children were rated for the ability to cope in a superior fashion with all problems. Scoring was based on social behavior, such as the ability to get the attention of an adult positively by touch, show, or tell, rather than by misbehaving or showing off, and on various cognitive skills, such as language ability and intellectual acumen.

On the basis of the results, the children were classified as A, B, or C. In these studies, a very competent child was classified as an A child. He copes in a superior fashion throughout the day in both social and nonsocial categories. The B child is obviously not incompetent, but he is not outstanding in any way. The C

child is least able to interact with adults. His social behavior is generally negative and his intellectual competence is the lowest.

In 1969, the project moved into the home. From another base group of children, Dr. White chose 39 A and C children with younger siblings. The object was to discover how the mother who had already raised one A child related to the younger sibling, and how her techniques differed from the mother of the C child. Mothers of A children were designated "A mothers," those of C children as "C mothers." The study did not follow through with the B children at this point, because the researchers were concerned with getting a sharply defined picture of contrasts in child rearing. Also, little consideration was given to the role the father plays, because, as Dr. White explains, the mother is the one who spends most of the time with the child during this period, and she has the greater influence on him.

"When we went into the home, we told the parents only that the observers were interested in how children develop and in their daily experiences," explains Barbara Kaban, a psychologist who has been with the project since 1966—first as a research assistant, then, since 1969, as assistant director. "The parents were not told that they had been assigned an A or C rating—and they received *no* advice from the observers."

The mothers were asked to ignore the researchers and to go about their normal routines—cleaning, laundry, shopping. "We would just tag along," says Ms. Kaban, the mother of a preschool child. "It took a few visits before the mother was able to ignore us completely; after a while we were just there." While only one observer went into each home, all staff members (there are at least 10 people working on the project at all times), including Dr. White, worked with the families because, as he explains, "we didn't want anyone to lose touch with any of the families and the process."

The 39 home environments were studied one day a week for six months of each year. Twenty were followed from the child's first to third birthdays and the others from the child's second to third birthdays. At various intervals, the children were scored for social behavior and

"By the age of three, children should have acquired the ability to understand most of the language they will use in ordinary conversations . . . ," says Burton White, Ph.D. "If a child has fallen significantly behind his peers by then, it's hard to turn him around."

were given nonsocial competence tests for such skills as language and intellectual competence. But the main task for the researchers was to study behavior patterns in the home. Using stopwatches to time interactions between mother and child and tape recorders for dictating their observations, the staff kept track of the home situation.

"In the first seven or eight months of life, virtually all children are treated similarly and develop equally," says Dr. White. "But at about eight months, several things happen that change the relationship between mother and child. From that time on, there are distinct and apparently important differences in the ways mothers treat children.

"At about eight months, the child begins crawling and exploring. He becomes a menace to himself and to household possessions. A little later, he begins to display negativism—he says *no* frequently and refuses to cooperate. These factors," says the researcher, "create a double-barreled tension to which mothers respond differently and thereby seem to affect the development of the child in fundamental ways."

In the home study, the researchers found that C mothers, like Betty, were prone to put children into playpens or restricted areas, both to keep the home neat and to keep the child out of danger. "However, when the child is cruising around and making clutter, there are two important things happening," says Dr. White. "First he is learning to master the use of his body, but, also, he is demonstrating his greater curiosity. Suddenly there is a whole new world to be explored with a variety of things to learn and discover, and this curiosity is what motivation is all about. It's curiosity that moves a child ahead under his own steam when he gets into kindergarten and school.

"Curiosity is at a very high level in just about every eight-month-old child, but it can be squashed. I've seen three-year-olds who are already flaccid or have had their interests channeled into narrow areas. We believe it's because C mothers cut the child off from the wonderful learning environment found in the home."

The A mothers, like Jennifer, on the other hand, are usually less worried about clutter and accidents. If a child wants to try and climb steps, and every child will, the C mother usually will put the protesting child into a playpen or crib or place a gate in front of the steps. The A mother, however, is likely to take a few minutes to stand by while the child tries to climb and will protect him from hurting himself.

"Climbing steps a few times each day gives the child a chance to learn to do it safely," Dr. White says, but adds, "If it costs a mother too much to give in to a child's interests frequently, forget it.

"There is a balance to all of this. The child also has to learn that mother isn't always going to be at his beck and call. Although the A mother will usually respond to a child's attention-getting device, sometimes she will be too busy and say so, and the child is getting a taste of the future. He also has to learn that he can't do anything he wishes. Firmness is an absolute necessity. When the child is misbehaving, the mother will discipline him firmly and consistently. If, for example, the child is throwing his food around, she will remove either him or the food from the table."

The research indicated that A mothers generally enjoyed relating to their child and liked having him nearby. During this critical, early learning period, they were what Dr. White calls "designers and consultants." As designers, the A mothers had safety-proofed and child-proofed their homes so that, as they moved from room to room, the child could stay nearby and still be free to explore and play. To child-proof the home, says the psychologist, the mother will do such things as move good books and valuable objects out of the reach of the child, leaving instead old magazines and playthings in their place. "Closet floors in the bedrooms are emptied of breakable or hazardous items so the child can rummage among shoes and other things that aren't easily damaged," he explains. "In the kitchen, where mothers spend a lot of time, sharp utensils and cleaning liquids and powders are taken out of cabinets close to the floor and replaced with objects that the child can play with, such as plastic containers and bottles, baby-food jars, and bottle caps." For the most part, the A mother allows the child to flit around among ordinary household items; if he becomes bored, she may introduce him to something different to help arouse his interest.

Because the child usually is playing near the A mother, she also has many op-portunities to act as a "consultant." The mother may stop her work when the child asks for attention: She pauses for 5 to 30 seconds to explain something that has caught his attention, then goes on with her chores. "She teaches spontaneously," says Dr. White, "not in the formal didactic way that we associate with the professional teacher. If a child wants help because he can't put a big block on a small one without its toppling, she might show how to reverse the operation, putting the little block safely over the big one and then adding a third block. She is not only showing the child how to solve the problem but is staying one step ahead of him."

The A mother is teaching on the fly, but her instruction is effective because a brief learning situation relates to what the child is interested in at the moment. Out of this give and take the child is learning how to gain an adult's attention and how to use the adult as a teaching resource, explains the project director. The mother's encouragement and enthusiasm spur him to explore further and continue to initiate learning situations.

The researchers found that during these learning sessions, the A mother usually talks to the child. "This seems to be how the child learns language during the early years," says Dr. White. "And he learns rapidly." At first the mother merely puts a label on things, "Ball...Dog...Table..." But, she usually stays one step ahead of the child. She might say, "Roll the ball." It would be too much, however, if she said, "Roll the ball to the dog and then get the ball and put it on the table." According to the psychologist, it's not important that infants be able to speak the words, but that they understand them and can follow simple directions such as, "Give the ball to mommy."

These brief but frequent language lessons are more effective than merely exposing the youngster to a lot of words—which is what happens when mothers go into lengthy speeches or use TV as a baby-sitting device. The Harvard team found that C children, with less language ability, received the bulk of their exposure to language from television, while A children got live language from their mothers.

"It's not that television hurts children, but that most young children are indifferent to it," says Dr. White. "I know that some studies claim that one- and two-year-olds watch a lot of television, but these have been based on reports from mothers. When we go into a home and observe the child, we find that he really isn't watching very much or very steadily, perhaps because he doesn't relate to the programming. There are a few children, two and three years of age, who watch 'Sesame Street,' but they are the exception."

The study also found that the mothers' reactions differed noticeably when their children, at about the age of 14 months, began exhibiting their independence and saying no. "The A mother was likely to divert the child's attention or to be compliant," explains psychologist Barbara Kaban. "But hearing children say no was a signal to C mothers that their children were showing signs of becoming brats. This was snuffed out immediately with disciplinary measures."

"This response may sound like good common sense," says Dr. White. "None of us want children to become bratty. What's wrong with this so-called commonsense thinking is that it doesn't tell the parents what is really developing in the young child.

"Negativism is normal, and, in balance, a healthy sign of the child's development. It tells us that the child is developing an increased social awareness of himself and his relationship to other members of the family."

On the basis of the in-home portion of the study, the Pre-School Project developed a set of guidelines for effective child-raising practices (see box, page 61). These guidelines, if implemented early enough, could make the difference between an A or C child, says Dr. White.

"The A child is the one who probably will be at the top of his class in school," explains Ms. Kaban. "He also will be fully competent to cope with social situations and other problems. The B child is the average youngster. He won't be incompetent, but he will not stand out in any way. The C child, by the time he enters school, is the one in obvious trouble."

According to Dr. Hunt, this development of the child's potential depends on the quality of experience the child has when he is very young. "The research is pointing out that the quality of experience is just as important as the child's hereditary constitution in determining the rate of his development," he explains. "And it's probably more important than a good many other things. Unless you get enough of the kind of circumstances that pull at a child's potential, it just doesn't come out," Dr. Hunt continues.

Although there are no hard statistics on the numbers of A, B, or C children in this country, Dr. White estimates that only about 10 percent are getting the best early education or best quality of experience. "Probably about 25 to 30 percent of the child population falls into the C classification," he explains. "This leaves a great chunk of Bs—and we think that many of these Bs and Cs could move up with better early education."

To see that more children receive a better early education, the project is moving into the next phase—teaching women to be better mothers. Working with parents of young babies, and even pregnant women, in the Boston area, Dr. White and his staff are trying to determine how mothers can effectively be prepared to work as "designers and consultants" to their children.

"The feedback looks good," says Dr. White although this phase of the program still is not complete. "We believe that most women, regardless of economic or educational level, are capable of doing a fine job with their children."

The fulfillment of this expectation, says the psychologist, holds great promise for future generations.

How to raise a competent child

by Barbara Kaban and Bernice Shapiro

photographs by Peter Jones

Barbara Kaban is assistant director of the Harvard Pre-School Project; Bernice Shapiro is administrative research coordinator.

Sam is a cheerful one-year-old. His father is a doctor; his mother is a lawyer who has decided not to practice while her children are young. Sam's older sister and two older brothers are school-age.

All four children have free run of the house. The dining room is used as a play room; toys turn up wherever the children play. Generally, Sam can find something to play with in whatever vicinity his mother is working. Although they are frequently in close proximity, Sam and his mother spend little time in exclusive concentration on each other. When Sam seeks her out for information or help, his mother responds quickly, favorably, and enthusiastically, but these interchanges seldom last more than a minute.

Even at the age of one, Sam is fairly independent. He will approach adults other than his mother for help; if necessary, he may seek aid from an older child. When he asks for help or attention, he really needs it. He doesn't often cling. Like all children, though, he knows how to whine and cling when it suits him.

When Sam can't find anything interesting to do, his mother will introduce an activity, but she expects him to carry on by himself. She may pull a chair over to the sink, fill it with water and some toys, and invite him to play there. She doesn't mind his splashes and mess. This may occupy him happily for half an hour. A safe stool stays near the bathroom sink, so that Sam may

The Harvard Pre-School Project affirms that mothering is a vastly underrated occupation

wash his hands easily when he has to. His mother enjoys giving him such opportunities to be independent.

Like other one-year-olds, Sam is very preoccupied with climbing. His house has hard wooden stairs, which could be dangerous to him. But his mother likes to take the time to let him climb while she stands nearby and watches. She also lets him use a small slide in the playroom, keeping an eye on him as he does so.

When Sam does something that bothers his mother —such as Magic Marking the wall—she responds quickly and consistently, making clear to him that he's out of bounds. She may also decide not to put Magic Markers out for him until he is older, avoiding difficulties for both of them.

Like all children, Sam likes to be where other people are.

"Gee, that's *great*," his mother may say when he shows her that he has fitted two parts of a toy together. She appreciates what he does, and recognizes its worth.

Even an independent child like Sam needs much praise and encouragement; Sam may approach his mother for some kind of response as often as twice every five minutes. The response she most often conveys is, "Yes—you're a worthwhile, competent person."

David is a well-developed one-year-old. He has no brothers or sisters. A housekeeper takes care of him during the day, while his parents work. The housekeeper is restrictive. She doesn't want David's mother to think she hasn't been cleaning the house, so she keeps him confined. She may allow him a whole room to himself, but she gates him into it, essentially putting him into an outsize playpen. David's playroom seems to be filled with every imaginable toy, but the toys are never found outside that room. ·

When David's mother is at home with him, she feels she should entertain him all day long. She decides what he will play with. She may decide to build an entire farm with him, and gets out all the little animals and blocks herself. David shows more interest in rolling a ball, but she insistently redirects him to the farm.

David's mother is nervous about his attempts to climb stairs, so she blocks them off with a gate.

At the end of one weekend, David colored his bedroom wall with his crayons. Both parents were angry. David had not meant to taunt them; it was simply that the uncrayoned wall was not precious to him.

Both Sam and David are often hugged and kissed. The difference is that when Sam has been thoroughly

comforted after a fall, his mother puts him down again. Roughhousing, hugging, and kissing are all part of Sam's day, but when he squirms to get off his mother's lap, she lets him down. David's mother often keeps him in her lap long after the squirming begins. She often carries him, too, when he doesn't need it.

Food plays a more prominent part in David's house than it does in Sam's. David's mother and housekeeper often give him food for comfort or distraction. It is as if food is being offered in place of the human response David is asking for in approaching an adult. He gets a cookie instead.

David is scarcely aware that adults can be an attentive audience. He seems accustomed to adult contacts as a random series of affectionate or hostile encounters. He is learning that the activities he initiates are not the valued ones.

The most effective mothers seem to perform the functions of designer and consultant for their children's lives...

For nine years, the Harvard Pre-School Project has been studying Davids and Sams. Its staff is trying to discover what it is that helps young children become competent. This report on the project contains suggestions and encouragement for all who live and work with young children; words of caution, too, for mothers who expect to work full time during the early child-rearing years.

Between the ages of eight and seventeen months, most children force a test of

their family's capacity to rear children. The primary burden in most cases falls upon the mother. The start of crawling at about eight months—together with the child's intense curiosity, his poor control of his body, his lack of awareness of common dangers and the value of objects, as well as his ignorance about the rights of others—cause a great deal of stress on the child's mother (and whoever takes her place when she is away).

In addition, at the end of the first year of life a baby begins to reveal a rapidly growing awareness of himself as an individual. This identity is largely shaped through social interchanges with his mother. These interchanges also appear to shape the child's basic orientation toward people in general. Through interactions with his mother, he seems to be acquiring his basic style as a human being.

What does all this mean for the development of the competent child?

We believe it means a great deal. Studying children's emerging abilities as we do, we are struck by the obviously overpowering influence of social and motivational forces on a child's learning experiences. The very competent children we have studied certainly require an appropriate physical environment to learn in the impressive manner they do; but the essential ingredient seems to be the complicated but understandable, direct and indirect, *human* contact—most often with mothers.*

Since our professional interest is educational, we concentrate our observations on those portions of the child's environment that seem to influence his learning process in the most fundamental way. Consequently, much of what will follow has to do with maternal behavior and its apparent effect from the ages of eight to seventeen months. One point that emerges is that mothering is a vastly underrated occupation.

We believe that most women are capable of doing a fine job with their one- to three-year-old children. Our study convinces us that an effective mother need not necessarily have a high-school diploma, let alone a college education. Nor does she need to have much money. In addition, it is clear that a good job can be done without a father in the home, or without a happy marriage.

Many of our most effective mothers do not devote the bulk of their day to rearing young children, since many of them are involved in pursuing interests of their own, or hold part-time jobs. What they seem to do—often without knowing exactly why—is to perform the functions of designer and consultant for their children's lives.

By that we mean they design a physical world (mainly in the home) that is beautifully suited to nurturing the burgeoning curiosity of the one- to three-year-old, and they respond appropriately when the child approaches them. These homes have many small, manipulable, visually detailed objects, some designed to be toys, others designed for other purposes (plastic refrigerator containers, baby-food jars and covers, shoes, magazines, television and radio knobs, and the like). There are things to climb, such as chairs, benches, sofas, stairs, as well as materials such as tricycles and scooters to nurture more mature motor skills.

In addition to designing a large mea-

We have studied families subsisting at a welfare level of income, with as many as eight closely spaced children, who are doing as good a job as the most advantaged families.

sure of the child's physical environment, an effective mother sets up guidelines for her child's behavior. These play a very important role in his development. She is generally permissive and indulgent: the child is encouraged in the vast majority of his explorations. When the child confronts an interesting or difficult situation, he often turns to his mother for help. Although she is usually working at some chore, she is generally nearby. When he goes to her, she usually—but *not always*—responds helpfully and

enthusiastically, occasionally providing an interesting, naturally related idea. These ten- to thirty-second interchanges are oriented toward the *child's* interest of the moment, rather than toward some need or interest of the mother. It is in experiences of this kind that we believe an infant's intrinsic curiosity is effectively expanded by these skillful mothers.

At times, under these circumstances, the child will *not* receive immediate attention. The effective mother does not always drop what she is doing to attend to a child's request. If the time is obviously inconvenient, she says so, giving the child a realistic sense that the world does not always revolve around him.

These mothers rarely spend five-, ten-, or twenty-minute stretches teaching their one- to two-year-olds, but they do an enormous amount of teaching "on the fly," and usually at the *child's* instigation. Although they may also volunteer comments, they primarily react to overtures by the child.

Effective mothers seem to be people with high levels of energy. The work of a young mother without household help is, in spite of modern appliances, very time- and energy-consuming. Yet we have studied families subsisting at a welfare level of income, with as many as eight closely spaced children, who are doing as good a job in child-rearing during the early years as the most advantaged families.

Although a mother's effectiveness is influenced by her material resources, her attitudes about the following areas are particularly important.

Life in general. A woman who is seriously depressed or unhappy about life probably cannot do a good job of getting her young child off to a good start. None of our successful mothers has such attitudes toward life, while some of our unsuccessful mothers do.

Young children. Some mothers don't really seem to enjoy their children during the one-to-three age range. They spend as little time as possible with them; when they interact with them, they don't seem to get much pleasure from the experience. Some of our mothers who do poorly fall into this category, others do not.

*The Pre-School Project has not studied fathers, but the findings and guidelines discussed in this article apply to anyone with major responsibility for child care.

However, all of our successful mothers seem to derive a great deal of pleasure from their children during this age range.

The formative role of the second year of life. Mothers seem to vary considerably in their opinion of the formative role of infancy. We doubt that many of our less effective mothers believe strongly that this stage of life has profound significance for development. On the other hand, not all effective mothers do either. It is our impression that many of our most effective mothers perform excellently without any measurable degree of commitment to the idea that infancy is a crucial period in a child's development. They seem spontaneously to grant their infants generous measures of attention and consideration.

Possessions. There is a fair degree of incompatibility between a strong desire to preserve the contents of one's home and the normal tendency toward non-malicious destructiveness in young children. The mother who is very concerned about her possessions, and insists upon leaving breakable items on display during this stage of her child's development, is going to have a difficult time. Three possible routes are open to her. She can, by the habitual use of playpens, cribs, and gates, physically prevent her child from contacting many items in the home. (We believe this route produces frustration and stunting of curiosity in children). She may allow the child the run of the house and attempt to prevent damage by stopping the child with words or actions when he appears about to break something. (This route is often unsuccessful because of the child's limited understanding of words, and the normal development of negativism. At the very best, it results in a mother who is very frequently saying, "no, don't touch that!") Or, she may allow the child to roam, and accompany him in an attempt at constant supervision combined with gentle redirection. (This route is very time- and energy-consuming, and few mothers can afford it).

Housekeeping. Very few of our effective mothers are meticulous housekeepers. A few are, but most of them seem to have accepted the idea that an infant and a spotless home are incompatible. The problem is often aggravated by a husband who insists on a spotless home. The paths a mother of an infant may take to maintain a spotless home are similar to those for the preservation of possessions, and the pitfalls are similar.

Safety. Every infant has the potential for self-injury. The danger is very real. Again, mothers vary widely in how they deal with danger. Most of the ways that reduce danger carry with them the real possibility of reducing the child's normal curiosity and development. There is some research that suggests that children have more built-in controls than we give them credit for. The work on depth perception by Gibson and Walk (1960), for example, suggests that by the time children begin to crawl, they can skillfully discriminate depth, and furthermore are inclined to avoid moving off safe positions and injuring themselves. There are certain African tribes that allow their infants access to sharp weapons and utensils, with no apparent serious injuries resulting. It is our impression that infants are generally far more careful about protecting themselves than we think. We do not mean to suggest that no caution need be exercised, but there is a midground in the treatment of the problem of safety. Some mothers are overprotective to the point where they seem to interfere with good development.

Let us add a few additional words about the resources necessary for excellent child-rearing. Perhaps the most basic necessary resource is energy. A second necessary resource is patience. An infant can be very tiring. He is usually slow in many ways, and this slowness, combined with his comparatively modest learning abilities and his tendency to persist in repetitive behaviors, can torment an adult. Without a deep love for her child, a mother may not be inclined to devote much energy and patience to him. She needs time with the child, but not as much as we would have thought when we began our study. Not only have we observed excellent mothers with half-time jobs, but, perhaps more importantly, our effective mothers who are home all day spend less than 10 percent of their time interacting with their infants.

In what we have learned, we find much to be optimistic about. We are convinced that we have witnessed the effective shaping of young lives and nurturing of learning abilities at the most important formative period. We think we have partially unraveled the process. Finally, it seems to us that most American families want very much to give their children an excellent "early education," and that most of them have resources to do so.   □

The Pre-School Project:
Stalking the competent child

How did the Harvard Pre-School Project go about studying and measuring the competence of preschool children?

Since we could not find a detailed description of healthy, well-developed six-year-old humans in the literature on human development, we decided to observe preschool children in their natural environment.

Beginning with as broad an array of preschool children as we could find—our original sample consisted of some 400 three-, four-, and five-year-olds from eastern Massachusetts—we eventually selected 41 children for further study. Half were judged very competent, able to cope consistently in a superior fashion with anything they encountered in daily life. The other half were judged to be free of gross pathology, but generally of very low competence.

We observed these children each week for a period of eight months, both at school and at home, gathering information about their typical moment-to-moment activities. At the end of the observation period, we selected the thirteen most competent children, and the thirteen least competent. After thorough staff discussions about their behavior, we compiled a list of social and nonsocial abilities that seemed to distinguish between the two groups. We made no attempt to include all the abilities of children. We concluded, for example, that differences in motor and sensory capacities between children of high and low over-all competence were generally quite modest.

The resulting list of distinguishing abilities repre-

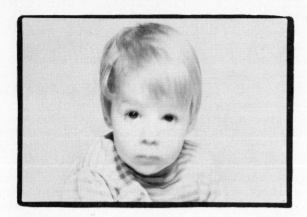

sents what we mean by competence in three- to six-year-old children.

Social abilities:

—To get and maintain the attention of adults in socially acceptable ways. To use adults as resources. To express both affection and hostility to adults.

—To lead and to follow peers. To express both affection and hostility to peers. To compete with peers.

—To show pride in one's accomplishments.

—To involve oneself in playing adult roles, or otherwise express the desire to grow up.

Nonsocial abilities:

—Verbal ability (to speak and comprehend).

—Intellectual ability (to sense dissonance or note discrepancies; to anticipate consequences; to deal with abstractions, i.e., numbers, letters, rules; to take the perspective of another; to make interesting associations).

—Executive ability (to plan and carry out multi-stepped activities; to use resources effectively).

—Ability to focus on two things at once (that is, the ability to sustain attention upon a task, and at the same time to monitor peripheral events).

Once we had a working definition of the competent six-year-old, we knew we had a basis for evaluating our eventual hypotheses about the role of experience in early development. For example, *using an adult as a resource* is an activity that almost all children engage in repeatedly, in one way or another, from the first months of life. The growth of each child's ability in that area can be monitored and assessed throughout the early years. Furthermore, the role of the mother as a potential resource appears to be of central importance.

Once we had described the distinguishing characteristics of the very competent six-year-old, we began to study the growth of these abilities. Our staff—numbering about twenty by now—came to a rather remarkable conclusion. *Our well-developed three-year-olds* (called 3A's) *performed more like four-, five-, and six-year-old A's than did our older poorly developing* (C) *children.* If we were to guess which group would have done better in first grade, had 3A's and older C's entered the following year, we would have chosen the 3A's over the 5C's and 6C's. This is not to say that 6C's have no abilities of consequence, but the general thesis seemed valid to us.

In the area of social competence, for example, we found 3A's routinely using adults as a resource in contrast to the C's of all ages, who demonstrated this ability far less often. Ability to concentrate on two or more things

simultaneously was a regular characteristic of A's regardless of age, but was rarely seen in C's.

The implications of our judgment about the remarkable level of achievement of some three-year-olds were most important for the project, and potentially for the field of early education. *If most of the qualities that distinguish outstanding six-year-olds can be distinguished in large measure by age three, the focus of the project could be narrowed dramatically, to the period from birth to age three.* Much of what we wanted to learn could be discovered by a close examination of the processes of development during the first three years of life.

The literature on human development during the first three years of life was the source of another judgment that shaped our efforts. Aside from extreme pathological cases, studies of infants from various socioeconomic backgrounds seem to indicate that developmental divergence does not become apparent until some time during the second year of life.

It appeared, then, that under the variety of early rearing conditions prevalent in contemporary American homes, differences in educability and over-all competence become quite substantial, in many cases, by three years of age. We therefore placed our focus on the second and third years of life.   — B.K., B.S. □

Pre-School Project guidelines for effective child-rearing

One result of the Harvard Pre-School Project's study has been the development of guidelines for the use of mothers of infants between five and seventeen months old. The guidelines that follow are being used in a training program for selected mothers in the Greater Boston area.

□ Provide access to as much of the house as possible, so that the child has maximum opportunity to exercise curiosity and explore his world.

□ Provide a wide range of materials for exploration. You don't have to spend a lot on toys. Children in this age range are fascinated by common household objects, such as plastic jars with covers, a big plastic container filled with interesting smaller objects, a baby-proofed kitchen cabinet filled with pots, pans, or canned goods.

□ Be available to your child for at least half of his waking hours. You don't have to hover over him con-

stantly, but you should be nearby to provide the attention, support, or assistance he may need.

If you are available and your child is given access to a large area and a wide variety of materials, it is inevitable that he will make overtures to you. Here are recommended ways of responding:

—As often as possible, respond promptly and favorably.

—Make an effort to understand what the child is trying to do.

—Set limits. Do not give in to unreasonable requests.

—As often as possible, provide encouragement, enthusiasm, and assistance.

—Use words as often as possible (ones your child will understand, or that may be a little hard for him).

—Use words to provide a related idea or two.

—Do not prolong the episode if the child wants to break it off. Such interchanges will often last less than a minute.

—Encourage "pretend" activities.

The above practices are related to the child's approaches to the mother. When they initiate interactions with their children, the effective mothers in the Harvard study usually follow these patterns:

—If the child seems bored, the mother will provide things for him to do.

—If the child is misbehaving, the mother will discipline him firmly and consistently.

—If the child is trying something new and potentially unsafe, the mother will monitor him rather than stop him (e.g., climbing stairs). Children are more careful than most people realize.

Here are some practices for mothers to avoid:

—Don't cage a child or confine him regularly for long periods.

—Don't allow your child to concentrate his energies on you to the point where he spends most of his time following you around or staying near you, especially in the second year of life.

—Don't allow tantrums to become habitual.

—Don't worry that your child won't love you if you say no from time to time.

—Especially from the middle of the second year, when your baby may start being negative, don't try to win every fight with him.

—Don't try to prevent the child from cluttering the house. It's an inevitable sign of a healthy, curious baby.

—Don't be overprotective, and don't overpower your child. Let him do what he wants as often as possible.

—Don't take a full-time job, or otherwise make yourself largely unavailable to the baby during this period of his life.

—If you can avoid it, don't bore your baby.

—Don't worry about the level at which he learns to read, count numbers, or say the alphabet. Don't even worry if he's slow to talk, as long as he seems to understand more and more language as he grows.

—Don't try to force toilet training. By the time he's two or three, it will be easy to do.

—Don't let your baby think the whole world was made just for him.

Reading Problems and Family Dynamics

Bruce B. Peck, Ph.D and Thomas W. Stackhouse, Ph.D.

Families in which one child is an identified problem reader were compared with normal families on a conjoint decision-making task. Reading-problem (RP) families took longer to reach a decision, spent a greater percentage of their decision time in silence, and evidenced fewer exchanges of explicit information and more irrelevant transactions. Results are discussed in terms of the communication atmosphere in RP families, a relationship between these exchanges and a child's reading disorder, and the RP child's role in the family system.

There are signs of a growing research interest in a relationship between family dynamics and children's school problems (Haley & Glick, 1972). Miller and Westman (1964, 1968), Miller, Westman, and Arthur (1966), and Peck (1970, 1971) investigated the possibility of a relationship between family interaction and a child's reading problem. Based on clinical-experiential data and psychotherapy contact, Miller and Westman (1964, 1968) found support for the idea that a child's reading disability is a condition of family homeostasis. Their observations of reading-problem (RP) families indicated that a reading problem in one child is symptomatic of an upset family system. Also, *both* parents and children appear to resist change in order to maintain this balance.

Peck (1970, 1971) argued that the RP child, as his contribution to the maintenance of the family system, has developed the *art of being stupid* – a skill which is similar to Feiner and Levenson's (1969) *compassionate sacrifice* and Haley's (1969) *art of being schizophrenic*.

These data and arguments suggest that RP families are similar in process to other "types" of problem families, i.e., the manifest RP pathology is a signal that the family as a whole is experiencing difficulty. Further, this system upset would be expected to show in the family's communication patterns – in the disturbed communications exchanged among the family members when they work together. This study is designed to pursue the "disturbed communication" hypothesis in families where one child is an identified problem reader.

Conjoint family decision making. The decision-making process is an effective medium for observing a family's communicative behavior. Winter and Ferreira (1969), in a series of studies, have used tape recordings of family decision-making sessions as a basic data source. With their results, they have developed the concept of *Family Pathology Cycle* (FPC) to explain the reduced communication effectiveness found in problem families which interferes with their decision making. The level of agreement among family members prior to a conjoint session (spontaneous agreement), the time required for a family to arrive at a decision

(decision time), the percentage of a family's decision time spent in silence (silent time), and the amount of clear, explicit information exchanged among family members are a few of the variables that contribute to the FPC.

Winter and Ferreira (1969) have shown that a continuum of problem families (neurotic, delinquent, schizophrenic), when compared with normal families, have a lower level of spontaneous agreement, take longer to make a decision, spend a greater percentage of their decision time in silence, and exchange a smaller amount of explicit information.

Explicit information exchange is a translation of Satir's (1964) system game, "Taking A Stand." This is a positive interpersonal interchange in which two or more persons exist as separate beings, free to be committed to his own wishes and still include the other. This rule allows for open negotiations on any issue in the context of basic trust and respect. In a family, the most effective platform for arriving at a conjoint decision would be for each person to "Take A Stand" on the specific issue.

However, problem families are conceptually and clinically observed to be notorious for poor decision making. They seem to be committed to not making a decision and devoted to confusion (Laing 1969, Haley 1959). This point has not been considered too clearly in previously family decision-making research. It has been assumed that the absence of explicit information is a key factor in the "disrupted" decision-making performance of problem families – not the presence of vague, inexplicit, ambiguous, irrelevant, and cryptic communications.

Even though destructive transactions have been widely discussed, they have not received significant empirical attention. The extensive exposure given these interpersonal activities indicates that they should be easy to identify in tape recordings of family sessions and that inter-rater reliability should be high. Thus, an additional purpose of this study is to test the hypothesis that destructive interchanges should appear more frequently in RP families than in normal families. Further, RP families are expected to be similar to other families caught in the *perpetuum mobile* of the FPC.

HYPOTHESES TO BE TESTED

Reading-problem families, in comparison to normal families (1) have a lower level of spontaneous agreement, (2) take longer to complete a decision-making task, (3) spend a significantly greater percentage of their decision time in silence, (4) evidence a smaller percentage of explicit information exchanges, and (5) manifest a larger percentage of system inputs that meet the criteria for System Games communications. There are more agree-placate,

attack-blame and irrelevant system game exchanges in RP families decision-making sessions (Satir 1964, Zweben & Miller 1968).

METHOD

The Families. Names of RP families were obtained from professional personnel in area school systems. Names of normal families were randomly drawn from area church and school directories. Ninety families (61 reading-problem and 29 normal) received an initial contact letter explaining that their help was needed for a family-opinion research project. Twelve normal families and 46 RP families declined to participate. Two families were eliminated after they had taken part in the experiment. In all, 30 families, 15 normal and 15 reading-problem, participated in this study.

Experimental subjects were Father-Mother-Son triads from intact families that had been together for at least two uninterrupted years. The son was between the ages of 9 and 13 and scored within the normal range of intelligence on available school data. With respect to the parent's age and educational level, family size, and father's occupational level, there were no significant differences between the two groups of families.

Reading problem criteria. Three factors were considered in defining the reading problem child: (1) The child's performance was unique such that he received attention from persons concerned with the treatment of reading disabilities. (2) Each child had experienced the usual sequence of educational events which should have provided him with an "opportunity to learn." (3) The child's reading retardation level was set at an observed reading score (Gates Reading Survey composite score) which was at least one grade below his expected reading grade as determined by the Bond and Tinker (1967) formula.

Experimental procedure. The procedure is similar to that reported by Ferreira and Winter (1968). Individual family triad members privately completed a 38-item Opinion Questionnaire (Mishler & Waxler 1968). In most cases in our study the RP child needed help. The second author read the questions and recorded the son's verbal choice.

After the questionnaires were completed, the family members were brought together in one room. They were instructed to arrive at a mutually satisfying decision for each of 20 items which had been selected from the privately completed questionnaires. These were items on which the family members had previously disagreed. They were, however, not told this fact; their differences were not revealed.

Finally, the family triad was left alone to discuss their choices and instructed to open the door to signal that they were finished. This session was tape recorded with the family's full knowledge.

Scoring procedure. The privately completed questionnaires were scored to determine the level of spontaneous agreement (SA) in the Father-Mother dyad and in the Father-Mother-Son triad prior to the conjoint session (Ferreira & Winter, 1968).

Two time variables were scored directly from the tape-recorded family sessions. *Decision time* was taken as the time in minutes spent by the family to complete the 20-item questionnaire. *Silent time* was defined as a percentage of the family's total decision time spent in silence. The percentage of silence was cumulated by a stopwatch. A reliability judge scored a random sample of 15 tapes for silent time as a check on the seeming coarseness of the procedure.

A Code Book* was developed as a guide for scoring the tapes and or training the reliability judge. It was structured on the basis of a central meta-message or rule for each System Game (Satir 1964, Zweben & Miller 1968). Explicit information, agree-placate, attack-blame, and irrelevant transactions were scored for each family's session.

The basic scoring unit was the speech or single, clear system input made by one family member. The first author and a reliability judge independently listened to the tapes until they each felt that they had accounted for the transactions that met the system games criteria. The judge scored a random sample of 14 tapes. Reliability was defined at the speech-by-speech agreement between the scorer and judge (inter-rater reliability).

RESULTS

Spontaneous agreement. An inspection of the means and standard deviatons for SA in the Father-Mother dyad ($\overline{X}_{RP}$ = 22.6, SD = 3.2; $\overline{X}_N$ = 23.4, SD = 3.0) and in the Father-Mother-Son triad ($\overline{X}_{RP}$ = 13.2, SD = 3.0; $\overline{X}_N$ = 13.8, SD = 3.0) reveals that they would not reach a criterion level of significance.

Decision time. The Mann-Whitney U performed on the decision time scores (X_{RP} = 37.09, SD = 13.81; X_N = 27.23, SD = 7.71) was significant beyond the .01 level (U = 52, n_1 = 15/n_2 = 15).

Silent time. A rank order correlation was run on the silent time scores for the original scorer and the 15 tapes scored by the judge. The reliability coefficient for the silent time scores was +.89. The Mann-Whitney U on the silent time scores (X_{RP} = 12.11%, SD = 7.12; X_N = 3.51%, SD = 2.48) was significant beyond the .01 level (U = 58, n_1 = 15/n_2 = 15).

System games. Table I shows the mean percent of the four system inputs for normal and RP families. The percentage is based on the total number of scorable acts for each family. The Mann-Whitney U for explicit information was statistically significant (U = 60, $P < .01$, n_1 = 15/n_2 = 15). An inspection of the agree-placate and attack-blame scores indicates that these differences would not reach an acceptable

---

A copy of the Code Book can be obtained from the first author (BP).

level of significance. The irrelevant scores Mann-Whitney U did reach a criterion level of significance (U = 62, $P < .01$, n_1 = 15/n_2 = 15).

Inter-rater reliability. Table II is a summary of the inter-rater reliability for each system game. The figures represent the percent input-by-input agreement between the original scoring and that of the judge. This based on a random sample of 15 tapes.

DISCUSSION

Normal and reading-problem families had the same level of spontaneous agreement. However, RP families took longer to complete the decision-making task and spent a greater percentage of their decision time in silence. The results also confirmed the expectations that RP families would evidence fewer explicit information and a greater percentage of irrelevant exchanges than normal families. Expected differences between the two groups on the agree-placate and attack-blame transactions were not significant.

The additional information provided by the system games results provide a more detailed picture of decision making in these two "types" of families. Normal families appear to be more efficient decision makers, not because they have higher SA, but because they exchange more explicit information, use fewer irrelevant transactions, and do not "waste" time in silence.

On the other hand, RP families appear to subscribe to the implicit rule, "We can handle only so much heat in our system and we will keep it cool." This rule is upheld by maintaining a high percentage of irrelevant transactions. Such a process could be called *irrelevant silent time* or *cool time*, "cool" in the sense that everyone is working to avoid the task of making a decision. Decision making requires confrontation, affect and direct statements of agreement and disagreement, i.e., "heat."

The combination of low explicit information, high irrelevancies, and extended decision time in RP families seems an operational definition of the family concept, *pseudomutuality* (Wynne et al. 1958). Reading-problem families appear to be caught in a pseudo-mutual impasse. The heat needed for

TABLE I. Mean percent of the System Games in normal and RP families.

SYSTEM GAME	Family Type	
	Normal	RP
Explicit Information	43.4%	26.5%
Attack-Blame	22.9%	22.3%
Agree-Placate	12.1%	15.5%
Irrelevant	19.8%	35.5%

TABLE II. Inter-rater reliability for each System Game.

SYSTEM GAME	Range (%)	Mean (%)
Explicit Information	82.2 – 98.0	89.5
Attack-Blame	58.0 – 91.5	80.7
Irrelevant	83.4 – 92.1	83.4

individuals to break out is invested in keeping the system cool by avoiding growthful conflict.

The above combination of communications is also related to the concept of *mystification* (Laing 1965). Mystification as a process is a technique for avoiding open, authentic disagreement through a misdefinition of the issue.

For example, RP families would often qualify the actual content, placing them in an irrelevant communication mode. From this base they would argue about arguing and often never reach a decision or confront each other (Peck 1970).

The system games results also suggest a definition of a normal family and confirm Mishler and Waxler's (1968) finding of "disrupted communication" in normal families. Normal families, in this study, used the irrelevant, attack-blame, and agree-placate games equally often, though less frequently than explicit information. Thus, in an environment fostering clear, explicit information exchange, the family members are free to use other games, yet not disrupt the decision-making process. In system games terms, a normal family is one in which the members do not avoid defining their relations with each other and are free to use any destructive game.

The communication atmosphere in RP families indicates that they tend toward being closed systems. Therefore, it would be expected that the learning potential of the child is invested in helping maintain the family system. Brodey (1968) has stated the problem very poetically:

> The family is the primal group in which learning how to learn begins. The child is taught how to learn before anybody is aware of teaching and the learning of the child how to learn teaches the parents how to teach as well . . . Then a family that teaches contact with what exists within it and around it and thus broadens its field of growth by teaching discovery. [p. 101]

Reading problem families apparently have taught the child how *not* to learn and the child has reciprocated by developing the *art of being stupid.* The RP family characteristically does not teach contact with what exists within it. This is evidenced by the lower percentage of explicit information exchanges. Further, since the educational process is equated with "teach discovery," it would be expected that children in such a family could develop reading and related school problems. Change and growth *via* learning are antithetical to the "way it is" at home. The act of going to school and achieving places the child in conflict with his family's process and his own identity as a family member.

Conversely, it is equally plausible to assume that the observed family dynamics are an adjustment to the presence of the RP child. Unfortunately, both interpretations presume a linear (if A then B) concept of causality, are mutually exclusive, and do not allow for the reciprocal, dialectical, ongoing nature of interpersonal systems such as families. The above results then are most useful in a discussion of the way in which these two groups of families operate. Future research using these procedures might be helpful to investigate whether family dynamics change as a function of remedial instruction for the child. Such an approach might clarify the relative contributions of the variables involved.

In summary, RP families apparently suffer from a process of reduced communication effectiveness that interferes with decision making. This is consistent with research using other "types" of problem families (Winter &

Ferreira 1969). Thus, there is good reason to argue that family concepts previously reserved for "schizophrenic" families are relevant to family processes in general. The fact that most early studies were conducted with families having a diagnosed schizophrenic member seems to have generated the view that something as "simple" as a school problem cannot be related to family dynamics.

Finally, these results indcate that a family-oriented approach to reading problems might be useful. Intervention into the family system could push it out of equilibrum, help free the RP child to learn through discovery, and release the parents from a painful bind. — *Lexington-Larpenteur Medical Center, 1124 W. Larpenteur Ave., St. Paul, Minn. 55113.*

ACKNOWLEDGEMENTS
This article is based on a dissertation study conducted with funds provided by the Graduate Research Council, Department of Psychology, Bowling Green State University. Esther Madaras, Marge Shoemaker, Suzanne Welty, Nanette Prosser, John Lustig, James Trautwein, Bruce Weatherly, and Dr. C. M. Freeburne are largely responsible for the administrative success of this project.

REFERENCES

Bond, G. L., and Tinker, M.A.: *Reading Difficulties: Their Diagnosis and Correction.* New York: Appleton-Century-Crofts, 1967.

Brodey, W. M.: *Changing the Family.* New York: Clarkson N. Potter, 1968.

Feiner, A. H., and Levenson, E. A.: The compassionate sacrifice: an explanation of a metaphor. *Psychoanal. Rev.,* 1969, 54, 553-573.

Ferreira. A. J., and Winter, W. D.: Information exchange and silence in normal and abnormal families, *Family Process,* 1968, 7, 251-256.

Haley, J.: The family of the schizophrenic: a model system, *J. Nervous and Mental Disease,* 1958, 129, 357-374.

Haley, J.: *The Power Tactics of Jesus Christ and Other Essays.* New York: Grossman, 1969.

Haley, J., and Glick, I.D.: *Family Therapy and Research.* New York: Grune & Stratton, 1972.

Laing, R. D.: Mystification, confusion, and conflict. In: I. Boszormenyi-Nagy and J. L. Framo (Eds.), *Intensive Family Therapy.* New York: Harper & Row, 1965.

Laing, R. D.: *The Politics of the Family.* Toronto: Hogarth Press, 1969.

Miller, D. R., and Westman, J. C.: Reading disability as a condition of family stability. *Family Process.* 1964, 3, 66-76.

Miller, D. R., and Westman, J. C.: Family team work and psychotherapy. *Family Process,* 1968, 5, 49-59.

Miller, D. R., Westman, J. C., and Arthur, B.: Psychiatric symptoms and family dynamics as illustrated by the retarded reader. In: I. M. Cohen (Ed.), *Family Structure, Dynamics and Therapy.* Washington, D.C.: Amer. Psychiatric Assn., 1966.

Mishler, E. G., and Waxler, N. E.: *Interaction in Families.* New York: Wiley, 1968.

Peck, B. B.: A communication analysis of family decision making in normal and reading-problem families. Unpublished doctoral dissertation, Bowling Green State Univ., 1970.

Peck, B. B.: Reading disorders: Have we overlooked something? *J. School Psychol.,* 1971, 9, 182-190.

Satir, V.: *Conjoint Family Therapy.* Palo Alto: Science & Behavior Books, 1964.

Winter, W. D., and Ferreira, A. J. (Eds.): *Research in Family Interaction.* Palo Alto: Science & Behivior Books, 1969.

Wynne, L., et al.: Pseudomutuality in the family relations of schizophrenics. *Psychiatry,* 1958, 21, 205-220.

Zweben, J. E., and Miller, R. L.: The system games: Teaching, training, psychotherapy. *Psychotherapy: Theory, Research & Practice,* 1968, 5, 73-76.

Des Moines Family Learning Centers

By MAUREEN MILLER
*Department of Community and Adult
Education, Des Moines, Iowa, Public Schools.*

Where can parents meet with other parents to come to grips with family concerns—a breakdown in communications, for example? Or where can groups of adults gather to seek answers to their personal challenges in dealing with topics such as alienation, self-acceptance, creative conflict?

Where can parents work side by side with their own children, preparing lessons, helping them learn? Where can parents, grandparents—adults of all ages finish high school or brush up on forgotten skills?

At Des Moines Family Learning Centers, people can do all these things and more. And, like the over 700 participants already served by the Centers, they can find that school at Family Learning Centers (FLC's) is unlike any classroom they ever remembered.

In an atmosphere of freedom, informality, sharing, and accessibility, the Centers offer adult education in several elementary school locations.

During the first three school years of operation (1972-75), the FLC project was federally funded under joint operation of the Department of Community and Adult Education of the Des Moines Public Schools and the Adult Education Department of the Des Moines Area Community College.

This school year, however, the Des Moines schools have adopted FLC, the first federally funded project the system has ever adopted formally.

The FLC project began with two Centers staffed by full-time specialists. The next year, four Centers were operating. The third year, with a much-tightened schedule and a lower ceiling on expenditures, six Centers were in force on a half-time basis with a half-time family learning specialist (FLS). One Center has now closed because of a population shift and a resulting decline in potential enrollees. Five centers are currently in operation.

The project involves parents, adults, and children in an educational process that includes both adult and elementary education. It offers to adult educators another answer to recruitment and retention of students and to elementary educators an effective means of involving parents in the education of their children.

Moreover, the Centers serve as hubs of school-community relations. They help tie in parent and community interest to the school through their easy accessibility and the variety of their programs. These include core FLC programs as well as classes arranged to meet each community's special requests. Some of the Centers receive "feed in" from school-community councils that look to Family Learning Centers as part of their overall focus on school operations.

The sharing, freedom, and informality are immediately apparent at the Centers. Shiny Parsons tables, colorful plaid davenports, and comfortable chairs are grouped in the discussion areas. Dining tables and chairs used for studying blend with the furniture islands, which store instructional material.

In this unstructured setting, learning is divided into two basic areas: the family block of education and the adult block of education.

The family block involves workshops on the principles of parenting and parent-child reading sessions.

Parents of all ages who are enrolled in the workshops gather weekly to tackle one common subject—"How Can I Be a Better Parent?" They zero in on a variety of topics, including "Helping My Child Feel Worthwhile" and "What To Do When Children Misbehave."

Comments from the parents indicate that the workshops help. "It was hard, real hard, putting these principles into practice, but they have paid off. My whole family situation has improved greatly!" said one mother.

Another said, "I no longer dislike being around my kids. I enjoy having them at home and don't dread school vacations."

The Family Learning Centers help tie in parent and community interest through their easy accessibility and the variety of their programs.

In addition to information learned from formal presentations, workshop participants gain much insight from informal group discussions. Various participants have said, "I thought I had problems, but when I came to the workshops, I realized my own troubles were minor." And, "It is comforting to know other parents are also having problems."

For the past two years, 10 workshops were offered and repeated cyclically throughout the year. This autumn, a new series of 30 has been adopted. The curriculum materials for these *Family Learning Center Workshops—A Series of Growth and Getting Along Together* consist of a moderator's outline and a package of worksheets pertaining to each topic. (These materials are available on request. Write to Dr. Gareld Jackson, Director of Community and Adult Education, Des Moines Public Schools, 1800 Grand Ave., Des Moines, IA 50307.)

The parent-child reading sessions involve parents in teaching their children according to each one's specific needs.

When a parent comes with a child, the Center specialist tests the child to determine individual needs. Then the parent is shown exactly what to do to boost needed skills.

Pretests (part of a packaged parent-child reading system) are given to determine the child's needs, which are then correlated with prescriptions showing the exact material parents can use to meet any of over 400 K-6 reading objectives.

Parents like these sessions. "I'm glad I can come to school and work with my child," one father said. "At home, we just never used to take the time, but we do now, for we realize how important it is!"

Both the parent-child reading sessions and the parent-discussion groups are under the direction of the family learning specialist, who serves in a managerial capacity at each Center. The FLS also moderates workshops for parents of preschool children, which, in some areas, are offered several times a year in cooperation with the school's Early Learning Center.

The adult block of education focuses on adults only. Some participants may be learning or brushing up on basic skills; others may be involved in an exciting language, logic, and comprehension program or a series of popular human relations workshops, *Hanging In There—Coping or "Copping Out."*

Adults may also be working in the high school equivalency program (known as GED). Instructors for these classes are from the Department of Community and Adult Education.

Coordinators from this Department also help arrange other adult education programs specifically requested by each community. As with the GED, these classes are held at times that do not conflict with the core Family Learning Center, a half-day operation. (The half-time FLS in each center handles the core programs, thus making the Centers also available for a variety of other activities.)

In the past two years, a family service specialist (FSS) has worked in all of the Centers, serving as liaison with legal, social, and psychological agencies whenever these agencies are the best-qualified to serve a client's needs. The FSS has also conferred with children; counseled adults; and assisted in recruitment of potential FLC participants, evaluation of program outcomes, and job placement for Center participants needing help in finding employment. Now, however, operating the five Centers on the smaller budget of the Des Moines schools precludes having these FSS services available this school year. The existing staff of Community and Adult Education has taken over the duties of the FSS. The five half-time family learning specialists are still at the Centers, however.

Various approaches have been used to spread the word about the FLC program. Publicity has ranged from home visits to media campaigns involving radio spots, news releases, and television spots. Other devices have included the use of fliers in churches, posters throughout the city, handouts sent home with children, and direct mailings. Teacher referrals to parents during conferences have also helped spread the FLC message. And during the past year, trained communication workers have made personal contact in their own neighborhoods.

From the beginning, the Centers have been known as "sharing places." There is sharing between teachers and FLC specialists as they discuss each child's progress, between school and parents, between school and community, and between the adult education and elementary school staffs. And there is sharing between parents and children.

As one thinks of the workshop participants all working together as a group, the statement of one father comes to mind: "The way I see it, when you help yourself, you help your child." □

Community Involvement in Metropolitan Nashville

By **JOHNELLA H. MARTIN,** *President,*
JUNE KENNEDY, *President-Elect, and*
GEORGE KERSEY, *Immediate Past-President,*
Metropolitan Nashville Education Association.

In the fall of 1970, the public school system of Nashville faced the first of two decisive federal court orders. The initial directive required full integration of each school's professional staff, thus eliminating predominantly black faculties and reassigning teachers so that all school faculties would be approximately 80 percent white and 20 percent black.

One year later came the second federal mandate: Schools were required to integrate, and no school was to have a majority of black students.

Carrying out this second mandate involved extensive crosstown busing, moving school opening hours up to as early as 7:00 a.m., and reorganization of about 100 schools (some were reorganized with only one grade; many, with just two; few elementary schools remained K-6).

Great community unrest resulted from these changes, and two political campaigns (one for mayor and one for U.S. Congress) aggravated the tensions. Both campaigns involved the same challenger who was opposing the incumbent each time and who made the federal court order his rallying point.

In both elections, the incumbents were reelected, which alleviated the growing unrest to some extent. However, as schools opened in September 1971, white parents picketed many of them, and students staged boycotts. In addition, Nashville's first large comprehensive high school opened, bringing together the students from at least three separate high schools.

Believing that substantive professional involvement is essential before any school system can make effective use of community involvement, leaders in the Metropolitan Nashville Education Association began working actively several years ago to improve the Metro Nashville Public Schools. They are committed to changes that will benefit the system, the teachers, and the students they teach.

Traditionally, teachers had looked to the PTA for community support. But implementation of the second federal mandate dealt this organization a stunning blow: Most PTA officers now found their children no longer attended the schools where they, the parents, had assumed leadership roles. Should they continue with their duties, or should they assume responsibilities in a new setting?

Local school staffs worked diligently to encourage parent participation in the affairs of the schools, making personal contacts, distributing newsletters, and organizing car pools.

Another factor in many secondary schools was the reorganization of the PTA. In recognition of the influence and the contribution students can make, parent-teacher-student associations were formed. These have proved valuable, not only in gaining the students' points of view but in increasing parent attendance at school activities. (Parents are almost always attracted to school events when their children take part.)

Despite all these efforts, some local schools lost their PTA units. Nevertheless, the PTA has survived in Nashville, and its voice is still heard in support of the public schools.

The court order placed other traditional programs in jeopardy. For a number of years, Metro Nashville Public Schools had scheduled parent-teacher conferences at the elementary level. On conference days, teachers were freed from student responsibilities to discuss with individual parents their children's achievements. This practice had proved worthwhile in promoting communication and understanding and in establishing rapport. With the neighborhood school no longer intact, could these conferences continue?

By using many of the methods that had ensured the PTA's survival (personal contacts, newsletters, car pools, and so on), the teachers and principals scored another victory for the schoolchildren of Nashville: Parent-teacher conferences are still alive and well.

Continuance of time-tested programs was a boon, but new efforts were obviously needed. In 1975, therefore, recruitment of community volunteers to serve in the public schools intensified. Under the leadership of former NEA President Helen Bain, a concerted campaign began to enlist volunteer help. Churches carried special inserts in their bulletins; press, radio, and television spots proclaimed the concept.

Since Metro Nashville Public Schools are divided into three districts (each with its own superintendent, but under one director of schools and one board of education), district committees were established to implement the program. These committees were to orient and train new volunteers.

(Students also serve as volunteers: Those from the senior highs and from Nashville's 11 colleges and universities, tutor low achievers on a one-to-one basis.)

It is too soon to make an evaluation, but if this program continues to operate as planned, with the program in each school built around the specific requests of each faculty, the verdict should be resoundingly favorable. Community people are in the schools giving service; but they are also able to observe and to report the experiences, problems, and achievements of pupils and teachers.

The goals of this program are best explained by its coordinator, Helen Bain: "Through the volunteer program, the people of Nashville will get to know and appreciate each other. It offers adults and children of different racial, ethnic, and economic backgrounds an opportunity to get acquainted and work together."

The results of another innovation, the Citizens' Advisory Committee, are being analyzed by professional educators. Originally proposed by the director of schools, the Committee was expected to encourage representative participation of citizens in the construction of the school budget and in defining priorities of the school program.

In some local buildings, the effort seems to be succeeding. Many elected teachers, principals, and lay citizens work together to establish priorities. This process continues at the district level. However, the central Committee has been a cause of concern. Its meetings have not invariably been represented by all racial, ethnic, or socioeconomic groups. The participants are well-meaning but busy people who receive most of their information from the central office staff.

Teachers and principals recognize the potential of the Citizens' Advisory Committee for supporting and contributing to the efforts of educators to achieve a better educational opportunity for pupils. Nevertheless, we believe that the Committee has been used as a tool against teachers and principals as they strive to obtain an appropriate salary schedule and a larger voice in curriculum decision making.

All programs are not universally approved, nor have all of them been properly evaluated. Just the same, Metro Nashville is proud that united effort has resulted in continued community support for the public schools. ☐

HOME-SCHOOL RELATIONSHIPS

Boise

By JO GOUL
*Specialist, Boise (Idaho) School
Volunteers, and Secretary, National
School Volunteer Program, Inc.*

"Thanks to her, we now have a complete bibliography of our multimedia kits for each of the teachers, catalog card filing is always up-to-date, and dozens of books get to the shelves much faster than they would if she were not helping."

"In the beginning I didn't want volunteers. Now I don't think I could get along without them."

The above quotes are comments from a librarian and a teacher about Boise, Idaho, school volunteers. Under the direction and guidance of professionals, more than 1,000 of these volunteers have responded to the invitation of teachers to help students in 37 Boise public schools.

Volunteers are not new to Boise or to education. The concept of volunteers in education is a deep-rooted one. In an earlier day in our nation, volunteers built schools, boarded teachers, and chopped wood for the school stove. School volunteer programs, as organized and coordinated activities, however, are relatively new.

Boise's program is similar in organization to the more than 3,000 other such programs in the nation. With the approval, cooperation, and financial support of the Independent School District of Boise, the Boise School Volunteer (BSV) office serves as the central coordinating agency for the recruitment, training, and placement of volunteers in the city schools.

The foremost aim of the program is to assist professional personnel in their efforts to provide maximum educational opportunities for all schoolchildren in the city. BSV tries to achieve this by relieving teachers of nonteaching tasks, giving special help to students with special needs, and enriching the curriculum by providing resources to the professional personnel.

School volunteers give their time, talents, and energies to help students develop a better self-image, become productive responsible citizens, and succeed academically.

Incidentally, they serve as public relations people, too. If there is a problem between school, home, and

Likes Its School Volunteers

community, volunteers may help bridge the gap.

The names of 300 persons who have specific interests or skills are on file in the BSV office. When these people, called Special Resource Volunteers, visit a class, they can bring enrichment to the curriculum and reinforce what students have been learning.

For example, for the past four years, a retired engineer, aided by his wife, has given more than 200 special resource presentations on American Indians and, in so doing, has thrilled students with his stories and collection of Indian artifacts—a collection which fills two 20-foot-long tables.

The five-year-old Boise program sponsors orientations, conferences, training sessions, a 15-hour workshop for volunteer reading tutors, a junior Great Books leadership training course, and social gatherings.

To a large extent, the success of the program is dependent on the local school volunteer coordinator. With the assistance of the BSV office, a community-wide Advisory Board, the principal, and the professional staff, the local coordinator serves as chairperson of the individual school program. The coordinator, who is usually a member of the board of directors of the PTA or other parent organization, attends faculty meetings and acts as a liaison between the community and school. The coordinator also stimulates parent- and community-volunteer involvement in the school and tries to interest teachers in involving volunteers in their class program.

All coordinators meet monthly with the BSV office and various members of the Advisory Board for orientation and problem-solving activities. After receiving requests for volunteers from teachers, they recruit them from their respective school communities. If volunteers are not available from the school community, the BSV office refers persons who have volunteered from the community at large.

Throughout the community, the BSV office recruits volunteers and makes the community aware of the program through the newspaper; television and radio; bumper stickers, tent cards, and posters; and slide presentations to groups, agencies, and organizations. In the local school community, the BSV office, the school coordinator, and various chairpeople recruit volunteers by sponsoring coffees, by sending fliers to parents through the students, and by telephoning.

A few Boise principals and teachers have been hesitant to involve the community in their schools. In criticizing the expenditure of $4,000 that the school district put into the volunteer program the first year, one principal stated: "Give me that money, and I will have the best program in the district." However, he was forgetting that the program serves all 37 schools, not just one, and that during the 1974-75 school year, the BSV office arranged for 846 resource presentations, each reaching 25 to 30 students.

If a volunteer program is to be successful, principals and teachers must want volunteers and know what they want them to do and why. Professionals may also need help in learning how to use volunteers effectively if the program is to benefit all involved.

Principals and teachers should be aware that they will be largely responsible for volunteer preservice and in-service training, requiring time and effort.

One volunteer states: "I feel most of the training has to come from the teacher. I also feel that the teacher-volunteer relationship makes a volunteer assignment successful or unsuccessful. I try to supplement what the teacher does and would hesitate to go into the classroom pushing my ideas. However, I do feel free to make suggestions and have been asked for my opinion."

Dependability of volunteers is sometimes the most important factor in teacher acceptance of them.

If occasions arise when a volunteer and a teacher cannot work together, the BSV specialist and the principal are the ones who deal with the problem. But, of course, any volunteer can be reassigned if either the teacher or the volunteer is unhappy about the working relationship.

As a result of its rapid growth, BSV has not had time to formally evaluate its accomplishments. Those involved in the program see a need for studies that would measure the extent of program acceptance by both students and professionals, student achievement, and any need for training of volunteers and professionals.

Despite various difficulties, however, school volunteer programs can do much to stimulate community interest, understanding, and support for education. This, in turn, can help pass bond issues, educate parents to their children's academic needs, and create more interest in the schools. □

Education for Parenthood

By **PAMELA KIRKLAND**
*Instructor, Exploring Childhood and
Psychology, Owensboro (Kentucky)
High School.*

Everything has its season; everything has its time, but time for the adolescent can be very frustrating and confusing. Having worked with young people for several years, I find this becoming more obvious every day. I see that this period of rapid change in our country is leaving its mark on the family as a unit and upon each individual within the family. I believe that we must look for ways to strengthen the ties of the family that are being torn by a fast-paced, seemingly apathetic industrial society.

Even in education, we have been failing our youth. With transmitting the culture and socializing the young as the central aims of education, we have left little time in the classroom for the students to discover their own feelings, needs, and frustrations.

During the summer of 1973, James Hilliard, the superintendent of our school system, and Duane Miller, the school psychologist, presented me with a program for high school students that was to be field-tested at 200 sites within the United States the following year.

The program, entitled Exploring Childhood, was funded and supported by three government agencies: the Office of Education, the National Institute of Mental Health, and HEW's Office of Child Development. The goals of the program include helping students to view childhood and adolescence as an important time for becoming a person, to develop confidence in their own identities, to understand their own beliefs and values, and to see how others experience the world.

Early on, we applied on behalf of the Owensboro

"When I completed the outfit by handing him the cane, I saw ➝ a burst of wonderful joy come over his face.

283

schools to participate in the testing of this program, and much to our delight we were accepted.

I have been teaching the program for three years. It expanded from 19 students at the start of the first year to 43 this year. The students are with me for two hours each day the entire school year.

The first nine weeks are devoted entirely to classroom activities. During this time, we study human growth and development, as well as desirable techniques for working with children. In these weeks, the students first begin to realize what the world is like for the child. For example, some of the activities involve making and placing on the classroom walls outsize figures of people, furniture, and animals to give students an idea of how the world looks to babies and small children.

After the students have stood next to these figures, they write down their feelings, describe how they would get the attention of someone whose belt buckle is at their eye level, or tell what it's like to look a dog in the eye! I think at this point they really begin to realize what a young child's world is like.

Within this nine-week period, I also prepare students for upcoming months of field observation and experience by engaging in role-playing situations and group discussions and by having children visit our classroom. These activities are followed by visits to various schools and grade levels for observations. Subsequently, each student spends about nine weeks working in each of three schools that have been selected to provide insight into a variety of factors such as socioeconomic class and into the characteristics of three different age groups ranging from four months to nine years.

Student field-placement sites during the past school year included five public schools (grades K-4), one private kindergarten, one private day nursery (ages four months through five years), and two special education classes, as well as private swimming classes for mentally retarded children.

The students go to the various field sites in a bus provided by the board of education. The fieldwork for each student includes one-and-a-half hours three days a week spent in direct learning experience at one of the field sites. This part of the program is unique, as it affords a real practicum in both seeing how well-qualified teachers work with children and in giving the students an opportunity to relate with young children and to observe them at work and play.

In the spring we spend about three months studying a variety of family group situations, such as the Israeli kibbutzim. During this time, we put up a bulletin board entitled We Are a Family. Each student brings in a picture of the family he or she lives with.

One of my objectives in the class is to help students deal with the reality of their own home and to take pride in their family. Aware that some students would be self-conscious about their family composition, I brought in a picture of my three children and me (I am now a single parent) and put it on the board. Within a few days the board was filled with pictures of students and various family members: one with grandparents, one with a sister and mother, one with parents and grandparents, one with 14 siblings and parents.

It was remarkable to hear students talking about the different compositions and sizes of families and the advantages and disadvantages of each.

An essential part of the program is the student journal, in which each student keeps a running account of classroom and field experiences. It is always rewarding to read the students' journals. Sometimes they make me laugh out loud, and other times they bring tears to my eyes. Let me give just one sample journal entry written by one of my senior girls:

October 31, 1974. Today I entered my field site all dressed for the holiday. It was Halloween, and all the kids were filled with excitement. They wore many different kinds of costumes. Some of the children who couldn't afford store-bought costumes wore paper sacks over their heads.

I arrived dressed as an old man with a big black hat and a coat and a cane. As I shook my cane at the children, I noticed a small black child with no costume whatsoever. I asked him if he would like to wear mine, and he jumped at the chance. I put the hat (about five sizes too big) on him. Then I helped him into the coat and rolled up the sleeves, which still came to his knees. When I completed the outfit by handing him the cane, I saw a burst of wonderful joy come over his face. What a thrill to have done a favor so rewarding as this. He was happy, and I felt as if he were my own.

Later on in the day the announcement came over the intercom that this little boy was the winner of the costume contest. He won a silver dollar, something he had never owned before. I also now own something (deep in my heart) that I never owned before.

The problems of the program have been few. I'd like to have more boys enrolled in the class, but the mistaken notion still seems to exist that a program involving child study is only for girls.

The rewards certainly far outweigh any problems I have had with the program. The principals and teachers we have worked with at the field sites have all been just great. I only wish they could read the student journals and realize the tremendous impact the program is having on my students' lives.

At this point, measuring the results of the program is difficult. There is some evidence that participating students come to understand the importance of childhood, the rewards and frustrations of parenthood, and the need for self-understanding. Doesn't this make it all worthwhile? □

XI. PEERS

The term peer is a quaint word signifying one's equal in rank, ability, or age. It has been taken over in America by behavioral scientists to refer somewhat technically and exclusively to peer groups, in the sense of a group of individuals of roughly the same age. The importance of the concept registered among educational psychologists during the 1930's, when psychiatrist Jacob L. Moreno invented the applied science of sociometry. Moreno demonstrated in *Who Shall Survive?* that the social perferences — telic bonds, he called them — of members of a group for one another could be diagrammed as network which depicted the interacting statuses and roles of peer group members. Moreno's technique, and a few elements of his theory, became a mainstay in educational and psychological research within a few years of his invention.

Peer group affiliations, interdependencies, and pressures are of importance because, as volumes of sociometric research have demonstrated, they *predict* and control a variety of behavioral outcomes for individuals, including school achievement. It is a truism that students learn as much or more from one another as they do from their instructors. Why might this be true, and what implications does it hold for reformulating conventional teaching and learning situations?

Social contact alone is both facilitating and depressing for learning of many kinds. There are types of learning tasks that are facilitated when people do them in mere proximity to one another. Similarly, there are a few types of learning tasks that are delayed or otherwise inhibited by the presence of other persons. When the stimulus of social contact is intensified through interaction, division of labor in the performance of shared activities, and group setting of standards, the stimulus is magnified in effect. When contact and interaction occur within a group of peers — that is, where there is some basis for mutuality, co-equalti,y and the attribution of significance to the other members — the stimulus becomes paramount. It can be exceeded in positive or negative reinforcement strength in an overall, gross way only by such competing sources of identification as *family* or other primary group membership.

All of this is generally true for peer groups of learners simply because of the psychological power latent in the combined processes of social comparison, social identification, group conformity, and fear of social rejection or isolation. These are processes which mediate between the abilities of the individual and his or her encounter with the task of learning a concept, a series of facts, or a skill.

The great importance of peer groups has been understood for centuries, wherever teachers and learners have gathered to study. The importance is by now so tacit, however, as to be overlooked by the exponents of common sense. The teacher stands before the group of students. The teacher requires recitation in the presence of a group of students. The students are graded competitively and their grades posted on the wall. These are all illustrations of the ways in which peer group influences are worked within classrooms, however unwittingly.

One of the tasks of educational psychologists is to reject what is tacit or to test it by making it more explicit. Thus, psychologists have experimented systematically for the last forty years with ability grouping, heterogeneous grouping, peer tutoring and peer counseling, and with using the very stuff from which sociometric attachments are formed as fuel for augmenting learning. The distance between convention and the frontier of knowledge in this as in many other instances is very great. Teachers go on standing in front of rows of alphabetically arrayed students. They go on grouping students on the basis of ability or decorum, or both. They persist in the custom of refusing to divide the labor of instruction among the members of the learning group in may schools. And, they assume that competitive grading of individuals aids learning.

Very gradually, however, the implications of experimental studies of group effects and peer group processes will begin to be absorbed by teachers and other publics. The paper by Roger T. Johnson and associates is included in this section because it expresses the way in which new knowledge can be used to redesign the conditions under which teaching and learning take place. As they conclude, "for optimum pupil motivation, it seems essential that teachers have the ability to structure cooperative classroom situations."

The article by Donald R. Rardin and Charles E. Moan shows how peer group data may be used by educational psychologists to explore dimensions of cognitive development. Their exploration invites speculation about the positive uses of peer interaction for designing learning tasks and for decisions about when to make effective use of psychotherapy. The article by Robert A. Dentler and Bernard Mackler illustrates the ways in which peer groups, espcially under conditions set by adults, may function to *depress* growth and development. The same state training school for retarded children could use the resources of peer groups to enhance growth, naturally.

Cooperation and Competition in the Classroom

Roger T. Johnson
David W. Johnson
Brenda Bryant

Most classroom work is structured so that individual pupils compete with one another for school marks and other rewards. Some pupils find competition compatible with their needs. Other pupils do not (1), and for them classroom work can be structured in ways that encourage cooperation rather than competition. The study reported here focuses on two variables. One is a personality variable. The other is a classroom structural variable. The personality variable focuses on the individual's center of control, which he may see as internal or external. The structural variable focuses on the attitude encouraged by the classroom structure—an attitude of cooperation or an attitude of competition. The researchers were interested in having pupils who externalized and pupils who internalized classify their classrooms as cooperative or competitive and to state their preference for classroom structure.

Much research has been conducted on the effects of cooperative and competitive structures on pupils' behavior in the classroom. A cooperative classroom structure may be defined as one in which the goals of the separate pupils are so linked that their goal attainments are positively related (2). Under purely cooperative conditions, an individual can attain his goal if, and only if, the individual with whom he is linked can attain his goals. When a pupil behaves in such a way as to increase his chances of attaining his goal, he increases the chances that the other pupils will also attain their goals. Deutsch (2) describes three psychological consequences of such a state. The first consequence is substitutability. Substitutability is present when actions of members in a cooperative relationship are interchangeable. If one member has engaged in a certain behavior, there is no need for others in the relationship to repeat the behavior. The second consequence is positive cathexis, which may be described as favorable evaluation. If the actions of one member in a cooperative relationship move the individuals toward their goal, his actions—and he as an individual—will be favorably evaluated by the others. The third consequence is inducibility, or receptivity to efforts to persuade. If the actions of one member in a cooperative relationship move the others toward their goal, they will be receptive to his attempts to induce them to engage in behavior that will facilitate his actions.

A competitive classroom situation may be defined as one in which the goals of the separate pupils are so linked that their goal attainments are negatively related (2). Under purely competitive conditions a pupil can attain his goal if, and only if, the others cannot attain their goals. In such a situation one may expect the oppositive of substitutability, positive cathexis, and positive inducibility.

Research on the effects of cooperative and competitive classroom structures reports three major findings:

1. Cooperation results in higher achievement than competition in studies involving some type of problem-solving (3-8). Results based on overall achievement on objective tests are not clear (2). When the task is simple drill, results may favor the pupil who works alone (9).

2. In the area of interpersonal skills, subjects in cooperative situations engage in more integrating behavior and less dominating behavior (10-12). They are described as being friendlier and more secure, as learning one another's names more easily and more rapidly, as being more satisfied, more attentive to—and more influenced by—what fellow members say. In contrast, the subjects in competitive situations are described as aggressive, obstructive, oppositional, and self-defensive (2).

3. Competition increases anxiety in pupils who are performing a motor-steadiness test (12). It is also reported that subjects in a competitively structured discussion are more anxious. They lose self-assurance, show more self-oriented needs, are less able in recitation and more dissatisfied with discussion. Pupils in a cooperatively structured discussion are described as less tense, more task oriented, more effective in working together, enjoying discussion, and covering more material (13).

On the basis of this research it may be concluded that a cooperative classroom structure, in comparison with a competitive classroom, will result in higher achievement in problem-solving, more positive interpersonal interaction among pupils, and less pupil anxiety. Such research, however, fails to take into account individual differences among pupils that may lead them to prefer a cooperative or a competitive classroom structure. It may be concluded that pupils who prefer individual competition will be most highly motivated in a classroom structure that encourages competition between individual pupils, and pupils who prefer cooperation will be most highly motivated in a cooperative classroom structure. In this study the individual-difference variable focused on what each child believed to be his locus of control.

In studies of the locus of control, subjects are classified into two categories: internalizers and externalizers. Internalizers generally attribute their successes or failures to themselves. Externalizers attribute their successes or failures to powerful others, fate, chance. The research on locus of control reports four major findings:

1. Internalizers demonstrate higher school achievement than externalizers (14-18).

2. In the area of interpersonal skills, internalizers are described as more successful in changing the attitudes of others (19) and measure higher on indices of social and personal adjustment (20). Externalizers exhibit less interpersonal trust (21).

3. Studies that compare the anxiety of internalizers and externalizers associate externalizers with greater anxiety and neuroticism (22-25). Butterfield (21) noted that internalizers adapt to situations better than externalizers do, especially when the situation arouses anxiety.

4. Cromwell and his associates (25) found results which suggest that when working on a task externalizers prefer to receive direction and help more than internalizers do.

The research on cooperation and competition and on locus of control led to three hypotheses:

1. Because of the traditional emphasis on individual competition in schools, it is hypothesized that the majority of the subjects interviewed, regardless of whether they are internalizers or externalizers, will perceive their classroom structure as competitive.

2. On the basis of the research which indicates that pupils in cooperative structures are more friendly, satisfied, secure, and attentive to one another than pupils in competitive structures, it is hypothesized that the majority of pupils, regardless of whether they are internalizers or externalizers, will prefer a cooperative classroom structure. However, when one compares the classroom-structure preferences of

externalizers and internalizers, there is reason to expect a difference.

3. The third hypothesis stems from the previously cited research which indicates that, in competitive situations, externalizers are more susceptible to anxiety than internalizers are, and that externalizers want to be directed and helped by others when working on a task, while internalizers want to accomplish the task by themselves. On the basis of these findings, it is hypothesized that more externalizers than internalizers prefer a cooperative classroom structure.

The children who took part in the study were from twenty sixth-grade classrooms in a suburban community of Minneapolis. All sixth-grade pupils available on the day of testing were screened by using the Intellectual Achievement Responsibility Questionnaire, which was developed by Crandall, Katkovsky, and Preston (16). This is a forced-choice test designed to determine whether in situations involving intellectual achievement children feel that control is internal or external. From each of the twenty classrooms the researchers selected the boy who was the most extreme externalizer and the boy who was the most extreme internalizer. The extreme internalizers and the extreme externalizers were those who were the most consistent in their answers in terms of these categories and therefore the most appropriate for this study. In screening internalizers and externalizers, the sex of the subject was found to have little relation to results on the Intellectual Achievement Responsibility Questionnaire. Therefore, boys were selected to facilitate another part of the research (26). Any child whose intelligence quotient was below 90 was eliminated from the study; only one child was eliminated on this basis. The resulting sample was made up of twenty externalizers and twenty internalizers. In general, the group of internalizing boys and the group of externalizing boys did not differ in intellectual level or social status. A more detailed description of the sample appears in Bryant's report (26).

To get data for the study, interviews ten to fifteen minutes long were held with each child. The test instrument used during the interviews was developed by the investigators. It was designed to measure the subjects' perception of the cooperativeness or the competitiveness of their classroom structure and to get information on whether they preferred a cooperative classroom structure or a competitive classroom structure. The instrument consisted of three pairs of photographs. One photograph in the pair depicted an aspect of cooperative classroom structure; the other photograph depicted competitive classroom structure. Each photograph was accompanied by a story two or three sentences long describing each of the situations picture. The pupils in the pictures and the classroom background in the pictures were held constant. Only the pupil activity varied. The stories focused on the specified variables and excluded interfering variables.

The three pairs of photographs and stories were based on Deutsch's (2) definitions of *cooperation* and *competition* and dealt with three subjects: interaction, substitutability, and positive cathexis. In one photo on interaction, pupils were conferring with one another and sharing ideas. In the other photo on interaction, pupils were working individually with no interaction. In one photo on substitutability, each pupil was doing part of the assignment, then their work was combined to complete the entire assignment. In the second photograph on substitutability, each pupil in a group completed the entire assignment individually. In the first picture on positive cathexis, one group of pupils was congratulating a pupil on his good idea, which contributed to the success of the entire group. In the second picture on positive

cathexis, the group continued to work while a pupil raised his hand to share his idea with the teacher privately.

During the interviews the photographs were displayed and the stories were read. Each child was asked, "Which is more like school?" After the subject made a choice, he was asked to explain why he had made the choice. The subject was then asked, "Which of these do you prefer?" He was again asked to explain his response. The same instructions were given to each subject. In each pair of stories and pictures, the order of presentation to the subjects was randomized to eliminate possible effects of order in the subjects' responses.

Table 1 reports the number of externalizers and internalizers who perceived their classroom as cooperative or competitive in structure and their preferences in structure. Each subject was classified in two ways: on his perception of his classroom as competitive or cooperative in structure and on his preference for classroom structure. Each classification was made by pooling the subject's responses on the three related aspects of cooperation and competition. If a subject's responses to the three aspects were not all competitive or all cooperative, he was classified on the basis of the majority of his responses. Thus, a subject was classified as perceiving a competitive structure if he responded with two competitive responses and one cooperative response when he was asked, "Which of these is more like school?"

The authors were interested primarily in the descriptive material made available by the interview, but have computed *p* values for the data using binomial tables (27) and 2 x 2 contingency tables (28). The authors have made their own interpretation of the data, but the reader is encouraged to examine the data and draw his own conclusions.

The first hypothesis deals with the subjects' perception of their classroom structure. As Table 2 indicates, only a minority of subjects perceived their classroom structure as cooperative: 20 per cent of the externalizers and 15 per cent of the internalizers classified their classrooms as cooperative, while 80 per cent of the externalizers and 85 per cent of the internalizers classified their classrooms as competitive. When the responses were combined, 17.5 per cent of the subjects classified their classrooms as cooperative and 82.5 per cent classified their classrooms as competitive. On the basis of binomial tables and a predicted result of .5, these results are significant at the .01 level and support Hypothesis 1.

Table 1. *Perceptions of, and Preferences in, Classroom Structure Reported by Externalizers and internalizers*

Locus of Control and Perception of Classroom Structure	Preference in Classroom Structure		
	Cooperation	Competition	Total
Externalizers			
Cooperation	4	0	4
Competition	11	5	16
Total	15	5	20
Internalizers			
Cooperation	3	0	3
Competition	8	9	17
Total	11	9	20

Table 2. *Number and Per Cent of Pupils Who Perceived Classroom Structure as Cooperative or Competitive**

	Perceiving Cooperation		Perceiving Competition		Total	
	Number	Per Cent	Number	Per Cent	Number	Per Cent
Externalizers	4	20	16	80	20	100
Internalizers	3	15	17	85	20	100
Total	7	17.5	33	82.5	40	100

* Significant at the .01 level on the basis of binomial tables and a predicted result of .5.

Table 3. *Number and Per Cent of Pupils Who Preferred a Cooperatively Structured Classroom or a Competitively Structured Classroom**

	Preferring Cooperation		Preferring Competition		Total	
	Number	Per Cent	Number	Per Cent	Number	Per Cent
Externalizers	15	75	5	25	20	100
Internalizers	11	55	9	45	20	100
Total	26	65	14	35	40	100

* Significant at the .01 level on the basis of binomial tables and a predicted results of .5.

The second hypothesis states that the majority of subjects, whether they are internalizers or externalizers, prefer a cooperative classroom structure. The data reported in Table 3 support this hypothesis ($p = .01$). When the information collected on the three aspects of cooperation-competition was pooled, 65 per cent of the subjects preferred a cooperative classroom structure. Their verbal comments indicated a belief that "working together" was "easier," "more fun," provides "more and better ideas," and results in a "better" product. The subjects who did not prefer a cooperative environment indicated a strong "work" orientation and confidence in the efficiency of "working alone."

The third hypothesis states that more externalizers than internalizers prefer a cooperative classroom structure. The results in Table 3 indicate general support for the hypothesis. When the responses to the three aspects of cooperation-competition were pooled, 75 per cent of the externalizers preferred a cooperative classroom while only 55 per cent of the internalizers did so. No subject who perceived himself in a cooperatively structured classroom preferred a competitive environment, as Table 1 shows. Subjects who perceived themselves in a cooperative structure form a small per cent of the total sample. The major share of the subjects preferred a cooperatively structured classroom, but perceived a competitive structure. Of the sixteen externalizers who perceived a competitive structure, eleven (69 per cent) preferred a cooperative structure. Of the seventeen internalizers who perceived a competitive structure, only eight (47 per cent) preferred a cooperative structure.

Although the difference in perception between internalizers and externalizers does not represent a significant diffrence at the .05 level of significance, the direction of the data is strengthened by the verbal responses of those internalizers who preferred to be in a competitively structured classroom. Their comments indicated confidence in their ability to achieve and lack of threat in working alone.

The results of this study have implications for the literature on locus of control and for the literature on cooperation and competition. In regard to locus of control, the pupils in this study who believe that the locus of control of their behavior is external prefer a cooperatively structured classroom. Cooperative situations produce less anxiety than competitive ones. It is more important for externalizers than internalizers to be in low-anxiety situations. Externalizers like direction and help in working on a task. Externalizers prefer interpersonal support in their environment. Thus,

cooperatively structured school situations may well promote the adaptation and the achievement of the externalizing pupil. Internalizing pupils seem to be able to adapt to either a cooperative structure or a competitive structure. Once they have adapted they tend to prefer the structure to which they have adapted. Yet 45 per cent of the internalizing pupils who perceived their classroom as competitively structured preferred a cooperative structure. Thus, even with internalizers a cooperative classroom structure may facilitiate achievement.

The research on cooperative and competitive classroom structures indicates that cooperative structures may be more promotive of problem-solving by pupils, of positive interpersonal interaction among pupils, and of lower levels of pupil anxiety than competitive structures. Yet most teachers seem to structure the classroom so that individuals complete with one another. The results of this study indicate that, for the most part, the pupils interviewed perceive their classrooms as competitively structured but prefer a cooperative structure. Externalizers show an especially strong preference for a cooperative structure.

No research has been done on the effects of compelling pupils to operate in a classroom structure they do not prefer. Yet it seems reasonable to assume that the degree to which a child prefers the classroom structure in which he operates will affect his motivation to achieve in the structure. One could speculate, therefore, that large numbers of pupils, internalizers and externalizers, are less motivated to achieve in the classroom than they could be if they were in a cooperative classroom structure. For optimum pupil motivation, it seems essential that teachers have the ability to structure cooperative classroom situations. Research in industrial settings indicates that as employee satisfaction goes up, performance on the job improves (29). If pupils' satisfaction with school can be increased by placing them in the type of classroom structure they prefer, it is possible that their performance on classroom tasks will improve and their disruptive behavior will decrease.

It is important that more attention be given in teacher training to the ways in which cooperation may be structured into classroom activities. The use of cooperative structures in the classroom does not eliminate competition. Much of the research on cooperation and competition in the classroom indicates that the most productive arrangement may be one that encourages competition between groups and cooperation within groups (30). Many behavioral scientists and educators would agree with Sexton (31: 268-69) when she wrote:

The present, highly competitive system of marks, exams and comparisons of all sorts should be replaced by other types of incentives to learn. If there is to be competition, emphasis should be on group rather than on individual competition. Marks and grades hurt more than they help; they discourage students from studying "hard" subjects or taking good but tough teachers; they discourage really independent and critical thinking.

REFERENCES

1. Philip W. Jackson. *Life in Classrooms.* New York, New York: Holt, Rinehart and Winston, 1968.
2. M. Deutsch. "A Theory of Cooperation and Competition," *Human Relations, 2* (April, 1949), 129-52.
3. J. C. Almack. "Mental Efficiency of Consulting Pairs," Ohio State University *Educational Research Bulletin, 10* (January, 1930), 2-3.
4. S. F. Klugman. "Cooperation vs Individual Efficiency in Problem-Solving," *Journal of Educational Psychology, 35* (January, 1944), 91-100.

5. M. E. Shaw. "Some Motivational Factors in Cooperation and Competition," *Journal of Personality, 26*
(June, 1958), 155-69.

6. S. C. Jones and V. H. Vroom. "Division of Labor and
Performance under Cooperative-Competitive Condi-
tions," *Journal of Abnormal Social Psychology, 68*
(March, 1964), 313-20.

7. H. Gurnee. "Learning under Competitive and Collaborative Sets," *Journal of Experimental Social Psychology,
4* (January, 1968), 26-34.

8. J. B. Maller. *Cooperation and Competition.* New York,
New York: Teachers College, Columbia University,
1929.

9. H. H. Anderson. "Domination and Integration in the
Social Behavior of Kindergarten Children in Experimental Play Situations," *Genetic Psychology Monographs, 21* (1939), 357-85.

10. Sing-chi Tseng. "An Experimental Study of the Effect
of Three Types of Distribution of Reward upon Work
Efficiency and Group Dynamics." Unpublished manuscript. New York, New York; Teachers College, Columbia University, 1952.

11. J. W. Julian and F. A. Perry. "Cooperation Contrasted
with Intra-Group and Inter-Group Competition,"
Sociometry, 30 (March, 1967), 79-90.

12. G. M. Vaught and S. F. Newman. "The Effect of Anxiety on Motor Steadiness in Competitive and Non-
Competitive Conditions," *Psychonomic Science, 6* (December, 1966), 519-20.

13. D. B. Haines and W. J. McKeachie. "Cooperative vs
Competitive Discussion Methods in Teaching Introductory Psychology," *Journal of Educational Psychology,
58* (December, 1967), 386-90.

14. J. S. Coleman, E. Campbell, C. J. Hobson, J. McPort-
land, A. M. Mood, F. D. Weinfeld, and R. L. York.
Equality of Educational Opportunity. Catalog Number
FS 5.238:38001. Washington, D.C.: Government Printing Office, 1966.

15. P. McGhee and V. C. Crandall. "Beliefs in Internal-
External Control of Reinforcements and Academic Performance," *Child Development, 39* (March, 1968),
91-102.

16. V. C. Crandall, W. Katovsky, and A. Preston. "Motivational and Ability Determinants of Young Children's
Intellectual Achievement Behaviors," *Child Development, 33* (September, 1962), 3.

17. V. C. Crandall, W. Katkovsky, and V. J. Crandall.
"Children's Beliefs in Their Own Control of Reinforce-
ment in Intellectual-Academic Achievement Situations,"
Child Development, 36 (March, 1965), 91-109.

18. W. L. Davis and E. J. Phares. "Internal-External Control as a Determinant of Information-Seeking in a Social
Influence Situation," *Journal of Personality, 35* (December, 1967), 546-61.

19. P. D. Hersch and K. E. Schiebe. "Reliability and Val-
idity of Internal-External Control as a Personality
Dimension," *Journal of Consulting Psychology, 31*
(December, 1967), 609-13.

20. J. H. Hamsher, J. D. Geller, and J. B. Rotter. "Interpersonal Trust, Internal-External Control and the
Warren Commission Report," *Journal of Personality
and Social Psychology, 9* (July, 1968), 210-15.

21. E. Butterfield. "Locus of Control, Text Anxiety, Reactions to Frustration and Achievement Attitudes,"
Journal of Personality, 32 (September, 1964), 355-70.

22. D. Watson. "Relationship between Locus of Control
and Anxiety," *Journal of Personality and Social Psychology, 6* (May, 1967), 91-92.

23. N. T. Feather. "Some Personality Correlates of External
Control," *Australian Journal of Psychology, 19* (December, 1967), 253-60.

24. E. Lichtenstein and S. Ketzer. "Further Normative and
Correlational Data on the Internal-External (IE) Control of Reinforcement Scale," *Psychological Reports,
21* (December, 1967), 1014-16.

25. R. L. Cromwell, D. Rosenthal, D. Shakow, and T. P.
Zahn. "Reaction Time, Locus of Control, Choice Behavior, and Descriptions of Parental Behavior in Schizophrenic and Normal Subjets," *Journal of Personality,
29* (December, 1961), 363-80.

26. Brenda Bryant. "Student-Teacher Relationships as Related to Internal-External Locus of Control." Unpublished thesis. Minneapolis: University of Minnesota,
1971.

27. E. S. Pearson and H. O. Harley (editors). *Biometrika
Tables for Statisticians, I.* New York, New York: Cambridge University Press, 1954.

28. D. S. Finney. *Tables for Testing Significance in a 2 x 2
Contingency Table.* New York, New York: Cambridge
University Press, 1963.

29. R. Kahn and D. Katz. "Leadership Practices in Rela-
tion to Predictivity and Morale." In *Group Dynamics:
Research and Theory.* Edited by D. Cartright and A.
Zander. New York, New York: Harper and Row, 1960.

30. David W. Johnson. *The Social Psychology of Education.* New York, New York: Holt, Rinehart and Winston, 1970.

31. P. Sexton. *Education and Income.* New York, New
York: Viking Press, 1961.

Peer Interaction and Cognitive Development

Donald R. Rardin
Charles E. Moan

81 children from 1 classroom each of kindergarten, first, second, and third grades were ranked on measures of popularity, cognitive and social development. The measure of social development, developed for this study, consisted of combined ratings from 4 measures: Reason for Friendship, Stability of Friendship, Names Not Known, and Congruency of Friendships. The 2 measures of physical concept development was conservation and classification. Piaget proposed that, during the grades studied, physical and social concepts are closely related to each other and are parallel in their development. He also proposed that various systems of cognition are becoming interconnected during this period and that peer interaction is a causal force helping to bring about this qualitative change in cognition. 2 hypotheses, based on these formulations, were examined. The first, that peer relations develop in a manner parallel to the development of physical concepts, was significantly supported. Both cognitive and social skills progress from kindergarten through the third grade in a similar manner. A second hypothesis was that a child's cognitive development would be directly affected by the quality of his peer relations, as judged by popularity rankings. Popularity was found to be closely related to social development, but its relations to measures of physical concept development were relatively minor.

It has been proposed by many developmental theorists that cognitive processes are highly interrelated and interdependent, while learning theorists generally propose processes which are comparatively independent and whose relatedness is an experiential function. The present study primarily concerns the former position and, in particular, cognitive development as proposed by Jean Piaget.

In Piaget's system, *structure* is seen as interposed and mediating between *content* and *function*. Briefly, function refers to the manner of cognitive progress; content refers to external behavior; and, structure refers to inferred organizational properties which explain why particular content occurs (Flavell 1963). Cognitive progress is possible through the interaction of assimilation and accommodation. Accommodative acts are always being extended to new and different features of the surround; and, to the extent that a newly accommodated feature can fit somewhere in the existing structure, it will be assimilated. Through assimilation, the structure is changed and further accommodative extensions are possible. Assimilation and accommodation have a cyclical relationship recurring at each level of cognitive development, at first undifferentiated and then progressively separated and coordinated.

The present investigation examines structure changes which Piaget infers to take place at about 7 years of age. He proposes that peer interaction is a major factor influencing these cognitive changes and that the social development of the child progresses in a manner parallel to and reflective of cognitive development (Piaget 1952). Accordingly, cognitive development takes place as self and world become differentiated and the accompanying coordination of assimi-

lation and accommodation lead to a state of objectivity and equilibrium (Piaget 1954). With such differentiation, there is a simultaneous process of the establishment of external reality and an inward process of self-awareness. Therefore, ontogenetic development may be viewed as a series of equilibrium (differentiation) achievements, applying not only to sensorimotor acts but also to symbolic manipulations, with the development of cognition at several levels simultaneously proceeding inward and outward from the boundary of self and milieu and the objectification of reality and the reduction of egocentrism proceeding parallel to the acquisition of self-perception (Flavell 1963; Piaget 1954).

Piaget has partitioned cognitive development and its structure evolution into three major stages: sensorimotor, operations, and formal operations. The period of concrete operations contains two major substages: *(a)* preoperational representations (ages 2-7) and *(b)* concrete operations (ages 7-11). The present investigation concerns the transition from preoperational representations to concrete operations and the assumption that cognition at all levels is the application of actions to the milieu, these actions becoming progressively internalized and less external and observable.

For example, the concrete operational child has an integrated system from which to operate, with the result that the contents of his world, through the imposition of his structure upon them, are placed in a perspective which takes into account the various facets of the system (Inbelder & Piaget 1958). This child then behaves for the first time in terms of an integrated network of possible actions, with the world beginning to be lawfully organized and thought achieving primacy over perception. Moreover, on the plane of representational thought, social relationships or coordination among individual minds evolves in the same manner as do space relations or object relations. Therefore, it is with the advent of concrete operations that it becomes possible for the child to objectively structure relationships among classes, relations, and numbers, while socially he acquires skill in interindividual relations in a cooperative framework. The acquisition of social cooperation and the structuring of cognitive operations are, then, two aspects of the same developmental processes.

The preoperational child, on the other hand, is most prominently characterized by his social egocentrism. Such egocentrism with its lack of introspection, its rigidity, and its lack of logical justification is not overcome simply by experience with objects and events but primarily through social interaction with peers. In the course of such interaction, especially conflicts and arguments, the child is forced to examine his own contentions (Piaget 1928). Therefore, experience, especially with peers, is needed to break down the egocentrism of the preoperational child in order to allow him to consider other perspectives. This "decentration" enables thought to escape the immediate and obvious and encourages the development of conceptual thinking derived from laws and commonalities, as in all true generalization. And, one of the most primary sources of such common laws is interpersonal cooperation and its verifying judgments.

The present investigation focuses upon peer exposure and socialization as they relate to cognitive development. Peer exposure is considered the independent variable; and socialization, directly related to the effects of popularity, the dependent variable. In addition, since social development is considered an integral part of cognitive development, their courses of progress should be parallel. Therefore, if Piaget's proposals are correct, progress into concrete operations should vary directly with the amount of peer exposure a child experiences. Further, as Piaget considers cognitive and affective reactions dissociable and parallel but interdependent, the more affectively positive the child's peer interactions are, the more he will seek and the greater will be his progress toward mastery of concrete operations. This study assumes then that the more popular children will receive more peer exposure.

Direct support for the hypothesis of a relationship between popularity and cognitive development comes from a study by Goldschmid (1968) in which she found popular peers to be more adept at conservation, while other investigations found emotionally disturbed and institutionalized children to be slower in achieving conservation (Goldschmid 1967) and slower at overcoming egocentrism (Neale 1966). Moreover, the predicted trend of social development is also reported in studies not conducted for the purpose of testing Piaget's proposals. Horrocks and Buker (1951), Horrocks and Thompson (1946), and Thompson and Horrocks (1947) demonstrated the trend of greater stability of friendships as children advance in school. Further, while Challman (1932) was unable to establish that friendships among preschool children were based on similarities of the children involved, Furfey (1927) found that similarities such as age, height, weight, and intelligence determine the selection of school "chums." These studies demonstrate some progress toward friendship based on autonomy and differentiation. In addition, Dymond, Hughs, and Raabe (1952) found that second graders place more value upon externals for friendship, while sixth graders more often emphasize personality factors. Such is congruent with the establishment of peer autonomy and with rising above field dependency and surface characterization, as older children should do. A later study (Byrne & Griffitt 1966) found that similarity of attitudes and consensual validation help to determine interpersonal attraction in fourth graders. This result is consistent with Piaget's propositions, and it would be expected that this effect would be observed less often in younger children.

Thus, since relevant studies indicated support for the expected course of social development in relation to cognitive development, the following hypotheses are offered for investigation:

1. The development of peer relations and interactions, as reflected by carefully designed and constructed measures of popularity and social decentration will, through the grade range (kindergarten through third grade) tested, parallel that of physical concept development.

2. The individual's progress in cognitive development, as reflected by two measures of physical concept development which assess the ability to classify and conserve, will vary directly with the affective quality of his peer relations.

METHOD

Subjects

Eighty-one children (20 kindergarten, 19 first, 21 second, and 21 third graders) in a school in a relatively small, homogeneous Wyoming town were *Ss*. Of these, there were 80 Caucasians, one Indian; 43 males, and 38 females.

Procedure

Each child was individually assessed on two cognitive measures of physical concept development to evaluate the ability to classify and conserve and presented with a task which resulted in a modified sociogram measuring social decentration and popularity.

Cognitive Measures

The first measure of cognitive growth was Form A of the Goldschmid and Bentler Concept Assessment Kit, assessing a child's ability for conservation (the ability to realize that properties such as weight, volume, etc., remain constant despite transformations such as shape or position). Form A consists of six conservation problems which include: two-dimensional space, number, substance, weight, and continuous and discontinuous quantity. The manual of the kit explains in detail the psychometrics of the test.

The second measure of cognitive development concerns inclusion or classification skills and follows a procedure developed by Kofsky (1966), who used tests which demonstrated six different, ordered levels of difficulty of classificatory logic. Three of these steps, occurring during the age levels of the present study and employed as measures of cognitive progress, were: *(a)* "a grasp of the elementary relations among objects and classes in a hierarchy including the knowledge that an object can belong to more than one class . . . which was demonstrated by . . . a majority of the six-year-olds"; *(b)* "conservation of hierarchy . . . and reclassification, which were performed successfully by most of the seven-year -olds"; and *(c)* "knowledge of inclusion which was apparent in most of the nine-year-olds." The actual tasks involve the ability to correctly manipulate a set of geometric blocks whose plane surfaces were either square, circular, or triangular and whose colors were red, blue, green, or yellow. The administration was the same as presented by Kofsky except that all tasks were presented in the same order to each *S*.

Modified Sociogram

This measure, a sociometric status procedure similar to that employed by McCandless (1957), with a retest after 6 weeks, involved presenting each child a picture of his class and asking him to show which three children he liked most (best) at that time. The procedure was modified and supplemented by questions attempting to ascertain reaction to present field, the basis of friendship in terms of reciprocity, and individual autonomy. Immature socialization, relative to other children, would be represented by: instability of friendships (based on retest); lack of interpersonal awareness, or egocentricity (based on how well the child is aware of others' feelings); and lack of individual autonomy (determined by basis of friendship and whether it is reciprocal).

After each child was individually presented a picture of his class, the following inquiries were made for scoring purposes:

This is a picture of your classmates, do you recognize them?
Can you show me some of your friends?
Can you show me the three friends you like the best? Why?
Which one of those do you like the very best? Why?
How long have you known him (or her)?
Where did you meet him (or her)?
Can you name all the children in the picture?
Which boy do you think most of the kids like best?
Which girl do you think most of the kids like best?

The question "'Can you show me the three friends you like best?" was repeated in a retest after 6 weeks. In both cases, *S* was to identify three individuals who were actual best friends, not three whom he would like to have as best friends.

Scoring

The conservation and classification measures were scored by ranking *Ss* once for the number of errors on the conservation task and once for the number of errors on the classification task. For ties, a mean rank was assigned for each group of tied individuals.

The popularity measure was obtained by counting how often a child was chosen by *Ss* as one of the three children in the class they liked best. Scores were assigned to each *S* according to how often he was chosen and were ranked as with the other measures.

From the questions concerning socialization, each *S* was ranked five times, using the following criteria: (1) reason for choosing best friend (Reason); (2) stability of friendships (Stability); (3) numbers of names of the children in the class that were not known (Names Not Known); (4) matching of friends chosen with each other (Congruency); and (5) ability to choose children which other children like best (Popularity Perception). The scoring methods for these five measures are as follows:

1. Reason scores were achieved by grouping reasons given by children into three categories: impersonal, personal, and interpersonal. The impersonal category was usually a fact of circumstance such as a cousin or living on a farm. The personal category includes personal actions such as playing with another child. The third category includes reasons which show awareness of the other child, for example, "He's nice," or "He's fun to play with." The *Ss* were given scores of 1, 2, or 3 depending upon into which group they were placed.

2. For Stability scores, *Ss* were grouped according to the number of friends on retest which were the same as on initial testing, 0, 1, 2, or 3.

3. Scoring for Names Not Known was achieved by grouping *Ss* according to number of children in their individual classes whose names were not known and assigning a score equal to that number, corrections being made for small differences in classroom size.

4. Congruency scoring was obtained by counting the number of matches between an individual's six choices of best friends (three on initial testing and three on retest) and their reciprocal choice of him as a best friend. The individuals were then scored according to the number of matches (0-6).

5. Popularity Perception scores were achieved from the answers to the questions concerning which boy and which girl *S* thought the other children in the class liked best. A *S's* choices were compared with the actual popularity rankings. Rankings then proceeded according to differences between the most popular and the one perceived as most popular for each *S*. The highest ranking was accorded to *Ss* whose choices for being most popular were in fact the most popular.

It was planned to rank *Ss* according to how they stated they met the child whom they liked the best, but almost every child replied that they simply met at school. The same applies to length of friendship. Therefore, these criteria were not included in data analyses.

In each of the five scored categories, *Ss* were ranked according to their scores, a mean rank being assigned to tide individuals.

RESULTS

The Kruskal-Wallis test, a nonparametric "analysis of variance by ranks" (Hays 1963), compared the population distribution of the various rankings (popularity measure, conservation task, classification task, and the five measures of socialization) across grades (kindergarten, first, second,

and third), as is shown in table 1, where H is referred to a γ^2 distribution with 3 *df* (Hays 1963).

All measures except Stability are significant, suggesting that the distributions of the various measures are not the same for each group. Stability approached significance with $p < .25$. Further, the comparison of grade means (table 2) demonstrates progressive gains from kindergarten through

TABLE 1

KRUSKAL-WALLIS COMPARISONS OF POPULATION DISTRIBUTION FOR ALL RANKINGS ACROSS GRADE LEVEL

Measures	Rankings
Classification	$H = 34.52***$
Conservation	$H = 29.18***$
Stability	$H = 4.95$
Names Not Known	$H = 22.19***$
Reason	$H = 16.77***$
Congruency	$H = 9.49**$
Popularity Perception	$H = 24.80***$

$** p < .05.$
$*** p < .01.$

TABLE 2

MEAN RANKS FOR EACH MEASURE AT EACH GRADE LEVEL

	K	1	2	3
Classification	63.0	46.6	34.4	21.6
Conservation	63.8	41.7	33.4	26.2
Stability	51.1	37.9	37.6	37.5
Name Not Known	62.2	36.3	35.2	30.9
Reason	56.1	43.0	39.7	26.0
Congruency	47.9	48.3	40.3	28.6
Popularity Perception	54.1	23.7	32.1	53.0

the third grade for all means except Popularity Perception and Congruency, although the Congruency measure progresses essentially as expected. All other rankings become progressively higher with successive grades (the rank of 1 being the highest possible).

In order to obtain a measure of socialization, the rankings for Stability, Names Not Known, Reason, and Congruency were combined into a single measure. The four ranks for each individual were summed, and the resulting combined scores were themselves ranked (table 3). Popularity Percep-

TABLE 3

MEAN RANKS OF THE SOCIALIZATION MEASURE FOR EACH GRADE AND COMPARISON OF ADJACENT GRADE-LEVEL MEANS FOR EACH COGNITIVE MEASURE

	K	1	2	3
Socialization	64.20	41.47	36.26	23.21

	GRADES COMPARED		
	K-1	1-2	2.3
Conservation	3.13***	1.17	1.04
Classification	2.21**	1.65**	1.78**
Socialization	3.06***	.67	1.80***

NOTE — For Z scores, ** $p < .05$ and *** $p < .01$.

tion was not included, since it was obviously measuring something different from the other four measures.

As can be seen from the mean scores for socialization, conservation, and classification, the measures progress in a similar manner from grade to grade. Figure 1 illustrates this similarity. For each measure, there is a progressive improvement from kindergarten through the third grade. Dunn's (1964) technique of "Multiple Comparisons Using Rank Sums" demonstrates that the majority of differences between successive grades, for each measure, reach significance (table 3). When classes which are two grades apart, rather than one, are compared, the differences are all significant.

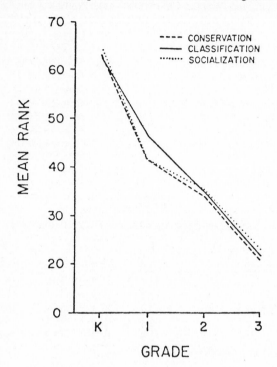

FIG. 1.—Mean ranks of the three cognitive measures for the four grades

Kendall's τ with ties, employed as a rank-order correlation method was used to examine the relations among conservation, classification, and socialization measures (Hays 1963). Table 4 shows the significance of the relationships among the three cognitive measures. All coefficients are significant at the .01 level. This significance, however, may be artificial because comparisons of the three measures with grade in school also have very significant τ coefficients (table 4).

While this again shows the similarity in function of the three measures, it also suggests that the correlation coefficients of their interrelations may only reflect their mutual relations with grade in school. If the rank-order correlations among measures are considered within grade level rather than across grade level, the levels of correlation are much smaller, as seen in table 5. Here, the coefficients among measures are smaller, and only in the first grade do they consistently reach significance. For the first-grade children, socialization correlates with a coefficient of .25 with conservation and with a coefficient of .31 with classification (significance at .05 and .01, respectively).

Socialization appears to function similarly to conservation and classification throughout the preceding statistical procedures. However, their actual relationships to each other are relatively minimal when measures are compared within each grade.

Kendall's τ was also used to examine the hypothesis that

TABLE 4

KENDALL'S COEFFICIENTS FOR THE THREE COGNITIVE MEASURES AND FOR THE COMPARISON OF COGNITIVE MEASURES WITH GRADE IN SCHOOL

	Coefficient
Socialization-conservation	.26***
Socialization-classification	.39***
Conservation-classification	.49***
Socialization and grade	.48***
Classification and grade	.47***
Conservation and grade	.50***

*** $p < .01$.

cognitive development, as measured, would vary directly with popularity. Table 5 lists the rank-order coefficients for popularity compared with each of the cognitive measures in each of the four grades. The levels of significance were determined by z scores corrected for continuity (Hays 1963). As can be seen, all the coefficients are in the predicted direction; but the relation of popularity to conservation or classification appears to be relatively minor, while the relation between socialization and popularity is consistent and reaches significance. During the first grade, the correlation coefficient reaches a high of .60.

TABLE 5

KENDALL'S τ COEFFICIENTS FOR RELATIONS AMONG COGNITIVE MEASURES WITHIN GRADES AND WITHIN-GRADE COEFFICIENTS FOR POPULARITY RANKINGS AND THREE COGNITIVE MEASURES

GRADE LEVEL	Socialization and Conservation	Classification and Conservation	Socialization and Classification
K	.046	.31**	.035
1	.25**	.36***	.31***
2	−.017	.21	.080
3	.37***	.10	−.081

MEASURE WITH POPULARITY

	Socialization	Conservation	Classification
1	.60***	.29*	.13
2	.47***	.07	.05
3	.25*	.16	.15
K	.11	.13	.27*

*$p<.10$.
**$p<.05$.
***$p<.01$.

In summary, the hypothesis that peer relations develop in a manner parallel to the development of physical concepts was significantly supported. Both cognitive and social skills were found to progress from kindergarten through third grade in a similar manner. The second hypothesis was that a child's cognitive development would be directly affected by the quality of his peer relations, as judged by popularity rankings. Popularity was found to be closely related to social development, but its relations to physical concept development were relatively minor.

DISCUSSION

As hypothesized, it was found in the present investigation

that the measure of socialization and measures of physical concept development (conservation and classification) increased progressively from kindergarten through the third grade and showed very significant differences between and extremely similar mean ranks within grades. The socialization measure was derived from a combination of four others (reason for friendship, stability of friendships, names of children in class not known, and reciprocity or congruency of friendships). Popularity perception had been planned as a fifth inclusion, but it was found that first-grade *Ss* received a higher mean ranking on popularity perception than kindergarten *Ss* and that second and third graders received progressively *lower* rankings than did first graders. These variable, unexpected results may be a function of children becoming more demanding of reciprocity of friendships as they become more adept in interpersonal perception. Thus, while there is much agreement as to which children are liked best in the first grade, this agreement declines in second and third grades, possibly because the first-grade children who *were* so popular cannot later be reciprocally close friends with all the children who like them. Therefore, in the later grades, "best friend" choices are spread out over more children. The measure of popularity in the present study did not reflect this interaction adequately for inclusion in the measure of socialization.

The second hypothesis, that cognitive progress varies with the quality of *S's* peer relations, is not clearly supported by the data. Rank-order correlations are quite significant when popularity and socialization are considered; but, when the rank-order correlations between popularity and conservation or classification are considered, only two of six resulting coefficients show a significant, but minimal, result. Indirect effects of popularity by ways of its effects upon socialization might be derived from correlations among socialization and conservation and classification. The correlations among the three measures themselves are highly significant if taken across grades, but significant results are primarily limited to the first grade if the correlations are taken within grades. The three measures all correlate highly with grade in school; and the relationship among the measures, across grades, may result from each of their relationships with age.

Therefore, social awareness appears significantly related to this measure of popularity, but neither popularity nor socialization has an important relation with the development of physical concepts. This latter statement, however, must be modified in view of the τ correlations of .25 between socialization and conservation and of .31 between socialization and classification (significant at the .01 and .05 levels, respectively)—both at the first-grade level.

There are other considerations possibly affecting these correlations. First, administrative differences might be important, since the three measures of this study obtained their information in different manners: *(a)* the conservation measure contained forced-choice questions; *(b)* the classification measure contained both forced-choice and open-ended questions; and, *(c)* the socialization questions simply solicited information rather than presenting problems and asking questions. Further, only in the first grade is there a wide distribution of scores within each measure—particularly the measure for conservation. In kindergarten, nearly all *Ss* miss every item of the conservation measure; and, already in the second grade, *Ss* are successfully answering most items. Thus, the comparisons of socialization and classification measures, which appear to span a broader grade and age range, with conservation are possibly distorted, because, at any but the first grade, they are being compared with the extreme ends of the conservation measure, where there is a very narrow range of difference.

It would be expected, therefore, that the most likly grade for significant correlations would be the first, as is the case. The importance of these correlations is that Piaget proposed that the various cognitive skills gained at this level reflect an underlying whole which, in part, determines these cognitive changes. The learning principles of behaviorism would predict more independent development. An argument might be put forth that only in the first grade are the correlations among measures significant and that even then the coefficients are small. An answer in support of a Piagetian view would be that, first, the significant results are found only at the first grade, which may be partially an artifact of the measures employed, and that, second, the interrelations among socialization, conservation, and classification *should* decline after about the age of 8. These are circumscribed skills which can be learned in their totality at this age and not open-ended skills which would be continually extended for years. Therefore, the independent variables and the relations among the skills themselves will function as such only while the skills are coming into being.

The hypothesis that cognitive development will vary directly with the affective quality of peer relations receives varying amounts of support, depending upon how the question is approached. If the present measure of socialization is accepted as a reflective measure of cognition (which the data concerning the first hypothesis appears to support), then, at least on this particular measure, the second hypothesis appears to support), then, at least on this particular measure, the second hypothesis reecives significant support with the following correlations between popularity and socialization: kindergarten, .11; first grade, .60 ($p < .01$); second grade, .47 ($p < .01$); and, third grade, .25 ($p < .10$). Direct evidence for the interrelationship of popularity with either conservation or classification was limited.

Grade level appears to show much greater influence as a common denominator with Kendall's τ correlations between grade and cognitive measures, being .48, .47, and .50 for grade and *(a)* socialization, *(b)* classification, and *(c)* conservation, respectively (all significant at .01). The closeness of these figures also lends further support to the first hypothesis.

There are three major areas of implication in this study: child-development theory, education, and psychotherapy. In the area of child development, there does indeed appear to be a qualitative change at the second grade, about 7 years of age, in cognitive processes. This change demonstrates many of the qualities which Piaget described as grouping of structure. Grade was the strongest common factor with the three measures in the present study. Popularity appeared significantly related to the three measures in the first grade, but, in general, its effects on conservation and classification were slight. Two possible conclusions would be that either (1) the popularity measure was not indicative of the amount of peer interaction a child experiences or that (2) the amount of peer interaction, which forces a child to examine his own contentions, affects physical concept development in only a minor capacity. It is presently felt that the popularity measure was consistent with Piaget's proposals and that the latter conclusion coincides with both the present data and Piagetian theories. The former conclusion would be open to further experimental investigation.

In the area of education, it appears that the best way to learn awareness of others is by having active exposure with them. If, in fact, this is a learned skill, it is an area which formal education is often accused of hampering. Highly structured, noninteractive classes during the early ages would appear to discourage this type of growth, with such also holding true at later ages and different levels of cognitive development. On the other hand, currently popular exercises such as "show and tell" would appear to encourage individual autonomy and awareness, and schools of the prototype of Summerhill would appear to develop socialization to its furthest degree. However, it also appears that the effects of peer interaction upon other areas of cognition is limited; for learning these concepts, it seems that adult-mediated direct exposure to them would be necessary.

Finally, in the area of psychotherapy, it would appear that group therapy before age 6 would have few, if any, therapeutic advantages. During the ages when concrete operations are being gained, a time when many children are seen in clinics because of difficulties experienced in adapting to the pupil role, careful consideration might be given to the use of peer groups in which peer interactions were encouraged. The socialization process, which peer interaction appears to aid (from data in the present experiment), would seem to be a benefit to such children; and the social skills learned at this age would obviously be very useful with regard to the child fitting into a classroom situation.

REFERENCES

Byrne, D., & Griffitt, W. A developmental investigation of the law of attraction. *Journal of Personality and Social Psychology,* 1966, 4, 699–702.

Challman, R. C. Factors influencing friendships among preschool children. *Child Development,* 1932, 3, 145–158.

Dunn, O. J. Multiple comparisons using rank sums. *Technometrics,* 1964, 6 (3), 241.

Dymond, R. F.; Hughs, A. S.; & Raabe, V. L. Measureable changes in empathy with age. *Journal of Consulting Psychology,* 1952, 16, 202–206.

Flavell, J. H. *The developmental psychology of Jean Piaget.* Princeton, N.J.: Van Nostrand, 1963.

Furfey, P. H. Some factors influencing the selections of boys' chums. *Journal of Applied Psychology,* 1927, 11, 47–51.

Goldschmid, M. L. Different types of conservation and non-conservation and their relation to age, sex, IQ, MA, and vocabulary. *Child Development,* 1967, 38, 1229–1246.

Goldschmid, M. L. The relation of conservation to emotional and environmental aspects of development. *Child Development,* 1968, 39, 579–589.

Hays, W. L. *Statistics for psychologists.* New York: Holt, Rinehart & Winston, 1963.

Horrocks, J. E., & Buker, M. E. A study of the friendship fluctuations of preadolescents. *Journal of Genetic Psychology,* 1951, 78, 131–144.

Horrocks, J. E., & Thompson, G. G. A study of friendship fluctuations in rural boys and girls. *Journal of Genetic Psychology,* 1946, 69, 187–198.

Inhelder, B., & Piaget, J. *The growth of logical thinking from childhood to adolescence.* New York: Basic, 1958.

Kofsky, E. A scalogram study of classificatory development. *Child Development,* 1966, 37, 191–204.

McCandless, B. R. Peer popularity and dependence on adults in preschool-age children. *Child Development,* 1957, 32, 511–518.

Neale, J. M. Egocentrism in institutionalized and noninstitutionalized children. *Child Development,* 1966, 37, 97–101.

Piaget, J. *Judgment and reasoning in the child.* New York: Harcourt, Brace, 1928.

Piaget, J. *The origins of intelligence in children.* New York: International Universities Press, 1952.

Piaget, J. *The construction of reality in the child.* New York: Basic, 1954.

Thompson, G. G., & Horrocks, J. E. A study of friendship fluctuations among urban boys and girls. *Journal of Genetic Psychology,* 1947, 70, 53–63.

THE SOCIALIZATION OF INSTITUTIONAL RETARDED CHILDREN

By Robert A. Dentler and Bernard Mackler

THE SOCIALIZATION OF INSTITUTIONAL RETARDED CHILDREN[1]

INTRODUCTION

In Goffman's terms, a state hospital and training school for mentally retarded children is one type of "total institution": A residential institution within which specially defined persons are grouped or aggregated for special purposes, and where customary divisions between the sleep, play and work patterns common to non-institutional life in communities are reorganized into scheduled uniformities. As Goffman notes.

> Total institutions . . . are social hybrids, part residential, part formal organization, and therein lies their special sociological interest. There are other reasons . . . for being interested in them, too . . . Each is a natural experiment . . . on what can be done to the self.[2]

This paper reports on the manner in which aides in one state hospital and training school for retarded children socialize newly arrived children toward the adoption of institutionally acceptable patterns of behavior. By socialization is meant the process by which the children are trained toward compliance with the

1. This research was supported in part by a grant from the Graduate Research Fund of the University of Kansas. The authors are indebted to Leland Miller, Max Siporin, Robert Sommer, Bernard Farber, Joseph Spradlin, Ross Copeland, and Charles Warriner for their comments and suggestions.
2. Erving Goffman, "Characteristics of Total Institutions", in *Symposium on Preventive and Social Psychiatry* (Washington, D. C., Walter Reed Army Institute of Research, Medical Center: Government Printing Office, 1958), p. 48.

demands made by agents in a particular environment. The analysis is restricted chiefly to the period covered by the first two months after entry into the institution. It is also restricted to consideration of what will here be defined as socialization toward compliance with management and interpersonal, in contrast to academic and medical, routines. Both sociologically and practically, the problem of institutionalization is "a most crucial one because it bears not only the problem of the effects of environmental change on performance and potential but on one of our society's major ways of handling . . . mental retardation."[3] The main questions addressed in this report are: (1) What routines of management are emphasized by aides in the institution, and how are these implemented? (2) What are some of the effects of institutional socialization on the interpersonal relations of children?

RESEARCH PROCEDURES

State School was selected for investigation for two reasons. First, State School is regarded by experienced practitioners in this special domain as a relatively "optimal" institution. Its physical plant, the qualifications of its staff, its aide training program, and its research program, have gained national attention for their excellence. Few state institutions for retarded children in the nation are considered superior to State School by the practicing professions. This provided some basis or assuming that, while no single institution could be representative of others, practices of aides at State School could not be attributed in some judgemental fashion to limited resources or "poor" standards. Secondly, the arrival of a group of new children, all assigned to a newly constructed cottage managed by experienced aides, offered a novel opportunity to study institutional socialization.

3. Seymour Sarason, *Psychological Problems in Mental Deficiency* (New York: Harper & Brothers, 1959), p. 626.

The 29 new boys, inhabitants of Cottage X, arrived at State School within a few days of one another. They ranged in age from six to twelve, with a mean of 9.6 years. Their mean IQ was 56, and all were classified tentatively by the staff as educable. Four fifths of the boys were diagnosed as exhibiting no noteworthy central nervous system pathology.

The boys and aides in Cottage X were observed by the authors for three weeks. Every hour of the day was observed, with emphasis given to the waking periods. The authors stationed themselves in corners of rooms, tagged along to meals, to the playground and the gymnasium. Most of the boys ignored the observers after the first two days, but about one third of them persisted with efforts to involve the "non-participating" observers in reading or writing mail to parents, in sharing in games or secrets, and in unelaborated physical contact. Thus the informal social relations of the boys were not left untouched or unaffected. A code for classifying observations was adapted from the scheme developed by Spiro[4], who studied children in an Israeli kibbutz. But observation was only partially systematic. Unique incidents, unanticipated types of interaction, and general insights were tape recorded together with as exhaustive a report on mundane matters as could be recalled immediately after leaving the cottage scene. More exact observations were also secured. These are reported elsewhere.[5]

To investigate the question of the effect of institutionalization on the interpersonal relations of the children, the authors devised sociometric tests that these children appeared capable of taking. Each child's photograph was mounted on a large but portable board with pins. The photographs were arranged randomly in six rows of five columns. At the close of their third week of observing, the authors established rapport with each child, one at a time, and administered the following questions in the privacy and comfort of a cottage bedroom:

Which boys would you most like to play with in the Day Hall?

Which boys would you not like to play with in the Day Hall?

Which boys would you most want to be (like)?

Which boys would you most like to work with in cleaning up the cottage?

The children responded with pleasure and apparent understanding to these questions. A minimum of *three* choices was elicited on each criterion.[6] Two weeks later, these sociometric questions were administered again. The arrangement of the pictures was changed and the tests were administered not in the cottage but in the hospital research unit.

ORGANIZATIONAL CHARACTER

State School may retain children against their will; yet, unlike state mental hospitals, State School is subject, under varying legal conditions, to the continuing agreement of parents or guardians. The terms of entry and release are more flexible than those common to institutions for adults. Children at State School may be released temporarily to vacation at home or undertake treatment or education elsewhere. A few are allowed access to the surrounding community. This flexibility is somewhat limited by the fact that, under law, entering children are defined as incompetent minors. This status naturally intensifies the custodial responsibility of State School.

The primary, manifest functions of State School are management, treatment, rehabilitation and education. As studies of other types of total institutions have demonstrated, these functions are somewhat incompatible[7,8]. Efficient custodial

4. Melford E. Sprio, *Children of the Kibbutz* (Cambridge: Harvard University Press, 1958).

5. Robert A. Dentler and Bernard Mackler, "Effects on Sociometric Status of Institutional Pressure to Adjust Among Retarded Children", submitted to *Sociometry* and Robert A. Dentler and Bernard Mackler, "The Porteus Maze Test as a Predictor of Functioning Abilities in Institutional Retarded Children", *Journal of Consulting Psychology*, 1961.

6. As a small internal check, we included the picture of a boy who did not live in Cottage X. Each child was asked to point to the picture of the boy who "Does not live in your cottage." Three fourths of the children identified this picture correctly. Incidentally, children were invited to point to their choices, eliminating the problem of unscrambling a verbal response.

care, for instance, militates against achievement of educational objectives. State School has changed during the last decade from a relatively single-purpose custodial hospital for adult epileptics to a multiple purpose institution. In the course of improvements in physical plant, reduction in patient load from one thousand to about three hundred, and of changes in external relations between the institution and the state, State School staff have given increasing priority to rehabilitative and educational goals. In spite of this marked change, as Zald has noted about other institutions:

> The actual degree of dominance of one goal over another is not wholly determined by the chartering agents. Even if they were to specify quite precisely the relative emphasis upon goals that were to be expected, the organization might not be able to realize this goal ratio. Depending upon its resources, structure, personnel, and clientele, the institution might be more or less successful in attaining its goals . . . The existence of the two major goals of custody and rehabilitation heighten the possibility of conflicting occupational role groups and the development of conflicting policies.[9]

The organizational dilemma of incompatible goals is complicated by the contrast between bureaucratic structure (or what Goffman refers to generically as formal organization in total institutions) and informal relations as these emerge wherever aggregates of persons eat, work, play and sleep in close extended proximity. State School constitutes a bureaucratic structure: It operates within a legally and administratively prescribed context of specialization, a hierarchy of authority, a system of rules, and with relative impersonality. Defined as patients, children at State School are expected to learn to behave in terms of rules established by the leadership within this structure. Blau has observed that

> Bureaucracy, then, can be defined as . . . an institutionalized method of organizing social conduct in the interest of administrative efficiency. On the basis of this definition, the problem of central concern is the expeditious removal of the obstacles to efficient operations which recurrently arise.[10]

Other functions are performed at State School but the primary task of the institution is the maintenance of efficient, safe routines for the management of patients defined as incompetent minors. State School has little if any difficulty achieving this objective at the level of the staff. The physical plant is relatively adequate, communication facilities are excellent and lines of authority established. From the point of view of the institutional functionary, the critical obstacles to efficient operations are various behavior patterns of patients.

Patients may be treated by nurses, psychologists and physicians, educated by teachers and ministers, and rehabilitated by a variety of therapists, but their day to day and night to night behavior is managed by residential cottage aides. The *initial* task of the aides is to prepare the new patient for accommodation to the institution. From the point of view of the professional staff, rehabilitation becomes possible principally when this accommodation has been achieved. Initially, therefore, virtually all interaction between staff and children is mediated by cottage aides. When a child in Cottage X was diagnosed by a psychologist, for example, the psychologist's secretary telephoned an aide at the cottage. The aide made an appointment note and, at the appropriate hour, called the child from his room, the cottage lounge or the play area, and walked him to the hospital office of the psychologist. After his hour in the hospital, the child is picked up by an aide and returned to the cottage. Later in his institutional career, the same sequence of

7. Erving Goffman, *op. cit.* and
Gresham Sykes, *Society of Captives* (Princeton, New Jersey: Princeton University Press, 1958) and
Meyer Zald, "The Correctional Institution for Juvenile Offenders: An Analysis of Organizational 'Character' ",
Social Problems, Vol. 8 (Summer, 1960). 57-67.
8. Ivan Belknap, *Human Problems of a State Mental Hospital* (New York: McGraw-Hill, 1956).
9. Meyer Zald, *op. cit.,* pp. 58-59.
10. Peter M. Blau, *Bureaucracy in Modern Society* (New York: Random House, 1956), p. 60.

events occurs, but the child is directed to make his own visit and return from the hospital to the cottage.

Managerial responsibility of the cottage aide during the first two to three months after a child's arrival is very extensive. It includes all aspects of the management of sleep, play, eating, participating in cottage cleaning and limited work routines, toilet and bath and dress habits, assistance with communications between child and family, discipline and superficial medication. Administrative regulations embrace these domains of responsibility, and the department of nursing bears the burden of maintaining periodic as well as emergency supervision. Exclusive of scheduled contacts with individual staff professionals and of the preparation of meals, however, the context of life in the early months is totally established and managed by cottage aides.

ROUTINES AND SOCIALIZATION

During the period of socialization, only a very few persons other than aides entered or left the cottage X. Nurses made periodic rounds. All but one of the nurses concentrated exclusively during visits on the paper reports, prepared by the aides, on tap at the aide desk inside the entry hall of the cottage. The one nurse paused sometimes to interact with the children. A recreation therapist stopped at the cottage to pick up groups of children for trips to the gymnasium. And on four occasions during three weeks, older boys from other cottages entered Cottage X to carry out housecleaning assignments. Excerpts from the notes convey an impression of the nature of the daily routine:

Two aides were on duty at all times. They woke the children, who sleep two to a bedroom and four to a bedroom in some cases, at 5:50 a.m. From 6:00 to 7:00, the aides helped the children wash, toilet, dress, and made their beds. At 7:00, the aides lined the children up in pairs at the front door of the cottage and directed them at a casual pace to the cafeteria. Shifts at the cafeteria are so arranged that no more than two cottage groups eat together at a time. At 7:45, the aides walked with the children back to the cottage. Inside the cottage, aides directed the boys into the television lounge, where they watched cartoons.

Between 9:00 and 9:15 a.m., the aides opened one of the toy closets in the day hall. Eight of the 29 boys moved out of the TV lounge and into the day hall. There was much drifting of boys between the two rooms. Infractions were frequent at this time; and individual boys were disciplined by being sent to their bedrooms. The drifting within the cottage continued until 10:00.

The chief aide assembled the boys in the day hall at 10:00. Each boy was told to take a chair at a table. The aide said, "Now it is time to have a talking session. Who remembers what we learned yesterday at the talking session?" M's hand went up. The aide said, "No, M told us what we learned the last time I asked. Who else knows?" G made a stab at an answer. Aide said, "No, that's not right." (I had attended yesterday's Talk Session but could not recall what had been learned, either). J tried. Aide said, "No, that's not right."

Four more children tried answers. Aide then outlined what we had learned: "First we learned no kicking and no pushing. Then, we learned we shouldn't go into the rooms of any other boys or bother their belongings. These are what we learned. Now we will have some cookies, because IC got some in the mail."

LB got a box out of the toy cupboard. Aide opened it and LB moved about the room giving each boy a cookie. The waste basket was set by aide in the center of the room. Aide said, "Take one piece and say thank you to L as he comes past."

The boys sat quietly at the tables. Aide said, "Ah, that is good. You are all learning to sit nicely and quietly in here. Now we will have our new thought for today. Our new thought is that we should have no wrestling or playing in the television room. We should play only in the day room. Can you remember that?"

The second aide entered and removed four boys — "For Music." They were sent to the department of music therapy. At 10:10, the chief aide said, "Keep in your seats and be quiet now. We've got about four minutes left. Sit down there now. This lasts until 10:15. Now who can tell me what we talked about that is new this morning?" The procedure described above was repeated identically.

At 10:15, aides directed the boys to the TV room. The set was turned on, this time to a soap opera. Drift between TV room and Day room continued and much disciplining was necessary. Non-conformers were punished by being sent to their bedrooms again. (On some days the children were allowed out of doors at this time in the morning to play on bikes, wagons and scooters.)

At 11:30 the children washed and dressed for lunch. They got ready for and walked to the cafeteria just as for breakfast.

After lunch, from 1:00 to 4:00, activities were diversified for the first time. Some children were sent to professional departments for evaluation, treatment, or classification. Others took naps for two hours, then played perfunctorily around the cottage.

At 4:30 the boys got ready for dinner. They washed up, toileted, then sat and watched TV or played in the play room. At 4:50, they walked (casually) in pairs to the cafeteria, eating and returning to Cottage X at 5:45. They took showers and assisted in cleaning the cottage rooms from 6:00 until 8:00. They sat in the Day room or watched TV for 45 minutes. Then they were seated at tables in the Day Room and given crackers and milk.

Contacts during the day with non-Cottage personnel included: three nurses on their rounds, one minister who came to observe for an hour, recreation therapist and cafeteria food servers.

HOW SOCIALIZING IS CONDUCTED BY AIDES

The critical demands of the institution, during the initial phase of socialization, were for conformity to routines, fulfillment of instructions from aides, and minimization of conflict with peers.

Management involves physical protection and "time filling". As the outline of the schedule suggests, blocks of time each day are unoccupied during the first three months after arrival. One task of the aide is to occupy this time. As Goffman has observed,

> In the inmate group of many total institutions there is a strong feeling that time spent in the establishment is time wasted or destroyed or taken from one's life; it is time that must be written off. It is something which must be 'done' or 'marked' or 'put in' or 'built' or 'pulled' . . . As such, this time is something that its doers have bracketed off for constant conscious consideration in a way not quite found on the outsde . . . Harshness alone cannot account for this quality of life wasted. Rather we must look to the social disconnections caused by entrance and and to the usual failure to acquire within the institution gains that can be transferred to outside life — gains such as money earned, or marital relations formed, or certified training received.[11]

Young children with mental ages between two and ten do not define their life situation this way. The children did not "mark time". Some had been separated from their parents with the expectation that they would be going to school, and as unintentional school failures in their communities, this was a powerful incentive. But for two months, no classroom experience was presented. One boy faced each day with the remark, "Today I go to school." Two or three times daily he would attempt to leave the cottage. Retrieved, he would explain, "I am going to school."

For the aides, who attended to the clock closely in scheduling events for the children and in waiting for their changes in shifts, management was a matter of socializing the children toward increased control. The cues employed were simple. They were repeated endlessly. Summed up they were, "Don't make noise, don't get into trouble, don't get into fights, just be quiet."[12] In achieving these controls, the primary techniques were *deprivation* and *seclusion*. If a boy did not "mind the

---

11. Erving Goffman, *op. cit.*, pp. 62-63.

aide," he was deprived in accordance with the extent of the deviation. Toys were taken away and locked up for a fixed period of time. Or the child was sent to his bedroom, or placed on a chair in a corner of an unoccupied lounge, or made to sit or stand on the "Naughty Bench," a stone settee that ran along one wall of the TV lounge. When a child was disciplined, the particulars of his infraction and the discipline taken were written on pink slips, to be circulated among staff departments and then filed in the child's records. Here are excerpts from the pink slips filed by aides:

> 8:10 p.m. H restricted to his room for 30 minutes for pulling down S's pajamas. Taken off restriction at 8:40.
>
> One day restriction: L would not stay in his room during nap time. D was crying and L went to his room and told him to shut up. Aide warned him several times, but L ignored this. D was crying for his mother.
>
> B was told plainly to stay on a restricted walk while on wheel toy. When he disobeyed, B was taken to room and kept there for 20 minutes. After release, B slipped out of cottage without coat and cap, was brought in and set (sic) on chair for 15 minutes.

The most severe technique was placement in the "psychiatric unit," a closed ward for "disturbed children," for a fixed period of time. For example, "M was placed in psychiatric unit at 5:30 p.m. for putting water in O's hat, then throwing this water all over O's bed and floor."

In addition to deprivation and seclusion, physical directives were used. For example, children described in their medical records as enuretic were wakened periodically about every hour and a half throughout the night and escorted by an aide to the toilet. According to a night aide, "No matter how careful we are, darn it, two or three of them wet or soil their beds anyway."

Rules were abundant and closely enforced. As Sykes[13] has noted of guards in prisons, aides have but a small number of privileges to mete out. Thus they tried to make privileges out of gratifications children customarily take for granted. Watching television was thus defined as a privilege in Cottage X. Efforts were made to ration periods when the set would be turned on. If the noise level seemed too high in the cottage, the set was turned off. Eating crackers and milk was made into a privilege, as was receiving the mail, playing with the wagons and bicycles, and listening to the phonograph.

To increase their stock of privileges, aides also *delegated authority.* Boys were chosen to sweep the hall, run messages, go to get the mail, and so forth. This was the aide's most powerful resource. But, only one fourth of the boys in Cottage X were capable of completing "trustee-type assignments," and these tended to be the boys least in need of socialization. Some aides employed physical affection as a reward. Conforming children were spoken to, hugged, petted, or played with briefly. This tactic became confused insofar as the children differed greatly in their degree of affective dependency. Demonstraton of affection was difficult to ration selectively. Some children took it from aides by hanging close by or pressing close, others got it by provoking reactions. Others avoided these forms of aide contact. Finally, aides regarded *drugs* as control agents. Aspirin as well as thorazine and other "tranquillizers" were believed to improve greatly the chances of developing a quiet, well behaved cottage. Upon the agreement of the professional staff, children in Cottage X were not placed on drugs during the course of our observations. Toward the close of the second week, aides began to resent this agreement. They felt their capabilities for improving control had been reduced substantially. Indeed, observation was cut short by a request from the medical department that drug programs be introduced at once.

---

12. That silence is valued at other state schools is suggested by a fictional yet documentary autobiography of a cottage aide in a state training school for the retarded. Martin Russ, *Half Moon Haven* (New York: Rinehart, 1959), p. 27.

13. Gresham Sykes, *op. cit.,* pp. 53-54.

To convey something of the quality of socialization in action, two fragments of observations are presented:

At 7:00 p.m., the children finished cleaning up the cottage, clean-up being the primary privilege extended on Home Night. The aides directed all but seven of the children in the TV lounge and to seats along the walls. Soon, individual children took chances at entering the center floor area of the lounge. They were controlled from the aide's desk. Aide C would call out, "Get back in your chair," "Get your feet off the chair, you," "Get back in your chair," "Go stand in the corner — you know you must stay in your chair," and so forth. Three corners of the lounge were used as punishment centers. At 7:40, one child, G, began to slump into sleep in his chair. The aide called out, "G, you get up here and go out and wash your face with water and wake up. It's not bedtime yet."

At 6:50, the aide said, having seated the children around the walls in the TV lounge, "If everyone is quiet now, we'll watch a little television." There was a brief uproar of glad approval from the boys. The aide walked to the set, hesitated till a silence came over the group, and then switched on the last ten minutes of a western, "The Rebel." For the next half hour, no more than four boys watched the TV screen at any one time. All other boys spent their time watching one another or the aide at the desk. At 7:05, child M came over and touched my mouth and chin and throat very gently and looked carefully at me. Aide C interrupted this at once: "Get back to your chair, M, at once!" M returned to his chair and began to cry loudly. Some of the boys around him began to mock his crying.

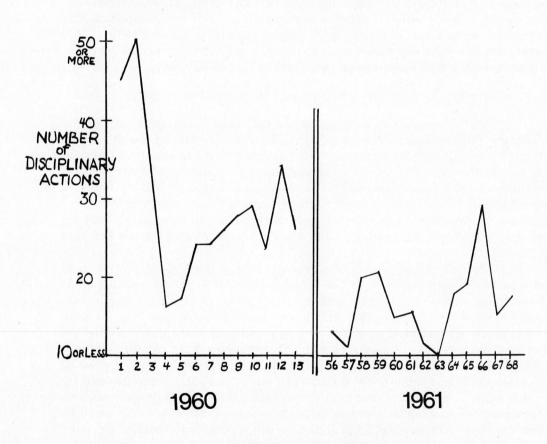

WEEK IN YEAR

FIGURE 1. GRAPH OF AIDE DISCIPLINARY ACTS
PER WEEK, INITIAL PERIOD (1960) AND LATER.

Figure I illustrates an aspect of the process of socialization through disciplinary action. Aide's pink slips reporting infractions of children and disciplinary action for two comparable time periods were summed in units of weeks for the 26 out of 29 boys who remained in State School for more than one year. The first period comprises the first thirteen weeks after the 26 had entered Cottage X. The second period consists of thirteen weeks in a comparable season of the following year. The points on the graph reflect dual behavior; namely, violations of cottage rules and disciplinary acts. Disciplinary acts by aides were not always responses to misconduct, however, as aides could define behavior as deviant or ignore it. Certainly, the two events were mutually interactive. The graph is interpreted here as representing trends in *degree of pressure* exerted by aides in maintaining control.

Pressure was most extreme during the first three weeks. In the fourth week, drug programs were initiated, and pressure was relaxed. This initial degree of pressure was never reintroduced, but the trend from the eighth to the thirteenth week suggests that disciplinary pressures were intensified periodically. An equilibrium was never achieved, but the data from the 1961 period suggest that sufficient control was established so that the degree of pressure became consistently lower. After one year, a level of control was realized under which most children appeared quiet, subdued and conforming. In the initial phase for example, no one boy received more than 13 per cent of the total number of pink slips, and the mean was 7 per child. A year later, two boys among the 26 received 47 per cent of all the pink slips, although the mean declined to 3 per child. There is some consistency over time in which individual boys were and were not disciplined. The correlation between ranked totals for the first and second periods is .34 (p < .05). Among the four boys disciplined most frequently in the second period, however, only one received more than average punishment in the initial period.

INTERPERSONAL RELATIONS AMONG CHILDREN

How were the socialization processes and the social behavior of the children in Cottage X interrelated? What were the social consequences for the children of adaptation to this new life situation? The instrument for exploring this question was sociometric choice. It was assumed that the status structure of any group is indicative of the values endorsed by the group; that structure is built around a reward system for conformity to norms; and that the choice status of individual members may be used as an index of social acceptance and of what is valued by the members. These assumptions echo the theory developed by Riecken and Homans[14].

In a previous report, the authors presented an analysis of the correlates of individual sociometric status[15]. It was found that, initially, the boys with highest choice status among the children received the most frequent disciplinary restrictions. In the second month after arrival however, the status structure changed. The boys who gained most in status were those who showed the greatest reduction in frequency of disciplinary action. The evidence from analysis of individual choice status supported the conclusion that the boys in Cottage X adapted progressively to institutional life through incorporation of the norms imposed by cottage aides. Rewards of status from peers were given increasingly to those boys who conformed with all routines or rather who stayed out of trouble. As these were the boys with minimal capabilities for effective action, that is, the most apathetic and retarded, the correlation between mental ability and declining status were extremely significant.

Friendship ties or mutual preferences are, like choice status, meaningful indicators of interpersonal relations. The emphasis on who is over or under-chosen,

14. Henry Riecken and George W. Homans, "Psychological Aspects of Social Structure," In *Handbook of Social Psychology*, Vol. II, Gardner Lindzey, ed. (Cambridge: Addison-Wesley, 1954), pp. 786-832.

15. Robert A. Dentler and Bernard Mackler, *op. cit.*

however, is replaced with an emphasis on the degree to which individuals are contained in or excluded from one or more subgroups and the degree to which a network of social sentiments has developed. A greater than chance number of reciprocal choices suggests that a group has developed solidarity. A lower than chance number suggests that barriers to interaction exist which reduce exchange of sentiments among members.

FIGURE 2. SOCIOGRAM OF COTTAGE X, FIRST MONTH.

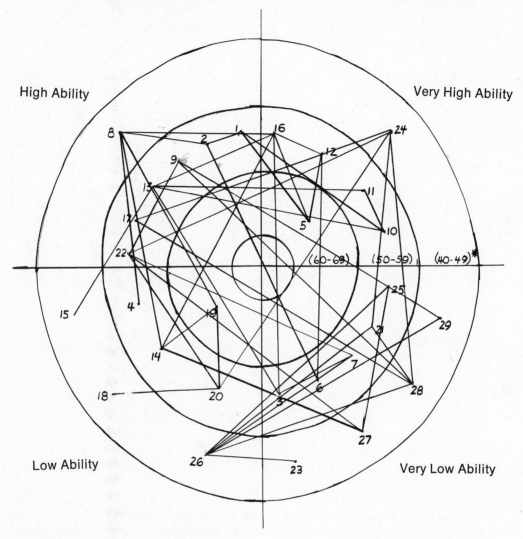

*Normalized Scores on Choice Status

In Figure 2 is presented a target type diagram of the sociometric structure of mutual relations between the 29 boys in Cottage X in its *first* month. The quadrants of the target contain boys grouped by level of functioning ability. The three bands of the target reflect level of individual choice status, with the most over-chosen boys located in the inner circle and the most underchosen in the outer circle. Figure 3 is an identical diagram based on sociometric responses in the *second* month. In both figures, the lines represent mutual ties or reciprocal choices between individuals.

FIGURE 3. SOCIOGRAM OF COTTAGE X, SECOND MONTH.

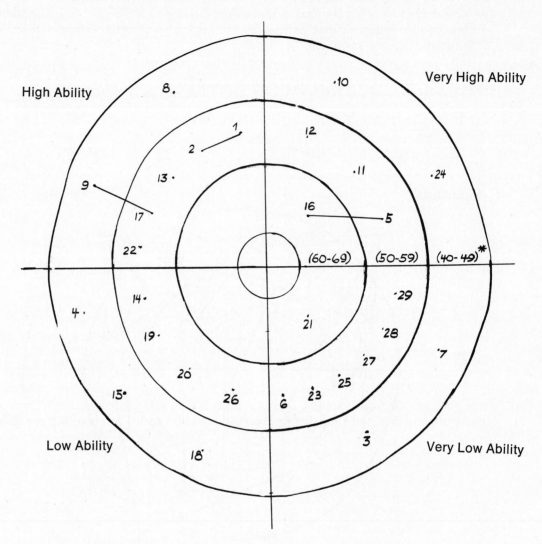

*Normalized Scores on Choice Status

The single most important datum of this study consists of the extreme contrast between the structure of interpersonal preferences in the two time periods. Using the three criteria of playmate, work mate, and identification preferences in a composite fashion, 45 mutual preferences occurred in the first month and three in the second.

Using the probability model recommended by Katz and Powell[16], Cottage X boys appear to have developed interpersonal ties in the first month that were greater than would be expected by chance. Figure 2 thus depicts a group structure that approximates a statistically expected structure. Figure 3, using the same model, is .02 points distant from the most extreme deviation from chance obtainable under conditions set by the choice questions. The extent of interpersonal reciprocation, in other words, is extremly close to the absolute and to probabilistic minima. There are far fewer reciprocal choices than would be expected by random choosing alone.

16. Leo Katz and James H. Powell, "Measurement of the Tendency Toward Reciprocation of Choice", *Sociometry*, Vol. XVIII (December 1955), pp. 659-664.

The contrast may be interpreted as evidence of *avoidance learning*. This process underlay the socialization practices and was witnessed frequently. The development of friendships depends on opportunities for socal interaction. For sentiment to develop, activities must be shared. Under the condtions imposed by aides, such activities became, over time, occasions for deprivation and seclusion. For example, here are illustrative excerpts:

> A new aide replaced Mr. Y this evening. While he was being introduced to a nurse and to the other aide, several boys, noting that the aides were not in direct control, began to wrestle playfully and teasingly near the TV lounge. P, who initiated this play, was observed by the old aide and placed for ten minutes in a corner of the lounge with his face to the wall.
>
> J and R were sitting on a couch watching TV. W was sitting with O nearby. J began to talk to R. Aide N said, "Hey, hush up," S and K were also seated together. On TV a western film was showing. About half the boys were watching it. Whenever any boy talked, aide N said, "All right, guys, get quiet." J got up and came toward O. Aide N said, "OK J, get up on the naughty bench and don't say a word." M had already been assigned to the bench. Soon J began to try to play with M. Aide N said, "I told you to get up there so you would stay out of *trouble* — and there you go again."
>
> K and G were playing, talking and giggling in the hall. Aide N said to them, "Keep still now." S and SY began playing with two small rubber balls that S brought out of his room into the corridor. They bounced them cautiously up and down for a mement. Aide N said, "You don't play ball in here. You know that." The activity stopped at once.
>
> B moved across the TV lounge and talked to me. Thereupon Aide B told him to sit down, face forward and "put your feet on the floor."

The change from the first to the second month reflects not the total absence of preferential interaction but the introduction of caution into social relations, the extreme restricton of what Moreno terms *social* expansiveness. The number of choices made declined from 308 or about 10 per child to 101 or about 3.5 per child in the second phase (although the instructions were the same each time and included an effort to obtain at least 9 choices per child).

DISCUSSION AND CONCLUSION

This research was conducted as an exploratory field study; findings are intended as material through which to generate hypotheses for further research. They pertain to the early phases of institutional socialization, to educable retarded children under 13 years of age, and to what was observed and measured in only one cottage in one institution.

The authors suspect that the latent function of the initial socialization process is to reorganize the self of the newly arrived patient. Through severe initial control over interpersonal relations among the children, the social responses brought in as part of the presenting culture are broken down. The result is a child obliged to accept peer as well as adult relations on terms specified completely by the institution, at which point the *colonized* patient may be rehabilitated.

From observing "Old Boys" briefly, the authors speculate that the system succeeds in fulfilling its objectives. The basic routines, once established, especially among the educable patients, are maintained indefinitely. Patients generally are prepared to re-enter the outside world with improved manners and greater independence in the tasks of eating, bathing, and the like. Furthermore, between the years from 13 to 21, academic education and vocational training are added to the patient's repertoire.

Through job training, which was observed, "Old Boys" develop job-centered attachments to peers. In the matrix of a work group, the adult social self begins to develop and gratification is increased. The ideal end product, the social outcome, we suspect, is a quiet, well mannered, even subdued young adult, demonstrably independent and able to earn a living.

The reorganization of a new patient is functional not only because it leads to colonization and thus guards against rebellion. The "stripping away" of older response sets is probably also *economical*. Goffman has demonstrated that this is the case in mental hospitals[17]. To move aggregates of persons through elaborate schedules across long periods of time, it is important that mechanisms be devised that are certain to reduce individual differences. Efficient, economical control may be obtained by increasing the stability or predictability of behavior. The mechanisms discussed are ones that assist in the reduction of differences, just as colonization leads toward uniformity of perception among the patients.

Whether individual potentialities would be realized more completely under a different process of socialization is a question that this report seems to pose rather sharply. This much of the question perhaps can be answered: the character of this total institution is incompatible with the goal of maximum fulfillment of indivdual potentialities. It is not incompatible with efficient management and rehabilitation toward limited participation and adult subsistence in the outer community.

17. Erving Goffman, *op. cit.*

XII. SCHOOLS

A school — a setting ostensibly established for the conduct of teaching, studying, and learning — is still a sometime thing in the world. Perhaps half of the world's living population has never gone to school. Over recorded history, perhaps nine in ten human beings who ever lived never went to school. Clearly, a school is *not* a necessary condition for any of the three events set forth above. And, there are those among us — such as Ivan Illich — as the article in this section by Joseph Featherstone reminds us, who argue that most schools in most parts of the world should be abolished as detrimental to learning and as economically unfeasible.

For most educational psychologists, however, schools continue to be of enormous importance for three compelling reasons. First, they exist in vast numbers as places that house the actors in the educational drama for six or more hours a day, five days a week, for better or worse. Second, as behavior settings, they influence the teaching-learning process in and of themselves. They are a weighty physical and organizational factor in the mysterious equations of growth and cognitive development. And third, they offer an extraordinary resource for study, research, and theory building.

The essay by Joan L. Roberts in this section demonstrates the first type of concern with schools as behavior settings. The Coleman survey of Equal Educational Opportunity, summarized in the article by Robert Dentler earlier in this book, revealed that, across a representative sample of more than 4,000 public schools in America, the *uniformities* far outweighted the variations. In outer and interior appearance and design, in arrangements of physical space, in formal and in informal organization of staffs and students, the schools he and his associates surveyed were more alike than a sample of railroad stations or post offices might be. Since that date in the mid-1960's, some diversification has taken place. Today, the eyes of parents can be stunned by open classrooms, carpeted corridors, pods, movable walls and portable bleachers, and a myriad of architectural and educational innovations. But these comprise, still, only a small fraction of the schools in the nation's 22,000 school districts. Roberts' essay shows from urban sources how these uniformities of setting and organization of staff and routine *shape* the education and social experiences of students.

With few exceptions schools do provide a place that is safe, warm, lighted, and comparatively quiet. They offer an alternative to the relative isolation of individuals within houses and apartments. They enable the possibility of teaching and learning, but this enablement is little more than a stage for the actors. If the stage includes neither playground nor gymnasium, there will be some obvious limitations placed upon motor skill learning, but with the exception of gross facility effects of this sort — a library's presence or absence, a music room, a shop room, for example — what is influential is the *social* and *instructional* context within the settings.

Measuring What Schools Achieve

Joseph Featherstone

A massive international study is shedding new light on one
of today's most sensitive questions:
What *really* accounts for differences in children's academic
achievement? Mr. Featherstone offers here a sensible
summary of recent research and speculation.

Throughout the 1960s an organization called the International Association for the Evaluation of Educational Research (IEA) surveyed the achievement of schoolchildren
in some 22 countries in mathematics and other conventional
academic subjects. The results of many of these surveys are
now being published, and recently a conference at Harvard
met to discuss what they mean. With cross-national samples
involving over 250,000 schoolchildren, the IEA researchers used the same sort of statistical procedures as those employed for the British Plowden Report, *Children and Their
Primary Schools;* by the sociologist James Coleman in his
report, *Equality of Educational Opportunity;* and by Christopher Jencks and his colleagues in their book *Inequality.*
The data add an interesting international dimension to the
long and often muddled debate over the relative effects of
home background and schooling on children's achievement
test scores.

On the whole, the IEA studies tend to confirm earlier
findings: Social class and family background seem more
important than schooling in accounting for differences in
children's achievement test scores. There's one major qualification, however: Schooling seems to be more important
in some subjects than in others. Both the Coleman and the
Plowden reports dealt with tests for verbal and mathematical
ability; the IEA surveys show significant school influence in
science, literature, and second language teaching. In the
case of literature particularly, the survey suggests that
schoolchildren pick up very distinctive approaches to discussing literary works. Those in Chile, England, and New
Zealand take an interest in matters of pure form; those in
Belgium, Finland, and the United States talk about themes
and content; those in Italy take an essentially historical approach. We don't know why. Nonetheless, the literature
survey suggests that responses to literature — and presumably to other parts of the curriculum not tested by these
surveys — may indeed be learned, and that the learning may
well be the result of different sorts of school experiences.

This would scarcely be an astonishing revelation were it
not for the heated current arguments over what schools can
do. The IEA data suggest that in certain kinds of subjects
schools do indeed make a big difference.

The most dramatic fact in the IEA surveys is the huge
gap in achievement scores between children in the wealthy,
developed nations and children in poor, developing nations.
Differences in reading scores among affluent nations are not
great, whereas reading scores in three developing nations —
Chile, India, and Iran — are so low that 14-year-old students
seem almost illiterate by comparison. In discussions at Harvard of the educational plight of the poor nations, two points
were stressed. The first was their need to build up some kind
of educational *system.* In developed nations a wide array
of formal and informal educational institutions have existed
for three or four generations, and egalitarian social policy
has slowly — with some glaring exceptions — narrowed

the range of differences between schools. This very systematization poses a new set of problems: standardization,
bureaucracy, overly rigid professionalization. Poor countries do not share this affluent malaise. A rural school in
Chile may have no books at all, and so the problem is not
how well or how soon children learn to read but whether
they will ever learn.

A second point made at the Harvard conference was that
however great the need for system, it is an open question
whether the models of schooling developed in the industrial
West are appropriate for developing nations. No developing nation has thus far established an advanced educational
system without exacerbating class and caste divisions, and
without according brain work a higher status than hand
work. This problem was debated in Bolshevik Russia in the
1920s; it is a pressing issue in China and many other poor
countries today. Ivan Illich and other proponents of deschooling and of a Tolstoyan nostalgia for rural life are
right when they warn developing nations not to adopt educational institutions that are ill-suited to the needs of a
majority of their people. And yet our counter-cultural as-
saults on schools and reading have a shallow and elitist
ring; there is something unedifying about the spectacle of
the jaded and overeducated rich preaching deschooling to
poor nations hungry for education. Representatives from
poor countries at the Harvard conference noted that literacy
and numeracy are coming to be reckoned as fundamental
human rights, and although warnings about an overelabo-
rated educational edifice are well taken, the problem remains: how to equip students in developing nations with
practical, functional skills such as the ability to read a newspaper, political pamphlet, or tractor repair manual.

In economically advanced societies, the tests of 14-year-
olds showed Japan, Hungary, and Australia first, second,
and third in science. (The pitfalls of cross-cultural research
were revealed when a Japanese gentleman politely pointed
out that the IEA survey overlooked the fact that Japanese
secondary school students attend school six days a week;
after momentary consternation, it was decided that this
probably did not alter the results significantly.) In reading
comprehension for 14-year-olds, New Zealand and Italy
were first and second, with the United States, Finland,
French Belgium, and Scotland all tied for third. (Some in-
novation-happy Americans were startled when a man from
New Zealand suggested that one reason for his nation's high
reading scores was the lack of abrupt changes of content
and direction in New Zealand reading programs.) The
United States ranked fifth in science; in literature its 14-
year-olds scored second.

Now, achievement tests are a limited art form. Each culture has distinct educational aims; all cultures want much
more for their children than a narrow range of skills that
can be measured by achievement tests. Mass cross-cultural
survey data probably should be taken with a pinch of salt.
For one thing, the tests ignore important differences within
each nation's educational system — most notably the proportion of students at a given age who remain in school to
be tested. (The tests were given to 10-year-olds, 14-year-
olds, and students in the last year of secondary school.)
Also some observers accuse the tests of a Western bias, and
it is true that students in poor nations are not as test-wise as
the examination-ridden children of affluent societies. Few
children in developing nations have ever even had the
dubious pleasure of facing a multiple choice test on which
the IEA surveys largely rely.

One illustration of why simple comparisons of test scores
in a "cognitive Olympics" don't mean much arises from
considering the US position in the science survey. Those

who remember educational debates in this country in the fifties will recall that Admiral Hyman Rickover and others used to argue that the highly selective, elitist science education in European secondary schools was far superior to the science education of American students in our more or less comprehensive high schools. Now it turns out that the admiral and other critics were wrong. More students in secondary schools does not mean worse, although the results look wretched enough at first glance: The mean science scores of American students are lower than those for any other developed nation. However, it makes no sense to compare the performance of average high school graduates in comprehensive secondary school systems like America and Japan with the selected students who sit for *baccalauréat* in France, because the American and Japanese students constitute a majority, whereas the French students are a minority. If instead of comparing all science students you instead look at the performance of the best, the highest-scoring 1, 5, and 9%, you discover that they score about the same as their top European counterparts. Thus in the United States which graduates over 70% of its students from high school, the scores of top science students come close to those of the best students in selective European educational systems graduating fewer than 20% of their students. The IEA data suggest that the performance of more able students is not hurt when masses of students are given access to comprehensive schooling. Traditionally those who argue for elite systems measure the quality of the surviving few; those who favor more comprehensive education focus on the quality of education given to all. Within the sharp limits of the conventional terms of achievement tests, the IEA scores are mildly reassuring on the first point for American educators, who, if they are candid, will confess that they have not squarely faced the second.

> "One point that keeps getting blurred in American debates is that the research that has been done does not show that schools make no difference. What it does show is that by certain crude measures schools are very similar to one another."

One other aspect of the science study is of interest: the clear advantage of boys in science across the board and across the world. Boys everywhere are more interested in science and do better on the tests. The gap widens as students grow older. Differences are most marked in physics and slightest in biology. The IEA science report hints here and there at innate sexual differences, but most of the scholars at the Harvard conference preferred the simpler hypothesis of sexual bias. (In reading comprehension and literature, girls did better than boys.) What has now been documented on an international scale is the degree to which much of science learning is a male preserve.

Because of the political situation within their own country, Americans at the conference were particularly concerned about the public response to this sort of research. One point that keeps getting blurred in American debates is that the research that has been done does not show that schools make no difference. What it does show is that by certain crude measures schools are very similar to one another.

We should not confuse discussions of the effects of schooling (about which we know very little) with research on the effects of differences between schools in a roughly uniform educational system.

As matters stand, the effects of schools on achievement tests are much alike — though their effects on the daily lives of the children who attend them may vary enormously. But matters may not stand still. Schools could change their ways of teaching, or — more plausibly in the current political climate — budget cuts and declining support for education might create significant differences between the schools that are adequately supported and those that are starved. The authors of *Inequality* speculated that if schools were shut down — or, presumably, if schools for the poor were to deteriorate markedly — what they call the "cognitive gap" between rich and poor and black and white would be far greater than it is now.

All the school research so far leaves unexplained a great deal of the variation in students' test scores. You may call whatever explains the leftover variation "social character," "as yet unmeasured characteristics of students, teachers, and schools," "luck," or perhaps even "love," as Lewis Carroll's Duchess might put it. Whatever you call it, it is a mystery to the researchers. Complex methodological issues lurk like carp beneath most statements about schools. Critics of the IEA surveys argue that the methods used inflate home effects and minimize school effects, a criticism that the economist Samuel Bowles and others have made of the Coleman Report and similar research. There was repeated questioning at the Harvard conference whether mass surveys of schooling have not reached the limits of their usefulness, and persistent complaints that particular research paradigms are too limited, covering over fundamental uncertainties with a misleading layer of numerical precision. Some educators argued that the IEA surveys' reliance on standardized achievement tests runs counter to a growing international trend promoting individuality, diversity, active learning, and a variety of styles of thinking among students. Educators in many countries are beginning to see education as lifelong, not as steps up an achievement ladder. Although the IEA data contained noncognitive items on student attitudes, a number of scholars were also critical of a basic neglect of values. There is certainly a need to look at education from perspectives of people not normally part of the research and policy system: children, teachers, parents, poor people. There was surprising agreement at the conference that the various goals different nations have for their schools are far too broad and complex to be settled by the crudities of mass testing.

This subdued emphasis on complexities — the sense of how little is actually known — is probably the most important thing for the public, policy makers, and practitioners to realize. By itself this ignorance constitutes a good argument for further research, research in a variety of modes. Yet many educational practitioners are coming to feel the same way about research as the exasperated student who, after taking yet another IEA test, wrote. "The money for this would have been better spent sending woolens to Africa." But as the process of framing educational policy becomes more self-conscious, the kind of research that is available and how it gets reported is important. The Plowden Report, for example, presented the British public with important quantitative research on the limits of schooling, along with qualitative material on classroom practice and educational philosophy that was of direct benefit to British practitioners. This combination is unheard of in this country, where educational discussions often manage to avoid the problems of practitioners altogether. It would be foolish pragmatism in our present state of basic ignorance to insist that all or even most educational research directly helps children and teachers, but it is not hoping too much that some of it will, and that some researchers will be willing to spend at least as much time working with teachers and children as Konrad Lorenz spends with his ducklings.

"This subdued emphasis on complexities—the sense of how little is actually known—is probably the most important thing for the public, policy makers, and practitioners to realize. By itself this ignorance constitutes a good argument for further research. . . ."

Part of the current animus against social science research on schools is the age-old desire to kill the messenger who brings unwelcome news. To the degree that these sorts of studies check the traditional American faith in the boundless power of schooling to effect fundamental social change, they perform a valuable service. For the dark side of the coin of our utopian faith is the despair that sets in when schools do not do the impossible. In this despairing mood, educators tend to exaggerate the baleful impact of research, forgetting the primacy of the political climate. Much of recent American writing on the effects of schooling was intended as a critique of liberal sentimentality about the power of schooling, on the part of scholars who imagined that liberals would continue to dominate educational policy; the research reads strangely in an era when policy is in the hands of conservatives intent on dismantling the social ser-

vices. It is, however, not the research itself, but the *Zeitgeist* that is mainly responsible for how particular findings get interpreted, emphasized, and acted upon. Arthur Jensen is, so to speak, always waiting in the wings, because the debate between conservative hereditarians and liberal environmentalists is perennial. It is only a political climate of despair and retreat from social commitment that puts the spotlight on him.

Meanwhile, in its endless concern for its schools, the American public might keep in mind two points made by one participant trying to sum up the IEA findings and other similar research. Home background is the best predictor of children's achievement scores, and yet the older students in school do successively better on the tests than the younger ones. The first point suggests the limits on the differences schools make; the second indicates that they may make a measurable difference on achievement test scores, as well as in more important, less readily measurable realms. Knee-deep in computer printout, and profoundly divided on many of the research issues, the scholars are still far from having resolved this key ambiguity.

Robert L. Ebel

WHAT ARE SCHOOLS FOR?

Perhaps, after all, they are where the young should learn useful knowledge.

When the history of our times is written, it may designate the two decades following World War II as the golden age of American education. Never before was education more highly valued. Never before was so much of it so readily available to so many. Never before had it been supported so generously. Never before was so much expected of it.

But in this eighth decade of the twentieth century public education in this country appears to be in trouble. Taxpayers are revolting against the skyrocketing costs of education. Schools are being denied the funds they say they need for quality education. Teachers are uniting to press demands for higher pay and easier working conditions.

College and high school students have rebelled against what they call "the Establishment," resisting and overturning regulations, demanding pupil-directed rather than teacher-directed education, and turning in some cases to drink, drugs, and delinquency. Minorities are demanding equal treatment, which is surely their right. But when integration makes social differences more visible, and when equality of opportunity is not followed quickly by equality of achievement, frustration turns to anger which sometimes leads to violence.

Surely these problems are serious enough. But I believe there is one yet more serious, because it lies closer to the heart of our whole educational enterprise. We seem to have lost sight of, or become confused about, our main function as educators, our principal goal, our reason for existence. We have no good answer that we are sure of and can agree on to the question, What are schools for?

It may seem presumptuous of me to suggest that I know the answer to this question. Yet the answer I will give is the answer that an overwhelming majority of our fellow citizens would also give. It is the answer that would have been given by most educators of the past who established and operated schools. Indeed, the only reason the question needs to be asked and answered at this time is that some influential educators have been conned into accepting wrong answers to the question. Let me mention a few of these wrong answers:

—Schools are not custodial institutions responsible for coping with emotionally disturbed or incorrigible young people, for keeping nonstudents off the streets or out of the job market.

—Schools are not adjustment centers, responsible for helping young people develop favorable self-concepts, solve personal problems, and come to terms with life.

—Schools are not recreational facilities designed to entertain and amuse, to cultivate the enjoyment of freedom, to help young people find strength through joy.

—Schools are not social research agencies, to which a society can properly delegate responsibility for the discovery of solutions to the problems that are currently troubling the society.

I do not deny that society needs to be concerned about some of the things just mentioned. What I do deny is that schools were built and are maintained primarily to solve such problems. I deny that schools are good places in which to seek solutions, or that they have demonstrated much success in finding them. Schools have a very important special mission. If they accept responsibility for solving many of the other problems that trouble some young people, they are likely to fail in their primary mission, without having much success in solving the rest of our social problems.

Then what is the right answer to the question, What are schools for? I believe it is that schools are for learning, and that what ought to be learned mainly is useful knowledge.

Not all educators agree. Some of them discount the value of knowledge in the modern world. They say we ought to strive for the cultivation of intellectual skills. Others claim that schools have concentrated too much on knowledge, to the neglect of values, attitudes, and such affective dispositions. Still others argue that the purpose of education is to change behavior. They would assess its effectiveness by examining the pupil's behavior or performance. Let us consider these three alternatives in reverse order.

If the schools are to be accountable for the performance of their pupils, the question that immediately arises is, What performance? A direct answer to this question is, The performance you've been trying to teach. But that answer is not as simple or as obviously correct as it seems at first glance. Many schools have not been primarily concerned with teaching pupils to perform. They have been trying to develop their pupils' knowledge, understanding, attitudes, interests, and ideals; their cognitive capabilities and affective dispositions rather than their performances. Those who manage

313

such schools would agree that capabilities and dispositions can only be assessed by observing performances, but they would insist that the performances themselves are not the goals of achievement, only the indicators of it. A teacher who is concerned with the pupil's cognitive capabilities and affective dispositions will teach quite differently, they point out, than one whose attention is focused solely on the pupil's performances. And, if performances are not goals but only indicators, we should choose the ones to use in assessment on the basis of their effectiveness as indicators. Clearly we cannot choose them in terms of the amount of effort we made to develop them.

But, if we reject performance goals, another question arises: What should be the relative emphasis placed on affective dispositions as opposed to cognitive capabilities? Here is another issue that divides professional educators. To some, how the pupil feels – his happiness, his interest, his self-concept, his yearnings – are what should most concern teachers. To others the pupil's cognitive resources and capabilities are the main concern. Both would agree that cognition and affect interact, and that no school ought to concentrate solely on one and ignore the other. But they disagree on which should receive primary emphasis.

In trying to resolve this issue it may be helpful to begin by observing that the instructional programs of almost all schools are aimed directly at the cultivation of cognitive competence. Pupils are taught how to read and to use mathematics, how to write and to express perceptions, feelings, ideas, and desires in writing, to be acquainted with history and to understand science. The pupil's affective dispositions, his feelings, attitudes, interests, etc., constitute conditions that facilitate or inhibit cognitive achievement. They may be enhanced by success or impaired by failure. But they are by-products, not the main products, of the instructional effort. It is almost impossible to find any school that has planned and successfully operated an instructional program aimed primarily at the attainment of affective goals.

That this situation exists does not prove that it ought to exist. But it does suggest that there may be reasons. And we need not look too far to discover what they probably are.

Feelings are essentially unteachable. They can not be passed along from teacher to learner in the way that information is transmitted. Nor can the learner acquire them by pursuing them directly as he might acquire understanding by study. Feelings are almost always the consequence of something – of success or failure, of duty done or duty ignored, of danger encountered or danger escaped. Further, good feelings (and bad feelings also, fortunately) are seldom if ever permanent possessions. They tend to be highly ephemeral. The surest prediction that one can make when he feels particularly good, strong, wise, or happy is that sooner or later he is going to feel bad, weak, foolish, or sad. In these circumstances it is hardly surprising that feelings are difficult to teach.

Nor do they need to be taught. A new-born infant has, or quickly develops, a full complement of them – pain, rage, satiety, drowsiness, vitality, joy, love, and all the rest. Experience may attach these feelings to new objects. It may teach the wisdom of curbing the expression of certain feelings at inappropriate times or in inappropriate ways. And while such attachments and curbings may be desirable, and may be seen as part of the task of the school, they hardly qualify as one of its major missions.

The school has in fact a much more important educational mission than affective education, one which in the current cultural climate and educational fashion is being badly neglected. I refer to moral education – the inculcation in the young of the accumulated moral wisdom of the race. Some of our young people have been allowed to grow up as virtual moral illiterates. And as Joseph Junell points out elsewhere in this *Kappan*, we are paying a heavy price for this neglect as the youth of our society become alienated, turn to revolt, and threaten the destruction of our social fabric.

This change in our perception of the function of the school is reflected in our statements of educational objectives. A century ago Horace Mann, Herbert Spencer, and most others agreed that there were three main aspects of education: intellectual, moral, and physical. Today the main aspects identified by our taxonomies of objectives are cognitive, affective, and psychomotor. The first and third elements in these two triads are essentially identical. The second elements are quite different. The change reflects a shift in emphasis away from the pupil's duties and toward his feelings.

Why has this come about? Perhaps because of the current emphasis in our society on individual liberty rather than on personal responsibility. Perhaps because we have felt it necessary to be more concerned with civil rights than with civic duties. Perhaps because innovation and change look better to us than tradition and stability. Perhaps because we have come to trust and honor the vigor of youth more than the wisdom of age.

In all these things we may have been misled. As we view the contemporary culture in this country it is hard to see how the changes that have taken place in our moral values during the last half century have brought any visible improvement in the quality of our lives. It may be time for the pendulum to start swinging back toward an emphasis on responsibility, on stability, on wisdom. Older people are not always wiser people, but wisdom does grow with experience, and experience does accumulate with age.

Schools have much to contribute to moral education if they choose to do so, and if the courts and the public will let them. The rules of conduct and discipline adopted and enforced in the school, the models of excellence and humanity provided by the teachers, can be powerful influences in moral education. The study of history can teach pupils a decent respect for the lessons in morality that long experience has gradually taught the human race.

Schools in the Soviet Union today appear to be doing a much more effective job of moral education than we have done in recent years. This fact alone may be enough to discredit moral education in some eyes. But concern for moral education has also been expressed by educational leaders in the democracies.

Albert North Whitehead* put the matter this way at the end of his essay on the aims of education:

> "The essence of education is that it be religious."
>
> "Pray, what is religious education?"
>
> "A religious education is an education which inculcates duty and reverence. Duty arises from our potential control over the course of events. Where attainable knowledge could have changed the issue, ignorance has the guilt of vice. And the foundation of reverence is this perception, that the present holds within itself the complete sum of existence, backwards and forwards, that whole amplitude of time which is eternity."

If these views are correct, moral education deserves a much higher priority among the tasks of the school than does affective education. But it does not deserve the highest priority. That spot must be reserved for the cultivation of cognitive competence. Human beings need strong moral foundations, as part of their cultural heritage. They also need a structure of knowledge as part of their intellectual heritage. What schools were primarily built to do, and what they are most capable of doing well, is to help the student develop cognitive competence.

What is cognitive competence? Two distinctly different answers have been given. One is that it requires acquisition of knowledge. The other is that it requires development of intellectual skills. Here is another issue on which educational specialists are divided.

To avoid confusion or superficiality on this issue it is necessary to be quite clear on the meanings attached to the terms *knowledge* and *intellectual skills*. Knowledge, as the term is used here, is not synonymous with information. Knowledge is built out of information by thinking. It is an integrated structure of relationships among concepts and propositions. A teacher can give his students information. He cannot give them knowledge. A student must earn the right to say "I know" by his own thoughtful efforts to understand.

Whatever a person experiences directly in living or vicariously by reading or listening can become part of his knowledge. It will become part of his knowledge if he succeeds in integrating that experience into the structure of his knowledge, so that it makes sense, is likely to be remembered, and will be available for use when needed. Knowledge is essentially a private possession. Information can be made public. Knowledge cannot. Hence it would be more appropriate to speak of a modern-day information explosion than of a knowledge explosion.

The term *intellectual skills* has also been used with a variety of meanings. Further, those who use it often do not say, precisely and clearly, what they mean by it. Most of them seem not to mean skill in specific operations, such as spelling a word, adding two fractions, diagraming a sentence, or balancing a chemical equation. They are likely to conceive of intellectual skills in much broader terms, such as observing, classifying, measuring, communicating, predicting, inferring, experimenting, formulating hypotheses, and interpreting data.

It seems clear that these broader intellectual skills cannot be developed or used very effectively apart from substantial bodies of relevant knowledge. To be skillful in formulating hypotheses about the cause of a patient's persistent headaches, one needs to know a considerable amount of neurology, anatomy, and physiology, as much as possible about the known disorders that cause headaches, and a great deal about the history and habits of the person who is suffering them. That is, to show a particular intellectual skill a person must possess the relevant knowledge. (Note well at this point that a person cannot look up the knowledge he needs, for knowledge, in the sense of the term as we use it, cannot be looked up. Only information can be looked up. Knowledge has to be built by the knower himself.) And, if he does possess the relevant knowledge, what else does he need in order to show the desired skill?

Intellectual skill that goes beyond knowledge can be developed in specific operations like spelling a word or adding fractions. But the more general (and variable from instance to instance) the operation becomes, the less likely it is that a person's intellectual skills will go far beyond his knowledge.

Those who advocate the development of intellectual skills as the principal cognitive aim of education often express the belief (or hope) that these skills will be broadly transferrable from one area of subject matter to another. But if the subjects are quite different, the transfer is likely to be quite limited. Who would hire a man well trained in the measurement of personal characteristics for the job of measuring stellar distances and compositions?

Those who advocate the cultivation of knowledge as the central focus of our educational efforts are sometimes asked, "What about wisdom? Isn't that more important than knowledge?"

To provide a satisfactory answer to this question we need to say clearly what we mean when we speak of wisdom. In some situations wisdom is simply an alias for good fortune. He who calls the plays in a football game, who designs a new automobile, or who plays the stock market is likely to be well acquainted with this kind of wisdom — and with its constant companion, folly. If an action that might turn out badly in fact turns out well, we call it an act of wisdom. If it turns out badly, it was clearly an act of folly.

But there is more than this to the relation of knowledge to wisdom. C. I. Lewis of Harvard has expressed that relation in this way:

"What schools were primarily built to do, and what they are most capable of doing well, is to develop cognitive competence."

> "...the school should not accept responsibility for the learning achievement of every individual pupil. ... If a pupil is unwilling or unable to make the effort required, he will learn little in even the best school."

Where ability to make correct judgments of value is concerned, we more typically speak of wisdom, perhaps, than of knowledge. And "wisdom" connotes one character which is not knowledge at all, though it is quality inculcated by experience; the temper, namely, which avoids perversity in intentions, and the insufficiently considered in actions. But for the rest, wisdom and knowledge are distinct merely because there is so much of knowledge which, for any given individual or under the circumstances which obtain, is relatively inessential to judgment of values and to success in action. Thus a man may be pop-eyed with correct information and still lack wisdom, because his information has little bearing on those judgments of relative value which he is called upon to make, or because he lacks capacity to discriminate the practically important from the unimportant, or to apply his information to concrete problems of action. And men of humble attainments so far as breadth of information goes may still be wise by their correct apprehension of such values as lie open to them and of the roads to these. But surely wisdom is a type of knowledge; that type which is oriented on the important and the valuable. The wise man is he who knows where good lies, and how to act so that it may be attained.*

I take Professor Lewis to mean that, apart from the rectitude in purposes and the deliberateness in action that experience must teach, wisdom in action is dependent on relevant knowledge. If that is so, the best the schools can do to foster wisdom is to help students cultivate knowledge.

Our conclusion at this point is that schools should continue to emphasize cognitive achievements as the vast majority of them have been doing. Some of you may not be willing to accept this conclusion. You may believe some other goal deserves higher priority in the work of the school, perhaps something like general ability to think (apart from any particular body of knowledge), or perhaps having the proper affective dispositions, or stable personal adjustment, or simply love of learning.

If you do, you ought to be prepared to explain how different degrees of attainment of the goal you would support can be determined. For if you can not do this, if you claim your favored goal is intangible and hence unmeasurable, there is room for strong suspicion that it may not really be very important (since it has no clearly observable concomitants or consequences to render it tangible and measurable). Or perhaps the problem is that you don't have a very concrete idea of what it is you propose as a goal.

Let us return to the question of what schools are for, and in particular, for what they should be accountable. It follows from what has been said about the purposes of schooling, and about the

cooperation required from the student if those purposes are to be achieved, that the school should not accept responsibility for the learning achievement of every individual pupil. The essential condition for learning is the purposeful activity, the willingness to work hard to learn, of the individual learner. Learning is not a gift any school can give. It is a prize the learner himself must pursue. If a pupil is unwilling or unable to make the effort required, he will learn little in even the best school.

Does this mean that a school should give the student maximum freedom to learn, that it should abandon prescribed curricula and course content in favor of independent study on projects selected by the pupils themselves? I do not think so. Surely all learning must be done by the learner himself, but a good teacher can motivate, direct, and assist the learning process to great advantage. For a school to model its instructional program after the kind of free learning pupils do on their own out of school is to abandon most of its special value as a school, most of its very reason for existence.

Harry Broudy and John Palmer, discussing the demise of the kind of progressive education advocated by Dewey's disciple William H. Kilpatrick, had this to say about the predecessors of our contemporary free schools and open classrooms:

A technically sophisticated society simply does not dare leave the acquisition of systematized knowledge to concomitant learning, the by-products of projects that are themselves wholesome slices of juvenile life. Intelligence without systematized knowledge will do only for the most ordinary, everyday problems. International amity, survival in our atomic age, automation, racial integration, are not common everyday problems to which common-sense knowledge and a sense of decency are adequate.*

Like Broudy and Palmer, I believe that command of useful knowledge is likely to be achieved most rapidly and most surely when the individual pupil's effort to learn is motivated, guided, and assisted by expert instruction. Such instruction is most likely to occur, and to be most efficient and effective, when given in classes, not to individuals singly.

If the school is not held to account for the success of each of its pupils in learning, for what should it be accountable? I would say that it should accept responsibility for providing a favorable learning environment. Such an environment, in my view, is one in which the student's efforts to learn are:

1. guided and assisted by a capable, enthusiastic teacher;
2. facilitated by an abundance of books, films, apparatus, equipment, and other instructional materials;
3. stimulated and rewarded by both formal and informal recognition of achievement; and
4. reinforced by the example and the help of other interested, hard-working students.

The first two of these aspects of a favorable

316

*C. I. Lewis, *An Analysis of Knowledge and Valuation* (LaSalle, Ill.: Open Court, 1946).

*Harry S. Broudy and John R. Palmer, *Exemplars of Teaching Method* (Chicago: Rand McNally, 1965).

learning environment are unlikely to be seriously questioned. But perhaps a word or two needs to be said in defense of the other two. First, what of the need for formal recognition and reward of achievement as a stimulus of efforts to achieve?

In the long run learning may be its own reward. But the experience of generations of good teachers has shown that in the short run learning is greatly facilitated by more immediate recognition and rewards. This means words of praise and of reproof, which good teachers have used from ancient time. It means tests and grades, reports and honors, diplomas and degrees. These formal means and occasions for recognizing and rewarding achievement are built into our system of education. We will do well to retain them, to disregard the perennial advice of educational reformers that such so-called extrinsic incentives to achievement be abandoned — unless, of course, we are also willing to abandon excellence as a goal for our efforts.

Next, what of the influence of classmates in either stimulating, assisting, and rewarding efforts to achieve, or disparaging and ridiculing those efforts? In the experience of many teachers these positive or negative influences can be very strong. Of course a teacher's attitudes and behavior can tend to encourage or discourage learning. But much also depends on the attitudes the students bring with them to the class. If they are interested and prepared to work hard, learning can be productive fun. If not, learning is likely to be listless and unproductive.

There may be some teachers with a magic touch that can convert an uninterested, unwilling class into a group of eager learners. I myself have encountered such teachers only in movies or novels. Surely they are too rare to count on for solving the problems of motivation to learn, especially in some of the more difficult situations. For the most part, motivation to learn is an attitude a student has or lacks well before a particular course of instruction ever begins.

Going to school is an opportunity, and ought to be so regarded by all pupils. The good intentions which led us to enact compulsory schooling laws have trapped us. School attendance can be made compulsory. School learning can not be. So some of our classrooms are loaded with youth who have no wish to be there, whose aim is not to learn but to escape from learning. Such a classroom is not a favorable learning environment.

The remedy is obvious. No upper grade or high school young person ought to be allowed in a class unless he wants to take advantage of the opportunity it offers. Keeping him there under compulsion will do him no good, and will do others in the class harm. Compulsory school attendance laws were never intended to create such a problem for teachers and school officials. Have we the wit to recognize the source of this problem, and the courage to act to correct it?

Let me now recapitulate what I have tried to say about what schools are for.

1. Public education in America today is in trouble.

2. Though many conditions contribute to our present difficulties, the fundamental cause is our own confusions concerning the central purpose of our activities.

3. Schools have been far too willing to accept responsibility for solving all of the problems of young people, for meeting all of their immediate needs. That schools have failed to discharge these obligations successfully is clearly evident.

4. Schools are for learning. They should bend most of their efforts to the facilitation of learning.

5. The kind of learning on which schools should concentrate most of their efforts is cognitive competence, the command of useful knowledge.

6. Knowledge is a structure of relationships among concepts. It must be built by the learner himself as he seeks understanding of the information he has received.

7. Affective dispositions are important byproducts of all human experience, but they seldom are or should be the principal targets of our educational efforts. We should be much more concerned with moral education than with affective education.

8. Intellectual skills are more often praised as educational goals than defined clearly enough to be taught effectively. Broadly general intellectual skills are mainly hypothetical constructs which are hard to demonstrate in real life. Highly specific intellectual skills are simply aspects of knowledge.

9. Wisdom depends primarily on knowledge, secondarily on experience.

10. Schools should not accept responsibility for the success of every pupil in learning, since that success depends so much on the pupil's own efforts.

11. Learning is a personal activity which each student must carry on for himself.

12. Individual learning is greatly facilitated by group instruction.

13. Schools should be held accountable for providing a good learning environment, which consists of a) capable, enthusiastic teachers, b) abundant and appropriate instructional materials, c) formal recognition and reward of achievement, and d) a class of willing learners.

14. Since learning cannot be made compulsory, school attendance ought not to be compulsory either.

Schools ought to be held accountable. One way or another, they surely will be held accountable. If they persist in trying to do too many things, things they were not designed and are not equipped to do well, things that in some cases can not be done at all, they will show up badly when called to account. But there is one very important thing they were designed and are equipped to do well, and that many schools have done very well in the past. That is to cultivate cognitive competence, to foster the learning of useful knowledge. If they keep this as their primary aim, and do not allow unwilling learners to sabotage the learning process, they are likely to give an excellent accounting of their effectiveness and worth. □

"No. . . high school young person ought to be allowed in a class unless he wants to take advantage of the opportunity it offers. Keeping him there under compulsion will do him no good, and . . . others . . . harm."

Little People in the Establishment: Small Groups in Bureaucracy

by Joan L. Roberts

Both teachers and students must exist within the context of an organization; consequently, their actions are strongly influenced by the procedures and traditions found in each local school and in the entire school system. Like all organizations, educational institutions develop different atmospheres by rewarding, encouraging, and emphasizing particular styles of life.

Aspirations and academic achievement of high school students are affected by the social atmosphere of institutions. The climates of eight different high schools, varying in the number of students from different social status levels, were investigated in one study. In the predominantly lower-status schools, the *proportion* of middle-class boys planning to attend college was significantly lower. Academic achievement was similarly affected. School climates clearly affect children's values, thus influencing their grades and goals. In the social structure of the middle-class school, peer groups were more fragmented because of greater control by both teachers and parents who emphasized their own educational values. Consequently, peer groups exhibited more discrimination between college and non-college aspirants than in the lower-income schools where attitudes toward schooling were largely irrelevant to assessments of each other:

In the Flats (lower-class schools), the boys who are disinterested in extending their education are well integrated in their classes. None of them are isolates and they are, in fact, far over-represented among leaders of their peers. In the Foothills, the most heterogeneous schools, college aspirations are irrelevant to social location. Those who do not want to go to college are stars and isolates in about the same proportion as those who do. In the Hills (middle-class schools), more of the non-college aspirants are isolated than in either Foothills or Flats. Relatively, then, terminal students are the social leaders in the lower economic strata. They gain social support from their peers, and, in turn, set the pace for them, without adopting the standards of success prevalent in the wider community of adults (Wilson, 1959, 1963).

Obviously, a classroom group can only be understood if seen as a part of a whole. Both in and out of school, human behavior occurs in a field or system of interdependent parts. The Gestalt or total configuration of the parts in relation to each other must be known in order to understand the meaning and functioning of any one component (Kohler, 1929; Koffka, 1935; Asch, 1952). This idea, though derived from studies of perception, applies to human organizations. The nature of small group interaction is best understood if seen as a part of a whole which is, in urban areas, a school system that has evolved into a massive, multi-layered bureaucracy. A bureaucracy in which strains between strata split apart people in different positions at various levels. It is an organization in which control over the size and composition of groups excludes teachers and students from decisions about their own classes. The classroom group continues to function in this situation despite a dangerously overextended system that intrudes directly into the classroom through administrative intervention or indirectly through rules and regulations governing the conduct of the thousands of groups.

The enormous size of the metropolitan school system can be grasped by realizing that over one and a half million children are enrolled in approximately 820 schools in the nation's largest school system (Sheldon and Glazier, 1965). This number of children in *one* organization, is larger than the population of any one of our cities, excluding the five largest, and nearly matches the population of Detroit, the first largest city, and exceeds that of the sixth largest city, Baltimore (United States Census Bureau, 1960).

Though exceptionally large, this school system typifies the population explosion combined with urban migration experienced nationally. One-sixth of the nation resides in our fourteen largest cities where ninety-seven percent of the national growth occurred during the nineteen-fifties (Ford Foundation Project, 1960). The expansion of school organizations in all major cities is inevitable, regardless of the absolute magnitude of growth experienced locally. For example, in New York City, the number of school children increased 23,000 *per year each year* during the past decade (Sheldon and Glazier, 1965).

Adapting Bureaucracy to Education

As organizations grow larger, division of labor leads to specialized departments or bureaus; each of these performs limited tasks required in handling masses of people. These departmentalized organizations acquire, out of specialization, the label, bureaucracies. Eventually routines and rules are devised by the officials who manage bureaucratic subdivisions. Uniform procedures become crucial to organizational functioning and regulations are inflexibly applied to *all* members at a particular level. Because the purpose of educational institutions is the highly individualized task of learning, uniformity and inflexibility should be avoided. The opposite has occurred; instead of avoidance, there has been acceptance of bureaucracy. Bel Kaufman, in her novel *Up the Down Stair Case*, shows what this does to the teacher and her group of students in circulars that exemplify bureaucracy in action:

Circular #1A
Topic: Organization
Please keep all circulars on file, in their order. Diligence, accuracy and promptness are essential in carrying out all instructions as to procedures.

Circular #5B
Topic: Teachers' Welfare
Please keep all circulars on file, in their order. Teachers shall be required to report to principals and principals shall be required to report to the associate superintendent for personnel and to the law secretary all cases of assault suffered by teachers in connection with their employment.

Circular #61
Topic: Homework Addendum

Please keep all circulars on file, in their order. We have had an epidemic of unprepared students. A student unprepared with homework must submit to his teacher, in writing, his reason or reasons for neglecting to do it. Please keep these homework excuses on file in the right-hand drawer of your desk.

To: All Teachers
The following material, and no other is to be placed in the center drawer of your desk in the room where your official class meets and locked up with key provided for the purpose. This material is to be kept locked up at all times except when in use by teacher or other authorized agent: roll book, attendance pads, absentee postal cards, seating plan, emergency slips, transcript sheets, program cards (in alphabetical order), consent slips, truant slips (blue), parent letters #1 (yellow), parent letters #2 (pink) extra-curricular credit cards, and lunch permits.

The school library is *your* library. All students are encouraged to use it at all times. Students on the library black-list are not to receive their program cards until they have paid for lost or mutilated books. The library will be closed to students until further notice to enable teachers to use it as a workroom for the PRC entries (Kaufman, 1964).

Callahan, in a historical analysis of school administration, documents how educators have adopted bureaucratic models from industry. In the business world, earlier in this century, classical organization theories were developed to provide models for efficient operation of industrial bureaucracies. One model was based on the idea of departmentalization in which large amounts of work of the same kind were brought together for maximal use of machinery and mass production. A second model was founded on the time study methods begun by Taylor, who broke down jobs to the most simple and least physically demanding units. Both approaches viewed the human being as a *passive instrument* required for production (March, *et al.*, 1958). This assumption and these formulations have guided educational leaders over the past decades (Callahan, 1962).

Transplanting these theories into education made administrators more concerned with the economic operation of an "educational plant" than with sound educational policy or solid intellectual values. Administrators came to see themselves as plant managers or business executives and children become products to be processed efficiently. Over time, the concern for efficient production and uniform tasks led to the preparation of administrators who presented doctoral dissertations such as "Analysis of Janitor Service in Elementary Schools" as evidence that they were ready to lead a school system.

The desire for inflexible routines in education was articulated by Harrington Emerson (1912), an early pioneer in time and motion studies, who outlined principles of scientific management in a speech to high school teachers of New York City. Included in his guidelines for educational efficiency were: Standard records, standard conditions, standardized operations, standard instructions, and standard schedules. A response to this talk was printed in a publication of the teachers the following month. It stated, ". . . we are privileged to feel so close a kinship between our problems and those of the business world around us."

Not only was standardization from business found acceptable, but assembly-line production was also considered appropriate. An eminent administrator earlier in this century wrote:

Our schools are, in a sense, factories in which the raw products (children) are to be shaped and fashioned into products to meet the various demands of life. The speci-

fications for manufacturing come from the demands of the twentieth-century civilization, and it is the business of the school to build its pupils to the specifications laid down. This demands good tools, specialized machinery, continuous measurement of production to see if it is according to specifications, and elimination of waste in manufacture, and a large variety of output (Cubberly, 1916).

Though attitudes toward business have changed, many current practices in schools observed originate with the incorporation of industrial organizational models. It is, therefore, not surprising to learn that lower-income children who face this factory model daily have actually coined the slang expression "warehouses" for the bad schools in their neighborhoods (Wylie, 1965). In very basic ways, students in "warehouses" are influenced by administrative stress on bureaucratic operation of efficient plants. Class size, for example, has been greatly influenced by earlier attempts to ape cost-cutting practices in manufacturing. Movement from class to class for very short time intervals, resulting in student loads of 150 to 200 each day for every teacher, is derived from a conveyor belt conception in which the entire "educational plant" was to be used all the time for maximal efficiency.

Unfortunately, the assumptions about human nature underlying business administrative principles are only partially accurate at best. Classical organization models assume that the average person has an inherent dislike of work, avoiding it, therefore, as much as possible. Because of this dislike, people must be controlled, forced, threatened with punishment or given extrinsic rewards to get them to do what the organization wants done (McGregor, 1960). Thwarting the real social needs of human beings by managerial practices based on these assumptions has brought about widespread hostility, apathy and rejection of the goals of management (Argyris, 1957). The adoption of similar control methods in education has brought similar results, particularly in urban schools.

This organizational approach also overlooks two basic facts: children are animate and learning is a qualitative process. In addition, two unique characteristics of members within the educational system are unacknowledged:

This organizational complex is different from the bureaucracies of business or industry in that the child has no choice but to go to school. Employees may choose to quit and go elsewhere. But the child is prohibited from doing the same thing. He remains in an institution which differs in another way from those of the non-academic world: his teacher is part of a profession, and, at the time, part of a bureaucracy. She is caught between the demands of giving full devotion and unlimited time to her career as a professional should and punching the timeclock or signing in every morning as a bureaucratic employee must (Roberts, 1967).

Children have no legal choice but to be "produced." Teachers have had to act as employees in a system rather than as members of scholarly disciplines. They have, despite their centrality to the organizational purpose, had to accept the lowest and least powerful level in the hierarchy of adult authority.

Distributing Power
In a bureaucracy, people are compartmentalized into different units to produce a common product. This results in a hierarchy of power and communication that is formalized in an organization chart describing who has power over whom and who communicates to whom about tasks. Theoretically, there should be a two-way flow of information both upward and downward. Frequently, however, one-way communication,

through directives, and one dimensional power, through decisions, flow downward. In such circumstances, power becomes centralized and communication upward is often blocked. Unequal power lines and blurred communication channels lead to stress between people at different levels. When teachers are unable to communicate their ideas to others, dissatisfaction with their work affects relations with students in their groups. Deutsch (1960) concludes from his research that:

> . . . the teacher is an essential part of the learning process, and when she is made—or feels she has been made—a super numerary in matters of policy and curriculum and in evaluation and discussion of teaching problems, she loses her initiative and interest in evaluating her own role. This must be true in any school context, but is particularly valid when the actual frustrations are so enormous, the problems so great, and the guidance so minimal as in these special problem schools. . . .

The teachers were interested in communicating with each other and in working out solutions to the problems they recognized. However, they saw no ready path of communication, either with each other or with the educational hierarchy. The teachers universally felt that they were excluded from a curriculum-planning and school organization role, that they lacked the respect of those higher in authority, and that their problems as teachers were not objectively viewed or seriously considered. In general, they felt under-utilized because they saw no way to enrich the school curriculum through the consideration or introduction of their own ideas and experiences.

Distribution of power to make decisions among different organizational levels is crucial in school systems. In all large systems, positions determine different sets of standards that are simply expectations of behavior required. These expectations define roles which specify behavior in relation to other roles that also prescribe interlocking actions. In the formalized school setting, various positions and associated roles involve highly specialized functions spelled out in detail. Role conflict for a person in any of these positions can occur if he holds two incompatible roles or if role expectations in one position are contradictory.

In urban school systems, superintendents are very likely to be caught in the middle between contradictory demands. In one study, superintendents disagreed with board members about budget recommendations, salary decisions, teacher-hiring procedures, teachers' grievances, and use of school facilities by community groups. Role conflict was resolved by some, the moralists, on the basis of the legitimacy of expectations; the expedients based decisions on the sanctions to be expected if demands were not met; the moral-expedients combined both approaches in resolving dilemmas (Gross, McEachern and Mason, 1958).

Regardless of the manner in which role conflict is resolved, it remains common in urban schools. For example, an administrator in one local school takes issue with a policy of the Board of Education:

> There is a gap between the attitude of the school system and that of the students and families toward illegitimate children. The family seems to accept and care for the children whereas the school requires the student's mother to transfer her daughter out of her school to a new one where she will be removed from the supposed shame of her position. Such shameful feelings toward illegitimacy exist perhaps in middle-class culture but not among the working class. The teaching supervisors, nevertheless, think they can protect the child by transferring her out of the school after she's had the baby. Often the girl wants to come back to the school she left because all of her friends are there. In addition, the school system requires the

withdrawal of a girl or boy who marries but permits the students who become pregnant and have babies to continue. This is another discrepancy between the school rules and the cultural realities.

This local administrator, like the superintendents discussed above, is in the middle of incompatible demands. He must, however, adhere to the policy dictated by those in authority over him. To do so makes little sense because it means that a child will be rewarded, in a sense, for not being married since she can finish school while her peers who marry cannot. When the principal enforces this uniform regulation, he sees himself rewarding the very behavior that the system does not wish to enforce.

Centralized authority sometimes results in policies that are unrealistic in the local situation. In this case, research indicates that the administrator's understanding of the problem of illegitimacy is more realistic than the formal policy set by the Board of Education. In one study of lower-class families in Washington, D.C., mothers accepted their daughters' illegitimate children even though they did not approve of the pregnancies (Lewis, 1961). One mother exemplifies this reaction:

> "I told him [her own husband] she ain't the first one who ever made a mistake and I was going to let her stay right here with me. I told Esther we would take care of her through this one, but no more babies before you're married."

With decreased awareness of local problems and increased distance from the situation, inflexible rules of bureaucracy may seem illogical or simply foolish. When these regulations do not coincide with local realities, trouble is ahead for both the teacher and her students.

Conflicting Roles

The local administrator may, therefore, also be the recipient of dissatisfaction from those beneath him, despite his proximity to the situation. One teacher says of administrators in his school:

> . . . there's no reason why youngsters should just disappear from classes during the course of the day. If a youngster is absent from his class when he has been marked present by his homeroom teacher, I make a point of trying to tell the homeroom teacher about the absence. If administrative control were tightened and if the kids were convinced that the teachers would really follow up on them if they decided to be truants during the day, lots of them would appear more regularly.

When communication of dissatisfaction upward is blocked, informal groups often form to discuss their feelings. One such group of teachers gather together to read an administrative policy statement they had just received:

> There is a great deal of bitterness expressed by the teachers which can be summed up in the statement of one of them who says, "That's all the supervisors need—another reason for blaming everything on the teachers."

In still another school, four teachers are listening sympathetically to the account of another. The observer records:

> They agreed with her in her perception of the administrative staff. All of them felt that the principal and his assistants were opposed to extracurricular trips and activities for the children.

When the whole system is strained with role incompatibilities, unrealistic policies, and blocked channels of communication, teachers' dissatisfaction will be certain to influence their work as leaders with their students. In a nationwide study of teachers, their ratings of superintendents, principals, and supervisors were highly correlated to their satisfaction with teaching children (Chase, 1951). In another study, the administrator, in particular, the principal, was the key to staff morale (Gordon, 1955). In still another study, teachers in schools with low morale had greater dependence on the principal than in schools with high morale (Becker, 1951). The organizational strains, particularly those between teacher and administrators within the local school, are crucial determinants of the satisfaction a teacher feels in her role in the classroom.

Often people in pivotable positions are caught between the pressures of those above and below them. In one sense, the principal can be compared to a foreman in industry. In both positions, the individual is a group member, prior to his selection to a position of authority, of those he is expected to lead. In both situations, the person is placed in power by those in authority over him and not by the persons with whom he previously worked. Consequently, such a person has double allegiance. The problem for a leader in a pivotable position is to resolve the allegiance to those under and over him at the same time. The principal comes from the ranks but is appointed by administrators and he is expected to carry out their directives. If the teachers disagree with these policies, where does he owe his allegiance? Eventually, he must give his loyalty to the administration because ultimate power resides there (Lieberman, 1956). The principal or his assistants who are in this role conflict may alienate their teachers who feel their concerns are not understood nor represented in the hierarchy.

Not all strains within the school bureaucracy occur vertically between higher and lower strata; horizontal stresses are apparent *within* each level. For example, the administrator in School No. 2 says:

In School No. 1 the principal there terrifies the children, In fact, he has the reputation of sitting in his office with the door locked so nobody can get to him. Here the door is always open for a child to come in. As a result, we have very little vandalism as compared to other schools.

Observers' comments corroborate this statement. For example, one observer notes:

This school is considerably less regimented—much less run as an army or a police state than School No. 1. . . . In this school, it seems to be less of a pattern that children are automatically sent to the assistant principal. Today I heard remarks made by children that would never have got by the people at School No. 1 without a scene being made. . . . The very fact that time can be given to observing informal groupings of children in this school indicates that the system here allows such groupings to operate more than in School No. 1 where such observations were more difficult.

Teachers, too, have attitudes toward other schools and teachers. For example, one teacher feels that:

". . . the reading scores worked up by the elementary school teachers are fraudulent. They try to push the children out of the school and in consequence give tests which involve guessing. Children on the fourth reading level as reported in their elementary school records, could not read the word 'dog' when I put it on the board in my class."

Within the *same* school, strains between teachers in coordinate positions also exist. Such strain is apparent in this teacher's comment:

When I see a fight, I'm not afraid to step in and break it up. But some of these teachers walk on as if they didn't see it. The other day, I broke up a fight in the school and was late getting my class dismissed—held up another teacher getting into the room. She was mad. I told her I had stopped to break up a fight, but she didn't care. She felt I should have considered her

needs first rather than those of the kids. Honestly, some of them think the whole school should be organized around them and they won't ever do *you* a favor.

The children, too, are aware of differences between schools and teachers in the system. One observer asked Shauna, a seventh-grader, what the school was like. She replied:

Oh, it's all right—better than it used to be. The school's not as bad as my cousin told me it would be.

One teacher reports that her students:

". . . are positive that I want to leave. They say to me, 'Why are you going to stay in a place like this?' The kids sense that people think that they are not very good and that the school is not very good and that any teacher who is nice wouldn't want to stay here."

Surviving in the System

The strains, both vertical and horizontal, in the system are often accentuated in areas where a school—whether good or bad—may be seen as inferior simply because of its location. Many of the strains, however, are inherent in any large bureaucracy that compartmentalizes people for different purposes. The teacher in New York City, for example, is one of 55,000 others, leading only a few classes among thousands located in approximately 600 elementary, 130 junior high and 90 high schools of differing varieties (Sheldon and Glazier, 1965). The autonomy of the teacher and her group becomes lost in the size of this straining and cumbersome bureaucracy.

Indeed, one cause of organization strain is the common feeling of teachers that they are merely "interchangeable units" in the system. For example, one teacher interviewed said:

I'm teaching math mainly this year but I'd like to teach French which is what I'm trained to teach.

Another way to shift teachers around with little reference to class needs or teacher preparation is through the use of non-licensed teachers who were more often observed teaching out of their major subject areas. In 1950, 94 percent of junior high school teachers held teaching certificates while in 1962, only 72 percent were licensed (Sheldon and Glazier, 1965). Still another way to provide persons to stand in front of a class is to substitute one teacher for another who is busy with other activities or absent from school. This frequently happened in classes observed. An observer noted, "This class has had four substitute teachers today."

Whether a regular or substitute, each teacher is assigned a group formed by administrative decision and continually influenced by organizational policy. The most obvious way the bureaucracy directly affects the life of the class is through required adhesion to routines and regulations. In some classes observed, the regulation that all students stand in unison and walk in line out of class caused teachers to lose as much as one quarter of their classtime in fruitless efforts to enforce a rule. In such situations, ". . . adherence to the rule, originally conceived as a means, becomes transformed into an end-in-itself" (Merton, 1940).

As organizations grow and set inflexible routines, the perpetuation of the system itself sometimes becomes more important than the original purpose for its existence. The development of a school bureaucracy is, theoretically, just a means of coordinating a large number of people to help some of them teach and others learn. The elaborate structure developed, however, requires a great number of specialists, who, sometimes, become so involved in their compartmentalized duties that the goal of learning is superseded by the papers, forms, rules, regulations, procedures, and policies originally intended to help the teacher and her learners. Here are some of the activities required:

> Program for Today's Homeroom Period
> (Check off each item before leaving building today.)
>
> Make out cards and seating plan
> Take attendance
> Fill out attendance sheets
> Send out absentee cards
> Make out transcripts for transfers
> Make out 3 sets of students' program cards (yellow) from master program card (blue), alphabetized and send to 201
> Sign transportation cards
> Requisition supplies
> Assign lockers and send names and numbers to 201
> Fill out age-level reports
> Announce and post assembly schedule and assign rows in auditorium
> Announce and post fire, shelter and dispersal drills and regulations
> Check last term's book and dental blacklists
> Check library blacklist
> Fill out condition of room report
> Elect class officers
> Urge joinning G.O. (Government Organization) and begin collecting money
> Appoint room decorations monitor and begin decorating room
> Salute flag (only for non-assembly or Y2 sections)
> Point out the nature and function of homeroom: literally, a room that is a home, where students will find a friendly atmosphere and guidance
> Teachers with extra time are to report to the office to assist with activities which demand attention (Kaufman, 1964).

Notice the time spent in one class on the maintenance of the school organization in which the group must function:

Mr. S devotes his attention to such things as collecting notes for absences. He says, "I keep these in my files. You never know when it may be important. Sometimes there is a court case and the school has to produce an official record of a pupil's presence or absence on a given day." He then begins checking to see if the boys have ties on. After that, he proceeds to collect money. He explains, "I use the fine system—if a boy doesn't have a tie on, it's five cents. And if I catch someone chewing gum, it's two cents." Next, he begins taking attendance and marking his book accordingly. While this is happening, one student brings him a paper to sign. He tells him, "If you are going to belong to the club, you'll have to watch your conduct. Otherwise, I won't let you belong." Polio slips are collected next. While these are being collected, a girl is at work at the blackboard in the back of the room making a chart of the names of pupils who are absent or tardy. While the teacher watches her, he comments, "The loudspeaker isn't working so the class won't participate in the morning exercises which still go on here despite court rulings." Mr. S then returns to the front of the room and compliments the students on the way they got started, saying, "Let's make the rest of the day perfect too. I'm not satisfied with the section sheet for the last two days." Then before beginning the lesson, he locks the doors to the closet in which coats and wraps of the children are hung.

Mr. S, like the average teacher in this school system, will spend approximately one hundred hours a year on these clerical duties in his homeroom. Add to this figure time spent in his other classes during the day, time involved in evaluating students' competence for organizational placement in classes and grades, and time in numerous other jobs such as hall or lunchroom duty. The amount of time spent by the teacher to keep the organization functioning "smoothly" grows while time for teaching shrinks. The irony is that "smooth" functioning of the bureaucracy becomes totally functionless when the child is not adequately taught. Teachers in this dilemma tend to feel bureaucratic pressures more than administrators. In one study, principals saw themselves as primarily interested in student learning but their teachers saw these administrators as stressing not the goal of the system but the maintenance of the organization (Singletary, 1951). In lower-income schools, teachers are even more negative and disillusioned; as indicated by the following fictionalized conversation between two teachers:

> Joe Dion shared my curiosity about what would happen to Danny. But he laughed at my folly to think the forms I wrote out on a week-end would serve any purpose. "They'll park him with Skally awhile—she runs a smooth room." said Joe, meaning her tendency to let disrupters out of the room. The police picked up one such kid this month over on the other side of Central Park—she'd let him out. He was trouble in class; she never worried about the truancy. "But forms—don't be naive, comrade. I used to write-up and follow-up too. Long ago. You miss the point—the forms are to keep you busy and out of the whole thing, not in it. Your form may wind all the way down to City Hall, it won't affect the poor kid. And, you may still get him back" (Green and Ryan, 1966).

When teachers perceive bureaucratic functioning as the system's foremost demand, some take on, over time, the characteristics of a "good" bureaucrat. Merton (1940) says:

> The bureaucrat's official life is planned for in terms of a graded career, through the organizational devices of promotion by seniority, pensions, incremental salaries, etc., all of which are designed to provide incentives for disciplined action and conformity to the official regulations. The official is tacitly expected to and largely does adapt his thoughts, feelings and actions to the prospect of this career. But these very devices which increase the probability of conformance also lead to an over-concern with strict adherence to regulations which induce timidity, conservatism, and technicism.

In 1932, Waller claimed that teaching developed inflexibility of personality, excessive concern with limited but well-defined status, didactic and authoritative manner, and uncreative minds. He concluded that these traits were found because of their survival value in the schools: "If one does not have them when he joins the faculty, he must develop them or die the academic death." Research thirty years later does tentatively suggest that teachers do change patterns of personal characteristics after exposure to the school setting. High deference, order and endurance characterize both veteran teachers and those enrolled in teacher-training institutions; however, students entering state universities for teacher preparation exhibit a different pattern of characteristics. After years of teaching, *all* teachers regardless of differences in initial training come to share the same three characteristics to a high degree:

> Somehow, through educational experiences the initial personality differences of teachers coalesce into a common personality pattern . . . teachers who have personalities like that of the veteran teacher are valued by principals. Yet apparently the more one becomes like the typical teacher in terms of need structure, the less likely one will be satisfied, feel effective, or have confidence in the principal's leadership. . . . The data reflect a real change in satisfaction, effectiveness and confidence as the teacher realizes more and more how far from ideal everyday teaching practices and school procedures really are (Guba,

Jackson, and Bidwell, 1959).

The traits most characteristic of teachers may not lead to satisfaction but they do lead to survival in a bureaucracy. Deference —yielding to the leadership and judgment of others—is necessary for a teacher who is relatively powerless in the system. Order—organizing one's work and personal life systematically —is fundamental to the teacher confronted with a multitude of rules and procedures. Endurance—working at a task until it is completed—is a requirement for any teacher faced with the bureaucratic demand to "process" up to two hundred children daily.

Teachers react in one of three ways: nomethetic—follow the rules of the institution; idiographic—stress the demands of individuals; or transactional—a combination of the two (Getzels and Guba, 1957). Mr. Williams, a teacher of six years in one school, reacts to the influence of the bureaucracy. Note his nomethetic reaction; concern with his position takes precedence over teaching.

The principal took me to the room of one of his better teachers. Class had already begun. He called W to the door, introduced us and then departed. The students were writing—answering questions on some Social Studies material. Mr. W began to tell me about the program at great length—in normal conversational tones so that all could hear. "They don't have social studies materials for these classes and I have to write my own. Recently we have been studying the Civil War and the Reconstruction. I work it all out so it coincided with Negro History Week. I try to improve the image these kids have of themselves. The children have recently completed essays on great Negroes. Here are two of them you can read." He then showed me some material on the bulletin board and continued talking. "Career Guidance pupils are those kids who have a history of truancy or they may be holdovers. Most of them are potential dropouts. They can be helped with reading. I work on reading three or four times a day. When the kids get up to better scores, I try to send them to normal classes and integrate them back into the school. But sometimes there's a hitch. The Board of Education hasn't worked some of these things out. It's no good to have programs like this unless the boys who improve can be rewarded." He goes on to tell me about himself saying, "I've been here six years but I want to teach in a high school." Mr. W has been talking with me for at least thirty minutes. I'm becoming increasingly embarrassed because I don't see how the children can concentrate. Mr. W obviously sees me as some kind of a supervisor. I say, "I don't want to interfere with your class. I'll just sit at the back."

Finally, the bell rings and the class stays for an English lesson. Mr. W passes out sheets that had five rules for the use of commas on it and some sentences to be punctuated according to each rule. He then calls on a child to read a sentence and punctuate it. The class is very passive. The students seem to vary in their ability to handle the material but on the whole they don't seem to do too well. Mr. W then begins to review nouns, adverbs and phrases. He has talked most of the time. His voice is getting louder as time goes on. Finally, he asks me if I have any comments. I reply, "No." But he asks again and finally puts me on the spot and I have to say something. I say, "I'm very interested in your work and enjoy being with you."

Mr. W is keeping them overtime to explain further the grammar. Finally, he lets them go to gym—but first writes a note explaining they were late because they were being observed by _____ (Observer #1) who had been brought in by the principal. He then says, "You kids have had a good experience in being observed. This will happen often when you get to high school."

I decide not to go to the gym class since I feel that I have really disrupted the normal working pattern of this class. As I am leaving, Mr. W says, "I hope you'll be able to say something good about the class to the principal." I explained my role more fully, "I'm a social scientist and I'm not here to judge you or your class. In fact, I make it a rule not to discuss what I observe with the principal or with anyone else at the school." Mr. W nevertheless thinks that I should report the good things. Again, I try to explain the reason for my presence and again state that I am not a supervisor.

Mr. Williams leads only classes that are low on the grade scale; in fact, this one is for "retarded" children. Within the school, there is often an informal prestige system that classifies teachers by the intellectual level or subject matter taught. Perhaps Mr. Williams' concern with authority is because he sees his position in the school structure as peripherally important when compared to teachers of more prestigious classes. Note how the informal prestige system operates in the decision of the next teacher observed:

She asks for volunteers at the end of the period to wax a door that had been newly stained. About half of the group volunteers to wax the closet door. But the teacher has second thoughts about removing students from their science class since it was "a major subject. If it were physical education or music, it would be all right." One student comments to a friend, "If it was gym, I wouldn't have volunteered."

Similarly, teachers instructing classes of higher intellectual ability often enjoy greater prestige. The beginning teacher seldom has any option regarding the school, grade, intellectual calibre or composition of class she will teach or even the location of school or classroom within the school where she is sent. With seniority in the system, the teacher begins to exert some control over her class assignments. When this happens, she frequently leaves lower-class areas for "better" schools elsewhere. If she stays, she is able to get a class of superior intellect. Thus, the newest and least experienced teachers are often found in schools in poor neighborhoods and in lower-ability groups. The teacher may be unenthusiastic about this placement in the system. Havighurst, for example, found that the greatest amount of teacher dissatisfaction was in schools in poor areas of Chicago (1964). Concomitantly, the greatest number of teachers who wanted to transfer to other schools were also, not surprisingly, to be found in these areas. Sexton, in her study of the Detroit school system, discovered—what is now typical of other cities surveyed—that the "difficult" schools were staffed with the least experienced and least qualified teachers (1961). In short, the bureaucratic selection and movement of teachers in the system through slow progress up the ladder creates problems in those schools where greatest help is needed.

The teacher is often in the unusual position of being a leader of a group which she did not choose and which did not choose her. It is not unusual for organizations to assign leaders without consent of those led. But it is unusual that followers are legally constrained to stay in the group to which assigned. The child, just as the teacher, often has little, if any, control over the school or classroom group he joins or the leader who directs it. One child interviewed exemplifies these restrictions:

". . . but once we had a good science teacher. I used to get 80's and 90's on the exams. A lot of the kids used to get high scores but when she left, we started getting 40's and 50's and we don't like the new teacher." Do you like the class? He replies, "No." Then why did you sign up for it? "I didn't sign up for it—it was just given to me."

Needless to say, this child's perception of the class or teacher may be entirely erroneous from an adult's view. But the point is that the child is assigned a class and kept in it by organizational decision. Watch the same rigidity of placement in the following conversation between a mother and the principal of one school:

A second mother appears with her daughter. This daughter has been bothered by one of the boys in the school and the girl wants to be transferred to another school. The principal says, "We can't transfer your daughter, at least not for some time." The girl says, "In the school I came from, I asked to be sent to the school I want to go to now, but they sent me to this school instead." The principal replies, "That is because you live in the district of this school." He then quietly reprimands the girl for not attending this school regularly. He attempts to find out if the girl was staying home to take care of her sister's new baby. The mother insists that this is not the case although it had been for a few days after the sister had come out of the hospital. The mother also indicates that she would see to it that her daughter attended school, but she is adamant about the transfer because of the boy who is pestering her daughter. The best that the principal could suggest was that they transfer the girl to another class.

Moving Along the Assembly Line

Uniform regulations apply to all children in a bureaucracy. His age locates him in the lock-step grade pattern which pushes him upward at regular intervals over more than a decade. Regardless of his intellectual capacity or social ability, the system allows little deviation in this pattern because the assumption underlying the organizational structure states:

. . . At each stage of an individual's development there are certain tasks, learnings, achievements, behaviors of which he is capable and which may be expected of him by society. From this is derived both the patterned progression through the school system and the section variations within each grade. 'Grade progression through the system is based on the allocation of a pupil to one grade for one year. . . . Pupils are graded and classified within a given grade level in accordance with standardized test results and teachers' estimates of ability and social maturity. . . . Teachers are advised to make every effort to identify the intellectually gifted by the end of the kindergarten year in anticipation of their later placement (Sheldon and Glazier, 1965).'

The age-grade system is a relatively recent organizational development. Prior to the end of the nineteenth century, children were expected to progress through readers at their own rates. A formal age-grade system developed partly in response to organizational size. Such a system meets the demands of the bureaucracy for orderly processing of children but it does not fit the needs of the teacher in her group nor of the children who are in it. The mental ages measured on standardized tests vary as much as four years in the first grade and eight years in the sixth grade (McNemar, 1942). This diversity in ability has been handled by sectioning each grade into supposedly homogeneous classes. These are traditionally formed by placing all those whose intelligence or achievement seem similar in the same group. Obviously, the present indices used to measure these two indicators and the indicators themselves are insufficient as measures of overall similarity. Presumably all types of learning are covered; yet research plainly indicates that group purpose determines whether homogeneity or heterogeneity is appropriate. Furthermore, the assumption underlying ability groups is that all should have about equal capacity; however, this is necessary only if uniformity in content, methods, and pacing are also assumed appropriate. Finally, there are social and psychological consequences that are detrimental

(Taba, 1962). Haggard (1957) found psychologically adverse effects on groups and individuals from the pressures for high achievement in gifted groupings. For those in lower sections, Clark (1965) concludes:

Children who are stigmatized by being placed in classes designated as "slow" or "dull" or for "children of retarded mental ability" cannot be expected to be stimulated and motivated to improve their academic performance. Such children understandably will become burdened with resentment and humiliation and will seek to escape the humiliating school situation as quickly as possible.

Sociologically, sectioning into homogeneous groups tends to perpetuate the social class and ethnic group divisions in society. Years ago Warner (1944) discovered that homogeneous classes reflected the community status system quite accurately; of fifty-three lower-income children, only six were in the top class, twenty-eight in the middle class and nineteen in the lowest class. The upper class children numbered eight in the top class, and one in the middle and lowest classes. Warner concluded that ability grouping teaches people to like being on their own status levels. As Taba says:

. . . it seems idle to talk about grouping in general. Manageable, productive, and dynamic learning groups can be put together only in the light of the specific purpose, the specific situations, and the nature of learning processes employed. . . . It seems clear also that multiple rather than single criteria need to be employed for designing groups. . . . Classrooms composed exclusively for expedience and convenience of scheduling can easily contain groups composed of human ingredients which are imposto manage. . . . The idea of reducing differences by homogenizing groups on a single basis is always an illusion. . . .

In one school, even the graded curriculum has been junked in favor of phases through which children can progress at their own rates of speed without worrying about which grade they are in. This experimental school has produced the following results:

The ancient shibboleth that all students are equal and should study the same phenomena and learn the same details has been thoroughly dissipated. . . . Our teachers have been compelled to abandon the mass of trivia which directs the way conventional classes are taught. I am referring to the monotonous practice whereby the teacher conducts a class by asking questions to which he has pat answers. . . . The most reassuring result has been the complete disappearance of discipline problems. . . . With students taking more responsibility for their own learning, we found that the conventional high school library was no longer appropriate. . . . When we took the limits off learning, many students began to ask for longer school hours (Brown, 1964).

Despite these innovations, the metropolitan school systems often remain locked in age-grades and homogeneous groupings. The system in which junior high schools were observed had, in fact, developed an elaborate subclassification of children within a grade. The wide disparity of age-graded classes were classified into common intellectual groupings. Thus, a child who is sent to the seventh grade—despite his intellectual capabilities—will be assigned to a class given a number or exponent which denotes it as superior, such as 7-1, or inferior, 7-21. Those with exceptional talent or exceptional lack of talent are given names such as Special Progress at the superior end or Special Adjustment at the inferior end. By the time the child is about six years of age, his placement by intellectual competence is begun. Children, just as teachers, develop their own prestige system on the basis of age or seniority and intellectual placement. Listen to one child talking to an observer:

The child informs me that he is the brightest boy in the class and then tells me his I.Q. score. I asked him how he knows he is the brightest boy and he says, "My teacher told me. My class is the one with the smartest kids."

These bright children, according to one observer, "have an elite place in the school system. They are a special group administratively and are considered to be such by others." Special treatment is accorded these few children in all schools observed:

". . . this is a class with special projects. . . ."

". . . I am doing an intensive job on giving them materials which will challenge their minds. . . ."

". . . this means a more intense subject content . . ."

". . . this group is a highly selected one and it is one that is able to get along admirably with the teachers. . . ."

Standards for entrance to these classes are quite high. One teacher does not feel his top class on the grade meets these standards. He refers to the class as a "supposed" talent class, saying:

". . . Many of the students are here because the class happens to be very small and they couldn't exactly permit that, so they has to toss in other kids who did not have the talent.

Since only about fifteen of every hundred students in the urban school system go on to college, what happens to the other eighty-five? A large proportion of them are placed in middle classes but a considerable number are found in the lowest levels on each grade level. For those considered exceptionally "dense" or deviant, there are also special classes. Placement to these classes is supposedly based on I.Q. scores derived from individual intelligence tests. Children in Classes for Retarded Mental Development (CRMD) are those with I.Q.s between 50 and 75. Children who deviate from the system are placed in Special Adjustment classes. And children who aren't "stupid" enough or "disturbed" enough to get into these classes simply end up in classes labeled 8-23 or 7-21, the lowest classes on the grade level. Theoretically, these classes with special names are ". . . established to avoid stigmatization of the child. Pupils attending these classes are accepted as part of the assembly and playground groups, as monitors and participants in other school activities" (Sheldon and Glazier, 1965). Again, theoretically, children are placed by intellectual competence. That those in such classes are neither integrated into the school activities nor placed by intellectual potential seems to be the opinion of one administrator who was interviewed:

. . . there are about fifty children in the program for the mentally retarded . . . they are segregated in one section of the building and share only one joint activity with other students. Brown says, "I don't think they should be in the building at all. But someone at 'headquarters' says we have to educate all the children so there isn't anything we can do. I feel that most of them aren't mentally retarded but rather have emotional blocks to learning. They could benefit from psychiatric care but that's not even available for the brighter kids so you can't expect it to be provided for this group."

The differentiation of children in these retarded classes in the social system of the school is not only marked by control of space in the school but also by time in terms of their class schedules.

In some ways this is the most overtly custodial program I have yet seen. The school day is shorter because they are dismissed earlier at the end of the morning and afternoon. Two periods are devoted to gym and one period to arts and crafts. The reading period in the morning and the "social studies" program in the afternoon are the only periods devoted to anything resembling the academic.

For children who deviate from institutional demands in their behavior there is also special treatment. Guidance classes are available for children who:

". . . have a history of truancy or who are holdovers. . . . They are potential dropouts."

According to another teacher, these classes—at least in one school—are not considered helpful by the students themselves:

. . . a number of the boys—about five or six—have been transferred to the career guidance class. This is a place where most of the kids don't want to go. They are afraid, for one thing, of being considered helpless and, for another thing, of the stiff corporal punishment applied by the career guidance teachers.

Still other classes are available for the youngster who is not behaving properly. For example, special classes for children with behavioral problems are provided by the school system. In a conversation with a teacher of one of these classes, the observer noted the wide variation in reading scores in the classes, to which the teacher responded:

". . . to some extent these classes are a dumping ground for kids who have trouble getting along. The adjustment classes stay put in one room except for gym and shop."

Again, we find that children who are "different" in some way from others in the system are controlled by the institution in a way that limits their space in the school in a manner similar to elementary school treatment of children.

Other classes, those with the lowest exponents on each grade level, are not as clearly differentiated within the social structure by obvious and overt control of location. Such classes are more integrated into the junior high pattern, following similar time and space movement of other children in higher classes. Though the placement is again supposedly on the basis of intellect, one teacher of such a group said:

"The class is extremely erratic. There are wide variations, for example, in their reading scores from the fourth year to almost the eighth." Why is this so? "It's related to discipline problems. In effect the class is a kind of a dumping ground for kids who get into trouble in their previous classes."

Still another teacher commented:

". . . 8-23 might be of interest to you because these are holdover students. All these students were held over from the previous semester and many of them present quite a discipline problem."

Finally, some children belong to non-existent classes—simply "paper classes." For example, in school No. 1, the observer records the following:

There are children who are said to be traveling with a class. These are children who get transferred out of the classes they started in for poor behavior, mental incapacities, or ability beyond the level of the class they are in. For one reason or another, *officially* they are in classes that have a special number but exist only on paper. Actually, they are part of other ongoing classes without ever having been transferred officially to these classes.

Children, regardless of the number or names given their

classes, are usually quite aware of the prestige system of their class placement in the school. One boy told an observer: "I want very much to be transferred out of this class. It's ruining my record. I want to learn."

One teacher in another study (McGeoch, 1965) says, "they want a lot of books to carry, to make it look as though they are smart. Of course, they know they aren't 'smart,' that they aren't in a bright class, but even carrying books they can't read helps a little." Words that are supposedly more palatable such as Adjustment or Guidance do not disguise the social system for the children. If anything, the jargon leads the child to lump together certain classes just as it leads the housewife to discover and then classify all boxes of soap as simply "big" when they are called King Size, Jumbo Size and Family Size. To the educational consumer, the child, low exponents and special names become labels that all mean classes which are for "dumb" or "delinquent" kids. The fact that these two categories can apply to the same class is also known to a child. Watch a guidance counselor use the threat of placement in a lower-level class with one youngster:

The counselor asks, "Are you on welfare? What does your father do? Where does he live? Why aren't you doing better in school?" After the child's muffled replies to each question, the counselor then says, "I'm beginning to think that the thing to do with you is to put you in a class where you *can play* all day long."

Institutionalizing Individuals and Groups

Ostensibly, the use of homogeneous groups is for the purpose of helping the child without slowing down classmates. As a result, the slow child should be less visible to his peers as lacking ability. Unfortunately, the system appears to work in reverse. In addition, the standards of intellectual calibre may be confused with behavioral indices. Obviously, the nature of the small group is drastically affected by grade and section placement policies. Still another way the organization may control the teacher and her group is to determine the actual size of the class. The range of class size is generally set by the administration without, and sometimes despite, teachers' recommendation. Even with insistent pressure from teachers' unions, class size is only reduced by one or two students in a number of cities. This reduction is somewhat short of the ideal size suggested by the next teacher:

I ask him about the problems of teaching in this school and the ways teaching here could be improved. He has one pat answer: "No class should be larger than fifteen." That is his solution to the problem. He is adamant about it, adding no other solutions.

Though other teachers may wish to offer other solutions, many would agree that their work as leaders with students is limited by the size of classroom groups. These groups, however, vary in size; some are standard—". . . There were about thirty students. . . . There were only twenty-six pupils in this class today. . . ." And a few were subdivided into separate sections for specialized instruction. For example:

. . . there were ten children in the class while the other half was busy at remedial reading, orchestra or other activities. . . .

. . . there were only eight students present. The teacher explains that this is a special class in reading. Part of the class has gone to another teacher.

For shop, the official class split into four groups. Two of these groups attended woodworking shops while the other two attended arts and crafts.

Teachers of groups that are involved in non-academic subjects are more likely to face large collections of children from several classes combined together. Teachers of children at either end of the intellectual continuum are more likely to have split classes, but for entirely different reasons. Classes of "limited intellect" are usually split into smaller groups for specialized work in reading. Classes considered bright are split into groups for diversified programs in foreign languages, vocal or instrumental music, and art. Thus, the bureaucracy determines group size in general and subgroup size by intellectual level. It also offers different educational experiences through control of curriculum. This control is partly caused by the size of non-academic classes in which children's participation is limited because of crowded conditions. In addition, the control of physical facilities and equipment indirectly influences curriculum in academic groups as well. In an upper-level class, one teacher says:

". . . . I want to show the film, 'The Valiant Years' which the Board of Education has, but the film will arrive too late. It shows some of the causes of World War I and I need the film for dramatization to increase interest. Dramatization and interest lead to better retention because it's associative. However, by the time the film comes, it will be too late. It will be merely review."

Unfortunately, using bureaucratic channels does not always lead to improved physical conditions. For example, here is the monthly report of:

Room: 304
Teacher: S. Barrett
Door off hinge.
Sliding wardrobe panel doesn't close: blackboard on it can't be used.
Book closet, back of room, broken; shelf splintered.
Window in back, right, broken.
Teacher's desk missing two drawers.
Radiator keeps clanging.
(Same conditions prevail as in last month's report, with addition of radiator. Hole in window getting bigger, though. Wind and rain blowing in. Also, glass crunching underfoot.) (Kaufman, 1964).

Still another way in which small group goals are influenced is through the amount of work done by students that is basically an extension of administrative tasks. Though less influential than poor physical conditions, a prime example of this is:

The art class gives its full period (a double session) to the production of posters for a program on music and art which has been planned by the staff.

Group goals can also be influenced by the demands of external examinations:

The teacher tells the students that for homework they are to work out problems 36 to 42 in their sample copy of the 1962 Regents Review Book. One student speaks up: "We've already done problems 36 to 42." The teacher replies, "My mistake." He then assigns other problems from the Regents Review Book.

Organizational control of learning activities through the demands of an external examination determine group goals for both teacher and learners. The system's influence extends, in addition, to the composition of small groups through control of distribution of sex and ethnic groupings to which children belong. Cutting across classes of all sizes, intellect, and curricular experience in all classrooms are these primary membership groups. Administrative policy within a school may accord differential treatment to children on the basis of sex membership. In school No. 1, for example, boys and girls are separated by administrative decision in many activities. Teachers indicate that:

Girls and boys have separate entrances into the building but are mixed together in the lines which go from class to class. The only rule there is to stay on the right.

Boys and girls have separate entrances into the lunch room.

In the pupils' cafeteria, they feed about two hundred early—the CMRD, Career Guidance, and Special Adjustment classes. About five hundred kids are fed later. The girls eat at one end and the boys at another.

Observers noted separation in assemblies, too:

In the assembly girls were seated on one side and boys on the other.

The auditorium has a number of children seated in it—boys and girls are sitting separately. At the appointed bell, the children leave in two single files. The girls come out one door and the boys come out the other.

The teacher lines up the girls first and then the boys to go to the auditorium in twos.

In schools where sex-separation is administratively demanded, the classroom groups are also more frequently arranged in the same fashion:

The class is not very orderly. Girls are sitting on one side and boys on the other. At the beginning of the period two of the boys sat in a girls' row. They were quickly and sharply put in their place and gave little argument about it.

The boys are seated in the first two rows and the girls, in the last two rows near the window.

In another school where there is no policy of sex segregation, the observers note:

Throughout the day there is not the rigid division by sex in seating patterns that is common in school No. 1.

Usually one sits next to someone of one's own sex. However, in this class there are two bi-sexual pairs.

No seating plan was arranged in this class but the boys were, for the most part, seated together apart from the girls.

In this school, in which sex segregation is not demanded by the administration, the children tend to gravitate—of their own accord—to others of their own sex. In the other sex-segregated schools the burden on the teacher to insure adherence to unnecessary rules regarding sex division seems a useless load. Since a wide variety of sociometric studies show that boys and girls show preference for members of their own sex when choosing seat companions or working classmates, administrative policy imposes superfluous regulation in school No. 1.

All schools, however, follow some pattern of sex-segregation by subject matter. For example:

Home economics is studied only by the girls. The only subject along these lines that both sexes take is tailoring. I feel that much of the hygiene course could be given to boys and girls together.

The next two periods are devoted to shop. The boys and girls separate for this. Aside from shop, all other classes today are co-ed, but in all classes the girls sit on one side of the room and the boys on the other side.

As mentioned previously, ethnic membership also cuts across small group lines and changes the nature of classroom member-

ship. In the schools observed, the effects of de facto segregation are abundantly evident. Despite plans to bus children out of the ghetto, to pair slum schools with those in other areas, and to make a multitude of other efforts to balance the racial composition of schools, children in the schools observed were primarily members of minority, lower-class groups. Some examples of this unequal ethnic distribution in classes include:

The class is about half Black and half Puerto Rican.

This morning there are twenty-one children present. All were Black except one who appears to be Japanese.

There are eighteen Black children in this split class.

One of the girls is a West Indian. A second is a Puerto Rican child. The remainder are Black Americans.

There are seven boys and four girls who are Black. The rest appear to be Puerto Rican.

Thirty-one children are present. Nineteen are boys and of this number, four are Black and the rest apparently Puerto Rican. There are eight Black girls, one Chinese girl and the rest of the girls seem to be Puerto Rican.

No other issue has been so important in education in the last few years as integration. No other problem has caused more difficulty in the urban metropolis for administrators. And no other problem has met with such lack of success, as seen in repeated failures to eliminate de facto segregation. The teacher, today, is still faced with a group of children who come from low-income areas and from ethnic minorities. When these children from various backgrounds meet together, there are a number of problems that have to be resolved in the classroom. Here is one such intergroup problem that ended up with the administrator:

Mr. S asks the girl and her mother what had happened. The girl was in tears. Yesterday, she apparently was hit by a boy in the school. She had evidently called the boy a name which referred to his color. It was a Puerto Rican vs. a Black epitaph. S listens to the girl's side of the story. According to her, she, as president of her class, was carrying the section sheet and one of the boys tried to grab it and hit her in the process. The principal then called in another boy and asked him to give his version and then later sent out for the boy who had been involved in the incident. All of the youngsters gave their conflicting views about what had happened. S then told the youngsters that the situation was over and ended. He told the girl that she should apologize to the boy for having called him a name and he told the boy that he should apologize to the girl for having hit her and taken the section sheet. The mutual apologies occurred and the whole matter was dismissed by the principal. Unfortunately, the youngsters' facial expressions left some doubts as to whether the incident was closed for them.

Both teachers and administrators must deal with a lop-sided ethnic distribution in classrooms because of a system and society which has yet to solve intergroup problems that are reflected in the children, whose behavior exhibits the stresses of segregated living. Until the school system can resolve the dilemma of unequal ethnic distribution, the teacher will continue to face the problems of class members who are not allowed to live and attend school in other areas.

These problems must be faced by each teacher *within* her own classroom since each class is only one of many similar small groups in the school. The school is, after all, a unique social system because, at base, it is simply a collection of many semi-autonomous groups of learners. These groups seldom engage in joint activity. When multiple groups do meet together, administrators usually affect each of them by first, taking the children from the classroom and second, determining what will happen to them while they are gone. Notice the reactions of some teachers and pupils to the disruption of their classroom groups:

The teacher says somewhat sarcastically to the students, "Thanks for telling me." The news of the trip was obviously new to her though the children apparently thought she already knew about it.

At 9:15, a man enters the room briefly and then leaves; the teacher says that he is a fellow teacher who is in charge of the assembly exercises. He wanted to get some of the students to practice for the installation services. "Seeing that I have a visitor, he decided not to ask the children to leave class. I'm very glad that you're here because it means that he won't take the kids away from my class today."

One of the boys complains that he has not had a chance to really get into the experiment or to understand what is going on. The teacher replies, "Do I call fire drills? I just work here."

Administrative policies about procedures which involve simultaneous movement and congregation of multiple groups create forced interaction of the school as a unit. Consider the effect on the next class:

While the students were writing, another bell sounded and this was the signal for the air shelter drill. Students immediately stopped writing and lined up. We went out into the hallway and waited a moment and then went down the steps from the fifth floor to the gymnasium at the bottom of the building. There was a great deal of noise in the hallway as all the classes were participating. The teacher remained in front of the class while en route downstairs. When we arrived in the gymnasium, all the classes were in orderly form and all the teachers were there to keep order. I asked the teacher how often they have these drills. He replied, "Since the principal is new here, we've had quite a few to orient the students to different kinds of drills. There is a fire drill, an air shelter drill and another drill which requires that the students leave the building."

The entire school or large portions of it may also be involved in another form of interaction for a common goal—assemblies—which are ostensibly arranged for the enjoyment and edification of students. Here are some examples of multiple group relationships in such gatherings:

I attended a seventh grade student assembly at which the student government officers were being inducted. The principal is speaking while most of the children are not paying attention. They are talking with each other or doing their homework.

On the stage a teacher is telling the children about selling boosters. The teacher is a ninth grade homeroom teacher who is promoting the ninth grade yearbook. The eighth graders generally sell ads or boosters within the community to help the ninth graders with their yearbook. The teacher says, "You will be ninth graders next year and will want the incoming eighth graders to do everything possible to help make your yearbook a success." He ends by adding, "The class which sells the most boosters will receive the largest party."

The principal goes to the stage and the group become very quiet. He gives the invocation and then the Color Guards with three flags walk to the stage and stand in the center while the group sings, "From the Halls of Montezuma," and gives the pledge of allegiance. Then the flags are placed on the stage and the children come back to their seats. The principal begins to reprimand some children in the back who are talking and tells some of them that they have no ties on.

In these assemblies very little participation from students is expected. Administrators plan, organize, and lead these gatherings. As might be expected, talking, homework, and administrators' remonstrations mark this lack of student involvement. Notice, also, that external rewards are used to get involvement. These are offered by a teacher—not a student. How do the students react to administrative rewards?

Some children are given individual commendation cards. At this point, discipline is extremely poor. There is a constant undertone while the guidance counselor on the platform attempts to announce the names of the various children who are to receive awards.

One class is announced as the winner of the award. There are boos and groans and laughter from the other classes. The president of the class walks to the platform and receives a commendation card from the assistant principal. Another class receives the Sanitation banner. The general attitude of the auditorium is still one of derision.

Though these gatherings of multiple groups are theoretically for the students, little student initiative is allowed and there is minimal student acceptance of adult rewards. The exception, of course, is the children in "high-ability" groups who are allowed to participate in more activities. The class presented next is in the bottom third of the seventh grade. Observe the confusion exhibited about administratively-controlled student government:

After a review of the test for the next day, the teacher asks the class, "Who is not in the Government Organization?" When almost half of the kids' hands were raised, he tells them, "Try to get some money in by Friday." One of the children asks, "Does the student government money go for Field Day?" Many of the boys seemed very confused by now about the use of money they were being asked to give. The teacher answers, "No, but you get a discount for Field Day." He then suggests that they earn forty cents over the weekend. Another student suggests that they earn a dime a day.

Though the school year is almost over, many of these children do not belong to the student government and are unsure about the activity of this body. Research findings suggest that children from middle-class backgrounds are much more likely to take major awards and honors in school activities (Abrahamson, 1952). Since inner-city schools are more homogeneous groupings of lower-income children, it would be hoped that here, at last, these children would have equal chance to excel. Evidently, administrative policy leads to involvement of those in upper-ability classes and again the majority of lower-class children are neglected (Sheldon and Glazier, 1965).

When administrative actions curtail student initiative, the functioning of each small group of learners is affected by creating a school climate which is not conducive to optimal student involvement. Research findings from a varied number of institutions suggest that personal activity in decisions and functions increases the morale of organization members (Anderson, 1959). Other studies indicate that people in central positions of power or importance in groups tend to be more satisfied and involved in the group's activities (Leavitt, 1951). If this is the case, it appears that the administrators conducting assemblies and the children from upper-ability groups who sing or walk in color guards in these meetings will be more involved than the majority of students who do nothing. In short, organizational influence in the form of limited authority and involvement of students can lead to a climate of low morale and limited identification with the school. This climate permeates the work of teacher and students in the small group.

Institutional control of students can be expressed in a large number of ways which directly or indirectly affect the teacher and her group. Regulations defining the activities allowed outside the classroom often create major strains within the class. As student autonomy decreases in the school, teacher authority increases, thus forcing added responsibilities. This control of student autonomy can be seen in the following observations:

These students are similar in that classroom doors are locked from the outside. . . .

At the door of the classroom, students are asked to line up. The classroom had been locked.

The students are not allowed to come into the front of the building. In fact, only one door is open and an older student is standing guard there.

The teacher says, "Two thirds of the class have lunch passes. These are permits to leave the school during lunch if the students want to."

Many of them had lunch passes with numbers on them. These lunch passes were distributed during the homeroom period when the children came back from their fourth period class.

Entrance into and out of the school can be strictly controlled by administrative policy. Movement between classes may also be influenced by the organization:

There is a regular system of having adults posted in the halls or outside of their classroom doors. Children are required to pass on the right hand side of the hall.

The formation of a double line before the end of the class period is required as one of the school's rules.

The teacher explains to the group, ". . . many of the monitors will not be traffic monitors any more. There will be only a few at the entrance to stairways. It is very important for you to continue walking close to the wall and in the right direction and on the assigned staircase. Otherwise the traffic in the hallways will become chaotic."

I ask Joan and another of her friends about the principals' contest in the schools, adding, "Are you going to vote?" They both say no, they did not like Mr. S. I asked why. Joan replies, "He is a little, short stump of a man who cuts off water. After he came into the school, he cut off the water on all the floors except the main office floor. Now if you want a drink of water, you have to go all the way downstairs."

Sometimes, when this control of students' movement from one group to another seems to falter, special efforts are expended to reinforce control:

Miss O says, "I don't know what I'll do when they try silent passing. I use the fact that the kids can talk in the halls to keep them quiet in the classroom. For example, I say, 'Hold it just a few minutes longer til we're finished. You can tell her outside.' This system will really be thrown away if they enforce silence in the halls, too."

The teacher says, "They're having an operation during the next period." What is an operation? "It's like an operation dragnet. All the kids found in the halls after a certain time allowed for passing are picked up and taken to the assistant principal's office. There is an entry made on their records." Does it work? "For a day or so." Another teacher comments, "It doesn't really work. The only thing that would make it effective would be to send the kids somewhere they really feared to go." The first teacher continues, "The children don't know about these operations ahead of time but the teachers—or at least those on patrol—are notified of them."

Here are some of the things that happen to children while en route from one class to another:

There are several children in the hall during this period. Some of them are obviously on legitimate errands such as carrying supplies to a shop-room. Questionable pupils are stopped and have to justify their reasons for being in the halls. One or two have wooden placards with room numbers on them indicating they had been excused for the bathroom.

While passing through the hall, I talk with Fred. He tells me he liked typing the best. He had had typing a year ago at another school. About this time, a teacher stopped Fred and then saw me and asked if Fred were with me. I indicated he was. Fred looked at the teacher as if to say, "So there."

Just as I had gone through the doorway leading into the main part of the building, I notice that my student escort is stopped by a male teacher. I hear the student say that he is with that teacher, meaning me. The teacher replies, "Oh, no you're not," Then he sees me looking and asks if the child is with me. I say that he is. This teacher is equipped with a long wooden pole, which, after he let my escort through, he began to use by beating the children back who were following us. He did this by hitting them on the head with the pole.

One boy came in and said, "Oh boy, Mr. S, don't ever send me out in the hall again." The teacher says, "What happened, son?" The student replied, "I was picked up and sent to the principal's office." To this the teacher replied, "Don't worry, I'll take care of it. You were out on legitimate business." The teacher then explains to me that this boy runs errands in the afternoon because he can't take a full day of school.

It is rather obvious that the nature of the interaction in a small learning group will be affected by the institutional norms outside it. Both teacher and children will be influenced by this regimentation. The teacher who attempts to develop more student autonomy in her class may find that children perceive this as free license to do what they want because the institutional norms of externally-imposed control are in such contrast to classroom norms of internalized control. Children may not be able to shift their expectations of authority to meet those of a less-authoritarian adult. Even if the teacher attempts to vary the institutional norms in her classroom, the various control mechanisms will continue to intrude into her activities thus nullifying much of her effort. Consider the following examples of teacher enforcement of institutional requirements:

. . . a second girl receives permission from the teacher and takes the wooden placard which permits her to go to the bathroom.

A student came into the class late and brought a letter to Mrs. R who reads it and then says, "It doesn't look like it's legal to me, but I haven't got time to look it over."

Mr. S is passing out consent slips for the children to attend a program in honor of the district superintendent.

The rules and regulations that govern the school as a whole must be adhered to by individual teachers. Lunch permits, wooden bathroom passes, consent slips for parents, excuses for tardiness, and various other forms and formalities are daily intrusions into the life of each classroom group. Moreover, the teacher must face the consequences if her groups do not use the right stairways or the right traffic lanes or the right doorways.

Intruding into the Classroom

Administrative intrusions may be more direct. Listen to the principals below talk over the public address system to students in their classrooms:

The pledge of allegiance is recited and the class then sings the last verse of "America." Following this, two announcements are made: first, those students selected for special musical programs "are selected because we know they can keep up academically." For the "special opportunity" of participating in the musical programs you do have to pay a price—that price is increased work at home. . . . "

The broadcast system is audible in the background, but no one is paying any attention. Finally, the teacher tells everyone to stand and face the flag. By then, the pledge is half over and no one participates. A few children sing "America."

The morning announcement comes over the loudspeaker. The principal stresses the need for better housekeeping, but concentrates on inter-period changes, and the "horsing around that goes on." He tells about a boy "horsing around" yesterday who tried to run away from him but was eventually caught. "From now on people causing trouble during the change between classes will not be let off with just a warning, but a notation will be made on their report cards. If you're going to do something wrong, you should expect to be punished for it. Running away will only postpone the punishment. We will shortly institute one silent passing a week. We have visitors coming today from _____ College. You shouldn't spoil your reputation in the presence of strangers. We're not freaks at _____."

These regularly scheduled intrusions are managed differently by various teachers. Harder still to handle are unscheduled "spot" intrusions:

Just after the child began his report on the Vikings, the talk is interrupted by an announcement over the loudspeaker. The principal intones, "Far too much time is spent in passing between classes especially prior to the last period." Children are then told to do this more rapidly and hall monitors are ordered to pick up stragglers.

At 2:55, there is a loudspeaker announcement of an invitation to a picnic to be held that day.

At 1:20, the loudspeaker comes on and interrupts the spelling test. A male voice says that the purpose of the interruption is to answer their question about Holy Day. "Tomorrow is not a Holy Day of obligation for Catholics so they are expected to come to school. On Holy Thursday, there is a mass every hour at the Catholic churches. Children may not be excused to attend mass after you have reported to the school. You may go in the morning to mass."

Administrative intrusion may be direct with personal, physical intervention—wanted or unwanted—into the classroom:

One child spills some paint on the floor. The teacher takes this in stride and proceeds to direct some children to help clean it up. While this is going on, the principal enters and immediately instructs one boy to help clean up. His instructions nullify those of the teacher, but she accepts the help of the additional child. After a few minutes more, Mr. _____ leaves.

Committees of children are working on compositions about their favorite games. The teacher asks two of the committee chairmen to report what they are doing. Two girls report—the first is allowed to finish but the second one is interrupted and sent back to her seat. The teacher then explains it all instead. The principal tells the girl who is interrupted, "You've left an 'o' out of monopoly."

About ten minutes before the bell rings, an exceptionally large man enters the room. When he enters, he looks around for a moment and then walks over to the windows and opens two or three very wide. He then returns to the back of the room where he stands and watches the class for about three minutes. The teacher continues his lecture and the students are exceptionally quiet during this time. When the assistant principal leaves, there is a sigh of relief and an undercurrent of talking.

In each case, the nature of the small group is changed by the administrative intervention. Whether usurping the teacher's role or supporting her flagging leadership by his authority, the administrators influence the children.

No group of human beings stands alone. They are always in relation to each other and to still other groups. School children in educational groups feel the influence of an immense bureaucracy through interventions both direct and indirect, affecting them and their teachers within the small groups called classes.

The most dramatic intervention into the classroom life is seen in the struggle for power contained in the neighborhood control conflict. All the strains among various levels in the system are evident in this battle. All the cleavages between the schools and the community are apparent in this conflict. In the middle of the furor, no children, no friends, no group, no teachers continue in a viable way. In the center of the adult maelstrom, classes are disbanded or regrouped into odd collections of stragglers. Pitting the teachers against the families, the end result is further deterioration in the classroom group and increased elaboration of the bureaucracy. Whether the system of public education continues to exist depends on the outcome of these conflicts. How and in what ways the bureaucracy will continue to intervene into the lives of students and teachers in classrooms in the question to be answered in the next decade.

Poor Kids and Public Schools

by Ray C. Rist

We began this study with the contention that myths die hard in America. If what we have seen in Attucks School is representative, we can add that inequality will also die hard. What we have found is an interlocking pattern of institutional arrangements descending from the macrolevel of the city-wide school system to the social and cultural milieu of a single school to the various stratification techniques employed by individual teachers in their classrooms. The outcome of this multileveled organization is ultimately expressed by comparing the experiences of the Tigers to those of the Cardinals and Clowns or more precisely, comparing the experiences of Laura to those of Lilly.

Throughout the various levels of the St. Louis educational system we found commonly shared assumptions about "how things really are." The basic tenets may be summarized as follows: Middle-class students can learn, lower-class students cannot; white schools are "good," black schools are "bad"; control is necessary, freedom is anarchy; violence works, persuasion does not; teachers can save a few, but will lose many; the school tries, the home will not; and finally, only the naive would dispute these beliefs, as the wise know. *The outcome of this set of attitudes, assumptions, and values is that the school as an institution sustains, in a myriad of ways, the inequalities with which children first come to school.* The school's response to issues of color, class, and control all mesh together to make two nets—one to catch winners and one to catch losers.

Teaching and Learning in Attucks School

A major goal of this study has been to demonstrate the means by which teachers' assumptions manifest themselves within the classroom setting. These assumptions transform themselves into expectations for individual children, with the result that differential treatment is accorded various members of the same class. The single most influential variable to which the teachers responded was the social class background of the student. Thus, the kindergarten teacher's expectations as to who would emerge within the class as a "fast learner" and who would emerge as a "slow learner" clearly delineated the middle-class students from their peers. It is important to reiterate that when the teacher made her seating assignments on the eighth day, she had no formal measures of academic ability or cognitive development to aid in her evaluation.

With both the first and second grade teachers, the process of within-class differentiation resulted in patterns of classroom organization not dissimilar from those of the kindergarten teacher. The latter two teachers, however, created their tracking systems not on the basis of subjective interpretations, but by evaluating the previous test scores and readiness material completed by each student. The end result of this "objective" placement of students in different groups was the reinforcement of internal class divisions instigated by the kindergarten teacher.

One outcome of within-class tracking was the creation of a pattern of segregation among the students based on the socioeconomic positions of their parents. Among those defined by the teachers as expected to learn were the students who came to school clean and neatly dressed, who came from homes intact and middle-class in attributes, who displayed interest in the teacher, continually sought interaction with her, and who quickly learned the routine of schooling. On the other side of the segregation barrier were the students who were often dirty and smelling of urine, who came from poor homes frequently headed by one parent, who did not seek interaction with the teacher and who never appeared to grasp the subtleties of the school routine. The relative impermeability of the top group through the various grades gave it a castelike character violated only once in two and a half years.

In the examination of specific classrooms, there emerged at least two identifiable interactional processes which operated simultaneously. Both occurred between teacher and student and both evolved four distinct stages. Using the kindergarten as an example, the first involved the teacher and the students sitting at Table 1. Initially the kindergarten teacher developed expectations for different students in her class, some of whom she believed met the criteria essential for future academic success. Second, she reinforced through mechanisms of positive differential treatment those particular characteristics deemed important and desirable in that select group. In turn, the students responded with the behavior which helped them from the beginning to gain the attention and support of the teacher. Thus, the Table 1 students perceived that verbalization was an ability that the teacher admired and so persisted with high levels of verbalization throughout the year. The cycle completed itself as the teacher again focused even more specifically on the Table 1 students, in whom she found the behavior she desired. The end of this process was the creation of an interactional scheme in which certain early forms of behavior exhibited by the students came to be permanent behavioral patterns, continually reinforced by the teacher.

A concurrent behavioral process went on between the teacher and students placed at Tables 2 and 3. These students came into the class possessing a series of attributes, both behavioral and social, which the teacher perceived as indicative of "failure" within her frame of reference. By reinforcing her initial expectations, she made it evident that she did not consider them similar or equal to the students classified as fast learners. Those marked as potential and probable failures responded accordingly. That is, because of the teacher's use of control, her lack of verbal interaction and encouragement, her allocation of a disproportionately small amount of her teaching time, and her various techniques of exclusion, this group of students withdrew from classroom participation. The final stage was the cyclical repetition of solidifying behavioral and attitudinal characteristics initially labeled unacceptable. Like the students in the first group, the anticipated failures were not objectively tested before they were tracked.

Generally, one might assume that the students in the class as a whole possessed the range of potentials and abilities necessary to cope with the demands and routines of schooling. Yet without ascertaining those potentials, the teacher responded on the basis of social class criteria which inhibited two groups of students from changing positions—those in the higher group who in fact did not have the potential and those in the lower groups who did. This analysis should not be misconstrued to imply that segregation resulting from ability tracking in the classroom on the basis of objective criteria would be acceptable. What I do suggest is that the teacher by her actions may have created a situation in which those in the higher group who might not have been expected "objectively" to perform at the high level came to do so and those in the lower group from whom one "objectively" would expect more came to give less: all in accordance with the teacher's expectations.

From a different perspective one might argue that the teachers in Attucks School created their tracking systems not because they believed their students to be so dissimilar that they required entirely different treatment, but because they were quite similar. That is, the teachers may have assumed that the conditions within the black community were so strongly inhibitive to the development of successful middleclass life styles that it became absolutely necessary to "'save" those few whom they perceived as having even the slightest opportunity. The patterns of classroom segregation were created to protect the high group from the lower groups, with their interests in the "streets," their use of "bad" language, and their lack of regard for school. One teacher, in fact, stated that the school had two types of students—those with "street blood" and those with "school blood." The pathos and the sense of the tenuousness of success in the black community that are evident in these assumptions are not entirely without foundation. As Jencks (1972b) has so amply demonstrated, the middle-class black father has less than half the opportunity of the middle-class white father to pass on the benefits of his position to his offspring, in terms of both occupation and income.

Within the classrooms, one of the seemingly inescapable consequences of the segregation systems was that the children themselves quickly picked up what it meant to be on one side of the barrier or the other. Each group of students began to emulate the teacher's treatment of the other. The high group followed the teacher in their ridicule, belittlement, physical abuse, and social ostracism of the lower groups. In short, middle-class students were learning, very early on, the mannerisms and techniques of how to deal with the lower class. The lower-class students displayed patterns of deference and passivity toward those of the high group. They seldom returned the ridicule in kind and infrequently began any sort of conflict with the high group. *Thus the middle-class students were learning to control the poor, and the poor students were learning to shuffle.* The classrooms became microcosms of the larger society in which cultural values were transmitted and put into operation so as to legitimate the attitudes and assumptions necessary for the perpetuation of inequality.

An important part of this transmission of cultural values is the definition given to the activities of major institutions. The current institutional arrangements in this society favor the affluent and discriminate against the poor. This holds true whether one examines patterns of political power, economic concentration, occupational mobility, or access to the goods and services available in the society. Those who benefit are not likely to clamor for change in the status quo. In fact, what often emerges is an attempt to rationalize the inequalities as natural, inevitable, and desirable. This, in fact, has occurred in American schools. The patterns of schooling function so as to reward the kinds of activities and interests characteristic of middle- and upper-income students while ignoring or negating the contributions of lower-class students.

The rationalizations for this inequality take the form of defending "standards" that are class based, of proclaiming a policy of "equal treatment for all" which does no more than reinforce inequalities, and of laying the onus for lack of success on the individual rather than on the institution. Such assumptions attempt to undercut demands for change in institutional arrangements by implying that the institution is, in fact, benign and that any tinkering would only be deterimental. The irony emerges when one comes to take an egalitarian position in defense of inequality. Such is the present state of American education.

It should be evident from all that has gone before in this study that teachers play the central role in establishing and perpetuating the system of classroom segregation. The consequences and ramifications of this are several. First, teachers

create for themselves a paradoxical position. On the one hand, they view themselves as teachers—as those who seek to aid children to learn of themselves and their world. Yet they respond to the socioeconomic differences in their students in a way that precludes for some the very opportunity for learning. They generate failure in some of their students while believing themselves to desire success for their charges. The way out of this dilemma for teachers and school systems in general is to assume that they have done all they can in the face of overwhelming environmental (and genetic) odds. As Kenneth Clark has noted (1969):

> Educational officials and teachers have been persuaded—and particularly have persuaded themselves—that the causes of the educational retardation of Negro children are not to be found in the quality of teaching or school supervision. They have explained this chronic problem in terms of the children's alleged personal deficiencies—hostility and aggressiveness towards authority, low attention span, lack of educational experiences prior to entering school, and low motivation for academic work. The parents are to blame, so the teachers say, because they have "no-books-in-the-home," Because they lack interest in their children's school achievement. Some educators seriously offered as an explanation of student retardation the fact that these parents "do not attend PTA meetings." They assert that the community is to blame because it suffers all the pathologies of ghettoes—it has dirty streets, over-crowded and deteriorated homes, and provides no model of academic excellence and reward for children.

Secondly, teachers may be fairly equal in their use of praise and reward with their students and still reinforce differences through use of control. The second grade teacher, for example, gave nearly equal amounts of verbal reward to the Clowns and to the Tigers. Yet the pervasiveness of control-oriented behavior toward the Clowns effectively thwarted a positive learning situation. One might only surmise what consequences the reversal of this situation would have had on patterns of performance within the class.

Third, the teachers' seemingly immutable assumption of the class-based differences in children was grounded not in an attempt to be malicious, but in their belief that "some can do it and some cannot." On one level it is possible to agree with the teachers that profound differences do exist between children because of environment, genetic endowment, and interaction between the two. However, the issue is not so much whether differences do exist, for there are few who would argue that children all come from the same mold, but what, in fact, one does with such information. If one responds in such a way as to assume that initial differences will be manifest as eternal differences, then a determinist theory of man results in classrooms where attempts at minimizing such differences are viewed as useless exercise. In such classrooms, the teacher can do little more than follow the "inevitable." If, though, a teacher acknowledges that children come to the classroom with differences, but that they also are capable of learning of their world, then the teacher-student relation becomes of immense importance in the pursuit of academic performance and cognitive development. The stagnation of tracking systems can be broken only by redefining what is supposed to happen inside classrooms.

The teachers did not acknowledge the adaptations made by the students placed in the lower groups as having any function in the making of "successful" students. Faced with ridicule from teacher and peers, receiving on occasion as little as one-sixth of the teaching time of the top group, and subject to continual control-oriented behavior, the students developed among themselves patterns of secondary learning, of infrequently giving the teacher the response sought, and often giving no response at all. Teachers saw these reactions as further evidence that the students were "not yet ready" to handle the material being taught to the high group. The reinforcement of the self-fulfilling prophecy persisted when teachers thus misinterpreted student behavior initially instigated, in part, as a reaction to their own behavior.

Finally, and in defense of the teachers, it has not been a contention of this study that the teachers observed in Attucks School could not effectively teach their students. In my estimation, they taught quite well. *Competence, however, is not the issue. The issue is the unequal accessibility to students of that competence.* Students who came to the classroom from middle-class homes experienced a positive and rewarding learning situation where they were given large amounts of teacher attention, were the subject of little control-oriented behavior, held as models for the remainder of the class, and continually reminded that they were "special" students. Hypothetically, if Attucks School had contained only those students perceived by teachers as having the traits necessary for middle-class status and future success, I would anticipate that the teachers would have continued to teach well, and in these circumstances, to the entire class. The consequences of reserving their teaching for those whom they believed were destined to become winners necessarily resulted in the avoidance of those destined to become losers. And losers are what they became.

What is to be Done? Reflections on Policies, Priorities, and Options

What follows is predicated upon one basic assumption: that an advocacy of the rights and freedoms of children supersedes the need to legitimate or perpetuate any educational institution touching their lives. Thus it is not the system that must be preserved, but the integrity of the child; not the administrative positions, but the environment for learning; and not the necessity of adapting for institutional survival, but the gaining and sustaining of individual freedom.

Asking the question, "What is to be done with American schools?" is like opening a Pandora's box. The alternatives may range from a return to "traditional" emphasis upon such skills as reading and writing, to the creation of "discovery centers" where children would be free to plot and chart their own courses in what they seek to learn, to the ultimate disbanding or disestablishing of schools as a distinct institution. There is, of course, the additional possibility of allowing schools to continue as they are. To provide some delineation for a discussion of options in American education, the following propositions are offered as a context within which various policies and programs might be evaluated.

First, the school as a state-financed institution requiring attendance will be with us into the indefinite future. This does not rule out the continued existence of private, parochial, or "alternative" schools. But the realities of large and increasingly powerful teacher organizations; of communities with tens of millions of dollars invested in buildings, equipment and supplies; of parents who want someone else to "teach" their children; and of an industrial society which utilizes educational credentials as a means to sort and categorize persons for different social class positions, all lead me to believe that the bureaucracy of public schooling will persist. Further, the chief means by which this bureaucracy has retained its clients has been compulsory attendance. I do not envision schools becoming so free as to offer children and parents the option of whether or not to attend.

Ivan Illich (1971) has argued that schools should be "disestablished" or else society should be "deschooled" so that learning ceases to be the scarce commodity held by a few and distributed at their discretion. The end result, Illich argues, of such differential access to "learning" is the perpetuation of inequality between those who possess it and those who do not. I agree with his critique of education as "commodity," but as Gintis (1972) has noted, there is yet a step beyond negating the current educational systems. A new synthesis is reached by recreating in such a manner as to transform their functions. Gintis suggests that it is irrelevant to speak of "deschooling" when American society chooses not to talk also of the means by which to "de-office," "de-factory," or more generally, "de-bureaucratize." He proposes that the issue is not whether schools are going to wither away, but whom they will serve. Gintis assumes, ". . . Schools are so important to the reproduction of the capitalist society that they are unlikely to crumble under any but the most massive political onslaughts." Thus, so long as the current institutional arrangements in schooling continue serving the ultimate stratification functions they presently do, the central arena for educational change becomes the political arena. Political, for the aim is not to abolish, but to transform so as to work toward the creation of a new social system. He notes:

> The only presently viable political strategy in education . . . is what Rudi Deutchke terms "the long march through the institutions," involving the localized struggles for what Andre Gorz calls "non-reformist reforms," i.e., reforms which effectively strengthen the power of the teachers vis-à-vis administrators, and of students vis-à-vis teachers. . . .
>
> In other words, the correct immediate political goal is the nurturing of individuals both liberated (i.e., demanding control over their lives and outlets for their creative activities and relationships) *and* political aware of the true nature of their misalignment with the larger society.

A second proposition, which follows in part from the first, recognizes that, as Jencks (1972b) has written, "schools serve primarily to legitimize inequality, not to create it." As was manifestly evident in Attucks School, the inequalities, for example, with which Laura and Lilly came to school were reinforced, not reduced. The social class configurations of the larger society were mirrored and affirmed in the patterns of organization within individual rooms. Jencks notes: ". . . Schools serve primarily as selection and certification agencies, whose job is to measure and label people, and only secondarily as socialization agencies, whose job is to change people." (p. 135)

A wide range of major research findings, including the Equality of Educational Opportunity Survey, a study of the ninety-one high schools included in the Project Talent survey, and the Census Bureau studies of social mobility and income distribution, all provided Jencks with evidence. Given the seminal importance of Jencks' work, it is crucial to recapitulate his major findings and implications for American education. They may be summarized in five points:

1. Access to the resources of schools is distributed quite unequally, being directly related both to social class position and length of time spent in school. Access also varies with race, whites benefiting more than blacks.

2. "We found that both genetic and environmental inequality played a major role in producing cognitive inequality. We also found that those who started life with genetic advantages tended to get environmental advantages as well, and that this exacerbated inequality. . . . We found no evidence that differences between schools contributed significantly to cognitive inequality . . ." (pp. 253-254)

3. The family background of an individual was more influential in determining how much schooling he received than either intelligence (measured by IQ) or quality of schooling.

4. The occupation one eventually attains is directly affected

by educational background, and educational background is influenced by family background. Thus family background becomes the more important of several factors ultimately influencing occupational status.

5. Education influences the options one has for first entering a particular occupation, but it does not have much effect on earnings or competence within that occupation.

The implications of these findings for the future of American education and for the issue of inequality in general create the basis for a third proposition: that reform within the schools can ultimately have only marginal effect on the inequality that exists outside schools. *Consequently, if one wishes to reduce the present inequality in American society, it is more advantageous to attack it directly than to attempt to ameliorate it through manipulating the institution of school, which is only tangentially related to the creation of that inequality.* If one wishes to make the situations of adults more equal in income, opportunities for mobility, and job security, then it is necessary to address oneself to the consequences of differential family backgrounds in terms of socioeconomic variables rather than school curricula, teachers' credentials, size of gymnasiums, presence or absence of language laboratories, number of foreign languages taught, and the like. As Jencks summarizes:

> There seem to be three reasons why school reform cannot make adults more equal. First, children seem to be far more influenced by what happens at home than by what happens in school. They may also be more influenced by what happens on the streets and by what they see on television. Second, reformers have very little control over those aspects of school life that affect children. Reallocating resources, reassigning pupils, and rewriting the curriculum seldom change the way teachers and students actually treat each other minute by minute. Third, even when a school exerts an unusual influence on children, the resulting changes are not very likely to persist into adulthood. (pp. 255-256)

Applying these findings to the realities of what occurred in Attucks School, the best hope for those who sat at the Clown table lies not in anything that might be done for them within the classroom (though for humane reasons alone, change is necessary), but what might instead be done about the social class position of their families in American society. It is here that Attucks School weaves itself into the national pattern of generating educational winners and losers. Schools do not exist as agents of change, but as institutions which have been created to sustain, reinforce, and affirm existing structural and ideological arrangements. They have been created to reflect this society, not to transform it. It should not be surprising, then, if the income differential between the top fifth and the bottom fifth of American workers is 600 percent, that schools would mirror such inequalities. The point is that inequalities in the political and economic spheres of this society intrude into the space of the schools and are there reinforced. Consequently, the elimination of massive differentials in income and salary, in the control of property and assets, in the accessibility of mobility, in the possibilities for securing meaningful employment, and finally, in the ability to pass on the benefits of one's labors to one's children must be dealt with as the political realities they are, and not as the pedagogical issues they are not.

If we accept the correctness of these three propositions— that compulsory public schooling will be with us for the foreseeable future; that the organizational arrangements inside schools legitimate current patterns of inequality, but do not create them; and that reforming schools does not necessarily imply dealing with the inequalities of the larger society—then we might consider the following implications. First, we can liberate ourselves from the shackling myths of what schools are supposed to be doing, both for the benefit of the students

and for the larger society. We can put down the notions that schools are the "great equalizer" that provides everyone equal access to the mobility escalators. Rather, we can recognize the realities of how schools reinforce social class differences and act to preserve the current arrangements. There is little possibility of transforming the schools to the point where they do not serve this legitimatizing function if it is not first acknowledged that in fact they do.

Second, given the central stratification functions which schools serve for our economic system, it may be the most we can hope for—short of a major restructuring of economic institutions—that schools be organized in such a way as not to exacerbate the inequalities present in the society. I seriously doubt that schools are in a position to overcome the current economic and political inequalities, but it may at best be possible to withdraw schools from their legitimizing function through such means as the refusal to label any child by whatever negative traits he or she might have and the refusal to establish tracking systems. These types of changes may not appear to be systemic, and they are not, with regard to the magnitude of inequality in American society. But then again, the schools are not at the root of adult inequality. Thus we arrive at the fact that resolving school problems does not present itself as necessarily an effective means to resolving societal problems.

Third, the foregoing allows us to begin to approach schools as an end in their own right, not as a mechanism designed to serve some alternative motives. We can begin to ask questions about how the time that children have to spend in schools should be organized so as to maximize the benefits for them. If schools are no longer assumed to have to provide the means to reach mobility escalators, because such escalators are not even primarily related to schooling, then what one does with twelve years of a child's life takes on a new dimension. Bereiter 1972), for example, suggests that we split the current elementary school system into two, one part of which will provide training in spelling, reading, calculation and writing, while the second will provide child care areas where the child is free to explore as he wishes without the pressure of an adult attempting to "teach" something. Once we disabuse our thinking of the mythical functions of schools, we can begin to meet the needs of children in a humane way that does not require them to be more than simply children.

As we give up our grand illusions, we can set goals which more realistically fit what can be accomplished by teachers and students doing something together. Perhaps the most basic goal would be to provide outgoing students with the necessary means to function in this society. I am thinking particularly of insuring that within those twelve years, children learn to write, to spell, to do arithmetic, and to read. In San Francisco a lawsuit has been brought against the city Board of Education by a youth who was graduated with a fifth-grade reading level from a city high school. A good argument can be made that if one is going to be forced to attend a school, then that school should be held responsible for accomplishing what it is supposed to do— in this case teaching a high school graduate how to read at the level of high school graduates.

Establishing this sort of criterion for schools would dramatically switch the emphasis from a concern with the initial *input* of the child, for instance, I.Q., social class background, and father's occupation, to the *output* of the school. In short, schools should be called upon during the years of their hold over students to equalize in basic areas of competence those initial inequalities in academic performance with which children first come to school. Schools may not be able to transform the occupational hierarchy of this society, but they can be expected to perform so that the children of low-status parents can read a book as well as the children of high-status parents.

There are no universal antidotes one can offer to insure that all schools will become humane and rewarding places in which teachers and students can spend time together. The task of the future will be to examine the schools, if necessary one by one, to ascertain the needs, the values, and the dreams of those who will be inside their walls. Charles Silberman (1971, p. 208) believes that such schools are possible:

> Schools can be humane and still educate well. They can be genuinely concerned with gaiety and joy and individual growth and fulfillment without sacrificing concern for intellectual discipline and development. They can be simultaneously child-centered and subject-centered. They can also stress esthetic and moral education without weakening the three R's.

I should like to think that the time is at hand for learning if Silberman is correct. Depending upon one's perspective, the current arrangements in schools are either working very well or not at all. If one believes that the recent graduate in San Francisco or Lilly in St. Louis deserves, nay, has the inalienable right to leave the school equipped to do what the schools say should be possible, then the current system is simply unacceptable. If we, as a society, choose to shake loose of false assumptions, surreal expectations, and the consequent crippling of many young participants, we can begin to create settings where, because it is the humane thing to do, children are respected; where learning is valued; and where equality is pursued. In short, we can strive to create a new synthesis of words and deeds.

Schools Do Make a Difference

reports the Philadelphia Federal Reserve Bank Study.

The following article presents highlights of a research study conducted by Anita A. Summers, senior economist, Urban Research Section, Federal Reserve Bank of Philadelphia, and Barbara L. Wolfe, economic consultant, Urban Research Section, and assistant professor of economics, Bryn Mawr College. Free copies of the full report of the study may be obtained from the Federal Reserve Bank of Philadelphia, Philadelphia 19105.

Do schools make a difference? Americans who traditionally cherish their beliefs in the power of public education have had precious little support for these beliefs in the past few years. Recent major studies seeking answers to questions about students' educational achievement have found the answers everywhere but in the school. James Coleman attributed student achievement chiefly to family background; Arthur Jensen, primarily to heredity and race; and Christopher Jencks, mainly to luck.

Now, however, on the basis of a study completed this year at the Department of Research of the Federal Reserve Bank of Philadelphia, the belief that schools can indeed make a difference is reaffirmed. Moreover, the major finding of the study holds that proper allocation and targeting of school resources not only promote student achievement but can help compensate for the disadvantages associated with poverty, race, and low ability.

The Federal Reserve study was conducted over a two-year period with a sample school population of 1,896 students in 150 elementary, junior, and senior high Philadelphia schools.

The study addressed this two-pronged question: Which school resources promote learning, and how should these resources be allocated to maximize the learning of various kinds of students? The researchers attempted to identify which resources make a difference to which types of student—high vs. low income, black vs. nonblack, low vs. high achiever.

Probably the key difference between this study and many earlier ones that attributed a student's academic performance almost entirely to family background is that Summers and Wolfe explored the question of the interaction between specific school resources and characteristics of specific types of pupils. Earlier studies investigated educational achievement in terms of averages for all students. Further, this study examined these interactions using data that were specific to the pupil. For example, the data were detailed enough to match pupils with their specific teachers.

The researchers believe that previous educational studies may have failed to uncover the full accomplishments of schools because few school inputs consistently benefit *all* students. (Yet, statistically, earlier studies posed the questions in a way that assumed this.) Low-income students, for example, may require a different dosage of certain school resources than high-income students do.

If averages are used, rather than an analysis that ties specific school characteristics to specific students, the averaging out allows the negative effects to offset the positive ones, and the real impact of what is happening is disguised, if not lost.

Summers and Wolfe believe that this analysis not only explains why so many earlier studies concluded that school resources have little effect on achievement but that it also points out the direction for increasing student achievement by targeting school resources. In short, they believe that increased learning can take place if school resources are targeted to those pupils who will benefit from them the most.

The researchers indicate that of course the socioeconomic backgrounds of students are important in regard to student achievement, but they contend that some adverse conditions that may be associated with such characteristics as race, income, or "low ability" can be ameliorated by what the schools can do. Socioeconomic characteristics are clearly *not* within the immediate control of the school, but many conditions affecting student learning clearly *are* in its control.

In choosing change in achievement scores as a measurable criterion, the researchers recognize the fact that parents want much more from schools than reading, writing, and arithmetic. Summers and Wolfe limited their investigations of student achievement to the basic skills, however, as the single most important function of formal education. To carry out the study, they used standardized tests in basic skills to measure student achievement.

Over a two- or three-year period, growth in student achievement in relation to a broad range of school resources and characteristics was examined with the object of searching out the impact of each on students with different abilities and traits. These findings are not to be regarded as conclusive, but rather as indicators of possible directional changes, since they deal with just

336

one sample of students over one period of time. In the following summary, 15 of the more relevant items covered in the full report are reviewed. Note particularly which items this study suggests do or do not make a difference and for whom.

Heterogeneous vs. homogeneous student body. A key finding of the study is that the proportion of either high achievers or low achievers in a school can have an impact on learning. Low achievers performed distinctly better when they were in schools with high achievers, whereas the presence of low achievers generally appeared not to interfere with the learning of high achievers.

For those in the middle, however, being with more low achievers than high achievers seemed to have a somewhat negative effect. In short, the intellectual composition of the student body directly affected learning, especially for low achievers. The more heterogeneous the composition of the student body was in terms of abilities, the better off most of the student body was in terms of learning.

Racial balance. The major finding here is that both black and non-black students seem to benefit academically when schools are more or less racially balanced rather than when they are more or less racially segregated. This is the study's main finding with regard to race, although certain variations appeared at different age levels.

Class size. The study found that smaller classes fostered achievement for disadvantaged students. (Other research suggests that smaller classes foster the cognitive and affective development of all categories of students.) Classes of 27 or fewer were particularly helpful for low-ability elementary pupils. Classes of 34 or more appeared detrimental to everyone. While low-ability students benefited the most from smaller classes, senior high English classes with fewer than 27 had the highest learning rates for students of any ability level. (It is important to keep in mind that these "numbers" reflect the reality of big-city systems. There is reason to believe that benefit would be derived from still smaller classes.)

Size of school. Smaller schools apparently mean increased learning, particularly for elementary and senior high students. Black elementary pupils and low-ability high school students seemed to benefit most from smaller schools.

Quality of teacher preparation. All elementary students in this study did better with teachers from higher rated colleges and universities—but especially those students in the low-income category. To evaluate teachers' colleges, the Gourman rating system was used. It is a method rating nearly all U.S. colleges and universities according to the quality of individual departments, administration, faculty, student services, and general characteristics, such as facilities and alumni support.

Teacher experience. Approximately one-third of the teachers in the study had three years or less of experience; one-third had more than three and less than 10; and one-third had 10 years of experience or more. The study specifically looked at the impact of teacher experience on students with different abilities.

The findings: Length of experience had a very different impact on high- and low-achieving students. High achievers at all levels seemed to do best with more experienced teachers; in junior high, English teachers with experience of 10 years or more were most effective with all students. However, in elementary schools, low achievers seemed to do best with new, relatively inexperienced teachers.

Teacher education beyond the bachelor's degree. In this study, teacher education beyond the bachelor's degree was not shown to be related to better student achievement. This suggests that much graduate study does not meet teacher needs. A more productive approach, perhaps, could be developed around in-service programs more related to these needs.

National Teacher Examination. Test scores in the National Teacher Exam seem to be virtually unrelated to teacher effectiveness and raise serious questions about their continued use.

Relationship between race of teachers and race of students. The study found no relationship between student growth and whether or not a teacher and student were of the same race.

Disruption. Harsh incidents involving various kinds of violence significantly lowered the achievement growth of high and middle achievers but had much less effect on low achievers. School policies that reduce the number of serious incidents would, in all probability, improve the learning of the higher ability students.

Dropouts. The greater proportion of dropouts a high school had, the less student growth there was, particularly for high achievers.

Remedial education. Remedial resources showed no particular difference for low-achieving children in this study. In general, the failure of remedial resources to show improvement in student achievement may be because they were aimed at other educational objectives or because they were employed too sparingly to produce growth—or because the data were not adequate to relate how much remedial education specific pupils received.

Head Start participation. The findings on Head Start participation *in relation to the stated goals of this study* are that the Head Start child arrived at the third grade at an improved level of achievement. Once at that higher level of achievement, no further increase in *rate* of learning emerged.

Physical facilities. General physical facilities of schools had little to do with student learning as defined in this study, although they may make a difference in terms of other educational goals.

Measurable characteristics of school principals. While there was a wide variation in the backgrounds of the principals in the schools studied, the variance in their experience, graduate degrees, and extra credits seemed to have no correlation with student achievement.

There are limitations to the Summers-Wolfe study, just as there are to all research studies. However, some of the findings of this study are particularly important.

The major finding is that certain school characteristics *do* make a difference in student achievement, and that, although many resources are effective for all students, many are effective only when targeted to specific types of students.

Disadvantaged students can be brought to learning rates closer to those of their more advantaged classmates if they have access to particular resources—smaller class size, for example. High-ability students can move even faster if certain resources—such as experienced teachers—are directed specifically to them.

Peer group characteristics influence student achievement. Indeed one of the most significant findings is that the more heterogeneous a student body is in terms of race and achievement, the better it will fare in learning basic skills.

In addition, the way school resources are allocated can have an impact on pupil performance. The findings suggest that a more precise definition of equal educational opportunity revolves around the goal of equal progress in achievement rather than equal funding. Equity then would relate to what students get from their education in terms of achievement growth rather than in terms of how much the school spends per student.

It appears that school resources can be used to attain greater equity in educational opportunity—that school policy *can* help in compensating the disadvantaged.

Without necessarily raising expenditures, educational productivity can be increased in many cases by shifting resources · into these areas that generate more growth.

Finally, the findings suggest an approach to accountability in which school administrators may well be expected to know which resources matter and then to execute their proper allocation as part of management responsibilities. Whole communities could benefit, and students might well have a better chance of reaching their educational potential. □

Some Reactions to the Study

The Summers and Wolfe study is particularly interesting and particularly important for several reasons. One is the kinds of questions it asks, another is the kinds of data it uses to answer the questions, and the third is the results it finds. On all three counts, the study makes advances on earlier work.

First, concerning the questions it poses: It asks about the effects on academic achievement of particular school resources, as other studies have done. However, it does not ask these questions for all groups of students alike, but for different kinds of students (high-achieving vs. low-achieving, high-income vs. low-income, etc.). The authors do not assume that a school resource has the same effect for all kinds of students.

A few studies have asked similar differential questions, but ordinarily only for the sexes (i.e., different effects for boys and girls) or for race (different effects for Blacks and Whites). Summers and Wolfe carry this differential-effect approach much further than it has been carried before.

Second, Summers and Wolfe use data that are a significant improvement over those used in most other studies—on three counts:

1. They are able to measure achievement *growth* of a student and examine effects on that growth, rather than merely achievement differentials at a single point among different students, as many studies do.

2. They have matched students with the teacher or teachers they had rather than with the average for all teachers in the school, as most studies have done. Consequently, they have more results about effects of teacher characteristics than any other study I know.

3. They have measured characteristics of each student's school to give measures of the school climate and the social composition factors which determine that climate.

I know of no other study that includes the richness of data of these three types.

Third, the study is refreshing because it relieves the dull sameness of most research on the effects of school resources, which find "little or no effects." It has become fashionable to find no effects of school resources on learning. But Summers and Wolfe *do* find some positive effects. In this, I see their study as a kind of starting point in the long and arduous task of finding and confirming specific effects of school factors on learning and of building a solid base of knowledge about what resources make a difference to children's learning and how they do so.

In a sense, previous studies have cleared away a large amount of conventional wisdom about school resources and learning, wisdom that when put to the test failed to pass. Now I believe that studies following and improving upon Summers and Wolfe's methods will be able to begin the more positive task of discovering what does make a difference.

Now for the results themselves. I will comment only on those that I feel should be taken with some caution. As I have implied above, I believe the results are generally

This study is an important step forward in the strategy for learning how schools affect achievement.

—James S. Coleman

sound and constitute an important development in our knowledge. However, they are a starting point rather than an end point. Just as previous studies that failed to find beneficial effects of various school resources should not have led to an immediate withdrawal of those resources, so these positive findings should not lead to immediate changes in their deployment.

There are several reasons for such prudence. One is that peculiarities of a particular sample can sometimes lead to results that appear statistically significant for that sample but that turn out differently in other samples. A case in point: David Wiley and Annegret Harnischfeger[1], using data from the *Equality of Educational Opportunity* survey, but only for Detroit and only for the sixth grade, found that the *time* students spent in school made a great deal of difference in achievement. But the effects disappeared in a reanalysis by Nancy Karweit[2] that included the remainder of the schools in the Detroit metropolitan area. Karweit also examined schools in four other large metropolitan areas and found no clear pattern. Nor was the Wiley/Harnischfeger finding confirmed in all taken together. Thus, the apparent finding disappeared when the sample was expanded beyond Detroit. This example should induce a note of caution into use of results from a single study, no mat-

ter how well conceived.

A second source of prudent caution lies in the general sharpening and strengthening process that occurs, sometimes on the part of authors, sometimes on the part of their interpreters, in going from statistical results to interpretations and implications. Several instances of this occur in the highlights of the study presented here, and I will mention a few.

One of these occurs in the statement on racial balance. The authors correctly state the complexity of their findings, but that is lost in the highlights as presented here, with a somewhat misleading result. The findings for black students in the sixth grade were that (as the highlights indicate in general) they did better in racially balanced schools. But in the eighth grade and in the twelfth grade, they did better in predominantly black schools. There were other complexities for the white students.

These findings do not bear out the consistency implied by the statement that "the major finding here is that both black and nonblack students seem to benefit academically when schools are more racially balanced." The upshot of this is, for me, that the different results at the different levels do not mean that opposite *effects* occur at these levels, but rather that neither result is to be taken seriously. It certainly does not mean, however,

as in the highlights presented here, that one result is to be taken seriously and the opposing result in the other grades is to be discarded.

On teachers' experience, a minor point: The result that "low [elementary] achievers seemed to do best with new, relatively inexperienced teachers" seems, in my examination of the technical report, to hold only for the very lowest achievers and again raises some doubts about replicability.

The only serious misstatement of results in the highlights besides that on racial composition, according to my examination of the statistical results, is in the statement of effects of disruption. The effects of disruption were examined only at the sixth and eighth grades. At the eighth grade level, there appeared to be no significant effects for high, medium, or low achievers. At the sixth grade level, there were strong *positive* "effects" of disruptive incidents on achievement of low achievers and considerably less strong negative effects on achievement of high achievers. This is not at all the way the highlights summarize the results, which, I should add, is consistent with the authors' own discussion of their results.

These examples illustrate the kinds of modifications, artificial consistencies, and plausibilities that can occur in the movement from statistical analysis to policy implications. They show the need for caution in applying research findings and the need for validation and confirmation of results from further studies. But they should not seriously detract from this study.

It is an important step forward in the strategy for learning about how schools affect achievement. Its results are starting points, and both the approach it uses (the questions it asks and the kinds of data it uses) and the results it finds are foundations that future work will build upon.

—James S. Coleman, *professor, Department of Sociology, Univer-*

[1] David E. Wiley and Annegret Harnischfeger. "Explosion of a Myth: Quantity of Schooling and Exposure to Instruction, Major Educational Vehicles." *Educational Researcher* 3:7-11, April 1974.

[2] Nancy L. Karweit. *Is Differential Access to School an Important Factor in Student Outcomes?* Report No. 195. Baltimore: Center for Social Organization of Schools, Johns Hopkins University, May 1975.

sity of Chicago; author of Equality of Educational Opportunity (The Coleman Report), *1966.*

This study indicates that certain school resources can and do have significant effects upon the academic achievement of some children. The resources considered are important but they fail to give adequate consideration to perhaps the most valuable resource that schools have: teachers. The degree to which schools do make a difference in the education of children is primarily the result of the teachers who staff them.

The study discusses the finding that the amount of education a teacher has beyond the B.A. makes no difference. It also indicates that the race of a teacher does not appear to be related to student learning. However, it cites evidence to indicate that some children perform better with teachers from higher rated colleges.

Many attributes can be ascribed to teachers but, from my point of view, two stand out as most important. The first and most important attribute is the attitude that individual teachers hold toward children. The second one is their expectations of children. These two factors have implications for the education of all children but are even more important for the youngsters who are low achievers.

According to Kenneth Clark, "A key component of the deprivation which afflicts ghetto children is that generally their teachers do not expect them to learn." The result, he says, is that "the child of whom little is expected produces little."

Low-achieving youngsters are often poor, from a minority group, or both. These are the children who need the attention and for whom teacher attitude is crucial. I believe that poor and minority children are failing in school, not because they are incapable but because schools do not design instructional pro-

grams that build on the cultural strengths of these children. Cultural difference is perceived as a deficit and is equated with inferiority.

By and large, teachers enter the classroom unprepared to teach children from varying cultural backgrounds. Preservice teachers must be trained not only to understand and appreciate cultural differences but also to develop instructional techniques and strategies appropriate for children who may differ from them culturally.

Attitudes and expectations are closely linked. When a child is perceived in a positive way and the teacher expectations are congruent with the perceptions, the overall effect upon the child can lead to greater academic gains.

In a recent study, I found support for the belief that perceptions can be changed through training. It is therefore both appropriate and necessary for teacher preparation institutions to assume the responsibility for developing positive attitudes about different cultural groups in prospective teachers. These attitudes will then encourage teachers to see the need for building the teaching process on the strengths and realistic needs of the members of these groups.

The type of training should receive much consideration. The program ought to provide students with an in-depth study of the history and cultural influences of the various ethnic groups within our society. Learning experiences and analyses of these experiences can provide an extra dimension to the training.

In addition to the type of training that is offered, the duration or

length of the training program is crucial. Teachers' perceptions can be altered over a period of one academic semester. More change might be forthcoming if they are trained for a longer period of time. Curriculums that are integrated with culturally related content must become a permanent part of the entire professional training program for preservice and in-service teachers.

The Federal Reserve Bank study found that black and nonblack students seem to benefit academically when schools are racially balanced. Racially balanced schools can produce positive effects for all students, but to disrupt the life-styles of black children only for the sake of accomplishing this kind of balance is unfair and racist. Heterogeneous grouping by race should not be seen as a must for academic achievement but as an extra benefit for furthering group understanding and interaction.

Schools must reallocate resources so that improved pupil performance and achievement become a reality. They will need to give priority to those resources that have the greatest impact on students. Because teachers are not only the largest resource the school possesses but also the most important one, an emphasis upon their training and retraining is crucial.

—**Gwendolyn C. Baker,** *assistant professor, School of Education, University of Michigan, Ann Arbor.*

When I first read about this study, my reaction was rather negative because I questioned how people with limited experience in the

This study should have relevance for school systems throughout the country.
—Daniel J. McGinley

schools could produce a valid report with such extensive implications. However, after studying the findings carefully and talking to Dr. Summers and Dr. Wolfe, I feel that the study is valuable and renders a real service to education.

I am deeply gratified that two economists using statistical methods have concluded that schools do indeed make a difference—a firm conviction of mine, based on 20 years as a teacher and as a school administrator.

Let me comment briefly on several conclusions from the study:

1. The finding that average and low-achieving elementary students do better in schools with more high achievers came as no surprise. We have known for years that students learn from a variety of stimuli. Certainly, the presence of high-achieving students should provide stimulus for learning.

2. The finding that low-achieving elementary school pupils do better in classes of fewer than 28 was to be expected.

3. Both school administrators and teachers would take it for granted that learning is greater in schools with fewer disruptions and fewer dropouts.

4. The finding that low achievers in elementary school seem to do better with new teachers than with experienced ones speaks to the question of what expectancy beginning teachers bring to the job and whether that expectancy diminishes as the years go by.

5. The full study found that for all types of students at all levels, there is a positive correlation between school attendance and growth in achievement. This indicates that not only do schools make a difference but that it is important to look for patterns of nonattendance. The implication for the elementary school is that if these patterns are detected early and are reversed, the student will benefit.

6. My personal experience bears out the finding that high achievers do best with experienced elementary and junior high school teachers.

7. I don't think there can be much argument with the finding, expressed in the full report, that average and high-achieving pupils will do better if they have high school English teachers who scored high on an examination in English.

8. Those who believe in the value of the new math and understanding mathematics will not be surprised by the finding, also in the full report, that junior high students do better who have been taught by teachers trained in the post-Sputnik/new math era.

In this period of shrinking financial support for public education, I believe that the findings of this study have important implications for educators. Certainly teachers and administrators cannot afford to overlook anything that has significant economic implications for school districts. For example, if, in fact, small schools are in many instances better places for children to learn than large schools, then we need to consider this when we plan expenditures.

If, as the data seem to indicate, elementary pupils will do better with better prepared teachers, then one course of action might be just to employ teachers from the higher rated colleges and universities. I believe that school districts must reject that option and instead make every effort to provide in their budgets adequate funds for district-sponsored staff development programs. The finding that teachers with higher degrees do not necessarily cause pupils to be more productive should cause school districts to place greater emphasis on developing their own programs of upgrading competencies of staff members.

The "no-effect" conclusion the study reached on remedial education (within the range of expenditures in Philadelphia at the time of the study) must be looked at in light of how much remediation has been given and of how early the problems needing remediation have been identified. Certainly, much more exploration into the question of teacher expectancy is greatly needed.

The measurable characteristics of school principals and their correlation with student achievement will require further study. Assuredly, there are more pertinent variables present among principals than those considered by Summers and Wolfe—experience, graduate degrees, and extra educational credits.

Basically, I believe that consideration has to be given in Philadelphia to these findings when we make decisions that affect both the school system and the individual school organization. I understand that statistically it is important to be able to replicate these findings to be sure of what they say. In the meantime, I believe we can take them in their present form and use them as additional pieces of data that will help us in making decisions that affect the schools. This study should also have relevance for other school systems throughout the country.

—Daniel J. McGinley, *president, Philadelphia Association of School Administrators.*

Replications of the study would . . . help to guarantee that schools continue to make a difference.
—NEA Research and NEA Instruction and Professional Development

The Federal Reserve Bank of Philadelphia study reaffirms that schools do make a difference. The conclusion that school resources, if used wisely, can make a difference in the achievement of students is refreshing even though we have serious questions about the use of standardized tests as the sole measure of student learning.

As was mentioned earlier, the study contrasts with other much-publicized, if not conclusive, research studies which maintain that a student's future success is due most importantly to his or her family background, racial heritage, or just plain luck—circumstances that schools can do little to change.

Anita A. Summers and Barbara L. Wolfe, who conducted the study, questioned the finality of those conclusions. They hypothesized and then supported the premise that school resources affect the achievement of different kinds of students in different ways. The idea that targeting different amounts of resources to different kinds of students can raise student achievement levels is implicit in that premise. To investigate their thesis, they followed 1,896 students through Philadelphia schools for two- and three-year periods, linking many variables to individual performance. Unlike most researchers, they did not rely on averages—a mathematical technique where positive effects of variables on the achievement of some students can be offset by the negative effects on other students.

We would like to see the *approach* used in this study replicated in various other school environments. The attempt to include and control variables commonly believed to affect student achievement is commendable, but we would like to see alternatives for standardized test scores used as measures of student achievement.

There are limitations to this study as there are in any research; the potential importance, however, mandates that its scope be broadened so that some of the conclusions can be reexamined in other settings. Summers and Wolfe recognize many of the limitations in their full report, and readers should keep these limitations in mind:

1. The students sampled were all from one big-city school system—and relatively limited within that population. To what extent are conditions in the Philadelphia school system representative of conditions in other school systems? For example, class sizes reported in this study are larger than the national average. Would it not be valuable, therefore, to look at class sizes in more typical school systems, using the Summers-Wolfe approach?

2. The study used only standardized tests as the measure of student achievement. Are there not other objectives in addition to achievement such as social and emotional growth? Are standardized test scores reliable and valid measures of achievement? If so, should they be the *only* measures used?

3. The design used required that all resource variables be quantifiable—an engineering model applied to education. The measures selected for some of the variables were questionable: Is the number of times a student misses school, for example, a good measure of mo-

tivation? Is any rating of a teacher's alma mater a satisfactory predictor of that teacher's effectiveness? Even though the Gourman rating appears to be related, can we still rely on it as a predictor, which is what we would do if we accept these results. Are there, indeed, more basic measures?

Furthermore, are not such important variables as classroom atmosphere, teaching methods, and curriculums—generally not quantifiable and thus missing from the study—related to achievement?

4. The design used in the Philadelphia study does isolate relationships between variables when they exist; relationships, however, do not necessarily show cause and effect. Does motivation cause achievement or does achievement cause motivation? If, in fact, disruption really does lower student achievement, may there not be, in turn, an underlying cause of disruption?

These four significant limitations may also have contributed to the conclusions that some variables such as physical facilities and the advanced degrees of teachers appear not to have direct effect on student achievement. Because of the limited nature of this study, these findings should not be viewed as conclusive. For these and other reasons, replications of the Federal Reserve study would add much to our knowledge about the effective use of school resources and would help to guarantee that schools continue to make a difference.

—NEA Research and NEA Instruction and Professional Development.

XIII. COMMUNITY AND CULTURE

A school is a behavior setting organized to transmit culture. It has a subcultural dimension of its own, as the preceeding section suggests, but it is above all a creation of the community and culture in which it is lodged. The factor of community includes the place, the population and the social structure that provide the school its immediate surrounding. The factor of culture includes the ways of living — the beliefs, standards, knowledge, technology, and daily prescriptions for living — that surround and imbed the network of communities that make up a society. Viewed from the perspective of culture, then, a school is one among many transmitters of culture content, with the transmission being mediated by the local community.

Modern educational psychology is comparative in theory and method. Its scholars seek to examine the similarities and differences in teaching and learning policies and practices from culture to culture and from community to community within a culture. Reports on international comparative studies of school achievement are included in an earlier section of this book. Here are included Rhea Menzel Whitehead's article on education in Maoist China and Maurice Gibbons' article on "Walkabout." Whitehead illustrates the study of cultural change in education and Gibbons demonstrates how content and methods in education are diffused across cultures.

When a culture and the communities within it are very stable over decades of time, schools tend to transmit the culture accurately and predictably. The content and methods of teaching both tend to become fairly standardized, with the only noteworthy variations appearing as a result of urban versus rural, and socioeconomic status variations, from locality to locality. When periods of less stability occur, content and methods may be found to be slightly out of phase: some schools will be found to strain forward over the arc of cultural change, moving a bit ahead of the local conventions. Others may be found specializing in the conservation of the past, and so on.

In periods of extremely rapid change, a single community will often generate a spectrum of types of schools — and even classrooms within schools — which is wide ranging in responses or reactions to change. The period of the 1960's illustrates this process in the United States. The civil rights revolution, the Beatles as expressive of popular culture revolutions, and the Vietnam War reverberated through the nation's schools. Students tended to diversify first, in clothing, social manners, and attitudes toward authority. Young teachers followed, as older teachers and school boards went in search of everything from repression to total adoption of the new youth culture. By 1970, after less than a decade of massive cultural change, it was impossible to gauge what was in or out of phase. Schools became less and less predictable and agreements about what should be transmitted — the matrix of the curriculum — dissolved before our very eyes.

This period was one of vast and profound experimentation with every aspect of educational form and content. The theories and tools of educational psychologists were employed as never before in the century of discipline, analyzing the changes and inventing alternatives to conventional teaching and learning. Simultaneously, old culture reactions to experimentalism were equally profound. The conventions of the neighborhood school became a national cause in resistance to the import of the civil rights revolution, and entire communities were detonated by such school issues as pledges of allegiance, codes of student discipline, school prayer, and the censoring of controversial textbooks.

As a result, the educational psychology of the future will be sensitive as never before to the factors of culture and community. The educator of the future will be open to the world of learning possibilities, just as she or he will know that schools are prospectively too important to be left isolated from the context of family, neighborhood, region, and place of work. Open education is expressive of this change, as classroom walls come tumbling down and as ideas from England and France permeate American schools.

HOW THE YOUNG ARE TAUGHT IN MAO'S CHINA

HONG KONG

Nearly everyone in the People's Republic of China seems to be involved in some form of education or re-education. Mao-thought study groups, literacy classes, part-time study programs for workers and farmers, and cadre schools for the re-education of government office workers supplement the usual schools. Throughout the country one has the feeling of a whole people intent on improving themselves. Their expressed purpose, however, is not monetary gain, higher position, greater prestige, or even individual satisfaction, but the following of Mao Tsetung's concept of serving the people.

It is impossible to understand Chinese education without an awareness of the role of Mao's thought. For him, practice is both the source and the test of all knowledge. At every level of Chinese education heavy emphasis is placed on the application of knowledge on the farm and in the workshop, the laboratory, and the factory. Experienced workers and farmers are called in to give practical lessons to students because education must be intimately connected with life so that it will be related directly to the pressing needs of society.

The continuing struggle between the exploited and the exploiters is also central to Mao's thought. Such "class struggle," says Mao, continues in China even today. And since the educational process takes place within the context of social struggle, there must be constant effort to combat exploitative thinking and action.

Mao believes, however, that man is the product of his social condition and that he has an almost infinite potential for re-education. As a result, the Chinese are confident that they can create a new man and a new society in which the needs of others come before those of self. They are determined to make education serve the majority of the people, rather than just a privileged few, and are trying to avoid the kind of elitist education they see evolving in the Soviet Union.

By 1966 Mao had concluded that a thoroughgoing revolution was necessary to eliminate the vestiges of elitism and special privilege that remained. That summer the Cultural Revolution exploded. Schools closed. The central Ministry of Education was dismantled. Teachers, administrators, and textbooks came under bitter attack. When the schools reopened more than a year later, they set out to translate into practice Mao's conception of the role education should play. Now, more than four years later, the Chinese freely admit that their educational revolution remains unfinished.

The thrust of the future, however, seems clear. More than ever, schools will reflect the conviction that education can never be neutral. "Abstract education that does not serve the politics of a given class does not exist in the world today," one teacher told me. This is a rephrasing of Mao's belief that within education, as in all of society, there is a constant struggle between the exploited and the exploiters. The Cultural Revolution, the Chinese say, has been a victory for the exploited. In place of academic authorities, workers and peasants, who are assumed to know best what kind of people are needed for socialist revolution and construction, now have overall direction of the schools.

Traveling in China, as I did this past summer, one feels that this "festival of revolutionization," as the Chinese refer to the Cultural Revolution, has brought a renewed vitality and consciousness to Chinese education. Young people are convinced that they are playing a role in the creation of the future of China and the world and appear to be motivated by the concept of service rather than by personal gains. No one is considered worthless; even the deaf-mute and the cripple can make a meaningful contribution to society. The values children are taught are pride in the new China as led by Chairman Mao, selflessness, modesty, a willingness to learn from others, perseverance in the face of difficulties, and determination to struggle against anyone or anything that hinders the creation of a new society.

How then do the Chinese translate this philosophy and spirit into classroom practice? Any attempt to generalize on the state of education in a country of 800 million—which claims to have no fewer than 150 million students—must be done with caution. The sprawling urban complexes of Shanghai, Peking, and Wuhan are as different

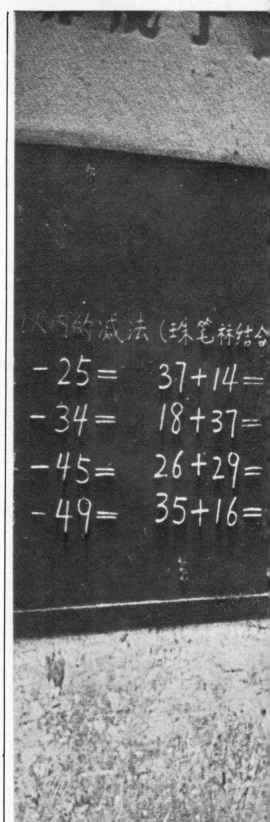

Classroom organization in China follows traditional patterns. Right, first-graders take turns on the large abacus, while their classmates work quietly at their individual desk models.

BY RHEA MENZEL WHITEHEAD

Mao: "Man has an almost infinite potential for re-education."

China hopes to create a new man for whom the needs of others come before those of self.

from the isolated villages of the northwest as New York City is from rural Mississippi. But some general changes can be identified. School courses have been shortened; textbooks are being revised. Greater flexibility in meeting local needs is encouraged. Emphasis on manual labor, pushed during the Great Leap Forward in 1958 but rejected during the early Sixties for lowering the quality of education, has returned. And other dimensions of the picture can be filled out from what is happening in individual schools.

Chen Hsien Primary School in Nanking, which I visited one sultry July day, is made up of a group of pleasant one-story classroom buildings surrounding a large courtyard. The din of children playing basketball, Ping-Pong, and a Chinese version of Drop the Hanky could have been that of an American school recess except for the political content to the game's song.

Classes in the school are large; I counted between forty-eight and fifty-six children to a room. While this is due partly to a continuing shortage of teachers and space, the Chinese do not consider a class of forty a problem. Children begin school at age seven for a five-year course, one year less than before the Cultural Revolution. The curriculum for the first three years includes politics, Chinese language, arithmetic, physical and military training, and "revolutionary culture" (music and art). Beginning in the fourth year, students learn English, natural science, agriculture, and industry.

Classroom organization is traditional, but the atmosphere varies considerably from room to room. I groaned inwardly at the classroom style of fourth-graders studying an essay on the revolutionary sculpture *The Rent Collector's Courtyard*, a scene of peasant exploitation. The class followed while the teacher animatedly read a six-page essay, occasionally wiping tears from her eyes. A period of rote reading and recitation followed. We heard well-rehearsed answers to questions about the nature of the oppression the peasants had endured. Students responded promptly and boldly, always standing when recog-

Workshops are an integral part of Chinese schools. Students not only repair school equipment but, as in the picture above, produce electrical wirings for 2,000 heavy trucks annually.

Children at a Nanking primary school play a Chinese version of Drop the Hanky—"The scene could have been an American recess but for the political content to the game's song."

nized. Discipline was impeccable, the students ignoring their visitors' presence completely. A bulletin board at the back of the classroom displayed the students' work—Mao poems they had copied. Other visual effects included a large world map, four political posters, and, as in all classrooms I observed, a small picture of Chairman Mao at the front of the room.

Fortunately, not all classes are so rigid. First-graders, each with an abacus on his desk, worked on two-column addition and subtraction problems. Children took turns demonstrating problem-solving processes on a huge abacus hung on the blackboard. The young teacher patiently explained and corrected when necessary. There was no automatic raising of hands, and youngsters helped each other in a quiet, relaxed manner.

In the past decade Mao has strongly advocated the abandoning of authoritarian teaching methods, and many articles in the Chinese press claim this is under way. Nevertheless, in conversations with the teachers, all insisted that in some subjects rote learning and class recitation were necessary, especially at the elementary level.

In other schools we did see children working in small clusters. Group dis-

cussions and evaluation have replaced memorization-type exams, the bane of traditional Chinese education. Class trips to historical shrines and museums are common and aid in developing a sense of China's past. Canton youngsters visit the Peasant Movement Institute, where Mao first started training revolutionaries. In Peking a fifth-grade class spent a whole week investigating life on a long avenue. Older shopkeepers told them stories of the past, when shops sold primarily foreign goods, workers had no rights, and ricksha pullers strained to deliver purchases to the wealthy few. Small class groups investigated different types of shops, houses, working conditions, and areas in need of improvement.

Many teaching techniques considered standard practice in America are regarded by the Chinese as individualistic and antisocial. Choice is collective rather than individual. Instead of exploring with finger paints or hammering abstract creations of scrap metal, Chinese first-graders remove the cork from bottle caps to facilitate their recycling. Others clean the streets, run errands for the elderly, make crystal radio sets and lantern slides, or learn sewing and barbering. The energy of the child as well as that of the adult is spent for the development of the nation.

Clearly, the most innovative part of Chen Hsien School is its workshops. Beginning at age eleven, children spend a half-day a week producing items actually used in bus production. Girls in flowered skirts hand-file grooves in metal plates for bus steps. Others electroplate, work machine presses, or make oil filters for carburetors. No fixed quotas are set. Such work is meant to instill respect for physical labor, reinforce lessons learned in math and science, and contribute to the school's operating funds.

Workshops are part of schools all over China. Following the principle of self-reliance, the Chinese are proud that shops are set up with minimal expense. Often nearby factories send workmen to the schools to help the students. And most urban primary schools also have garden patches where youngsters learn how to grow vegetables.

Most cities maintain specialized schools, such as the Canton deaf-mute school where I saw acupuncture used along with more traditional forms of treatment, or a Sian arts training school where eleven- and twelve-year-olds enter a program of disciplined dance and musical instruction. New schools are also being established for the education of the mentally handicapped.

Since the Cultural Revolution, decentralization and relaxation of "state standards" have allowed a great deal more local control of schools, both urban and rural. Communist China has always relied heavily on private, run by-the-people schools to provide supplementary school places. These schools have sometimes come in conflict with official regulations on academic standards, school hours, and age requirements. Many begun during the Great Leap were later closed. More recently, they appear to be flourishing anew.as factories, neighborhoods, and rural brigades organize their own schools. Education in China, incidentally, is not free. Almost all students pay a rather insignificant fee of from 3 to 8 yuan per year ($1.20 to $3.20 in U.S. money).

Rural primary education continues to expand rapidly and flexibly. In one Inner Mongolian region, itinerant teachers ride horseback to points where one to five students gather in the homes of herdsmen or in the fields. Spring and autumn holidays allow pupils to care for new lambs and work during the harvest. Classes focus on animal husbandry, agriculture, first aid, and acupuncture along with basic literacy training and cultural information. Several provinces report that universal primary education has been "basically introduced."

A firm principle of rural development has been self-reliance. But self-reliance alone will not help the countryside overtake the cities. Chinese whom I met seemed aware of the problem and spoke of the need to further equalize resources. Yet the "spirit of the pauper" cannot be considered unhealthy for a developing nation with limited resources. It is inspiring to be shown buildings made from local stone and straw, desks and benches made from bricks and stone, without encountering the familiar Asian attitude of "this must not be as good as you have in America."

Before the Cultural Revolution, the discrepancies in opportunity between city and rural youngsters were even greater at the secondary than at the elementary level. Middle School No. 33 in Peking, formerly a British-run missionary school with a chapel and swimming pool, remained an elite boys' school with strict entrance exams until 1966. Despite attempts to include manual labor in the curriculum, the emphasis remained on academic studies and university preparation. The curriculum, amazingly, varied only in superficial detail from what one might find in academic secondary schools anywhere in the world.

Now it is a coeducational institution accommodating all neighborhood youngsters who complete their primary studies. Students study politics, Chinese language, math, English, physics, chemistry, agriculture, health science, history, geography, and athletics and also prepare performances of revolutionary songs and dances. The curriculum, as in all urban middle schools, has been reduced from six years to five. Students spend one month at a Peking low-voltage electrical appliance factory, another on a farm, besides time in the school-run factory located on the premises. Getting students out of school and into factory and farm work offers the opportunity for a close partnership among students, workers, and peasants. Yet some of the factory's production plans do not integrate well with on-the-spot teaching of more theoretical lessons; therefore, the school's own workshops are important. Students not only repair desks and renovate water boilers but also produce electrical wirings and fluid brake lines for 2,000 heavy-duty trucks annually.

Many urban schools have set up rural branches where students live for periods varying from a month to a year. Students of these schools build houses, dig fish ponds, and sink wells, all the time studying related math and physics. Chinese authorities are hoping to equip urban youngsters with skills and attitudes applicable to life in rural areas, where many of them will eventually settle.

None of China's secondary school graduates now go straight to the university. Upon graduation they spend at least two years at manual labor—in the factory, on the farm, or in the army. Most will remain workers or farmers indefinitely; a few, estimated at 100,000 compared with 900,000 before the Cultural Revolution, will be selected by their working units for further education. It is hoped that this process will eliminate the "three-door students," those who have gone straight from the door of the home, to the door of the school, to the door of the office, where they become bureaucrats who have little contact with real life or ordinary people.

Rural secondary schools are frequently part of an integrated seven- or nine-year school system (five years elementary, two or four secondary). Although many rural children, especially in the remote districts, still do not go beyond the primary level, current programs of expansion augur well. The students' practical work emphasizes agricultural experimentation and the development of farm mechanization. Meanwhile, spare-time education is still considered necessary for some. In one mountainous Fukien commune of fifty-two villages, for instance, secondary schools hold midday and evening classes for those busy with other chores.

Chairman Mao has said: "The question of educational reform is mainly a question of teachers." Viewed with suspicion as harborers of bourgeois ideas, especially the emphasis on intellectual development, teachers were severely criticized during the Cultural Revolution. Yet very few have actually been removed from their posts. The overwhelming majority are depicted as wanting to transform their outlook

Mao: "The question of educational reform is mainly a question of teachers."

Politics permeates all subjects, even language lessons (English is in, Russian is out). Nine-year-olds in Nanking perfect their pronunciation by reciting thoughts from Mao.

and are encouraged to "study well; make progress every day."

In Liu Ling, near the old revolutionary base of Yenan, one teacher talked of how her previous teaching had been motivated by an unconscious assumption that the bright student was superior. She had felt great pride in students' intellectual achievements and led bright pupils to avoid manual labor. Others she subconsciously regarded as inferior. Now her first goal is to cultivate her students' concern for people and the environment.

Chinese authorities admit that the doubling of school enrollment since 1966 has created a situation in which both the numbers and standards of teachers are inadequate. Young people with middle school experience and demobilized servicemen are given a training course of three to twelve months and then are used to augment the teaching force. Workers and peasants themselves are often used as part-time or temporary instructors to give political and practical lessons.

On-the-job training is pursued intensively. To tackle specific problems, mobile teaching groups tour areas setting up seminars on map reading and surveying for secondary math teachers. The staff at one teachers' training college held a twenty-day course for all eighty teachers of one commune to dis-

cuss common problems. Correspondence courses are becoming popular. "Tutoring stations" are set up on a city- or countywide basis. Here teachers meet regularly to exchange experiences, gather supplementary aids, and collaborate in the writing of reference materials. In keeping with the Maoist view of knowledge, new methods and materials are not private but are to be as widely disseminated as possible. Some areas have instituted a "teachers' study day," when teachers on a swing basis are given one day a week away from classes to help in a factory or on a farm and to pursue solutions to professional problems.

Part of the Chinese teaching style is to publicize models for emulation. The exemplary teacher is one who consistently battles for the cause of mass education, who modestly accepts criticisms from students, workers, and peasants, and who regularly takes part in productive labor. He develops a close relationship with his students and sets high educational and political goals for himself as well as for them. He treats students with patience and commends rather than scolds. Just because a pupil is considered a problem is no reason to "write him off." Mao Tse-tung's thought encourages thorough investigations into causes and patient help to the person who is trying to change.

Teachers have cooperated with workers and farmers to produce academically and politically sound new textbooks. In retrospect, pre-Cultural Revolution texts appear surprisingly free of political content. Today, politics domi-

nates language lessons (English is in; Russian out). In one school I heard nine-year-olds reciting "I am a Little Red Guard"; in another "Sunflowers [the people] always face the red sun [Chairman Mao]." Arithmetic problems illustrate class exploitation. "Calculate how much rice poor Auntie Hsia was cheated out of when the crafty landlord weighed her rice in an extra heavy jar." History texts concentrate on the Chinese Communist Party and liberation struggles of the world's oppressed. Teachers said the books we saw last summer were "experimental," always under review. The simple paperback form in which materials are produced facilitates revision.

The "old" has not been eliminated with one stroke, however. That which can "serve China" is retained. Graceful girls perform Tibetan folk dances, the music and movement traditional, the words in praise of Chairman Mao. School children trudge through Peking's ornate Imperial Palace, learning to cherish the historic treasure as the product of the labor of the working man. The Sian Red Cultural Troupe sound much like Juilliard students, but the skills these budding musicians learn will be used in revolutionary opera and ballet.

The Chinese are making herculean efforts to erase those aspects of their educational heritage that gave special privilege to the educated, often the sons of the rich and powerful. Throughout China one meets young, confident leaders in factories and communes. No longer do workers and peasants feel inferior to the university-trained. The Chinese people have made great strides toward creating a new, indigenous, collectivized educational system to meet China's needs. They are determined to avoid developing an overeducated elite with no function to perform in society, such as that which Western-style education has created in many developing nations. Although the Chinese describe their far-reaching educational experiment as turning "the whole country into a great school of Mao Tse-tung thought," the problems they are grappling with are universal. □

Rhea Menzel Whitehead is a consultant for the National Council of Churches. Since 1961 she has lived in Hong Kong, and last summer she visited the People's Republic of China with a delegation from the Committee of Concerned Asia Scholars.

WALKABOUT:

Searching for the Right Passage From Childhood and School

By Maurice Gibbons

A year ago I saw an Australian film called *Walkabout* which was so provocative —
and evocative — I am still rerunning scenes from it in my mind. In the movie, two
children escape into the desert-like wilderness of the outback when their father, driven
mad by failure in business, attempts to kill them. Within hours they are exhausted, lost,
and helpless. Inappropriately dressed in private school uniforms, unable to find food or
protection from the blazing heat, and with no hope of finding their way back, they seem
certain to die. At the last moment they are found and cared for by a young aborigine,
a native Australian boy on his walkabout, a six-months-long endurance test during which
he must survive alone in the wilderness and return to his tribe an adult, or die in the
attempt. In contrast to the city children, he moves through the forbidding wilderness
as if it were part of his village. He survives not only with skill but with grace and pride
as well, whether stalking kangaroo in a beautiful but deadly ballet, seeking out the subtle
signs of direction, or merely standing watch. He not only endures, he merges with the
land, and he enjoys. When they arrive at the edge of civilization, the aborigine offers —
in a ritual dance — to share his life with the white girl and boy he has befriended, but
they finally leave him and the outback to return home. The closing scenes show them
immersed again in the conventions of suburban life, but dreaming of their adventure,
their fragment of a walkabout.

The movie is a haunting work of art. It is also a haunting comment on education. What I find most provocative is the stark contrast between the aborigine's walkabout experience and the test of an adolescent's readiness for adulthood in our own society. The young native faces a severe but extremely appropriate trial, one in which he must demonstrate the knowledge and skills necessary to make him a contributor to the tribe rather than a drain on its meager resources. By contrast, the young North American is faced with written examinations that test skills very far removed from the actual experience he will have in real life. He writes; he does not act. He solves familiar theoretical problems; he does not apply what he knows in strange but real situations. He is under direction in a protected environment to the end; he does not go out into the world to demonstrate that he is prepared to survive in, and contribute to, our society. His preparation is primarily for the mastery of content and skills in the disciplines and has little to do with reaching maturity, achieving adulthood, or developing fully as a person.

The isolation involved in the walkabout is also in sharp contrast to experience in our school system. In an extended period of solitude at a crucial stage of his development, the aborigine is confronted with a challenge not only to his competence, but also to his inner or spiritual resources. For his Western counterpart, however, school is always a crowd experience. Seldom separated from his class, friends, or family, he has little opportunity to confront his anxieties, explore his inner resources, and come to terms with the world and his future in it. Certainly, he receives little or no training in how to deal with such issues. There are other contrasts, too, at least between the Australian boy and the urban children in the movie: his heightened sensory perception, instinct, and intuition, senses which seem numbed in them; his genuine, open, and emphatic response toward them in saving their lives, and their inability to finally overcome their suspicious and defensive self-interest to save his. And above all there is his love and respect for the land even as he takes from it what he needs; and the willful destruction of animals and landscape which he observes in disbelief during his brushes with civilization.

Imagine for a moment two children, a young native looking ahead to his walkabout and a young North American looking ahead to grade 12 as the culminating experiences of all their basic preparation for adult life. The young native can clearly see that his life will depend on the skills he is learning and that after the walkabout his survival and his place in the community will depend upon them, too. What meaning and relevance such a goal must give to learning! What a contrast if he were preparing to write a test on survival techniques in the outback or the history of aboriginal weaponry. The native's Western counterpart looks forward to such abstractions as subjects and tests sucked dry of the richness of experience, in the end having little to do directly with anything critical or even significant that he

anticipates being involved in as an adult – except the pursuit of more formal education. And yet, is it not clear that what will matter to him – and to his community – is not his test-writing ability or even what he knows about, but what he feels, what he stands for, what he can do and will do, and what he is becoming as a person? And if the clear performative goal of the walkabout makes learning more significant, think of the effect it must have on the attitude and performance of the young person's parents and instructors, knowing that their skill and devotion will also be put to the ultimate test when the boy goes out on his own. What an effect such accountability could have on our concept of schooling and on parents' involvement in it!

For another moment, imagine these same two children reaching the ceremonies which culminate their basic preparation and celebrate their successful passage from childhood to adulthood, from school student to work and responsible community membership. When the aborigine returns, his readiness and worth have been clearly demonstrated to him and to his tribe. They need him. He is their hope for the future. It is a moment worth celebrating. What, I wonder, would an alien humanoid conclude about adulthood in our society if he had to make his deductions from a graduation ceremony announcing students' maturity: speeches, a parade of candidates – with readings from their yearbook descriptions – a formal dinner, expensive clothes and cars, graduates over here, adults over there, all-night parties, occasional drunkenness and sexual experience or flirtation with it, and spray-painting "Grad '74" on a bridge or building. For many it is a memorable occasion – a pageant for parents, a good time for the students. But what is the message in this celebration at this most important moment of school life and in this most important shared community experience? What values does it promote? What is it saying about 12 years of school experience? The achievement of what goals is being celebrated? What is it teaching about adulthood? How is it contributing to a sense of community? What pleasures and sources of challenge and fulfillment does it encourage the young to pursue? And if our alien humanoid could look into the students' deepest thoughts, what would he conclude about their sense of readiness to live full and independent lives, to direct their own growth, to contribute to society, and to deal with the issues that confront us as a world – perhaps a universe – citizenry? I think his unprejudiced conclusions would horrify us.

In my opinion, the walkabout could be a very useful model to guide us in redesigning our own rites of passage. It provides a powerful focus during training, a challenging demonstration of necessary competence, a profound maturing experience, and an enrichment of community life. By comparison, preparation and trial in our society are incomplete, abstract, and impersonal; and graduation is little more than a party celebrating the end of school. I am not concluding that our students should be sent into the desert, the wilderness, or the Arctic for six

"The walkabout could be a very useful model to guide us in redesigning our own rites of passage. It provides a powerful focus during training, a challenging demonstration of necessary competence, and an enrichment of community life."

MAURICE GIB-
BONS is professor of
education, Simon
Fraser University, Bur-
naby, British Columbia.
A frequent contributor
to education journals,
he is also the author of
several books. The most
recent of these is In-
dividualized Instruc-
tion: An Analysis of
the Programs (Teachers
College Press, 1972).

"Success in our lives depends on the ability to make appropriate choices. Yet, in most schools, students make few decisions of any importance and receive no training in decision making or in the implementation and reassessment cycle. . . ."

months – even though military service, Outward Bound, and such organizations as the Boy Scouts do feature wilderness living and survival training. What is appropriate for a primitive subsistence society is not likely appropriate for one as complex and technically sophisticated as ours. But the walkabout is a useful analogy, a way of making the familiar strange so we can examine our practices with fresh eyes. And it raises the question I find fascinating: *What would an appropriate and challenging walkabout for students in our society be like?* Let me restate the problem more specifically. What sensibilities, knowledge, attitudes, and competencies are necessary for a full and productive adult life? What kinds of experience will have the power to focus our children's energy on achieving these goals? And what kind of performance will demonstrate to the student, the school, and the community that the goals have been achieved?

The walkabout model suggests that our solution to this problem must measure up to a number of criteria. First of all, it should be experiential and the experience should be real rather than simulated; not knowledge about aerodynamics and aircraft, not passing the link-trainer test, but the experience of solo flight in which the mastery of relevant abstract knowledge and skills is manifest in the performance. Second, it should be a challenge which extends the capacities of the student as fully as possible, urging him to consider every limitation he perceives in himself as a barrier to be broken through; not a goal which is easily accessible, such as playing an instrument he already plays competently, but a risky goal which calls for a major extension of his talent, such as earning a chair in the junior symphony or a gig at a reputable discotheque. Third, it should be a challenge the student chooses for himself. As Margaret Mead has often pointed out – in *Growing Up in Samoa,* for instance – the major challenge for young people in our society is making decisions. In primitive societies there are few choices; in technological societies like ours there is a bewildering array of alternatives in life-style, work, politics, possessions, recreation, dress, relationships, environment, and so on. Success in our lives depends on the ability to make appropriate choices. Yet, in most schools, students make few decisions of any importance and receive no training in decision making or in the implementation and reassessment cycle which constitutes the basic growth pattern. Too often, graduation cuts them loose to muddle through for themselves. In this walkabout model, teachers and parents may help, but in the Rogerian style – by facilitating the student's decision making, not by making the decisions for him. The test of the walkabout, and of life, is not what he can do under a teacher's direction, but what the teacher has enabled him to decide and to do on his own.

In addition, the trial should be an important learning experience in itself. It should involve not only the demonstration of the student's knowledge, skill, and achievement, but also a significant confrontation with himself: his awareness, his adaptability to situations, his competence, and his nature

as a person. Finally, the trial and ceremony should be appropriate, appropriate not as a test of the schooling which has gone before, but as a transition from school learning to the life which will follow afterwards. And the completion of the walkabout should bring together parents, teachers, friends, and others to share the moment with him, to confirm his achievement, and to consolidate the spirit of community in which he is a member. Keeping these features of the walkabout analogy in mind, let us now ask the question, What might a graduation ceremony in this mode be like in a North American high school?

The time is September. The place, a school classroom somewhere in the Pacific Northwest. Margaret, a student who has just finished grade 12, is making a multimedia presentation to a number of relatives, over 20 of her classmates, several friends from other schools, some teachers, the mayor, and two reporters she worked with during the year. Watching intently are a number of younger students already thinking about their own walkabouts. Margaret has been thinking about this moment since grade 8 and working on her activities seriously since the night the principal met with all the grade 10 students and their parents to outline and discuss the challenges. Afterwards she and her mother sat up talking about her plans until early morning. She is beginning with the first category, *Adventure,* which involves a challenge to her daring and endurance. The film and slides Margaret is showing trace her trip through the Rockies following the path of Lewis and Clark in their exploration of the Northwest. Her own journal and maps are on display along with a number of objects – arrowheads and the like – which she found enroute. The names of her five companions – she is required to cooperate with a team in at least one, but no more than two, of the five categories – are on display. In one corner of the room she has arranged a set of bedroom furniture – a loft-desk-library module, a rocking chair, and a coffee-table treasure-chest – designed, built, and decorated as her work in the *Creative-Aesthetic* field. On the walls are photographs and charts showing pollution rates of local industries which she recorded during the summer and used in a report to the Community Council. The three newspaper articles about the resulting campaign against pollution-law violators, and her part in it, are also displayed to give proof that she has completed the third category, *Community Service.*

Margaret, like many of the other students, engaged in a *Logical Inquiry* which related closely to her practical work. Her question was, What structural design and composition has the best ratios of strength, ease of construction, and economy of materials? Using charts of the various designs and ratios, she describes her research and the simple experiment she developed to test her findings, and she demonstrates the effectiveness of the preferred design by performing pressure tests on several models built from the same material. After answering a few questions from a builder in the crowd, she shows how the problem grew out of her studies in architecture for the *Practical-Vocational* category. Passing her sketch books around and several summer-cabin designs she drew up, she goes on to describe her visits to a number of architects for assistance, then unveils a model of the summer camp she designed for her family and helped them build on their Pacific Coast property. Slides of the cabin under construction complete her presentation. A teacher asks why she is not performing any of the skills she developed, as the challenge requires, and she answers that her committee waived that requirement because the activities she chose all occurred in the field.

As Margaret's friends and relatives gather around to congratulate her, down the hall Ken is beginning his presentation with a report on his two-month *Adventure* alone in a remote village in France where he took a laboring job and lived with a French family in which no one spoke English. The idea arose during a discussion of his proposal to travel when the teacher on his committee asked him to think of a more daring challenge than sight-seeing in a foreign country. A professor in modern languages has been invited by the school to attend the presentations, converse with him in French, and comment on his mastery. Later, with his own guitar accompaniment, Ken will sing a medley of three folk songs which he has composed himself. Then, to meet the requirements of the *Community Service* category, he plans to report on the summer-care program which he initiated and ran, without pay, for preschool children in the community. The director of the local Child Health and Welfare Service will comment upon the program. Finally, Ken will turn to the car engine which stands, partially disassembled, on a bench at the back of the room. His *Logical Inquiry* into the problem, "What ways can the power output of an engine be most economically increased?" is summarized in a brief paper to be handed out and illustrated with modifications he has made on the display engine with the help of a local mechanic and a shop teacher. He will conclude his presentation by reassembling the engine as quickly as he can.

If we entered any room anywhere in the school, similar presentations would be under way; students displaying all kinds of alternatives they selected to meet the five basic challenges:

1. *Adventure:* a challenge to the student's daring, endurance, and skill in an unfamiliar environment.

2. *Creativity:* a challenge to explore, cultivate, and express his own imagination in some aesthetically pleasing form.

3. *Service:* a challenge to identify a human need for assistance and provide it; to express caring without expectation of reward.

4. *Practical Skill:* a challenge to explore a utilitarian activity, to learn the knowledge and skills necessary to work in that field, and to produce something of use.

5. *Logical Inquiry:* a challenge to explore one's curiosity, to formulate a question or problem of personal importance, and to pursue an answer or

solution systematically and, wherever appropriate, by investigation.

We would learn about such *Adventures* as a two-week solo on the high river living off the land, parachute drops, rock climbing expeditions, mapping underground caves, an exchange with a Russian student, kayaking a grade three river to the ocean, scuba-diving exploits, sailing ventures, solo airplane and glider flights, ski-touring across glaciers, a month-long expedition on the Pacific Crest trail, and some forms of self-exploratory, meditative, or spiritual adventures. We would see such *Aesthetic* works as fashion shows of the students' own creations, sculpture and painting, jewelry, tooled leather purses, anthologies of poetry, a humor magazine, plays written and directed by the author, a one-man mime show, political cartoons, a Japanese garden featuring a number of home-cultivated bonsai trees, rugs made of home-dyed fibers, illuminated manuscripts, gourmet foods, computer art, a rock-group and a string quartet, a car-body design and paint job, original films, a stand-up comic's art, tapes of natural-sound music, and a display of blown-glass creatures.

In the *Service* category students would be reporting on volunteer work with the old, ill, infirm, and retarded; a series of closed-circuit television hookups enabling children immobilized in the hospital to communicate with each other, a sports program for the handicapped, a Young Brother program for the retarded, local Nader's Raiders kinds of studies and reports, construction of playgrounds, hiking trails and landscaped parks, cleanups of eyesore lots, surveys of community needs and opinions, collecting abandoned cars to sell as scrap in order to support deprived families abroad, shopping and other trips for shutins, and a hot-meals-on-wheels program for pensioners. In the *Practical* realm we might see demonstrations of finely honed secretarial skills, ocean-floor plant studies, inventions and new designs of many kinds, the products of new small businesses, a conservation program to save a locally endangered species, stock market trend analyses and estimates, boats designed and built for sale, a course taught by computer-assisted instruction, small farms or sections of farms developed and managed, a travel guidebook for high school students, a six-inch telescope with hand-ground lenses and a display of photographs taken through it, a repair service for gas furnaces and other home appliances, and a collection of movie reviews written for the local suburban newspaper. And we would hear about *Logical Inquiries* into such questions as, How does a starfish bring about the regeneration of a lost arm? What does one experience when meditating that he doesn't experience just sitting with his eyes closed? What is the most effective technique in teaching a dog obedience? How do you navigate in space? Does faith-healing work, and if so, how? How many anomalies, such as the ancient Babylonian battery, are there in our history and how can they be explained? What folk and native arts and crafts have developed in this area? What are the 10 most important questions man asks but can't answer? What is insanity —

For the young person who has just finished twelfth grade, a graduation ceremony in the walkabout mode might include demonstrations of competence in five basic challenge categories: adventure, creativity, service, practical skill, and logical inquiry.

"The approach suggested here reflects what many innovative teachers have pointed out to me: that real change does involve new freedom for students, but that independence must be combined with a vivid personal goal and a framework within which the student can pursue it."

where is the line that separates it from sanity? and, What natural means can I use to protect my crops most effectively from disease and insects? All day long such presentations occur throughout the school, each student with his own place and time, each demonstrating his unique accomplishment, each with an opportunity to be successful in his own way.

At the end of the day the families, their children, and their friends meet to celebrate this moment. The celebration takes a variety of forms: picnics, dinner at a restaurant, meals at home – some cooked by the graduating students – and buffets which all guests help to provide. In some instances two or three families join together. The ceremonies are equally varied, according to taste and imagination; some are religious, some raucous, some quite quietly together. In each the student is the center of the occasion. Parents and guests respond to the graduate's presentation. Teachers drop by to add their comments. And the student talks about his plans for the future. Some may find ways to announce the young person's entry into a new stage of independence and responsibility, helping him to clarify and pursue his next life goal. To conclude, there may be a school or community celebration to which all are invited for music, singing, and dancing. The only formal event would be a presentation of bound volumes of the student's reports on their accomplishments to the principal and mayor for the school and the community libraries. My own preference would be to include, also, some ritual experience of the family being together at the moment of its coming apart, or some shared experience of life's mystery; perhaps a midnight walk or coming together to watch the dawn – the world beginning again, beginning still.

Far-fetched? I don't think so. It is true that Margaret and Ken appear to be exceptional students. So many colleagues identified them as atypical that I almost added a Charlie and Lucy of much more modest accomplishment. But it seems to me that our expectations are conditioned by student performance in courses. In fact, we have no idea what they may be capable of when the same energy and ingenuity that has gone into our system for teaching them subjects is transformed into a system for supporting their own development of their own potential. How far they can and will go along any particular path they choose may be limited, over the years, only by their ability to conceive of it as possible and our ability to confirm it. Besides, we are concerned here as much with depth as with range, as much with the quality of the students' experience as with the manifest products of their effort. One experience of true caring for another without expectation of reward, one experience of breaking through the confines of one's own believed limitations, one mystery unraveled, are the seeds of all later commitment and growth, and are worth cultivating with everything at our disposal. The purpose is not just to stimulate an impressive array of accomplishments, but to enable students to find

out who they are by finding out what they can do, and to confirm the importance of that most essential human work.

Nor is it far-fetched to think of schools adopting a program to accomplish these ends. The concept is flexible. Any school or community may adapt this proposal to its own circumstances by choosing different categories of achievement, different plans for preparation in school time, a different manner of demonstrating accomplishment, and a different kind of ceremony. The basic principles – personal challenge, individual and group decision making, self-direction in the pursuit of goals, real-world significance in activity, and community involvement at all stages of preparation and conclusion – can be accomplished in a variety of ways. It is true that a decade ago such a proposal was unthinkable. The importance of grades and the singular pattern of schooling for achieving them were so general it appeared impossible and impractical to break out of the system. Since the educational troubles of the sixties, with the rise of a responsible radicalism and the appearance of a number of technological and humanistic alternatives, many schools have successfully broken from old patterns to search for forms of education more appropriate for our times.

Some innovators, however, have merely put old content into new programs – for instance, by translating courses into assignment sheets and letting the student work through them at his own pace. Some changes – in the freest of free schools, for example – eliminate all content and directive instruction, relying instead on the student's discovery of his own program. Unfortunately, such laissez faire approaches too often create a leadership and authority vacuum in the classroom, one that students are unable to fill. The approach suggested here reflects what many innovative teachers and administrators have pointed out to me: that real change does involve new freedom for students, but that independence must be combined with a vivid personal goal and a framework within which the student can pursue it. If we remove the structure of subjects, disciplines, courses, lessons, texts, and tests, it is essential that we develop superstructures which will support the student's efforts to create a structure of his own. Autonomy, like maturity, is not a gift but an accomplishment of youth, and a difficult one to attain. This walkabout proposal describes one possible superstructure. For students who are already developing elements of their own programs – in open area elementary schools and interdisciplinary secondary humanities programs, for example – an appropriate walkabout would provide a clear, long-term goal and open the way for the school and community to develop a support structure as the student's need for assistance in pursuing his goal intensifies.

Preparation for the walkabout challenge can be provided in various degrees of intensity, depending upon how committed the school staff is to creating a curriculum which focuses upon personal development.

YOUR OPINION IS SOLICITED

Would a walkabout work in your school system? Would you be interested in helping develop a walkabout program or in participating in one? Can you suggest improvements upon Mr. Gibbons's ideas?

If the answer is yes to any of these questions, please fill out and return the postal card insert, inside back cover of this Kappan.

1. It can be an extracurricular activity in which all planning and work is done during out-of-school time.

2. It can be one element of the curriculum which is included in the schedule like a course, giving students time for planning, consultation, and training.

3. It can be the core of the grade 12 program, one in which all teaching and activity is devoted to preparing for trial.

4. It can be the goal around which a whole new curriculum is designed for the school, or for a school-within-the-school staffed by interested teachers for interested students.

If the school is junior secondary — this concept can readily be adapted to elementary schooling, too — students and parents should be notified of the graduation trial upon entry in grade 8, perhaps by a single announcement with an accompanying descriptive brochure. Trial committees — including the student, the parents, and a teacher — should be organized for meetings, likely as early as grade 9, to guide the student's explorations of possible challenges, so that serious planning and the preparation of formal proposals can begin in grade 10. To make the nature of the walkabout vivid, the committee should involve students in a series of "Experience Weeks" during which they would be out of school pursuing activities, first of the school's design and later of their own design, as trial runs. During these early years the student could also benefit from association with "big brothers" in the school, older students in more advanced stages of preparation who can help their younger colleagues, with considerable benefits for themselves as well. The committee would also be responsible for helping the student make his own choices and find the resources and training necessary to accomplish them; and by their interest, they would also help the student to develop confidence in his decisions and commitment to his own goals. A survey of student plans during any of the senior years would give the staff the information necessary to plan the most useful possible training, which could be offered in mini-courses — one day each week, for instance — or in a semester or a year-long curriculum devoted to preparation for trial. If students were required to write a two-page report on each challenge, a collection of these reports could provide an accumu-

lating resource for younger candidates as well as a permanent "hall of accomplishment" for graduates. In such ways the walkabout challenge could also become a real focus for training in such basic skills as speaking, writing, and use of the media. These are only a few of the ways this proposal can be implemented and integrated with other aspects of school life.

But colleagues and parents with whom I have discussed the idea raise a number of problems potential in the walkabout challenge. What about the inequality that exists between students who have great resources for such walkabout activities at home and students who have few resources at their disposal? What about the risks involved for students on their own in the city and the wilderness? What if competition among students to outdo each other drives them to traumatic extremes or failure? On the other hand, what if students don't want to be bothered? How can we account for differences in ability; that is, how can we distinguish the apparently modest accomplishment that is a severe challenge for one student from the apparently grand accomplishment which is actually a modest challenge for another? These are not fantasy what-ifs, but the real concerns of those who want to anticipate and eliminate as many liabilities as possible. They deserve consideration.

Such questions point to basic issues; motivation, risk control, support, and assessment. In each case resolution depends upon close communication and cooperation among students, parents, teachers, and other members of the community. Students will be motivated by the personal challenge, but it will be essential for all the adults to confirm the importance of these challenges by their interest, concern, and involvement. Counseling by the parent/teacher committees will be essential to help students to clarify their personal goals and to help them decide on activities which stretch, but do not threaten to break, their spirit. But, since this walkabout is a growth experience, I must emphasize that appropriate counseling must help the student to clarify *his* goals and should not be advice giving or demand making. Failure, except where health and safety are seriously threatened, can also be a growth experience for persons who have accepted responsibility for their decisions and actions.

When risk is involved, as in the *Adventure Challenge,* communication and cooperation between home and school will be extremely important. The risk and liability must clearly be the student's, accepted as such by him and his family. But the adults should then help the student to eliminate all unnecessary dangers from the adventure and to develop the knowledge and skills which will make him the master of the dangerous situation he is planning to enter. If his challenge involves scuba diving, for instance, they should be sure that his equipment is adequate, that he has received professional training and certification for free diving, and that he has arranged for a skilled companion to accompany him. The adult committee can also be of

"[Certain] questions point to basic issues: motivation, risk control, support, and assessment. In each case resolution depends upon close communication and cooperation among students, parents, teachers, and other members of the community."

"I am interested in the walkabout challenge because it promises what I most want for my own children. No one can give life meaning for them, but there are a number of ways we can help them to give life meaning for themselves."

assistance in helping students to arrange for necessary resources, such as scuba-diving equipment, in order to equalize the support each of them has available. However, the student with too many readily available resources is as much a problem as the student with too few — in terms of this proposal, at least. A more appropriate solution to the support issue would make the acquisition of resources the student's responsibility, no matter how much was available to him from parents — earning money for equipment and courses, scrounging materials, finding economical ways to travel — so that any achievement is more clearly and completely his own.

A spirit of competition among students attempting to outdo each other could easily emerge. Of course, competition is already a driving force in schooling. The difference is that there is only one kind of contest and one way to win in school competition, and the basic finishing order is quite clearly established after 12 years — usually, after the first year. In the walkabout experience proposed here each student chooses goals and activities which are important to him. Each will be different. Comparison will be difficult and somewhat pointless, particularly if the adult/student committees maintain focus on the student's personal growth through challenging himself rather than others. Everyone can be successful. To be an appropriate part of this learning/growing experience, any assessment must be the student's own judgment of the quality and importance of what he has done. The responses of many people during trial will provide participants with feedback on their progress, as will the audience at their final presentations and the guests at the evening ceremonies. Marks, grades — any comparative evaluation — would be disastrous. The competition is with one's self, not others. The pride is in the confirmation of competence, not superiority. The satisfaction is in the recognition by others of what one has proven to one's self: "I can accomplish. I can become. And therefore I can look forward with hope and anticipation." In these ways the issues of motivation, risk, support, and assessment can be converted from potential problems to beneficial elements of the program.

If there are problems to overcome, the effort required will be repaid by a number of benefits for the student and for the school. The school — any concerned adult — can have no higher aspiration for young people than assisting them to develop a profound sense of their own worth and identity. To reach this state, the young must find their way through the stormy clouds of self-doubt until they win the higher ground of confidence where greater clarity is possible. Getting there requires autonomy, initiative, and industry; three aspects of competence essential in the quest for identity — personal accomplishments which cannot be given or demanded, only nurtured. I believe the trial described here provides a framework for nurturing such development. The individual can clarify his own values and his goals. He can make decisions about his own directions and efforts. He can explore his personal resources by testing them in action. Curiosity,

inquiry, and imagination will take on new significance. He will see the uniqueness of his emerging accomplishments and abilities gain greater recognition than his adaptation to the norms of school and peer behavior. The student can learn to work intimately with a small group on a real and significant task, and can learn from them how his contributions are perceived. With goals clearly in mind, he will be encouraged to initiate his plans and see them through to fulfillment even though obstacles challenge his resourcefulness. And having reached these goals, he may take justifiable pride in the competencies he has developed as well as the things he has achieved. In schools where students are directed, dependent, and ultimately have no personal rights, such an opportunity to earn respect and dignity on their own terms would be a significant advance. Most important, the student will not only have begun to clarify his life goals through these challenges, he will have experienced the cycle by which life goals are pursued. His graduation can thereby be transformed from a school ceremony marking the end of one self-contained stage to a community celebration marking his transition to an independent, responsible life. It can be a celebration of a new stage in the flow of his becoming a person. The school also seems likely to reap a number of benefits from the walkabout challenge program: a boost to school spirit; an opportunity to establish a new, more facilitative relationship between staff and students; a new focus for cooperation with parents and the rest of the community; a constant source of information about what is important to students — and parents; a means of motivating and focusing learning for everyone, particularly younger, beginning students; a constant reminder of the relationship between education and living; and a device for transforming the nature of schooling to combine freedom and responsibility, independence and clearly directed effort. And most important, it will enable us to communicate to our younger generation how important their growth and accomplishment is to us. In fact, the success of this concept depends on that communication.

I am interested in the walkabout challenge because it promises what I most want for my own children. No one can give life meaning for them, but there are a number of ways we can help them to give life meaning for themselves. Central to that meaning is their sense of who they are in the scheme of things and their confidence that, no matter what the future holds, they can decide and act, that they can develop skills to be justifiably proud of, that they can cross the most barren outback with a certain grace and find even in simple moments a profound joy. I hope that by exploring what they can do and feel they will come to know themselves better, and with that knowledge that they will move through today with contentment and will look forward to tomorrow with anticipation. I think a challenging walkabout designed for our time and place can contribute to that kind of growth. □

Meta-Issues of the Future

by Willis W. Harman

Thus far we have looked at manifest trends and countertrends and have examined several aspects of the alternative futures among which we, as a society, are in the process of choosing. In a fundamental sense, choosing the future involves choosing a set of beliefs and values to be dominant. Because the current issues in the dissidence of youth and minority groups may be assumed to be indicators of the choices with which the society is faced, I have previously examined these in some detail. Various bits of evidence pointed to the possibility of a conceptual revolution in process and I have looked at those.

I am now ready to summarize what out of all this is directly relevant to educational policy. Let me, first of all, introduce a useful concept for my discussion, "choice point." By choice point is meant a point or period in time when the society as a whole makes a commitment of psychic, human, and economic resources in a particular direction. The associated decisions are multifold and are diffused in level (political, institutional, and value-belief), in time, and in space (some in Washington, some in other capitals, some in Wall Street, etc.). Some are made with awareness; others may be made by default, or with relaive unawareness of making any decision at all. The choice is not necessarily the result of a major decision by any one identifiable agency, but rather derives from an aggregate of decisions made more or less simultaneously (in the long-term historical sense) by different elements of society. An example would be the choice to provide some sort of old-age security, which took the form of numerous state and federal laws and amendments, and a host of less identifiable decisions by unions, committees, employers, etc.
by default, or with relative unawareness of making any decision at all. The choice is not

I have argued that the United States is presently at such a choice point, in moving toward either what I have termed the "second-phase" industrial society or the "person-centered" society. It is obvious that no one in the White House or anywhere else will actually make such a decision. But in effect, through a multiplicity of decisions made by such groups as the Congress, the Pentagon, local school boards, and industrial management, the choice is being made. At one level a decision may have to do with pollution of a local river, at another with the structure of regional government, at another with the values taught in the schoolroom. The form of education in the future will be much affected by which way society chooses to go. On the other hand, educators themselves have the opportunity to affect this choice, at least in part. For, just as the beliefs and values of a society determine the kind of educational system it chooses to have, so does the educational system affect what beliefs and values are either perpetuated or changed.

An important component of this choice rests in the decision of how to handle the current forces of political dissent and insurrection that consist particularly of our youth and minority groups, since the issues posed by these groups are in considerable measure the same as those involved in the larger choice. The possibility of a conceptual revolution, which I examined earlier, is also involved in this choice, and as I have also shown, is intimately connected with the youth revolt. In addition, I showed that the premises of the Perennial Philosophy are compatible with the "person-centered" society, although not demanded by it.

Now let us look at the changes in society one more way before I summarize how all of this relates to education. From all of the trends and alternative futures and revolutionary issues there emerge some meta-issues, or "issues behind the issues." I shall single out four. These meta-issues may seem to be at the level of questions about the nature of the good life and the good society. And indeed they are. But they are also implicit in such questions as what shall we do about local control of schools, drug use in high schools, student rebellion over school rules, sensitivity training, Black Studies programs, the role of vocational education, the quality of ghetto schools, new career ladders for minority-group teacher candidates, and person-centered curricula. Indeed, the choice the society as a whole makes on these meta-issues will determine in considerable measure what courses the schools will be able to take on the more specific issues.

357

Thus, far from being theoretical and impractical, these meta-issues are the important ones to keep an eye on. I select four as being among the most crucial. I label them as four "crises," using the word in its root meaning as a turning point, and recognizing that they may not merit the connotation of emergency that is often associated with that word. These issues are the key to the "unsolvable macroproblems" mentioned earlier. They are a crisis in human image, a crisis in authority, a crisis in economic values, and a crisis in pluralism.

THE CRISIS IN HUMAN IMAGE

I have already noted, in discussing the possible conceptual revolution, that a conflict exists between the basic premises of democracy—that man is, by virtue of his transcendental nature, endowed with reason, will, and a valid sense of value—and the reductionistic, deterministic, and physicalistic premises of the behavioral-science, sociopolitical theory that our universities impart to their annual crop of budding sociologists and political scientists.

The young social scientist is taught a sociology that has shifted away from its earlier emphasis on the semiphilosophical "humanities" approach to an emphasis on techniques and empirical studies. Man is implied in these latter studies to be a creature of his drives, habits, and social roles, and in whose behavior reason and choice play no decisive part.

In psychology this point of view is likely to be made even more explicit to the student, with consciousness considered an inconsequential accompaniment to behavior governed by external stimuli and instinctive urges. His political science tends to focus on the processes by which public policies are made, and to be relatively unconcerned with their contents. Amid the modeling of society and governments and the measurement of attitudes, population movements, organizational trends, and political behavior, little attention is given to the historically significant questions relating to man, his condition, and his destiny.

On the other hand, the concept of a transcendental, choosing, ultimately responsible self is essential to the entire theory of democratic government. It underlies the assumption that the criminal is responsible for his act (while recognizing through the provision of rehabilitation opportunities that his antisocial traits may have their roots in environmental conditioning). It is basic to the assumption in the judicial process that the judge can meaningfully make a normative judgment. Matson (1964) has cogently analyzed the consequences of overemphasizing the objective perspective in political affairs (as contrasted with a complementary relationship between objective and humane perspectives).

Drucker (1939) was one of the first to sound the demise of the image of Economic Man: "The belief in the desirability and in the necessity of the sovereignty and autonomy of the economic sphere is disappearing; and with the belief, the reality. . . . It is the characteristic feature of our times that no new concept lies ready under the surface to take the place of Economic Man." Such a new image may be emerging now.

Mendel (1969) speaks of the rejection of the image of Economic Man by youth as "the Great Refusal against that pitiful caricature of man created by five centuries of urban, technological, and scientific progress—*homo economicus*. The essential accusation of the Great Refusal is directed against the subordination of human experience to the economic processes of the consumer society and its increasingly more absurd products, to the aggressive militarism that at least in our case has become so tightly interwoven with this society, and to the gigantic, impersonal organizations through which it all functions."

The ramifications of this conflict go much further than has been indicated so far. The kind of educational system and educational goals a society sets up, the way it handles the problem of poverty, the priorities it gives to aesthetic considerations, the extent to which it considers its citizens' needs for communion with nature, the uses of leisure it fosters—all these aspects and many more are affected by the image of man held by the society. Currently in our society a potent emerging force pushes for a change in that image, in the direction of transcendent man; but thus far the power remains on the side of the reductionists.

THE CRISIS IN AUTHORITY

If the issue of the image of man is crucial but unobtrusive, the issue of authority is immediately and obviously before us. Recent decades have witnessed the hastening erosion of the authority of the parent, the teacher, the scholar, the church, the law, and the state. Today's youth deeply question the meaning of the nation's policies and apparent aims. We need only to remind ourselves of the changes, within a generation or two, in the connotations of the military uniform, the American flag on foreign soil, the policemen's badge, the draft card, and patriotism.

This issue essentially concerns the balance between authority based on power and authority based on voluntarily given respect. The central fact of today is that a significant fraction of the population, largely blacks and youth, have concluded that established authority on national and local levels is illegitimate—that is, it does not adequately represent their interests, and it is not based on trust, nor on a general consensus.

Varied is the speculation as to how this erosion of legitimacy of authority came about. Flacks (1969) lists and analyzes its possible origins and correlates; his list, supplemented by a few items from other sources, includes:

1. Widespread decline of commitment to "middle-class values" and to the capitalist ethic, while political and institutional elites continue to represent themselves in those traditional ways

2. Rapid growth of a sector of the middle class whose status depends on high education rather than on property, and who tend to be critical of traditional capitalism and skeptical about the sanctity and benevolence of established authority

3. Child-rearing practices by that group, and by significant minority cultures, that have cultivated doubts about established authority

4. Extension of education, leading to increased feelings of competence, self-esteem, efficacy, and potency, which in turn emphasize self-awareness rather than socialization as a suitable guide to behavior

5. Transformation of the American family in the directions of greater equality, encouragement of self-expression and autonomous behavior, and fewer parental demands for self-discipline

6. The Prohibition experience in particular and, more generally, widespread disregard of laws restricting private sexual behavior and of other sumptuary laws

7. Stringent punitive laws regulating marijuana usage, while such usage is considered by a rapidly increasing minority (adults as well as youth, teachers as well as students) to be a desirable substitute for the cocktail (a repetition of the Prohibition experience)

8. Increased distrust by Negroes, arising from liberal promises they view as unkept, and from experiences that repeatedly reinforce their conviction that the system is biased against them

9. Harrassment of blacks and hippies by police

10. Reaction to the unpopular draft and to the "immoral" Vietnam war

11. Specific incidents of dishonesty (e.g., 1959 television quiz show scandals, Eisenhower's denial of U-2 spying, Stevenson's U.N. denial of Bay of Pigs plans)

12. Lowering of faith in integrity of scholars and scientists (because of university involvement in military research, "quantification" and "dehumanization" of the social sciences, misinformation they have provided regarding marijuana and LSD)

Flacks provides several generalizations about the problems of maintaining the legitimacy of the authority structure:

1. Individuals tend to attribute legitimacy to authority when the exercise of that authority is perceived as beneficial to groups, individuals, or values to which those individuals are committed. Legitimacy tends to be eroded if members of minority subcultures experience a persistent pattern of inequity, or if groups perceive significant discrepancies between their goals and those of the larger society.

2. Attribution of legitimacy is a function of trust, which in turn depends on such matters as the objectivity of the authorities in mediating conflicts, the implementation of equality before the law, the openness of the political system to dissenting views, the trustworthiness of statements made by national leaders, and the degree to which officially espoused policies are actually implemented.
3. Individuals tend to attribute legitimacy to authority if they perceive a generalized consensus supporting legitimacy.
4. A person's sense of competence, potency, and efficacy is related to his response to different kinds of authority. Persons with a low sense of competence will tolerate authoritarian power; for those with high competence the legitimacy of authority depends on the degree to which they have access to the decision-making process, or believe that their judgments are taken seriously by their superiors, or have the freedom to shape their own situations without reference to higher authority.

These considerations suggest that the development of a sense of legitimacy of established authority and the restoration of the image of America as a provider of moral leadership and as an advancer of civilization are among the most urgent national educational tasks of today. They are tasks not just for the schools, but for the law enforcement agencies, for the political leadership, and for the polity as a whole.

THE CRISIS IN ECONOMIC VALUES

This crisis requires only brief mention here. The essential issue is the extent to which economic values shall be de-emphasized and values that are *noneconomic,* at least in the strict sense, shall be a part of our operative (as contrasted with declared) values. The issue is central to resolution of the revolutionary ferment. It becomes specific in spelling out the goals for program budgeting, in listing the benefits in a cost-benefit analysis, in evaluating achievement of educational objectives, in deciding what kinds of educational experiences shall be offered out of public funding, or in planning for continuing education. If one is persuaded that education has any capability at all to change values, the issue becomes a crucial one for the schools: What values shall be fostered?

THE CRISIS IN PLURALISM

A simple society can have a single culture; a complex modern civilization such as the United States cannot. Thus the question is not whether we shall have a multimodal culture with a variety of behavior patterns and norms in different socioeconomic, educational, religious, and ethnic groups—no doubt we shall. Rather, the real question is whether we have have mutual hostility and exploitation of weaker groups by stronger ones, or whether we shall have mutual respect and cooperation among diverse groups.

In a recent essay entiled "Psychology and the Social Order," Lawrence Frank wrote about the challenge of this issue:

A social order which tolerates such wide-ranging pluralism of norms must seek unity through diversity. This means recognizing and cultivating differences while simultaneously enlisting people's loyalty and allegiance to a core of conduct and relationships. Only education and persuasion, not force, can build a social consensus out of these massive and varied elements. . . . Social change and improvement must come through the concept of a population composed of individual personalities. . . . Instead of relying chiefly upon legislation, as in the past, we (must) begin to think how each person may become self-consciously aware of his role as a participant in his social order.

The issue of pluralism with respect to subcultures arises in the educational world most directly over such specific questions as Black Studies programs and community control of schools. In broader form it lies behind the more specific issues in teacher strikes and student rebellions.

We need your advice

Because this book will be revised every two years, we would like to know what you

think of it. Please fill in the brief questionnaire on the reverse of this card and mail it to us.

Business Reply Mail

No postage stamp necessary if mailed in the United States

First Class
Permit No. 247
New York, N.Y.

Postage will be paid by

Al Abbott
Editor-in-Chief
Harper & Row Publishers Inc.
College Dept.
10 East 53rd St.
New York, NY 10022

Educational Psychology

EDUCATIONAL PSYCHOLOGY: CONTEMPORARY PERSPECTIVES

I am a ___ student ___ instructor

Term used _____ 19 ___

Name _____

School _____

Address _____

City _____ State _____ Zip _____

How do you rate this book?

1. Please list (by number) the articles you liked best.

_____ _____ _____ _____ _____

Why? _____

_____

2. Please list (by number) the articles you liked least.

_____ _____ _____ _____ _____

Why? _____

_____

3. Please evaluate the following:

	Excell.	Good	Fair	Poor	Comments
Organization of the book	___	___	___	___	_____
Section introductions	___	___	___	___	_____
Overall Evaluation	___	___	___	___	_____

4. Do you have any suggestions for improving the next edition?

_____

_____

_____

5. Can you suggest any new articles to include in the next edition?

_____

_____

_____

_____

_____

_____

_____

Thank you very much

76 77 78 79 9 8 7 6 5 4 3 2 1